W9-CYB-823

OTHER A TO Z GUIDES FROM
THE SCARECROW PRESS, INC.

The A to Z of the Jacksonian Era and Manifest Destiny

Terry Corps

The A to Z Guide Series, No. 67

THE SCARECROW PRESS, INC.
Lanham • Toronto • Plymouth, UK
2009

Published by Scarecrow Press, Inc.
A wholly owned subsidiary of
The Rowman & Littlefield Publishing Group, Inc.
4501 Forbes Boulevard, Suite 200, Lanham, Maryland 20706
http://www.scarecrowpress.com

Estover Road, Plymouth PL6 7PY, United Kingdom

British Library Cataloguing in Publication Information Available

Library of Congress Cataloging-in-Publication Data

The hardback version of this book was cataloged by the Library of Congress as follows:

Corps, Terry, 1962–
    Historical dictionary of the Jacksonian era and Manifest Destiny / Terry Corps.
        p. cm. — (Historical dictionaries of U.S. historical eras ; no. 6)
    Includes bibliographical references.
    1. United States—Politics and government—1829–1837—Dictionaries. 2. United States—History—1815–1861—Dictionaries. 3. United States—Territorial expansion—History—19th century—Dictionaries. I. Title. II. Series.
    E381.C84 2006
    973.503—dc22   2006000647

ISBN 978-0-8108-6850-2 (pbk. : alk. paper)
ISBN 978-0-8108-7016-1 (ebook)

Contents

Editor's Foreword

Although in some sense every historical era is transitional, this characterization applies particularly well to the period encompassing the Jacksonian Era and the Age of Manifest Destiny. During these two decades, government became stronger and more active and the two-party system was consolidated. The still fairly simple, largely agricultural economy became more sophisticated, increasingly driven by manufacturing and commerce, and banking was given a more solid foundation. Last, but certainly not least, the country gradually stretched across the continent, soon reaching from sea to sea. This was obviously to the good, and would prove useful in the future. Considerably less positive was the treatment of Native Americans and millions of slaves. And most threatening for the nation was the reinforcement of sectional divisions which would ultimately culminate in the Civil War. Thus, this relatively short span from 1829 to 1849 under five presidents—Andrew Jackson, Martin Van Buren, William Henry Harrison, John Tyler, and James Polk—deserves considerably more attention than it usually receives.

The *Historical Dictionary of the Jacksonian Era and Manifest Destiny* fills an important gap in the growing series of Historical Dictionaries of United States Historical Eras and should be read in conjunction with its closest neighbors. Like the others, it starts with a chronology that charts the major events of the period, from one year to the next. The introduction sums it up more broadly, following the major trends and also focusing on events under each administration. The main section remains the dictionary, with hundreds of entries on important persons, not only the leading politicians and government officials but also some in the economic, social, and cultural spheres, and other entries on significant events, institutions, and issues, plus some which give the flavor of the times. It concludes with a bibliography, a particularly comprehensive one this time, so that readers can find more information on aspects of particular interest.

This volume was written by Terry Corps. Born and bred in Great Britain, where he still lives, he studied at Durham University and also the Ohio State University. He has devoted his career to American Studies. Dr. Corps first taught American history at York St. John College, where he was ultimately in charge of the American Studies program. Since then he has also taught at the Universities of Durham, Sheffield, and Leicester. From the outset he specialized in the period covered by this book, writing his doctoral thesis on the Jacksonians and navigation and presently researching U.S. commercial policy in the 1840s.

Jon Woronoff
Series Editor

Reader's Note

The *Historical Dictionary of the Jacksonian Era and Manifest Destiny* is organized so that entries are arranged alphabetically. The reader can also more fully explore a topic by using the cross-references provided in most entries, which are printed in boldface type. More information available on the same or related matters is provided at the end of an entry (or occasionally, in the case of longer entries, at the end of the most relevant paragraph) under *See also*.

Chronology

1829 **1 January:** The marriage of John Eaton to Peggy O'Neill Timberlake creates scandal among Washington society and lays the foundations for Cabinet wrangling and the "Eaton Affair." **19 January:** Andrew Jackson leaves Nashville en route for Washington, D.C. for his inauguration. **11 February:** Andrew Jackson arrives in Washington. **4 March:** The inauguration of Andrew Jackson seems to herald a new democratic era, with mass public involvement in the proceedings both at the Capitol and the president's house. The new president's message, however, promises reform only in a very general sense and does not propose radically new approaches to the economy and society. **9 March:** Office of postmaster general is given Cabinet rank. **17 May:** Death of jurist and statesman John Jay. **25 August:** Jackson offers to purchase Texas from Mexico, the first of many attempts to secure that region for the United States, amidst Texan revolution, worsening U.S.-Mexican relations, and ultimately annexation and war. **8 December:** Jackson's first annual message lays out possible future directions for his administration, with proposals for Indian Removal and for a constitutional amendment allowing distribution of surplus revenue, as well as hints that he will favor a reduced tariff, that he will support internal improvements only on certain terms, and that he has doubts as to the constitutionality and efficacy of the Second Bank of the United States. **29 December:** Samuel Foote's resolution on public land sales sparks off the Webster-Hayne debate in the Senate. Efforts by southern and western senators to forge a joint understanding on issues of importance to each section respectively, notably the tariff and public lands, leads to more heady discussion of slavery and the very nature of the Union.

1830   Introduction of the rotary steam press. **January:** Continuation of the Webster-Hayne debate. **February:** Representative George McDuffie of South Carolina attempts to lower tariff duties, but is defeated in the House. His effort reflects the anxiety among many southerners, and South Carolinians in particular, that the level of protective tariff duties imposed by the 1828 "tariff of abominations" be reduced. **April:** The *Book of Mormon* is published, introducing the world to the revelations made to Joseph Smith and leading to the establishment of the Church of Jesus Christ of Latter-Day Saints at Fayette, New York. **6 April:** The Mexican government bans further settlement in Texas by American citizens. **13 April:** At the Jefferson Birthday dinner, President Jackson challenges the stance of extreme states' rights elements and nullifiers with his toast, "Our Union: it must be preserved." From this point on it becomes publicly clear that Jackson is not going to sympathize with the nullifiers' position and that Vice-President John Calhoun is unlikely to receive his support for the succession. **26 May:** Congress passes the Indian Removal Act. **27 May:** Congress passes the Maysville Road bill, which is vetoed by President Jackson. The veto seems to signify his growing intolerance of internal improvements projects that benefit private corporations, although his administration will continue to oversee large amounts of federal money given in support of projects meeting clearly constitutional priorities. **28 May:** President Jackson signs the Indian Removal Act. It heralds the official attempt to persuade Native American tribes to remove, peacefully if possible, by means of treaty agreements offering them land in the further West. **29 May:** A Preemption Act is passed and signed. It gives squatters rights to purchase their land on preferential terms. **31 May:** President Jackson vetoes the Washington turnpike bill, but approves the Cumberland Road Act, further clarifying his position on what type of improvements projects can receive federal funding. **15 July:** A treaty regarding lands in Wisconsin and Illinois is signed with the Sac and Fox tribes. Although accepted by most in the tribes, the return of some two years later to the lands they left would spark off Black Hawk's War. **11 September:** A meeting in Philadelphia of Anti-Masonic delegates from 11 states represents both the emergence of a new national political force and also the first national party convention. **5 October:** Trade with the British West Indies is proclaimed open after Louis McLane settles long-standing maritime issues with the British government in London. **December:** The *Washington Globe*, edited by Francis Blair, is established as the new organ for the Jackson administration, replacing Duff Green's *U.S. Telegraph*.

1831   Alexis De Tocqueville begins his tour of America which lasts
until 1832. **1 January:** First publication of *The Liberator,* William
Lloyd Garrison's influential abolitionist newspaper. **February:** Thomas
Hart Benton introduces a Senate resolution opposing any attempt to re-
charter the Second Bank of the United States. It hints at a residual sense
of unease about the place of the national bank in the American political
economy and suggests that any later attack on the Bank would receive
sympathetic support from some. **18 March:** The U.S. Supreme Court
rules in the case of *Cherokee Nation vs. Georgia,* Chief Justice John
Marshall denying that the Court has any jurisdiction over this "dependent domestic nation." **20 April:** Announcement of Jackson's first major
Cabinet shake-up. After the tensions created by the Eaton Affair, Martin Van Buren and John Eaton volunteer to resign their posts making it
near impossible for three other Cabinet members to resist the president's call for them to resign as well. **June:** Martin Van Buren goes to
London as U.S. minister to Britain, his consolation prize for supporting
Jackson and the Eatons during the Eaton Affair. **4 July:** Death of former President James Monroe. **4 July:** The United States minister in
France signs a treaty, ratified in February 1832, settling long-standing
spoliation claims. Unfortunately the deal only resolves the dispute on
paper, as several French administrations fail to raise the money to meet
their commitment. Several more years of diplomatic pressure and saber-
rattling are required before the money is eventually paid. **4 July:** First
singing of the patriotic hymn "America." **21 August:** Nat Turner's
slave revolt in Southampton County, Virginia, causes grave disquiet in
the slave-holding South about the security of their institution and the
possible influence of abolitionist propaganda in fomenting slave rebellion. From this point on, most southern efforts to rid themselves of
slavery are sidelined as a more vigorous pro-slavery defense emerges in
challenge to the perceived threat of abolitionism. **26 September:** The
Anti-Masonic Party holds the first national party nominating convention, in Baltimore, choosing William Wirt as their presidential candidate. **December:** The Choctaws migrate from Mississippi.

1832   **6 January:** Founding of the New England Anti-Slavery Society, later to become the Massachusetts Anti-Slavery Society. **25 January:** The Senate rejects Martin Van Buren's nomination as minister to
Britain, by the casting vote of Vice-President Calhoun. **3 March:** The
Supreme Court rules in the case of *Worcester vs. Georgia,* upholding
the position of the Cherokee tribe and its missionary supporters against
the state of Georgia. The Court is powerless to enforce its ruling without the support of the president, and Jackson prefers to stand by the

policy of the state and by his own policy of Indian removal. **13 March:**
A bill to re-charter the Second Bank of United States is introduced into
the House of Representatives, heralding the beginning of the Jacksonian
era's wars over banking and currency. The Bank's supporters hope that
President Jackson will either be swayed by his Cabinet to accept the
new charter, with its amendments to assuage constitutional qualms
about its operations, or will fear the political consequences of vetoing
the bill in a presidential election year. **6 April:** The Black Hawk War
begins, when Black Hawk leads members of the Sac and Fox tribes
back to lands in Illinois. **9 May:** Treaty of Payne's Landing provides
for the removal of those Florida Seminoles approving the treaty to lands
west of the Mississippi River. **21 May:** The Democratic Party meets in
Baltimore, to nominate Martin Van Buren as their vice-presidential
candidate for the 1832 election. **28 June:** A cholera epidemic hits New
York City—over 2,200 die. **3 July:** Congress passes the bill to re-
charter the Second Bank of the United States. **7 July:** Andrew Jackson
vetoes the Bank re-charter bill, citing his constitutional doubts about the
right of Congress to create such an institution, but also warning of the
corrupting influence of chartered private corporations. His action and
words begin the battles over banking that will shape much of the political agenda of the remaining Jacksonian era, at both national and state
levels. **14 July:** Tariff Act of 1832 is passed, making significant downward revisions in the tariff schedule. Supporters of nullification in
South Carolina do not consider its reductions adequate. **21 September:**
Treaty of Fort Armstrong ends the Black Hawk War. **25 October:**
Cholera epidemic reaches New Orleans—6,000 die. **14 November:**
Death of Charles Carroll of Carrollton, the last surviving signatory of
the Declaration of Independence. **19 November:** South Carolina Nullification Convention meets. **24 November:** The Nullification Convention adopts the Nullification Ordinance, stating South Carolina's intention to declare null and void the tariffs of 1828 and 1832. It ushers in
the most serious sectional crisis since the debates over Missouri's en-
trance to the Union, with the federal government pitted against a single
state, although with the possibility of other sympathetic southern states
supporting South Carolina if force is used against it. **10 December:**
Jackson issues his Nullification Proclamation, putting forward a strong
unionist line in denial of South Carolina's right to nullify the tariffs.

1833   Disestablishment of the Congregational church in Massachusetts. Invention of the Colt revolver, to be patented three years later. **26
February:** House passes the compromise tariff bill. **1 March:** Senate
passes the compromise tariff bill. **2 March:** Jackson signs the compro-

mise Tariff and Force Acts. The former legislates for staged reductions of tariff duties over the next 10 years and seems likely to mark a significant enough challenge to the principle of protective tariffs to be satisfactory to South Carolina's nullifiers. The Force Act gives the president powers to enforce the tariff should that state continue to oppose its implementation. **11 March:** Re-convening of South Carolina Nullification Convention. **15 March:** Nullification Convention revokes its nullification of the tariff. **18 March:** Nullification Convention declares the Force Act nullified. However, since its acceptance of the tariff means the federal government no longer needs to use the Force Act's powers, this act is purely symbolic and the nullification crisis comes to an end. **1 April:** Texan settlers resolve upon an independent route, in defiance of Mexican rule. **1 October:** President Jackson initiates the next phase of the bank war by beginning the implementation of a policy of depositing federal revenues with state banks instead of with the Second Bank of the United States. This action alarms supporters of the Bank, in both the president's own party and the opposition, and also begins to raise concerns about Jackson's use of executive powers. **3 December:** Oberlin College is established, becoming the first co-educational college in the United States. **4 December:** Establishment of the American Anti-Slavery Society, the first national abolitionist organization. **26 December:** Henry Clay presents resolutions to the Senate, censuring President Jackson for his removal from office of Secretary of the Treasury William Duane and for the "removal" of federal deposits from the Second Bank of the United States.

1834   Michel Chevalier tours America. He will record his experiences in *Society, Manners, and Politics in the United States*. **January:** Riots at the workings of the Chesapeake and Ohio Canal result in President Jackson sending federal troops to police the outbreak, on 28 January. This goes against the usual image of Jackson as a man sympathetic to the interests of the laboring classes. **28 March:** The Senate passes Henry Clay's censure resolutions against Jackson's conduct as president. **4 April:** The House of Representatives passes four anti-Bank resolutions, demonstrating that Jackson's attack on the Second Bank has much potential support within the country and Congress. **15 June:** First settlement in Idaho is established at Fort Hall. **21 June:** Cyrus McCormick's reaper is introduced to the agricultural world. **28 June:** The Coinage Act is passed, changing the ratio of gold to silver from 1:15 to 1:16. **30 June:** Congress establishes the Office of Indian Affairs, formalizing arrangements that have been in place since 1830. **4-12 July:** New York anti-abolition riots take place, revealing the limits of support for abolitionism at this time as well as a strong strain of racist violence, since African-Americans are targeted at the same time. **11 August:** The burning of the Ursuline convent in Charlestown, Massachusetts, reveals strong strands of anti-Catholicism and considerable suspicion of the closed world of Catholic monastic life.

1835 Alexis De Tocqueville's *Democracy in America* is published. Oberlin College admits African-American students. **January:** The redemption of the national public debt raises questions of what to do with surplus federal revenues in the future, as receipts from customs duties and land sales continue to rise. Although for many distribution of the surplus is the answer, the economic panics of 1837 and 1839 will make the question largely irrelevant once more, as federal revenues collapse. **30 January:** Assassination attempt on President Jackson. **20 May:** The Democratic nominating convention at Baltimore selects Martin Van Buren as the party's presidential candidate for the 1836 election. **6 July:** Death of Supreme Court Chief Justice John Marshall. **August:** Riots in southern states against "incendiary" abolitionist mail make clear that the slave South will not sit idly by in the face of this new challenge. They also propel Congress and the Jackson administration into measures to prevent the distribution of such mail in the future, in order to preserve sectional harmony. **21 October:** The New York Anti-Slavery Society is founded. **29 October:** At a Democratic Party meeting in New York City the radical Equal Rights element defies attempts to shut down proceedings and block their participation, by using "Locofoco" matches to illuminate a darkened hall. The name sticks and comes to be representative of radical Democrat groups in the city. **November:** The second Seminole war begins, as U.S. troops seek to defeat this tribe's resistance to their removal from Florida. A difficult and bitter conflict ensues that will last until 1842. **29 December:** The Treaty of New Echota arranges the removal of compliant Cherokee natives across the Mississippi. Many Cherokee, not party to the treaty, refuse to be bound by its terms and will only be removed by deception or, later, by force.

1836 The Washington Monument is started in Washington, D.C. The Second Bank of the United States is re-chartered as the United States Bank of Pennsylvania and remains, under the direction of Nicholas Biddle, one of the largest financial institutions in the country. The 10-hour day is instituted in the Philadelphia naval yard. **30 January:** Death of Betsy Ross, maker of the first official Stars and Stripes flag. **23 February to 6 March:** The Mexican siege of the Alamo in Texas ends in defeat for the Texan rebels defending the mission house, with the death, among others, of Davy Crockett and Jim Bowie. However, their resistance both aids the long-term success of the Texan revolution and provides a symbolic, near mythic, rallying point for Texan and, later, American patriotism. **2 March:** Texan rebels declare independence from Mexico. **14 March:** The Senate passes the first "gag" rule preventing its consideration of abolitionist petitions about slavery in the District of Columbia. Although criticized by abolitionists and their political representatives as being a violation of the rights of free speech and petition, the rule, and its successors, reveal the willingness of most party politicians to subdue the slavery issue in a search for sectional harmony and national party unity. **21 April:** The victory of the Texan army at San Jacinto leads to the winning of independence from Mexico. **10 May:** A final settlement of the spoliation dispute with France is reached, as the French government successfully raises the money necessary to meet its obligations made in the treaty of 1831. **23 May:** Death of jurist and statesman Edward Livingston. **26 May:** The House of Representatives passes its first "gag" rule preventing its discussion of abolitionist petitions. **15 June:** Arkansas becomes the 25th state of the Union. **23 June:** The Deposit-Distribution Act is passed. It increases the number of deposit banks allowed to receive, hold, and pay out federal revenues and modifies the regulations under which they operate. It also provides for the first implementation of the policy of distributing surplus federal revenues to the states, although economic panic the following year brings an early suspension of the policy as federal surpluses slump. **28 June:** Death of former President James Madison. **2 July:** Congress passes the Post Office Act, making the office a formal part of the federal government subject to much closer financial supervision by both the Treasury and Congress. It also reforms some of the Post Office's working practices in an attack on corruption and inefficiency. **4 July:** Congress passes an act reforming the Land Office. It provides for a shake-up in the structure of agencies dealing with federal lands and also increases the number of officials working in this growth area of government business. **11 July:** The Specie Circular, issued by the Treasury, demands that all land purchases from the federal government have to be made with metal currency. **14 September:** Death of Aaron Burr. **22 October:** Sam Houston becomes the first president of independent Texas. **27 December:** Death of Texas patriot Stephen Austin.

1837   Samuel Morse patents the telegraph. However, it will be another seven years before a working telegraph line is ready for testing.

16 January: The Senate expunges its resolutions of March 1834 censuring President Jackson's conduct in relation to banking and the Treasury Department. Democrats make voting to expunge or not a test of party loyalty, with Democratic-controlled state legislatures putting pressure on their senators to vote for the president. Some that do not do so feel they have to resign as a result and put their case before their electorates. **26 January:** Michigan becomes the 26th state in the Union, but only after some dispute over its boundary with Ohio in the "Toledo War." **14 February:** The Supreme Court rules in the case of *Charles River Bridge vs. Warren Bridge.* By supporting the right of the Massachusetts state government to award a charter to a company seeking to construct a new bridge over the Charles River, Chief Justice Taney's case seems to open the way for state governments to intervene in the economy to allow competition and to promote the public good. **3 March:** After some delay the Jackson administration, on behalf of the United States, recognizes Texan independence. Previously it had been reluctant to do so, for fear of allowing the question of the expansion of slavery to arise, especially before the 1836 presidential election. **3 March:** A restructuring of the Supreme Court adds two justices. **4 March:** Inauguration of Martin Van Buren. **6 March:** The "Dade Capitulation" sees the cessation of hostilities by many Seminoles in Florida's Second Seminole War and preparation for their removal. Others, led by Osceola, continue the struggle. **10 May:** New York banks suspend specie payments, as the panic of 1837 begins to bite. Many noteholders and depositors are keen to redeem their money and banks suspend to avoid being caught with insufficient specie to meet these commitments. **15 May:** President Van Buren issues a proclamation for Congress to meet in special session in September, mainly to propose solutions to problems arising from the suspension of payment of specie by banks. **7 July:** The abolitionist editor Elijah Lovejoy is murdered in Alton, Illinois. Although only one of a string of episodes of anti-abolition violence over the years, this is certainly one of the most notorious, causing outrage among the abolitionist community. **25 August:** When leading Texans start to suggest the possibility of becoming part of the United States, President Van Buren announces his opposition to a policy of annexing the republic of Texas. He shares the same fears of sectional tension that caused his predecessor to delay recognizing independent Texas in the first place. **4 September:** Congress meets in special session to deal with the ongoing financial crisis. Although minor relief measures are passed, the main administration measures of an Independent Treasury and a bankruptcy bill are blocked. **October:** Capture of Osceola and other Seminole chiefs opposing U.S. troops in the

Second Seminole War. **November:** Revolt against British authority in Lower Canada, led by Louis Joseph Papineau. **8 November:** Mount Holyoke opens its doors to become the first lasting women's college in the United States. **5 December:** The Mackenzie revolt against British authorities in Upper Canada receives sympathetic and practical support from Americans across the border in New York. **29 December:** The *Caroline* incident in waters of the Niagara River between New York state and Canada leads to diplomatic tension. The seizure of an American-owned vessel and the death of an American citizen cause outrage among already sympathetic Americans and make border relations even tenser.

1838   **5 January:** The United States declares neutrality in the wake of the *Caroline* affair. Subsequently, U.S. army trouble-shooter Winfield Scott will be instrumental in turning this official neutrality into less tense relations on the border. **26 January:** Tennessee becomes the first state to pass laws relating to the prohibition of alcoholic beverages. **17 April:** As New York banks announce their decision to resume specie payments, suspended since May 1837, the immediate crisis of the panic of 1837 is relieved. **May-June:** Those Cherokee remaining in Georgia begin the "Trail of Tears" in their removal across the Mississippi River. Poor weather, bad administration, and a less than true commitment to any humanitarian motives behind removal make this one of the most notorious and damaging episodes in U.S.-Native American relations in human terms. **21 May:** Opposition groups succeed in securing a joint resolution of Congress rendering the 1836 Specie Circular inoperative. **4 July:** Iowa is granted territory status. **18 August:** Departure of Charles Wilkes' U.S. South Seas Exploration expedition. After many years and several trans-Pacific voyages, as well as a circumnavigation of the globe, the expedition will return with valuable examples of flora and fauna as well as vitally important information from maritime surveys. **3 September:** Frederick Douglass escapes from slavery. This begins his emergence as one of the most important abolitionists of African origin. **October:** Mormon wars take place in Missouri. After several years of tense relations with the Missouri public and state authorities, when Joseph Smith arrived, the community at Independence is attacked and eventually driven from the state. **21 November:** The United States issues a second statement of neutrality in the face of growing border unrest with Upper Canada, this time after the retaliatory burning of the *Sir Robert Peel* by American recruits sympathetic to the Canadian rebels.

1839   The anti-slavery Liberty Party is founded, the first avowedly abolitionist political party. After their experience in Missouri the Mormons settle in Nauvoo, Illinois. **1839-1845:** Anti-rent wars take place in New York State against the remnants of semi-feudal land-holding practices. These continue until the murder of a deputy sheriff precipitates greater attention and momentum toward a more liberal state constitution. **12 February:** The Aroostook "war" begins in territory disputed by Maine and New Brunswick. Rival lumberjacks and militia forces confront each other and raise the possibility of Anglo-American conflict. Pacific stances by both national governments, backed by diplomatic intervention on the ground by Winfield Scott, lead to an easing of the tension. **29 May:** Death of Jacksonian ideologue William Leggett. **28 June:** L'Amistad episode begins, when mutinying slaves on an illegal Spanish slave-trading voyage bring the vessel into American waters. Despite the stance of the Van Buren administration in favor of returning the slaves to their supposed owners in Cuba, abolitionists come to the support of the rebels and block their return through legal actions. The episode proves a testing ground for abolitionist distaste for the international slave trade. **9 October:** Nicholas Biddle's United States Bank of Philadelphia suspends specie payments, as the panic of 1839 hits. The bank's action is followed by most banks in regions to the south and west of New York City and heralds a long-term economic depression. **6 December:** The Whig Party convention, at Harrisburg, Pennsylvania, nominates former War of 1812 General William Henry Harrison as the party's candidate for the presidential election of 1840, in preference to Henry Clay. It suggests the Whigs are keen to play on the same heroic imagery that helped to win the presidency for Andrew Jackson. Harrison's candidacy begins a campaign better known for its "hard cider" and "log cabin" slogans than for its treatment of major issues.

1840   **23 January:** The Senate passes the Independent Treasury bill, proposing the official "divorce" of federal revenue deposits from all banks. **31 March:** Congress enacts a 10-hour day for federal employees. This represents a significant step forward for those laborers employed by the federal government. **1 April:** The Liberty Party's nominating convention is held at Albany, New York, and selects former slaveholder, but now confirmed abolitionist, James Birney as its presidential candidate. **5 May:** The Democratic Party convention is held at Baltimore. It nominates Martin Van Buren as its incumbent presidential candidate. **30 June:** The House passes the Independent Treasury bill. **4 July:** President Van Buren signs the Independent Treasury Act, which, after three years of blocked attempts, finally represents a legislative triumph for his administration's key policy. **12 November:** The Macleod affair threatens to reignite the border tensions created by the *Caroline* incident. A British officer boasting of involvement in the actions against American citizens on the vessel is arrested and charged in New York. As the state government refuses to back down in the face of federal pressure, there is genuine fear of war, as both sides seem ready to make military preparations. Only Macleod's acquittal and release ease the immediate tension.

1841   Establishment of the Brook Farm community in Massachusetts, inspired by Transcendentalist, and later Fourierite, principles. **4 March:** Inauguration of William Henry Harrison. The public gathering for the ceremony matches that for Andrew Jackson 12 years earlier. Harrison marks this change in party control of the executive branch by pledging to be more respectful of the rights of Congress and generally to limit his use of the powers of the president. Significantly he says he will not run for reelection in four years' time. **5-6 March:** Appointment of Harrison's Cabinet. It signals his desire to be his own man rather than the puppet of Henry Clay. **9 March:** The Supreme Court rules in the *L'Amistad* case. It declares that under Spanish law international trade in slaves is illegal and that, as such, *L'Amistad* slaves, on a voyage from Africa to Cuba, were being carried illegally. The Court orders that they not be returned to Spanish or Cuban possession. **4 April:** William Henry Harrison becomes the first president to die in office. After some debate as to his true status, John Tyler succeeds to the presidency and assumes the full powers of the office. **9 April:** Tyler outlines his likely course of action in an address. He calls for peace and honor in international affairs, but worries Whigs by his apparent concern to maintain states' rights in the face of attempts to enlarge the powers of the federal government and by his refusal to support the primacy of Congress over the president. Nor does he disavow the prospect of a second term. **10 April:** Horace Greeley founds the *New York Tribune*. **May:** Overland migration to California begins. **7 July:** Henry Clay assumes effective leadership of the Whig Party by outlining his proposals for legislation in Senate resolutions to the special session of Congress. **6 August:** Congress passes a new Bank bill. To be based in Washington, the proposed Bank's powers to issue notes and to establish branches in the states seem likely to run up against the opposition of the president. **13 August:** Congress repeals the 1840 Independent Treasury Act. **16 August:** President Tyler vetoes the Bank bill, while accepting repeal of the Independent Treasury. **19 August:** Congress passes the federal Bankruptcy Act. **4 September:** Congress passes the Preemption and Distribution Act. The latter element includes a clause suspending distribution of federal surpluses should tariff duties rise above levels of 20 percent. **9 September:** President Tyler vetoes a revised Bank bill, against both the advice of his Cabinet and expectations that the new version would meet his objections to the bill earlier in the session. **11 September:** President Tyler's inherited Cabinet, excepting Secretary of State Daniel Webster, resigns in protest at his Bank vetoes. **13 September:** President Tyler appoints a new Cabinet, generally accepted to be more talented than their predecessors as well as more loyal to the president's political principles. **27 October:** The *Creole* begins its voyage between two slaveholding U.S. ports. An uprising on board the vessel leads to a landfall in the Bahamas where the slaves are freed. Despite the efforts of the British authorities and abolitionists in America, the view that the *Creole* was involved in a legal domestic coasting trade prevails, with the result that, although the slaves are not returned, compensation is eventually paid to their owners and Britain agrees to accept that any similar episodes will lead to the return of slave property. **October to November 1842:** Dorr's Rebellion takes place in Rhode Island, pitting critics of the state's antiquated constitution in unofficial electoral and ultimately violent opposition to the established government.

1842   Oregon fever begins, with overland trails taking migrants to the Pacific Northwest coast. The Supreme Court rules in the case of *Prigg vs. Pennsylvania*, relating to the issue of fugitive slaves. The Massachusetts Supreme Court rules in the case of *Commonwealth vs. Hunt*, countering earlier interpretations of trade unions as illegal combinations. Mexico invades independent Texas. **24 June:** Congress passes the "Little Tariff" bill to tide the federal government over the immediate threat of losing its revenue from import duties. **29 June:** President Tyler vetoes the "Little Tariff" on the grounds that it contravenes a clause of the Distribution Act of 1841 by not suspending distribution at the same time as maintaining duty levels above 20 percent. **9 August:** The Webster-Ashburton treaty is signed in Washington. It resolves a number of outstanding Anglo-American issues, including the Maine boundary dispute and disagreement over other sections of the American-Canadian border as far west as Michigan, new terms for extradition, and joint involvement in policing the illegal international slave trade. At the same time, accompanying exchanges of letters provide grounds for agreement on the *Caroline* and *Creole* incidents and impressments. The most significant omission from the list of issues resolved is the question of the exact border in the Oregon territory, which will require further diplomacy to conclude. **30 August:** Congress passes the 1842 Tariff Act which President Tyler signs, but only after his veto of another version earlier in the month forces Whigs to abandon the attempt to maintain distribution while raising duty levels above 20 percent. The episode provides yet more ammunition for Whig attacks on their vice-president become president. **23 November:** Rhode Island responds to Dorr's Rebellion by implementing a new state constitution.

1843   The Millerite movement begins, leading to formation of the Adventist Church in 1845. **8 May:** Daniel Webster resigns from President Tyler's Cabinet. Already isolated from the regular Whig Party, Webster finds it difficult to square his position with Tyler's increasingly strong stance for the annexation of Texas. His departure removes a force for moderation within the Cabinet and opens the door to even more concerted efforts for annexation. **28 May:** Death of lexicographer Noah Webster. **June:** Formation of the nativist American Republican Party. **5 July:** Settlers in Oregon country adopt their own constitution for provisional government. Their action puts even more pressure on diplomats in their search for a solution to the disputed border with Canada.

1844   The Southern Methodists split from their northern brethren over the issue of slavery. The schism represents a worrying sign of the power of this sectional issue to divide otherwise like-minded Americans. **27 February:** Death of banker and political figure Nicholas Biddle. **28 February:** A gun explodes on the U.S.S. *Princeton*, killing among others several Cabinet officers and narrowly avoiding endangering the life of the president. **4 April:** Death of architect Charles Bulfinch. **12 April:** After a long stop-start process a treaty of annexation is signed by Texas and the United States. **1 May:** The Whig Party nominates Henry Clay as their presidential candidate in the forthcoming election. **6 May to 8 July:** Nativist riots take place in Philadelphia. **24 May:** The first public telegraphic message is sent and received. **29 May:** The Democratic Party nominates "dark horse" candidate James K. Polk for the presidential election. **8 June:** The U.S. Senate rejects the Texas annexation treaty. Its action forces the Tyler administration to seek an alternative method of acquiring Texas, without the need of a two-thirds majority in the Senate. **15 June:** Charles Goodyear receives a patent for vulcanization of rubber. **27 June:** Mormon founder Joseph Smith is murdered by a mob in Illinois. It sparks off the mood that will lead the Mormons on the great march across the continent to Utah. **3 July:** The Treaty of Wanghia is signed with China, establishing certain trading rights for American merchants. **3 December:** The "gag rule" against congressional consideration of abolitionist petitions is finally lifted. **4 December:** James Polk wins the presidential election.

1845   Southern Baptists split from northern brethren over the issue of slavery, reinforcing the impression left the previous year by the schism in the Methodists. Publication of Frederick Douglass' *Narrative of the Life of Frederick Douglass, an American Slave.* **23 January:** Congress establishes a national presidential election day. In future this will be the Tuesday following the first Monday in November. **2 March:** A joint congressional resolution authorizes the president either to offer Texas immediate annexation or to negotiate a new treaty of annexation. **3 March:** President Tyler chooses to offer Texas immediate annexation and statehood. **3 March:** Florida attains statehood, becoming the 27th state. **3 March:** A congressional vote on funding for naval vessels becomes the first example of legislative overriding of the presidential veto. **4 March:** Inauguration of James K. Polk. **28 March:** Mexico breaks off diplomatic relations with the United States in response to the annexation resolution. **8 June:** Death of former President Andrew Jackson. **July:** First appearance of the term "Manifest Destiny" in John O'Sullivan's *United States Magazine and Democratic Review.* **10 September:** Death of Supreme Court Justice Joseph Story. **10 October:** Opening of the U.S. Naval Academy at Annapolis. **13 October:** Texas ratifies statehood by popular vote. **29 December:** Texas is finally formally admitted as the 28th state.

1846   New York adopts a new constitution. Maine becomes the first state to adopt statewide prohibition of alcohol. Congressional legislation founds the Smithsonian Institution. **10 February:** The Mormons leave Nauvoo, Illinois, at the start of their great trek across most of the continent to the future territory and state of Utah. **April:** Hostilities between U.S. and Mexican troops break out on the Texas-Mexican border. **4 May:** Michigan abandons capital punishment. **13 May:** U.S. Congress declares war on Mexico. **14 June:** Outbreak of the Bear Flag revolt in California, as American and Hispanic settlers rebel against the Mexican government. **15 June:** After many years of diplomatic stalemate on the issue, the Senate ratifies a treaty establishing the present-day boundary between Oregon and Canada. It represents a compromise of earlier demands made by Polk and leads to claims by some that his administration is less willing to take a stand in favor of northern expansionist interests than it is for southern ambitions in the Southwest. **August:** Debates on measures to prosecute the Mexican War and to pay for any resulting territorial acquisitions precipitate the Wilmot Proviso, which proposes that slavery not be allowed to spread into any lands gained from the war. **6 August:** Passage of the Independent Treasury Act creates a system much like that established in 1840, only this time it will last well into the 20th century. **21 September:** General Zachary Taylor's capture of Monterrey ends the first phase of the war with Mexico. **6 December to 13 January 1847:** U.S. troops and Bear Flag rebels complete the conquest of California, culminating in the treaty of Cahuenga. **12 December:** A treaty with New Granada is signed, securing U.S. right of way across the Isthmus of Panama. It will be ratified on 3 June 1848, establishing long-term potential for railroad and canal routes through the isthmus. **28 December:** Iowa attains statehood as the 29th state.

1847   **19 February:** In debates on territorial organization in the Senate John Calhoun asserts the right of slavery to spread into all newly acquired territories. **22-23 February:** Zachary Taylor's victory at the Battle of Buena Vista ends the war in northern Mexico. **1 July:** Issue of the first U.S. postage stamps. **21-24 July:** The Mormon emigrants arrive in the Great Salt Lake valley and found Great Salt Lake City as the capital of their newly created state of Deseret. **14 September:** After a dramatic march from the Gulf coast port of Vera Cruz, winning several battles against far greater numbers, U.S. forces under Winfield Scott capture Mexico City. It is the victory that effectively ends the Mexican War's military phase.

1848   **24 January:** Gold is discovered near Sutter's Fort. **2 February:** Treaty of Guadalupe Hidalgo is signed, bringing the Mexican War to a conclusion. As well as resolving most of the precipitating causes of the war regarding Texas and its borders in America's favor, it secures the territorial acquisition of California and the wider Utah and New Mexico territories. **11 February:** Death of artist Thomas Cole. **23 February:** Death of former President John Quincy Adams. **10 March:** The U.S. Senate ratifies the Treaty of Guadalupe Hidalgo. **29 March:** Death of John Jacob Astor. **25 May:** Mexican Congress ratifies the Treaty of Guadalupe Hidalgo, which becomes effective on 4 July. **26 May:** The Democratic Party nominates Lewis Cass for president. **29 May:** Wisconsin attains statehood as the 30th state. **7 June:** The Whig Party nominates Zachary Taylor for president. **19-20 July:** A convention for women's rights takes place at Seneca Falls. Several hundred delegates attend and receive Elizabeth Cady Stanton's Declaration of Sentiments, using the Declaration of Independence as its model in calling for expanded women's rights. **9 August:** The Free-Soil Party, a coalition of anti-slavery elements from the Liberty Party and the anti-slavery extreme of both regular parties, nominates Martin Van Buren for president. **13-14 August:** Congress passes and President Polk signs a bill organizing Oregon as a territory where slavery will be prohibited. **7 November:** Election of Zachary Taylor. **5 December:** Polk accelerates the Gold Rush by mentioning the discovery of gold in his annual message to Congress.

1849   Death of former first lady Dolley Madison. **3 March:** Minnesota is established as a territory. **3 March:** Establishment of the Department of the Interior. **4 March:** Inauguration of Zachary Taylor. **15 June:** Death of former President James Polk.

Introduction

The 20 years that made up the Jacksonian Era and the Age of Manifest Destiny, 1829 to 1849, witnessed the United States poised on the brink of modernity. In most respects the nation seemed to be caught up in a transition from its birth status as an independent, but geographically limited, country at the time of the War for Independence to the nascent global superpower of the late 19th century.

As the age began it was only three years since the nation's Golden Jubilee had witnessed the near providential death of both John Adams and Thomas Jefferson on Independence Day, 1826. Five years later to the day James Monroe, the last president to have personal experience of politics in the immediate aftermath of the war, passed away, while a further five years on the father of the Constitution and Monroe's predecessor as president, James Madison, joined him. Perhaps most symbolically of all, and to an outburst of national mourning in black-edged newspapers, Charles Carroll of Carrollton, the last surviving signatory of the Declaration of Independence, after November 1832 survived no more.

The personal stories of some of the leading figures of the Jacksonian period only emphasize the sense that a new age had begun for the United States. Of the era's presidents, only the first, Andrew Jackson, had anything like direct experience of the independence struggle against Britain, and that only as a teenager skirmishing in defense of his home and family against British troops. William Henry Harrison had been but a boy during the war, while Martin Van Buren was the first president, and John Tyler and James Polk the second and third respectively, to have been born after the signing of the Declaration.

1

Interspersed among these signposts back to the past were the seeds of a later, more modern age to come. Jackson's presidency alone saw the birth of three future Gilded Age presidents, James Garfield, his succeeding Vice-President Chester Arthur, and Benjamin Harrison, who as grandson of William Henry represented the most visible personal link between the two ages. A fourth, Grover Cleveland, was born only two weeks after "Old Hickory" departed the White House, while William McKinley, born in 1843, would be the first to serve as president in the 20th century. Perhaps more significant in view of the largely business-driven fortunes of the United States in the second half of the 19th century and beyond were the births between 1835 and 1839 of the three most prominent financial and industrial figures of their age, Andrew Carnegie, J. P. Morgan, and John D. Rockefeller. Meanwhile, in the space of a month in 1847 two of the men who would revolutionize modern living, Thomas Edison and Alexander Graham Bell, were born.

Of course many of this later generation, as well as their immediate predecessors, were men and women for whom one event, the Civil War, defined their lives. Most of those who lived through, or who were born in, the period 1829 to 1849 would go on to experience the impact of the war in one way or another, and some of the war's most famous personalities began their rise to prominence during the extended Jacksonian age. Leading wartime politicians cut their teeth in the local and national party battles of the age, while many of the military leaders of both Union and Confederate armies gained extensive, if not always relevant or valuable experience, in the war against Mexico. And in a strangely parallel fashion, both rival Civil War presidents, Abraham Lincoln and Jefferson Davis, were at one time on the point of being caught up in the Black Hawk War in Illinois in 1832.

Had the Jacksonian era represented merely a passive bridge between the climactic events of the War for Independence and the Civil War and the acceleration in modernization that followed, it is unlikely that it would have attracted the range of historical investigation that it has over the years. But of course, far from being inert in the subsequent development of the United States, this period played a crucial role in the process, introducing and enhancing many of the forces that would make America modern. It also witnessed the emergence and reinforcement of many of the sectional tensions that would ultimately tear the nation apart in 1861, tensions at first successfully subdued by politicians of the day, but tensions eventually allowed to crash out of control by the end of the 1840s to the extent that in 1850 many Americans for the first time had genuine cause to fear for the future integrity of their nation.

Historians have long debated just how far the United States had moved along the road to modernity by the end of the 1840s, how it got there, and the degree to which the majority of the population of the time considered this a welcome development. In one of the more recent syntheses of the period, Charles Sellers portrays the era as one of triumph for a newly dominant liberal bourgeois ideology.[1] In this thoroughgoing political and social revolution, the vanguard of liberal capitalism utilized religion and education, political influence and reform activity to channel the nation and large swathes of its population into support for a political economy underpinned by the forces of the marketplace. Challenging this near conspiratorial view of the history of the age, in which significant elements of the population were seemingly persuaded to act in defiance of their own best interests and earlier doubts about market values, other historians such as Daniel Feller have painted a picture of much less contested social and economic change.[2] In their view, Jacksonian Americans embraced opportunities for personal economic and cultural advancement with genuine enthusiasm and vigor.

Whichever of these two interpretations is preferred, both are founded on the premise that Americans were experiencing a degree of change that foreshadowed later accelerated moves toward modernization. Encouraged by individual entrepreneurial efforts and by specific improvements in transportation, Jacksonians displayed levels of geographical mobility high even by American standards. While for some this meant pursuing specific dreams, for others it meant escaping either the harsh conditions of overcrowded American rural districts such as New England, or a range of European environments. They moved in the hope of finding something better in the further American West or in the burgeoning urban centers of northeastern coastal America and of the Midwest.

This movement of people both exploited and nourished the growth of cities such as New York, Boston, and Philadelphia in the East and Cincinnati, Cleveland, St. Louis, and the emerging Chicago in the West. In the process a distinctively new form of urban lifestyle was nurtured, affecting nearly one fifth of the nation's population by mid-century and an even greater proportion of around one third in the more heavily urbanized northeastern states. Alongside the emergence of a significant urban sector, although not always directly connected to it in a spatial sense, came development in manufacturing industry in both quantitative and qualitative terms. Higher levels of production and of value of manufactured goods accompanied the introduction of new types of products and, especially, new methods of production and means of organizing manufacturing labor, which directly affected the working lives of many American men and women.

In the face of the great triumvirate of American modernization, immigration, urbanization, and industrial development, it is easy to overlook the fact that the United States remained during the Jacksonian era a predominantly rural nation, with the majority of its families involved in agricultural pursuits. Here too, though, the outreach of change and modernization was quite marked, as wider expanses of the nation's agricultural regions found themselves within range of the influence of the market. Of course there was considerable variety of experience, depending on proximity to urban centers or transportation links and on personal tastes and circumstances, including the simple fact of how long one's farm or plantation had been established. But more and more agricultural units were increasingly managed according to the demands and opportunities of the marketplace, with choice of types of crop and livestock and other production decisions being made on such grounds. This whole process also proved an expansive affair, as more families and farmers sought more land to escape to or to exploit, and as, generally, the federal government facilitated their aspirations through a policy of easy access to land.

There were losers as well as winners in the story of agricultural expansion. For some the push into either the further West or urban settlements represented a flight from earlier failed efforts. They at least, though, had had the chance to try, whereas the experience of a significant minority of inhabitants of American lands pointed out the racially defined limits of American agricultural opportunity. The place of slavery in the southern economy and its push into the Southwest blighted the lives of millions of African-Americans. Meanwhile two aspects of federal government support for rural expansion affected Native Americans and Hispanic Mexicans. A concerted policy of "Indian Removal," driven by white demands for access to land and mineral resources, pressured many Native American tribes into leaving long-established areas of domicile. American expansionism, both popularly and officially manifested, created a new ethnic dynamic in the far Southwest, effectively, if indirectly, establishing a new racial minority by the addition of a significant Hispanic element to the rich cultural mix of the American population.

Of course expansion itself provides one of the major themes of early American history and during this period it reached its zenith in marking out another dimension of the nation's later destiny, although one to be overshadowed in the medium term by a more portentous contribution to American history. At times the American people pushed at and beyond the geopolitical limits of the United States, consolidating earlier settlements in Mexican Texas and establishing new communities in Mexican California and the disputed Oregon territory. Ultimately the U.S. government would support these populist expressions of the nation's Manifest Destiny by respectively annexing the newly independent Texas in 1845, taking California (as well as New Mexican territories) in 1848 as the spoils of the Mexican War, and settling with Britain an agreed boundary in Oregon in 1846. While the long-term legacy of these acquisitions included access to both a wealth of land resources and Pacific maritime facilities, more immediately the successful filling out of the modern contiguous United States was what caught the eye. The addition of a further half-million square miles represented the conclusion of an 80-year-long geopolitical expansion that had converted the narrow band of Atlantic colonies into a continental power, and the superpower of the future. With the federal government having already pursued diplomatic efforts in East Asia, the prospect of American influence spreading into Pacific as well as Atlantic oceans now lay ahead. Ironically, though, expansion's legacy in the longer term could so easily have been lost to its impact in the short term, as it became intimately caught up in sectional tensions emerging over the future place of slavery within the growing nation.

Until the 1840s the Jacksonian political system more or less successfully accommodated any significant dispute arising from both the rise of the direct ideological assault on the peculiar institution by the abolitionists and a more strident pro-slavery defense. Even the issue with potentially the most power to disrupt relations between North and South had been subdued by the efforts of the Jacksonian era's immediate predecessors, who had set out terms under the Missouri Compromise for the admission of new states within the 1803 Louisiana Purchase territory as either free or slave. Under the terms of the Compromise, and of the earlier Northwest Ordinance, the westward push of the American people had found political expression in the organization of a new band of territories and states up to the Mississippi River and beyond. Even the prospect of first a greater number of free states still to be created from the Louisiana territory, and then the actual admission of the annexed, already slave, state of Texas did not seem immediately to raise concerns about where the balance of power between states free or slave would lie.

Yet the possible, and then actual, acquisition of new territories from Mexico raised questions the political system proved less capable of answering. Here, against the new background of generally more heated views on slavery, was an issue that was likely to unite each section in opposition to the other: northerners against the thought of further extending an abhorrent institution; southerners against both the idea that they were being told by northerners that they could not expand slavery westward and, if that northern will were upheld, the prospect of a politically more dangerous free state preponderance in Congress. This stand-off, against the background of yet one more expression of the popular expansionist drive, the 1849 California Gold Rush that brought an immediacy to the need to organize the new territories, propelled the United States into its most serious sectional crisis to date just at the point when the era of Manifest Destiny came to an end. If not yet inevitable, the Civil War had its most important origins in the political decisions made with regard to territorial expansion and organization in the late 1840s.

Moreover, within five years of 1849 the very political system that had struggled to contain signs of sectional tension during the Jacksonian era had fallen victim to that same sectionalism, with the result that one of the strongest remaining ties between North and South was lost. In this way the era set the scene for the coming drama of the Civil War, just as its economic and social developments laid the foundations for America's subsequent rise to a position as a modernized continental superpower.

Political Developments

The election of Andrew Jackson in 1828 seemed to represent to some degree the political manifestation of the same trend toward modernization. The active involvement of huge crowds at Jackson's inaugural festivities, which so scared many conservative observers of the day while enthusing many other Americans and subsequent historians, seemed to demonstrate the arrival of a much more open, popular style of politics, often given the label "Jacksonian Democracy." If truth be told, Jackson was far more the beneficiary of greater levels of democratic opportunity and behavior than he was their herald, but sure enough the American people, albeit mainly white men, were more directly involved in the political process than any previous generation. Some men, and more significantly women, attempted a form of direct political action by signing and sending petitions in support of reform causes, such as moves to keep the Sabbath special, opposition to Indian removal, and abolition. Men and, again, growing numbers of women were caught up in the activities of electioneering campaigns which reached new levels of popular participation in the form of rallies, picnics, songs, and slogans. Most obvious of all was the high proportion of eligible voters who participated in large numbers in all elections, but especially in the tightest battleground wards in presidential election years.

While there was undoubtedly a direct relationship between the accelerated social and economic change of the era and this growing popular involvement in political processes, it took leaders and institutions to forge the link and to channel people's energies. So it was then that parties became the focal point of so much of the political activity of the day, whether it was in their electioneering efforts or in growing levels of voter loyalty and party discipline in legislative circles, trends that have earned for this development the label "second party system." Even as the era began, the Anti-Masonic Party demonstrated the power of parties to influence the electorate through their rhetoric and choice of issues. The Anti-Masons inspired a groundswell of popular enthusiasm for politics in parts of New England, New York, and Pennsylvania and in most of those places would help to channel new support into the growing Whig opposition to Jackson's administration. The Whigs themselves developed quickly as a party in the mid-to-late 1830s, coming to match Jackson's Democrats in their ability to organize and to mobilize popular support. But of course it was Jackson himself, together with the organization around him, who did most to shape the political landscape of the whole era. His energetic approach to the presidency, in his management of the administration and use of the veto in particular, suggested a new dimension to presidential power. It was a dimension that scared many, and perceived "executive tyranny" along with Jackson's choice of economic, financial, and fiscal policies defined much of the domestic political debate for a generation and sustained the second party system until it came under increasing pressure from sectional issues in the late 1840s.

Jackson, Van Buren, and the Second Party System

If the 1829 inauguration seemed to mark the arrival of a new closeness between the American people and their highest elected representative, then this was a relationship that Andrew Jackson did much to cultivate. Having been cheated out of their popularly acclaimed choice of a military hero for president in the 1824 election by a combination of multiple candidates, the electoral system's need for a majority winner, and a series of political (if not necessarily corrupt) bargains in the House election that crowned John Quincy Adams in 1825, now the people in 1829 had seemingly got the right man in the person of Jackson and he had no desire to let them down. Time and again, he would use his sweeping electoral success in 1828, and that in 1832, to justify his actions in the name of the people who had voted for him. He translated the fact that he, as president, was the only political figure to be elected from across the entire national constituency into a claim that he alone represented the will of the whole nation when assessing the constitutionality or suitability of important pieces of congressional legislation. He also explained his approach to federal patronage in terms of his responsibility to the will of the people. Although his own removal of about 10 percent of federal officers during his eight years in the White House did not constitute a significantly greater commitment in practice to the idea of rotation of office-holders than demonstrated by other presidents, his claims that such removals would help to keep officers honest and closer to the people, helping to break down signs of entrenched privilege, no doubt sounded a popular message.

Ironically for a president so personally energetic in his approach to executive affairs, it was an issue relating in part to his control over his administration that represented the first significant crisis of Jackson's presidency. As early as the Inaugural Ball a number of the most prominent Washington wives began to snub recently nominated Secretary of War John Eaton and his wife Peggy, whose marriage had aroused scandal and accusations of immorality because of rumors about widowed Peggy's behavior in the absence of her first husband. As several other Cabinet officers and their wives were among those shunning Peggy, the "Eaton malaria," as it came to be called, imposed considerable strain upon Jackson's administration. The president stood by the couple, whose circumstances resonated with a man whose own marital status had once been called into question, and Jackson insisted that his Cabinet members socialize with the Eatons, even taking time out of Cabinet meetings to force his point home. In the face of growing disruption to the administration, it took the offer of Secretary of State Martin Van Buren, a Jackson loyalist, to open the door to the resignation of the entire Cabinet in April 1831 and end the crisis.

Had the Eaton Affair been only about the politics of personality and morality it would have been destabilizing enough. However, interwoven with those influences were others, potentially more threatening in that they raised questions about relations between the different sections of the Union. Rightly or wrongly, Jackson suspected the hand of Vice-President John Calhoun behind the campaign against the Eatons, believing that it formed part of an attempt to wrest for Calhoun more influence within the administration, to smooth his way to the presidential succession, and to improve the prospects for a resolution of the sectionally-charged issue of the protective tariff along lines more favorable to the interests of his home state of South Carolina and other extreme opponents of the protective principle. As such the affair seemed to fit into a context of a first presidential term in which political debate continued to emphasize responses to sectional pressures or regionally identified interest groups more than party lines. In the 1829-30 congressional session the Webster-Hayne debate emerged out of discussions over the speed with which western lands should be made available for sale. The likes of Thomas Hart Benton and Robert Hayne flirted with the possibility of establishing a stronger alliance between southern and western states in the pursuit of mutually satisfactory policies, before Daniel Webster provoked Hayne into taking debate into the more dangerous territory of the relationship between the South and the rest of the Union. Meanwhile, on the question of federally-funded internal improvements the president had to decide between his western support base's preference for such projects and his own ideological and political qualms about sanctioning either specific developments or the general principle of federal financial backing for them. In a couple of stand-out cases, including the Maysville Road bill of 1830, Jackson decided to apply his veto, but the overall record of his administration in terms of an increased level of federal spending on improvements suggests a degree of inconsistency at worst or at best a willingness to appeal to clearly interested groups. Far more consistent, as well as geared to distinct southeastern and western interests, was Jackson's stance on Indian removal. Whether it was his sympathetic position alongside the state government of Georgia in its efforts to pressure the Cherokee into conforming to state-imposed laws or into leaving the state, or his own administration's efforts to negotiate and implement treaties with native tribes, Jackson remained committed to the policy of removal. Indeed the Indian Removal Act of 1830 was perhaps the single most significant piece of administration-inspired and backed legislation throughout his two terms in office.

However, it was the tariff that remained the most important issue in the early years of Jackson's administration, if only because in the winter of 1832-33 it brought the United States to the brink of its worst sectional crisis to date. The president's past history on this issue was checkered, mirroring the complexity of debate between different interest groups in different sections of the nation. Now as president the messages Jackson sent out on the principle of protection were mixed, although there were signs that he was beginning to develop a resolve in favor of reducing tariff levels. In part this was in response to what was an increasingly dangerous sectional dimension to the issue, as extreme opponents of protection in South Carolina advocated the sanction of nullification as the only way of manifesting their view. As congressional efforts to modify the tariff initially failed to make progress in 1830-31 and then resulted in the revised tariff of 1832 that proved unsatisfactory to the nullifiers, South Carolina's electorate voted in favor of defiance. A special convention declared its intention to nullify the tariff and set in train the nullification crisis. Faced with this challenge to the nation's integrity, Jackson held firm to the Union and asserted his duty to enforce federal laws in full. At the same time he hoped a further revision of the tariff would act as a carrot to tempt South Carolina away from its nullification stance, a hope that was fulfilled when the compromise tariff of 1833 passed Congress, satisfactory enough to allow South Carolina to revoke her nullification ordinance. Yet the threat of disunion had been very real, with talk of armed militias in Charleston, the threat of federal military force, and noises from other southern states to the effect that, while they may not support nullification itself, they would find it difficult to stand by should a sister state be "invaded" by federal troops.

Yet even before the compromise tariff brought an end to the immediate nullification crisis and seemingly defused the tariff as an issue of sectional significance, indeed even before the crisis itself broke out, Jackson had set a different tone for the politics of his second term. When confronted with an attempt by supporters of the Second Bank of the United States to push through an early congressional re-charter of the institution in the summer of 1832, Jackson viewed it as a challenge to his expressed suspicions about the power of the Bank and also as a thinly veiled attempt to force him to support it or risk losing the presidential election later in the year. Calling the bluff of the National Republicans and the Bank's backers, Jackson vetoed the re-charter bill and set in train a series of debates at national and state level over the place of banking in the nation's political economy, debates that would last well into the 1840s. Taking his victory over Henry Clay in the presidential poll as evidence of popular support for the veto and a mandate for further action, Jackson's administration carried on the battle by means of a decision to deposit future federal revenues with selected state deposit banks instead of with the Bank. Supporters of the administration also broadened their attack to the overall system of credit and paper money, with calls for a currency based much more firmly on metallic coinage. Jackson helped to implement this with a series of Treasury circulars demanding payment of a range of federal dues in hard money only. Meanwhile, at state level the debate was translated into battles over the very existence of banking in some places, and in others over the degree of freedom within which banking institutions should operate.

Consistent approaches to the banking issue between state and federal levels are suggestive of growing coordination along party lines. This occurred at an organizational level but also to some extent within the electorate, as voters related issues arising from the bank wars to their own fears and aspirations in the context of economic and social modernization. Jackson's attack on the Bank helped to tighten flabby party allegiances, with opponents of the Bank and of other banking institutions gravitating to the president's Democratic Party, while supporters of the credit system, including some former Jackson loyalists, lined up in the ranks of the emerging Whig opposition, as each new assault on banking caused greater anger. In addition to their appeal to those more committed to the credit system, the Whigs proved attractive to many, especially in the South, who found Jackson's use of the veto and other methods in handling the banking wars most alarming after his recent strident response to nullification. So it was that alongside the more obvious debates over economic policies party politicians battled over the role of the presidency itself, with successful attempts in 1834 by the Senate opposition to censure Jackson's dominance over the Treasury during the removal of the federal deposits, a censure that was finally expunged by Democrats in the dying days of the administration.

If party lines were beginning to firm up over questions of economic policy and executive tyranny, then in 1836 at least this did not translate into a straight two-way race for the presidency. In part reflecting the regional distinctions between different groups of Whig supporters, and perhaps in part drawing on memories of the manner in which Jackson had lost the 1824 election, the Whigs offered the electorate three candidates to vote for instead of the Democratic Martin Van Buren. Van Buren, though, carried with him the momentum of the Jacksonian administration and won the election by a comfortable majority. As one of the former president's closest advisors, it was to be expected that Van Buren would carry forward the same kind of agenda. The main focus of his presidency was the completion of the task of cutting the final ties between the federal government and private banking institutions. Administration supporters in Congress repeatedly strove to pass bills establishing the federal government's own system for handling and storing its revenue deposits, in place of the state bank deposit system that had prevailed since 1834. Ultimately they succeeded with the creation of the Independent Treasury, although only in 1840, and only at the cost of yet one more defection of "conservative Democrats" into a working alliance with the Whigs.

Ironically by the time the Independent Treasury Act had been passed, a similar, but informal, system had been in sporadic operation since 1837, as economic panics in that year and again in 1839 had left few banks in fit shape to act as receivers of federal funds. Unfortunately for the Van Buren administration, the panic of 1839 also left the painful legacy of a long-term depression that would help determine the outcome of the 1840 election. Accusations of mishandling the economic fortunes of the country combined with further claims of executive tyranny to weaken Van Buren's chances of reelection. He was faced this time by a single Whig candidate, William Henry Harrison, a former territorial governor, legislator, U.S. minister to Colombia, and, like Jackson, a military hero. In a campaign in which the electioneering hullabaloo reached heights never seen before, Harrison swept into the presidency with a majority of over 150,000 votes.

Tyler, Polk, and the Erosion of the Second Party System

In spring 1841, as it would do on several later occasions, fate served the Whig Party badly. Faced with the opportunity and challenge of using presidential and congressional power to redress the Jacksonian economic policy legacy, as well as tackling the worst impact of depression, the party lost its new figurehead when Harrison died after only one month in office. Vice-President John Tyler's route to the White House, from the ranks of southern states' rights Whigs, did not bode well for party unity on key issues. In a special congressional session in the summer of 1841 initial agreement witnessed in the repeal of the Independent Treasury Act collapsed as Tyler vetoed successive Whig national bank bills, while later in the year his own proposal for a new central fiscal agency got nowhere. The following year the president outraged his nominal party once more by allowing a new tariff bill to pass only with a clause discontinuing the policy of distribution of surplus federal revenue, another favorite Whig measure.

As most Whigs remained true to their party's heritage, best symbolized by their expected presidential candidate for 1844, Henry Clay, Tyler was virtually written out of the party. As early as September 1841 all but one of his Cabinet resigned, while the following year there was talk of impeachment. Increasingly Tyler relied for advice on other states' rights Whigs and even on Democrats. Still ambitious for reelection, he also cast about for a significant new issue which would allow him to stand out as a possible third force in 1844, and his selection of the annexation of Texas was both portentous and by one measure well chosen. The danger lay in the possibility that debate over the admission of one, or possibly more, slave states carved out of Texas could arouse latent northern hostility to the idea of extending the nation's slave domain. Andrew Jackson and especially Van Buren had steered away from the issue for precisely that reason, and now the two leading parties' front-runners, Van Buren and Clay, made public their continued reluctance to consider annexation for fear of its impact upon national party lines and upon sectional harmony. But Tyler was correct in his assessment of Texas as a vote-winner, because annexation caught the popular mood. Sadly for Tyler he would not be the one to benefit, as the Democrats jettisoned the reluctant Van Buren in favor of the avowedly expansionist James Polk, whose advisors eventually persuaded Tyler of the futility of carrying on his campaign. In a desperately close election, Polk's stance on expansion and a continuation of the Jacksonian economic policy legacy won out over Clay.

Despite the apparent influence of the new-style issue of Texas upon the election's outcome, the old Jacksonian economic agenda continued to play a significant role in party affairs. Local debates over banking policy dragged on and the Polk administration proved energetic and successful in carrying the agenda through on the national stage. The 1845-46 congressional session saw the passage of a new Independent Treasury Act and a downward revision of the tariff, an issue which since the replacement of the expired 1833 compromise act by the tariff of 1842 had come to be viewed more in party than in sectional terms. Polk even mirrored his Tennessee predecessor in vetoing a number of improvements bills.

Nevertheless, one of the consequences of the annexation of Texas would provide the force that began to erode the established lines of the second party system. The popularity of expansion itself was still something that evoked a largely partisan response, Democrats being more in favor of both the annexation of Texas and pressure for war with Mexico than were the Whigs. However, once war with Mexico broke out, politicians were faced with the prospect of further territorial acquisitions and with difficult questions as to how to organize any such new territories, slave or free. As such, rather than being the issue that in itself brought about significant political changes, expansion proved to be a catalyst, raising the specter of slavery-driven sectionalism that would define those changes.

Prior to the Mexican War sectionalism for the most part remained a lurking presence beneath the surface of party politics. Just occasionally, especially in the South, party allegiance was chosen in response to an assessment of a party's or a candidate's position on slavery-related issues. But generally politicians from both Democratic and Whig parties agreed on the wisdom (politically if not morally) of sweeping sectional issues to one side, with gag rules in Congress, support for southern states in their obstruction of abolitionist mail, and the previously mentioned reluctance to annex Texas. The most overt manifestation of a sectional force within national politics was the Liberty Party, an abolitionist body that performed weakly in the 1840 and 1844 presidential elections. The Wilmot Proviso, offered as a House amendment to a bill raising funds for the prosecution of the war with Mexico, helped to change all that. It encapsulated the one approach that seemed to unite most northern opinion on an issue relating to slavery, the sense that it was wrong, for whichever of several reasons that different northerners might give, to allow a further expansion of slavery. For the latter part of Polk's term, debates over war prosecution and then, in turn, territorial acquisition and organization would be dominated by the central question of whether slavery would form a part of any newly acquired lands and by the subsidiary questions of how northerners and southerners would respectively prohibit or provide for the expansion of slavery.

These questions put enormous strain on the Whig and Democratic parties, since they threatened to supplant issues that northern and southern members of both parties could agree on with others that would divide them. The process was not an immediate one, as many northern members of each party, including "Cotton" Whigs and Hunker Democrats, found enough, by interest or inclination, to make them want to keep working with their southern brethren and so did not push the slave expansion issue. For other northern "Conscience" Whigs and for many northern Democrats, however, that issue was more important, and many of each bolted their regular parties to join up with elements from the Liberty Party in forming the "free soil" coalition behind the 1848 presidential candidacy of Martin Van Buren. In yet another tight election it was the Democratic candidate Lewis Cass who lost out, as strong showings by free-soilers in a number of key states, including New York, eroded his support and allowed the Whig nominee, Zachary Taylor, to squeeze into the White House. Yet four years later it would be the Whigs who suffered more from the continuing pressure of the sectional issues generated by expansionism in the era of Manifest Destiny, marking the effective end of the age of the second party system.

Economic Trends

Viewed as a whole, this period seemed to demonstrate its place in a steady, if modest, rise in the economic fortunes of the United States. As a nation of expansive tendencies, both geo-politically and in terms of population mobility, it was only to be expected that many of the main economic indices would mark an upward trend. A first sign of this is provided by the most visible local manifestation of the federal government, post office branches, whose numbers doubled in the course of the period, as the postal network spread to cater to increases both in population and in areas of habitation and cultivation. The American population also nearly doubled over these 20 years, from 12,866,020 in 1830 to 23,191,876 in 1850, and the open door to the outside world encouraged an accelerating level of immigration as the 1840s succeeded the 1830s. Land sales were buoyant, topping one million acres annually throughout the period, and contributed to rising output figures for every main agricultural product, with corn and cotton exhibiting the biggest proportional growth, over two-fold in the case of the latter. Agricultural production still dominated the outward-going portion of American overseas commerce and here too the picture was one of a 20-year period marked by an overall rise in the value of exported goods.

Indicators provided by some of the newer forms of economic activity undertaken by Americans also reveal a record of overall growth. Although by no means a new phenomenon, as the influence of the Erie Canal, completed in 1825, demonstrated, transportation improvements added to the mobility of the population and of its economic output. The newest addition to the growing network of transport facilities was the railroads, whose mileage shot up from a mere 29 usable miles in 1830 to over 9,000 by 1850. Extractive industries, such as lumber and coal in particular, experienced increases in production of between two- and five-fold over the 20-year period, while the manufacture of raw goods like pig iron and finished textiles, shoes, and metal products also underwent significant growth.

Proportionally these sectors of the economy were the fastest growing, with non-farm workers doubling in numbers while those laboring on farms rose by just under double. This relative shift of workforce into commercial and manufacturing pursuits represented one way in which Americans experienced part of the broader "market revolution" the country was undergoing during this period. For those men and women new to such employment the adjustment would have been dramatic, with altered daily routines and levels of personal independence in the workplace. But others too found shifts in manufacturing practice disorienting, as changing forms of ownership and organization within business demanded new approaches to work from workers as well. Many felt their skills and control over finished products threatened by shifts in work practices that separated different parts of the production process between different workers. Much of the organized trades union activity of the time reflected this sense of loss of skilled workers' autonomy. Meanwhile for other workers, in textiles and shoe production in particular, there came the first experience of factory-style production that added a spatial element to the sense of loss of control over their working environment.

It must be remembered that agricultural labor still represented the biggest share of the workforce in 1850, numbering over seven and a half million compared to over two and half million in non-farm occupations. Changing economic priorities had the power to affect America's agricultural classes as well, as many found themselves increasingly caught up in the opportunities, but also dangers, of a speculative, credit-driven economy. Farmers and planters borrowed to expand their activities, to buy new land, to buy new labor, and to increase their productive capacity.

Had the economy provided a reliable pattern of growth, this kind of activity would have been fine, but the mid-1830s to early 1840s actually witnessed a picture of far more fluctuating economic fortunes than a simple comparison of statistics between 1830 and 1850 can reveal. Fired in part by favorable trends in international currency flows, in part by the excitement of the age, Americans indulged in an orgy of speculative activity in the middle third of the 1830s. State governments invested heavily in improvements projects; individuals bought land in ever-increasing amounts, with land sales rising to over 20 million acres in 1836; and banks fuelled both by expanding their loans and issues of paper currency. Such a frenzy could not last forever and when international forces resulted in the contraction of foreign credit to American merchants and in the outflow of specie, the speculative bubble burst. A panic in 1837 brought closure to many banks and caused merchants in particular economic pain. A further, more damaging panic in 1839 left the longer legacy of a four-year depression that meant long-term problems of cuts in manufacturing production and urban unemployment. Nearly every economic indicator fell to around or below its 1830 levels and only slowly would the economy recover to a position of modest and steady growth again by the mid-1840s.

Social, Ethnic, and Cultural Developments

Economic pressures, whether the immediate impact of depression or the longer term influence of the market revolution, added to the sense that society was undergoing some form of marked transition. Predictably, the modes of responding to these changes were many. Some converted their hopes or frustrations into partisan allegiance, choosing to view the Whigs and Democrats as respectively the saviors of economic opportunity or the best defense against the wiles of the credit system. Trade unions articulated many workers' grievances but often struggled to operate in the harshest of economic conditions. Meanwhile, others found different, more or less formal, means of expressing their aspirations and fears in this fluid society.

On 30 January 1835 the failure of Richard Lawrence's pistols to fire properly saved Andrew Jackson from becoming the first president to be assassinated in office, but the event nonetheless was a shocking reminder of the potential for violence in American society. This was not, of course, a new phenomenon and Jackson himself was no stranger to resorting to legal, unofficial, and ritual violence to resolve political or personal problems. Even the language he used in the context of the war against the Second Bank betrayed this violent streak, with threats to kill the monster before it killed him. While not endemic to American society, violence certainly figured large in a variety of forms, ranging from lynching and dueling as expressions of ritualized personal justice to rioting among laborers working on improvements projects such as canals. Most worrying for some was the level of violence, and crime generally, in the emerging cities of the nation, which seemed to reflect something about the nature of urban life and the type of people attracted to living it. Gang warfare bedeviled parts of New York City, while on a more organized level it seemed that some otherwise respectable folk were not above using riotous crowds as a tool in the articulation of their hostility to groups like abolitionists, African-Americans, and the foreign-born.

At times it seemed as if violence was no less than the extreme manifestation of a series of broader cultural battles feeding off the increasingly diverse make-up of the American population. Once again the success of the Anti-Masonic movement had demonstrated the potential for mobilizing large numbers of people against anything that appeared different or threatening to a personally held view of what American-ness might mean. The experience of the indigenous Mormon religion, driven further and further west by local prejudice and occasional violence, hinted at the same trend. Meanwhile, as immigration inflated the numbers of alternate ethnicities and religious denominations in the 1830s, so nativism reared its head in the form of small political movements dedicated to restricting immigration and the rights of recently arrived immigrants. Debates occurred over the place of the Catholic Church in matters such as education, with prominent figures such as Archbishop John Hughes standing up to defend the rights of his fellow Catholics. More ominous were the occasional outbursts of violence, such as attacks against symbolic targets like the Ursuline convent in Charlestown near Boston in 1834, and the anti-immigrant riots in Philadelphia 10 years later. Altogether this trend seemed to presage the more extensive nativist outburst of the late 1840s and early 1850s, which saw the rise to considerable political prominence of the Know-Nothing Party in reaction to the even greater levels of immigration of the mid-1840s. Moreover it was not entirely surprising that anti-Catholicism formed part, at least, of Manifest Destiny's justification of expansion into the Southwest.

Violence against abolitionists and African-Americans constituted another side to this cultural battle. Individual abolitionists such as William Lloyd Garrison and, fatally, Elijah Lovejoy, and their printing offices, were targets for frequent attack, while few would have dared to venture into the South where they were branded as criminals. Southern states, with the eventual compliance of the federal government, had already allowed mob action to prevent the distribution of incendiary abolitionist publications through the U.S. mail. Founded on suspicions of the racial implications of any successful abolitionist campaign, however unlikely that might have been, such actions again represented the extreme expression of political and social attitudes that both tolerated the continuing existence of slavery and reduced African-Americans to an inferior position in society. Although not sharing the outright denial of personal freedom endured by their southern brethren, African-Americans in the North also suffered from racial prejudice and legal discriminations imposed upon them by state governments. Ironically one of the strongest impulses behind northern acceptance of campaigns to stop the further spread of slavery was the desire to keep new territories white, free of people of color as much as free of slavery.

But of course the greatest example of discrimination, and of a form of violence toward African-Americans, was slavery itself. Rising from around two million in number at the beginning of the period to over three million by the end, African-American slaves constituted a significant part of the mostly agricultural labor force of the South. Indeed, the expansion of plantation agriculture into the trans-Appalachian territories and states of the Southwest was mirrored in the march of slavery, which in turn fueled the internal slave trade, considered by many critics of slavery as one of the most obnoxious aspects of the peculiar institution. While the experience of individual slaves would have varied between plantation and small farm, between agricultural and industrial or urban establishments, and even according to the personality of their owner or hirer, the fact of enslavement itself remained the era's greatest violation of American and human rights.

Not far behind came the treatment of Native Americans, along with Hispanic-Americans, the other functional victims of Manifest Destiny. The federal government's support for rural expansion brought with it perhaps the most concerted efforts the nation had yet made to remove Native Americans from eastern districts in the face of Euro-American settlement. In longer-established states such as Georgia tribal groups, including most infamously the Cherokee, shared the experience of any number of other tribes in the more obvious frontier environments of Florida, the Southwest, and Upper Midwest in being forced to surrender possession of their land. Often the result of fraudulent treaty arrangements, at times implemented at the point of a gun, and in the case of the Florida Seminole carried out after a period of prolonged and bitter conflict, this "Indian removal" allowed white Americans to exploit previously inaccessible agricultural land and mineral resources. In exchange Native Americans received lands in a new Indian territory beyond the Mississippi River, where in the space of a generation they would come under similar pressures once again.

Violence, while to a degree a reaction to aspects of social change in the era, to some seemed to be symptomatic of that change itself. As such it was one of many things that generated other cultural responses of both a spiritual and practical nature.

Religion provided for many the emotional and social strength to confront, and in some cases, benefit from the transformations that were going on around them. While this period heard the death rattle of established state religion, personal religious enthusiasm reached new heights as America continued to experience the impact of the Second Great Awakening. Camp meetings in the South and West and inspirational evangelical preachers in more developed and developing regions attracted people in their thousands to revived Methodist, Baptist, and Presbyterian denominations. At its extreme fringes this trend gave rise to new religious groups like Joseph Smith's Church of Latter Day Saints and millenarian sects. In preference to the popular emotionalism of revived religion, others turned to the intellectual comfort of Unitarianism and transcendentalism, with their emphasis on self-education and disciplined thought. Both trends produced examples of groups isolating themselves from society in pursuit of their vision of a better way of living, whether it was Mormon attempts to establish their own towns and eventually a colony in Utah, or the efforts of those at Brook Farm, Oneida, or other settlements to create alternative and exemplary communities to inspire the rest of society to improve its ways.

Religion and communitarian movements formed part of a more general spirit of improvement that prevailed during the period. While the democratic tone of the age and, for some, economic opportunities in themselves promised a great deal, there were still many Americans who believed that there was scope for managing things in a way more beneficial to their view of a better American society for all. Writers such as James Fenimore Cooper, Ralph Waldo Emerson, Henry David Thoreau, and Herman Melville warned variously of the dangers of developing democracy and of too much economic development. Labor activists and workingmen's parties called for more equitable access to the fruits of economic growth, while others hoped to forestall the accelerated rise of the manufacturing sector by means of a liberal land policy. While the Jacksonian Democrats' suspicions of economic privilege and of the influence of the credit system allowed them to tap into some of those ideas, the Whigs, generally, leaned toward another strain of reformist thinking derived from revived religion's emphasis on personal behavior as the buttress of social stability. Reformers banded together in voluntary associations to campaign for improvements in education and changes in the provision of prison and asylum facilities as a way of helping to enhance individuals' capacity for self-improvement. They also promoted the distribution of Bibles and religious tracts and the faithful keeping of the Sabbath to encourage religious perspectives, while attacking intemperance, sexual vice, violence in personal and national affairs, the woeful treatment of Native Americans, and, of course, the institution of slavery as examples of the worst excesses of personal behavior allowed to go to the bad. Often seen as part of a broader effort to mold the American people into good, disciplined, and productive citizens, no doubt these reformers did view their work as promising to contribute to a better moral development of American society.

One particularly distinctive feature of the reform tradition during the Jacksonian age was the involvement of women in the largely middle-class membership of its associated bodies. These women were in no way representative of the majority of American women, who toiled alongside their husbands on the family farm or the slave-master's plantation, who increasingly labored in workshops or factories, or who worked as domestic servants in urbanizing America's growing number of middle-class homes or in the plantation house. But greater family wealth and social hostility to women having an economic role left increasing numbers of middle-class women with more time, outside that still taken up by the continuing demands of motherhood, to become more directly involved in public affairs. While some women participated to an increasingly open degree in party political matters, their most overt involvement came in the activities of religious and reform groups, as signers of petitions and memorials, and occasionally as prominent speakers or activists, like the Grimké sisters and Dorothea Dix. The fact of their involvement and prominence, but also the limits of both, was marked by debates over the role of women in abolitionism, something that actually contributed to organizational splits at the movement's national level. This in turn gave rise to a new, if sporadic, campaign for women's rights themselves, culminating in this period in the Seneca Falls convention's Declaration of Sentiments and calls for full political rights for women. The fact that the achievement of these on a national level would not occur for another 70 years demonstrated that this period marked only another step, and a fairly short one, in the long march toward greater official equality for women in American society.

Foreign Affairs

In its foreign relations as in so much of its domestic development the United States seemed to be steering a course from older priorities to new directions. Much of the nation's business was concerned with resolving issues left outstanding after direct and indirect American involvement in the affairs of Europe, and especially that continent's conflicts. At the same time greater attention was given to relations with the rest of the American continent, with hints of a desire to extend American influence beyond into the Pacific. Bridging both of these fields of interest were the diplomatic implications of popular expansion, in itself a long-term trend in American foreign policy but now taken forward into new areas and culminating in the outbreak of war with Mexico in 1846.

The Jacksonian era inherited three main types of diplomatic issues with the old world powers, and in most cases the American government proved successful in resolving these in a satisfactory fashion. The first formed part of efforts made since independence to win for the United States as full and as fair as possible a participation in matters of overseas trade and navigation. The Jackson and Van Buren administrations completed existing negotiations with European powers and initiated new ones in a push to secure equal treatment for American goods and ships in the ports of Europe. One particular example of this involved a deal reached in 1830 to reopen trade with Britain's colonies in the western hemisphere, American producers finding rather more to celebrate in their renewed access to West Indian trade than did many American shippers. The Tyler and Polk administrations carried on these efforts, seeking to reduce Europe's import and transit duties by means of treaties of commercial and navigation reciprocity. More straightforward in concept, if not always in accomplishment, were negotiations to secure financial redress for American citizens whose property interests had been damaged during the Napoleonic wars. Jackson secured deals with Denmark, Sicily, Portugal, Spain, and, after a rather more protracted and tense relationship, with France. The final aspect of unfinished business involved tidying up America's boundaries, especially with Britain's North American provinces. The Webster-Ashburton treaty of 1842 finally settled boundaries, or in some cases the agreed means by which to establish an agreed boundary, between New Brunswick and Maine, and between those parts of Canada adjoining New York, Vermont, Michigan, and the Minnesota territory. Finally, after some heated rhetoric and more cautious diplomacy, the Polk administration in 1846 reached a compromise settlement of the boundary line through the Oregon country.

In the cases of both Maine and Oregon the energy of American citizens in settling in disputed territories complicated the natural confusion generated by development in a cross-border environment. Nor were these the only examples of popular mobility pushing forward the likely foreign policy agenda of the United States. Such migration into Texas made it harder for the U.S. government not to recognize the eventual independence of the Lone Star state, many Americans naturally sympathizing with men and women of U.S. origins in their struggle for survival against Mexico. Meanwhile, although not inevitable, annexation was very much more likely for the reason that Texas had such a strong Anglo-American identity. It seemed feasible that early Anglo-American settlement in California would exert the same sort of pressures, adding to the existing tension over Texas in worsening U.S.-Mexican relations in the mid-1840s.

Popular and official expansionism, while itself not a new phenomenon in American history, did reflect certain more recently emerging trends in U.S. foreign affairs. A strong feature of the justification for American involvement, first in Texas and then in California, was the expression of concern that if the United States did not act then Euro-

pean powers, such as France and, especially, Britain, would gain too
much influence in those territories. The same Monroe Doctrine-style
claims helped to mold efforts at commercial diplomacy with Latin
American states, with American diplomats determined that American
commercial and financial interests in the developing trade with the
southern continent should enjoy conditions at least no worse than former colonial powers and other European states. Finally, expansion
seemed to tap into a sense that to a degree American interests were developing beyond even its eventual Pacific coast. Between 1838 and
1842 the U.S. South Seas expedition combined official scientific and
nautical exploration of much of the Pacific rim with less official assessment of possible port facilities in the Oregon and California territories, a sign that for some the Pacific coast was a tempting prospect from
a maritime point of view. Already there was some significant American
trade with the Orient and the Jackson administration had sponsored two
special diplomatic missions under the command of Edmund Roberts to
investigate the possibility of more formal commercial relations with a
number of Asian states, expeditions whose outcome of treaties with
Siam and Muscat demonstrated more intent than success. In 1843-44
the Tyler administration's efforts proved more successful, with the
signing of a treaty with China putting American traders on similar
terms to those enjoyed by their leading rivals. While it was as yet early
days, the foundations of an American presence in the Pacific were being laid.

The Mexican War

Elements of nearly all the main preoccupations of American foreign
policy makers in the era were mixed into the increasingly tense relations with Mexico that culminated in the declaration of war between the
two countries in May 1846. American citizens had long-standing claims
for damages against the Mexican government, the satisfaction of which
formed a non-negotiable part of the unfulfilled instructions of U.S. minister John Slidell when he went to reopen diplomatic relations with
Mexico in the winter of 1845-46. Even before the Texan independence
struggle and then annexation of the former Mexican province completely changed the map of the American Southwest, there had been
disputes over the exact location of the U.S.-Mexican boundary. Annexation merely shifted the disputed border southward and made the
problem more immediate, as again indicated by Slidell's instructions.
But of course annexation represented far more than that, being symbolic

of the popular and institutional expansionism of the United States in this era of Manifest Destiny. It had been individual and group settlement by American citizens in Mexican Texas that had set the context first for independence and then for annexation, Mexico's response having been to cut off diplomatic relations with the United States. In the same way the presence of American traders in New Mexico and especially of settlers in California seemed likely to encourage any covetous feeling the U.S. government might harbor toward those Mexican provinces. Again, the Polk administration gave official expression to such views, by offering to accept those territories in exchange for U.S. government assumption of the responsibility for paying off the claims of American citizens. The offer only added to the offense already taken by the Mexican government at annexation and Texan claims on the boundary issue and led to Slidell's mission being rebuffed. It was left to Mexico's attempts to defend its concept of the border in the face of the presence of Zachary Taylor's troops to precipitate the outbreak of the war.

The swift and successful prosecution of both the New Mexican and Californian theaters of the war suggested that the Polk administration was well prepared for its outbreak. Troops quickly took New Mexico in August 1846 and marched on to join up with naval forces in the subduing of Mexican resistance in California by January 1847. Part of this involved official military support for the Bear Flag rebels who, in a way similar to Texan antecedents, had already revolted against the Mexican government, but it was most likely that American agents had already played an unofficial part in helping to foment the rebellion in the first place.

Fighting in the heart of Mexico proved the most important theater of the war, if only in the sense that it would be success or failure here that would determine the war's ultimate outcome and the prospect of holding onto any territories as part of the resultant peace settlement. At the war's opening Taylor held down and pushed back the initial offensive efforts of the Mexican army in northeastern Mexico, bringing campaigning there to an effective and successful conclusion at the battle of Buena Vista in February 1847. It was eventually left to the commander-in-chief of the U.S. army, Winfield Scott, to undermine the resistance of the Mexican regime with a dramatic offensive march from Vera Cruz to Mexico City, which he occupied in September 1847.

Even as Scott's campaign progressed the opening rounds of peace talks had begun, but the fall of the capital precipitated the final capitulation of the Mexican government and their acceptance of the terms secured on 2 February 1848 in the treaty of Guadalupe Hidalgo. To the personal cost of the man who signed the treaty, Nicholas Trist, those terms no longer reflected the full ambitions of the Polk administration, which was leaning toward the idea of demanding even greater territorial concessions. Even so, success in securing official Mexican recognition of the annexation of Texas with the Rio Grande as the agreed boundary, territorial cessions of New Mexico, Utah, and California territories for $15 million, in exchange for U.S. assumption of American citizens' damage claims to a total of around $3 million, represented a substantial achievement to set alongside Polk's domestic policy successes.

Nevertheless, triumph came at a price. Over 13,000 Americans died in this most forceful expression of Manifest Destiny, not to mention many more Mexicans. While arousing passionate support from many Americans, the war had its opponents, ranging from those Whigs who voted against the declaration of war and then reluctantly supported it once it started, to those for whom this war above all others was unjustifiable, claiming that it was being fought in the name of expansion of the peculiar institution of slavery. Henry David Thoreau was even prepared to go to jail, albeit briefly, after refusing to pay taxes toward a civil government whose goals he opposed. But most costly of all was the dangerous undercurrent to that outcome of the war that on the surface offered the greatest long-term legacy of economic benefits, the acquisition of territories. In their efforts to ensure that otherwise desirable territorial expansion would not be tainted with the stain of slavery, and to counter claims to that effect, supporters of the Wilmot Proviso propelled levels of sectional tension to new heights, raising the odds that the more immediate legacy of the Mexican War would be the American Civil War.

Notes

1. Charles Sellers, *The Market Revolution: Jacksonian America, 1815-1846* (New York: Oxford University Press, 1991), chaps. 11-12 passim.

2. Daniel Feller, *The Jacksonian Promise: America, 1815-1840* (Baltimore: Johns Hopkins University Press, 1995), xiv.

The Dictionary

– A –

ABOLITIONISM. Abolitionism was the distinctive direction taken by an increasing number of **anti-slavery** figures in the 1830s. Although there were many different strands to the argument against the existence of **slavery**, drawing on a range of political, religious, and economic principles, at the heart of them all lay the belief that because there was no justification for slavery it should be abolished immediately and without compensation to the slaves' owners. Many abolitionists took their stand on the **evangelical** conviction that morally slavery was indefensible and that therefore it was a question of converting the sinning slaveholders to the view that they should abandon the institution. To fail to do this would make non-slaveholders, in both North and South, equally sinful. For many, immune to the racist strain of opinion that marked other anti-slavery approaches as well as society as a whole, there was also genuine concern for the slaves themselves.

These perspectives influenced both the techniques the abolitionists adopted to convey their message and also their response to a variety of means of reducing the grip of slavery. Although their writings gained prominence from the early 1830s onward, arousing southern fears about the dangers of an agitated slave population, it was from 1834-35 that the abolitionists really came into their own, with propaganda campaigns which took their message to the very heart of the problem and to the national political capital. Abolitionist publications rained into southern states, calling on slave-owners to give up their stake in the institution and impugning their moral character if they did not. This provoked hostile reaction to what came to be dubbed **"incendiary mail."** At the same time abolitionists flooded Congress with petitions calling for that body to take action against slavery in areas where there was no doubt about the national legislature's constitutional right so to do, notably in the District of Columbia. Again, wider political reaction was negative, with the campaign to institute **"gag rules"** in Congress.

On other specific issues abolitionists were keen to support actions that would assist in the material improvement of individual slaves' prospects. They supported moves to ban the international **slave trade** and backed those slaves involved in mutinies or landings on free British islands in the Caribbean. They opposed the use of Fugitive Slave laws and, like their Quaker influences since the early days of independence, some abolitionists put their words into action by helping runaway slaves to escape via the "underground railroad," especially in the 1840s. However, while they could support some aspects of a broader anti-slavery agenda, such as preventing the spread of slavery into new territories, abolitionists condemned the ambitions of the **American Colonization Society** as being neither adequate nor morally acceptable in meeting the problem posed by the existence of slavery. See also *AMISTAD*; *CREOLE* CASE; *ENTERPRISE* AFFAIR.

The public prominence of abolitionism in the 1830s owed as much to institutional development as to its message. Its significant emergence can be dated to the establishment by **William Lloyd Garrison** of the *Liberator*. The movement was given institutional strength by groups such as the **American Anti-Slavery Society**, as well as a number of strong local- and state-based organizations. The financial support of a number of wealthy individuals such as the **Tappan** family also aided the abolitionists in their propaganda efforts, although as with all institutions this made them prone to uncertainty when hard times hit, as in the **panics of 1837 and 1839**. Overall they recruited a fairly narrow range of very committed supporters, numbering some 160,000 between 1833 and 1840. Their main constituency was among middle-class New Englanders and Quakers, but there were also elements to be found where New Englanders had settled further west, such as in western parts of New York and in Ohio. Significantly, women made up a large proportion of the rank and file membership, while Americans of African descent also played an active role in the movement. *See also* NEW ENGLAND ANTI-SLAVERY SOCIETY.

The later 1830s saw the abolitionists suffer a split in membership, as some, such as **James Birney**, Arthur and Lewis Tappan and **Theodore Weld**, came to the conclusion that moral persuasion alone could not succeed in bringing about a gradual and legal end to the institution of slavery—their views came to be represented in the **American and Foreign Anti-Slavery Society** and the **Liberty Party**, which called for more action through national political institutions. Toward the end of the 1840s, after the Mexican War, many of these would be attracted into the **free soil** movement. In the meantime, extremists of the moral suasion school, such as Garrison, moved in the opposite direction, attacking the Constitution which defended the institution of slavery and calling into doubt the value of the Union itself.

Such attacks on the nation's political foundations only made even more unpopular the message some abolitionists were trying to put across. Indeed from the very start their activities had made them a despised group, not only in the South, but often equally so in the North, where their calls offended the desire for sectional harmony and order, the strong prevailing sense of racism, and ironically the very optimistic view that the United States stood for special values of freedom. This unpopularity in turn generated a rash of anti-abolitionist activity, especially between 1834 and 1836, usually in the form of urban riots against them, against their presses, and against free African-Americans, sometimes, as in the case of **Elijah Lovejoy**, with fatal consequences. Notwithstanding their relatively small numbers and the opposition they generated, abolitionists were influential in shaping a growing sense of distaste of slavery among many northerners and in heightening the growing sense of North-South **sectionalism** during the era.

ADAMS, CHARLES FRANCIS (1807-1886). This son of **John Quincy Adams** assumed a political importance of his own in the later 1840s. Born in Boston and educated at Harvard, Charles Francis Adams undertook legal training in **Daniel Webster**'s law office before being admitted to the Massachusetts bar in 1829. After a flirtation with the Massachusetts **Anti-Masonic Party** in the early 1830s he hesitantly moved toward the ranks of the **Whigs**, although never feeling entirely comfortable there. Adams always leaned to the **conscience Whig** side of the party, as his **anti-slavery** views caused him to oppose **Texas annexation** and, while in the Massachusetts legislature in the early 1840s, to support his father's campaign against the three-fifths clause of the Constitution. His background and political leanings took him to the height of his political career in this period when he was nominated as the vice-presidential candidate of the **Free Soil** Party for the **election of 1848**. In addition to his political career Adams was also a writer and left a marvelous historical legacy in editing the papers of some of his illustrious ancestors, including his grandparents, John and Abigail Adams.

ADAMS, JOHN QUINCY (1767-1848). Adams, a member of the famous Massachusetts family and son of the second president of the United States, made his most immediate mark on the Jacksonian era by being the defeated incumbent in the **election of 1828**. Even his successful elevation to the presidency four years earlier in the infamous election of 1824-25 helped to shape developments that would follow. Along with unpopular policy choices as president, charges of political impropriety connected to his election, most notably of a **"corrupt bargain"** with **Henry Clay**, went a long way to explaining the growing strength of the political alliance and popular support which carried **Andrew Jackson** to the White House in 1829.

However, his influence did not stop there as, unlike most retiring presidents, Adams was not to remain a private citizen. After three years in semi-retirement he was persuaded to reenter national politics as a representative from the Plymouth district of Massachusetts, defeating his **Jacksonian** opponent comfortably. This heralded 17 years of service as an "independent" onlooker upon the partisan politics of the era. Although his outlook and defeat made it impossible for Adams ever to join the ranks of the **Democratic** Party, his association with the opposition **Whigs** was rarely more than notional. He considered **William Henry Harrison** a poor candidate for the presidency and would later assail **John Tyler**'s performance in vetoing the "**Little Tariff" bill of 1842**.

Adams' status and experience still made him a prominent figure in national affairs. He was a suitable choice for a range of organizational positions, including chair of the Foreign Affairs and Manufacturing committees at various times and, temporarily at the start of the first session of the 26th Congress in 1839, chair overseeing the organization of committees. It was inevitable that Adams would become involved in some of the prevailing big issues in national politics. He helped to shape the **tariff of 1832** and also made clear his opposition to the Jackson administration's policy of **"removing" federal revenue deposits** from the care of the **Second Bank of the United States**. In 1842 his support for a more **protective tariff** came out second best to his enthusiasm for the policy of **distribution** as expressed in the **Preemption and Distribution Act of 1841**. In 1846

Adams shocked many in the Northeast by supporting calls for the United States to acquire all the disputed territory in **Oregon**. He also chaired the committee overseeing the receipt of the bequest of James Smithson through to inspiration of the **Smithsonian Institution**.

However, Adams' second political career was marked most for his championing of a range of causes associated with the growing **anti-slavery** movement of the North. His personal conviction was reflected in 1840, in his legal advocacy of the *Amistad* mutineers before the Supreme Court, and he also opposed the awarding of any compensation to their Spanish owners. Politically, although Adams never embraced an all-out **abolitionist** position on **slavery**, he was prepared to fight the institution in all areas where he considered it constitutionally appropriate. He was a consistent opponent of measures to **"gag"** the consideration of anti-slavery petitions in the House and he supported a campaign to remove the Constitution's clause allowing slave population to be counted (as three-fifths) in the apportionment of congressional seats and electoral college votes. Both of these Adams regarded as reflective of the ability of a slave power conspiracy to promote southern, slaveholding interests through the federal government, and it was in this light too that as early as May 1836 he opposed **Texas annexation**. This stance would be carried over into his opposition to the declaration of war against Mexico, although once the country was at war he did vote for financial appropriations for its prosecution. How Adams would have responded to the U.S. acquisition of territories as a result of the war will never be known, as he died from a stroke while in the House in February 1848, just before the Treaty of **Guadalupe Hidalgo** was considered by the Senate. *See also* MEXICAN WAR.

ADMINISTRATIVE REFORM. On arriving at the White House President **Andrew Jackson** instigated a program of administrative reform, which would continue under his immediate successors. Such reforms had been very limited in number and scope in the previous 50 years, and changes in the size of the United States, its business, the speed of transportation, and general technological development now made action essential. Reform can be seen as part of Jackson's drive for greater efficiency and financial **retrenchment**, but was also symptomatic of his wish to act as a new broom, as seen elsewhere in his attitude to **rotation in office**. A combination of congressional and executive action brought changes in the main Cabinet offices, such as the **War** and State Departments, as well as a number of subsidiary offices, including the **Post**, **Patent**, and **Land Offices**, and a newly created **Office of Indian Affairs**. For example, the State Department in 1836 was reorganized into eight bureaus, of which only two actually dealt with foreign affairs, leaving the others to handle domestic matters such as arch. .es, library, and copyright issues. **Martin Van Buren**'s term saw further reform of the Post Office and War Department, and also efforts to improve operational practices within the Navy, cutting its budget between 1837 and 1839. The latter provided a springboard for more substantial **naval reform** during the **John Tyler** administration. The very end of the period would witness the continuation of this trend with the creation of the **Interior Department**.

AGASSIZ, LOUIS (1807-1873). Agassiz was a Swiss-born naturalist who traveled in the United States in 1846 after receiving a grant from Prussia to study the continent's flora and fauna. After giving a series of lectures at the Lowell Institute, two years later he gave up his position as professor of natural history at the University of Neuchatel to become professor of natural science at Harvard College. Here Agassiz founded the Museum of Comparative Zoology. Among his explorations of the North American continent were travels in the Lake Superior area in 1848.

AGRICULTURE. This was an era in which the United States remained heavily agricultural in the nature of its economic balance, and this was only likely to remain the case given the period's experience of western **expansionism** and settlement, opening up still more agricultural land. Although there were signs that the coastal Northeast was beginning to see a shift to a greater importance for **manufacturing**, each section of the nation was still primarily agricultural in its balance of population and creation of wealth. Nevertheless the style of agriculture differed from section to section, whether it be in the type of crops cultivated or of animals cared for, the degree of commercialized production, or, most explicitly, in the nature of the labor force, with the use of **slavery** in large areas of the South.

Nor was agriculture a static economic phenomenon. Popular mobility largely took place in search of new agricultural beginnings, extending the total agricultural domain of the nation. The **transportation revolution** can be seen mostly as servicing the needs of agricultural communities, while even the development of manufacturing was interpreted by many as a positive boon, providing a market for both the food and raw material products of American agriculture. In the process a greater number of those involved in agricultural production came to be touched by the effects of what historians have labeled the **market revolution**. As pressure to grow more crops, more efficiently, increased so technological change began to alter agricultural practices with improved plows, threshers, and reapers like that of **Cyrus McCormick**. Exploration and science also helped to forge new directions in farming development, with agricultural societies helping to diffuse their findings. *See also* CORN; COTTON; DAIRY FARMING; HEMP; HOGS; RICE; SHEEP; SUGAR; TOBACCO; TRUCK FARMING; WHEAT.

ALABAMA LETTERS. The first of these letters, to a newspaper in Tuscaloosa in July 1844, represented **Henry Clay**'s public modification of his stance on **Texas annexation**, as previously laid out in his **Raleigh letter**. In response to **Democratic** claims that he was against annexation entirely, Clay said he supported it in principle, but did fear that it might endanger the Union by alienating northerners who regarded it as a measure designed to strengthen the position of **slavery**. Stung by continued criticism from the South, he modified his position further in a second letter in which he said he would support annexation as long as it could be done without dishonor or war. Northerners should not worry about the implications for the spread of slavery, since, Clay stated, slavery was bound to become extinct eventually anyway. Although the latter sentiment further alarmed southerners and the overall impression Clay left was one of vacillation, the letters did work in shoring up his southern support to some extent, as it became increasingly clear that most southern **Whigs** might support annexation.

ALABAMA PLATFORM. This was the stance on the issue of **slavery**'s extension into new territories adopted by the Alabama state **Democratic** Party's convention in 1848. Introduced by William Yancey, it demanded the outright protection of slavery and its right to expand into new territories, in direct challenge to those proposals, such as the **Wilmot Proviso**, or an extension of the **Missouri Compromise line**, or **popular sovereignty**, which variously insisted upon, or potentially would have resulted in, the prohibition of slavery from some or all of the territories.

ALAMO. A mission building located near San Antonio, which became one of the most important symbolic sites in the fight for **Texan independence**. The Alamo had been occupied by **Jim Bowie** and loyal Texan troops as a potential defensive position in December 1835, and Bowie was later joined by **William Travis**, who assumed command.

In March 1836 a garrison of under 200, including in their number Bowie and **Davy Crockett**, delayed a strong Mexican army under **Santa Anna** for almost two weeks before being overwhelmed and killed to the last man. However, in the process several hundred Mexicans were killed and it is usually thought that the resistance at the Alamo both hindered Santa Anna's military progress and proved inspirational to later Texan actions.

ALBANY REGENCY. This was one of the first party political machines in the United States, dominating New York **Democratic** politics by means of party discipline, regular conventions, and tactical use of political **spoils**. The Regency flourished between 1820 and 1850 and gave rise to some of the most prominent politicians of the day, including **Martin Van Buren** and **William Marcy**. Indeed, Van Buren is credited with creating the Regency in order to run Democratic politics in New York while he was serving in the Senate, and it was he who was largely responsible for taking the Regency into the coalition of supporters behind **Andrew Jackson** in the **election of 1828**. Although the Regency did not initially reap the reward of federal offices in the state, Jackson choosing personal favorites and even sympathizers of **John Calhoun** in New York City in particular, as the president's term proceeded the drive for party regularity afforded the Regency growing influence over New York appointments. Although its power continued into the 1840s, it was weakened considerably by the splits between **Hunkers** and **Barnburners**.

ALCOTT, AMOS BRONSON (1799-1888). The father of popular author Louisa May Alcott, of *Little Women* fame, Alcott was in his own right an important figure in education and thought. Born in Connecticut, in the 1820s through 1832 he was an itinerant teacher, despite lacking any formal qualifications. He settled in Boston in 1833 where the following year he founded the "Temple School." Here Alcott strove to implement ideas on education expressed in his 1830 *Observations on the Principles and Methods of Infant Instruction*. His views on children were liberal, believing all to be born good and only needing an appropriately stimulating environment in which to flourish. As such he opposed corporal punishment. Ultimately Temple School failed in 1838, as did another a year later, in part because of Alcott's decision to admit an African-American pupil. In addition to his thinking on child-rearing and education he was attracted to the reform agenda, being a prominent **abolitionist**, and he steered a varied religious course, veering from **Unitarianism** toward a flirtation with **Transcendentalism**. In 1844-45 Alcott established an ultimately failing cooperative community at Fruitlands near Harvard.

ALLISON LETTER. In the face of uncertainty about his political record, given the largely military nature of his career to date, **Whig** presidential candidate **Zachary Taylor** issued this public letter in April during the campaign running up to the **election of 1848**. In it he countered evidence of his non-partisan past record by asserting that he was a Whig, albeit a moderate one, and would support any policies made by a Whig-controlled Congress on issues such as the **tariff**, currency, and **internal improvements**. Taylor's stance was made clear as a response to Whig fears of a repeat of their experiences under President **John Tyler**.

"ALL MEXICO." This emerging movement in 1846-47 took the geopolitical expression of **Manifest Destiny** and military success in the **Mexican War** to their logical conclusion, that the fruits of that war should include pretty much all of Mexico. It played on Mexico's choice to continue fighting and to block peace moves as giving ample reason for the United States to demand more territory. It proved a popular impulse that caused some major politicians, including **James Polk**'s Secretary of State **James Buchanan**, to support it. The impulse was opposed by **Whigs**, by **John Calhoun**, and even by Polk himself, although by the time **Winfield Scott** had taken the Mexican capital the president perhaps did favor more territorial acquisition than he had originally aimed for. The "All Mexico" claim was regarded as dangerous to the prospect of successful peace negotiations since, in the face of Mexico's understandable reluctance to concede all its territory, only further conflict and total victory would have delivered it. As it was, the movement peaked at the moment the Treaty of **Guadalupe Hidalgo** arrived in Washington, with 11 senators voting in favor of a treaty amendment proposed by Jefferson Davis pressing for a more extensive surrender of land by Mexico. However, fearing that this would prolong the war and potentially jeopardize the gains already made, six of the 11 were prevailed upon to support successful passage of the final treaty without the amendment, effectively ending the immediate relevance of the "All Mexico" impulse.

"ALL OREGON." This was the extreme expression of **Manifest Destiny** as it related to the Pacific Northwest coast of America in the first half of the 1840s. Prior to the **Oregon Treaty** settling the dispute with Britain over the boundary line through that territory, many

Americans expressed the desire that the line should be drawn along the **54° 40′** parallel, giving the United States the entire area under dispute. Although **John Tyler** advocated the demand in his 1843 annual message, the impulse derived its support mainly from **Democrats** from old Northwest states who were successful in having it adopted in their party's platform for the **election of 1844**. As well as drawing on genuine feelings of Manifest Destiny it was thought to provide a useful sectional balance to the demands made for **Texas annexation** at the same time. With individuals such as Secretary of State **James Buchanan** long in favor of an "All Oregon" settlement, it was hardly surprising that at various times in the tricky negotiations with Britain **James Polk**'s administration put this forward as their demand, both by direct communication with the British representatives and through press releases in the *Washington Union*. In Congress supporters such as David Atchison, William Allen, and **Lewis Cass** also proposed resolutions in support of "All Oregon" and called for urgent investigation of American military readiness should war be needed to achieve it. Polk's eventual willingness to accept a lesser compromise over the Oregon boundary threatened his private relations with some of these supporters and indeed with his own secretary of state, and although the treaty was accepted by the Senate over their opposition, many "All Oregon" supporters remained bitter at their apparent abandonment by the president and his seemingly greater willingness to support a southwestern expansion agenda.

ALLSTON, WASHINGTON (1779-1843). Allston was an important painter, credited with introducing the **romantic** art movement to the United States. Born in South Carolina and educated at Harvard, like so many native-born American artists of his day he traveled and worked largely in Europe. His most famous work, *Belshazzar's Feast*, was in progress throughout the Jacksonian era, interrupted by the need to produce smaller works on commission in order to make a living. However, some commissions Allston did not accept for political reasons, his dislike of **Andrew Jackson** causing him to turn down the opportunity to portray the Battle of New Orleans on the Capitol's rotunda in 1830. Allston was also among the early teachers of **Samuel Morse**.

"AMERICA." This national song, sung to tune of the British national anthem, was written by clergyman Samuel F. Smith in 1832 as a patriotic hymn by the name "My Country, 'tis of thee." It came close to becoming an American national anthem in this period.

AMERICAN AND FOREIGN ANTI-SLAVERY SOCIETY. This **abolitionist** organization was founded by the **Tappan** brothers in 1840 to represent a more gradualist approach to the attack on the institution of **slavery**. Its supporters had also fallen out with the **American Anti-Slavery Society** over the presence of **women** in active abolitionist ranks and the linking with abolition of the cause of women's suffrage.

AMERICAN ANTI-SLAVERY SOCIETY. This **abolitionist** organization was founded in Philadelphia by delegates from state and local abolition societies in December 1833. Their intention was to promote on a national level the new direct approach to the attack on **slavery**. By 1840 there were some 1,600 auxiliary bodies of the Society, with a membership of over 100,000. Its leading lights included **William Lloyd Garrison**, the **Tappan** brothers, Lewis and Arthur—the society's first president—and **Theodore Weld**. The Society developed a professional approach to its activities, with a network of agents across the North and an organized series of pamphlets and lecture tours to diffuse its ideas. It was one of the first bodies to use the power of **women** in its campaigns and it also drew upon the support and experiences of freed and fugitive slaves. Its main preferred tactic, of sending a large volume of abolitionist publications to the South, aroused the ire of southerners and provoked direct reaction against this "**incendiary mail.**" The mailing campaign's lack of substantial success weakened the society's impetus somewhat and its financial support withered in the wake of the **panic of 1837**. However, even after some leading members broke away to found the **American and Foreign Anti-Slavery Society**, the Society continued to represent an important arm of the abolition movement after 1839, including prominent figures such as Garrison, **Wendell Phillips**, **Lucretia Mott**, and John Brown.

AMERICAN COLONIZATION SOCIETY. This **anti-slavery** organization was founded in 1816 to provide for a gradual and compensated approach to the removal of **slavery** from the United States, by freeing slaves, shipping them to their ancestral continent, and paying compensation to their former masters. By the mid-1820s the Society had established the colony of Liberia for freed slaves on the west coast of Africa, with its capital Monrovia named after the American president of the time. The Society at this stage was supported by some later full-blown **abolitionists** such as **Benjamin Lundy** and **William Garrison**, as well as by many of the more prominent political figures of the time, including James Madison, Thomas Jefferson, James Monroe, **Henry Clay, Andrew Jackson, John Marshall, William Crawford,** and **Daniel Webster**. Politicians found colonization a more palatable (if not entirely realistic) approach to the **sectional** issue of slavery, not least because among the Society's supporters were numbered some southern slaveholders, in whose opinion it offered a solution to predicted future problems arising from the racial mix in a society of white former owners and freed slaves of African heritage.

However, in the 1830s the influence of colonization waned. It became clear that for many southerners the Society's activities were just a way of removing already free African-Americans rather than a part of a long-term campaign to rid the nation of slavery. In addition to this compromise of the Society's aims, in the 1830s it was squeezed from both sectional extremes: from southern **pro-slavers,** for whom any hint of hostility to slavery was anathema; and from abolitionists who considered colonization an inadequate and unfair approach to resolving the slavery question. Moreover, most free African-Americans were hostile to it as well. Although never entirely dropped as an idea—in 1832 Clay included colonization as one of the uses to which federal revenue **distributed** to the states could be put—it was soon overwhelmed by abolitionist calls for more drastic measures to end the institution of slavery. Ultimately inconsistency in its founding ideas, as well as practical problems such as a shortage of funds, meant that the Society proved of negligible influence in eroding the institution.

AMERICAN SYSTEM. This combination of policies designed to strengthen and diversify the United States economy, with a view to lessening its dependence upon foreign markets and suppliers, was most famously advocated in 1824 by **Henry Clay**, in the wake of the War of 1812 and the depression of 1819, both of which seemed to highlight the need for this kind of program. The main components of the system included a strong national bank; **protective tariffs** for domestic **manufacturing**—to lessen need for manufactured imports and to create home markets for raw materials and for the food needed to feed manufacturing workforces; and **internal improvements** projects, financed both federally and locally, to facilitate transportation of goods around the growing home market. The system's advocates enjoyed their greatest prominence during the administration of **John Quincy Adams**, between 1825 and 1829, in which Clay as secretary of state proved especially influential. However, the system continued to provide the inspiration for much of Clay's own political career throughout the 1830s and for the approach of the two political parties with which he was associated, the **National Republicans** and the **Whigs**.

At the same time the American System provided a focus for much of the criticism of nationalist approaches to federal governance and of accelerated economic development, with elements of the system being challenged, amended, or outright dismantled during the **Democratic** administrations of the 1830s. There were **tariff reductions in 1832 and 1833**, vetoes of improvements measures such as the **Maysville Road bill** in 1830 and the **Bank bill veto** in 1832.

This hostility caused Clay in particular to shift the emphasis of some of the system's elements. Constitutional qualms about federal funding of improvements could be met by molding the system to include the policy of **distributing** federal revenues to the states for them to apply to improvements projects of their choosing. Although still sympathetic enough to the idea of a national bank, Clay accepted the need to work more closely with the **deposit bank** system in the later 1830s. Even so the system remained a strong dream to many and some Whigs pinned their hopes on the election of **William Henry Harrison** and Whig congressional successes in 1840 as the harbinger of good prospects for all elements of the system. However, the choice of **John Tyler** as vice-president and his accession to the office of president after Harrison's death created tensions as he was a known opponent of the system. This, and the subsequent victory of Democrat **James Polk** in the **election of 1844**, represented the final nails in the coffin of the system insofar as this period was concerned.

AMERICAN TEMPERANCE SOCIETY. This **temperance** organization was one of the most successful reforming groups of the 1830s and 1840s in terms of membership numbers. However, its success in attracting members was never converted into effective moral persuasion of others to moderate or to give up their drinking, with the result that the Society, like other temperance groups, began to push for state and local legislation to discourage drinking.

AMISTAD. This celebrated episode had implications for the illegal international **slave trade** and attitudes toward **slavery** in the United States. In June 1839 the "slave" cargo of an illegal Spanish slaving ship, *Amistad*, mutinied during the final leg of a voyage that had carried them from Africa to Cuba. The vessel was waylaid by a U.S. warship off Long Island and was towed to New London in Connecticut, where the cause of the mutineers was taken up by **abolitionists** and their legal representatives. Calls came from Spain and the Spanish owners of the vessel for the return of their property, including the illegal slaves, on the grounds that the final leg of the voyage had been between two Cuban, and hence Spanish, ports, making them subject to Spanish rather than international maritime laws.

Martin Van Buren's administration concurred in this view and ordered the return of both ship and slaves without any need for recourse to legal action. When suits were brought on behalf of the mutineers a Connecticut court also agreed with the Spanish interpretation of the case, treating the slaves as salvage. However, the local federal court challenged this view, seeing through false claims that the mutineers were Cuban and declaring them to be free, on the grounds that even by Spanish law they should not have been carried from Africa in the first place.

When Van Buren refused to enforce this ruling, planning instead to extradite the mutineers to Cuba, the case was taken before the Supreme Court, where **John Quincy Adams** defended them. In 1841 the Court ruled that the slaves should be considered free on the grounds given by the original federal court, namely that under Spanish law the international slave trade was illegal. In the absence of a further ruling that it was the responsibility of the federal government to return them to Africa, the transportation of the remaining freed "slaves" back to their homeland was paid for out of leading abolitionists' pockets. Although a personal triumph for the freed Africans, and apparently a success for Adams and the abolitionist groups who sponsored him, the fact that the courts made constant reference to Spanish legal precedent rather than any grounds for attacking slave status in general on the basis of natural law, limited the **anti-slavery** impact of the episode.

ANTI-MASONIC PARTY. This political party emerged at a local level in 1827-28 out of the **Anti-Masonry** movement culture and became a strong national third party beside the **National Republican** and **Democratic** parties in the late 1820s and early 1830s. After growing success in state elections in 1830, with shares of just under 50 percent in some cases, the party decided to run its own candidate against **Andrew Jackson** in the **election of 1832**. After its first three choices, the Mason **Henry Clay**, the non-Mason **John Calhoun**, and **John McLean** all refused to issue statements hostile to Freemasonry, the party instead nominated **William Wirt** as its candidate for the presidency, with Amos Ellmaker as his running mate. Although Wirt only carried the state of Vermont, the party as a whole did win a good number of seats in the House of Representatives, some 10 percent of those it contested. Meanwhile, in state elections the party won good local victories in states like Rhode Island and New York and it even controlled the state governments in Vermont and Pennsylvania for a number of years.

In addition to the significance of its ideas and its status as a third party, the Anti-Masonic Party is often viewed as having popularized the business of party politics. It combined many of the emerging organizational and electoral tools championed by the Democrats with a campaigning style which owed much to the crusading zeal of **evangelical religion**, in the process becoming a genuine mass democratic movement. In addition it is credited with a number of procedural innovations, such as the first national convention at Philadelphia in 1830 and presidential nominating convention at Baltimore in 1831. These, and the rule that the successful candidate needed three-quarters of the votes, were seen as a better way to choose electoral candidates than the more secretive caucus-based methods that had prevailed to that time.

The popularity the party generated has been interpreted as a significant reason for the rise in electoral fortunes of the **Whig** Party, which would absorb many of the new voters politicized by the Anti-Masonic Party. Although the party was just as likely to challenge local National Republican as well as Democratic establishments, it was most lastingly influential in areas such as southern New England, Pennsylvania, and New York, providing one of the main conduits through which mass popular opposition to Jackson and the Democrats was channeled into the newly emerging Whig Party. Certainly many Anti-Masonic leaders began to play practical political games in order to win office, cooperating with the opposition to Jackson. As a result the party pretty well dissolved as a separate entity in 1834 when most of its leaders were absorbed into the Whig Party, the latter coming to share much of the same religiously inspired approach to political issues like **temperance**, education, **sabbatarianism**, and even **slavery**.

ANTI-MASONRY. This movement culture arose in upstate New York in the mid-to-late 1820s, in reaction to the supposed influence of **Freemasonry**. It was sparked off by the disappearance of William Morgan, allegedly murdered by Masons after he had threatened to expose details of their practices. There were also suspicions of the apparent complicity of local and state authorities as they dawdled in bringing to justice those suspected of Morgan's disappearance or murder. Appealing to **evangelized**, mainly rural communities, which responded to attacks on the alleged immorality and sacrilege of the Masons, Anti-Masonry broadened into a movement popular among all who were suspicious of exclusiveness, oppression, and the "establishment," whatever that might be in any particular locality. The ensuing Anti-Masonic campaigns through the efforts of newspapers, churches, and **anti-slavery** elements led to support for local political candidates who espoused Anti-Masonic views. From here it was a small step to the formation of the **Anti-Masonic Party**.

ANTI-PARTY FEELING. This was the longstanding conviction that partisan politics provided the antithesis of good politics and upright government. The argument ran that too great a reliance on party was thought to encourage demagoguery, corruption of officeholders, exploitation of the appointments system for the benefit of cronies and political supporters, and an insistence on party discipline. All of these undermined the sense that allowing men chosen on the basis of their natural talents to make independent decisions was the best means of ensuring proper debate in legislative circles and appropriate policy-making. Predictably, as the first party to rely more heavily on partisan organization and techniques, whether in elections or in government, the **Democratic** Party came in for greatest criticism from its opponents along these lines. In the campaign for the **election of 1836** in particular, the **Whig** attack was informed by an anti-party strand. It also formed part of the debate over the **Independent Treasury**, when **Conservative Democrats** railed against the use of party discipline to try to push the measure through. However, in both instances this was probably more tactical than a genuinely held principle, as Whigs would use many of the same party methods as the Democrats did, in 1840 and beyond.

ANTI-RENT MOVEMENT. The late 1830s and early 1840s witnessed a series of violent outbursts in parts of New York state that represented the final challenges to older, near feudal forms of land tenure. Issues of particular annoyance to tenants were the expectation that they should pay regular tributes to their landlords in the form of produce, money, or their own labor, and the payment of a fee when they sold on leasehold lands. Riots in 1839 and 1845 were denounced and pacified respectively by governors **William Seward** and **Silas Wright**, but the movement generated enough momentum to attempt to elect its own governor in 1846, while in the same year a state constitutional convention prohibited the establishment of any new feudal tenures, a move that quickly encouraged the conversion of old-style leases into new terms as well.

ANTI-SLAVERY. The general sense held by many Americans, initially in both North and South, that **slavery** was an unfortunate and ideologically inappropriate part of the American racial, political, social, and economic landscape. It held within it a whole range of responses to slavery, including individual and state efforts to emancipate slaves in northern states in the period before the Jacksonian era, individual acts of manumission in the South, and proposals for the compensated "repatriation" of slaves as espoused by the **American Colonization Society**. **Abolitionism** also fell within a broader definition of the spectrum of anti-slavery opinion, although the views, ambitions, and tactics of abolitionists were more extreme than those espoused by the majority of those who found slavery distasteful.

For some at the time, and subsequently for historians, anti-slavery came to assume a stricter definition, clearly distinct from abolitionism. This anti-slavery agenda was the mainly northern opposition to the expansion of slavery into those territories where it did not already exist. In part this opposition was founded on political motives, shaped by the desire to ensure that no or fewer new slave states would enter the Union bringing with them more representatives, senators, and electoral college votes for the slavery-based South. That region was felt already to be overrepresented because of the three-fifths clause in the Constitution which gave slave states higher representation in proportion to their voting public than free states enjoyed. Not surprisingly the anti-slavery stance ran head-first into the southern desire for a greater number of slave states and their resultant extra representative clout. As such anti-slavery became part of an increasingly **sectional** struggle, where the power of the federal government was sought for the purpose of pursuing issues, either directly related to the future of slavery or to others where it was felt that one section was thwarting the interests of the other. However, there were also moral and, especially, racial dimensions to the anti-slavery opposition to slavery's expansion, with some sharing the earlier sense of outrage at the existence of slavery and others themselves sharing, or pandering to, a mass view that western territories should be kept pure for white settlement.

As a political force, this brand of anti-slavery had been placed on the backburner by the **Missouri Compromise** of 1820-21, which had made provision for the status, free or slave, of all existing territories.

However, anti-slavery rose to prominence once more because of the **expansionist** drive during the 1840s, being intimately bound up with debates over **Texas annexation**, it being a state with slavery, and with the subsequent **Mexican War**, the fruits of which would re-awaken the issue of how to organize new territories. The anti-slavery view found expression in the **Wilmot Proviso** of 1846 and the **Free Soil** coalition in the **1848 election** campaign, and it would inform debates over the future territorial status of the **Oregon** and **New Mexico** territories. In sectional terms it was the one issue most likely to prove popular among northerners and to unite them in a way genuinely threatening to the interests of the South.

ARKANSAS, STATEHOOD. Arkansas entered the Union as the 25th state on 15 June 1836. Having attained separate territorial status in 1819, popular settlement had really taken off there in the late 1820s after agreements to remove branches of the Osage, **Cherokee**, and **Choctaw** tribes. From a level of just under 15,000 in 1820 the population rose to 50,000 by 1835, allowing the territory to petition for statehood. A convention framed a state constitution, which was accepted in the form received by Congress, albeit only after some debate about its clauses on **slavery**. Although all accepted that Arkansas would be a slave state, **anti-slavery** critics like **John Quincy Adams** queried clauses that forbade the state legislature from ever freeing slaves and from excluding slave importation from other states. From the point of view of maintaining the balance between different sections of the country it is interesting to note that the admission of Arkansas was mirrored on same day by the congressional act admitting **Michigan** to the Union although it would not be until January 1837 that that state actually entered the Union.

AROOSTOOK WAR. This bloodless crisis in 1838-39 represented a potentially dangerous deterioration of the **Maine boundary dispute**. In the face of stalled diplomatic initiatives, events in the disputed Aroostook valley took on their own momentum, as lumber interests on both sides of the border tried to take matters into their own hands. In 1838 New Brunswick lumberjacks entered the disputed territory, causing Maine authorities to send a posse to deal with what they considered trespassers. In response to this the governor of New Brunswick threatened to use force to expel the posse. Although the U.S. government had already made its own land grants in the area, Britain now began its own surveys and seized a U.S. land agent in February

1839. Both state and provincial governments sent militia troops and confrontation seemed a strong possibility.

Under considerable pressure to support the action of Maine, President **Martin Van Buren** instead adopted a conciliatory approach, condemning both the trespassing lumberjacks and the Maine authorities for taking things into their own hands without properly consulting either Washington or the governor of New Brunswick. He even suggested that he would support New Brunswick's action against the Maine posse, although not to the point of conceding anything over the ownership of the disputed territory, a question that remained to be decided by official means. To deflate the crisis both governments agreed that the Maine militia should withdraw, that New Brunswick should not try to force out the posse from Maine, and that in the future both local authorities should take joint responsibility for policing trespass. And while Congress authorized a 50,000 strong force to deal with the crisis, it too generally backed Van Buren's pacific approach.

To put flesh on this skeleton of agreement Van Buren ordered his successful trouble-shooter, General **Winfield Scott**, to the Aroostook region. He called meetings between the two parties and got them to agree to withdraw troops from the disputed territory. By effectively succeeding in having the agreement between Van Buren and the British government implemented by the parties on the ground, Scott brought to an end the immediate threat of war. However, further tension would remain as long as no solution to the dispute over territory was found, and when in late 1840 the Maine government, backed by several other U.S. states, called for the expulsion of British troops from the disputed area, some in Britain considered this as tantamount to a declaration of war. This resurgence of the dispute only pointed out further the need for the settlement that would eventually come about in the **Webster-Ashburton Treaty**.

ASSASSINATION ATTEMPT. An unsuccessful attempt was made on the life of President **Andrew Jackson** on 30 January 1835, by Richard Lawrence, a house painter. His pistols failed to fire properly.

ASTOR, JOHN JACOB (1763-1848). This German immigrant of poor background entered the Jacksonian age as one of the wealthiest Americans of his day. Astor carried on his economic pursuits in the far West until his retirement in 1834, when he sold off his fur trading interests there, but he still paid more than a passing interest in **expansion**. In 1835 he backed a settlement in Wisconsin, only to see it fail three years later. Even in retirement Astor maintained a prominent position, overseeing the construction of the Astor House hotel in New York City, which was opened in 1836. He was also an important philanthropist, giving money to the Astor library, the forerunner of the New York Public Library. He died leaving an estate of $20 million.

AUDUBON, JAMES (1785-1851). This ornithologist and artist, born in Santo Domingo, moved via France to the United States in the first decade of the 19th century. Audubon was most renowned for his numerous works illustrating the native birds of North America. Published originally in Edinburgh, Scotland, *The Birds of America*, four volumes of plate illustrations produced between 1827 and 1838, was accompanied by the *Ornithological Biography*, five volumes of commentary, written between 1831 and 1839. Later these two works came to be combined into a single publication, between 1841 and 1844, under the name *Birds of America*. Audubon had traveled extensively in North America in pursuit of materials for his illustrations, in 1829 to 1830, and again between 1831 and 1834, before settling permanently in the United States in 1839. He made one last research trip up the Missouri River in 1843 for his final work on *The Viviparous Quadrupeds of North America*, which was published between 1845 and 1854, despite the fact that severe illness and old age began to limit his activities from the mid-1840s.

AUSTIN, STEPHEN (1793-1836). This American of Virginian birth and Missourian background was among the first legal Anglo-American settlers in Texas, after periods of sojourn in Arkansas and Louisiana. An important landowner in his own right, Austin was a cautious advocate of moves toward **Texan independence**, having earlier been satisfied that Texas should stand as a separate state within Mexico. In 1833 he was delegated to go to Mexico City to call for self-government for Texas, and when rebuffed wrote to his colleagues urging them to go ahead anyway. For this action he was arrested and imprisoned for two years. When released in 1835 he joined the Texan revolution, first as a commander of volunteers and then as a commissioner to the United States government. Austin ran for the office of president of the newly independent republic of Texas in September 1836, but lost and instead served as secretary of state in **Sam Houston**'s Cabinet until his death.

– B –

BACHE, ALEXANDER (1806-1867). Although originally trained in a military career, this Philadelphian became a scientist and educator, specializing as a physicist and astronomer. Between 1828 and 1836 Bache served as professor of natural philosophy and chemistry at the University of Pennsylvania, before moving on to the presidency of Girard College between 1836 and 1842. He was also a leading figure in the American Philosophical Society and the Franklin Institute and a regent of the **Smithsonian Institution**. In 1843 Bache was appointed superintendent of the U.S. Coastal Survey, and in the following two years served on the Lighthouse Board and the Office of Weights and Measures. In all these posts he strove to professionalize the application of science to a range of activities. As an educational reformer he supported free public education in Philadelphia.

BADGER, GEORGE (1795-1866). Badger was a North Carolinian who followed a political course from Federalist leanings, through support for **Andrew Jackson**, to the **Whig** Party, helping to win his state for that party in the **election of 1840**. In 1841 **William Henry Harrison**, against the will of the Whig Party's leading figure **Henry Clay**, appointed Badger to the position of secretary of the navy in order to ensure a representative of the South Atlantic states in his Cabinet. Banking was the issue which seemed to shape his political career, since it was Jackson's attack on the **Second Bank of the United States** which caused Badger to desert him in 1834, while seven years later **John Tyler**'s veto of the **1841 bank bill** precipitated his resignation from the Cabinet along with most of his colleagues. Badger remained a significant figure in the North Carolinian Whig Party and in 1846-48 completed an unfinished term in the Senate. While there he expressed a Whiggish hostility to the **Mexican War** and when considering the Treaty of **Guadalupe Hidalgo** unsuccessfully proposed an amendment abandoning any thought of territorial acquisition from the war. He would be one of 14 who voted against the treaty in its final form. Despite some unlikely views, for his section, on slavery's expansion, including an acceptance that the **Wilmot Proviso** was a constitutional means for determining the issue, he was successful in securing reelection in 1848. *See also* CABINET RESIGNATION, 1841.

BALDWIN, MATHIAS (1795-1866). Baldwin was a manufacturer who played an important role in the development of several branches of engineering but who is best remembered for his contribution to the **railroad** industry. Born in New Jersey and serving an apprenticeship in Pennsylvania, he began working in jewelry-making and then textiles- and printing machinery and hydraulic processes. He next progressed to working on the development of stationary steam engines. In 1831-32 he built *Old Ironsides* for the Philadelphia, Germantown, and Norristown railroad, one of the first steam locomotives built in the United States for transportation purposes. The locomotive factory bearing his name became one of the most famous and significant producers of steam trains in the century to follow, selling to both domestic and overseas markets. Despite falling upon hard economic circumstances during the **panic of 1837**, taking a decade to clear his debts, Baldwin proved a generous philanthropist. He also dabbled in local politics and served on the Pennsylvania constitutional convention in 1837, taking a firm position against any thought of **suffrage** restriction.

BALTIMORE AND OHIO RAILROAD. This project represented one of the first efforts to build a **railroad** in order to challenge the influence of **canals** (and especially of the **Erie Canal**). Conceived in the late 1820s, and with its foundation stone laid by Charles Carroll of Carrolton in 1828, the Baltimore and Ohio was a system of tracks linking Baltimore with Washington and with the Maryland and Virginia backcountry. By 1830 the first section of track, some 13 miles to Ellicott Mills, was completed, with further progress to Frederick, Maryland, by the following year. The line reached Harpers Ferry, Virginia, in 1834 and a year later tracks were ready to begin services between Baltimore and the nation's capital. By 1842 the line was completed as far as Cumberland. Although initially using horse-drawn carriages, the Baltimore and Ohio was one of the first to promote the use of moving steam locomotives, giving trials to among others *Tom Thumb*. The railroad was also notable for being the first to convey a president, **Andrew Jackson**, who traveled by one of the company's trains in 1833.

BANCROFT, GEORGE (1800-1891). One of the most prominent men to emerge from the age, Bancroft combined an early career as a schoolteacher with work as a historian and politician for the **Democratic** Party in Massachusetts. After being educated at Harvard and Göttingen in Germany, he had founded a school in Northampton in 1823. He worked there until he began writing his *History of the United States* in 1831, publishing the first three volumes in 1834,

1837, and 1840 respectively. This work marked Bancroft out as one of the greatest of the **Romantic** historians. Combining close use of primary sources with a good narrative he conveyed a history of America shaped by the ordinary people's struggle for freedom. This sympathy for the people's sound judgment extended to his personal beliefs. Although willing to engage in a range of speculative financial pursuits and being himself aristocratic by temper, with friends among the Boston elite, he did favor the influence of a "natural aristocracy" of talent rather than breeding.

These views marked Bancroft out as one of the few Boston intellectuals who leaned toward the party of **Andrew Jackson**, and despite connections with the Boston **Workingmen's** Party (in 1830 he was elected to the Massachusetts legislature by them—he declined to serve), with the **National Republicans** (he attended their convention in Worcester, Massachusetts in 1831), and with the **Anti-Masonic Party**, by 1832 he was clearly aligned with the **Democrats**. He wrote articles sympathetic to Jacksonian aspirations, attacking the **Second Bank of the United States** in the *North American Review* in 1830-31, and he would continue to write for Democratic journals such as **John O'Sullivan**'s *Democratic Review* and the *Boston Quarterly*. Bancroft formed part of Marcus Morton's faction within the Massachusetts Democratic Party, opposing the leadership of **David Henshaw**. Indeed, in 1835 Bancroft proved unsuccessful in a challenge to Henshaw's position as party candidate for state governor. However, three years later he was rewarded with the position of Collector of the port of Boston when the Morton faction prevailed over Henshaw. He would later fail to win the gubernatorial election in his state in 1844.

It was in the 1840s that Bancroft attained national political prominence. At the Democratic nominating convention for the **election of 1844**, he attended as a supporter of the candidacy of **Martin Van Buren**, but, fearing that the New Yorker would lose out to **Lewis Cass**, switched his support to **James Polk**. Indeed it is almost certainly the case that Bancroft was one of those delegates who put forward **Young Hickory**'s name in the first place. His reward was the Cabinet position of navy secretary, in which post he helped to establish the Naval Academy at Annapolis and gave orders for naval support for the **Bear Flag revolt** in California. As further reward for his loyal service he was appointed to his long-cherished position of U.S. Minister to Great Britain in 1848. Throughout his career he put loyalty to party foremost and in 1848 demonstrated this once again when, despite **Barnburner** leanings and personal support for Van

Buren, he backed Cass, the regular Democratic candidate for the presidency.

BANK BILL AND VETO, 1832. In 1832 **Andrew Jackson** refused to approve a bill re-chartering the **Second Bank of the United States**, passed by Congress four years before the Bank's old charter was due to expire in 1836. The veto was presaged by doubts expressed in Jackson's earlier annual messages to Congress and by attempts by among others **Thomas Hart Benton** to introduce congressional resolutions against re-charter. But supporters of the Bank had brought forward the re-charter effort in order to call Jackson's bluff, in anticipation that he would not risk so rash an action as a veto in the year of his potential reelection. Negative committee reports on the Bank's conduct were generally sidelined, although the Bank's supporters did introduce amendments into the new charter, in the hope of meeting some of the criticisms being brought forward. The new charter would only last for 15 years, the nation's president could appoint a director to the board of each of the Bank's branches, and the Bank's branching and note-issue powers would be limited.

Despite comfortable majorities in the bill's favor in Congress, Jackson stood firm and vetoed the re-charter bill, primarily on the grounds of his strong constitutional doubts as to whether Congress had the power to establish a national bank. The president was vindicated by the failure of the bill's supporters to override the veto in Congress and by success in the **election of 1832** that followed. In the process Jackson set down new standards for use of the presidential veto, more as an instrument of executive law-making (or breaking), with the result that he opened himself up to accusations of **executive usurpation**. The precedent set by his action and the rhetoric he used in his **bank veto message** also shaped the battleground for subsequent **bank wars** and for political developments leading to the emergence of the **second party system** over the course of the next decade.

BANK BILL AND VETO, 1841. **Henry Clay**'s presentation of a bill to charter a new national bank reenergized the **bank wars** at a national level. In line with his long-term policy preference for a national bank as part of the **American System**, Clay hoped to make use of the **Whig** Party's success in both presidential and congressional **elections in 1840** to press through a new bank in the **special session** of 1841, in the process bringing full circle national policy on the issue after **Andrew Jackson**'s **bank veto** in 1832 and the demise of the **Second Bank of the United States** in 1836. Clay's proposal, put forward in direct challenge to the Treasury-sponsored **Fiscal Corporation bill**, was for a bank, based in Washington, D.C. and created by the national government, unlike the rival bill which would have had Congress establish the fiscal corporation as a function of its position as the governing body within the District of Columbia. Clay's proposal gave to the bank unfettered power to establish branches in the states.

Unfortunately for Clay, not all Whigs shared his desire for such a bank and, most significantly of all, President **John Tyler** had advised that such a contentious issue should be given more time for debate and had warned that he would veto any bill which gave him grounds for constitutional qualms. The power of the national government to create a bank with unchecked branching powers was precisely the sort of thing that gave him such doubts. Others suspected Clay of having purely political motives, seeking to strengthen his position within the Whig Party at the expense of the president, either by succeeding in passing the bill or by being in a position to attack Tyler should he veto it. Nevertheless, after fierce debate which saw attempts led by Tyler Whigs and former **Conservative Democrats** to restrict the bank's power to establish state branches, Whig majorities in the Senate and House passed the bank bill in late July and early August 1841 respectively. It ended up including the slight modification that individual states could legislate against a branch being established in their jurisdiction. But still the power to create branches was fairly strong, since a state's consent to the establishment of a bank branch was to be assumed unless, and until, the next elected state legislature voted against the branch, and even then Clay insisted on a further proviso that Congress would have the power to overrule any specific state refusal, should it deem this necessary and proper.

This proved too strong a power for Tyler, who, against the advice of his Cabinet, vetoed the bill on the grounds that the branching powers were unconstitutional. Thereafter the bank bill crisis shifted to consideration of the Fiscal Corporation bill, originally proposed by the Treasury and then amended by Congress. The whole episode created great anger within Whig ranks, especially as Clay had been mistakenly informed that Tyler would accept the bill as originally passed. Rather than strengthening the president's position, as Tyler thought it would, his veto led to fragmentation among Whigs, the **Cabinet resignation** of fall 1841, and Tyler's drumming out of the party.

BANK OF THE UNITED STATES. *See* SECOND BANK OF THE UNITED STATES.

BANK VETO MESSAGE. The message accompanying **Andrew Jackson**'s veto of the **bank bill of 1832** has come to be regarded as something of a polemic in which he and his closest advisors, such as **Amos Kendall** and **Roger Taney**, set out many of the principles underlying their philosophy of government, society, and the economy. For them, as well as simply being unconstitutional, the **Second Bank of the United States**, as chartered, represented a dangerous private monopoly despite being a national institution. Its stockholders, including foreign elements, potentially were in a position to corrupt the government by association. Moreover, the Bank was accused of acting prejudicially against Americans in southern and western states for the benefit of those in the Northeast. Generally the veto message encapsulated **Jacksonian Democracy**'s self-proclaimed attack on privilege, elitism, and aristocracy, and rang with great appeal to the many Americans who were suspicious of the direction in which the **market revolution** was taking the country and of the ways in which many politicians and businessmen were managing that revolution.

BANK WARS. For many contemporaries and historians the wars over banking were the defining political battle of the Jacksonian era. They were sparked off when **Andrew Jackson** issued his **bank veto of 1832**, an action that ushered in a period of conflict between his administration and the **Second Bank of the United States**. Further battles in the wars were Jackson's **removal of the federal deposits** from the Bank's control, in favor of a new system of state **deposit banks**, and **Nicholas Biddle**'s retaliatory contraction of credit, the latter action only serving to harden Jackson's stance still further and to increase the unpopularity of the Bank. The whole affair aroused passions on both sides, especially for those opposing the Bank, who reflected upon its earlier apparently pernicious influence in the panic of 1819. Moreover, for many the affair played on their suspicion of all banks, reinforcing their sense that banks were the creation of legal privilege, that through their control of the **credit system** they allowed a few to make artificial wealth at the expense of the many, and that banks generally represented a corrupting influence in society.

The result was that in the late 1830s debates over banking started to define the political agenda at both state and national levels, especially in the wake of the **overbanking** of the mid-1830s and the **panics of 1837 and 1839** and their consequences. **Democrats**' responses to these developments ranged from banning banks altogether, through regulating state banks more stringently in terms of their activity in issuing notes, to the idea of creating a monopoly for state-run banks.

Whigs on the other hand preferred free banking measures, by general incorporation laws. In so doing they adopted the idea espoused by some Democrats that specially chartered banks were impolitic, but were willing to offer the opportunity to create banks under much laxer terms of regulation than Democrats were prepared to accept. To some extent the wider hostility of many Democrats to all banks was mirrored at the national level, with attempts during the administrations of **Martin Van Buren** and **James Polk** to create an **Independent Treasury** by which to divorce the federal government from all private banking institutions. The Whigs carried the fight on into the late 1830s and 1840s with attempts initially to defend the deposit bank system once it came under attack from Independent Treasury proposals, and later to reinstate some form of national bank, with the **bank bill of 1841** a prominent example.

As well as providing a framework of issues that shaped the political narrative of the 1830s and much of the 1840s the banking issue, with its accompanying debates over currency and **executive usurpation**, played an important part in the emergence of the **second party system**. These issues forced politicians of both parties to consider where their party stood, causing the defection of many from one party to the other. This happened more commonly with supporters of Jackson, as each new shot in the battles gave Jacksonian supporters first of the national bank, then of the credit system generally, and finally of state banks, reason to feel more comfortable allied with or in the ranks of the emerging Whig Party. The banking issue also helped to create a truly national party system, with two-party politics emerging over banking issues in states and communities where previously party splits had been limited. Finally it brought new levels of popular involvement in the political issues of the day, as the people's experiences, positive and negative, came to be interpreted in terms of the impact of banks, of the credit system, and of the broader **market revolution**.

BANKRUPTCY ACT, 1841. Debate over this issue, already much discussed since the early days of the new nation, was given extra urgency by the level of debt and bankruptcy in the wake of the **panics of 1837 and 1839**. In 1837 **Martin Van Buren** had called for a bankruptcy law for corporations, hoping that the threat of punishment after a short period of suspension of specie payments would help to check the excessive issue of notes by banks and generally impose upon them some degree of responsible control. However, the House Judiciary Committee dismissed his proposal and the president did not repeat his call for it in the 1837-38 congressional session. He again suggested it in his 1839 annual message, in the wake of the panic of 1839, this leading to a full debate on a bankruptcy bill in 1840. This time southerners of both parties joined with northern **Whigs** in opposing such a bill, largely on the grounds of concern over **states' rights**. In the **special session** of summer 1841 the Whigs sponsored a measure, supported by both **Daniel Webster** and **Henry Clay**, providing for voluntary and compulsory bankruptcy, this time excluding banking corporations from its provisions. It was passed by the Senate in July 1841 but only passed the House after a log-roll in which western and eastern representatives agreed to support each other on bankruptcy and **distribution** respectively. As proof of its largely emergency nature, however, the act was repealed 18 months later.

BARING, ALEXANDER (1774-1848). Baring was a member of the British Baring bank company as well as a member of Parliament for various constituencies at one time or another. He also had served as president of the Board of Trade in 1834, which had enhanced his interest in foreign economic issues and Anglo-American relations in particular. In 1842, as Lord Ashburton, he was appointed special representative to the United States, sent to Washington to treat on a range of outstanding Anglo-American issues, in particular the **Canadian boundary**. Married to an American and being a personal friend of U.S. Secretary of State **Daniel Webster**, who had carried out some legal work for the Baring company, Baring was a highly suitable candidate for the job. Their good working relationship culminated in the **Webster-Ashburton Treaty** and several accompanying exchanges of letters, which successfully resolved most of the issues.

BARNBURNERS. These were a faction of the New York **Democratic Party** in the 1840s, associated with **Silas Wright** and **Martin Van Buren**. They leaned to their party's more radical side in their hostility to banks and to an increased state debt, opposing the more conservative line adopted by their rivals, the **Hunkers**. During the **James Polk** administration they formed part of a bitter struggle for official preferment in the patronage battles over Cabinet, state, and local positions. Although Polk was keen to keep the Barnburners sweet, nothing he offered seemed quite good enough for them, reinforcing the sense that he favored their Hunker rivals instead. Later in the decade they became involved in the evolving **free soil** movement. In 1848 the Democratic national convention refused to seat the Barnburner delegation, and so they met in a separate state convention in Utica.

There they nominated Van Buren for president and played a part in moves to establish him as the Free Soil candidate for the **election of 1848**. Polk's response was to attack them by making showcase removals of some of their number from office, notably **Benjamin Butler**.

BARNUM, P. T. (1810-1891). This Connecticut-born showman began his working life as a shop clerk and newspaper editor, before embarking on his career of sensational demonstrations from the mid-1830s. His first real money-spinner came in the form of a slave who was reputedly the nurse of George Washington. Then in 1842 Barnum founded his American Museum in New York, based on Scudder's American Museum purchased the previous year. It was now that he was introduced to his most famous exhibit, General Tom Thumb, whose tours in America and, in 1844, to England helped to make Barnum's fortune. He returned to New York City and a life of celebrity in 1848.

BARRY, WILLIAM TAYLOR (1785-1835). Barry was a Kentuckian attracted to the **Andrew Jackson** banner in the 1820s. He was motivated by his hostility to his fellow Kentuckian, **Henry Clay**, especially in the wake of the **"corrupt bargain"** accusations, but Barry was also sympathetic to the anti-bank, debt relief movement that afforded Jackson so much western support. He was a friend of two of that movement's important backers in Kentucky, **Amos Kendall** and **Francis Blair**, and would sponsor the latter's establishment of the administration newspaper organ, the *Washington Globe*, with official patronage. At the beginning of Jackson's first term Barry was considered as a possible nominee for a seat on the Supreme Court, but instead very early on replaced Jackson's first postmaster general, **John McLean**, effectively exchanging places with him as McLean became a justice. At the Post Office Barry became the first in his position to attain Cabinet status, but he was to become the focus of accusations of applying the principles of the **"spoils system"** too liberally in granting the significant levels of patronage at his disposal. In addition, his later tenure brought further concerns about growing annual deficits, poor record-keeping, and, at worst, suggestions of outright personal corruption. Under pressure of legislative scrutiny, with both **Whig**-dominated Senate and **Democrat**-dominated House producing hostile reports of the management of his department, Barry declared his readiness to resign in 1835.

That he had remained in office so long no doubt owed much to his stance as a Jackson loyalist. Barry was the only officer to survive the first major **Cabinet reshuffle** in 1831, by remaining loyal to Jackson, **John Eaton**, and **Martin Van Buren** and hostile to **John Calhoun** throughout the **Eaton Affair**. Also, although personally lukewarm to the decision to attack the **Second Bank of the United States**, he supported Jackson throughout, out of personal loyalty and out of the conviction that the attack would bring electoral benefit to their party. He died *en route* to Spain, where he had been appointed U.S. Minister after his resignation from the Post Office.

BEAR FLAG REVOLT. This popular revolt against Mexican rule in **California** became entangled with the U.S.-**Mexican War** in 1846-47. In January 1846 rebels of mainly American origin, although with some Mexican settlers as well, rose up in the Sacramento valley and proclaimed the separate Bear Flag republic at Sonoma. The rebels joined up with explorers **John Frémont** and **Kit Carson**, and later with U.S. forces fighting the Mexican War, headed by **Commodore John Sloat**. This U.S. involvement disgruntled Mexican Californians who now revolted in turn against the Bear Flag rebels and reestablished Mexican control in southern California. But this resistance was ended when **Stephen Kearny** took Los Angeles in 1847 and forced the Mexican capitulation at **Cahuenga**.

BEECHER, CATHARINE (1800-1878). The daughter of **Lyman Beecher**, Catharine was an important figure in her own right in the fields of education and reform of the role of **women**. After working in Hartford, Connecticut, in a school she had founded in 1823, she moved on in 1831 to establish a succession of other schools for young women in Cincinnati (when her father moved to the city to work at the **Lane Seminary**), Quincy (Illinois), Milwaukee, and Burlington (Iowa). As an experienced teacher she was well qualified to produce a series of educational textbooks and at one point collaborated on the writing of the **McGuffey Eclectic Readers**. Meanwhile, her 1841 publication *Treatise on Domestic Economy* issued a call for what would now be called "domestic feminism," assigning a strong place for women in domestic affairs and an ancillary role in wider society. Generally she advocated a more powerful role for women of her time, including specifically the running of family finances, although this would be instead of participation in more traditionally productive activities, many of which were now being carried out by men in the context of paid employment. In her *Suggestions Respect-*

ing Improvements in Education (1829) and *Essay on the Education of Women* (1835) she stressed the importance of women being well educated in order to be able to raise their children more effectively.

BEECHER, LYMAN (1775-1863). Beecher was the famous father of famous daughters, Harriet Beecher Stowe, author of *Uncle Tom's Cabin* among other works, and **Catharine Beecher**. A Yale graduate and Presbyterian clergyman, he served as pastor of the Hanover Street Church in Boston until 1832, before moving to Cincinnati where he became president of the **Lane Theological Seminary** as well as pastor of the Second Presbyterian Church of Cincinnati, a post he held until 1842. In the theological disputes of his day Beecher fell into the "New School" of Presbyterian doctrine. Convinced that spiritual redemption had the power to transform both the individual and society, he supported a full range of the reform movements emerging out of the religious revivalist fervor of his time, including the American Bible Society, the Tract Society, the American Temperance Union in 1840, and **anti-slavery** movements such as the **American Colonization Society**. That said, he opposed outright **abolitionism** as a danger to national unity, and it was his refusal to countenance abolitionism at Lane that led to the departure of **Theodore Weld** and the establishment of **Oberlin College**. Beecher's staunch anti-**Catholicism** was thought to have contributed to the attack on the **Ursuline convent** in Charlestown in 1834.

BELL, JOHN (1797-1869). Bell's political career mirrored the experience of many whose early allegiances were strained by the policy choices and personal ambitions of the age. As a Tennessean senator and representative in Congress between 1827 and 1841 he started as a firm supporter of **Andrew Jackson** and of several of his early measures. In 1830 he backed the joint package of **Indian removal** and vetoes of **internal improvement** measures such as the **Maysville Road bill** and two and half years later he approved Jackson's stance in the **Nullification crisis**, being among the few **Democrats** who supported the passage of the **Force Act** in February 1833. However, he only reluctantly backed Jackson's decision to veto the **bank bill of 1832** and it would be the issue of banking, and specifically the **removal of the federal deposits**, which prompted his drift away from the president in 1834. Later that year he defeated the Jacksonian candidate in the election for speaker of the House, a position he contested on a regular, if not always successful, basis in the years to follow.

Bell began to lead **Whig** moves to challenge **Martin Van Buren**'s presidential aspirations in Jackson's home state of Tennessee, backing the southern Whig candidacy of **Hugh Lawson White** in 1836 and **William Henry Harrison** in 1840. As a reward for these efforts he was appointed to the position of secretary of war in Harrison's Cabinet, but resigned a few months later along with most of his colleagues in response to **John Tyler**'s vetoes of the **bank bill** and **fiscal corporation bill** of 1841. After six years out of national office, during which time he continued his personal struggle against the Democratic Party in Tennessee by opposing the ambitions of his bitter rival **James Polk**, he returned to Congress in 1847 for the first of two terms as a senator. His greatest political moment would come after this period in 1860 when he stood as the presidential candidate of the Constitutional Union Party, albeit unsuccessfully. *See also* CABINET RESIGNATION, 1841.

BENEVOLENT EMPIRE. This was the name applied to a range of voluntary interdenominational associations that emerged out of the **evangelical** fervor of the second quarter of the 19th century. For many evangelical preachers, a key sign of God's grace was a person's benevolence to others. This created an activist approach to the individual and to society as a whole, with the aim of saving sinners or creating social conditions and attitudes which made it more difficult for sin to flourish. Drawing on most Protestant groups, but especially from the ranks of Presbyterians and **Congregationalists**, benevolent reform was manifested in a variety of bodies. Among the key examples to share this approach were the American Bible Society, the American Tract Society, the American Education Society and Sunday School Union, and various home and foreign mission societies. However, later reform movements such as the **abolitionists**, **temperance** societies, and other groups targeting dueling and excessive public entertainment were also inspired by the same guiding ideas.

BENNETT, JAMES GORDON (1795-1872). Bennett was a Scottish migrant who made his way to the United States via Canada, to become one of the most influential newspaper editors of his day. Together with James Watson Webb he developed the Jacksonian party organ, the *New York Courier and Enquirer*, in 1829, but then resigned when Webb sided with the opposition party in 1832. Three years later Bennett established the *New York Herald*, an example of the **"penny press."** The standard of the paper's journalism and news coverage, allied to a degree of sensationalist reporting, made it an instant success with high circulation levels. Among other innovations he introduced was the use of dedicated correspondents based in Europe to supply international news. At this time Bennett was noted for his apolitical, non-partisan approach to presenting news and editorial comment, this reflecting his own political meanderings as he supported, over the course of time, **Democrats Andrew Jackson** and **James Polk** and **Whigs William Henry Harrison** and **Zachary Taylor**. He did find a political constant, though, in his support for American **expansion**, believing that **Manifest Destiny** reflected the nation's best interests.

BENTON, THOMAS HART (1782-1858). Benton was an important political figure of the Jacksonian age, whose *Thirty Years View* of events in the Senate has proven an invaluable source for scholars studying the era ever since. With a background in North Carolina and Tennessee, Benton moved to Missouri and represented his new state in the Senate between 1821 and 1851. His own policy preoccupations dovetailed nicely with the developing political agenda of the early Jacksonian period, allowing him to become one of the most influential administration leaders in Congress.

Benton was a particularly strong advocate of **land policies** to make disposal of federal lands a quicker and cheaper process for true settlers. But more significantly at virtually every point in the **bank wars** and battles over financial policy he found himself leading **Democratic** efforts in Congress: as early as February 1831 he had proposed resolutions advising against any re-charter of the Bank; he supported **Andrew Jackson**'s initial attack on the **Second Bank**'s re-charter move; he stood firmly in favor of **"hard money,"** being keen to increase the amount of specie in circulation in the economy, and to this effect pushed for a congressional resolution demanding that certain levels of payments to the federal government be payable only in specie; and, when that failed, he helped Jackson draft this measure as an executive-ordered **Specie Circular** in July 1836. These efforts earned Benton his enduring nickname of "Old Bullion." He also supported the **bankruptcy** bill in the midst of the **panic of 1837**, and backed **Martin Van Buren**'s administration's attempts to create a system for depositing federal revenues in an **Independent Treasury**. However, in a clear expression of his priorities Benton opposed the **Polk** administration's **1846 Independent Treasury** bill on the grounds that it allowed for too great an element of federal paper currency.

While never entirely sure of his personal relationship with Jackson, after an earlier fracas, Benton proved a loyal supporter of both the Tennessean and Van Buren. As the new decade dawned the removal of both these figures and **Whig** electoral successes in 1840 left Benton struggling to adjust to a changing political landscape. He worried about the rise of new issues and of former rivals such as **John Calhoun**, which seemed to threaten the party system and **sectional** harmony of the 1830s. Although personally in favor of **expansion**, as revealed by his support for a tough stand in talks over **Oregon** and his disappointment when the **Webster-Ashburton Treaty** failed to settle that matter, Benton opposed the accelerated drive toward **Texas annexation** during **John Tyler**'s term, suspecting that it was inspired by a combination of the president's personal ambition and a slaveholders' conspiracy. He was prominent in opposing the annexation treaty when it came before the Senate in 1844 and, after helping to defeat the treaty, it was Benton who proposed the resolution in the Senate that annexation should not take place until a new treaty had been negotiated.

Although personally lukewarm to the **Mexican War**, Benton's stance on that issue came to be mixed up with familial issues, as he was unhappy with the treatment of his son-in-law **John Frémont** and his own failure to be made a lieutenant-general in the U.S. army in order to help with the peace negotiations. Not surprisingly he voted against the Treaty of **Guadalupe Hidalgo** when it came before the Senate. As Congress struggled to deal with the sectional consequences of the territorial acquisitions of the war Benton strove for moderation, opposing both the **Wilmot Proviso** and extreme calls for the aggressive expansion of **slavery** into the territories. Ultimately this caused him to maintain his loyalty to the Democratic Party, for although he initially supported the candidacy of Van Buren for the **election of 1848**, he chose to back the decision to nominate **Lewis Cass** rather than to follow Van Buren into the ranks of the **Free Soil** coalition.

BERRIEN, JOHN (1781-1856). Berrien was a wealthy Georgian planter whose political background lay first in the Federalist Party and then as a Senate supporter of **William Crawford**. It was through this latter association that Berrien swung into **Andrew Jackson**'s coalition during the campaign for the **election of 1828**, expressing his distaste for a number of aspects of the administration of **John Quincy Adams**. As a jurist, and perhaps more importantly as a strong supporter of the policy of **Indian removal**, he appealed to

Jackson as a candidate for the office of attorney general, that department likely to be busy handling the legal ramifications of the removal question. He served in that office until the break-up of the Cabinet in the wake of the **Eaton Affair**. He had refused to have anything to do with **Peggy Eaton**, arousing the president's ire, but perhaps more significantly his background and attitudes on the **tariff, states' rights**, and **slavery** inclined him toward Vice-President **John Calhoun** and against **Martin Van Buren**, this being equally likely to have weakened his standing in the president's eyes. After completing negotiations with the **Cherokee** tribes, he resigned under considerable personal pressure in June 1831, and would soon be seen enlisting in the **Whig** camp, running losing campaigns for the Senate in 1833 and 1837 before finally winning elections to that body in 1840 and again in 1846. While in the Senate he belied some of his earlier principles and his sectional background by following a fairly regular Whig Party line in favor of policies such as **Henry Clay**'s **bank** and **distribution bills of 1841** and the **tariff of 1842**, while opposing **Texas annexation, James Polk**'s approach to the **Oregon** boundary, and the **Mexican War**.

BIDDLE, NICHOLAS (1786-1844). Although never in elective office Biddle was one of the most influential opposition figures in the Jacksonian era. As president of the **Second Bank of the United States** from 1823 to its demise as a federally chartered institution in 1836, he was in the forefront of the most significant policy and party battle of the period. It was his efforts to secure the re-charter of the Bank that precipitated the first phase of the **bank wars** of the decade, when **Andrew Jackson** vetoed the congressional bill to re-charter. From that point on, Biddle pursued a range of policy options that pushed the struggle over the Bank to still more bitter levels. It is much debated whether he acted on the basis of his assessment of economic necessity or out of a desire to apply political pressure after Jackson's decision to **remove the federal deposits**, but Biddle's decision in 1833 to rein in the actions of local banks by calling upon them to redeem their notes in full caused a short-lived economic panic and only further roused the anger of the president, making the battle in part a personal one in Jackson's eyes.

Even after the Bank lost its federal status, Biddle continued to exercise influence as president of the **United States Bank of Pennsylvania**. In the midst of the **panic of 1837**, when most of the banks of the Northeast were forced to suspend specie payments, Biddle awoke painful memories of his earlier actions of 1833-34 by calling for banks to refrain from resuming the payments. His hope was that the economic impact of such a stance would increase the political pressure for a rescinding of the **Specie Circular** and for the abandonment of plans to divorce federal revenues from all banks. Finally in the **panic of 1839** Biddle's bank was forced to suspend specie payments again after he failed to manipulate cotton prices to keep the economy solvent. In the wake of this he gave up his presidency of the Bank in 1839, but remained central to its management until its demise in 1841, even being arrested (but later exonerated) on charges of criminal conspiracy connected to the Bank's declining fortunes. Late in his life Biddle hankered, unsuccessfully, for a diplomatic posting from **William Henry Harrison**'s administration, preferably to Austria, and supported **Texas annexation**, having made considerable investments in land in that state.

BINGHAM, GEORGE CALEB (1811-1879). This Virginia-born painter moved to Missouri in 1819 and it would be there that he settled down to his career in art, after brief periods studying in Philadelphia at the Pennsylvania Academy of Fine Arts in 1837 and in New York City in 1838. He specialized in painting western scenes for eastern audiences, usually portraying his subjects in a lyrical and serene form, such as in *Fur Traders Descending the Missouri* (1845), the *Jolly Flatboatmen* (1846), and *Raftsmen Playing Cards* (1847). He also served as a **Whig** member of the Missouri legislative body.

BIRNEY, JAMES (1792-1857). Birney was notable as the man who in 1840 ran as the presidential candidate of the first explicitly **abolitionist** political party, the **Liberty Party**. A man of Kentuckian roots, he was the son of a slaveholder who had lived in Alabama for some years. In 1832 he sold his inheritance of slaves and returned to Kentucky, later moving to Ohio, New York, and Michigan. Initially he favored a more moderate approach to the **slavery** question and had acted as an agent of the **American Colonization Society**, before being converted to support for the more immediate form of abolitionism preached by **Theodore Weld**. Birney established the Kentucky Anti-Slavery Society before his move to Ohio where he published the Cincinnati abolitionist newspaper *The Philanthropist* in 1836. In 1837 he became executive secretary of the **American Anti-Slavery Society**. By the late 1830s he had begun to fall out with **William Lloyd Garrison** over the issue of **women**'s rights. As Birney was also calling for direct political action on the slavery question he was a fitting choice when nominated for president by the Liberty Party's convention at Albany in April 1840. He secured 7,000 votes in the ensuing election. Four years later, after he had worked as a land agent in Michigan for three years, losing in that state's gubernatorial election in 1842, he ran for the presidency again, securing more than 63,000 votes this time around.

BLACK HAWK (1767-1838). A Sauk chief, by the native name Ma-ka-tae-mish-kia-kiak, Black Hawk had been a consistent opponent of continuing American **expansion** into the Midwest and of the resultant **Indian removal**. Having repudiated a number of earlier treaties which had ceded lands in Illinois, and having fought alongside the British in the War of 1812, in 1832 he led followers back into lands supposedly ceded to the United States in the wake of the war. His action aroused the hostility of local American settlers and precipitated the **Black Hawk War**. Black Hawk himself was captured and sent to Washington to meet President **Andrew Jackson**. Thereafter Black Hawk settled on an Iowan reservation with the remnants of his tribe, until his death.

BLACK HAWK WAR. This was one of several examples of violent resistance to the policy of **Indian removal**. In 1830 the federal government signed a treaty with the Sac and Fox tribes, designed to secure their removal from their traditional lands in northwest Illinois and southwest Wisconsin to new lands in Iowa. Although many had accepted this cession, after the harsh winter of 1831-32 **Black Hawk** of the Sauk tribe led some 2,000 followers back to Illinois, with the aims of planting crops and forging a military alliance with other tribes such as the Winnebagos. The Illinois government response was to raise a militia force that fired on Black Hawk when he attempted to surrender. The ensuing native retaliation sparked off the conflict, as regular U.S. army troops, led by Henry Atkinson, combined with 4,000 in militia units, led by Henry Dodge, to chase down starving natives. Black Hawk himself continued attacking frontier settlements but at the same time was making suits for peace, approaches the Americans simply ignored. After some 15 weeks, Black Hawk was defeated in late July 1832 and then early in the next month most of the remaining natives were slaughtered trying to cross the Mississippi River, leaving the 150 survivors to join their tribes in Iowa. The war ended when Black Hawk surrendered at Prairie du Chien. While the war ensured the future pacification of the region, encouraging the safer development of the community of **Chicago**, for many since then the war was most notable for the presence of **Zachary Taylor**, and future Civil War presidents Jefferson Davis and Abraham Lincoln among those who prepared to fight in the U.S. ranks.

BLAIR, FRANCIS PRESTON (1791-1876). A Kentuckian journalist and politician, of Virginian birth, Blair became a leading figure in the **Democratic** Party. His earlier stance in Kentucky on a number of the telling economic and social issues arising out of the depression of 1819 made him attractive to **Andrew Jackson**, and in 1830 he was called to Washington to found and edit the administration's organ, the *Washington Globe*. Blair would also go on to edit the *Congressional Globe,* the paper of record for the proceedings of Congress, as well as to fight with other editors for the lucrative government printing contracts of the day. He was known as a member of Jackson's **Kitchen Cabinet**, influential in shaping and reinforcing the president's attitudes toward banking and currency issues. Blair continued his advocacy of the Democratic Party throughout the rest of the period although with varying degrees of influence. The *Globe* remained the party's main organ during **Martin Van Buren**'s presidency, supporting its moves toward the **Independent Treasury**, and then it proved active in criticizing the **Whig** administration of **William Henry Harrison** and **John Tyler**, although, under pressure from Jackson, Blair did refrain from attacking Tyler once he had been welcomed back into Democratic ranks in 1844. **James Polk**, though, doubted Blair's loyalty and pressured him into selling his paper, facilities, and even circulation list to a new administration organ, the *Washington Union*. Even so, despite **free soil** sympathies, Blair remained loyal to the Democrats in the **election of 1848**, supporting **Lewis Cass**, even if he was willing to blame Polk for the party's defeat in that contest.

"BLOODY BILL." *See* FORCE BILL.

BLUFFTON PROCLAMATION. *See* RHETT, ROBERT.

BOARD OF EXCHEQUER. This was the proposal of the **John Tyler** administration, in December 1841, for an institution to fill the void left by the repeal of the **Independent Treasury** and by the vetoes of the **bank** and **fiscal corporation bills** during the **special session** of 1841. The final draft was made by **Daniel Webster**, after earlier work by Secretary of the Treasury **Walter Forward**, with advice from the rest of Cabinet, in particular Secretary of War **John Spencer**. Instead of a private national bank, the bill outlined a federal government agency based in Washington, D.C., with a five-man Board, consisting of the secretary of the treasury, the U.S. treasurer, and three president-appointed commissioners. It would establish up to two agencies in each state, throughout the country, which would be able to handle the public moneys, and, subject to state government approval, to hold up to $15 million of specie deposits, with power to issue certificates against them. The Board itself could also issue $15 million of **Treasury notes**, but would not have the power to compete with state banks in the making of loans. The Board would have no legislated duration of existence, allowing future Congresses to amend or repeal it at will. Despite support from Webster and some **Whigs** in Congress, the outright hostility of **Henry Clay** condemned the measure to failure. Using familiar arguments that the Board would become another weapon of **executive usurpation**, despite assurances and safeguards to the contrary, his followers joined with **Democrats** in tabling the proposal and finally voting it down in January 1843.

BOOK OF MORMON. This religious work, published in Palmyra, New York, in 1830, inspired the start of the growth of the distinctively American religion of **Mormonism** and still forms the centerpiece of the Church of Latter Day Saints. It represented the translation by **Joseph Smith** of a series of revelations, received, he claimed, on a number of gold plates. Running to almost 600 pages in its first version, it presented both a history of a number of emigrants from Jerusalem to the Americas around 600 B.C. and of their continuing progress in the New World, and religious teachings on the role of individual free will and the importance of America's destiny. It is seen by most to complement, rather than contradict, the central teachings of Judeo-Christian scripture.

BOWIE, JAMES (1799-1836). Jim Bowie was an American-born pioneer who in 1828 settled in Mexico, acquiring sizable lands in the vicinity of San Antonio. He became a naturalized Mexican citizen in 1830, but would be prominent in the **Texan** revolution, fighting in early skirmishes in 1832 and, after a brief sojourn in Louisiana in 1833-34, becoming a colonel in the rebel army in 1835. Most famously he was a member of the besieged and defeated garrison at the **Alamo**.

BRANCH, JOHN M. (1782-1863). This wealthy southern planter became an important figure in the early administration politics of **Andrew Jackson**'s first term. He was a North Carolinian, with experience as both governor and senator of that state. He entered the Jackson coalition from the wing of the Republican Party that supported **William Crawford** and upheld that group's usual distaste for the presidency of **John Quincy Adams**, not least because of the way he had won the election of 1824 by an alleged **"corrupt bargain."** As a man with a strong support base in his own state, and as a personal friend of both Jackson and of his close advisor **John Eaton**, Branch seemed a suitable candidate for Cabinet office, and he was duly nominated as secretary of the navy by the victorious Jackson. Like many of his colleagues he fell victim to the **Eaton Affair**, his wife having snubbed **Peggy Eaton** as early as the day of Jackson's inauguration. Although Jackson was reluctant to drop Branch from his Cabinet, the secretary resigned, bitterly attributing the whole matter to the influence of **Martin Van Buren**, whom he publicly accused of having manipulated the affair as a means of reducing the influence of **John Calhoun**'s supporters in the Cabinet. After leaving the Cabinet, Branch served a single term in Congress in 1831-33 before entering the ranks of the **Whig** Party in his state. Although he lost the 1838 gubernatorial election in North Carolina, in 1843 he won appointment from **John Tyler**'s administration as territorial governor of **Florida**, in which post he helped move forward the campaign for statehood.

BROOK FARM. This communal organization was established in 1841 near West Roxbury, Massachusetts, as the Brook Farm Institute of Agriculture and Education. It was inspired by **Transcendentalists** in Boston, such as **George Ripley**, one of its key founders. Early residents included **Nathaniel Hawthorne** and Charles A. Dana, while other associates included **Margaret Fuller, Amos Bronson Alcott, William Ellery Channing, Ralph Waldo Emerson**, and Theodore Parker. Brook Farm's guiding principles included economic cooperation above selfish competition, and between 1843 and 1845 it was organized along the more disciplined and prescriptive lines of Fourierite communities under the influence of Albert Brisbane. From 1845 onward it was the place of publication of *The Harbinger* journal. Brook Farm suffered a destructive fire in 1846, and the lasting impact of that combined with poor finances, weak leadership, and popular opposition to bring an end to the community in 1847.

BROWNSON, ORESTES (1803-1876). This self-educated Vermont-born author and clergyman journeyed through a number of denominational affiliations during the period. In 1832 he abandoned Universalism for **Unitarianism**, and four years later he formed his own church, the Society for Christian Union and Progress. Shortly afterwards Brownson mingled with New England intellectuals, including members of the **Transcendentalist** and communitarian movements, and then shocked many by converting to Roman **Catholicism** in 1844. As a writer he was prominent as editor of the *Boston Quarterly Review* from 1838 to 1842, and then, after a two-year interlude in which it was merged with the *Democratic Review*, he took it over once more as *Brownson's Quarterly Review*. In 1836 he published his first book, *New Views of Christianity, Society, and the Church* and four years later *The Laboring Classes*.

In works like the latter Brownson demonstrated concern for the condition of working Americans, a topic of constant interest to him, although his analysis of it did not always remain consistent. Initially he believed in the power to exhort the individual to self-improvement, but latterly, especially in the wake of the **panic of 1837**, he attributed the cause of workers' poverty more to the influence of associated wealth than to individual immorality. Brownson began to attack accumulated ownership and the factory system and advocated instead a system of mass proprietorship as the best means of elevating the community as a whole. Politically he also shifted allegiance as the years went by, with support at various times for **Workingmen's parties** and the **Democrats**, before disillusionment with the way the majority had voted in the **election of 1840** caused him to lean toward **John Calhoun** and his defense of minority rights.

BRYANT, WILLIAM CULLEN (1794-1878). Born in Massachusetts, Bryant developed into one of the country's leading poets. He was most renowned for his early poetry, the collection *Poems* from 1832 being among the best examples of his work. Bryant was also an able journalist who, after moving to New York in 1825, became an editor of the *New York Evening Post*. He rose to the position of chief editor of the newspaper by 1829 and later became a part-owner of it. He also wrote for **John O'Sullivan's** *Democratic Review*. Bryant's support for issues such as minimal government, **free trade**, free speech, and the rights of workers aligned him with the Jacksonian movement, and he supported **Andrew Jackson** and **Martin Van Buren** both as presidents and in their efforts in opposition to the **Second Bank**. At the same time, though, Bryant's preference for **abolition** sat less comfortably with his support for the **Democratic** Party, a state of affairs that only became more pronounced in the 1840s. He was happy enough to support the candidacy of **James Polk** in 1844 but was alarmed by the party's platform commitment to **Texas an-**

nexation. Four years later it was only Bryant's sense of duty and loyalty that caused him to remain in support of the regular party candidate, **Lewis Cass**, rather than backing a candidate more in line with his **anti-slavery** views.

BUCHANAN, JAMES (1791-1868). Although best known as the president whose term of office witnessed the descent of the United States into extreme **sectionalism** and southern secession, James Buchanan's significant political career took off in the Age of Jackson. After an early legal career and service in the War of 1812 he had entered the House of Representatives in 1821, remaining there until 1831 when he was appointed U.S. minister to Russia. During his two years in that country he signed a significant **commercial treaty** in 1832, which opened up trade concessions to American shippers in the Black Sea. On his return to the United States Buchanan represented Pennsylvania in the Senate until 1845, preferring to remain there rather than accepting two offers of more senior office, the position of attorney general from **Martin Van Buren** in 1839, and then a seat on the Supreme Court from **John Tyler**.

While in the Senate Buchanan was a solid **Democratic** supporter, although his personal views and constituency pressures did not always allow him to support administration measures. Throughout his career his origins in a state strongly supportive of the **protective tariff** made his position on that issue a difficult one. In 1830 his fears that **Andrew Jackson** would veto the **Maysville Road bill** caused him to withhold his support from the **Indian removal bill**, while during Van Buren's term Buchanan's personal preference for a divorce of federal government funds from banks was outweighed by instructions from the Pennsylvania state legislature that he should vote against the **Independent Treasury**. Buchanan did, however, support measures counteracting the influence of **abolitionists**, namely the "**gag rules**" in Congress and actions against **incendiary mail**. And much later, when in **James Polk**'s Cabinet, he was the main advocate of extending the **Missouri Compromise line** across the whole continent as the means of determining the status, free or slave, of future states.

Indeed, the peak of Buchanan's career during this period came in 1845 when Polk appointed him secretary of state. Previously, when in the Senate, for a time as chair of the Foreign Relations Committee, Buchanan had had opportunities to express his views on international relations. In 1842 he had been critical of the **Webster-Ashburton Treaty** for surrendering too many points to Britain. But he did support expansion, and with **Texas, Oregon,** and relations with **Mexico** high up on the agenda this placed him in a crucial position at a momentous period. That said, he still had to perform a difficult balancing act between his own and his office's natural tendency to caution and what Polk and his own image in the eyes of a potential electorate in 1848 might demand. So, while Buchanan initially warned against pushing Britain too far over Oregon, toward the end of that ultimately successful negotiation he adopted a more extreme position. Also, although keen to keep the peace with Mexico as long as possible, when the war neared its conclusion he was among those supporting calls for **"all Mexico."**

Throughout his tenure in the State Department Buchanan had problems working with Polk, who very much tried to run foreign policy himself. Buchanan was the Cabinet officer who had most disputes with the president, and on several occasions he threatened to resign, two times being near to accepting a Supreme Court position instead. Part of the tension between the two was no doubt founded on Buchanan's thinly veiled ambition for the party's presidential nomination in 1848, the thwarting of which brought an end to his personal journey during the period.

BUCKSHOT WAR. This political revolt took place in Pennsylvania in 1838, when both main parties contested the results of the election to the state House of Representatives. A mob forced several legislators to flee from the statehouse in Harrisburg, before the governor sent in the militia to quell the rioters. No violence ensued and the crisis was resolved when some **Whig** members joined with **Democrats** to organize the new House.

BUENA VISTA, BATTLE OF. This was the battle that virtually ended the northern Mexico theater of the **Mexican War,** in February 1847. Although it was not a decisive victory on the ground, **Zachary Taylor** did manage to hold at bay General **Santa Anna**'s Mexican army of over three times the size of his own 5,000-strong force, inflicting twice as many casualties as he suffered. He forced the Mexican general to retreat, leaving U.S. forces in control of northern Mexico and restricting Santa Anna's ability to aid in the Mexican prosecution of the war further south. Taylor himself took no further action in the war, being condemned for the battle by **James Polk**'s administration, and shortly afterwards he requested his leave from further active service.

BUFFALO FREE SOIL CONVENTION. This nominating convention during the run-up to the **election of 1848** represented the official beginning of the **Free Soil Party**, the first political party based around expressly **anti-slavery** views. Meeting in August of that year, the convention drew upon **Barnburners**, after their state convention at Utica, other antislavery **Democrats, Liberty Party** supporters, **conscience Whigs**, and "free soilers" coming from the **People's Convention** in Columbus. Those elements coming from the two main parties were unhappy with the nominations of the Whig candidate **Zachary Taylor** and Democrat **Lewis Cass** respectively, the former a southerner, the latter a northerner whose policy of **popular sovereignty** offended the anti-slavery view that **slavery** should not be allowed to spread further at all. The convention attracted delegates from 17 states, including the slave states of Maryland, Delaware, and Virginia, and nominated **Martin Van Buren** and **Charles Francis Adams** on a platform of the **Wilmot Proviso**, free land, federal abolition of slavery where it had the power so to do, and a slogan of "free soil, free speech, free labor, and free men." In addition the convention called for cheap postage, federal aid for **internal improvements**, a **tariff for revenue**, and a homestead law.

BULFINCH, CHARLES (1763-1844). This famous early American architect's influence stretched right up until his retirement in 1830. After following the usual course for American artists, of travel in Europe, he had returned to the United States to participate in the design of many important public buildings, including most famously the Massachusetts State House and the U.S. Capitol. He saw the latter through to its then completion in 1830, with the rotunda, the western portico, and the surrounding landscaping bearing the influence of his ideas. At the same time he designed the Maine state house in Augusta, completed in 1832.

"BURNED-OVER DISTRICT." This area of western New York was a very distinctive and important cultural region during the era. So labeled by **Charles Grandison Finney**, because it had been so frequently scorched by evangelical revivals in the early 19th century, it nurtured many Protestant religious groups and figures and associated reform impulses, as well as some of the more distinctive cultural and spiritual movements of the time, such as the **Anti-Masons** and the **Mormons**. The region was prone to such a development in part because of the rapid economic and social change wrought by the **market revolution**. This brought new class and gender relations creating tensions that revived religion could help to relieve, and it gave rise also to acquisitive businessmen seeking religious justification for their wealth and newly influential positions in society. But the area was also opened up physically by the **transportation revolution** brought by the **Erie Canal**, as it was settled heavily by New Englanders and found itself flooded with preachers such as Finney himself and with religious literature disseminated by various **benevolent** groups. The combination of economic development, revived religion, and also Anti-Masonic influence made this one of the most solid **Whig** regions in the nation.

BUTLER, BENJAMIN (1795-1858). After sitting in the New York legislature between 1827 and 1833 Benjamin Butler was appointed to **Andrew Jackson**'s Cabinet as attorney general in 1833. He held the position for the rest of Jackson's presidency and the first year of his former law partner **Martin Van Buren**'s, at one point, between October 1836 and March 1837, serving as acting secretary of war as well. During this time Butler backed the administration's efforts at **Indian removal** against legal challenges and also supported the policy of **removing the federal deposits** from the **Second Bank**. After leaving the Cabinet by his own choice, he returned to his home state where he became district attorney for southern New York from 1838 to 1841.

Throughout, Butler was considered a radical Jacksonian, favoring **"hard money"** policies to regulate the issue of small notes by state banks and supporting a separation of banking and governmental bodies. He also was somewhat rare in being a **Democrat** who leaned toward a more interventionist position on some of the religiously-inspired issues of the day, such as **temperance** and **Sabbatarianism**. These views, allied to his engrained sense of loyalty to Van Buren, located him within the **Barnburner** faction of New York Democracy, a stance that embroiled him in the factional battles of the 1840s. Having ultimately come round to supporting **James Polk** for **election in 1844** after being one of Van Buren's main flag-bearers at the party's nominating convention, Barnburners hoped that Cabinet office, and preferably the position of secretary of state, would be Butler's reward. When only offered the War and then the Treasury Departments Butler turned them down, believing this to be the course of action the Barnburners would have desired of him, in the process only reinforcing their sense of being sidelined as an influence within the party. Although Butler did accept a position as district attorney, four years later he again backed Van Buren to the last, this time working with other Barnburners for his nomination by the **Free Soil** coalition. The price Butler paid was removal from office by Polk in September 1848.

BUTLER, WILLIAM O. (1791-1880). This Kentucky-born lawyer and army officer was a protégé of **Francis Preston Blair**. He served his state in the House of Representatives between 1839 and 1843, before fighting under General **Zachary Taylor** in the **Mexican War**. Toward the end of that conflict Butler was appointed to replace **Winfield Scott** as commander-in-chief, with the authority to assist **Nicholas Trist** with the business of signing a peace treaty. When he found Trist had already done so, all Butler could do was send both agent and treaty back to the United States. As a military man with ties to the more radical side of the **Democratic** Party he seemed to offer a potential factional balance on the party's ticket and so was nominated as **Lewis Cass'** running mate for the **election of 1848**.

– **C** –

CABINET RESHUFFLE, 1831. This occurred in the wake of the **Eaton Affair** that had left **Andrew Jackson** less than satisfied with the behavior and political leanings of the majority of his Cabinet. Ironically the reshuffle could only take place when the two members who had given the president fewest grounds for annoyance, **Martin Van Buren** and **John Eaton** himself, first offered to resign in April 1831, although the loss of the latter as supporter and secretary of war was easier to stomach after Jackson's cherished **Indian Removal** bill had been passed the previous year. Jackson then asked **John Branch**, **John Berrien**, and **Samuel Ingham** to resign as well, leaving **William Barry** as the sole Cabinet survivor. There has been some debate as to why the reshuffle took place nearly a year after the Eaton Affair had lost its main impetus but the likely reason was that Jackson was certain by 1831 that he wanted to be rid of the influence of Berrien, Branch, and Ingham, who seemed to be working against his reelection in favor of **John Calhoun**.

The new Cabinet, eventually put together by August 1831, was considered generally to be a more talented group, including **Louis McLane**, **Edward Livingston**, **Lewis Cass**, **Roger Taney**, and **Levi Woodbury**. Although Jackson was personally very pleased with the outcome which rid him of a disobedient Cabinet and gave him a chance to stab at what he regarded as Calhoun's influence, the fact

that three of the former Cabinet members all made bitterly and publicly clear that they had been forced out by the president did create
both political uproar and doubts as to whether Jackson's reputation
would survive the various layers of explanation given for the change.
It also prefigured later charges of **executive usurpation** that would
be leveled against him.

CABINET RESIGNATION, 1841. John Tyler inherited his first set
of Cabinet members from **William Henry Harrison** in April 1841,
deciding to keep them on as his advisors for fear of creating even
more uncertainty than the death of his predecessor and the succession
had already created. Although the Cabinet was heavily populated by
Henry Clay men who might be expected to disagree with Tyler on
substantive issues, the president and Secretary of State **Daniel Webster** hoped to steer a middle course between Tyler's own more
states' rights element of support and the more extreme Clay **Whig**
element. Initially things seemed set fair as the Cabinet backed the
administration's **Fiscal Corporation bill** in the **special session** of
1841. However, when Tyler vetoed first Clay's **bank bill** and then a
modified version of the Fiscal Corporation bill, all but two members
of the Cabinet resigned in September 1841.

Those leaving admitted that they blamed Clay for pushing the
bank issue too far too fast, but then also cited Tyler's change of mind
on apparently agreed bills and his failure to consult with them prior to
his second veto as the reasons for their decision to quit. No doubt
they also knew that Clay's influence within their party would make
their position untenable if they decided to stay. A further member,
Francis Granger, also resigned but only on the grounds that it was
the will of his state's congressional delegation that he should go. Of
the original Cabinet only Webster decided to remain in office, mainly
in order to continue tricky negotiations with the British government,
although he also cited good personal relations with Tyler and his
state's approval as other reasons for not resigning. It is generally
agreed that the new Cabinet was the most talented of Tyler's numerous Cabinet combinations, Secretary of the Treasury **Walter Forward** excepted.

CAHUENGA, TREATY OF. This instrument was signed by **John
Frémont** in 1847 to bring to an end the Mexican resistance in **California**, securing both the success of the **Bear Flag revolt** and U.S.
conquest of that territory during the **Mexican War**.

CALHOUN, FLORIDE (1792-1862). Floride, wife of **John Calhoun**, played a vital part in the parlor politics of the early **Andrew Jackson** presidency. In the opening days of the administration she was one of the first Cabinet ladies to refuse the social advances of **Peggy and John Eaton**, snubbing the couple at the inaugural ball, and, despite receiving a visit from them, deciding that she would not give her approval to their marriage by paying a return visit to their household. Although by no means the only one involved in the **Eaton Affair**, the fact that Floride was the vice-president's wife, and he such a prominent figure anyway, threw suspicion upon her husband in terms of his role, his motivation, and his loyalty to the president. This sense was only reinforced by the fact that before John Eaton's appointment as secretary of war Floride had been prepared to socialize with his wife.

CALHOUN, JOHN CALDWELL (1782-1850). Calhoun was a major player in the politics of the era, drawing on a long career in legislative and executive roles in the previous two decades. As **Andrew Jackson**'s running mate he remained in the vice-presidency, having also served in that capacity under **John Quincy Adams**. Much debate exists as to the degree of influence Calhoun exercised in Jackson's first term, and in whose name, but it was clear that initially he had high hopes of being the president's successor and that he strove to increase his influence in the president's Cabinet, with the likes of **Samuel Ingham, John Branch**, and **John Berrien**. When it became clear that Calhoun and the president did not see eye to eye on most matters, but especially on **nullification**, Jackson used knowledge of Calhoun's attitude toward him in debates on the **Florida expedition report** and growing tension in the Cabinet arising from the **Eaton Affair** to make a public split from his vice-president and to purge the Cabinet of his followers. In 1832 Calhoun resigned the vice-presidency and returned to his home state of South Carolina before reentering national political office as senator in the 1832-33 session. There he remained until 1843 when he resigned to cultivate his chances of presidential **election in 1844**, and it was only when it looked as if his hopes of nomination had disappeared that he accepted the office of secretary of state from **John Tyler**, whose administration he had already influenced behind the scenes to a considerable degree. After eventually choosing to support **James Polk** in 1844 Calhoun returned to the Senate once more in 1845, where he served for the rest of the period.

A brief skeleton description of his career barely serves to illustrate Calhoun's significance in the period, whether as an actor in his own right or as the catalyst for the actions of others. The keynote to understanding his work is the recognition that he always tried to do the best for his state and, more broadly, the southern section. While earlier in his career this had caused Calhoun to adopt a fairly nationalist approach to federal powers, by the late 1820s he was convinced of the need to restrict the federal government's influence as part of a defense of minority and **states' rights**. At first his presence as vice-president and the hope that he would one day become president himself convinced extreme states' rights elements that there was a chance that their views on issues such as **slavery** and the **tariff** would prevail. But as Calhoun's star fell, so then they turned instead to his more extreme resort of nullification, as expressed as early as 1828 in Calhoun's **South Carolina Exposition**. Calhoun's return to the Senate was to enable him to champion his state's interests during the **Nullification crisis** and it is unlikely that South Carolina would have accepted the **compromise of 1833** had he not been involved in its construction.

From that point on Calhoun defended what he perceived as the interests of the South in the Senate. This caused him to alternate between support and opposition for measures proposed by the administrations of Jackson and **Martin Van Buren** depending on how far they could be squared with states' rights principles. Initially Calhoun could be found alongside those **States' Rights Whigs** who opposed President Jackson for his apparently unbounded use of **executive** powers. Yet on the issue of the **Independent Treasury** Calhoun found himself aligned with Van Buren in favor of a measure that would take regulation of banks out of the hands of the federal government—indeed he would oppose the Independent Treasury bills of 1838 and 1839 because they compromised that principle too much. Calhoun's states' rights stance even caused him to oppose federally implemented measures to block the distribution of **incendiary mail** in the South, preferring that this be left to the individual states. Generally, though, he now more openly defended slavery, championing it with the **proslavery** argument that it was a positive good.

In the changed political environment of the 1840s Calhoun clearly linked the issue of slavery with **expansion**. As secretary of state he defended **Texas annexation** in the **Pakenham letter** on the grounds that it would help to safeguard American slavery, a communication that ironically may have contributed to the defeat of the annexation treaty in the Senate. Although he was only a reluctant expansionist, preferring that northern **anti-slavery** opinion not be aroused at all, once it did become an issue Calhoun adopted a most strident stance by insisting on the right of the South to extend its institution of slavery into all new territories gained in the **Mexican War**. As such he set down one of the competing demands that would dominate the growing **sectional** crisis at the end of this period and beyond. *See also* CABINET RESHUFFLE; JEFFERSON BIRTHDAY DINNER.

CALIFORNIA, ACQUISITION. This Mexican province on the Pacific coast of North America proved an attractive focus for American settlement in the 1830s and especially the 1840s, when the first overland migrations began to take place. Almost inevitably the presence of Americans in the region sparked off official U.S. interest in the territory, which would propel it into the contentious diplomatic and later military developments in the relationship with Mexico in that decade.

During the presidency of **John Tyler** there were signs that the U.S. government was beginning to take very seriously the prospect of securing California. In part this was the result of reports from the **U.S. South Seas Exploring expedition**, which highlighted how attractive the region was and how it might provide American naval and mercantile vessels with useful port facilities on the Pacific coast. As the United States negotiated with Britain over the future boundary in the **Oregon** territory, British representatives even suggested that it might encourage Mexico to offer part of California, including San Francisco, to the United States, in order to allow U.S. diplomats to soften their demands for access to ports further north in the disputed Oregon lands. While many in the Tyler administration would have supported such a deal, there was no way that the Mexican government, already at loggerheads with the United States over **Texas**, would countenance it. As a range of forces brought the two neighbors closer to war, it became clear that California would form a desirable military objective for the United States. Indeed, in one bizarre occurrence a naval captain, Thomas ap Catesby Jones, did actually seize Monterey for a day believing war to have broken out in October 1842, only to abandon it and apologize the next day.

While this episode signaled the end of serious official approaches from the Tyler administration (although **John Calhoun** did send **Duff Green** to Mexico in 1844, apparently with California on the shopping list), the settlement of trappers, traders, and farmers continued and ultimately generated the dynamic for U.S. conquest of the territory. Having already offered to purchase California, **James Polk** seized the opportunity to support the **Bear Flag revolt** when the **Mexican War** broke out in May 1846. U.S. naval and land forces under **John Sloat**, **Robert Stockton**, **Stephen Kearny**, and **John**

Frémont came to the aid of the Bear Flag rebels and then occupied California for the United States, securing the surrender of Mexican elements by the **Treaty of Cahuenga**. The whole of California, both Upper and Lower, became one of Polk's wishes for any peace treaty, with Upper California as a non-negotiable demand. Indeed, the latter did form part of the land settlement at the end of the war in 1848 by the Treaty of **Guadalupe Hidalgo**.

CALIFORNIA, TERRITORIAL STATUS. Even before the formal acquisition by the United States of the former Mexican province of Upper California in the Treaty of **Guadalupe Hidalgo** in 1848, in his annual message to Congress in December 1847 President **James Polk** had advised of the need to consider a form of territorial government for California. Initial progress in debates about its entry to the Union was thwarted by their complexity and the concurrent discussions over the admission of the territories of **Oregon** and **New Mexico**. The discovery of gold at Sutter's mill and the ensuing rush of prospectors to California only increased the need for some kind of organized government, including possible immediate statehood. Various options were debated in 1849, including one combining California in a single state with New Mexico. Polk preferred the option of a separate California. However, the question of statehood now became caught up in the dangerous tensions resulting from the **pro-** and **anti-slavery** disagreement over the expansion of slavery, with the result that no arrangement could be agreed upon before the end of Polk's term. Eventually California would enter the Union as a free state in 1850.

CAMPBELL, ALEXANDER (1788-1866). This important religious leader was born in Ireland, moving to the United States in 1809, where he would eventually settle in the western part of Virginia. As first a Presbyterian and then a Baptist Campbell was a combative thinker who was prepared to debate the significance of religion with members of other denominations such as the **Mormons** and **Catholics**. But it was as the founder of the Disciples of Christ in 1832 that he achieved his lasting influence. This primitive form of Christianity was based on literal interpretations of the Scriptures, views Campbell put forward in a range of magazines and in his most important doctrinal work, *The Christian System*, published in 1839. A year later Campbell founded Bethany College to train others in his religion. For a brief moment Campbell also had a role in the politics of his state, calling for the elimination of **slavery** at the Virginia constitutional convention in 1830.

CANADIAN BORDER. The exact location of the boundary between the United States and British possessions in North America remained an issue of contention from the signing of the Treaty of Paris at the end of the War for Independence in 1783 all the way through to the Jacksonian era. Several specific disputes arose to create tension between the two countries and to vex their diplomatic representatives. In Maine there was the **Aroostook war**, while the common borders between Canada and New Hampshire, New York, Vermont, and Michigan all threw up disputes in this era. Subsequent to the Louisiana Purchase the far northwestern boundary in the **Oregon** territory also came to the attention of diplomats of the age. In addition to topographical differences the presence of American sympathizers also occasionally helped to assist or to foment rebel movements in Canadian provinces, as would happen in the *Caroline* affair and the so-called Patriot War across the Michigan border in 1838. Most of these issues came to a head in the late 1830s when many even considered them likely cause for war between the two nations. As it was, cautious diplomacy would calm immediate threats to peace and bring settlement to most of the outstanding border disputes, in the Northeast by means of the **Webster-Ashburton Treaty** in 1842 and in the Northwest by a treaty on Oregon in 1846.

CANALS. The Jacksonian era fell at the end of the main period of canal-building in the United States, with inspiration from the success of the **Erie Canal**, completed in 1825, still proving influential. Indeed, as well as proving the desirability and feasibility of canals, the Erie provided impetus in the very practical way of training a group of engineers, surveyors, and builders, including millwrights and masons, qualified to take forward the great project of canal-building. These were supplemented by a labor force made up heavily of **immigrant** Irish laborers working for low rates of pay, which accounted for occasional outbursts of **labor** disorder at canal sites in the period. By 1830 it was estimated that over 10,000 miles were already built or planned, made up from over 100 actual or prospective canals, while between 1816 and 1840 over 3,000 miles were actually constructed. Canals were financed either by private resources, most particularly when serving an individual industry's needs or when traversing already settled areas, or by state sponsorship (in the form of land grants, subsidies, and stock issues) when building a canal was seen as having a developmental role in opening up an area to new settlement. The latter tended to be less successful than the former, but all canals struggled in the **panics of 1837 and 1839** and resultant depression up to 1843, which hit midwestern canal developments especially harshly. In 1838 Congress suspended aid to canal corporations and construction came to a virtual standstill. Although very few canals made money for their investors, the Erie being the major exception, they still played an important part in the **transportation revolution** with its concomitant effects, helping goods and people to move around more quickly and generally more cheaply. *See also* CHESA-PEAKE AND OHIO CANAL; LOUISVILLE AND PORTLAND CANAL; MIAMI AND ERIE CANAL; OHIO AND ERIE CANAL; WABASH AND ERIE CANAL.

CAROLINE **AFFAIR.** This tense episode in Anglo-American relations was sparked off by local New Yorkers' responses to rebellions which developed in Lower and Upper Canada in November-December 1837. Rebels in Upper Canada, under the leadership of William Mackenzie, had been receiving support from American sympathizers, often in the form of supplies carried over the Niagara River. Some New Yorkers even joined the rebels, aiding in the seizure of Navy Island in Canadian territorial waters. British protests to the U.S. government about this action were superseded in December 1837 when loyal British-Canadian troops captured and destroyed the *Caroline*, a privately owned American vessel engaged in supplying the rebels on the island. In the process one American citizen was killed and several others taken prisoner, all in American territorial waters.

Despite the predictable sense of outrage among many Americans and increases in sympathy for the Canadian rebels and in Anglophobia, **Martin Van Buren**'s administration agreed with Britain that a pacific approach was the best option, with the hope of discouraging such border incursions in future. In January 1838 U.S. army commander **Winfield Scott** left for the border to restore order. He succeeded in persuading American recruits to the rebel cause to give up their position on Navy Island and, by leasing all available boats, he managed to stop the provisioning trade. Van Buren helped the process by denouncing the behavior of the American recruits and declaring U.S. neutrality. He also suggested new laws to enforce neutrality commitments upon private individuals, which Congress passed in March, allowing civil authorities to prevent land- or river-based trade in supplies to rebels within neutral countries. These laws proved effective later in the year when more recruits arose supporting the rebels and a British vessel, the *Sir Robert Peel*, was burned in retaliation for the *Caroline*. The local authorities did act to discourage the recruits, which, together with further declarations of neutrality, helped to ease relations with Britain.

However, this did not mark the end of the affair, as the Van Buren administration's call for redress for damage to the *Caroline* and for Canadian infringement of American territorial waters met with a British refusal. The tension was heightened still further by the associated **Macleod affair** in 1840. It would be another two years before the matter would be finally resolved, when in an exchange of letters made at the same time as (but not forming part of) the **Webster-Ashburton Treaty** of 1842 the British expressed regret and made an indirect apology for the destruction of the *Caroline*. Throughout the whole episode the Van Buren administration, and then **John Tyler**'s, had adopted as pacific an approach as possible and seemed determined not to allow things to degenerate to broken relations or even war. In the context of other **Canadian border** disputes and difficult Anglo-American issues, however, the *Caroline* affair represented a potentially dangerous matter.

CARSON, KIT (1809-1868). Born Christopher Carson in Kentucky, Kit moved to Missouri with his family before running away to roam the further West, eventually settling in Santa Fe in the early 1840s. By that time he had become a leading frontiersman and scout, who had been engaged in many explorations and who would get caught up in the **Mexican War**. After serving on and leading expeditions to the far West in the 1830s, he acted as guide to three **John Frémont** expeditions: in 1842-43 to Wyoming; in 1843-44 to California and Oregon; and in 1845-46 to California again. On the latter Carson fought alongside Frémont and **Stephen Kearny**, assisting the **Bear Flag** rebels and then helping to establish U.S. control in **California**. As with so many **Manifest Destiny** pioneers Carson became a near legendary figure to Americans, but he was also generally respected by all ethnicities for his honesty, loyalty, and courage.

CASS, LEWIS (1782-1866). Cass was born in New Hampshire and then studied and practiced law in Ohio, before becoming military and then civilian governor of the Michigan territory between 1813 and 1831. His experience in dealing with Native American affairs provided a good background for his next position, secretary of war in **Andrew Jackson**'s Cabinet between 1831 and 1836. In the latter year Cass resigned that post to become U.S. minister to France, serving until 1842 when arguments with **Daniel Webster** over the **Webster-Ashburton Treaty** and about international agreements to police the **slave trade** forced him to resign once more.

His strident Anglophobia at a time of tense Anglo-American relations, his commitment to **Texas annexation**, and his firm stand on **Oregon** earned Cass genuine popularity, and together with his opposition to a national bank, to **internal improvements**, and to **distribution** put him in the running for the **Democratic** Party's presidential nomination for the **election of 1844**. At the party's convention neither he nor his main rival **Martin Van Buren** could secure the necessary majority to win the nomination, but it was Cass' star that was clearly rising before **James Polk** was chosen as the dark horse candidate.

When Cass entered the Senate to represent Michigan between 1845 and 1848 he was clearly being viewed as a strong presidential candidate for the **election of 1848**, especially when Polk announced his decision to serve only one term. Cass' moderate line on the question of **slavery** expansion, expressed in the **Nicholson letter**'s advocacy of **popular sovereignty**, alarmed the more radical elements of the Democratic Party and his successful nomination caused the bolt of **Barnburner** elements from the party's convention and eventually into the ranks of the **Free Soil** coalition. How far this contributed to his defeat in the election proper is debatable, but his loss of New York State undoubtedly owed something to the Barnburner defection and that state's electoral college votes would have swung the election his way.

CATHOLICS. This large religious minority experienced quite dramatic developments during the period, both in terms of its numbers and its legal and cultural position within American society. The 1830s began to witness the first major growth in Catholic numbers, as German and Irish **immigrants** entered the country, to the point that there were some 200 Catholic schools by 1840, supporting growing populations in the Northeast and Midwest in particular. However, it was in the 1840s that Catholicism experienced massive growth, as Irish immigration in particular rocketed.

While some states removed restrictions on office-holding which had previously barred Catholics, culturally their experience was more negative. Some **nativist** groups impugned the loyalty of Catholics, portraying them as part of a dangerous Papist plot to overthrow Protestant America. These attitudes occasionally translated into violent reprisals, such as the **Ursuline convent** fire and the **Philadelphia ri-**

ots. Catholics also suffered by association, as a degree of anti-Catholicism was later mixed into the less savory side of **Manifest Destiny** in its analysis of Hispanic cultures in the American Southwest and Mexico. Separate education for Catholics was an issue that aroused nativist hostility and Catholics also found themselves viewed with suspicion because of their failure to join in the reform fervor that swept across so many Protestant denominations. The preference of Catholics for a more individualistic approach to personal morality and moral issues brought them squarely into opposition to the moral reform agenda and inclined them to be attracted politically to the **Democratic** Party which tended to eschew such reforms.

CATLIN, GEORGE (1796-1872). This Pennsylvania-born lawyer found fame after turning to painting in 1823. After a modest career as a portraitist working in Washington Catlin won great acclaim for his body of work illustrating various aspects of Native American tribal life. Between 1829 and 1838 he painted some 600 works of this kind, including representations of 45 different tribes, many of whom he had spent time living with between 1832 and 1838. Catlin went on to exhibit his collection and in 1841 he published his *Letters and Notes on the Manners, Customs and Condition of the North American Indians*. Throughout his work he displayed a sympathetic approach to what he considered a dying native way of life, but he also shared the common desire to Christianize a noble race. Accordingly his portrayals were both realistic but also heavily romanticized. Catlin's work could also be controversial, as was notably the case with his particularly noble representation of **Osceola** at the height of the **Second Seminole War**.

CENSURE RESOLUTIONS. These represented the legislative embodiment of the claims of **executive usurpation** made against **Andrew Jackson** by his opponents in the Senate, headed by **Henry Clay**. The resolutions focused specifically on Jackson's refusal to accept his Cabinet's and congressional advice on the banking issue. In particular it was Jackson's decision to **remove the federal deposits** as a way of further prosecuting his war on the **Second Bank of the United States** which sparked off the censure campaign. Passed after three months of debate, in March 1834, the resolutions asserted that the reasons given by the administration for the removal of the deposits were inadequate. They also censured the president for the way in which he had replaced William Duane with **Roger Taney** as secretary of the treasury, after the former refused to implement the removal policy. They claimed that it was that officer's, and not the president's, responsibility to take such a decision, and that, as the secretary was answerable to Congress and not to the president, then Jackson had had no right to act as he had done. Similar resolutions proved impossible to pass in the House, though, where Jackson's supporters held a majority, and subsequent attempts to **expunge** the Senate's resolutions would provide a significant test of party loyalty in later sessions.

CERRO GORDO, BATTLE OF. This battle of the **Mexican War**, fought during **Winfield Scott**'s march from Vera Cruz to the Mexican capital, took place on 17 and 18 April 1847. The U.S. army of over 8,000 troops confronted the Mexican army of 12,000 under **Santa Anna**, shortly after his retreat from battle against **Zachary Taylor** at **Buena Vista**. It proved a stunning victory for Scott, as American casualties numbered less than a third the total of 1,200 inflicted upon the Mexicans and as Santa Anna was forced to flee.

CHANNING, WILLIAM ELLERY (1780-1842). Born in Rhode Island and educated at Harvard, Channing served as pastor of Boston's Federal Street **Congregational Church** between 1803 and 1842. He was most influential in leading the liberal **Unitarian** breakaway from Congregationalism's more extreme Calvinist tenets, helping to set up the American Unitarian Association in 1825. In works like "Self-Culture" (1838) he advocated a religion in which greater emphasis was placed on a rational than on an imaginative approach, with the main aim being elevation of the individual soul. His hope for all to be able to fulfill their potential led to Channing's support for a range of reform initiatives including public education, **temperance**, pacifism, **labor** reform, and **anti-slavery** action, though never to the extent of all-out **abolition**. His influence earned him the title "Apostle of Unitarianism" and stretched beyond his immediate denomination to other groups such as the **Transcendentalists**.

CHASE, SALMON P. (1808-1873). This New Hampshire-born lawyer and statesman became famous as one of the first prominent **anti-slavery** politicians. After working as a teacher in Washington, D.C. Chase moved to Ohio in 1829, where as a lawyer he helped to codify the state's statutes. He soon got involved in practical efforts to attack **slavery**, becoming famous for his legal defense of fugitive slaves in Ohio. He also warned of the influence of **pro-slavery** groups in the formulation of federal government policies and opposed the expansion of slavery, slavery in the District of Columbia, and the domestic **trade in slaves**, all classic elements of an anti-slavery stance. With such views it was no surprise that Chase became a leading figure of the **Liberty Party** in Ohio and eventually joined the **free soil** movement, helping **Benjamin Butler** to write the party's 1848 platform at their **convention in Buffalo**.

CHARLES RIVER BRIDGE vs. WARREN BRIDGE. This significant legal case gave the Jacksonian appointee as chief justice of the Supreme Court, **Roger Taney**, the opportunity to rule against monopoly privilege. Although the ruling was made in 1837, the case had first come before the Court six years earlier in response to wrangling between two bridge companies in Massachusetts. In 1828 the state legislature had chartered the Warren Bridge Company to build a second bridge across the Charles River between Boston and Charlestown, to be toll free in six years. The company running the existing toll bridge claimed that the act challenged their bridge's monopoly right, transferred to them by state charter from an earlier ferry crossing over the river, and that the state legislature had thereby infringed the contract clause of the U.S. Constitution.

Taney and the majority of largely Jacksonian appointees ruled specifically that the earlier monopoly rights for a ferry should not have been transferred to a bridge. They also supported the general right of states to regulate and encourage economic activity, saying that it was in the public's favor for Massachusetts to enact a law that may damage the interests of a few, if it were in anticipation of wider economic benefit. As a result of the case, future grants of state monopolies were often only made with the proviso that states could revoke some or all of them at a later date. Moreover, the apparent support of the idea that any question of interpreting such rights should be weighed in the public's favor is usually seen as having encouraged the growth of competition in transportation and industrial development. At the time others, including Justice **Joseph Story** and the old bridge company's advocate, **Daniel Webster**, denounced the ruling as a dangerous attack on charter, and hence property, rights.

CHEROKEE. This famous Native American tribe, one of the "five civilized tribes," assumed a central part in the Jacksonian era's battles over **Indian removal**, generating political and legal struggles and ultimately being caught up in one of the most notorious episodes of maltreatment of natives in U.S. history. Despite the fact that many Cherokee lived settled and "civilized" lifestyles with their own written language, sharing many of their white neighbors' planting and slave-holding interests, their native racial status counted against them and was unlikely ever to win them favor among white settlers. The settlers' hopes of buying land from the Cherokee also seemed likely to be thwarted by the fact that they still held tribal land in common. When gold was discovered on Cherokee lands in Georgia in the late 1820s, white prospectors rushed in and it was only a matter of time before the Cherokee became victims to the pressure of white settlers' influence upon both the state and federal governments.

Already, from 1817 onward, some Cherokee had been moved to the western part of Arkansas by the federal government, some trading in those lands for others further west still, in 1828. Now the Georgia state government passed laws, effective from June 1830, to deny Cherokee rights within the state. Rather than give way, either by accepting the impact of the laws or by removing themselves to the further West, the remaining Cherokee and their white sponsors opted to contest Georgia's actions in the courts and won a significant victory in the case of *Worcester vs. Georgia*. However, here they fell victim to the unwillingness of **Andrew Jackson** to back their cause, as he refused either to protect them with federal troops against immediate violent reprisal or to call for the implementation of the Supreme Court's ruling. For a variety of reasons his course was entirely predictable. In the face of pressures to oppose the more extreme **nullification** stance of South Carolina and his political rival **John Calhoun**, Jackson was prepared to back the rights of a state in Georgia's case, by specifically denying the right of the Court to intervene against state jurisdiction over Native Americans within their borders. He was no doubt anxious to curry favor with southerners on this **states' rights** issue. But, of course, he was also already committed to a policy of Indian removal and so was clearly sympathetic to the interests of the state and its white settlers.

Indeed, his administration now attempted to use its powers under the 1830 removal law, first to encourage removal of Cherokee individuals and then, after that proved to be largely unsuccessful, with only about 200 leaving, to sign a removal treaty with a minority portion of the tribe. However, the majority still refused to go, and it was only when the leader of the opposition, **Coowescoowe**, was away from the tribe that the treaty party, with the support of some of the earlier opponents, was prevailed upon to sign the further Treaty of **New Echota**. This treaty was now taken as officially representative of the whole tribe's view and the Cherokee were forced to give up all their remaining eastern territories within three years. Their physical removal, on the infamous "**trail of tears**" in 1838, would mark their final departure from Georgia.

CHEROKEE NATION vs. GEORGIA. This Supreme Court case was the first of two landmark cases generated by **Cherokee** resistance to the attempts of the state of Georgia to abolish their separate government and laws and to annex remaining lands that the Cherokee claimed had been guaranteed to them as a "nation" by earlier treaties in which they ceded other lands. It came about as Georgia sought to enforce laws passed in 1828 over Cherokee lands, in support of large numbers of white settlers who had moved there in a gold rush of 1829. Chief Justice **John Marshall**'s ruling, in 1831, was that the Cherokee were neither citizens nor a foreign nation, but rather a "domestic dependent nation" with no distinctive and separate constitutional rights, and that as such the Court had no jurisdiction over them. This rebuff led to an alternative legal approach culminating in the case of *Worcester vs. Georgia.*

CHERUBUSCO, BATTLE OF. This was one of several **Mexican War** battles forming part of **Winfield Scott**'s triumphant march on the Mexican capital. Taking place in August 1847, together with the battle at **Contreras** the battle at Cherubusco accounted for the loss to **Santa Anna** of one third of his army's strength. The two battles forced Santa Anna to offer a temporary armistice during which initial peace negotiations took place.

CHESAPEAKE AND OHIO CANAL. This was seen as one of the great national **internal improvements** projects of the era when it was conceived and started in the 1820s. Planned initially to run from Georgetown to Cumberland around the Potomac falls, it proposed ultimately to provide a **canal** link between the nation's capital and the Ohio River, and as a sign of its importance it received financial support from the states of Virginia, Maryland, and Pennsylvania, as well as from the federal government. Construction on the canal began on Independence Day, 1828, but it was beset with engineering difficulties, labor shortages and unrest, and with competition from the **Baltimore and Ohio railroad** that claimed access to some of the planned route. Nevertheless, sections were opened as they were completed, with Harper's Ferry being reached in 1834. However, in the face of tunneling problems and financial difficulties, it would be a further 16 years before the canal reached Cumberland. By that time the canal's railroad competitors were much further advanced, with the result that it was decided to abandon a planned continuation of the canal to Pittsburgh.

CHICAGO. A fort located at the position of the future city on Lake Michigan was rebuilt in 1816 but for the next 20 years settlement was sparse, at least until there had been further removals of Native Americans, such as in the aftermath of **Black Hawk's War**. As the community's growth was spurred on by harbor improvements and by the start of construction of a canal, civilian settlement started to accelerate from 1833, to the point that by 1837, when the city was incorporated, the population had grown to some 5,000. The city continued to grow steadily and at the very end of the period received a major boost from the 1848 completion of the Illinois and Michigan canal which linked Chicago with both the Mississippi River system and the eastern seaboard.

CHICKASAW. The Chickasaw were one of the "five civilized tribes," in their case originally residing in northern Mississippi and neighboring territory in Alabama, Kentucky, and Tennessee. After many years of gradually ceding their territory by treaty, in the 1830s all the surviving members of the tribe were forced to relocate to the Oklahoma territory. They attended a meeting in Tennessee in the summer of 1830 at which they were offered terms of allotment and removal under the **Indian removal** act of earlier that year. They signed a provisional treaty in August, but only on condition that suitable lands were found for them. Once those lands were not forthcoming, they were offered a further allotment treaty two years later, which started the process by which gradually they sold their lands and moved west, most having done so by 1837.

CHILD, LYDIA MARIA (1802-1880). Born in Massachusetts, Lydia Child went on to become a prominent campaigning writer. In the 1820s she wrote novels and also children's stories, such as those published in the *Juvenile Miscellany* between 1826 and 1834. She was also an educator, running schools as part of her effort to promote a role for **women** as creators of the right environment to educate children properly. Although she clearly perceived that women had a vital role in society and she wrote extensively on topics pertaining to women, including *The Frugal Housewife* (1829), *The Mother's Book* (1831), and a *History of the Condition of Women in Various Ages and Nations* (1835), she did not at this stage push a strongly feminist agenda in the groups she worked with. Among these were those who attacked the treatment of the **Cherokee** natives, and especially the **abolitionists**. In 1833 she and her husband, David Lee Child, wrote one of the first anti-slavery books in America, *An Appeal in Favor of That Class of Americans Called Africans*, and they would go on to edit the **anti-slavery** newspaper, *The National Antislavery Standard*, from 1840 to 1849. They also allowed their home to be used as part of the underground railroad assisting the escape of fugitive slaves.

CHOCTAW. The Choctaw were one of the "five civilized tribes," in their case originally living primarily in southern Mississippi. From 1817 onward the federal government engaged in a policy of moving them from east of the Mississippi River to the western part of Arkansas. Although some remained in Mississippi, in 1825 others traded their lands to move further west still. In the early years of **Andrew Jackson**'s administration the Choctaw remaining in Mississippi became the first focus of attempts to implement removal under the terms of the **Indian Removal Act** of 1830. Although initially the tribe's leaders, unlike those of the **Chickasaw**, refused to attend a meeting in Tennessee, in September 1830 they did meet with Secretary of War **John Eaton** at Dancing Rabbit Creek in Mississippi where they were prevailed upon to sign a treaty under the terms of the act. Choctaw families were offered the chance to take up allotments of land in Mississippi, but it was expected that most would then sell it in order to remove from that state altogether. The ensuing sales of land and removal provide a first example of the limits of the administration's humanitarian concern for Native Americans. Fraud, and the willingness of federal authorities to overlook it, caused most Choctaws to lose out in the land deals. Then a government drive to cut costs combined with harsh winter conditions and a cholera epidemic to produce appalling conditions on the trail during the three main removals in 1831-33. By 1842 most of the Choctaw tribe had been relocated west of the Mississippi.

CHOLERA EPIDEMIC. In June 1832 the United States was struck by one of several dire epidemics to hit the country in the 19th century, this time Asiatic cholera. Of major cities only Boston and Charleston escaped it ravages, while some 3,000 died in New York and 4,000 in New Orleans. It had virtually disappeared by 1833, but not before giving fuel to some less charitable analyses of its causes, ranging from blaming the larger numbers of immigrants from poorer backgrounds entering the United States to condemning the moral weakness of many Americans already there. Certainly the epidemic was fostered by the cramped conditions in America's growing urban areas, with their inadequate public health facilities. A further outbreak of the disease hit port cities in 1848, killing 5,000 in New York, before spreading across the country through the transportation network.

CLAY, HENRY (1777-1852). Already a significant player in legislative and executive matters before the period, Henry Clay remained one of the most important figures of the whole Jacksonian era. His career began with significant legislative triumphs and as early as 1816 he would be one of the founding members of the **American Colonization Society**, a body he would preside over from 1836 to his death. As a leading member of the **National Republican** and **Whig** Parties, Clay seemed to be a perennial presidential contender, only to lose both the elections he actually contested, in 1832 and 1844, and to be considered an unsuitable candidate in 1840 and 1848, ironically the only two elections won by his party. So it was that purely in terms of personal ambition the era was a massive disappointment to Clay. He was left to influence affairs either from a position of private correspondence with fellow party members or more commonly from the Senate where he represented his state of Kentucky for most of the period between 1831 and 1842 and again at the very end of the era. Even here, though, his numerous attempts to influence the policy-making agenda were often thwarted by the realities of partisan politics.

Clay entered the era as the retiring secretary of state and, like his executive chief, **John Quincy Adams**, suffered the political consequences of accusations of **"corrupt bargain"** that were thrown at him for the way he attained that position in the first place. Despite the taint of these charges, Clay was clearly considered the leading National Republican, and then Whig, of his time, largely responsible for the **American System** of policies that came to be associated with both parties. His advocacy of the **Second Bank of the United States** and the **protective tariff** would bring him into the forefront of the major political battles of **Andrew Jackson**'s administration.

Together with Bank president **Nicholas Biddle** Clay pushed for the early re-charter of the institution, only for their efforts to be thwarted by Jackson's **bank veto**. If their strategy had been one of finding an issue with which to beat Jackson in the **election of 1832**, then it backfired, as the still popular Jackson defeated Clay easily. Moreover, Jackson only used the election result as a sign of popular disapproval of the Bank, making that institution's position untenable after 1832 and weakening the political standing of those, like Clay, associated with it. Indeed, by the end of the 1830s Clay was forced into the public position of supporting the **deposit bank** system against proposals for an **Independent Treasury** rather than pushing for another national bank. However, the speed with which he advocated a bank bill in the **special session** of 1841 indicates that it was still his preferred option, and made only more bitter the experience of suffering yet further vetoes, this time at the hands of the nominally Whig President **John Tyler**.

As a supporter of the protective tariff Clay was also involved in the **Nullification crisis**, working with **John Calhoun** in formulating a **compromise in 1833**. This, too, removed from political debate an issue upon which Clay would have expected to lead in Congress, at least until 1842 when he did at least see a more protective tariff enacted. Even this, though, came at a high price, as Congress had to suspend another Clay-preferred policy of **distribution** to pass the tariff. Ironically Clay had only come out in support of distribution once Jackson's **Maysville Road veto** made direct federal funding of **internal improvements** politically less viable.

Despite all these setbacks Clay remained the leading figure in the opposition to Jackson and his successor **Martin Van Buren**. It was around Clay that efforts coalesced to **censure** Jackson for **executive usurpation**, and even though his failure to secure the Whig nomination for 1840 was a great disappointment to him, he still hoped to influence matters from the Senate (turning down the offer of Cabinet office from **William Henry Harrison** to stay there) and to lay the basis for a successful campaign in 1844. Yet again, though, a shift in the political agenda left Clay high and dry. As **expansion**, and especially the **Texas annexation** became the top issues of the day, he struggled to reconcile his presidential ambitions with his hope of playing down issues that he believed endangered both the unity of the national party he depended on and good sectional relations. His equivocation on the Texas issue, in the **Raleigh** and **Alabama letters**, lost him support in both South and North, and assisted **James Polk** in winning the election.

Clay remained out of office between 1842 and 1849 and was not considered a real contender for nomination in 1848 as he was too old and had demonstrated his detachment from the newly emerging issues of the day. He would return to the Senate in 1849 to play a part in the debates leading to the 1850 legislative measures that temporarily resolved the growing **sectional** crisis, but even in this his role was not as great as is sometimes suggested. It seemed to mark a fitting conclusion to a great career, yet one that always seemed to deliver less than promised.

CLIFFORD, NATHAN (1803-1881). Clifford was a New Hampshire-born lawyer who went on to become a prominent **Democratic** politician from the state of Maine. He entered national politics as a representative in 1839, after periods as a state legislator between 1830 and 1834 and as state attorney general between 1834 and 1838. After Clifford left Congress in 1843, **James Polk** appointed him federal attorney general in 1846, and he served in that post until March 1848 when Polk sent him to Mexico as one of the special envoys to secure a treaty to end the **Mexican War**. During the war Clifford had been one of those keen to push for more territorial gains from Mexico.

COFFIN HANDBILL. This pamphlet was used by anti-Jackson followers in the **election of 1828** to throw doubt on **Andrew Jackson**'s fitness for the office of president. It seemed to illustrate Jackson's rash and violent nature by featuring a dozen coffins of men allegedly killed by him, including six militiamen hanged during the Creek wars of the previous decade.

COLE, THOMAS (1801-1848). This English-born artist moved to the United States in 1819 where he became one of the pioneers of the **Hudson River School**, producing work based on his experience of living in the upstate region of New York. These included particularly fine landscapes such as *The Oxbow* (1836) and *In the Catskills* (1837). Cole's choice of subject fit with his wider principles, the portrayal of a wilderness untainted by the worst features of modernizing America demonstrating his distaste for much of the rapid change of the era. In his painted work, as well as in poems and essays, he also revealed a suspicion of democracy and bemoaned the apparent influence of **Andrew Jackson** in undermining older republican values. Throughout his career Cole struggled to resolve his contradictory intentions of producing a realistic portrayal based on a close scrutiny of nature and of infusing his work with an elevated sense of meaning through the use of his imagination. To some extent he resolved this dilemma when he chose to work on entirely imagined allegorical scenes, such as in the *Course of Empire* (1833-36) and the *Voyage of Life* (1839-40).

COLONIZATION. *See* AMERICAN COLONIZATION SOCIETY.

COLT, SAMUEL (1814-1862). Colt was born in Hartford, Connecticut and had a fairly unremarkable early life at school, working in his father's bleaching establishment and then as an apprentice sailor. However, it was during his time at sea that he developed an interest in explosives and gunpowder and that he made his first wooden model of the revolver that bears his name and would make his fortune. On his return from sea, in 1836, Colt took out a patent on his revolving firearm and established a company to manufacture it. At first his business was unsuccessful, bankruptcy in 1842 demonstrating that he had failed to convince people of the need for such a weapon in peacetime. However, the outbreak of the **Mexican War** brought a government order for 1,000 revolvers, which allowed him to establish a new and ultimately successful factory. Colt also dabbled with other inventions, including underwater mines, and undertook some manufacture of cable for underwater telegraph links.

COMMERCIAL TREATIES. The negotiation of commercial treaties represented a major, if routine, diplomatic initiative of the era. Alongside attempting to guarantee secure conditions for American citizens trading abroad through the establishment of consular offices and legal rights, the main thrust of commercial diplomacy was to secure as favorable terms as possible for American export products and shippers in foreign ports. The level of success was usually dictated by the degree to which the treating partners were willing to concede terms to U.S. negotiators. So then when it came to duties imposed on American goods entering other countries treaties normally only granted such goods the same terms as enjoyed by the "most favored nation." One significant exception was the treaty with the **Zollverein**, which offered the United States unique reductions in import duties in return for reciprocal favors. "Most favored nation" terms were also secured for American vessels entering the ports of most of America's trading partners, with the **Treaty of Wanghia** winning this condition in the important trade with China in 1844. But U.S. negotiators also had considerable success in extending the right of American ships entering a foreign country's ports to be treated on the same terms as the vessels of that country, a principle known as reciprocity in navigation when the United States offered the same terms in exchange. Treaties with a substantial number of countries secured this right for American vessels, either trading directly from the United States or indirectly from a third country. Altogether such treaties helped to reduce the burdens on American traders and to guarantee their competitive position against rivals. *See also* OVERSEAS COMMERCE.

COMMONWEALTH VS. HUNT. This 1842 ruling in the Massachu-setts courts represented a significant early legal gain for the cause of organized **labor**. Previously efforts to encourage workers to join **trade unions** had been treated as criminal conspiracy, but as a result of this ruling, in favor of the Boston Journeymen Bootmakers Soci-ety, the criminal conspiracy charge was no longer deemed constitu-tional. The Massachusetts precedent caused the criminal conspiracy interpretation to be outlawed in other states as well.

COMPROMISE OF 1833. This was the accommodation that resolved the crisis posed by the threat of **nullification** in the winter of 1832-33. It was the work of, among others, Senators **Henry Clay** and **John Calhoun**, the latter having just returned to the Senate after resigning as vice-president. Its essential component was the passage of the **tar-iff of 1833**, which enabled South Carolina to back down from its ex-treme stance on nullification. The fact that the bill set out rules for the adjustment of duties over the next 10 years seemed to make possible the relegation of the tariff as a threatening **sectional** issue for the du-ration of that period. The compromise is also often seen as establish-ing an unsteady alliance between Clay and Calhoun in opposition to **Andrew Jackson**, as Calhoun and his followers supported Clay's land revenue **distribution** bill which passed at the same time as other elements of the compromise (albeit to be vetoed by the president). However, the compromise cannot be seen as their work alone, as it took Jackson's own role, support for the **Force bill**, and indeed the support for the tariff from many Jacksonians, to allow the whole package to succeed.

CONGREGATIONAL CHURCH. This Protestant denomination was the enduring heir of the Puritan religious tradition and, once the **Uni-tarians** split away, the last remnant of New England's strict Calvin-ism. Intimately bound up with the region's colonial and state gov-ernments throughout their history, Congregationalism lost its last buttress of state support in 1833, when Massachusetts abandoned the Standing Order by which towns were allowed to tax their citizens to support public worship by paying Congregational church ministers. Nevertheless, despite the attractiveness of alternative denominations such as the Baptists and Methodists, the Congregationalists still exer-cised disproportionate influence on public life through their involve-ment with moral reform groups and efforts to spread religious teach-ings through **benevolent** societies.

CONSCIENCE WHIGS. These were a group within the ranks of the **Whig** Party in New England, and in Massachusetts in particular, which leaned to an **abolitionist** or **anti-slavery** position on the increasing number of issues about **slavery** reemerging in the 1840s. Conscience Whigs tended to come from older, established families, and would form an important part of the **Free Soil** coalition. They opposed the southern slaveholder **Zachary Taylor** as the Whig candidate for the presidential **election of 1848**, and one of their own number, **Charles Francis Adams**, received the vice-presidential nomination of the Free Soil Party in that year.

CONSERVATIVE DEMOCRATS. This label refers to an element of the **Democratic** Party that supported state banks and **paper currency** in the midst of the **bank wars** of the later 1830s and early 1840s. Although some pro-bank Democrats continued to work within the party, such as the **Hunker** faction in New York, the label Conservative Democrat is more precisely and distinctively applied to those Democrats in many states who refused to work with the national party's lead on issues relating to banking and currency. Led by **Nathaniel Tallmadge** of New York and **William Rives** of Virginia they opposed the stances adopted by **Andrew Jackson** and **Martin Van Buren** on the **specie circular** and the **Independent Treasury** and instead cooperated with **Whigs** on such matters at both national and the local level, allowing the Whig opposition to block several administration measures from the 1837 **special session** onward. They even developed their own newspaper organ, *The Madisonian*, to put forward their alternative position.

Their actions weakened the Democratic Party as it approached the **election of 1840**, and indeed by 1839 there were signs of conservatives such as Rives abandoning their party altogether and officially joining the Whigs. However, the limits of this new alignment were reached when **Henry Clay**'s Whig supporters attempted to charter a new national bank in the first year of **John Tyler**'s term, many conservatives opposing the **bank bill of 1841** and supporting the president's plans for a much more limited national **fiscal** agency. Indeed, Rives would become one of Tyler's close advisors for the rest of his term.

CONTRERAS, BATTLE OF. This **Mexican War** battle took place on 19-20 August 1847, as part of **Winfield Scott**'s march on Mexico City. Although yet again outnumbered the U.S. army secured a good victory, inflicting 1,500 casualties for the reported loss of 60 men.

Together with the battle of **Cherubusco**, the Mexican defeat prompted **Santa Anna** to offer a temporary armistice.

COOPER, JAMES FENIMORE (1789-1851). Cooper was the first really professional American writer, producing throughout the period as well as during the years before. His prolific output fell into many different genres. He is most famous for his Leatherstocking Tales, best known through the earlier *Last of the Mohicans*, but with many of the same characters also appearing in two novels written during the Jacksonian era, *The Pathfinder* (1840) and *The Deerslayer* (1841). In these Cooper deals with the relationship between Americans and their wilderness environment and other ethnicities. He also produced several works of maritime fiction, such as *The Water Witch* (1831), an interest extended to his *History of the Navy of the United States* in 1839. His travel writing was another prominent form, the fruit of several years traveling in Europe in the late 1820s and early 1830s.

When Cooper returned to the United States, moving to New York City in 1833 and then to Cooperstown in 1834, he found his home country a much changed place, an experience which inspired some of the most penetrating social and political critiques of his time, notably *The American Democrat* (1838), *Home as Found* (1838), and *Homeward Bound* (1838). In these he still clung on to an optimistic belief that Americans had the capacity for being better than the people of other nations, but at the same time expressed disgust at what he perceived to be American society's demagoguery, lack of good taste, fickleness, greed, corruption, fraud, and prejudice. In the 1840s Cooper remained mostly at Cooperstown, producing still more novels such as *Satanstoe* (1845), *The Redskins* (1846), and *The Crater* (1848).

COOPER, PETER (1791-1883). Cooper was a New York-born manufacturer, who made his first fortune from a glue factory and then went on to diversify with the Canton ironworks in Baltimore in 1828, coal and iron mining, and the manufacture of wire and cable. He left his most lasting mark in 1829-30 by designing *Tom Thumb*, the first American steam locomotive, which operated on the **Baltimore and Ohio** railroad.

COOWESCOOWE (1790-1866). Also known as John Ross, from the Scottish side of his parentage, this **Cherokee** chief became one of the most fervent opponents to **Andrew Jackson**'s policy of **Indian re-**

moval. Ironically in the light of what followed, Coowescoowe had earlier in his life fought alongside Jackson against the **Creek** and at the battle of New Orleans in 1815. Although only one-eighth Cherokee himself, Coowescoowe rose to the position of principal chief of the majority eastern branch of the Cherokee in Georgia. Here he struggled to lead the resistance against a white encroachment sponsored by the state government and tolerated by Jackson's administration. After refusing to negotiate terms for his tribe's removal under the auspices of the 1830 Removal Act, Coowescoowe rejected both a treaty signed by a minority of the tribe and then the Treaty of **New Echota**, signed by some of his followers in his absence. He maintained his opposition to the very last possible moment, before being forced to lead his tribe to new territories west of the Mississippi in 1838-39 on the "**trail of tears**." Although challenged by civil war, eventually by 1844 he became chief of the united Cherokee nation under a new constitution that he had helped to draft.

CORN. This native, staple crop of North America was grown extensively across the corn belt region from Ohio to Iowa and also in states further south. National production rose steadily during the period, with a figure of 378 million bushels in 1839 climbing to 592 million bushels a decade later. Corn was used for food, mainly among the poorer groups in society, and as meal for livestock, and was also distilled to make whiskey. Although corn was important in those northern states where it was grown, as late as 1839 it was the South that was the main producer of the crop. Indeed, in that region it actually accounted for more acreage and a greater number of agricultural units than did **cotton**. However, although cheap to produce, the very low prices it fetched meant that it remained a convenience crop servicing other activities on farms rather than a seriously successful cash crop in its own right.

"CORPORAL'S GUARD." *See* KITCHEN CABINET.

"CORRUPT BARGAIN" CHARGE. This accusation represented an important part of the impetus behind **Andrew Jackson**'s movement toward the **election of 1828**, giving the candidate and his supporters a serious grievance that energized their campaign. The charge arose from the circumstances of **John Quincy Adams**' elevation to the presidency four years earlier, by means of selection in the House of Representatives after the failure of the electorate to produce a majority winner in terms of electoral college votes. The fact that Jackson had won a majority of the popular vote as well as the highest number of electoral college votes made Adams' subsequent victory tantamount to robbery in Jackson's supporters' eyes, and caused them to search around for a guilty party. The fact that the supporters of the fourth candidate, **Henry Clay**, had ultimately backed Adams, and that Clay had subsequently been appointed secretary of state, the traditional route to the presidential succession, suggested that Clay had sold out for personal advancement. The likelihood was that Clay would have supported Adams anyway, especially when he received assurances that Adams would abandon his New England-derived opposition to federal support for **internal improvements**. If there was a bargain then this was probably it, as Adams did indeed come out in support of improvements in his inaugural, while at the first opportunity they got New Englanders in Congress began to support the **National Road** project they had previously opposed. Nevertheless, the more damaging "corrupt bargain" charge stuck, tarnishing Adams' own reputation prior to his reelection effort in 1828 and haunting Clay's campaign in the presidential **election of 1832** and even the one in **1844** as well.

COTTON. In terms of income generated, cotton was the key **agricultural** product in antebellum America, accounting for over half the nation's exports during the period. Of course it was most closely associated with the South, and with southwestern states in particular, where it was grown in a range of types on most sizes of agricultural establishment, ranging from the small family-run farm to plantations based upon **slavery**. More and more people got involved in the production of cotton in this period, with the result that the volume produced rose from over 730,000 bales in 1830, to around 1.3 million bales a decade later, and to nearly 2.5 million bales in 1849. Of course its significance was not production-driven alone, its value being due to the fact that it provided the raw material vital to the burgeoning textiles manufactures of Britain and the rest of Europe and of the northeastern United States. Cotton's role in the export economy was so prominent that any rise and fall in demand for it could influence the economic health of the whole nation, as in the mid-1830s when British demand pushed up prices by 50 percent compared to 1830. However, when credit tightened, causing British demand for cotton to drop, the price of cotton fell and the basis for many speculative hopes was crushed. Merchants who had gambled on cotton prices remaining high faced bankruptcy, while many planters, in the Southwest in particular, were left with debts they could not pay. As such cotton played a significant contributory role in the coming of the **panic of 1837** and the longer-term depression of 1837-43.

COTTON WHIGS. This label is most accurately applied to northern **Whigs** in the 1840s whose belief in the status quo, in property rights, and in the Union caused them to abhor the potentially disruptive **sectional** message of the **abolitionists**. As a group, including the likes of **Daniel Webster**, **Edward Everett**, Robert Winthrop, Rufus Choate, and **Millard Fillmore**, they tried to maintain good relations with their economic and party allies in the South, Whig southern planters, which accounts for the use of the "cotton" moniker. In order to avoid damage to their party's national solidarity and to inter-regional economic links they tried to oppose or avoid policies likely to cause offense to the South and strove to interpret others, such as **expansion**, in non-sectional terms. The label is also used by some historians, less accurately, to refer to southern Whigs.

CRANDALL, PRUDENCE (1803-1890). This educator and reformer of Rhode Island Quaker stock became something of a *cause célèbre* among those **abolitionists** keen to offer genuinely equal opportunities to African-Americans. In 1831 Crandall established a school for girls in Canterbury, Connecticut, and outraged many of her white patrons by taking the radical step of admitting an African-American girl to the school. Two years later she decided to open a school exclusively for black girls, attracting an enrolment of 15-20 students. Local white opinion was outraged and pressure of various forms was brought to bear to force Crandall to close down the school. There were physical attacks on the school and threats against her person, as well as resort to old vagrancy laws to challenge the school's legality. Ultimately Connecticut produced its Black law that forbade the establishment of any school enrolling non-resident African-Americans and that insisted that any school for African-Americans could only operate with the consent of the local community. Crandall was charged with violating this law and, although supported in court by leading abolitionists, she was found guilty in October 1833. She would later be released on appeal on a technicality but she had to abandon her school in the face of further physical intimidation. She would go on to open another school in Illinois in 1842.

CRAWFORD, WILLIAM HARRIS (1772-1834). Crawford was secretary of the treasury under James Monroe and one of the presidential candidates in the 1824 election. At one time considered a frontrunner for the presidency for 1828, he was persuaded to stand down from the campaign by assurances that **Andrew Jackson** was a safe alternative, capable of uniting old Republican groups in North and South. As such Crawford's following constituted a significant portion of the growing electoral coalition for **Old Hickory**. Crawford went on to serve as a circuit judge in Georgia from 1827 to 1830 before retiring because of ill-health. He played one further significant part in the course of Jackson's administration, by leaking a letter to Jackson that convinced the latter of **John Calhoun**'s opposition to his conduct as an army officer in Florida. This helped stoke Jackson's anger over the **Florida report**, and contributed to the breakdown in relations between president and vice-president.

"CREDIT SYSTEM." The first third of the 19th century had witnessed a significant modification in the way the credit system operated. Previously credit had been granted on a short-term basis, either by banks in the Northeast and West or by merchants in the South, allowing businesses and individuals to make purchases on the basis of promises to pay when they had earned income. Now as larger projects such as transportation improvements required greater levels of financing, there was an increase in long-term credit. This provision made capital less liquid and increased the danger that banks would not be able to honor their notes with specie. This was clearly displayed in the **panic of 1837** when the ability of banks to make such loans was badly restricted as lenders became reluctant to tie up their capital for long periods. The late 1830s saw the emergence of specific savings banks designed to accumulate the reserves necessary to make longer-term loans, institutions whose activities came to be handled by stock exchanges, while in the 1840s insurance companies also became a major provider of long-term credit. Politically the credit system was one of several aspects of business to be brought together for ideological attack by the more radical elements of the **Democratic Party**, who portrayed it as just one more way in which the privileged **"money power"** lined its own pockets at the expense of the producing classes.

CREEK. The Creek, one of the "five civilized tribes," had been among the strongest Native American groups south of the Ohio River, residing in parts of Georgia and Alabama. However, following defeat by General **Andrew Jackson** in the War of 1812, the Georgian Creek endured a long series of land cessions until 1828 when, under pressure from Governor George Troup, they gave up all their remaining lands in the state and moved to the Indian territory which later became Oklahoma. Those remaining in Alabama signed a treaty in March 1832 in line with the **Indian Removal Act** of 1830. Although on the surface this seemed to guarantee their position by allotting lands to individuals in place of the old tribal land possession, in fact, as in so many other cases of removal, it only made them more vulnerable to fraudulent land grabs and gave them individual insecurity of holding rather than collective security. Many now chose to leave and were removed by means of private companies whose practices made the removal experience one of inadequate provision and much discomfort. Those who refused to leave were marched out in chains. By 1837 some 15,000 had been removed.

CREOLE **CASE.** This was another case, similar to that of the *Enterprise*, arising out of an uprising of **slaves** on board an American vessel transporting slaves between ports in two slaveholding states, Norfolk, Virginia and New Orleans. When the slaves landed the *Creole* at Nassau in the Bahamas in 1841, all but the mutiny's leaders and murderers were declared free by the islands' British authorities. The ensuing refusal of the British government to hand over the slaves created a crisis with the U.S. government, as the official American interpretation was that the vessel's involvement in the coasting trade made it immune to British colonial law. **Abolitionist** opinion, both in the North and in Britain, which condemned any **trade in slaves**, demanded that Britain stand by the actions of the island's authorities. Meanwhile southern anger at the refusal to return the mutineers put equal pressure on Secretary of State **Daniel Webster**.

He eventually decided to ask for compensation rather than the return of both the mutineers and the other freed slaves, and, in an exchange of letters, agreed with Britain the means by which such circumstances would never be allowed to happen again. Specifically, governors of British islands were not in the future to interfere with American coastal slave traders driven to their islands by accident or by force. The episode also sharpened debates over extradition terms included in the formal **Webster-Ashburton Treaty**, making murder and piracy, among others, clear extraditable offenses. Meanwhile the freed slaves from the *Creole* were never returned, their role in the whole affair being marked ultimately in 1853 by a grant to their owners of over $100,000. The episode allowed opportunity for more public discussion of slavery and the coastal slave trade, with **Joshua Giddings** making a very public stand on the issue.

CRITTENDEN, JOHN J. (1787-1863). This lawyer and statesman was educated at the College of William and Mary before returning to a political career in the state of his birth, Kentucky. In early battles over banking and finance Crittenden aligned himself with groups that favored the **Second Bank of the United States,** opposing the likes of **Amos Kendall** and **Francis Blair.** It was not surprising, then, that he began to lean toward support for **Henry Clay** and became one of his closest lieutenants in the **Whig** Party. After serving as U.S. district attorney in Kentucky under **John Quincy Adams** and then as his state's secretary of state up to 1834, Crittenden began a fairly lengthy period in the Senate, between 1835 and 1841 and 1842 to 1848, in the second term replacing Clay after the latter's resignation. In between, **William Henry Harrison** appointed him federal attorney general in 1841, only for Crittenden to resign with most of the rest of **John Tyler**'s Cabinet later that year. That said, he had worked hard to reconcile Tyler and Clay Whigs behind a **bank bill** they could all agree on and had counseled Clay not to push the president too hard. Once back in the Senate Crittenden adopted the expected Whig line of opposing both the **Texas annexation** and the declaration of the **Mexican War,** if not the latter's prosecution once it had begun. His loyalty to Clay remained unchallenged until the very end of the period when he considered his fellow Kentuckian unsuitable for presidential nomination in 1848 and so supported the candidacy of **Zachary Taylor** instead. Crittenden took over the office of governor of Kentucky in 1848, before reentering national politics as **Millard Fillmore**'s attorney general in 1850. *See also* CABINET RESIGNATION, 1841.

CROCKETT, DAVID (1786-1836). Davy Crockett was a renowned frontiersman and Tennessee representative between 1827 and 1831. He was a friend of **Andrew Jackson** but parted company with the president over **land policy** and **Indian removal,** so that when he returned to Congress in 1833 he did so as an opposition representative. After a second defeat for reelection in 1835 Crockett moved to **Texas** where he died in the defense of the **Alamo** in 1836. His death only enhanced the folk hero status that he had earlier helped to create by touring the eastern states with his autobiography in 1834.

CUBA. In the wake of the **Mexican War,** some extreme **expansionists** turned their attention to the Spanish island of Cuba. Pushed by the likes of **John O'Sullivan** and Stephen Douglas in spring 1848, President **James Polk** gave provisional support to the idea of purchasing and annexing the island and discussed the proposal with a divided

Cabinet, **James Buchanan** opposing and **Robert Walker** strongly supporting the idea. Rejecting any thoughts of military action to support or foment a revolt on Cuba, it was agreed to assure Spain of good U.S. intentions and to offer $100,000,000 should it be willing to sell the island. Spanish refusal to do so brought an end to any such prospect.

CUSHING, CALEB (1800-1879). This Harvard-educated lawyer, politician, and statesman from Massachusetts experienced a volatile career in national politics. After electoral defeats in 1832 and 1833 Cushing served in the House as a **Whig** between 1835 and 1843. He always leaned to the more conservative wing of that party, worried by **Democratic** attacks on property in banks but equally expressing sympathy for southerners in the face of **abolitionist** threats to their **states' rights** and property. In the period 1841 to 1844 he gained notoriety among Whigs for his support for **John Tyler**, although Cushing's earlier course ought to have made predictable this preference for an equally conservative figure. He acted as one of Tyler's "corporal's guard" of advisors, attacking regular Whig attempts to bring the executive branch to heel and denying that those behind the "**Whig manifesto**" were truly representative of their party. Cushing's reward was higher office, with Tyler attempting to have him appointed as secretary of the treasury, but three times on the same day the Whig-dominated Senate threw out the nominations. Instead Cushing had to be content with the role of special representative to China, leaving in 1843 and returning two years later with the 1844 **Treaty of Wanghia**. By then he had become a Democrat and on his return he supported the **Mexican War**, even leading his own regiment into action. He would be the defeated Democratic candidate for governor of Massachusetts in elections in 1847 and 1848.

– D –

DAIRY FARMING. Dairy farming became an increasingly important northern **agricultural** pursuit, especially in those more eastern states which suffered a relative decline in their position in the nation's overall balance of commercial **wheat** cultivation. Dairy production began to be founded upon a more commercial basis from the 1820s onward and by 1840 was worth about $33.8 million. The states of New Hampshire and Vermont became specialist dairy producers, while Massachusetts, Pennsylvania, New York, Ohio, and Virginia also witnessed significant dairy production in both milk and cheese. The introduction of "milk trains" in the 1840s facilitated the faster transportation of that product to **urban** markets and served to increase the commercialized basis of dairy farming.

DALLAS, GEORGE MIFFLIN (1792-1864). Dallas was born in Philadelphia, educated at Princeton, and became a leading Pennsylvanian **Democrat**, holding a range of local and national offices before the culmination of his career as **James Polk**'s vice-president. He began to come to prominence as mayor of Philadelphia from 1828 to 1829, and then as U.S. district attorney for eastern Pennsylvania between 1829 and 1831. Two years in the Senate were followed by two as his state's attorney general, by which time some were even considering him in terms of a possible presidential nomination for the **election of 1836**. His one-time rival, **Martin Van Buren**, appointed Dallas to serve as U.S. minister to Russia and on his return in 1839 offered him the attorney general's position, which Dallas declined.

Although Dallas' earlier career had not always seen him fully in line with Jacksonian policies (he had acted as a counsel for the **Second Bank** and, although advising **Nicholas Biddle** against attempting re-charter in 1832, had voted in favor of the bill and for overriding Jackson's **bank veto**), by the late 1830s he was considered a sound Democrat and a suitable northern balance on the presidential ticket with Polk in 1844. That he had family ties to the arch expansionist **Robert Walker** and himself supported the **Texas annexation** also made him attractive. Dallas' term as vice-president was notable for patronage battles with his Pennsylvanian rival **James Buchanan**, and for the casting votes he gave in favor of the administration's **tariff bill of 1846**, a stance that caused him to lose political credibility in his home state, which preferred a **protective tariff.**

DANA, JAMES DWIGHT (1813-1895). Born in Utica, New York and graduating from Yale in 1833, James Dana was a scientist with interests in geology, mineralogy, and zoology. After publishing his *System of Mineralogy* in 1837 he was appointed to serve on the **U.S. South Seas exploring expedition**. Upon his return he was employed for a lengthy period producing numerous reports of his findings, including the *Report on Zoophytes* (1846) and the *Report on the Geology of the Pacific* (1849). In addition Dana co-edited the *American Journal of Science* from 1846 and three years later was appointed professor of natural history at Yale.

DANA, RICHARD HENRY (1815-1882). This writer and lawyer born in Cambridge, Massachusetts, is most famous for *Two Years before the Mast*, published in 1840, an account of his experiences on a sailing ship voyage from Boston to California and back via the Cape Horn route. It proved influential in exposing the conditions faced by many American sailors and generated calls for reform of practices such as flogging. Dana's experiences also inspired him to become interested in the legal aspects of maritime life, as revealed in *The Seaman's Friend* of 1841. On returning from his voyage he graduated from Harvard and was admitted to the bar, becoming a lecturer on law, politics, and patriotism. In the 1840s Dana dabbled in politics, becoming an important **anti-slavery** figure, being present at the founding of the **Free Soil** Party.

DAVIS, ALEXANDER (1803-1892). This New York-born artist and architect grew up in New Jersey and the state of his birth, before starting to work in the printing trade, where he developed the skill of producing drawings and engravings of buildings. From here it was a short step to becoming an architect and, as part of the Greek revival movement in American architecture, Davis was responsible for the design of a number of significant public buildings. At first employed by, and then the partner of, **Ithiel Town** between 1829 and 1835 and again between 1842 and 1843, he formed what was effectively the first professional architecture business in America. Together with Town, among others, Davis helped to design the New York Customs House (begun in 1833), the North Carolina State Capitol (1833), the Illinois State Capitol (1837), and the Virginia Military Institute. He also designed many private homes and villas, which work gave rise to his publication of *Rural Residences* in 1837.

DEERE, JOHN (1804-1886). Deere was born in Vermont, and later moved to Illinois. A blacksmith by trade, he is best known for improvements he made to the design of the plowshare and for the farm machinery manufacturing company he developed on the back of his invention and reputation. The key feature of his plowshare was its facility for cleaning itself as it cut through the soil, an important innovation for farmers on the heavier soil lands of the prairies. The company bearing Deere's name was founded in 1837 and underwent a considerable expansion in Moline, Illinois, in 1848.

DELAWARE, NEW CONSTITUTION. The state of Delaware ratified a new constitution in 1831. Contrary to the hopes of many that it would address the disparity between changes in population and the apportionment of representatives to the state's three counties, its provisions mainly applied to the judiciary.

DEMOCRACY IN AMERICA. This important work by **Alexis de Tocqueville**, researched during a trip in 1831-32 to investigate America's penal system, remains one of the classic examinations of American society of any age From his own observations and from interviews with a wide range of individuals including prison officials and Supreme Court justices, farmers and businessmen, de Tocqueville produced a work investigating the administrative and legislative institutions of the United States, as well as their impact upon popular manners and habits. It was published in two volumes in France and translated into four volumes in English, between 1835 and 1840. In it de Tocqueville was generally supportive of an American system that allowed the best of European ideas to flourish. At the same time he warned of the danger of democracy becoming tyrannical in its own right, with the majority constantly endangering the rights of the minority. He hoped that the absence of an institutionalized aristocracy in America could be compensated for by the influence of the law, religion, family, and voluntary associations. At the same time he warned that specialization in **manufacturing** functions would create inequality between employers and employees.

DEMOCRATIC REVIEW. Fully entitled the *United States Magazine and Democratic Review*, this periodical publication was founded by **John O'Sullivan**, with the backing of **Benjamin Butler** and **Henry Gilpin**. **Andrew Jackson** was the first subscriber and in some ways the *Democratic Review* can be seen as the intellectual organ of the **Democratic** Party of the 1840s. It attracted writers of the caliber of **Nathaniel Hawthorne, Henry Longfellow, George Bancroft, John Greenleaf Whittier, William Bryant**, and **James Paulding**, all drawn by O'Sullivan's skilful editing and talent-finding. The *Democratic Review*'s columns were the first to include the term **"manifest destiny"** in writing, in an 1845 article entitled "Annexation."

DEMOCRATS. The Democrats were the most successful and resilient of the main political parties that made up the **Second Party System** of the broader Jacksonian era. They drew on roots in the Republican and Democratic-Republican parties, gradually coalescing around the figure of **Andrew Jackson** in the run-up to the **election of 1828**. Although initially the Democrats did appear heavily dependent upon

Jackson's personality as their central focus, it is clear that his appeal touched on certain ideological undercurrents and helped to sustain a much more cohesive party, and one which only became more cohesive as the 1830s, and that decade's key policy battle, the **bank wars**, progressed. This cohesion was allied to effective organization from local to national level, as the Democrats enthusiastically accepted the value of parties as a way of organizing political activity and used the tools of party to good effect, notably patronage, the press, and populist electioneering techniques.

The result was electoral triumph throughout the two decades, most notably in the presidential **elections in 1828, 1832, 1836, and 1844**. As the new policy agenda of **expansion** and debates over the extension of **slavery** began to force their way forward in the 1840s, the party did begin to lose some of its discipline. Major factions displayed discontent with the party's nominations for 1844 and 1848, and in the latter election many bolted the party to support the **Free Soil** candidacy of former party star, **Martin Van Buren**. However, the majority remained loyal and took the party into the 1850s as the strongest remaining national political party.

Almost inevitably in the American political system there were individual, regional, and local variations in Democratic ideas and policy stances, but the common core was strong enough to make it possible to identify the party's main outlook. Seeing themselves as the heirs of the Jeffersonian political tradition, they expressed support for democratic principles and the common man and for a philosophy of limited government. This meant opposing any artifice that might benefit a few at the expense of the many, such as special government charters for economic interest groups or too great a level of **protective tariff** that might help some but only at the cost of disadvantaging others. They expressed a preference for a currency based upon **hard money** as the most natural means of exchange, another sign of their hostility to artificial promotion of economic development, which they considered potentially corrupting of American morals. Culturally they were more likely to oppose the reform impulse of revived religion, betraying an element of anti-clericalism, and they were more open to the interests of **immigrant** groups. In this sympathy for outsider groups, among whom they might possibly include white Southerners, the Democrats revealed an element of what would now be termed multiculturalism. However, it should be stressed that in their case this did not stretch to include other races, such as Native Americans and both free and enslaved African-Americans, both these groups generally suffering as a result of Democratic policies. Overall, though, it would be fair to sum up the Democrats as a party that, in most cases, preferred to offer individuals the opportunity for self-determination rather than imposing upon them an agenda determined by government or by reformers.

DEPOSIT AND DISTRIBUTION ACT. This act of June 1836 was passed in Congress by **Whigs** and more conservative members of the **Democratic** Party. Its two main components, regulation of the **deposit bank** system and **distribution** of surplus revenue, both had been at one time favored policies of President **Andrew Jackson**, but the way the former was presented and the fact that Jackson had now come out against distribution brought the president close to a veto of the bill. However, a number of amendments made the deposit bank side of the bill palatable and important enough for him to sign, even with distribution attached.

The main element of the deposit system part of the bill was a proposal to limit the amount of federal funds that could be deposited in each deposit bank, in effect necessitating an increase in the number of banks. Such an expansion (which in practice turned out to be one from 33 banks to 81) replaced the original Jackson administration proposal for only one deposit bank in each state and territory, and caused the president to fear that having more deposit banks would only amplify the problems he increasingly associated with all banks. The act also stipulated that only those banks that paid specie on demand could be selected as deposit banks, a clause that had dramatic consequences when so many banks suspended specie payments during the **panic of 1837**. The administration made the bill more acceptable by having inserted a clause insisting that deposit banks only receive or issue notes worth $5 or above, that figure to rise to $20 by the end of Jackson's term, in an effort to promote a **hard money** currency circulation.

The distribution component of the act provided for a federal reserve of $5 million but any further surplus from customs and land sales revenues would be dispersed to the states in quarterly installments, proportional to their populations. Many states committed their share to assist in paying for education and **internal improvements** but, as in the case of the deposit bank element, the panic of 1837 would later affect the implementation of the act, by undermining federal revenues so much that there was no longer a surplus to distribute, causing the final installment to be suspended.

DEPOSIT BANKS. These were the state banks chosen by **Andrew Jackson**'s administration to act as repositories of federal funds, after the **"removal" of the federal deposits** from branches of the **Second Bank of the United States** in 1833. Initially, in October 1833, there were seven such banks (two in Boston, three in New York, one in Philadelphia, and one in Maryland), or "pet" banks as political opponents labeled them after it appeared that the administration was more likely to choose banks run by **Democrats** even though many others met the administration's own financial and procedural criteria for selection. Alarmingly, the practices of some of the selected banks seemed similar to actions criticized in the case of the Second Bank. As a greater proportion of federal business came to be done with the deposit banks and as the Second Bank neared its final demise, the number of deposit banks rose to 22 by January 1834 and to 33 by June 1836, while under the influence of the 1836 **Deposit and Distribution Act** the total number rose to the high 80s in November 1836. This later expansion in numbers came about in the face of Jackson's opposition, as he worried about the danger that even more deposit banks would increase the risks of corruption, let alone of economic mismanagement. This concern was no doubt exacerbated by the fact that in places it also proved necessary to lodge deposits with banks run by political enemies.

The 1836 act was also the culmination of efforts to introduce tighter regulation of the deposit banks in response to their greater numbers and potentially greater influence. Certainly the fact that they now received and held the larger share of federal deposits, at a volume increased by a boom in federal land sales, only served to raise both the pressure on and the temptation to deposit banks to increase loans and note circulation. Successive secretaries of the treasury had kept a close eye on their operations, demanding reports and insisting on a limited lending policy. **Levi Woodbury** even used the New York branches as a check on other state banks, in the same way as the Second Bank had once operated. Now the 1836 act attempted to check over-issue of loans and paper money, by putting a bottom limit on the value of bank notes receivable by deposit banks and by denying deposit bank status to any institution that suspended paying specie on demand. Ultimately this provision kicked in during the **panic of 1837**, causing all but five of the deposit banks to be banned from receiving federal deposits. Even when many resumed specie payments some remained disqualified because in the intervening year, in order to provide some means of circulation in the absence of specie, they had had to issue smaller notes than acceptable under the terms of the 1836 act. **Whig** attempts in 1838 to revise the small note clause were defeated by Democrats in Congress.

The impact of the panic on the deposit bank system reinforced an interesting shift in political stances. Whigs, initially opponents of the deposit bank system, now defended it against the proposed **Independent Treasury** scheme of **Martin Van Buren**'s administration. Convinced of the ability of the Treasury to supervise its own funds, in the absence of enough qualified state banks, many Democrats were more comfortable with the notion of a divorce of the federal government from banks, in preference to retaining the deposit system which might fail again.

DEPOSITS, REMOVAL OF. *See* REMOVAL OF FEDERAL DEPOSITS.

DIAL, THE. This journal, established in 1840 by, among others, **George Ripley**, **Ralph Waldo Emerson**, and **Margaret Fuller**, aimed to provide a vehicle for the publication of the verse and philosophy of the **transcendentalists**.

DICKERSON, MAHLON (1770-1853). This New Jersey politician and statesman was educated at Princeton and had interests in the law and manufacturing before entering political life. Dickerson had served as governor of his state in 1815-17 and then as senator from the latter year to 1833, before attaining national prominence as secretary of the navy between 1834 and 1838. His friendship with **Martin Van Buren** helped him to secure and retain this position, despite the fact that he was a strong supporter of the **protective tariff** and probably a consistent backer of the **Second Bank** throughout. Eventually Dickerson resigned under a cloud of criticism from many who thought him inefficient, and certainly he bequeathed to his successors the necessity for much work of **administrative** and **naval reform**.

DISTRIBUTION. This was the label given to a series of measures designed to provide the states with a share of federal revenue to spend on projects of their choice. Distribution was proposed as a sidestep to constitutional objections to direct federal funding of and chartering of **internal improvements** projects in individual states where a clear national or maritime interest was not evident. It assumed a variety of forms, including proposals that a proportion of all federal land sales revenue be distributed at any time or, after the paying-off of the **national debt**, a proportion of the federal surplus. As proposals usually included an element of proportionality linked to states' populations, distribution tended to be favored by northeastern states that would benefit disproportionately from the measure. Western states feared they would get less and demanded that they get special favors such as a share of federal land within their own borders for themselves before any sale and division by the federal government, but generally they worried that distribution might be used to justify higher land prices. Southerners tended to oppose distribution as liable to encourage higher **tariffs**.

Distribution had a checkered political and legislative career. **Andrew Jackson** proposed the measure in his first annual message, by a constitutional amendment should it initially be deemed unconstitutional, but by 1831-32 he had turned against it. Instead distribution came to be associated more with **Henry Clay** and the **National Republican** and, later **Whig**, parties, who saw in it a method of supporting internal improvements after Jackson's **Maysville Road veto**. Specific legislative proposals came in 1831 from Secretary of the Treasury **Louis McLane**, to sell lands to states in which they lay, with the proceeds being distributed among all the states, and then in 1832 in a land bill, by which 15 percent of land sales revenue would go to the state in which land was situated. Neither succeeded in Congress although the Senate did pass the latter. Clay's distribution bill of 1832 proposed that 10 percent of federal lands sale revenue go to the state where the lands lay, while the remaining 90 percent would go into a common pot to be shared out among all the states proportional to population. As the bill also stipulated that land prices should be kept high, it seemed likely that it would meet with strong opposition, but in 1833 it was passed, southerners voting in its favor as part of the **compromise of 1833**. This time, though, it was President Jackson who blocked distribution with his pocket veto, on the grounds that it militated against cheaper federal land prices.

Even when distribution was successfully passed and approved by presidents, its impact proved short-lived. Although implemented by the 1836 **Deposit and Distribution Act**, distribution was suspended by the **special session** of Congress in 1837, as the nation reeled from the effects of the **panic** of that year and as the federal government needed more revenue. In the process many states were embarrassed by debts taken out in anticipation of the surplus enabling them to pay them off, and throughout the rest of **Martin Van Buren**'s term Whigs continued to press for the reintroduction of distribution as the most appropriate way to alleviate this problem of state debt. Clay did succeed in getting the **Distribution and Preemption Act** passed in

the special session of 1841, but only a year later the practical implementation of the measure was terminated yet again as it fell victim to
a clause which abandoned distribution in the event of tariff duties rising above 20 percent, as they did in the **1842 tariff**. An attempt to
pass a separate bill allowing distribution to continue even though duties were rising above that level was thwarted by **John Tyler**'s
pocket veto.

DISTRIBUTION AND PREEMPTION ACT OF 1841. Passed in the
special session of 1841, this bill represented the successful effort of
Henry Clay to log-roll his preferred policy of **distribution** through
Congress on the back of another issue. Indeed, in addition to support
from those favoring **preemption**, Clay drew upon the supporters of
the **Bankruptcy Act** that also passed at the same time. The act had
two main elements. The preemption component provided for permanent extension of the terms of an 1830 act which gave settlers the
right to stake a claim to surveyed land prior to purchase and to buy up
to 160 acres at the cheap price of $1.25 an acre. The distribution ele-
ment was put forward in the form of a grant to the states of federally-
owned land, with some 500,000 acres going to each new state. Ten
percent of the revenue from the sale of those lands would go to the
state in which the land was located while the remaining 90 percent
was to be divided among all the states on a proportional basis linked
to population. However, the distribution of land revenues was made
conditional upon tariff duties remaining at or below the 20 percent
level prescribed in the **tariff of 1833**, a nod to the fears of **John Tyler** and other southerners that distribution would be used as an excuse
to push tariff rates higher to make up for the loss to the federal government of some of its land sales revenue. In this form President Tyler was prepared to approve the act, hoping that distribution would
help to pay off state debts. However, in practice distribution was only
to be implemented for a short time, as pressure to raise **tariff duties
in 1842** triggered its suspension.

DIX, DOROTHEA (1802-1887). Born in Maine, Dorothea Dix was a
schoolteacher who became one of the most influential philanthropists
and reformers of the age. Upon her return from a trip to England,
where she became familiar with the work of prison reformers, she
visited literally hundreds of prisons, asylums, poorhouses, and hospitals in the North and Upper South. The result was a dogged campaign
for major reform in the care of the insane, stated most notably in a
memorial to the Massachusetts state legislature in January 1843, but

repeated in approaches to several other state governments as well. Dix also wrote *Prisons and Prison Discipline* in 1845 to convey her views. Her work directly influenced the creation of six new hospitals and also reforms in older ones, but she failed in an attempt to secure public land from the federal government to back the development of asylums for the mentally ill.

DONELSON, ANDREW JACKSON (1799-1871). Donelson was the nephew of **Rachel Jackson** and a loyal supporter of her husband and his fellow Tennessean **Andrew Jackson**, from the time he acted as his aide during the first Seminole war in Florida through to the former president's death. From 1829 to his resignation in 1836 Donelson served officially in the General Land Office while acting as the president's private secretary, helping to draft state papers and annual messages. He would survive in this role despite the difficulties he and his wife **Emily** experienced during the **Eaton Affair**. Donelson's later political career was served mainly in significant diplomatic pursuits. He was chargé to Texas in the last months of **John Tyler**'s administration, continuing into the early period of **James Polk**'s. In this position his cautious approach helped to counter the more clumsy efforts of even more extreme **Texas annexationists** and to coax Texans into final agreement to annexation. He moved on to the position of U.S. representative in Prussia before returning to edit the *Washington Union* in 1849, a post for which he had been considered as early as the start of the Polk administration.

DONELSON, EMILY (1807-1836). Emily was the wife of **Andrew Jackson Donelson** and part of the wider family community of President **Andrew Jackson**. When Jackson entered the White House recently widowed, Emily stepped into the breach and effectively became his hostess. Although doing sterling service for most of the period she and her husband were in Washington, there were periods of tension notably during the **Eaton Affair**, when Emily refused to socialize with **Peggy Eaton**. Indeed this led to a period spent at home in Tennessee before she reluctantly agreed to resume her Washington role in September 1830.

DONNER PARTY. Made up mainly of two families, led by George Donner, this party of 89 settlers became stranded in the Sierra Nevada Mountains in 1846 after problems had delayed their migration from Illinois to **California**. As they reached the mountains late in the migration season, the party split up and severe weather killed, in all,

44 of their number, while the others were forced to resort to cannibalism in order to survive. This turn of events has afforded the episode notoriety ever since.

DORR, THOMAS (1805-1854). Dorr was a Harvard graduate and prominent Rhode Island lawyer, who became famous to history as one of the leaders of the 1841-42 popular revolt that bears his name. Already in the 1830s he had served in Rhode Island's government, first as a **Whig**, before rejecting their policies in the **bank wars** and lining up on the more radical, **Locofoco**, wing of the **Democratic** Party. In 1841 Dorr helped to organize the People's Party, demanded a liberalization of the state's political practices, and suggested how in his draft of a new constitution. It bore the hallmark of his Locofoco views, providing for free suffrage, the secret ballot, an independent judiciary, the removal of restrictions on voting on the grounds of country of birth, educational reform, and limits to special privileges. In the **Dorr Rebellion** proper he was elected governor of a shadow government in April 1842, but then fled after the revolt's failure in the face of threatened state and federal military force. Dorr returned to Rhode Island in 1844, only to be arrested, convicted, and sentenced to life imprisonment. He spent 20 months in jail before being released and then continued his support for the Democratic Party. He was pardoned in 1851.

DORR REBELLION. This political rebellion took place in Rhode Island in 1841-42, as the state struggled to adapt its institutional framework to changing social and economic realities. In the face of **immigration** and a growing **urban** population the state's government, still based on its original royal charter, seemed increasingly inadequate. For example, it limited certain legal privileges to propertyholders. More importantly it restricted the **suffrage** to propertyholders and their oldest sons, and to annual rent-payers. The effect of these stipulations was that in some areas, such as Providence, as many as 95 percent of white males were excluded from voting, while for the state as a whole almost half the white male population could not vote. The existing constitution also disproportionately represented the population of rural areas at the expense of the expanding urban districts.

After the established government refused to set up a constitutional convention, some Rhode Islanders took matters into their own hands. In October 1841 they drafted their own People's Party constitution, including white manhood suffrage, legislative reapportionment, and other reforms. Although it was produced by a completely unsanctioned convention, the people of Rhode Island hailed the draft. However, the state government rejected it and produced its own Freeman's constitution, a modification of the old charter. This clearly failed to meet the mood of the times and the people of the state rejected it in a popular vote, before proceeding to elect **Thomas Dorr** as governor of a rival state government in spring 1842. The formally elected governor, Samuel King, was reelected by the officially sanctioned means, and both the state's supreme court and **John Tyler**'s administration refused to recognize the People's constitution. Tyler did refrain, though, from sending military support to the state government, on the grounds that no actual violent revolt had taken place.

However, after a failed attempt by Dorr and his followers to seize the state arsenal and offices, King sent out the militia and this time Tyler did warn the rebels to disperse or be faced with federally approved militia action. In the face of this opposition the rebels surrendered without any hope of success. These events precipitated further modification of the Freeman's constitution, with a widening of suffrage levels, and eventually this succeeded in securing a favorable popular majority, **Rhode Island's new constitution** coming into effect in May 1843. On a national level, although criticized from both extremes for his performance during the rebellion, later investigations found that Tyler's conduct had been exemplary, as he avoided jumping to extreme responses to the developing situation in Rhode Island.

DOUGHTY, THOMAS (1793-1856). This lithographer and painter is often regarded as foreshadowing the development of the **Hudson River School** of painters. Doughty was born in Philadelphia and worked as a leather currier until he turned to a popular and successful career in painting from 1816 onward. He became one of the first native-born Americans to specialize in landscapes, his common subjects being the Adirondack and Catskill Mountains and the Hudson River valley, in works such as *In the Catskills* (1836). Doughty was noted for his light, almost primitive, treatment of subject, such as in his 1835 work, *In Nature's Wonderland*. At various times in his career he worked from Philadelphia, Baltimore, and Boston, even establishing a painting school in the latter city.

DOUGLASS, FREDERICK (1817-1895). Frederick Douglass was a slave, born in Maryland by the name Frederick Bailey. He demonstrated considerable initiative and native resistance to **slavery** by forming a secret school in 1833 and a self-improvement society for his fellow slaves in Baltimore. But it was his successful escape from slavery, on his second attempt in 1838, which propelled him into historical consciousness as one of the great African-American opponents of slavery. After settling in Massachusetts, within three years Douglass entered the ranks of **abolitionists** when he gave an off-the-cuff address to an **anti-slavery** convention at Nantucket. As a result he was engaged by the Massachusetts Anti-Slavery Society to give lectures and to assist with the underground railroad. It was during this period that he produced *The Narrative of the Life of Frederick Douglass* (1845), whose autobiographical character soon made it an abolitionist classic. Between 1845 and 1847 Douglass spent time in England to evade the fugitive slave laws, and there his increasing reputation led to money being raised to buy his freedom. On his return he settled in Rochester and again helped to conduct an underground railroad station, as well as editing an anti-slavery newspaper, the *North Star*.

DURAND, ASHER (1796-1886). Durand was an artist who combined careers in painting and engraving. Although more renowned for his painting, it was his engraving which sustained him professionally until 1835. He produced engravings of many prominent Americans and also proved influential in the design of American banknotes. After 1836 Durand made painting his profession, with both portraits and landscape studies of the Hudson River valley and New England becoming his common output. He had been one of the early members of the **Hudson River School** in the 1820s and was also a founder of the National Academy of Design, serving as its president from 1845 to 1861. *Old Oak* (1844) and *Kindred Spirits* (1849) were his most famous paintings during the era.

– E –

EATON, JOHN HENRY (1790-1856). Eaton was a Tennessee colleague of **Andrew Jackson** and one of the founders of the coalition of support behind **Old Hickory** prior to the **election of 1828**. He became one of the central figures in the early part of Jackson's first administration, being a member of the **Kitchen Cabinet** and serving as secretary of war between 1829 and 1831. He was chosen for the office in part because Jackson knew he could trust Eaton on the question of **Indian removal**, a key issue for the president and one which the War Department was expected to play a major part in, and, indeed, after the passage of the 1830 Removal Act Eaton did engage in various treaty negotiations in an effort to implement its terms with several native tribes. However, Eaton's name is best remembered for his role in the **Eaton Affair**, it being the furor over his marriage to **Peggy Eaton** that led to tension in the Cabinet and ultimately to the resignation of all but one of its members.

For Eaton resignation did not mean retirement from public life, as he soon became president of the **Chesapeake and Ohio Canal** Company, holding office at the time when Jackson sent federal troops to quell **labor** unrest among the company's workforce. Eaton also continued to hold public office, first as governor of the Florida territory in 1834-35, and then as minister to Spain in 1836-40. On his return to the United States he supported the **Whig** candidate **William Henry Harrison** in the **election of 1840**, a sign that he had never been keen on **Martin Van Buren** and that he had grave doubts about the stance of the Jackson and Van Buren administrations during the **bank wars**. Indeed only near Jackson's death was Eaton fully reconciled to his former favorite.

EATON, MARGARET "PEGGY" (1796-1879). Formerly known as Peggy O'Neill, after her Washington landlord father, and then by her married name from her first husband, John Timberlake, this was the wife of **John Eaton**, whom she married in 1829. Because of rumors about a relationship with Eaton while still married to Timberlake, Mrs. Eaton was shunned by fellow Cabinet officers' wives and by much of Washington society. Significantly **Andrew Jackson** and **Martin Van Buren**, both widowers and as a result under less pressure from female associates, felt able to continue socializing with her. For Jackson there was also a painful resonance of the circumstances of his own marriage to **Rachel**, who herself had backed Peggy, and the president supported the Eatons to the last, both prior to and after their marriage. Peggy stuck by John throughout the ensuing **Eaton Affair** which split Jackson's administration, and went on to serve as an effective governor's and minister's wife in Florida and Spain respectively.

EATON AFFAIR. The Eaton Affair, arising from the, to some, scandalous marriage between Secretary of War **John Eaton** and his wife **Peggy** and from rumors about her earlier romantic adventures, came to have significant implications in the early politics of the **Andrew Jackson** administration. Influenced by the advice of Presbyterian preachers John Campbell and Ezra Stiles Ely, many Washington wives shunned the married couple as early as the inaugural ball in March 1829 and pressured their husbands into doing the same. Not only did their behavior undermine the usual protocol of Washington entertainment and society, but, as **John** and **Floride Calhoun** and several of the members of Jackson's Cabinet were involved, it also took the affair to the very heart of the government. The president was very close to the Eatons and had appointed John in the War Department for the advice he would offer on the key issue of **Indian removal**. The accusations also brought back unhappy memories for Jackson of how his own marriage to **Rachel** had once been criticized and made the affair a more personal one for him. It distracted him from the business of government as he tried to convince Cabinet members of the innocence of both Eaton partners and he even held special Cabinet meetings to discuss the matter. He also tried to force the Cabinet wives to call on Mrs. Eaton and was greatly angered by their continued snubbing of the Eatons.

Had the affair remained solely a social matter it would have been unsettling enough, but Jackson came to see it as part of an attempt to pressure him into sacking Eaton. As early as autumn 1829 the president suspected that it an effort by Vice-President Calhoun to discredit Jackson for the appointment of Eaton (a man who had voted for the hated **1828 tariff** of abominations) and to reinforce his position with the Cabinet with a view to a possible presidential challenge in 1832. Whatever the motivation, Jackson found it hard to work with his Cabinet and it took the **Cabinet reshuffle** of April 1831, which purged its Calhounite influence, to bring an end to the immediate political influence of the Eaton Affair. Even then, though, the affair affected how the reshuffle turned out, as Jackson refused to order his friend Eaton to resign first on a point of principle, leaving **Martin Van Buren** to offer to resign in order to allow the president to ask the other Cabinet members to relinquish their positions also. A bitter conclusion followed as one of the departing Cabinet officers, **Samuel Ingham**, blamed his removal on his refusal to socialize with the Eatons, provoking John Eaton into challenging him to a duel. Only after both families left Washington could the affair be said to be truly over. Overall it had upset the smooth running of government in the early years of the Jackson administration and had lasting significance by increasing the political stock of Van Buren, who as a widower felt less social pressure to avoid the Eatons, while that of Vice-President Calhoun fell.

ELECTION, PRESIDENTIAL, 1828. The 1828 election heralded the Jacksonian era by bringing to the White House the man around whom most of the policy and party developments of the next two decades would revolve. But as well as bringing about the election of **Andrew Jackson**, this campaign witnessed a number of innovations in electioneering that would change the business of politics in America forever.

The campaign began early, itself something of a novelty, as supporters of Jackson prepared to avenge their hero's defeat in 1824-25 at the hands of what they called a **"corrupt bargain."** Hoping to recreate an old political alliance between Republicans in North and South, organizers like **Martin Van Buren** and **Thomas Ritchie** strove to build a strong coalition with Jackson and his western support base. Theirs was a major effort in party organization, with resort to close committee correspondence as well as many populist tactics, such as public meetings, barbecues, and parades. In addition to the bitterness about 1824, Jackson's followers played on his popularity as a military hero and portrayed him as the people's choice, in stark contrast to **John Quincy Adams** whom they represented as being suspicious of popular government. They also hoped to exploit growing alarm at the nationalist direction of the Adams administration. In response the Adams men tried to defend his record in office and predictably warned, in propaganda like the **Coffin handbill**, that a military chieftain such as Jackson was a dangerous candidate for the presidency. It was a bitter and often personal campaign fought in handbills and the columns of an increasingly partisan newspaper press, involving salacious charges on both sides, such as rumors about Jackson's premarital relationship with his wife, **Rachel**, and about Adams' alleged activities as a pimp for the Russian tsar.

Jackson won the election by 178 electoral college votes to 83, and a popular majority of nearly 150,000 out of 1.15 million votes cast. The total number of votes was three times higher than that cast in 1824, with a turnout averaging 56 percent, but rising to over 70 percent in hotly contested states, and 90 percent in certain key localities. Jackson drew heavily upon supporters in the newly opening South and West of the country, as well as in the crucial states of New York and Pennsylvania. Adams' successes occurred mainly in the northeastern corner. **John Calhoun** was successful in retaining his office as vice-president.

ELECTION, PRESIDENTIAL, 1832. This was a landmark election in that all the main parties selected candidates by national nominating conventions, the **Democrats** choosing a vice-presidential candidate and the **National Republicans** following the lead of the newcomer **Anti-Masonic** Party in selecting their presidential nominee. Indeed, the fact that a major third party was running a candidate was also something of a novelty. However, despite the presence of the Anti-Masons and the importance of other issues, such as **Andrew Jackson**'s policy of **Indian removal**, the **tariff**, the **spoils system**, and foreign affairs, to many the election became something close to a referendum on the issue of the **Second Bank of the United States**. The election followed soon after Jackson's **bank veto**, pitting the president against his main contender **Henry Clay**'s continued support for the Bank. But the debate perhaps focused more on the ideological implications of the bank veto: Democrats stressed the dangers of political and moral corruption posed by the Bank and its supporters, while National Republicans warned of the dangers of **executive usurpation** which the veto seemed to exemplify.

The popular vote certainly seemed to back the Jacksonian view and to demonstrate continuing trust in the president's personal strengths to withstand the threat from the Bank. Jackson won by 219 electoral college votes to Clay's 49, with South Carolina's 11 of the remaining votes going to their own candidate, **John Floyd**, and Vermont's 7 to the Anti-Masonic candidate, **William Wirt**. As in 1828 Jackson's popular majority over his main opponent was huge, over 200,000, while the national turnout remained about the same as four years earlier, at 55 percent. As well as remaining strong in the South and West and competing effectively in the Mid-Atlantic, Jackson's followers also started to meet with success in New England, winning two states there. His close advisor **Martin Van Buren** became vice-president.

ELECTION, PRESIDENTIAL, 1836. The 1836 election saw **Martin Van Buren** take up the reins of the **Democratic** Party from the hands of his predecessor **Andrew Jackson**. Although Van Buren was virtually the personal choice of the departing president, his nomination was confirmed by the party's national convention. This distinguished him from his three main rival candidates, the **Whig** Party's **Daniel Webster**, **Hugh Lawson White**, and **William Henry Harrison**, who were selected in the Northeast, South, and West respectively, in the hope that each would win enough votes off Van Buren locally to prevent him from securing the necessary electoral college majority. As in 1832 South Carolinians ran (and voted for) their own candidate, this time **Willie P. Mangum**. No single issue seemed to dominate the election campaign, although for many it was a chance to vote for or against the record of the previous eight years, on economic issues in particular. In the South debate also arose over exactly where Van Buren stood on the issue of **slavery**, and a further strand of campaigning involved criticism by each party of the other's party stance or tactics. Whigs played to some extent on **anti-party** feeling, while Democrats warned that the Whig nomination strategy might cause a repeat of the circumstances in the 1824-25 election that produced the alleged **"corrupt bargain."**

The Whig strategy, such as it was, failed, with Van Buren winning 170 electoral college votes, to a combined Whig total of 113 (Harrison's 73, White's 26, and Webster's 14). Van Buren's popular vote was less convincing than that of his predecessor, totaling just over 25,000 more than his rivals' combined vote. Turnout rose slightly, to around 58 percent. While in part due to the strategy adopted by the Whigs, the results did suggest that the trend witnessed in 1832, of both parties becoming competitive prospects throughout all regions of the country, had continued. Van Buren won four out of six New England states, while Whigs picked up more southern and western support than before, including the state of Tennessee. This development was a significant part of the emerging **Second Party System. Richard Mentor Johnson** won the vice-presidency, but only in the House of Representatives after Virginia's refusal to vote for him in the popular election left him one vote short of the necessary majority.

ELECTION, PRESIDENTIAL, 1840. This election was one of the most famous of its time, and perhaps in American history, in particular for the way it was conducted. For the first time the **Whig** Party embraced the more populist electioneering methods of their rivals, using mass meetings and catchy labels and slogans such as **"log cabin," "hard cider,"** and **"Tippecanoe and Tyler too."** Whig **women** became involved in the election process far more than had ever been the case before, and the Whig candidate, **William Henry Harrison**, was the first to electioneer in person in the presence of the public.

Indeed, it had been because of his potential popularity as a military hero, in the mold of **Andrew Jackson**, and his strong showing in the **election of 1836**, that Harrison had been nominated by the Whig Party's national convention in preference to **Henry Clay**. Standing against Harrison was the incumbent President **Martin Van Buren**, and despite the dramatic style of the campaign, his record in office did contribute significantly to the outcome of the election. The Whigs were able to charge Van Buren with **executive usurpation** (as evidenced by the **Independent Treasury** and **militia reform** proposals) and with responsibility for the economic problems accompanying the **panics of 1837 and 1839** and the resultant depression, blaming **Democratic** attacks on the banking and **credit systems** as blocks on economic progress. As an alternative, the Whigs presented themselves as the advocates of congressional authority and a one-term presidency and as the champions of economic opportunity and progress for all through sensible banking and currency policies.

The power of the Whig message carried Harrison through to a victory by 234 college votes to 60, the 53 percent of the total vote he won giving him a popular majority of around 150,000. Both parties easily secured more votes than they had in 1836 as turnout rose to an impressive 80 percent. Van Buren's seven states included five in the South and Illinois and New Hampshire, while in four states, including New York and Pennsylvania, the margin was narrow enough that a shift of only 8,000 voters would have delivered the overall election to him. Meanwhile the **Liberty Party** represented a new face to politics, the first avowedly **abolitionist** political party, but it only secured around 4,000 votes. The **States' Rights Whig John Tyler** was elected as a southern foil for Harrison, a significant choice in view of subsequent events, as Harrison's early death propelled his running mate into the White House.

ELECTION, PRESIDENTIAL, 1844. This was the first election in which the reemerging issues of **expansion** and **slavery** made a significant impact on party politics. The drive for **Texas annexation** proved the key issue and indeed it is likely that **John Tyler** and his advisors were so keen to proceed with it because they saw in it a potentially popular platform for his renomination either as an independent candidate or as the candidate of the **Democrats**.

Even when it became clear that it would not help Tyler overcome other, stronger reasons for not nominating him, Texas continued to affect the choices and campaigning of the main parties. Both original front-runners for their parties' nomination, Democrat **Martin Van Buren** and **Henry Clay** for the **Whigs**, felt they had to make a statement on Texas in response to Tyler and both suffered to varying degrees as a result of their agreement not to push for annexation. The Democrats, perhaps more in tune with the popular mood of **manifest destiny**, failed to deliver a majority nomination for Van Buren when he refused to abandon sectional conciliation in favor of a more pro-

Texas line and so the party nominated **James Polk** instead, who combined reliable Democratic economic principles with an expansionist agenda on both Texas and **Oregon**. Meanwhile Clay's equivocation on Texas, between the **Raleigh** and **Alabama letters**, demonstrated that he was neither ideologically nor temperamentally suited to meeting the challenge of a strongly expansionist rival. The campaign was not only about Texas, as Clay suffered some particularly vicious personal attacks and as debate also raged on the more traditional party issues of **distribution**, the currency, and **executive usurpation**. But certainly the election did seem to signal the beginnings of a change in the main issues of electoral and partisan politics in the 1840s.

It was also a pretty tight affair as Polk won by 15 to 11 states, and 170 to 105 electoral college votes. His 8,000 popular vote margin of victory over Clay might have looked different had over 60,000 not voted for **James Birney**, who had again run for the **Liberty Party**. Indeed it is possible that Birney's candidacy did affect the outcome of the election in New York, one of two states Polk won by less than a majority, and one that was vital in swinging the final result his way. However, there were also suggestions that a growing **nativist** tendency of Whigs in that state was causing them to lose ground to the Democrats anyway as the latter appealed more to the **immigrant** vote. Clay's equivocation on Texas no doubt lost him some southern votes, allowing Polk to win eight southern states, although not his home state of Tennessee. **George Mifflin Dallas** was the successful vice-presidential candidate.

ELECTION, PRESIDENTIAL, 1848. The 1848 election was notable for being the first presidential election in which voters all across the country voted on the same day, following legislation to that effect passed in January 1845. However, it was more significant in witnessing the continuing stress placed upon the **second party system** by the issues of **expansion** and **sectionalism**.

As had happened four years earlier it was the **Democrats** who displayed the greater amount of turmoil at the nomination stage. Numerous factions supporting different candidates and, increasingly, viewpoints on the issue of slave expansion attended the party's convention at Baltimore in May 1848. When **Lewis Cass** was chosen as the party's candidate, standing on the proposal of **popular sovereignty**, which opened up the possibility of the extension westward of **slavery**, **anti-slavery** Democrats such as the **Barnburners** bolted from the party and joined with others at the **Buffalo convention** to create the **Free Soil** Party, with former Democratic President **Martin Van Buren** as presidential candidate. The **Whigs**, too, lost some activists and supporters to the Free Soil Party, but generally were more successful in uniting behind their choice of candidate, the **Mexican War** hero **Zachary Taylor**.

This time around the internal divisions within the Democrats combined with the popularity of a military hero to deliver the election to the Whigs. It was close again, though, as the main party candidates each won 15 states, giving Taylor an electoral college majority of 36. As four years earlier, the election probably turned upon New York where Van Buren ran second ahead of Cass, allowing Taylor to take the state and the election as a whole. This was one of three states where the Free-Soilers came second, the others being Vermont and Massachusetts, and generally they performed well in New England and the Northeast, securing over 10 percent of the national vote. The Democrats maintained their strength in the Northwest, while the Whigs ran strongest in the mid-Atlantic states and in the South. **Millard Fillmore** was Taylor's successful running mate.

EMERSON, RALPH WALDO (1803-1882). Emerson was the famous Massachusetts intellectual, educated at Harvard Divinity School, whose essays and poetry placed him in the forefront of the **Transcendentalist** movement. With a background in teaching he became a **Unitarian** minister at Boston's Second **Congregational** Church in 1829, a post he gave up three years later out of doubts about the miraculous element behind some of the sacraments. Following the death of his wife and a brief European tour Emerson returned to the United States to become a renowned lecturer and writer, producing many significant essays and addresses as well as major works like *Nature* in 1836, which is seen as setting out the course other transcendentalists would follow. In this and later addresses such as "The American Scholar" and "Address at Divinity College" he outlined his ideas of self-reliance and intuitive experience, expressing the view that nature had everything necessary for individuals to teach themselves, and he warned against the strictures of both formal religion and majority democracy, which endangered individuals' capacity for fulfilling their own personal growth. However, two volumes of essays published in 1841 and 1844 revealed by this stage his declining optimism and an increasing pessimism about the capacity of humans to transcend their circumstances. At the same time Emerson also wrote for *The Dial* and took over from **Margaret Fuller** as its editor between 1842 and 1844. His first volume of poems was published in 1846, while in 1847 he went on his travels again, touring and lecturing in England until 1848. His lectures on *Representative Men* were published in 1849. Emerson was a major figure in American letters, championing the emergence of an independent American literary tradition, free of too great a European influence. He also affected the thinking of a great number of Americans, including philosophers and writers, as well as other groups such as the **abolitionists**.

***ENTERPRISE* AFFAIR.** This diplomatic incident arose out of international efforts to ban the **slave trade** on the high seas. In 1835 the *Enterprise*, an American vessel carrying slaves in the coasting trade between two U.S. ports, was blown off course to Bermuda, where **slavery** had recently been abolished. The island's British authorities freed the slaves on board the *Enterprise*, and, unlike on earlier occasions before their own abolition of slavery, refused to pay any compensation. The American government countered with the claim that international law backed its view that the fact that the vessel had been involved in a domestic coasting trade made it immune from British colonial legislation and that the slaves should have been returned or their owners compensated. **John Calhoun** went even further in March 1840, calling upon the Senate to condemn Britain's actions as contrary to the law of nations. The Senate adopted Calhoun's resolutions without a negative vote, albeit with 11 abstentions. Indeed **Martin Van Buren**'s administration and most in Congress were fairly united behind the legality of their case, which would be used again in the *Creole* episode shortly afterwards. Ultimately, in 1853, compensation was secured for the owners of the *Enterprise* slaves.

EQUAL RIGHTS PARTY. *See* LOCOFOCOS.

ERIE CANAL. The Erie Canal, already completed as the Jacksonian era began, remained one of the great engineering feats of the age. Running 363 miles between Buffalo and Albany, it demonstrated the impact that **internal improvements** such as **canals** could have as part of the **transportation revolution**, continuing to influence economic, but also social, cultural, and political developments, for many years after. It gave great impetus to the development of the region immediately around the canal, assisting in the spread of people and ideas into the **Burned-Over District** of western New York and beyond. Meanwhile it enhanced the position of New York City as the main trading center of the nation, mainly because the canal reoriented the trade of much of the upper and middle Midwest onto a northeasterly route away from the Mississippi River. The Erie also proved inspirational to a host of other such improvements and left a practical bequest in the form of a generation of civil engineers who went on to head other projects throughout the nation. At the most basic financial level the canal also proved of great benefit to the state of New York, as the canal fund, raised from revenues from the canal's operation, proved a lifeline in times of difficulty such as the **panics of 1834 and 1837** and the **New York City fire** of 1835.

While there were plans in place to improve and enlarge the Erie Canal, which were implemented from 1836 onward (although not to be completed until 1862), the canal's orbit of influence was widened by the construction of several satellite canals and railroads. The Cayuga and Seneca Canal bridged the 27 miles from the Erie to those two lakes, while the Chemung Canal, chartered in 1829 and largely complete by 1833, carried that route through from Watkins Glen at the southern tip of Seneca Lake to Elmira near the northern Pennsylvania state line. Meanwhile, also in 1833, the Keuka Canal linked Seneca Lake with Lake Keuka (or Crooked Lake). The Chenango Canal, finished in 1836, ran between Utica on the Erie and Binghamton on the Susquehanna River, and the Genessee Valley Canal, chartered in 1836, survived the difficult economic times of the later 1830s to create a further link through the Genessee River valley to the Allegheny River. Finally, the area to the north of Albany came to be served by the Champlain Canal, which underwent construction throughout the period. Altogether these feeder canals enlarged the field of influence of the Erie Canal system and increased its economic impact.

EVANGELICAL RELIGION. The second quarter of the 19th century witnessed a strong evangelical movement in the United States, with revivals in northern rural and urban communities, camp meetings among Methodists and Baptists in southern and western regions, and organizations like the American Bible Society and the Sunday School movement all committed to increasing the numbers of believers. A strong part of evangelical belief, especially among Presbyterians and **Congregationalists**, was the perfectibility of human beings, and so a major co-development was the emergence of a reforming impetus, both in individuals trying to make their own lives more moral and in demands for private and public initiatives to improve the well-being of others and society as a whole. Targets such as drink, **slavery**, **Indian removal**, dueling, **Sabbath infringement**, poverty, and disability all gave rise to groups sharing this perspective. Evangelical religion proved particularly attractive to **women**, to whom it promised independence and moral authority in the home. It also helped to salve the conscience of successful businessmen who could claim that their efforts at leading righteous lives and at encouraging others to do so were signs of divine favor. Incidentally it also justified their attempts to impose a degree of social control over their workforces. Apart from **temperance**, southern evangelicals did not share so fully in the reform impulse arising from evangelical religion.

EVERETT, EDWARD (1794-1865). This Massachusetts statesman, educated at Harvard, made a career as a **Unitarian** clergyman, educator, and editor of the *North American Review* before going on to represent his state in Congress between 1825 and 1835. Although fairly independent in his early political career, Everett gradually swung into opposition to the policies of **Andrew Jackson**'s administration. He abhorred **Indian removal** and supported the **Second Bank of the United States** against Jackson's **bank veto** and **removal of the federal deposits**. By 1836, when he became governor of Massachusetts, Everett was a **Whig** supporting other Whigs' reform proposals, such as **Horace Mann**'s education plans and the creation of the state board for education.

After losing the governor's position, Everett's friendship with **Daniel Webster** earned him the reward of the position of U.S. minister to Great Britain, serving in London throughout the joint Harrison/Tyler administration and turning down **John Tyler**'s offer of the mission to China in 1843. Notwithstanding the malicious influence of **Duff Green**, Everett was able to maintain peaceful relations between the two countries, providing a solid British foundation for the success of the **Webster-Ashburton Treaty**. Moreover, although his proposal for a solution of the **Oregon** boundary issue was turned down by Robert Peel at the time, it effectively became the basis of the eventual treaty signed in 1846. On his return to the United States Everett served as president of Harvard College between 1846 and 1849, before resuming political and diplomatic activity in the 1850s as a **cotton Whig**, serving as **Millard Fillmore**'s secretary of state for one year, and later as a vice-presidential candidate of the Constitutional Union Party.

EWING, THOMAS (1789-1861). Thomas Ewing served as a Whig senator from Ohio in the 1830s, opposing the key financial policies of **Andrew Jackson**'s administration, such as the **removal of the fed-**

eral deposits and the **Specie Circular**. Indeed, he went so far as to defy his state government in backing moves to **censure** President Jackson. In 1841 **William Henry Harrison**, on the advice of Daniel Webster, appointed Ewing as secretary of the treasury and **John Tyler** adopted him along with the rest of the Cabinet. Ewing worked hard to forge some sort of compromise on the bank issue during the 1841 **special session**, with his own **fiscal corporation** proposal becoming part of the bargaining. Therefore he had extra cause to feel frustrated and betrayed when Tyler vetoed even that bill and so he joined in the **Cabinet resignation** of September 1841.

EXECUTIVE USURPATION. Charges of executive usurpation became an important part of the **Whig** attack upon the **Democratic** Party and the behavior of its presidents **Andrew Jackson** and **Martin Van Buren**. Borrowing ideas born in opposition to the monarchy in Britain (hence the party name Whig, the traditional opposition to the executive in that country), the executive usurpation line proved useful in tying together different strands of the Whig Party in a common stance: northern reformers could point to Jackson's defiance of the Supreme Court in response to the *Worcester vs. Georgia* ruling as one example; southern **States' Rights Whigs** could warn of the dangers inherent in Jackson's **Nullification Proclamation** and his support for the **Force Act** as another; while opponents of the trajectory of Democratic banking and financial policies had a whole range of actions to refer to as illustrations of usurpation, including the **Bank veto**, the **removal of the federal deposits**, the **Specie Circular**, and the **Independent Treasury** proposals to make the executive branch responsible for supervision of the federal government's revenue. Even more minor matters, such as **militia reform**, could be interpreted in the same way, these being portrayed as just one more threat to popular liberty and to the nation's well-being.

The Whigs went beyond simply condemning their opponents on such grounds, such as in the attempt to **censure** Jackson for his banking policy in 1833-34. They also made executive usurpation the focus of some of their constructive proposals, with **William Henry Harrison** pledging to hold the presidency for only one term, to use the veto discriminately if necessarily at all, and to consult fully with Congress over such appointments as it had a particular interest in, such as the secretary of the treasury's position. It was hardly surprising then that use of the executive usurpation charge also informed Whig attacks on **John Tyler**, whose vetoes hampered their party pledge to reform presidential power. There were even some who considered impeaching the president for his behavior in office. But the party as a whole now called for a single-term presidency, greater congressional control over key appointments, and limits to the veto power. In spring 1842 **Henry Clay** proposed, unsuccessfully, a constitutional amendment to change the margin needed for a congressional override of the veto from two thirds to a simple majority.

EXPANSIONISM. Expansion and the motives behind it have been a long-standing trend in American history, especially its earlier years. However, expansionism, whether in the form of popular movement across the North American continent or in the geopolitical growth of the United States, had perhaps its greatest moment in the 1830s and especially the 1840s. Motives of land hunger, a desire for western port facilities, and, at the tail end of the period, a gold rush generated the first major population shift of European Americans beyond the immediate Mississippi River valley, across the Plains and the Rocky Mountains, to California and Oregon. Running parallel to this movement, and on occasions driven by it, was the federal government's successful acquisition of territory, filling in most of the remaining area of the nation's current-day continental landmass, through the annexation of **Texas**, by a settlement of the border line between **Oregon** and British North America, and by the military spoils of **New Mexico** and **California**.

As well as responding to popular and commercial motives for more lands, the process of acquisition was inspired by a range of political and ideological impulses, including: a desire to spread the benefits of American democracy or to preserve the essentially agricultural makeup of the American population; feelings of racial and cultural superiority over Native and Hispanic-American groups; and a continuation of the Monroe Doctrine suspicion that European powers might try to become more involved in the American West. Altogether these came to be wrapped up in the idea of **manifest destiny**, which was used to explain and justify the process of expansion.

Although generally a very positive outcome for the long-term fortunes of the United States, if not for all groups within it, expansionism had other immediate and medium-term consequences. Inevitably the drive for expansion helped to shape the diplomatic stance of the United States, especially in its relations with Britain over the **Canadian border** and Oregon, and with Mexico over Texan annexation and later events running up to the **Mexican War**. It provided a further issue for debate between and within political parties about the desirability and speed of acquisition of new territories and their eventual settlement. And it ushered in the specter that had so haunted earlier generations of American statesmen, the question of the future status of **slavery** in any newly won territories, as witnessed in debates over the **Wilmot Proviso**. Indeed, ultimately expansion would provide the **sectional** issue that generated the main impetus toward the Civil War.

EXPUNGING OF CENSURE. In January 1837 supporters of **Andrew Jackson**, led by **Thomas Hart Benton**, succeeded in having expunged from the congressional record the Senate resolutions passed in 1834 **censuring** the president for his actions with regard to **removal of the federal deposits**. To Jackson the resolutions had represented a stain of dishonor and immediately after their passage he had complained of them in a special message to Congress. At that stage the Senate refused to have this protest included in their journal of proceedings, but Jackson's call did spark off a campaign at state level to order senators to vote for expunging the resolutions. For some, including Jackson, it became something of a test of party loyalty, with **Democratic** state legislators demanding that their state's senators either surrender their posts if they had voted to censure Jackson in the first place or now support efforts to expunge the censure. Although not universally successful, with the campaign failing in Tennessee, Pennsylvania, and Maryland, other states did pass resolutions so ordering their senators. One example was Virginia, whose censorious senators were eventually both forced to resign. In the process, with elections ousting other offending senators as well, the campaign did throw control of the Senate back into the hands of the Democrats, who took the opportunity to amend the record just before Jackson left office, having a thick black line and the word "expunged" drawn through the journal's page.

– F –

FAIRFIELD, JOHN (1797-1847). John Fairfield was a **Democratic** politician who served as governor of Maine at the crucial period of the **Aroostook War**. After working as a court reporter for his state's supreme court, he went on to represent Maine in Congress between 1835 and 1838. However, it was during his two terms as governor, 1838-39 and 1841-42, that Fairfield assumed a prominent position in national affairs. In his first term he supported legislative decisions to use the state militia against what were seen as intrusions from New

Brunswick, and even called for federal military support during the Aroostook crisis, rather clumsily warning President **Martin Van Buren** that he could not guarantee the state's future political support for the Democrats if help were not forthcoming. Fairfield was again at the helm during the final resolution of the **Maine boundary dispute**, reluctantly accepting the deal worked out in 1842 in the **Webster-Ashburton Treaty**. After leaving the governor's mansion Fairfield went on to serve his state in the Senate between 1843 and 1847, some even considering him a possible vice-presidential candidate in 1844. However, his defense of the freedom to petition Congress about **slavery**, and his own **anti-slavery views**, made him unacceptable to most of the Democratic Party.

FALKLANDS ISLANDS DISPUTE. This minor diplomatic incident occurred in 1831 when an Argentinian officer who had occupied the islands seized three American vessels. **Andrew Jackson** sent a U.S. frigate in reprisal and threatened to deport the whole population of the islands. Two years later, when British naval forces captured the islands, Andrew Jackson went against expectation, his own Anglophobia, and the principles of the Monroe Doctrine by turning down Argentinian calls for assistance against the British.

FAREWELL ADDRESS. Drafted on behalf of **Andrew Jackson** by Chief Justice **Roger Taney**, this statement, published in 1837 after the president's retirement from office, provided a summary justification of the course his administration had taken on issues such as the **tariff, internal improvements**, and especially the **bank wars**, currency, and finance. Its keynote was the danger posed by artificial interference in economic matters to the benefit of privileged classes and the **"money power."** As such Jackson asserted that he was not against commerce, improvement, or **manufacturing** *per se*, but he did rail against any measures that seemed to give certain individuals or corporations favored treatment, whether it be by charter privileges, special tariff duties, or grants of federal money for improvements. These "corrupting" measures allowed those groups to flourish at the expense of the incorruptible self-reliant farmers, planters, and laborers who worked for their own rewards, and who, in terms similar to Thomas Jefferson's "Blessed are those who labor in the earth" expression, would be more fit guardians of American democracy and economic development. At the same time, Jackson expressed absolute faith in the Union and the Constitution and hoped that Americans would accept their diversity on issues like **slavery** and would retain the moral standing to operate successfully according to the tenets of the Constitution.

"54° 40′ OR FIGHT." This saber-rattling slogan formed part of the posturing in the background to diplomatic attempts to resolve the dispute over the boundary between the United States and British North America in the **Oregon** territory. As early as 1843 a convention held in Cincinnati, discussing the Oregon issue, had called for the line of latitude at 54° 40′ to be the boundary, which would effectively have given the whole of the disputed area to the United States. Although frequently linked to the **Democratic** campaign of 1844, it is now generally accepted that its adoption as a slogan post-dated the election, with **James Polk** making use of it in his inaugural address. Most importantly it came to represent the extreme view of the **"All Oregon"** movement, among the likes of William Allen, **Lewis Cass**, and Stephen Douglas.

FILLMORE, MILLARD (1800-1874). Fillmore was a self-educated lawyer from the **Burned-Over District** of New York who rose to political prominence in the midst of the **Anti-Masonic** movement. He ran successfully for the state legislature in 1828, and then sat in the House from 1833 to 1835 and from 1837 to 1843. By these latter terms he had joined the **Whig** Party and proved a strong supporter of **Henry Clay**, keen to compromise the issue of **slavery** as the price of keeping the Union together. By the 1840s Fillmore was beginning to assume a greater prominence in legislative matters. As chair of the House Ways and Means Committee he played a key role in the passage of the protectionist **tariff of 1842**, which superseded the **compromise tariff of 1833**. After his hopes of the Whig vice-presidential nomination for 1844 were thwarted, he ran instead as their candidate for governor of New York, only to be defeated by **Silas Wright**. However, three years later Fillmore secured the greatest victory ever by a Whig in New York by winning election as the state comptroller of finances. His vote-getting capacity, allied to his continuing friendship with Clay, made him an ideal choice to balance the Whig ticket for the **election of 1848**, when Clay was again frustrated in his hope for the presidential nomination by the choice of **Zachary Taylor**. Taylor's victory in the election placed Fillmore one step away from the White House and of course he would succeed to the presidency after Taylor's death in 1850.

FINNEY, CHARLES GRANDISON (1792-1875). Finney was a liberal Presbyterian theologian and prominent **evangelist** who exercised a remarkable influence on the religious lives of large numbers of Americans. He was born in Connecticut but moved to New York early in his life, beginning training to become a lawyer before starting to preach in the mid-1820s. Finney brought to his ministry a passionate belief that people could be saved by conversion rather than only by predestination, and his revival meetings became dramatic and famous affairs. His influence spread among most Protestant denominations along the corridor of the **Erie Canal**, in new urban developments such as Rochester in 1830-31. But he also preached in established eastern cities like Philadelphia, Boston, Wilmington, and New York, where he served as pastor of the Second Presbyterian Church in 1832. Civic leaders supported his efforts as likely to improve the morality of citizens and workers, since part of the conversion process was a willingness to evidence continuing moral worth through the performance of good deeds, including self-reform and reform to assist others. So it was that this reform impulse brought Finney into contact with the **Tappan** brothers, Arthur and Lewis, **abolitionists** both, who helped him to establish the Broadway Tabernacle in 1835-37. This facility enabled him to carry on his evangelizing work in the East even after he was appointed professor of theology and pastor at **Oberlin College** in Ohio from 1835 onward. These associations strengthened his abolitionist views, although the sense remains that he still was more concerned about saving souls than slaves themselves.

FISCAL CORPORATION BILL, 1841. As the **Whig** Party sought to capitalize on its success in the presidential **election of 1840** and gains in congressional polls, the creation of a new central agency to impose greater control over banking and financial matters swiftly rose to the top of their agenda. Both **William Henry Harrison** and his early successor **John Tyler** recognized that such a body was necessary in the economic circumstances and politically essential to the Whig Party's credibility, and this bill, presented to the **special session** of Congress by Secretary of the Treasury **Thomas Ewing** in June 1841, was the administration's response.

　　Rejecting the advice of some of his southern friends for a states-created association of controlling banks, Tyler instead backed his Cabinet's plan of a single bank based in Washington, founded upon Congress' power to legislate for the District of Columbia. This mode of establishment, along with limited power to establish branches (only in those states which gave their permission), seemed to meet constitutional doubts raised about both earlier national banks, doubts that Tyler shared. Both the central body and any branches could receive deposits and could discount notes, while the Washington branch would act as the fiscal agent of the federal government. The federal government would hold 20 percent of the stock; the states, proportional to population, would hold one third of the stock, while the rest would be open for public subscription.

Despite some support for it, especially among moderate Whigs such as **Daniel Webster**, the proposed agency was criticized for not being strong enough, especially in its dependence upon states' permission to allow the development of branches. Others called for it to be located in a proper financial center rather than Washington. In the face of such criticism it was no surprise when the bill was sidelined as Congress instead considered a **bank bill** presented by **Henry Clay**.

But when Tyler vetoed that bill, the administration measure seemed a suitable fall-back position for Whigs keen for passage of any kind of bill that the president would approve, especially as it appeared to meet exactly the qualms Tyler had expressed about Clay's bill. After discussion with the president, an adjusted bill was drafted, combining elements of both Clay's and Ewing's proposals and thought to meet most of Tyler's objections, by abandoning the power of local branches to discount notes. This alternative bill was passed in September 1841, only for Tyler to return it with his veto, on the grounds that some of its original and amended details were now giving him further cause for concern. In particular he objected to this version's establishment of the bank under Congress' power as national authority rather than as government for the District of Columbia, and he also feared that the measure's allowance of bills of exchange could be used as a back-door method of implementing a note-discounting function. Tyler's veto precipitated an irreparable split within his party and the mass **Cabinet resignation** of September 1841.

"FIVE CIVILIZED TRIBES." *See* CHEROKEE; CHICKASAW; CHOCTAW; CREEK; SEMINOLE.

FLORIDA EXPEDITION REPORT. This report, written in the aftermath of **Andrew Jackson**'s conduct in the first Seminole war in Florida (1817-19), assumed political importance at the beginning of his administration in the context of increasingly fraught relations with his vice-president, **John Calhoun**. Jackson's incursion into Spanish Florida to pursue fleeing Seminoles and his execution of two British traders had sparked off an international incident and forced James Monroe's Cabinet to assess his actions. While Monroe and **John Quincy Adams** backed the future president, Calhoun, who was secretary of war at the time, joined the rest of the Cabinet in condemning Jackson's conduct.

For several years it was believed that Jackson was unaware of Calhoun's position, but even after rumors started to circulate in 1824-25 it did not prevent Jackson from accepting Calhoun as his running mate in the **election of 1828**. When in 1829 the one-time secretary of the treasury of the Monroe administration, **William Crawford**, sent Jackson more concrete evidence of Calhoun's stance, still the president did not seem to act on it. However, it did provide him with ammunition to use against Calhoun should he become disloyal, and after the **Jefferson Birthday dinner** revealed publicly the growing tension between the two men, Jackson requested further information from Crawford and in May 1830 used the Florida report as a pretext for splitting with his vice-president.

Throughout the whole episode Jackson displayed considerable political skill, choosing as his weapon an issue connected to relations with Native Americans, which would reinforce his standing in the South and West. He also waited until the end of a congressional session to act, so that Calhoun's use to him as presiding officer in the Senate was no longer so important. Calhoun was rather more clumsy, publishing his correspondence on the matter in the *United States Telegraph* in an effort to make the president look weak. However, this only served to complete the estrangement between him and the president.

FLORIDA STATEHOOD. Florida had been pushing for statehood for some time, and, amidst the **Second Seminole War**, drafted a constitution in 1838. However, that conflict and the hard times endured in the wake of the **panic of 1839** delayed Florida's admission as a state until March 1845.

FLOYD, JOHN (1783-1837). Floyd was a Virginian politician and proslavery advocate who supported the coalition of **Andrew Jackson** in 1828. However, it was clear that he came from the **John Calhoun** wing of that coalition, and gradually he became more disillusioned with Jackson. After failing to get official preferment from **Old Hickory** Floyd became governor of Virginia, but it was really after the

Nullification crisis that he expressed his disenchantment, like many other **states' rights** supporters, by enlisting with the **Whig** Party in opposition to Jackson. However, his most prominent moment came when South Carolinians first nominated him and then awarded their 11 electoral college votes to him in the **election of 1832**.

FORCE ACT. **Andrew Jackson** requested the Force Act as an accompaniment to the **compromise tariff of 1833**, in the midst of the **Nullification crisis**. Passed in March 1833 mainly by **National Republican** and northern **Democrat** legislators (most southerners abstaining in a willingness to reach a compromise to the whole crisis), it authorized the president to use federal facilities such as floating customs ships to enforce the tariff, while federal troops were to intervene only if South Carolina confiscated property or itself resorted to violent force in its threat to nullify the **tariffs of 1828** and **1832**.

Although designed as a sword to be used only as a back-up to the olive branch of the compromise tariff, many regarded the act as a dangerous growth of federal and executive power in relation to the individual states. This was especially so in the South where, even before the act's passage, states like Virginia, North Carolina, Alabama, and Mississippi refused to accept it. As a parting shot in the crisis, after accepting that the tariff of 1833 would go into operation, South Carolina nullified the Force Act in a display of principle, an act of defiance ignored by a federal government relieved that the more apparently substantive issue of the tariff had been resolved, leaving no grounds for use of the Force Act anyway. Nicknamed the "Bloody bill" by some, the Force Act had a longer-term impact in reinforcing the growing view that Jackson was tyrannical and supported a theory of government dangerous to **states' rights**. It helped give rise to a group of southern **States' Rights Whigs**, including several who had been counted among Jackson's earlier supporters.

FORREST, EDWIN (1806-1872). Forrest was one of the first great American actors. He was born in Philadelphia and trained to be an actor from an early age, reaching the top of his profession with classical performances and modern productions on tour across the United States and in Britain. His influence became so great that he was able to sponsor play-writing competitions to produce plays with roles constructed especially for him. Forrest also had ties in the radical **Democratic** community of New York City, with the likes of **William Leggett**, whose newspaper the *Plain Dealer* he supported and whom he later helped to clear his debts. Forrest even visited **Andrew Jack-**

son at the **Hermitage** while on tour. However, he turned down offers to run as a **Tammany**-backed candidate for Congress. His rivalry with the British actor William Charles Macready led to the emergence of rival support factions and Forrest's followers in the radical community were in part implicated in the Astor Place theater riots in New York City in May 1849, in which 22 died.

FORSYTH, JOHN (1780-1841). This Georgian statesman and party politician, having served in the House and as governor of his state in 1827-29, was a loyal supporter of **Andrew Jackson** during a term in the Senate between 1829 and 1834. On the key issues of the **bank wars** and **Indian removal** Forsyth very much saw eye to eye with the president and his loyalty also stood the test of the **Nullification crisis**, during which he opposed the nullifiers and backed the administration, even to the point of being one of only two Democratic Senators from the South to vote for the **Force Act**. His reward was appointment to the position of secretary of state from 1834 to 1841, during Jackson's latter years in the White House and throughout **Martin Van Buren**'s term. In that office Forsyth proved excellent at the social duties of the State Department and an able administrator, helping to bring reform of the department's activities. Although by inclination an Anglophobe, he brought moderation and a pacific approach vital at a time of considerable tension between the United States and Britain, over the **Aroostook war** and the *Caroline* incident. For some, Forsyth would have made a good running mate with Van Buren in 1840 but he withdrew himself from the contest for the nomination.

FORT HILL ADDRESS. Taking the form of a letter to **James Hamilton**, the governor of South Carolina, in July 1831, this is usually regarded as the clearest (and first public) statement of **John Calhoun**'s views on **nullification** as a solution to the problems of the **protective tariff** and consolidated federal power. It set out a series of recommendations for dealing with an issue like the tariff: from a constitutional amendment demanding ratification by three-quarters of the states of any law nullified by one; through revision or abandonment of existing tariff laws; failing that, to nullification of the law and, in the most extreme cases, secession by any state offended by such a law.

FORTY-NINERS. This was the nickname of immigrants to **California** in 1849, following the discovery of gold in the Sacramento Valley and **James Polk**'s publicizing of the find in his 1848 annual message. The Forty-Niners either went by the sea routes around Cape Horn or to and across the Panama isthmus, or directly by land across the Plains and the Rockies. They came from the United States, but also from as far away as Latin America, Europe, and Asia.

FORWARD, WALTER (1788-1852). Born in Connecticut, Forward moved via Ohio to Pennsylvania where he made his political career. In 1828 he supported **Andrew Jackson**, but within a few years Forward had opted for the **National Republicans** and then the **Whigs** instead. Indeed, in 1840 he served as presiding officer at the Whig Party's national convention, and the next few years would be ones of official preferment. First Forward turned down a district attorney position in favor of one in the Treasury as first comptroller of the currency. Then after the fall-out of the **Cabinet resignation** of 1841, John Tyler chose him to replace Secretary of the Treasury **Thomas Ewing**. Forward's two years in office were less than inspiring and he came to be regarded as inactive or, worse, incompetent, which put pressure on his Cabinet colleagues to bail him out. In 1843 he was persuaded to retire, to return to a career in the law. His final public fling came with a diplomatic posting to Denmark from **Zachary Taylor**'s administration in 1849.

FOWLER, ORSON (1809-1887). Along with his brother Alonzo, Orson Fowler became one of the leading advocates of phrenology in the United States, making a living from reading the patterns of bumps on people's heads. Trained initially for the ministry, he brought a near religious zeal to the study of phrenology, seeing in its power to encourage self-improvement similarities with religion, education, and other reforms. In 1835 he settled with his brother in New York City, and three years later they founded a phrenology museum in Washington, D.C. They also published the *American Phrenological Journal* in 1842, which Orson edited. He also supported a number of other reform trends such as hydrotherapy, dress reform, and penal reform.

FRAZEE, JOHN (1790-1852). Born in New Jersey, Frazee's childhood was a mixture of self-education on the family farm and of periods indentured to a neighboring farmer and apprenticed to a builder. While with the latter he started carving stone for decorative purposes, which encouraged him to enroll at the American Academy of Art in 1824 to become a sculptor proper. Frazee was one of the first and leading American proponents of carving portrait busts in materials such as marble. Among his main works were a bust of John Jay for Congress in 1831 and others of **Daniel Webster, Joseph Story**, and **John Marshall** for the Boston Athenaeum in 1834. However, his artistic career was not wholly successful and he also spent periods as site architect for construction of the New York Customs House and even as a customs inspector between 1843 and 1847.

FREEMASONRY. This fraternal association, derived from English roots but present in North America since colonial times, was thrust into the limelight by the William Morgan affair and the rise of **Anti-Masonry**. In the face of this movement, the number of Masons in the United States was decimated, especially in eastern and middle states, as individuals resigned and Masonic lodges were disbanded. This was despite the fact that a large number of significant politicians of the period were Masons, including President **Andrew Jackson** himself. However, the association started to recover its popularity and numbers in the 1840s.

FREE SOIL PARTY. This political party of the late 1840s had as its main founding principle opposition to the extension of **slavery** into new territories obtained in the **Mexican War**. The party began to coalesce in 1848, drawing leaders and support from the **Liberty Party** but also from both main political parties as neither would endorse the **anti-slavery** stance of the **Wilmot Proviso**. It appealed to **Conscience Whigs** from New England and to the more radical wing of the northern **Democrats**, including factions such as the **Barnburners**.

After preparatory meetings at the **People's Convention** in Columbus, Ohio, and the Barnburners' Utica convention, the party's **convention at Buffalo** nominated the Barnburners' champion **Martin Van Buren** as their candidate for the **election of 1848**. As well as opposition to slavery extension, they stood for homestead legislation, **internal improvements**, and a **tariff for revenue**. Although their practical success was modest, winning counties rather than whole states, the fact that Van Buren won over 10 percent of the popular vote, almost exclusively centered in northern states, demonstrated that the Free Soil Party, or a similarly sectional party in future, could mobilize significant electoral support. However, the party never did fully succeed in attracting all the anti-slavery elements from the two main parties, and after 1848 the party's support ebbed away. It was particularly badly hurt when most of the New York Barnburners returned to the ranks of the Democratic Party in 1849.

FREE TRADE. This was the view of political economy that favored as little interference by government as possible, allowing unencumbered economic intercourse between individuals and nations. In the Jacksonian era this perspective stood as a polar opposite to support for the use of **tariffs** for the protection of American domestic interests such as **manufacturing**. It also extended to a preference for **hard money** instead of artificial **paper currency**.

FRELINGHUYSEN, THEODORE (1787-1862). This New Jersey politician came to be known as the "Christian statesman" for his support of political causes pressed by the reforming religious groups of the age. Frelinghuysen held a number of political posts in the name of the **National Republican** and then **Whig** parties, in New Jersey as attorney general to 1829 and as mayor of Newark from 1836 to 1839, and nationally as a senator between 1829 and 1835. He is best remembered for his condemnation of the treatment of Native Americans, of the kind witnessed in **Andrew Jackson**'s **Indian removal** policy and its application toward the **Cherokee**. His religious leanings led Frelinghuysen to support the American Bible and Tract Societies in their drive for preservation of the **Sabbath** and in their calls for a national fast day. He was also for **temperance** and supported the **American Colonization Society**. But in addition he proved a regular opposition man as well, defending the **Second Bank**, whose president Nicholas Biddle was a personal friend. Frelinghuysen would also stand fast against pressure from his state legislature to support moves to **expunge the censure** resolutions against Jackson. After his stint as mayor he became chancellor of New York University, a post he would hold until 1850, but he also made one last major appearance on the national political stage when he was nominated as **Henry Clay**'s running mate for the **election of 1844**.

FRÉMONT, JOHN C. (1813-1890). Born in Savannah, Georgia, Frémont made his reputation as an explorer of the far West and as an army officer during the **Mexican War**. He served in the corps of engineers, which afforded him the opportunity for extensive exploration of America's western lands on mapping expeditions, beginning in the upper Midwest in 1839. Then Frémont led several expeditions into Oregon, mapping out the **Oregon trail** in 1842, and reached California in his 1843-44 expedition and again in 1845. On one occasion he symbolically and provocatively raised the American flag, in a show of the spirit of what could be labeled **"manifest destiny"** and in defiance of continuing negotiations with Britain about the exact location of the northern U.S. boundary in the **Oregon territory**. This political side to Frémont's work carried on into his **Californian** expeditions, as he was served with orders to be ready to help seize the region for the United States should war with Mexico break out, orders he found easy to carry out since he was probably already fomenting rebellious attitudes in the territory. As the war broke out he served as military commander in northern California, giving assistance to the **Bear Flag** rebels as well as leading regular U.S. armed forces. Frémont participated in the seizure of Los Angeles in January 1847 and then secured the Treaty of **Cahuenga**, which effectively ended Hispanic resistance in the territory.

His appointment as civil governor of California by **Richard Stockton** brought a bitter taste at the end of Frémont's war experience, as he refused to follow orders from **Stephen Kearny**, who had fallen out with Stockton. Frémont was court-martialed and although cleared on charges of mutiny was found guilty of insubordination. He resigned his commission, while his father-in-law, the politician **Thomas Hart Benton**, never forgave President **James Polk** for his failure to back the war hero fully. After the war Frémont returned to the activities which had earned him his nickname "pathfinder," surveying possible routes for a transcontinental railroad via the Rio Grande, before taking up in earnest a career in politics, as the first senator from the new state of California, a major step toward his later nomination in 1856 as presidential candidate for the new Republican Party.

FULLER, SARAH MARGARET (1810-1850). Margaret Fuller was a reformer from Massachusetts who became a central figure in the **transcendentalist** movement as well as a strong advocate of equal rights for **women**. Between 1835 and 1839 she excelled as a teacher at the Temple School in Boston and the Green Street School in Providence, her specialist subject being languages, and it was her work as a translator that introduced her to the writings of the German transcendentalist thinkers. Her friendship with **William Ellery Channing** and **Ralph Waldo Emerson** also propelled her toward transcendentalism. Fuller was perhaps best known for co-founding the transcendentalist magazine *The Dial* in 1840, which she edited for the next two years. But she also organized special gatherings for the intellectual and social development of women, and these provided much of the inspiration and material used in her *Woman in the Nineteenth Century*, published in 1845. She also served as literary critic for the *New York Tribune* between 1844 and 1846, publishing some of her famous critical essays in *Papers on Literature and Art* in 1846. In

1846 Fuller left the United States to travel in Europe. While in Rome she married an Italian nationalist leader and became involved in the revolution of 1848. She died in a shipwreck on her return journey to America in 1850.

– G –

GADSBY'S NATIONAL HOTEL. This hotel, opened in the late 1820s, was situated on Pennsylvania Avenue in Washington D.C. and became a frequently used place of residence for visiting congressmen. Even **Andrew Jackson** stayed at the hotel on his initial arrival as president-elect in 1829, in the process setting something of a precedent, as several later presidents-elect, including **William Henry Harrison**, also stayed there prior to their inaugurations.

GAG RULES. The gag rules were a series of procedural motions adopted between 1836 and 1844, designed to block consideration of the growing number of **abolitionist** petitions reaching Congress. The House rule, introduced initially by the South Carolinian Henry Pinckney, automatically laid on the table such petitions, affirming that their main request, an end to **slavery** in the District of Columbia, would be inexpedient. Meanwhile the Senate, on the suggestion of **James Buchanan**, voted to receive the petitions but then to reject them immediately and automatically. Two years later both houses repeated their gags, and a two further years after that, in 1840, the House tightened its stance by resolving that it should not even accept such petitions in the first place.

The fact that the gags passed so often, with the support of most southerners but also of many northerners, especially **Democrats**, demonstrated that many were anxious to prevent the subject of slavery and abolition being put on the national public record, in order to avoid tension disruptive to the health both of the nation and of the developing **second party system**. In the face of this obstruction abolitionists increased their efforts in sending calls for abolition of slavery in the District and added to them other petitions calling for the termination of the gags themselves. As time went by there were signs of increasingly **sectional** voting on the gag resolutions, as northerners became less willing to take a stand on keeping slavery out of national debates for the sake of harmony, when they believed southerners had aroused the very same issue with their growing pressure for **Texas annexation**. Opponents of the gags, most prominently **John Quincy**

Adams, declared them an unconstitutional infringement of the right to petition, adding to the list of crimes committed by the southern slave power this obstruction of free speech. In the face of such claims the gag rules were finally lifted in the House in 1844, by a vote of 108 to 80.

GARRISON, WILLIAM LLOYD (1805-1879). Born in Newbury-port, Massachusetts, William Lloyd Garrison entered the printing trade as an indentured apprentice. From an early age he displayed sympathies with the oppressed and soon he rose to become the most prominent **abolitionist** of his day. After publishing *The Genius of Universal Emancipation* with **Benjamin Lundy** in Baltimore in 1829, Garrison progressed away from that journal's gradualist **anti-slavery** view. In his *Thoughts on African Colonization*, published in 1832, Garrison turned against the idea of **colonization**, claiming it actually helped to cement the position of **slavery** in the American South. But it was as founder and editor of the *Liberator*, first issued in January 1831, that he first really made his mark, espousing the inflexible view that slavery was evil and that a complete and immediate emancipation was necessary. He carried such beliefs into organizational efforts, helping to found both the **New England** and **American Anti-Slavery Societies** in 1832 and 1833 respectively, and writing the latter group's Declaration of Sentiments. Garrison also sent pamphlets to the South to confront slaveholders and to convert them to the proper path.

His strident views frequently got him into trouble. While still in Baltimore in 1830 only the financial intervention of **Arthur Tappan** released Garrison from jail after he faced charges of libel, an incident that caused him to return to his native New England. Even there he found himself unpopular with politicians who preferred a more cautious approach to the slavery question and with anti-abolition groups that issued several threats against his life. Even within abolitionist circles Garrison's views were not always appreciated and his stance on **women**'s rights contributed to fractures within the anti-slavery movement and to the creation of the **American and Foreign Anti-Slavery Society**. Shortly afterwards, in 1841, he became president of the American Society, remaining in that post for the next 22 years.

Garrison's extremism only grew in the face of events in the 1840s, by which time he had come close to denouncing the Union itself, burning the Constitution as a "covenant with death" in 1840 and calling for the peaceful secession of the free states from the Union. It was hardly surprising that he opposed the **Mexican War**, almost to the point of treasonous calls for an American defeat in order to avoid the possibility of spreading the slavery system westward. However, it was concern for the millions of African-Americans in bondage and the many others who suffered from discrimination, although notionally free, that really preoccupied Garrison and caused him to work on their behalf in any way he could, supporting reform movements such as **Prudence Crandall**'s educational efforts as well as abolition per se.

GENIUS OF UNIVERSAL EMANCIPATION. This **abolitionist** newspaper was established in Baltimore in 1829 by **Benjamin Lundy** and **William Lloyd Garrison**. The latter's editorship brought him to prominence as an abolitionist leader.

GIDDINGS, JOSHUA (1795-1864). Joshua Giddings was a lawyer and legislator, born in Pennsylvania but serving in Ohio, who was one of the first openly **abolitionist** members of Congress. He first served between 1838 and 1842, resigning in the latter year to test the popularity of his **anti-slavery** views, as expressed in resolutions inspired by the *Creole* case, denouncing **slavery** and the coastal **slave trade**. Despite the fact that the House had censured his attempt to introduce the resolutions, his constituency clearly backed him and re-elected him for the first of nine more terms in the House. In several other ways Giddings carried the fight against slavery into legislative circles, backing **John Quincy Adams** in efforts to rescind the **gag rules**, calling for the abolition of slavery in the District of Columbia, and opposing both **Texas annexation** and the **Mexican War**. Giddings had also opposed the **Second Seminole War** on the grounds of his largely discredited claim that the war was in part an effort to capture runaway slaves who had gone to live with the Seminole, either to return them to their masters or to send them to Oklahoma and compensate their masters. Although a **Whig** for most of the first part of his legislative career, he clearly leaned to the **Conscience Whig** group and would join the **Free Soil** coalition in 1848.

GILMER, THOMAS (1802-1844). Gilmer was a Virginian, who removed to Missouri but later returned to his native state in 1824, where he developed his political career, also working as a lawyer and newspaper editor. From 1834 he was a **States' Rights Whig**, having followed the course of many appalled by the behavior of their former favorite, **Andrew Jackson**, in the **Nullification crisis** and **bank wars**. Gilmer held a range of state offices, including governor in

1840-41, before entering the House, where he was drawn to the group surrounding fellow States' Rights Whig **John Tyler**. Indeed, Gilmer claimed to be the president's most important advisor, and certainly he helped to shape the fate of some of the key elements of the Tyler administration. He was a strong proponent of the **bank veto in 1841** and he backed Tyler against efforts to override the veto and against subsequent Whig attacks on his position. By 1842 Gilmer was effectively a **Democrat**, campaigning to retain his seat for that party, and it was also clear that he was leaning closer to the figure of **John Calhoun**. Nevertheless, his support for **Texas annexation** clearly helped him retain Tyler's confidence and early in 1844 the president made him his secretary of the navy. However, only two weeks later Gilmer died in the U.S.S. *Princeton* disaster.

GILPIN, HENRY (1801-1860). This Pennsylvanian lawyer, editor, and statesman reached the peak of his career as **Martin Van Buren**'s attorney general from 1840 to 1841. In the previous decade Gilpin had served as one of the federal government-appointed governors of the **Second Bank of the United States**, providing a critical perspective on the Bank's president, **Nicholas Biddle**, whom he regarded as a tyrant in his dominance over the Bank's board. After several years as a U.S. district attorney in Pennsylvania Gilpin moved to his Cabinet position, having time to be involved in only one really significant case before the change in administration in 1841. It was he who put the administration's case in the *Amistad* affair, upholding the decision to return the mutineers against claims that they should be freed.

GOODYEAR, CHARLES (1800-1860). Born in New Haven, Connecticut, Charles Goodyear belied a lack of formal education to become the inventor of one of the most useful products of the modern era, vulcanized rubber. He had worked with his father in a hardware store and had spent time in and out of debtor's prison trying to ride out fluctuations in economic fortune in the 1830s. For several years he had tried to improve the quality of rubber, even buying the patent of an unsuccessful rival who had experimented with the use of sulfur in the process. By accident, in 1839, Goodyear found that high temperatures allowed rubber and sulfur to fuse in a way that made the rubber less susceptible to changes in property under extremes of temperature. He received a patent for his discovery of vulcanization in 1844 and of course set the rubber industry on its way to becoming a multi-million dollar concern.

GOUGE, WILLIAM (1796-1863). Gouge was a newspaper editor from Philadelphia who became one of the most influential economic thinkers and writers of his age, especially among followers of the **Democratic** Party. Up to 1831 he edited the *Philadelphia Gazette* and then between 1834 and 1841 served under various secretaries of the treasury as a clerk. His *Short History of Paper Money and Banking in the United States*, published in 1833, was very important in popularizing the "**hard money**" case among Jacksonian thinkers, reinforcing hostility to **paper money** and corporations as examples of artifice in economic pursuits, likely to assist a few at the expense of many others and to create a divided society. **Andrew Jackson** and others used Gouge's ideas in their attacks on the **Second Bank** and on paper money, while in office Gouge supported both the **Specie Circular** (which he would have preferred to be more all-embracing) and the **Independent Treasury** scheme.

GRADUATION. Graduation was one of several **land policies** designed to encourage settlement of lands in the West and as such to appeal to western voters. By its terms the price of federal land was graduated, becoming cheaper the longer land remained unsold. With support from **Andrew Jackson**'s administration and especially its main western flag-bearer, **Thomas Hart Benton**, it was hardly surprising that several attempts were made to pass graduation into law. However, in both the 1829-30 session of Congress and in 1832, it ran into opposition from southern congressmen and **National Republicans**, and failed to pass. In 1837 **Martin Van Buren** came out in support of graduation, partly in the hope of winning western support for his financial reforms, but the House rejected it yet again in both 1838 and 1840.

GRANGER, FRANCIS (1792-1868). Granger, born in Connecticut and educated at Yale, went on to become a minor **Whig** leader in New York and a player in the bitter administration politics at the start of **John Tyler**'s presidency. After a legal career he had entered New York politics as an **Anti-Mason**, running unsuccessfully as a fusion candidate for the Anti-Masonic and **National Republican** parties in the 1830 and 1832 gubernatorial elections. In between failing in efforts to get the Whig vice-presidential nomination in 1836 and the gubernatorial candidacy in 1838, Granger served in the House in 1835-37 and 1839-41. **William Henry Harrison** appointed him as postmaster general, in which post Granger engaged in a fair amount of **spoils system** style appointments, before joining the mass **Cabinet**

resignation in September 1841. He was exceptional, though, in taking the decision only after advice from his state's congressional delegation. On his resignation he returned to the House for another term.

GREELEY, HORACE (1811-1872). Although born in New Hampshire, Greeley found fame as a newspaperman in New York City, establishing the weekly *New Yorker* in 1834. He also made his way through association with two of the leading **Whigs** in his state, **William Seward** and **Thurlow Weed**, helping the party's campaign activities with later publications *The Jeffersonian* in 1838 and *The Log Cabin* in 1840. Greeley's most famous publication was the *New York Tribune*, established in 1841 as a cheap but serious Whig newspaper, which he would edit throughout the 1840s and beyond. He supported a number of important reform and policy trends in his time, including campaigns to end capital punishment, for **women**'s rights, and for **temperance** in both alcohol and tobacco use. Although not in favor of **abolition**, Greeley was hostile to **slavery** and opposed the **Mexican War** as part of what he and others conceived to be a slaveholders' conspiracy. This stance, together with a range of preferred economic policies that combined support for a **protective tariff** with opposition to accumulated wealth and monopoly and a desire for fair opportunity for settlers in the West and the development of **agriculture**, would attract him to the ranks of the Republican Party after this period. Greeley was perhaps most renowned for a comment made in the midst of the **1839 panic** and depression, when he counseled the unemployed not to go to New York where there was no work to be had, but to "Go to the Great West" instead.

GREEN, DUFF (1791-1875). Green was both a prominent and a shadowy figure in the national politics of the era and made some very influential, if not always positive, contributions to the politics and diplomacy of his day. He came from a Kentucky and Missouri background, as a land speculator and newspaper editor, and first received national attention when he moved to Washington D.C. and established the *United States Telegraph* in 1825. Coming initially to the coalition behind **Andrew Jackson** through its Calhounite wing, Green's *Telegraph* became the main organ of the Jackson administration and he also served as printer to both congressional houses. But it became clear that his loyalties lay more with Vice-President **John Calhoun** than with the president, Green's daughter having married Calhoun's son, and, after the *Telegraph* had been dropped in favor of the *Washington Globe*, Green supported Calhoun by printing correspondence relating to the **Florida report**. Never as overtly in favor of **states' rights** as Calhoun was and never a nullifier, Green supported **Henry Clay** and **Hugh Lawson White** in the presidential **elections of 1832 and 1836** respectively, and then supported the ticket of **William Henry Harrison** and **John Tyler** in the **election of 1840**. He was never reconciled to **Martin Van Buren** in the same way that Calhoun was over the **Independent Treasury**.

In the meantime Green had given up the *Telegraph* in 1836 to concentrate on a range of business investments, including transportation, mining, and industrial pursuits in addition to his landed interests. But in 1841 he resumed his unofficial public career, when Tyler sent him to Britain as his personal agent. Green remained there until 1843, returning later that year for a stay until 1844. While in Britain his Anglophobia and unofficial activities caused no end of trouble to the regular minister **Edward Everett**. Claiming to have official status, Green attempted to negotiate commercial treaties with various British officers and then presented these to Everett and the State Department almost as *faits accomplis*, although they had no formal standing whatsoever. He also pushed the Calhoun and **Abel Upshur** line on **Texas**, fostering the impression that Britain would be a threat to the United States and to **slavery** if annexation did not take place as soon as possible. He would carry on this stance in 1844 while serving as consul to Galveston, where his self-promotion in both personal and economic terms generally made him unpopular among those he dealt with, including the Texan president Anson Jones.

GREENOUGH, HORATIO (1805-1852). Greenough was born in Boston and educated at Harvard. He is generally considered to be the first professional American sculptor. He was well traveled in Europe and indeed spent much of his career working from a studio in Florence, Italy. As well as busts of leading figures of the day, including **Henry Clay** and Lafayette, Greenough produced a number of public works. In 1833 he received a commission for a statue of George Washington to stand in the Capitol, a job which took eight years to complete, but the finished item was so heavy that it had to be placed outside instead, before going to a more permanent home in the **Smithsonian Institution**. He also produced a sculpture called *The Rescue* between 1837 and 1851, which features on the portico of the Capitol.

GRIMKÉ, ANGELINA (1805-1879). Angelina was one of two sisters from the South Carolinian plantation of Beaufort who shocked their section by moving north to become active **abolitionists**. Although she was younger than her sister **Sarah** and moved to Philadelphia to become a Quaker eight years after her, in 1829, Angelina proved the more forceful in shaping their later lives and careers. After a period as a teacher in Philadelphia she began to make a name writing abolitionist materials, starting with a letter that **William Lloyd Garrison** printed in the *Liberator* in 1835. The following year she wrote "An Appeal to the Christian Women of the South" in which she argued that slavery degraded all **women**, whatever their color. Two years after that, in 1838, she produced "Reply to an Essay on Slavery and Abolition" and in 1839, with her husband and fellow abolitionist **Theodore Dwight Weld**, whom she had married also in 1838, "American Slavery as It Is." Throughout she called for the outright and immediate abolition of slavery and promoted the role of women in pushing for those goals. When the latter viewpoint attracted criticism she joined her sister in defending women's rights as well, with her "Appeal to the Women of the Nominally Free States" in 1837. However, after her marriage her public activity waned as she spent more time helping her husband run a school in New Jersey.

GRIMKÉ, SARAH (1792-1873). Sarah was the older of the two South Carolinian sisters who made the dramatic move of leaving their home state plantation at Beaufort to move to Philadelphia, in her case in 1821. There she became a Quaker and an advocate of a range of reforms, including temperance, peace, **women**'s rights, but most famously **abolition**. Sarah remained unmarried and was never entirely happy among Philadelphia's Quaker community, which she felt discriminated against African-Americans. She moved to New York City in 1836 where she produced "Epistle to the Clergy of the Southern States," the start of a career writing about and talking in public about slavery. Like her sister **Angelina**, when criticized for breaking conventions of gender, Sarah replied by defending her position as a woman in her "Letters on the Equality of the Sexes and the Condition of Woman," published in 1838. She tended to be the less forceful of the two sisters and ended up following her sister and brother-in-law to work in their school in New Jersey.

GRUND, FRANCIS (1798-1863). Grund was a Bohemian who settled in the United States in 1827 after a period spent in Rio de Janeiro. In his new home he taught in schools for five years, but also dabbled in party politics, proving useful to both parties as a direct communicator with German-speaking voters. After supporting **William Henry**

Harrison in the **election of 1840,** Grund was rewarded with a range of diplomatic postings, as special agent and consul to a number of ports on the North Sea and Baltic coasts, including Bremen and Antwerp. However, he frequently made himself unpopular with the local population as a result of his occasionally unruly behavior and self-serving activities. Alongside this minor political and diplomatic career, Grund served as a commentator on American life, and it is for this facet that he is best remembered. Two works, mirroring **De Tocqueville**'s *Democracy in America*, stand out, *The Americans* in 1837 and *Aristocracy in America* in 1839. In these he proved a cheerful advocate of the United States and generally approved the democratic tone of life in his adopted country.

GRUNDY, FELIX (1777-1840). Grundy was a Tennessee politician on the **Democratic** side of the party divide, having been involved in political action against the **Second Bank of the United States** in Kentucky earlier in his career. At the start of the Jacksonian era he sat in the Senate as an ally of both **John Calhoun** and **Andrew Jackson,** but he turned against the vice-president when his **nullification** views became too extreme. Indeed Grundy was one of the few southern senators who voted for the **Force Act** in 1833. Although clearly an administration man, on occasion personal and constituency pressures caused him to oppose Democratic Party measures. For instance he personally disliked the **bankruptcy** measure of 1837, while the Whig-controlled Tennessee state legislature ordered him to oppose divorce measures leading to the **Independent Treasury.** Even so Grundy was viewed with sufficient regard to be appointed **Martin Van Buren**'s attorney general in 1838, before returning to the Senate once more in 1839. The following year he gave the keynote speech at the 1840 Democratic convention in an effort to underline the sense of continuity from Jackson to Van Buren, and his influence even stretched to the future president, **James Polk,** who had undertaken his legal training in Grundy's law office.

GUADALUPE HIDALGO, TREATY OF. The treaty was the product of a tortuous process of negotiation, beginning in August 1847 and culminating in early 1848, but eventually was approved and brought to an end the **Mexican War** with the United States. The chief U.S. negotiator, **Nicholas Trist,** had defied several sets of orders in continuing with peace talks after he had been advised by his government to press for greater gains from the defeated Mexico and even after he had been recalled. But, as one set of orders also called upon him to take back to the United States any treaty he may already have signed, so then **James Polk**'s administration was duty bound to consider this agreement when Trist arrived in Washington with it, even though it did not meet their more extravagant demands, including perhaps "**all Mexico**" in the eyes of some Cabinet members.

Despite this unpromising background, the Polk administration feared that rejecting the treaty would seem in bad faith since it did secure most of what had been demanded when the war broke out. It also worried that to reject the treaty would increase the possibility of the war lasting even longer, to greater levels of criticism and unpopularity than had been the case before, and perhaps with stalemate or failure as the ultimate outcome. So Polk presented the treaty to the Senate for approval, where with minor amendments it passed by a non-partisan vote of 38 to 14 in March 1848. The treaty survived efforts from both extremes calling for it either to include more territorial gains or none at all, and in the end moderates in both **Whig** and **Democratic** parties, concerned that the war finish sooner rather than later, prevailed in ratifying the treaty. The Mexican congress followed suit in May of the same year.

By the treaty's terms the United States annexed **California** and received the New Mexico and Utah territories, lands totaling more than five million square miles, for a payment of $15 million. Mexico also recognized **Texan annexation** by the United States, with the Rio Grande as the established border. The U.S. government agreed to protect certain rights of Mexicans living in the conquered territories, including their religious rights, although the Senate struck out a further provision respecting Mexican property rights. Mexico did retain Baja California and a land bridge to that region from rest of Mexico. The U.S. government also assumed responsibility for the payment of claims of American citizens against the Mexican government, amounting to over $3 million.

– H –

HALE, JOHN P. (1806-1873). This New Hampshire politician fluctuated in political loyalty early in his career, swinging from the **National Republicans**, via the **Workingmen's Party**, to the **Democrats** while serving in his state government. Between 1834 and 1841 Hale was the Democrat-appointed U.S. district attorney for New Hampshire and then went on to serve his state in the House of Representatives between 1843 and 1845. It was during this period that he began to demonstrate more overt **anti-slavery** views, voting in favor of scrapping the **gag rules** and opposing **Texas annexation**, with the result that the New Hampshire Democratic Party declined to reselect him. Instead, a combination of **Whigs**, independent Democrats, and **Liberty Party** men returned him to the Senate for a term between 1847 and 1853. There, Hale continued to counter the influence of the slave power in Congress, in particular in his opposition to the **Mexican War**, and he revealed himself to be the first overtly anti-slavery senator. In October 1847 the Liberty Party nominated him as their presidential candidate for the **election of 1848**, but when that party amalgamated with the **Free Soil** coalition, Hale dropped out of the race in favor of **Martin Van Buren**.

HALE, SARAH (1788-1879). Sarah Hale was born in New Hampshire and worked as a schoolteacher before marriage brought her 10 years of motherhood and domestic duties. After the death of her husband she took up writing professionally, first with poetry and then novels and children's writing, including the verse "Mary had a little lamb," published in the 1830 collection *Poems for Our Children*. In 1828 she was appointed editor of the Boston *Ladies' Magazine*, the first literary periodical targeted at **women**. Then in 1837, when Louis Godey bought out the *Ladies' Magazine*, Hale became literary editor of *Godey's Lady Book*, moving to Philadelphia in 1841 to carry out her duties. She proved an immense success, increasing the circulation of the *Lady Book* to 40,000 by 1849. In addition, she used this non-political periodical to advocate a number of reform causes, including education for women and general female advancement, although she never pushed for women's suffrage.

HAMILTON, JAMES (1786-1857). This South Carolinian was educated in Rhode Island and Massachusetts before returning to his native state to become a planter, lawyer, and leading **states' rights** politician. After opposing the administration of **John Quincy Adams** Hamilton mirrored the personal journey of **John Calhoun** into opposition to **Andrew Jackson** during the **Nullification crisis**. In 1830 he was elected governor of his state and as a fervent nullifier he was prominent in organizing the campaign in favor of calling the nullification convention in October 1832. Hamilton himself presided at the convention, before being replaced as governor so that he might take personal command of the state militia in response to any violent federal reprisal. Ultimately, though, he was prepared to accept the **compromise tariff** that helped to end the Nullification crisis. After the crisis Hamilton returned to his state's senate, but from then on he concentrated most of his efforts on a range of personal economic pursuits, as a director of the Bank of Charleston and as a speculator in lands in South Carolina and Texas. The latter interests actually involved him in public affairs once more, and he played a part in securing the Dutch government's recognition of **Texan independence**.

HARBORS AND RIVERS BILLS AND VETOES. Congressional consideration of a number of bills relating to river and harbor facilities afforded **James Polk** the opportunity to express his constitutional and budgetary opposition to the principle of federally funded **internal improvements**, in the same way as had his mentor **Andrew Jackson** with the **Maysville Road bill** veto. Strong support from the **Whig** Party and from many western **Democrats** pushed harbors and rivers bills through in both congressional sessions between 1845 and 1847. The first bill provided for coastal improvements across the country, but met with the president's veto, issued out of concerns for the bill's budgetary and **sectional** implications, but also the constitutional qualm that many of the improvements were clearly local in nature and did not relate to any port or harbor involved in overseas trade. A vote to override the veto received a narrow majority but not the necessary two-thirds.

In the following session culminating in March 1847 Congress passed another wide raft of appropriations, totaling half a million dollars, for projects throughout the country, concealed in a bill to continue certain improvements works in Wisconsin. This bill Polk pocket-vetoed. Although the veto message associated with the pocket veto, but not sent until December 1847, gave clear indications that Polk would continue to oppose any such improvements, Congress again considered more measures, either tacked onto other appropriation bills, such as the routine civil and diplomatic bill, or in independent form. However, the president's threat to veto even the former bill with any such extras attached caused the House to abandon that log-roll, while the campaign for a separate harbors and rivers bill finally ran out of steam in that session. Nevertheless the public mood across wide stretches of the country was still in favor of improvements, and meetings such as the Chicago **Rivers and Harbors convention** gave vent to such demands as well as frustration with Polk's use of the veto.

HARD CIDER CAMPAIGN. This was one of several labels applied to the campaign for the **election of 1840**. Initially it had been a

Democratic writer who had described the **Whig** candidate **William Henry Harrison** as so uncommitted to the race that he would stand aside for a pension, a log cabin, and barrel of hard cider. However, the label proved more popular than critical and soon cider barrels were forming part of the campaign iconography of the Harrison camp. Although apparently clashing with the anti-drink stance of many Whig supporters, cider was viewed more favorably than distilled spirits by **temperance** groups, and it evoked a nostalgic glow of domesticity and good times. Not surprisingly the distribution of cider, sweet for temperance folk and hard for the rest, also helped the Whigs win popularity among the electorate.

"HARD MONEY." Hard money was another name for the metallic coinage which the Constitution stipulated had to be the basis for all currency in circulation in the United States. But in this period "hard money" also came to be used as a label for those who expressed hostility to the over-issue of **paper money** or indeed to the use of paper money at all. Drawing on ideas of men like **William Gouge**, the "hard money" stance played on the same fears of artificial interference in the economy that sustained the anti-bank position in the **bank wars**. Democratic politicians such as **Andrew Jackson, Martin Van Buren**, and **Thomas Hart Benton** translated "hard money" views into policies limiting the acceptability of paper notes of low monetary value. Examples of these policies included clauses in the **Deposit and Distribution Act of 1836**, the **Specie Circular**, and proposals made during the debates on the **Independent Treasury** that the federal government work only with metal money (or, at most, with notes issued by the Treasury itself). Van Buren even toyed with the idea of a constitutional amendment allowing the federal government to ban banks from issuing notes of small denomination, but this idea was rejected out of fears for **states' rights**. However, several states did themselves choose to prohibit state-chartered banks from issuing notes under $5.

HARDING, CHESTER (1792–1866). This New Hampshire-born artist came from humble origins, moving from work in sign- and house-painting to portraiture. After many travels in the West, Washington, D.C., and Philadelphia as an itinerant portrait painter, Harding settled in Boston in 1823, where he developed a flourishing portrait business. His early work, including several versions of **Daniel Webster**, **Henry Clay**, John Randolph, and Stephen van Rensselaer, earned him a good reputation and commissions for later works such as a portrait of **John Marshall** for the Boston Athenaeum. Harding was also present at the famous Virginia Constitutional Convention of 1829, where he painted former presidents James Madison and James Monroe among others. Later he would be patronized by Amos and **Abbott Lawrence** in Boston.

HARRISON, WILLIAM HENRY (1773-1841). Harrison won his greatest fame as a presidential candidate twice over for the **Whig** Party and, after a triumph in the second of his campaigns, as the shortest-serving president on record. His early public life mirrored that of his **Democratic** predecessor **Andrew Jackson**, with a military career and a reputation as a fighter of Native Americans. His victory at the Battle of **Tippecanoe** in 1811 won him a nickname that would be prominent as a campaign slogan in the **election of 1840**. Despite his Virginian birth it was as an Ohioan politician that Harrison later rose to a new public awareness, with terms in the House and Senate, as well as elected office in the Ohio state legislature. He also served the **John Quincy Adams** administration as minister to Colombia. After Jackson removed him from that post Harrison retired to a less than successful farming career, but still kept an eye on politics, just as some of his old anti-Jackson colleagues considered his military reputation a possible vote winner.

In the **election of 1836** Harrison was the most successful of the three Whig candidates, garnering a good popular vote in the Northwest and taking 73 electoral college votes. This relative success marked him out as a strong candidate for the next election in 1840 and he won out in securing his party's nomination over **Henry Clay** and **Winfield Scott**. Although not strongly connected with the traditional Whig policy on a national bank, Harrison clearly supported measures to promote the **credit system** and enterprise, such as **paper money**, and said he would not object if Congress did pass a new bank bill. It is usually thought, though, that the populist **"Log Cabin"** **campaign** of **hard cider** and slogans, reinforced by the difficult economic conditions that prevailed during the administration of his rival **Martin Van Buren**, proved more important in winning Harrison the election than did any stance on policies.

On arriving at Washington he wrote his own inaugural address, promising a less intrusive executive power and, ironically, only a single term in office, a stance in line with Whig attacks on **executive usurpation**. Even before Harrison's tragically early death, only one month into office, there were signs that his presidency would not be as harmonious as many Whigs hoped, as he appointed a Cabinet of his own choosing rather than of men loyal to the party's legislative figurehead, Clay. Indeed the sense is that **Daniel Webster** was far more influential in the selection of the Cabinet. There were also reports that Harrison was opposed to allowing Clay too great involvement in affairs. The president died of pneumonia in April 1841, in part the result of having delivered the longest inaugural address on record, without a coat on.

HAWTHORNE, NATHANIEL (1804-1864). This Massachusetts-born novelist was one of the most famous of his generation and part of the traditional canon of American literature. After studying at Bowdoin College in 1821-25, Hawthorne devoted himself to writing but really only attained public acclaim over a decade later, when some of his tales were published in *Twice-Told Tales* in 1837, a mixture of historical and allegorical sketches. Previously he had edited the *American Magazine of Useful and Entertaining Knowledge* in 1836, and he had also written *Peter Parley's Universal History* in 1837. This limited success still did not make his writing career financially viable and so with the help of his friend, future President **Franklin Pierce**, Hawthorne took up a **Democratic** appointment as a weigher and gauger in the Boston custom house between 1839 and 1841. In the latter year he returned to writing and spent a six-month period at the **Brook Farm** communal society, before marrying and settling down in Concord in 1842, where he spent a comfortable four years. During this time he published a second series of *Twice Told Tales* in 1842 and *Mosses from an Old Manse* in 1846, in which several of the tales revealed his obsession with secret motivations such as guilt and pride. Money remained a problem, though, and in 1846 he took up a position as surveyor at the Salem custom house, only to lose the post when the **Whigs** came to power in 1849.

HAYNE, ROBERT (1791-1839). Hayne was a leading **states' rights** spokesman from South Carolina, prominent as a senator in the run-up to the **Nullification crisis** and then during the crisis itself as governor of his state. In the **Webster-Hayne debate** of 1830 he had taken up the cudgels for the South (and West), defending **slavery** and states' rights against the attacks of **Daniel Webster**. Hayne resigned his Senate seat in 1832 to allow **John Calhoun**, recently resigned as vice-president, to enter the upper house. Meanwhile Hayne was elected to replace **James Hamilton** as governor of their state and led it throughout the immediate Nullification crisis. He supported the nullification convention's adoption of the **Nullification Ordinance**, and, when **Andrew Jackson** proved determined to enforce the **tariff laws**, Hayne called for the raising of 10,000 state troops to meet the threat. At the same time he exercised a degree of restraint, preferring the militia to remain on alert at their homes rather than calling them to Charleston where they might have been considered a provocative presence. After the end of the crisis Hayne gave up the governor's position, but later would become mayor of Charleston between 1835 and 1837. He also pursued a career as a **railroad** promoter, keen to develop a rival line that would put Charleston in a position to challenge New York's domination of commerce from the West. The result in 1836 was the Louisville, Cincinnati, and Charleston Railroad, of which he became president, but in face of the **1837 panic** only a few miles of this line were built.

HEMP. Hemp was one of the first cash crops in American **agricultural** development and proved important to the early economic progress of states like Kentucky and, later, Missouri. The crop was harvested for the raw material needed in the manufacture of rope.

HENRY, JOSEPH (1797-1878). Henry was a physicist, born in New York, who became professor of natural philosophy at the College of New Jersey (now Princeton) between 1832 and 1846. In the latter year he was appointed the first secretary and director of the **Smithsonian Institution** and supported a vision of it as a research center of potentially international renown. As a scientist in his own right Henry's main field of interest was in the physics of electricity, as well as in astronomy and molecular structure. His discoveries covered much of the same ground as those of Michael Faraday but, with the exception of electromagnetic self-inductance, Henry gained little credit for being first, because of Faraday's earlier publication of his findings. However, on a practical level Henry's investigations in electrical and electromagnetic fields led to advances in telegraphic communication and he designed an early version of an electric motor. A very religious man of Presbyterian background, he advocated a rational approach to religion and supported Darwinian views on evolution.

HENSHAW, DAVID (1791-1852). Henshaw was a leading Massachusetts **Democratic** politician of the 1820s and 1830s, serving as **Andrew Jackson**'s collector of the Port of Boston from 1829. As director of a number of companies, including railroads, he supported the **removal of the federal deposits** for the benefit of state banks. However, having enlisted with the Democratic Party only after being rebuffed by the **National Republicans**, Henshaw always leaned more to the conservative wing of the Democrats, and this, on top of his preference for **John Calhoun**, lost him some favor with other Democrats, especially when he tried to push the cause of Calhoun in Massachusetts at the expense of **Martin Van Buren**. It was not entirely surprising when **John Tyler** appointed Henshaw as secretary of the navy to replace **Abel Upshur** in 1843, but his nomination was rejected by the Senate.

HERMITAGE. The Hermitage was **Andrew Jackson**'s estate near Nashville and even when president he holidayed there every other summer, before retiring to it in 1837. The plantation's heart was originally a log cabin but this burned down in 1834. The building that replaced it survives to this day.

HICKS, EDWARD (1780-1849). Hicks was a leading folk artist of the early 1800s, with an artistically naive primitive style. He was also a Quaker preacher, a cousin of Elias Hicks who inspired the emergence of the "Hicksite" Quakers, and Edward considered his art a useful craft to inform people about faith, rather than a way of making money. Hence his works were often based on biblical themes, including his most famous series of works on the *Peaceable Kingdom,* worked on from the 1820s onward. He also painted copies of others' works in his own style and produced some interesting farm-scapes in the 1840s.

HILL, ISAAC (1789-1851). This New Hampshire Jacksonian newspaper editor and politician had joined other supporters of **William Crawford** in their switch to **Andrew Jackson**'s camp for the **election of 1828**. Although his appointment as second comptroller of the Treasury was rejected in 1829, Hill became one of Jackson's **Kitchen Cabinet** until moving to fill **Levi Woodbury**'s Senate seat between 1831 and 1836. He was a strong supporter of the attack on the **Second Bank of the United States**, being the only New England Senator to vote against the Bank's re-charter, and he would go on to back the **removal of the federal deposits**. He was a most interesting individual who, despite a physical disability, pursued an active political life as Senator and then as governor of New Hampshire between 1836 and 1839. He was also a successful businessman, conservative in nature, yet he supported radical policies and championed the poor in his speeches. Although he was appointed receiver-general at the Boston

Sub-Treasury under the **Independent Treasury** scheme, he was never as loyal a follower of **Martin Van Buren** as he had been of Jackson and by the 1840s he was backing **John Tyler** and **John Calhoun**. Tyler appointed him to the Navy's new Bureau of Provision and Clothing in 1844, but the Senate rejected his nomination.

"HIS ACCIDENCY." This nickname was given to **John Tyler**, behind his back, in a comment on his status as the first vice-president to succeed to the presidency. The novelty of the situation and a lack of interpretative clarity over exactly what the Constitution laid down by way of succession meant that beneath the nickname's comic tone lay very serious questioning by some as to whether Tyler was truly president or merely the vice-president acting as president. Moreover, his actions in office only served to reinforce the sense that he was a man out of line with the electoral choices the public had made in 1840.

HOGS. Helped by the ready availability of **corn** as feed, the rearing of hogs remained an important livestock business in the period. At this time hogs were usually driven to market in cities on the eastern seaboard, but toward the end of the period centers for meat production started to develop in western cities such as Cincinnati and later Chicago.

HONE, PHILIP (1780-1851). This famous New York diarist of the period 1828 to 1851 left a lively record of the era's political and social developments which has proven invaluable for historians ever since. Once an auctioneer and formerly mayor of New York in 1825, Hone was also a **Whig** publisher, opposing the **bank war** policies of **removal of the federal deposits** and the **Independent Treasury**. He was not a great man of the people, revealing a **nativist** tinge in his suspicions of **immigrants** and also feeling free to accuse **Andrew Jackson** and later **Martin Van Buren** of rabble-rousing.

HOUSTON, SAM (1793-1863). Houston made his name as a frontier hero and later as an American settler in **Texas**, before becoming one of the leaders of that state's independence struggle. A Virginian by birth, he had grown up in Tennessee and followed that state's most famous citizen, **Andrew Jackson**, during the war of 1812, fighting mainly against the **Creek**. After the war Houston undertook legal training and then served his state in the House of Representatives and as governor in the 1820s. With a record of considerable sympathy to the Native Americans, born of a period of virtual adoption by the **Cherokee** (whose interests he represented in Washington), in 1832 Houston was appointed by Jackson to negotiate with Comanche natives in order to secure safer conditions for American traders in Mexican Texas. Houston chose to settle there himself and when the war for independence began he became commander-in-chief of the Texan forces. His victory at **San Jacinto** was the battle that ended the war, and soon afterwards he became the first president of the independent Texas for two terms, serving from 1836 to 1838, and again for three years after 1841, sandwiching a period as member of the Texan Congress.

Houston's views on annexation by the United States fluctuated, depending on his assessment of what was politically possible, especially in the U.S. Senate. He most probably supported annexation *per se*, indeed twice offering it to **John Tyler**'s administration in 1842. However, he was not prepared to push for annexation at any cost and in the summer of 1843 dropped the idea, fearing that if it were attempted but then rejected, Texas would also lose British encouragement of the promising signs that Mexico would recognize the state's independence. When hints of Mexico's more sympathetic stance had waned, Houston was willing to pursue annexation once more, although he had left office by the time it was finally approved and implemented. When Texas attained its statehood Houston was elected as one of its first senators, serving as a **Democrat** to 1859.

HOWE, ELIAS (1819-1867). This Massachusetts inventor labored in his father's saw and grist mills before going on to work for an instrument and watch maker. It was while with a manufacturer of machinery for cotton mills that Howe began designing a sewing machine, for which he received a patent in 1846. Although forced to market his invention in England, he returned to the United States in 1849 to fight patent infringements by, among others, Isaac Singer.

HUDSON RIVER SCHOOL. This was the first significant group of landscape painters to emerge in the United States, flourishing between the mid-1820s and mid-1870s. The school earned its name from the fact that many of its number lived and worked around the Catskill Mountains region of New York and in particular along the Hudson River itself. Theirs was a romantic view of nature, represented in a form that paid close attention to detail. The school also reflected and reinforced a nationalistic view of America's wilderness environment. Leading artists among the group's ranks were **Thomas Cole, Thomas Doughty**, and **Asher Durand**.

HUGHES, JOHN JOSEPH (1797-1864). This Irish-born immigrant moved to the United States in 1816, where he became an ordained priest in Philadelphia in 1826. Hughes became a prominent figure in **Catholic** circles, publishing the *Catholic Herald* in 1833 and backing Catholic emancipation. After several failed nominations for the episcopacy in 1829, 1833, and 1836, he became bishop of New York in 1842 and eight years later would become the first archbishop of New York.

Hughes was no stranger to controversy, either with folk of his own religion or Protestants. He attacked the influence of lay trustees in the structure of the American Catholic Church and eventually secured state legislation removing control of church property from them, giving title to it to the bishop instead. He also defended Catholicism against extreme Protestant attacks at all levels, especially outbursts of **nativist** violence. He strongly condemned nativist riots in New York and Philadelphia, which he warned could lead to more general violence. Hughes supported both the secularization of public schools in 1841 in order to lessen the influence of Protestant teaching, and the development of separate Catholic parochial schools to the same end, to give Catholic children the chance for an education that might support their religion rather than attack it. As a sign of Hughes' significance, in the run-up to the **Mexican War James Polk** consulted with him and with the bishop of Missouri, to assure them that his actions were not motivated by any hostility to the Catholic religion. Hughes even volunteered to go to Mexico to carry this message to the Mexican government but his offer of service was not taken up.

HUNKERS. This was a faction emerging in the late 1830s in the New York **Democratic** Party, which, unlike the **Conservative Democrats**, chose to express their conservatism and opposition to their party's more radical financial policies from within its ranks. This resulted in a bitter factional rivalry with the **Barnburners**, over the **spoils** of office, as well as over policy choices on issues such as state debt, state banks, **canal** developments, and, nationally, the **Independent Treasury**. Having supported **James Polk**'s nomination for the **election of 1844**, the Hunkers were generally more successful than their rivals in securing patronage favors, notably in the president's appointment of **William Marcy** as secretary of war. Meanwhile in New York the factional wrangling was such that the Democratic Party almost ceased to operate in the period 1844-48, creating grave problems for the Barnburner governor **Silas Wright** and contributing to his defeat in the gubernatorial election of 1846. The prominence of the Hunkers within national circles reached its highpoint in 1848 when they stuck by the presidential nomination of the regular party candidate, **Lewis Cass**, which caused many Barnburners temporarily to flee the party.

– I –

IMMIGRATION. This era witnessed the peak of what historians subsequently labeled the "Old Immigration," the first wave of large-scale immigration to the United States, primarily from countries in northern Europe. Freed from the trammels of war and with clearer sea-lanes, the growing populations of Europe looked to America as a place for a new start, on occasions propelled by crisis moments such as the great Irish famine in the mid-1840s. Although the 1830s saw fairly steady levels of immigration, with annual figures ranging between 20,000 and 80,000, it was the 1840s which witnessed the first example of mass immigration into the United States, only three years of that decade seeing a figure of less than 100,000 and the last three years topping 200,000 annually.

Throughout the period Europeans made up the vast majority of immigrants and their proportion of the total only increased as the 1840s progressed. Within this wider continent's supply there were changes in the balance from different countries, with immigrants from the island of Ireland forming the biggest group throughout and becoming increasingly so in the 1840s, to the point that they made up a majority of immigrants from Europe and even of all immigrants in the latter years. Migrants from the various German states remained at a level with those from Great Britain for the first half of the 1830s before growing to become clearly the second highest group overall. There were also significant levels of immigration from Scandinavia, France and the Benelux countries, the West Indies, and British North America.

Depending on their origins and time of arrival, the composition of immigrant groups varied, as did the range of occupations they entered. While males usually constituted a majority, family groups were common, and a high proportion of those arriving were between the ages of 15 and 40. The Irish in particular entered the ranks of physical labor on improvements and construction sites and in **manufactur-**

ing establishments in cities. Their concentrated numbers, living conditions, and different religion made them easy targets for **nativist** criticism. Large numbers of Germans and Scandinavians became farmers in the north-central midwestern states, and proved less immediately threatening to the sensibilities of native-born Americans, although in some western cities a growing German-born population alarmed some.

Immigration reached such high levels during this period that it began to become a political issue for some Americans. The **Democratic** Party proved far more sympathetic to the growth of white diversity, pushing for rights to citizenship and suffrage for recent immigrants. Some **Whigs**, as well as expressly nativist groups, called for restrictions on immigrant rights, fearing their religious differences and their cultural opposition to many of the reform trends of the day, such as **temperance**. It was hardly surprising, then, that Irish and German voters tended to fall into the ranks of the Democrats.

INAUGURATION OF 1829. This was an event that did much to increase the popular conception of **Andrew Jackson** as a man of the people. Huge numbers attended Washington that day, with up to 20,000 listening to him take the oath of office and make an unimpressively inaudible address, this being the first time these formalities were conducted outside on the east portico of the Capitol. Many of the crowd then followed the new president to and into the White House, cramming its rooms in the search for refreshment and spectacular entertainment. Jackson himself had to leave and only when food and drink were taken outside was the accidental damage to the interior of the building prevented from going still further. This inauguration, like so many other aspects of the Jackson presidency, set the short-term example for others to follow, and **William Henry Harrison**, that other general, albeit less heroic in record than **Old Hickory**, also addressed hordes of upward of 50,000 as he inaugurated the **Whig** revolution in government in 1841.

INCENDIARY MAIL. This was the label given to the large amount of **abolitionist** literature sent to the South by groups such as the **American Anti-Slavery Society** in the mid-1830s. The preaching tone and general subject matter of the material aroused the hostility and outrage of many southerners, who responded practically on a number of levels, especially after a large volume of such mail was sent in 1835. Some simply resorted to violence, as mobs intercepted the mails, in the case of Charleston with the connivance of federally-appointed postmasters. Other southern postmasters refused to distribute the mails, while southern legislatures made it a capital offense to distribute incendiary mail, and called on northern states to assist in preventing the flood.

On a national level too, the abolitionist campaign met with opposition. **Andrew Jackson** considered the publications wicked and unconstitutional, even proposing congressional legislation specifically banning their circulation in the South. Together with his Postmaster General **Amos Kendall** he refused to discipline postmasters for their interception of abolitionist mail and declared that the mails would be closed to any incendiary publications forbidden by state law, allowing local justices of the peace to decide what was to be considered abolitionist and therefore fit for burning. Jackson's call for legislation banning the mails was rejected on the grounds that it would give too much power to the federal government, but **John Calhoun** proposed an alternative bill more in line with southern **states' rights** sensibilities and with what was actually transpiring by means of executive action. A bill to this effect, allowing postmasters to abide by state laws, was passed by the Senate for a third reading in June 1836 with Vice-President **Martin Van Buren** at one stage using his casting vote in the Senate in its favor. However, the fact that this bill did not pass a final vote suggested that many northerners were worried about its implications for freedom of speech. Nevertheless, the postmaster general's order continued and even some loyal northern **Democrat** postmasters complied, refusing to allow the mails to be used for the conveyance of abolitionist leaflets from their jurisdictions.

INDEPENDENCE, MISSOURI. This town was established in 1827 as a local agricultural center, attracting mainly southern settlers. It soon became the setting-off point for many of the great trails out to the West. Its fame grew when **Joseph Smith** visited it in 1831 and declared it to be the site of the **Mormon** "Zion," where Jesus Christ would return. Many Mormon settlers arrived, setting up churches, a school, stores, and newspapers. However, under pressure from local people and the Missouri state government the Mormons abandoned Independence in the late 1830s, moving instead to Illinois.

INDEPENDENT TREASURY ACT, 1840. The proposal for an Independent Treasury represented a continuation of the **bank wars** as **Martin Van Buren** became president in 1837. In part it was inspired by the belief that the federal government should only be directly interested in its own financial affairs and did not need the banking powers necessary to regulate foreign or domestic exchanges through currency manipulation. The proposal also emerged out of the practical and ideological reaction to the apparent failure of the **deposit bank** system during the **panic of 1837**. By the terms of the **1836 Deposit Act** banks that suspended specie payments during the panic were not allowed to hold federal funds. Even when banks began to resume specie payments in 1838, many could only deal in notes of small denomination and so again by terms of the 1836 act still could not handle federal deposits. In response the Treasury felt compelled to keep federal funds in the customs houses and land offices where they had first been received, demonstrating that it was feasible for Treasury offices to hold federal money on deposit. Even without this practical demonstration the deposit bank suspensions also made it more likely that radical **Democratic** anti-bank views would prevail within the party, blaming banks rather than economic circumstances or Jacksonian policies for the panic and backing the view that it would be best for the Treasury to hold its own funds in the future.

Although Van Buren introduced the idea of the Independent Treasury to the 1837 **special session** of Congress, it took another three years of debate and several defeats before such a measure was passed in June 1840 and signed by the president in July. Two main areas of controversy shaped congressional consideration of the bills that followed.

The first was the structure of any Independent Treasury. In 1837 supporters of the first bill fought off proposals either to select state banks as Treasury depositories, using special dedicated vaults and not being able to use the deposits for their own commercial purposes, or to create a new bureaucracy of special sub-treasury branches to hold the deposits. Instead, for simplicity's sake, deposits would be kept by local revenue collectors when they received them from the usual sources of land sales and tariff duty payments. The 1838 version of the bill would have established extra mechanisms for the Treasury to hold its own funds. Four receivers general were to be added to the U.S. Mints and to the Treasury itself as places of deposit, but the bill would also have allowed use of special deposit banks in the absence of adequate Treasury facilities nearby. These two bills, and a third, were defeated in Congress before the version that was eventually successful, in June 1840, created a structure of sub-treasuries across the nation to hold and disburse federal funds.

Ultimately more important in delaying the passage of the bill was the second contentious issue, the question of what forms of currency would be accepted by any Independent Treasury. Debate raged between those who regarded this as an opportunity to extend the "**hard money**" approach of the Jackson administration and those who asserted that even an Independent Treasury should have some responsibility for ensuring the nation's currency and credit supplies and the health of the banking system. Van Buren's line, as supported by **John Calhoun**, who found himself back in line with the Jacksonians on this issue, was to accept **paper notes** only under very clear conditions that would help to check the worst excesses of currency inflation by state banks. The House blocked this proposal in 1837 and such was the disagreement over the measure that even when the specie-only restrictions were removed in the 1838 and 1839 versions, both bills failed to pass. Only after the **panic of 1839** again seemed to demonstrate the failings of state banks did enough support finally build up to allow passage of the bill in June 1840, with a clause stating that after a four-year interim period treasury offices would accept only specie as payments.

The long road to the bill's passage, during which Van Buren had even contemplated using executive powers to establish the Independent Treasury, helped to delineate further the **Second Party System**. For the more radical wing of the Democratic Party it offered yet another rallying point in the march toward a fairer economy. Some termed it a second declaration of independence, allowing a return to a political economy more in accord with the initial desires of the founding fathers, before it had been corrupted by the Hamiltonian financial system and by a growing dependence upon economic cycles apparently dominated by British policy. However, many **Conservative Democrats** were uncomfortable with the direction of the policy and joined with the **Whigs** in defending the deposit bank system against the administration's proposals. Together they did not accept that deposit banks were responsible for the economic crisis and felt it more sensible to allow federal revenue to be kept in banks where it could be used to support the prudent extension of credit. Indeed in rhetorical terms the battle over the Independent Treasury became one between hard money and the **credit system**, between deflation and careful inflation of the currency, and this allowed Whigs to jettison, at least publicly and temporarily, their dependence upon calls for a new national bank as their main economic policy.

Following the transition from the Democratic Van Buren administration to the Whig administrations of **William Henry Harrison** and **John Tyler**, the act became a target of Whig leaders, such as **Henry Clay**, who were determined to reinstate some form of national bank. President Tyler also condemned the Independent Treasury for failing to provide either a sound currency and plentiful credit supply or a strong banking system, and so he agreed that its repeal was a suitable goal at the special congressional session of 1841. Although the pro-Bank element failed to achieve their ambition, thanks to Tyler's **Bank bill vetoes in 1841**, they could agree on repealing the Independent Treasury, in August 1841. In just over a year of existence it had done little to bring financial stability, and certainly it had not stopped the issuing or receiving of paper money by the federal government.

INDEPENDENT TREASURY ACT, 1846. This measure was similar to the **Independent Treasury Act of 1840**, although this second act succeeded in setting up a fiscal system that would survive until 1913. **James Polk** adhered to the radical **Democratic** line of opposition to both a national bank and a system of **deposit banks**. Therefore, partly out of principle and partly because it helped to keep the more radical elements of his party sweet, it was hardly surprising that when he became president he was keen to reintroduce an Independent Treasury to replace the system of state bank depositing to which the previous administration had returned almost by default after the repeal of the 1840 act and **John Tyler**'s **bank veto** in the summer of 1841.

Polk called for a new Independent Treasury in his annual message of 1845 and a bill was introduced on behalf of the administration in March 1846, proposing the establishment of vaults for the deposit of money paid to the federal government, those funds to be disbursed as and when necessary. By the standards of the time, and indeed of similar debates in the 1830s, the passage of the measure proved remarkably uncontroversial, but the absence of passionate debate did not mean its passage was swift, as procedural wrangling held it up in both houses before it passed on lines of strict party voting in August 1846. **Whigs** did contest one significant amendment which provided that after 1 January 1847 deposits would have to be in specie, although **Treasury notes** would be deemed an acceptable alternative. However, the Whig argument that the system would keep specie locked up in government vaults rather than in useful circulation, thereby causing a deflation of the currency, was to no avail against the strength of the administration forces. The bill passed and with it was created a system of federal sub-treasuries, based in Boston, New York, Philadelphia, Charleston, New Orleans, and St. Louis.

INDIAN REMOVAL ACT, 1830. The issue of Indian removal was one of the most significant in the early years of **Andrew Jackson**'s administration and certainly represented one that was closest to the heart of the president himself. Of course the nature of the relationship between European Americans and the many Native Americans who lived in neighboring lands was a long-standing problem and one that would persist for as long as geopolitical and popular **expansion** remained a key American trend. Some 100,000 Native Americans lived in Indiana, Illinois, and the Michigan and Wisconsin territories to the North and in Georgia, Alabama, Mississippi, and the Florida territory in the South, while the next band of territory further West also had its complement of native tribes. All these represented a challenge to European Americans desirous of fresh lands on which to settle. Jackson's experience of dealing with native tribes afforded a greater degree of urgency to the whole issue and generally gave support to the view that Native Americans should be moved out of areas settled primarily by whites. Certainly he backed measures in states like Georgia, Alabama, and Mississippi to get Native Americans resident within their boundaries to conform to state law or to get out.

The 1830 act provided further evidence of Jackson's stance as well as the mechanics of future Indian removal. It empowered the president to reach agreements with various tribes for their removal, giving up their eastern lands in exchange for others in an Indian territory created west of the Mississippi. Any wishing to stay would be subject to state laws and would have to own their land as individuals rather than as tribes in common. The act also initially allocated $500,000 in federal funds for carrying out negotiations to this effect and then for implementing the process of removal itself.

The final success of the act gave evidence of Jackson's political acumen, since it only passed narrowly in the face of considerable resistance on the part of opposition legislators and would probably have met with defeat had the president not kept enough western representatives on his side by delaying his **Maysville Road veto** until the day after the House voted on Indian removal. The act also gave the president an issue with which to buttress his western and southern support at a time when the latter in particular was under threat on the **tariff** and **nullification**. Such political intent, along with economic and racial motives, probably weighed heaviest in explaining Jackson's and ultimately Congress' support for the measure, and certainly **Indian removal**'s **implementation** seems to lend little support to claims made at the time that the policy could be justified as part of an effort to allow Native Americans the chance to be peaceful and become civilized in a protected environment away from white neighbors. *See also WORCESTER VS. GEORGIA.*

INDIAN REMOVAL IMPLEMENTATION. Indian removal during the Jacksonian era represented the continuation of the policy of gradually pushing back the Native American frontier, now under the terms of the 1830 **Indian Removal Act** as well as by individual state actions. Although often seen as serving the interests of **expansionist** elements in the South and Southwest, where the most famous removals took place, in the process buttressing the political position of **Andrew Jackson**'s administration, there were also plenty of removals of less numerous tribes from the more northerly Midwest. In all some 30 tribes were relocated by the end of the 1830s as the policy was continued into **Martin Van Buren**'s term, with some 70 treaty agreements being signed with the likes of the Shawnee, Ottawa, and Wyandot from Ohio, the Kickapoo, Chippewa, Peoria, Winnebago, Potawatomie, and Sauk/Fox tribes from Illinois and Indiana, the **Cherokee, Creek, Choctaw,** and **Chickasaw** from southeastern states, and the **Seminole** from the Florida territory.

Normally the negotiation of a removal treaty was conducted under the auspices of the Department of War, with some secretaries such as **John Eaton** getting directly involved. Money was then provided to cover the practical business of moving the Native Americans and providing for them in their new homes. However, progress was rarely as smooth as this, as elements of many tribes opposed removal or rebelled against agreements both old and new. Both the **Black Hawk War** and the **Second Seminole War** resulted from such difficulties, while the experience of the Cherokee, both in the run-up to and during the **"trail of tears"** itself affords the most notorious example of how implementation of the policy rarely lived up to some of the more principled reasons given for it. Several tribes suffered from inadequate facilities and from a decision to travel in the worst possible weather, with the result that their removal experience was uncomfortable at best and tragic at worst.

As a result earlier political opposition to Indian removal was reinforced. **National Republicans**, especially from the Northeast, had already opposed the 1830 act and in the campaign running up to the **election of 1832 Henry Clay** attacked the policy as a whole as well as specific treaties signed for the removal of individual tribes. The moral reform elements of the **Whig** Party called for a fairer approach to Indian removal, and the forces of **benevolent** Christianity constantly criticized the Jacksonian approach.

However, removal continued into the 1840s and in the latter part of that decade **James Polk**'s administration boasted of several treaties by which yet more land was acquired for white expansion and celebrated the fact that earlier removals seemed to have been accepted by those tribal members who had initially opposed them. Increasing numbers of tribes took up residence in the region west of Iowa, Arkansas, and Missouri, but the administration refused to countenance the creation of permanent settlements there, no doubt in recognition of the likelihood of later generations of white settlers having ambitions on such lands. But this later period did see the federal government support the establishment of manual labor schools in Indian territory, as well as boarding and district schools, which altogether educated nearly 4,000 Native American youths.

INGHAM, SAMUEL (1779-1860). This Pennsylvanian congressman, who served in the House between 1823 and 1829, became **Andrew Jackson**'s first secretary of the treasury between 1829 and 1831. Ingham's was a slightly anomalous position in that he came from a manufacturing background and a state which strongly supported the **protective tariff**, yet he leaned in political allegiance toward **John Calhoun**, who was becoming a leading advocate of **nullification**. His known favor for Calhoun also got him into trouble during the **Eaton Affair**, when his wife was one of the first to shun **Peggy Eaton**. As Ingham refused to give up his post, the president effectively told him to resign when the Cabinet was broken up in June 1831. Ingham went one step further in defending himself in public, printing correspondence in the *United States Telegraph* explaining why he had had to go, an action that precipitated a further personal crisis with **John Eaton** who challenged him to a duel. The duel never happened and Ingham managed to leave Washington alive.

INTERIOR, DEPARTMENT OF THE. At the very end of the period, on 3 March 1849, this was established as the sixth Cabinet department. It combined several branches, including the **Office of Indian Affairs**, the Office of the Census, the General Land Office, and the Pension Office.

INTERNAL IMPROVEMENTS. In the expanding and developing nation that was Jacksonian America, the question of how to encourage the movement of people and goods around the country figured high in the economic and political decision-making of the day. Apart from the obvious technological decisions to be made, such as which types of transportation to use and along which routes, significant political issues arose over how to fund such improvement projects in the first place and how to support them in the era's times of financial hardship. Throughout the period, private investment and state and municipal authorities played the major part in their sponsorship and development. But since the end of the War of 1812 many Americans had supported federal funding of improvements. It formed a significant plank of **Henry Clay**'s **American System** and President **John Quincy Adams** had also come round to favoring the policy. However, local jealousies and more significantly constitutional doubts generated considerable opposition to such federal participation, an opposition that found a home in the coalition of support for **Andrew Jackson**. For Jackson the trick would be to keep the latter viewpoint sweet, while not abandoning the idea of improvements to which he, as a westerner, was fundamentally sympathetic.

When Congress, in its first session of Jackson's presidency, passed six improvements bills, some federal in nature, some private or local, the president was forced to take a stand that would set out his administration's priorities from the start. The **Maysville Road veto** seemed to tip the balance toward opponents of improvements, as Jackson made clear that he would not support privately chartered improvements corporations, institutions that proposed to charge tolls, or measures that would increase the **national debt**. His veto was upheld, as was that of a bill to extend the Washington turnpike in Maryland. He also pocket-vetoed a bill to improve the Louisville river navigation and a lighthouse bill. At the same time, however, he allowed through two more important improvements bills, a general survey for potential future federal projects and an extension of the **National Road** west from Zanesville, Ohio. Moreover, his later support for spending on genuinely national projects, such as lighthouses and rivers and harbors, meant that federal expenditure on internal improvements actually rose in the 1830s, with Jackson's administration witnessing a doubling of annual improvements expenditure compared to that of Adams.

Despite this fact, after the Maysville bill veto debate shifted to finding alternative ways of channeling federal money to improvements projects, by means such as **distribution**. Moreover, in the panic conditions of the later 1830s attention became focused more on how to bail out improvements companies struggling in the hard times. Nevertheless, constitutionally approved improvements did still form a part of federal spending into the 1840s and aspirations for a transcontinental railroad, floated as early as 1844-45 by the likes of

Stephen Douglas, also relied on the prospect of federal funding. Others continued to call for improvements to other facilities but ran into the opposition of **James Polk** when he regarded them as constitutionally inappropriate, as illustrated by his vetoes of **harbors and rivers bills**. Polk, as Jackson before him, did lose some of his western (and especially his northwestern) support base as a result of his vetoes. *See also* CANALS; *CHARLES RIVER BRIDGE VS. WARREN BRIDGE*; RAILROADS; RIVERS AND HARBORS CONVENTION; TRANSPORTATION REVOLUTION.

IOWA, STATEHOOD. What became the state of Iowa in December 1846 had previously been part of three broader territories. After belonging to the Michigan territory until 1836 and then the Wisconsin territory, the Iowa territory, which included Minnesota and parts of the Dakotas, was established in July 1838. Settlers were attracted by tales of fertile land and, as government policy began to oversee **Indian removal** in the area, so the white population rose from fewer than 100 in 1832 to nearly 40,000 by 1840. The first public land surveys began in 1837 and in the following year two land offices were set up. A former governor of the state of Ohio, Robert Lucas, served as the first territorial governor, while the territorial legislature met initially at Burlington, before moving to Iowa City. After two attempts to get voters to support statehood ran into their opposition to the extra burden of taxation needed to sustain a state government, a constitution was finally ratified and statehood confirmed in 1846.

IRVING, WASHINGTON (1783-1859). From the first this American author's output raised him to a status of international renown. Born in New York City, Irving's early career combined writing with work in commercial pursuits, including periods spent abroad, something that prepared him for a spell in the late 1820s when he served in the U.S. legation in Spain (where he found inspiration for his 1832 work *The Alhambra*), and then, between 1829 and 1832, as secretary to the U.S. legation in London. He returned to the United States in 1832 and spent time traveling in the West, garnering experiences that would be reflected in some of his later works, including *A Tour of the Prairies* (1835), *Astoria* (1836), and *The Adventures of Captain Bonneville, USA* (1837). In 1838 **Martin Van Buren** offered him the position of secretary of the navy but Irving turned it down, the post going to his close friend **James Paulding** instead. In 1842 Irving was appointed to the position of minister to Spain, staying there until 1846 when he returned to live out the rest of his days in New York State.

– J –

JACKSON, ANDREW (1767-1845). Andrew Jackson was in every sense the central actor of the political drama of the Jacksonian era, not only giving his name to the age but dominating the personal and party developments and policy agenda for a 20-year period. As well as serving as president for two terms **Old Hickory** was a close friend and persistent advisor of his virtually hand-picked successor **Martin Van Buren**, while the career of President **James Polk** so mirrored his Tennessee forerunner that he came to share a common nickname, **Young Hickory**. The political party which emerged from the original coalition of support for Jackson may have changed considerably in its leadership and support groups as the period went on, but retained the label **Jacksonian Democrats** for most of the period, so great was Jackson's stamp of influence upon its development. Whether loved or feared, Jackson was the dominant figure of his time.

Jackson had risen to prominence through frontier legal activities and especially in a military career as a fighter of Native Americans and as victor over the British at the Battle of New Orleans in 1815. The popularity this record afforded him lasted throughout the rest of his political career, and although his record in fighting the **Creek** and the **Seminole** in the late 1810s stained his reputation in the eyes of some keen to find something to criticize him for, overall his military reputation served him well and left a legacy for other military heroes, such as **William Henry Harrison, Winfield Scott,** and **Zachary Taylor,** to follow. After periods as governor of the Florida territory and as a senator for Tennessee, the people got their opportunity to demonstrate their love for the man when Jackson ran for the presidency in 1824. His popular vote and electoral college return were the highest of the candidates standing, but without a college majority, he had to put his name up for election in the House of Representatives where he was defeated by **John Quincy Adams** in the subsequent ballot. This defeat, an apparent overturning of the popular will by the machinations of politicians, only increased the sense that Jackson was truly the man of the people, and this, together with the feeling of outrage he and others shared at what was termed a **"corrupt bargain"** between Adams and **Henry Clay,** gave him sufficient impetus to sweep to victory in the **election of 1828**.

Jackson's presidency was marked by much activity and dispute, making his the most energetic and talked-about administration for years. The **Eaton Affair** and Jackson's lack of trust in the loyalty of some Cabinet members, who seemed to lean less toward him than to

Vice-President **John Calhoun**, produced a major **Cabinet reshuffle** in 1831. Prior to that Jackson had relied rather more on an unofficial collection of advisors than had been the case with earlier presidents, to the extent that some labeled it his **Kitchen Cabinet**. Meanwhile in 1833-34 there was further upheaval as Jackson lost two secretaries of the treasury as a result of disagreements over the policy of **removal of the federal deposits**. By reputation, if not always by deed, the Jackson administration was seen as something of a new broom, cleaning out government posts by means of "**rotation of office**," albeit with clearly partisan intentions at play as officers operated within a kind of "**spoils system**." The president seemed most keen on **administrative reform** as part of efforts at government **retrenchment** and at reducing the **national debt**. In one final, if less desirable way, Jackson set a precedent for his successors, as an early example of a president who underwent an **assassination attempt**.

Although his stance on particular policies sometimes took a little time to develop, Jackson left no doubt that he viewed the office of the president as having an active and inspirational role, with a duty to shape the legislative landscape if it were constitutionally appropriate. His administration saw developments across a wide range of issues, most actively in relations with Native Americans and in matters connected to the economic development of the United States. **Indian removal** proved the one area of policy where Jackson sought to offer a really constructive (if not always morally acceptable) lead, while in a series of vetoes of **internal improvements** bills and, most famously, of a bill to re-charter the **Second Bank of the United States** he established economic and especially financial policy as a major field for political debate. Subsequent aspects of the **Bank wars**, such as the removal of the deposits and the **specie circulars** demonstrated his willingness to make the most of his office's powers and brought upon him partisan attacks for his "**executive usurpation**." But throughout, Jackson justified his actions on the grounds that he alone represented the American people as a whole, as his popular reputation and election victories in 1828 and 1832 seemed to confirm. He considered himself, the people, and the Union inseparable, as best witnessed in his forthright stance during the **Nullification crisis**. Predictably his actions also generated hostility, which helped to mold the overall political landscape, with the rise of a clear **second party system** being shaped largely by support for or opposition to Jackson and his policy stances.

After he left Washington, Jackson remained influential in the circles of his own political party, as only befitted a man whose stamp of authority was so great. He continued to advise Van Buren, supporting his stance in persisting with the Specie Circular and in pushing for the **Independent Treasury**. It was also highly significant, if regrettable to Jackson, that he felt he had to abandon his support for his successor in the run-up to the **election of 1844**, when Van Buren seemed not to favor **Texas annexation**. Although Jackson, when president, had delayed recognition of **Texan independence** until his very last day in office, fearing the **sectional** difficulties it might have raised earlier, he definitely supported the idea of annexation itself and ultimately supported, in James Polk, a candidate who would back annexation while remaining safe on other issues central to his own political record. To the very end his influence shone out as Polk consulted with him about his Cabinet appointments and as Jackson supported the choice of the *Washington Union* as the new administration organ at the expense of his old advisor **Francis Blair**'s *Washington Globe*.

JACKSON, RACHEL (1767-1828). Rachel Donelson had met **Andrew Jackson** in Nashville when the future president was boarding at her mother's house. At this time she was married to Lewis Robards, and her husband's jealousy led to a personal crisis that resulted in her fleeing for Natchez with Jackson as her protector and ultimately securing a divorce from Robards. Rachel and Andrew married, and then remarried after it became apparent that her divorce was not finalized, a set of circumstances that would haunt the couple in later years. Indeed, doubts about the divorce and the significance of this for her initial period of marriage with Jackson generated many rumors that would form the basis of political slander, the trigger for several of Jackson's later duels. Jackson also attributed Rachel's early death, soon after his victory in the **election of 1828**, to the level of slander directed at them during the campaign. The treatment of his wife's reputation not only angered Jackson but also increased his considerable sympathy for **John** and **Peggy Eaton** when they faced similar accusations during the **Eaton Affair**.

JACKSONIAN. This multi-faceted label is used generally to describe the era in which **Andrew Jackson** served as president (1829-37) or flourished as a leading military and political figure (1815-45), and is also applied to the American people at large during that era. More specifically, and more usefully to historians, the term covers any follower of President Jackson or members of the **Democratic** Party.

JACKSONIAN DEMOCRACY. This term is commonly used to convey the sense that in some way the advent of **Andrew Jackson** to the presidency heralded a shift in the relationship between the American people and their elected officials. While the impression is often given that this involved an opening up of the political process, and while there was indeed some **suffrage extension** during the era, this was more the result of increased active popular participation in politics than it was of a legal loosening of political restrictions. Certainly the popularity of the leading figure of the age, Jackson himself, the growth of the **second party system**, and the range of issues debated during the period (and the way they were packaged for popular consumption) inspired more people to vote than had ever been the case before. This, and the fact that Jackson and his party assumed for themselves the mantle of the party of the people, led to the association of Jackson with a growth of democracy in America. The label Jacksonian Democracy has also been used to encompass the era's general sense of progress and reform, ranging from voting changes, calls for **women**'s rights, educational and prison reform, through humanitarian campaigns, to new intellectual currents as well. As with the term **Jacksonian**, the label is sometimes applied more narrowly to the **Democratic** Party.

JALAPA. This Mexican town was occupied in April 1847, the day after the battle of **Cerro Gordo**, as part of **Winfield Scott**'s **Mexican War** march from Vera Cruz to Mexico City.

JEFFERSON BIRTHDAY DINNER. On 13 April 1830 a group of old Republicans and **Jacksonians** met to celebrate the former president's birthday at a dinner attended by most of the leading members of the U.S. government. It was strongly suspected at the time that the organizers of the event were hoping to use it to strengthen the relationship between the southern and western elements in **Andrew Jackson**'s coalition of support, with a view to creating a political alliance that would serve the best interests of both sections. Jackson himself was encouraged to believe that the dinner had been organized by southern **states' rights** elements in order to draw him into clear support of their position, in the hope that the president would take as favorable a stance on issues like the **protective tariff** as he had done on Georgia's policy toward the **Creek** and **Cherokee**. Instead, though, the dinner became the occasion when Jackson set his stall out in opposition to **nullification**, when he responded to toasts put forward by the nullifier **Robert Hayne** and others with his own toast:

"Our Union: *it must be preserved.*" Vice-President **John Calhoun** rose to the challenge, with his own, less succinctly put toast, "The Union: next to our liberty most dear. May we always remember that it can be preserved only by distributing equally the benefits and burthens of the Union." Regardless of the intentions, real or suspected, of the dinner's planners, the event served to reinforce Jackson's suspicion of his vice-president and strained relations between the majority of the president's followers and the more extreme states' rights elements within his support coalition. It proved one of the precipitating causes for the more public rift between Jackson and Calhoun, as played out in the publication of correspondence relating to the **Florida report**.

JERVIS, JOHN (1795-1885). Jervis was one of the leading civil engineers of the age, involved in most of the types of improvement and construction projects that were so important at the time. Born in New York State, he underwent a fairly basic self-education before becoming an apprentice to the chief engineer on the **Erie Canal**. Jervis went on to work for a number of **railroad** companies, such as the Delaware and Hudson and Mohawk and Hudson lines, involved not just in planning and building track, but also in designing steam locomotives, such as the *Experiment* in 1832, at that time the fastest to be built in the United States. In 1836 he took on the project of constructing the Croton aqueduct, for supplying water to New York City, which was completed in 1842, and then he moved on to become chief engineer of the Hudson River railroad.

JESUP, THOMAS SIDNEY (1788-1860). Jesup was born in Virginia but grew up in Kentucky, before entering a long career in the U.S. army. After serving in the War of 1812, he spent the majority of his career as quartermaster general, with a brief, but significant, interruption for active service, when he helped to put down a revolt of **Creek** natives in Alabama. He was then appointed by **Andrew Jackson** to command the armed forces in the **Second Seminole War** in December 1836, making effective strides in the war by capturing **Osceola**, albeit under a flag of truce, and by winning the battle of Okeechobee. Jesup was eventually removed from his post in May 1838 after his calls for peace talks were rejected. In a more prosaic fashion he also contributed to the winning of the **Mexican War**, it being his organization of supplies that kept the army on the move. He took part in the final march from Vera Cruz to Mexico City with **Winfield Scott**.

JOHNSON, CAVE (1793-1866). This Tennessee politician had a long record of association with Presidents **Andrew Jackson** and **James Polk**. Johnson had served with **Old Hickory** in the War of 1812, before turning to the common combination of careers as tobacco farmer, lawyer, and politician, with two periods of service in the House of Representatives, in 1829-37 and in 1839-45. As the close friend of Polk he had helped work for his nomination in 1844, and Johnson's reward was to be appointed postmaster general in 1845. He remained a close personal friend of the president in social circles but was probably the least vociferous of Polk's Cabinet officers. Nevertheless he was considered an honest and efficient postmaster general, overseeing **Post Office reform** and the massive growth of facilities required by an expanding nation. In the process Johnson had considerable patronage power, with many appointments to new offices at his disposal, and he also indulged in a degree of **spoils system** politics, with many of the 14 percent of removals being the replacement of **Whigs** by **Democrats**.

JOHNSON, RICHARD MENTOR (1780-1850). Johnson was a Kentuckian of legal and military background who rose to become vice-president during the administration of **Martin Van Buren**. Renowned as the man who had killed Tecumseh at the Battle of the Thames during the War of 1812, he owed a great deal to his reputation among westerners as a valuable fighter of Native Americans. From 1819 to 1829 Johnson served as a senator before spending the next eight years in the House of Representatives, where he proved loyal to the **Andrew Jackson** administration as much out of ambition and party sense as out of support for particular policies. For example, while he voted for the original **Maysville Road** bill in 1830 he chose not to support efforts to override the president's veto. Two of his particular favorite legislative subjects were support for the abolition of imprisonment for debt and opposition to **sabbatarian** efforts to suspend postal services on Sundays. As Van Buren's running mate in the **election of 1836** Johnson was regarded as a controversial figure, many finding distasteful his choice of a mulatto woman as his partner. However, this did not prevent him winning the vice-presidential election, albeit as the only vice-president to win by a House ballot, having failed to secure a majority of electoral college votes. After a fairly undistinguished term, even within the limits of his office, Johnson was Van Buren's defeated running mate in the 1840 election, and then retired to private life, only to be briefly considered by some as a candidate for 1844.

JUDICIARY ACT. This act, passed in March 1837, was in part a response to numerous calls for judicial reform by **Andrew Jackson** in his annual messages. It increased the number of Supreme Court justices from seven to nine and, in recognition of the failure of the existing appeal court provision for a nation in the process of expanding westward, it created two new appeals circuits for the western states.

– K –

KANE LETTER. This letter was sent to John Kane by **James Polk** during his campaign for **election in 1844**. Kane was a prominent Philadelphian and a member of **George Dallas'** faction of the Pennsylvanian **Democratic** Party, and the letter was intended to placate supporters of the **protective tariff** in that state. Already the Democratic platform had been equivocal on the issue, and Polk's claim in the letter that he had no objections to a **tariff for revenue** providing some incidental protection, even if he opposed protective tariffs *per se,* could easily have been interpreted as being friendly to the idea of protection.

KEARNY, STEPHEN (1794-1848). Born in New Jersey, Kearny became a serving army officer, with experience in the New York militia and the regular army in the War of 1812. During later frontier postings he assisted in the construction of forts and rode several of the overland trails to the West, such as the **Oregon Trail** in 1845. This experience put Kearny in a good position when the **Mexican War** broke out. He was appointed brigadier general and commander of the Army of the West, starting his campaign by conquering New Mexico in August 1846. After setting up civil government at Santa Fe, he moved to assist **Robert Stockton** in capturing Los Angeles in 1847. However, his relations with Stockton and his ally and appointee as military governor of California, **John Frémont**, were not good and Kearny exercised his seniority of post by having Frémont court-martialed and forcing him to resign. Kearny in turn became governor of California and then in 1847 was appointed civil governor in Veracruz and Mexico City in occupied Mexico. However, soon after further promotion he died of an illness he had picked up during the campaign.

KEMBLE, FANNY (1809-1893). This English actress, born Frances Anne Kemble, had a famous career as the "Queen of Tragedy."

While on tour with her father in America for the first time in 1832, she met and married an American in 1834, upon which she retired to lead a life as the wife of a plantation owner. Her 1835 *Journal of Frances Anne Butler* and 1838-39 *Residence of a Georgian Plantation* offered a realistic and critical portrayal of **slavery**, and after hearing **William Channing** speak she became sympathetic to the **abolitionists**. She was also becoming frustrated by American rules on marriage which had encouraged her husband to try to suppress her writings, and, after two trips back to Europe to escape and to convalesce, she divorced him and resumed a professional career as a dramatic reader.

KENDALL, AMOS (1789-1869). Kendall was a man of Massachusetts and New Hampshire roots who moved to Kentucky at the age of 25. After a period as tutor to **Henry Clay**'s children, he became a newspaperman, beginning to edit the Frankfort *Argus* in 1816 and taking that paper into the ranks of the Jacksonians in the mid-1820s. Kendall's own experience and that of many of his neighbors during the hard times of the late 1810s and early 1820s generated in him a hostility to the **credit system**, banking, and the **Second Bank of the United States** in particular. It was this hostility that would make him so influential a figure in **Andrew Jackson**'s administration during the **bank wars**. From a relatively obscure post as fourth auditor at the Treasury, Kendall became a member of the **Kitchen Cabinet** and helped to write several of Jackson's great public papers, including annual messages and the **Bank veto message**. After 1835 he served as postmaster general for both Jackson and **Martin Van Buren** and strove to bring greater efficiency to the Post Office. He retired for reasons of ill health in 1840, but also in order to edit the *Extra Globe,* a Van Buren campaign paper, from whose columns he continued to support the administration's flagship policy, the **Independent Treasury**, which he hailed as a second Declaration of Independence. After his political retirement Kendall worked largely unsuccessfully as a journalist and claims agent and then in 1845 he became **Samuel Morse**'s business manager and represented him in a number of patent cases, in the process of which he made himself a very wealthy man.

KENNEDY, JOHN PENDLETON (1795-1870). After an unrewarding legal career, this Baltimore-born member of the famous Pendleton family of Virginia was freed by an inheritance to pursue a double career as a writer and partisan politician. Under his pen-name of Mark Littleton he became one of the most important southern writers of the age, mixing with other authors such as **Edgar Allan Poe**. His works *Swallow Barn* (1832), *Rob of the Bowl* (1838), and *Horse-Shoe Robinson* (1838) revealed him to be a perceptive commentator on southern, and especially Virginian, society, albeit with a stereotypically sympathetic view of **slavery** as the best condition possible for African-Americans. He also wrote political satire, notably in *Quodlibet* in 1840, preparation for some of the more bitter polemical attacks he would make during his own, brief, political career.

His family background, his early legal career, and then two marriages brought Kennedy into direct contact with the mercantile and manufacturing communities of Maryland, and in 1838 to 1839 and 1841 to 1843 he represented these in the House. As a supporter of **John Quincy Adams**, **Henry Clay**, and the **American System** he naturally fell into line with the **Whig** Party and became one of their most active partisans while in Washington. Kennedy attained most notoriety for his scathing attacks on **John Tyler** after his various vetoes, being influential in moves to condemn the president in the **Whig Manifesto**. He would also write a two-volume *Defense of the Whigs* in 1844 in reply to Tyler's own response to his earlier attacks, a sign of the depths to which their personal relations had sunk.

"KING ANDREW I." This critical nickname for **Andrew Jackson** was used by the **Whigs** as part of their charge of **executive usurpation** against him, portraying the president as similar to a tyrannical monarch whose excesses required vigilant monitoring.

KITCHEN CABINET. This originally derisive name, bandied about by opposition newspapers like the *United States Telegraph*, was used to describe the small coterie of unofficial advisors and lesser government officials that **Andrew Jackson** consulted instead of his Cabinet proper, especially at times in the period 1829-31 when the **Eaton Affair** caused him to suspend regular meetings with the Cabinet. Among his key advisors were **Isaac Hill**, **Frank Blair**, **William B. Lewis**, **Andrew Donelson**, and **Amos Kendall**, as well as Cabinet-members proper **John Eaton** and **Martin Van Buren**. The reshuffle of the real Cabinet in 1831 did lessen the need for its unofficial rival as Jackson brought men more of his own stamp to office. Nevertheless the shift to fighting the **bank war** after 1832 caused him to rely once more on figures outside the Cabinet, especially Kendall and Blair. Throughout, though, the established Cabinets operated in the way they had for many years previous, carrying out the executive duties assigned to each office, and it was only in a more advisory capacity that other figures beyond the Cabinet's official ranks were consulted.

The peculiar circumstances of **John Tyler**'s accession, with an inherited Cabinet, encouraged him also to use a "kitchen cabinet" of sorts, and certainly the "Corporal's Guard," as it was called, did provide him with alternative advice, especially from the Virginian **states' rights** angle. Several members of the "Corporal's Guard" went on to become Cabinet members in their own right, although apparently offering greater loyalty to **John Calhoun** than to the president himself.

– **L** –

LABOR. As the United States underwent the massive changes wrought by **manufacturing** development and by the **transportation** and **market revolutions**, it was inevitable that American workers in all fields also experienced significant upheavals in their lives and working environments. Whether it was individuals or families laboring on their own or rented farms, migrant farm laborers, or **slaves** on establishments of various sizes, many **agricultural** workers witnessed major changes in the type of work they were doing and the commercial pressures under which they worked. So-called "unskilled" workers found their labor in great demand as the nation embarked on a dramatic period of **internal improvement**, with the building of **canals** and **railroads** and other construction projects, but this did not guarantee either that working conditions were good or that employment was stable.

Of course the term labor is traditionally more closely associated with manufacturing occupations and in these too workers in this era experienced if anything greater levels of change. The growth of manufacturing industry, its diversification into a number of different working environments, such as the "putting out" system and the factory style, and an increasing separation of skills, all confronted American workers with new patterns of daily work and altered relationships with their employers. Skilled artisans, faced with the introduction of machinery, underwent a degree of de-skilling with the result that they were now more likely to be considered wage laborers, often working on piece rates, having less in common with their masters than was previously the case, and having fewer opportunities for personal advancement. There was even change in the very nature of the workforce, as factory villages like **Lowell** employed predominantly **women** and then immigrant workers, while other manufacturing communities marshaled the labor of whole families.

On top of problems inherent in these kinds of labor usage, such as issues relating to safety, insecurity of employment because of seasonal variation, long hours and low wages, the period's economic fluctuations also brought difficulties for American workers. Wages tended to rise less quickly than prices in the inflation years of the early 1830s, while the **panics of 1837** and **1839**, with their accompanying depression through to the early 1840s, brought considerable hardship for urban workers in particular, with unemployment of up to one-third in cities like New York.

In the face of these specific problems and the longer-term changes, American workers sought a variety of ways to put forward their views. Two in particular prevailed in an organized form: **trade unions** and wider **Workingmen's movements**, which adopted respectively either more traditional union tactics in workshops and factories, or local political activity. However, organized labor had considerable limitations, especially in times of particular economic hardship like the late 1830s when the threat of unemployment caused many to accept whatever working conditions were necessary to keep their jobs. Moreover, trade unions rarely represented the mass of semi- or unskilled workers in free employment, let alone those in bondage. On occasions these less skilled workers resorted to other more traditional, and violent, forms of protest, such as in flour riots in New York City in early 1837 and several examples of rioting in canal works, to say nothing of the variety of methods of resistance adopted within slave communities.

Confronted with this variety of activity politicians of both main parties proved sympathetic rather more in word than in deed. Most promised policies that would benefit the interests of laborers, and the **Democrats** in particular shared much of the ideological background of Workingmen's groups. However, few politicians supported labor's more active methods and **Andrew Jackson** was the first president to use federal troops to intervene in a strike action, when violence broke out on the workings of the **Chesapeake and Ohio canal** in Maryland. *See also COMMONWEALTH VS. HUNT.*

LADD, WILLIAM (1788-1841). This New Hampshire-born sea captain became prominent as a promoter of international peace, denouncing all wars if not totally eschewing reasonable levels of force in self-defense. Ladd became a Congregational minister in 1837 and clearly drew upon the general pool of religiously-based reform of the age. He was most famous for founding the American Peace Society in 1828, while his *Essay on a Congress of Nations* in 1840 proposed international bodies that predicted the League of Nations and United Nations.

LAMAR, MIRABEAU (1798-1859). This Georgia-born statesman became one of the leading figures in the newly independent **Texas**. In his home state he had served as private secretary to Governor George Troup, and came to share his **states' rights** and anti-Native American views. Lamar edited a states' rights newspaper and in the wake of the **Nullification crisis** came out in strong opposition to **Andrew Jackson** after the president inspired the passage of the **Force Act**. However, after failing to win electoral office in his home state, Lamar moved, via Alabama, to settle in Texas in 1835, permanently from March 1836.

As a fighter during the Texan revolution he gained a good reputation, being appointed commander-in-chief temporarily, and commanding the cavalry at the battle of **San Jacinto**. After terms as secretary of war to an interim president, and then as attorney general and vice-president under **Sam Houston** in 1836, Lamar himself became president of Texas for two terms between 1838 and 1844. His term in office was marked by some early reform attempts such as the establishment of a public school system, but overall his presidency was something of an expensive disappointment, as he added $5 million to the public debt of $2 million he inherited. He was known most for his stance on international affairs, having some success in achieving European recognition of Texan independence. He also took a particularly aggressive stance toward both Native Americans and Mexicans in his effort to defend the new state's territory, but in the process he provoked Mexico to acts of retaliation. Initially his view of a strong and independent Texas made him cool to the idea of **annexation** by the United States but after he left office he came round to supporting it and later fought for his new country in the **Mexican War**.

LAND OFFICE ACT. This act represented the culmination of a series of **administrative reforms** in an important policy area, given the significance of **expansion** and the volume of land sales during the era. Expansion and **Indian removal** swamped the existing general land office and its procedures with a much increased workload and demonstrated the grave need for change. In March 1833 a minor reform was instituted, relieving the president of the duty of signing every land patent, a special clerk being appointed to sign his name for him. Further reform followed when Ethan Allen Brown replaced Elijah Hayward as commissioner of the Office, bringing with him more watertight practices, and also recommendations for reforms that Congress eventually implemented in this act in July 1836. It provided for a shake-up in the structure and number of layers of office in the Land Office, and an increase in the body of employees to handle the growing workload of the times.

LAND POLICY. This was a period when land policy was rarely out of the public attention, from the **Webster-Hayne** debate right through to policies for lands in new territories acquired from Mexico. This was hardly surprising given the wresting of Indian lands into white ownership and the acquisition of territories by annexation and conquest, but also vital was the American public's sheer hunger for land, as revealed in the level of federal land sales in the mid-1830s in particular. This not only made it an issue linked very closely to the aspirations of the American people as well as to the future economic development and health of the nation, but also one that accounted for a significant share of public revenue, rising to some 48 percent in 1836, after a two-year period which had seen returns from land sales over three times and then five times higher than they had ever been in any one year prior to 1834.

One series of suggested policies, most directly associated with **Democratic** politicians and their western elements in particular, such as **Thomas Hart Benton**, was intended to encourage settlement and a speedy disposal of public lands. Western states, keen to attract more settlers, tended to favor cheaper or even free dispersal of land but they also supported a **graduation** of land price, so that lands became cheaper the longer they remained unsold, a move which would have lessened the point of eastern states opposing generally cheaper land prices. Supporters of land settlement also tended to support **preemption** as a way of rewarding families who improved lands before actually buying them.

Others opposed this more liberal approach and regarded western lands as a resource to be carefully marshaled, both for development's sake and as a long-term revenue source. As such, land policy also came to be tied up with debates over the policy of **distribution** of federal revenues, with **Henry Clay** supporting careful land sales to provide a revenue to distribute, while **John Calhoun** adopted a southern **states' rights** view that federal lands should be surrendered to the individual states in which they lay. Ironically, **Andrew Jackson**'s **Specie Circular** of 1836, which was in part designed to counteract the excessive speculation in land by private companies using **paper money** in the 1833-37 period, probably made it even more difficult for genuine land settlers to purchase land since they would not have enough hard currency to do so.

LANE THEOLOGICAL SEMINARY. This Presbyterian college was founded near Cincinnati in 1832, assisted by finance from the **Tappan** brothers. Its first president was **Lyman Beecher**, who regarded it as an instrument of religious revival on the frontier. However, from its earliest days it attracted extreme **anti-slavery** supporters, such as **Theodore Weld**, and this threatened the stability of the Seminary's position. So extreme were some of the public lectures on the issue of **slavery** that they were banned, causing most of the Seminary's first class of students to go to **Oberlin College** instead. Even so Lane was one of several colleges which gave real energy to the **abolitionist** movement, providing many graduates who went on to become abolitionist thinkers and leaders.

LARKIN, THOMAS (1802-1858). This Massachusetts-born merchant moved to North Carolina before abandoning his trading interests there to settle at Monterey in California in 1831. There Larkin developed a number of business interests including a flour mill and a general store. His local prominence made him a suitable candidate to take on the sensitive position as U.S. consul in the port in 1844 and in that context he was influential in encouraging the U.S. government impulse to acquire **California**. As a secret agent for **James Polk**'s administration from October 1845, Larkin also followed orders to back Californian "**Bear Flag**" rebels in the event of a war breaking out between the United States and Mexico. After the successful military campaign in California, which incidentally Larkin benefited from by supplying U.S. troops, he joined **Robert Stockton** in announcing the annexation of California to the United States in July 1846.

LAWRENCE, ABBOTT (1792-1855). Lawrence was a member of an important Massachusetts mercantile family, initially involved in the import trade but later diversifying into trade in American textiles. Ultimately in the 1830s he would also invest in textiles manufacturing and in 1845 went on to join with several industrialists in buying the site of the manufacturing community in Massachusetts that bears his name. Lawrence also served as a politician, whose support for **sabbatarianism** and for economic policies designed to promote economic activity clearly aligned him with first the **National Republican** and then the **Whig** parties. He sat in the House in 1835-37 and 1839-40, backing the efforts of **Henry Clay** against rivals like **Daniel Webster** and **John Tyler**. Some even considered Lawrence a potential running mate for **Zachary Taylor** in 1848, but his prospects were thwarted by the opposition of Webster and his own state's **Conscience Whigs**, who opposed the nomination of **Cotton Whigs** to both presidential and vice-presidential candidacies.

LEGARÉ, HUGH (1797-1843). After studying law at Edinburgh, Scotland, Legaré returned to his home state of South Carolina to pursue activities in law, journalism, and politics. His early career was marked by his founding of the *Southern Review*, which he also edited, and by a term as attorney general for his state in 1830-32. He rose to prominence as a **Unionist** during the **Nullification crisis**, which won him the reward from **Andrew Jackson** of the office of U.S. chargé to Belgium between 1832 and 1836. Legaré returned to take a seat in the House of Representatives, 1837-39, by which time a combination of his views on **states' rights** and his support for economic enterprise was pushing him toward the **Whig** Party. He opposed **Martin Van Buren**'s **Independent Treasury** proposals as likely to stifle economic activity and he campaigned for the Whigs in 1840. This support, and his background views, made Legaré a suitable choice for **John Tyler**'s Cabinet once **His Accidency** had succeeded to the presidency, and he served first as attorney general between 1841 and 1843 and as interim secretary of state. Indeed many considered him to be the president's closest Cabinet colleague, and he came to share his support for **Manifest Destiny** and for American naval and trading advances into the Pacific Ocean. He died suddenly from an illness.

LEGGETT, WILLIAM (1801-1839). Leggett was an influential thinker and writer for the **Jacksonian** movement, bringing to the **Democratic** Party the opinions of the radical **Locofoco** faction of New York City. After a career in the navy he had become a journalist in the late 1820s, serving as assistant editor to **William Cullen Bryant** on the *New York Evening Post*, before founding his own *Plain Dealer* in 1836-37. Leggett's radicalism stemmed from a libertarian approach that viewed all government intervention in the economy as likely to serve the interests of a corrupt and corrupting aristocracy at the expense of most other people. Hence he supported **free trade** and **hard money**, while opposing the **Second Bank of the United States**

and other chartered monopolies. At the same time he supported the right of working Americans to join **trade unions** and even defended the rights of **abolitionists** to speak.

LEWIS, WILLIAM B. (1784-1866). Although born in Virginia Lewis gained fame as a friend and supporter of **Andrew Jackson** in Tennessee and on his military campaigns as **Old Hickory**'s quartermaster. He proved an important advisor during Jackson's early political career and helped to shape his victory in the **election of 1828**. As second auditor of the Treasury he lived in the White House and acted as one of the **Kitchen Cabinet**. Lewis also proved loyal to the president during the **Eaton Affair**, but his personal friendship did not mean total agreement on policy, as he favored re-charter of the **Second Bank of the United States** and opposed the **removal of the federal deposits** when it occurred. Nevertheless he still remained loyal to the president and to **Martin Van Buren**, having worked for the latter's succession to the vice-presidency and then to the presidency itself in 1836. Although by the end of 1841 Lewis was no longer a leading player, he still managed to hold onto his post, acting in an advisory capacity to **John Tyler**. Loyal to his friend to the very end, Jackson pleaded with **James Polk** to retain Lewis in office, but the new president finally dismissed him in 1845.

LIBERATOR, THE. This **abolitionist** newspaper, published by **William Lloyd Garrison** in partnership with Isaac Knapp, began publication in Boston in January 1831. Although its circulation never rose above 3,000 it proved very influential through to its closure in 1865, probably being the leading organ of abolitionism and attracting contributions from many of the most prominent abolitionist writers of the period. It helped to shift the emphasis of **anti-slavery** to the more immediatist approach and it provided the mouthpiece through which Garrison made some of his more extreme calls for ending the Union with slaveholders in the South.

LIBERTY PARTY. The Liberty Party was the first major political party to place issues connected with **slavery** at the heart of its agenda. It started life in western New York and Massachusetts as a pressure group trying to ascertain the views of leading politicians on matters of importance to the **anti-slavery** movement, such as **abolition**, the treatment of fugitive slaves in northern states, and even issues of racial discrimination in the North. But, led by **James Birney** from November 1839 and bankrolled by **Gerrit Smith**, and later supported by **Lewis Tappan** and others in the **American and Foreign Anti-Slavery Society**, it began to run its own electoral campaigns in the hope of influencing the political system in a more direct way. The Party's leaders believed that the abolitionists' approach of moral suasion was failing to effect significant change, as the treatment of **"incendiary"** abolitionist literature and the **"gag rules"** had demonstrated. Meanwhile anti-abolition rioting in the North and the fate of abolitionist editors such as **Elijah Lovejoy** had exposed the inability and unwillingness of the political system to protect the antislavery movement. So then the Liberty Party acted in part to try to change the system in order to guard against its domination by Southerners and their northern allies. The Party's main targets were those things that seemed to tie the federal government to the slave regime: slavery in the District of Columbia; slavery in the territories; the fugitive slave law; and the three-fifths constitutional clause allowing southern states to count slaves as partial people for the purpose of calculating representation in Washington.

The Party's electoral highpoint came in the period 1840 to 1846. In April 1840 delegates from six states met in a convention at Albany and nominated Birney as their presidential candidate for that year's election, a contest in which he won around 7,000 votes. He ran for the presidency again in 1844, attacking the two main parties' candidates, **Henry Clay** and **James Polk**, the latter for his clear support for **Texas annexation** and Clay for his developing ambiguity on the topic. While never having a chance of winning the election, the Party did increase its presidential vote nine-fold compared to four years earlier, and its vote in New York may well have tipped that state and the election into the Polk camp. The Party's level of support was creditable considering it did not represent even a majority of those opposed to slavery. The fact that it stopped shy of outright abolition and was resorting to political action in the first place made its activities distasteful and inappropriate to other leading abolitionists like **William Lloyd Garrison**.

But the same things that disenchanted some abolitionists probably made the Party less likely to offend other voters who found slavery distasteful, and so its support continued to grow, the Party securing more than 74,000 votes in congressional elections in 1846. The following year the party nominated the anti-annexation Democrat **John Hale** as its candidate for 1848, already a sign of its willingness to expand its appeal, but then many of the party's followers, such as **Salmon Chase**, felt even further broadening was necessary and they assisted in the formation of the **Free Soil** Party in 1848, dropping Hale as a separate candidate. In exchange for supporting the Free Soil candidate, former Liberty Party men were promised that the new party's platform would include a commitment to abolish slavery wherever it was in the power of the federal government so to do, and with this deal the separate existence of the Liberty Party effectively ended.

LIGHTHOUSE BILL VETO. *See* INTERNAL IMPROVEMENTS.

"LITTLE MAGICIAN." This nickname for the political organizer and president **Martin Van Buren** arose out of his apparent ability to manipulate people and events behind the scenes, almost as if by magic and in secret.

LITTLE TARIFF BILL, 1842. This measure was considered in summer 1842 as a stop-gap solution to potentially embarrassing problems arising from the implementation of the **compromise tariff of 1833**. By the terms of the latter there would be a leveling of all import duties to 20 percent that summer, too precipitate a drop on many items according to some, while others even questioned whether duties could be collected at all after the end of June 1842. As full consideration of a brand-new tariff was likely to go on beyond that deadline, many **Whigs** believed that the federal government could be left without one of its major sources of revenue, with the result that it would fail to meet its obligations. Although some regular Whigs might have enjoyed the embarrassment that this would bring to **John Tyler**'s administration, and had opposed earlier relief measures for that very reason, the prospect of federal employees not being paid was too dangerous to risk and so they considered this temporary measure to resolve the dilemma.

The solution, at one level, was quite obvious, as the bill proposed to postpone the 1833 act's final reduction of duties until 1 August 1842. What made this sensible proposal controversial was a specific clause providing for the continuation of **distribution** of surplus federal revenue, even though some tariff duties would remain above 20 percent, in direct contravention of a provision in the previous year's **Distribution and Preemption Act**. Although debate in Congress focused mainly on this element of the bill, it passed. However, President Tyler was not willing to countenance the bill's failure to suspend distribution and vetoed it, an action that only added to Whig frustration with **His Accidency**. Unable to override the veto, Whigs watched as the final duty reduction did come into force, but their worst fear did not materialize as customs collectors did continue to collect duties. The debate over duty levels and distribution would carry over into debates leading to the **tariff of 1842**.

LITTLETON, MARK. *See* KENNEDY, JOHN P.

LIVINGSTON, EDWARD (1764-1836). This scholar, legalist, and statesman was born into a long-established New York family and was educated at Princeton. After a career in law and service in the War of 1812 as **Andrew Jackson**'s *aide de camp* Livingston moved to New Orleans where he became a planter and helped to draft Louisiana's legal code. With early leanings to the Federalist Party, he served his adopted state in the House of Representatives from 1823 to 1829 and then in the Senate from 1829 to 1831. Despite his vote to override Jackson's veto of the Washington turnpike **internal improvements** bill and his support for the **Second Bank of the United States**, Livingston was appointed secretary of state in 1831. In that office he made significant progress with the issue of **spoliation claims**, but most importantly his more nationalist viewpoint came to prominence during the **Nullification crisis** when he helped to draft Jackson's **Nullification Proclamation** in response to the actions of South Carolina. In 1833 Livingston went to France to serve as U.S. minister until 1835, before retiring to the family estate in New York where he died the following year.

LOCOFOCOS. The Locofocos, officially known as the Equal Rights Party, were a radical splinter group of the New York **Democrats**, usually regarded as representing members of the urban working classes. Taking on many of the ideas of earlier **Workingmen's parties**, as developed by the likes of **William Leggett** and Ely Moore, the Locofocos strongly opposed government-granted monopolies, the **Second Bank of the United States**, and banking in general, while supporting a "**hard money**" currency. Their name emerged from events at **Tammany Hall** in October 1835. When the Equal Rights group tried to continue with a meeting previously dominated by pro-Bank Democrats, their opponents adjourned proceedings and turned off the gas lights, forcing the more radical elements to use "locofoco" matches to light candles. Although this occurrence only confirmed Locofoco hostility to the regular party organization, few took the final step of leaving the party. Those who did lost federal patronage for their newspaper organ, the *New York Post*, but they were soon reabsorbed within the Democrats when **Martin Van Buren** made clear his own "hard money" and anti-banking credentials. This union caused the name "Locofoco" to become a nickname, used by the **Whigs** to pour scorn on the Democratic Party as a whole.

"LOG CABIN" CAMPAIGN. This was one of several labels applied to the **election of 1840** in recognition of the use of the "log cabin" slogan in support of the **Whig** candidate, **William Henry Harrison**. It was originally the **Democrats** who portrayed Harrison as so lacking in ambition as to be happy to live in a log cabin and drink **hard cider**, but the Whigs turned this image around, leaving the positive and comfortable impression that their candidate was one of the people, living a simple frontier existence. This bore very little relation to Harrison's true background, as he had not been born in a cabin and had never lived in the one portrayed in campaign literature as being near his current residence. But Whigs did succeed in using the image to persuade the electorate that Harrison offered a more traditional republican alternative to the **executive usurpation** of **Andrew Jackson** and **Martin Van Buren**'s administrations.

LONG, CRAWFORD (1815-1878). This Georgia physician is considered the first surgeon to have used ether as an anesthetic, during eight operations between 1842 and 1846. However, because his account of his work was not published until 1849, Long lost out to **William Morton** in the claim to be first, Morton having publicly announced his use of anesthetic in 1846.

LONGFELLOW, HENRY (1807-1882). Born in Portland, Maine, and educated at Bowdoin, this poet interspersed travel in Europe with phases of teaching modern languages at Bowdoin from 1829 to 1835 and at Harvard from 1836 to 1854. His first volume of poetry, *Voices in the Night*, was well received in 1839 and he followed this with *Ballads* in 1841, including the "Wreck of the Hesperus." This period also saw him complete *Poems on Slavery* in 1842, the long narrative poem *Evangeline* in 1847, and *The Seaside and the Fireside* in 1849. Longfellow also wrote works of prose such as *Hyperion* in 1839 and *Kavanagh* in 1849. His most famous output emerged just after the Jacksonian era concluded.

LOUISVILLE AND PORTLAND CANAL. As early as the 1790s a **canal** had been contemplated as a way of circumventing the problems posed by the Louisville falls on the Ohio River. Before this period

Kentucky, in partnership with the federal government, had sanctioned the canal's construction so that boats would be able to by-pass the falls, and, for the cost of just over $1 million, it was completed in 1830. It proved a financial success and in the next 11 years its income exceeded the initial cost of construction. However, a bill for further federal finance of the project was one of several **internal improvements** measures vetoed by **Andrew Jackson** in 1830.

LOVEJOY, ELIJAH (1802-1837). Born in Maine, Lovejoy was educated at Princeton theological seminary and became a "new school" Presbyterian minister in 1833. He advocated a range of reform causes, including **temperance** and a **nativist** anti-Catholicism. However, it was as a newspaper editor that he came to prominence, moving to St. Louis to produce the *Times* and the *Observer*, newspapers that annoyed the local community with their **anti-slavery** tone. Under threats of physical violence Lovejoy moved to Alton, Illinois, where he would suffer the attacks that would write his name into the historical record. After enduring several assaults when he wrote articles offensive to the neighborhood, including a defense of an African-American who had been lynched, he was killed on the fourth occasion a mob attacked his printing press in November 1837, after his calls for the establishment of an auxiliary branch of the **American Anti-Slavery Society** in Illinois. Lovejoy's death proved inspirational to many **abolitionists** and sparked off anger among those who felt that it represented the most extreme infringement possible of the freedom of speech and of the press by **slavery**'s supporters.

LOWELL. This city, located in northeastern Massachusetts at the junction of the Merrimack and Concord Rivers, was incorporated in 1836. It had developed as a center of textiles manufacturing and indeed was named after Francis Cabot Lowell, a pioneer in that industry from Waltham, Massachusetts. Many considered it a model industrial town, and the condition of its workforce, in particular its mill girls, was much celebrated. President **Andrew Jackson** himself waxed lyrical about the conditions for workers in the city, during a visit in 1835. However, Jackson's rosy impression and the city's reputation as a whole were somewhat exaggerated. Indeed by the 1830s pressure of competition was causing employers to increase workloads, to extend working hours, to cut wages, and even to change the very nature of the workforce by starting to employ Irish immigrants. Designed originally to avoid many of the pitfalls of England's industrial revolution, Lowell had itself assumed many of the same problems, with the result that some of its workers, including **women**, resorted to organized **labor** activity.

LUNDY, BENJAMIN (1789-1839). Lundy was an early **anti-slavery** associate of **William Lloyd Garrison** in Baltimore, involved with him in publishing the *Genius of Universal Emancipation*. Lundy was born in New Jersey but had lived in Virginia and Ohio, before setting up in Baltimore. Although he was influential in pushing Garrison a little further down the **abolitionist** road, he differed in method, preferring a more gradual approach and **colonization** as the best ways of ending **slavery** and resolving the race issue at the same time. Attacked and left for dead by slave traders during a trip to the South, he published only sporadically through the 1830s, writing both for other papers and for his own, before starting up the *Genius* again in 1839. Lundy's work, including the 1836 pamphlet on *The War in Texas*, helped to develop the idea that a slave-holders' conspiracy was partly responsible for the drive to create an **independent Texas** and then bring it into the United States, and proved influential with **John Quincy Adams** in his attacks on the slave power.

LYON, MARY (1797-1849). Mary Lyon was an educator, born and educated in Massachusetts. In 1834 she retired from a teaching career of her own in order to raise funds to found a **women**'s college, out of the conviction that women should have the right to be educated to the same level as men, both for their own sense of self-improvement and to produce good wives, mothers, teachers, and missionaries. She was successful to this end and in 1837 established Mount Holyoke College in Massachusetts, with a curriculum that followed that of Amherst College. She also tried to keep costs low so that women from less well-off backgrounds could enroll at the college. Lyon was president of Mount Holyoke from 1837 to 1849.

– M –

McCORMICK, CYRUS (1809-1884). After a childhood with little formal education this Virginian worked with his father, an ironworker and maker of agricultural implements. Cyrus McCormick succeeded where his father had failed, in inventing the successful reaping machine that made both his fame and fortune. The McCormick reaper was first displayed in public in 1831 and received its patent in 1834. Initially McCormick did not produce the reaper for sale, preferring to work at the family ironworks while trying to perfect its design. But when the **panic of 1837** brought hard times to his family, McCormick began selling reapers and then in 1844 licensed manufacturers to produce it for him, in order to reach a wider market. However, when their work proved less than satisfactory, McCormick opened his own factory for the manufacture of the reapers in Chicago in 1847. His invention proved vital to greater efficiencies in agricultural development and many of the innovations he incorporated in the reaper's design remain basic to similar machines to this day.

McGUFFEY, WILLIAM (1800-1851). McGuffey was an educator and writer born in Pennsylvania and became best known for his editions of *McGuffey's Eclectic Reader*. Although lacking much in the way of formal education, his self-teaching and capacious memory allowed him to make great strides in the educational field. While still but a boy himself he taught in schools in Ohio and Kentucky, before going on to graduate from college in 1826. By this time McGuffey was already teaching at Miami University, Ohio, and soon had risen to the positions of professor of ancient languages and head of the department of mental philosophy and philology. In 1833 the Cincinnati publishing company Truman and Smith invited him, in place of their first choice **Catharine Beecher**, to produce a reader aimed at a western market, and the concept of the *Eclectic Reader* was born. While producing the first texts McGuffey became president of Cincinnati College, in 1836, and three years later became president of Ohio University. After an altercation with the local town of Athens he resigned this post in 1843 and then two years later became professor of moral philosophy at the University of Virginia, in which post he saw out the rest of his professional life. By this time his personal involvement in the series of *Readers* had ended, in 1843.

McGuffey was also a Presbyterian minister, and his own fairly conservative views on social issues and doctrinal matters are evident in the moralizing tone of the *Readers*. He was also interested more generally in the cause of education and during his time in Ohio helped to establish the state's public school system.

McGUFFEY'S ECLECTIC READER. **William McGuffey** originally produced this series of four primary school texts between 1836 and 1837. Although designed to encourage reading, the *Readers'* mixture of moral tales, fables, and extracts from literature also made them likely to imbue children with religious, moral, and patriotic lessons as well, and this made them enduringly popular to the extent that they went from strength to strength in the period and indeed later in the 19th century as well, being used in some 37 states. Throughout their production there were questions as to the authenticity of their authorship, some of the work being attributed to other members of McGuffey's family, and other elements being declared plagiarized. Indeed an out-of-court settlement seemed to acknowledge this and resulted in some of the *Readers'* contents being amended. After the first two editions McGuffey's own involvement ended and others took on the work of making the revisions that kept the series fresh and popular, from the third edition in 1844 onward.

McKAY TARIFF BILL. This attempt at **tariff** reduction in 1844 proved unsuccessful, as its modest reductions of many duties failed to meet with the approval of either extreme southerners or manufacturing groups. However, more moderate groups hoped it would form the basis of later attempts to bring about tariff reform during **James Polk**'s administration, a hope in turn thwarted by more wholesale reductions made by **Robert Walker**'s **tariff of 1846**.

McKENNEY, THOMAS (1785-1859). This Maryland man rose to significance when he was appointed by **John Calhoun** to oversee Native American matters in the 1820s and he is usually considered to have been the first equivalent to commissioner of Indian affairs. McKenney was a humanitarian paternalist who believed in educating and civilizing Native Americans, although such aims could be achieved, in his view, by removing Natives from white pressures and allowing them to develop in their own separate space. Through the federally-funded New York Board for the Emigration, Preservation and Improvement of the Aborigines of America he advocated the **Indian removal** cause in the late 1820s, and he proved a useful ally, at first, to **Andrew Jackson**'s own push for removal. Indeed, McKenney helped with the progress of the **Indian Removal Act** through Congress in 1830, although as a **National Republican** he never fully enjoyed Jackson's trust. Eventually he argued with Jackson and **John Eaton** over the mechanics of removing the **Cherokee** and was dismissed by the president in August 1830, in part for being too sympathetic to the natives. Although hopeful of holding office in later **Whig** administrations, McKenney received none and spent his time publishing his *History of the Indian Tribes of North America*, between 1836 and 1844.

McLANE, LOUIS (1786-1857). This Delaware politician and states-man of Federalist roots became one of the foremost administrative figures of the Jacksonian era. After a period in the navy and a legal career, McLane had entered politics as a supporter of **William Craw-ford** before attaching himself to **Andrew Jackson**'s star. After three years in the Senate, between 1827 and 1829, McLane served as U.S. minister in London in the early Jackson years, playing a constructive role in the resolution of the dispute over the **West Indian trade**.

He returned to Washington to become secretary of the treasury between 1831 and 1833 at the crucial time of consideration of the fu-ture of the **Second Bank of the United States**. He was a firm sup-porter of the Bank, produced an executive report strongly in its favor, and tried to act as a channel of communication between Jackson and the Bank's president, **Nicholas Biddle**, proposing modifications in the new charter that might make it acceptable to **Old Hickory**. De-spite this stance McLane retained Jackson's favor and again proved influential in the **Nullification crisis**, advising the president on how to respond to South Carolina and sponsoring the administration's Verplanck tariff bill as an attempt to find a compromise in Congress. Soon after, he moved to the State Department, serving as secretary of state until 1834, even though he again opposed the most significant administration policy of the time, the **removal of the federal depos-its**. But by then he was becoming more disenchanted with the ad-ministration and especially with the influence of his former friend **Martin Van Buren**, who he thought had abandoned him. McLane left the Cabinet and would never speak to the New Yorker again.

Now he became a leading business figure, holding the presiden-cies of both the Morris Canal Company in 1835 and the **Baltimore and Ohio Railroad** in 1837. McLane remained in the public eye and was still held in some regard, so much so that both **John Tyler** and **James Polk** offered him executive posts: Tyler, the State Department in autumn 1841, which he turned down; Polk, a return to his first po-sition of national significance, as minister to London, which McLane accepted, serving from 1845 to 1846. Here again his careful and con-ciliatory approach helped to ease the two countries through a crisis, this time over **Oregon**. Polk also considered McLane a potential sec-retary of state when it seemed that **James Buchanan** might resign, but the latter eventually did not do so. At the very end of the period, in 1848, ill-health prevented McLane from performing one last act of national service as one of the commissioners to convey the ratified Treaty of **Guadalupe Hidalgo** to the Mexican government.

McLEAN, JOHN (1785-1861). This politician, administrator, and jurist was born in New Jersey but rose to prominence in Ohio. McLean had served three presidents as postmaster general by the time he relinquished the post in favor of **William Barry** shortly after the start of **Andrew Jackson**'s administration, having fallen out with his new boss over patronage. Instead he moved to a position on the Supreme Court for the rest of this period and beyond. Despite his judicial role McLean remained a perennial presidential and vice-presidential outsider throughout the period. He was considered by some as a possible **Democratic** successor to Jackson should he decide not to run in 1832. In the same year McLean received but turned down the **Anti-Masonic Party**'s nomination. Over a decade later some still considered him a possible presidential candidate, for the **Whigs** in 1844 and for the **Free Soil Party** in 1848. In the mean-time **John Tyler** had invited McLean to join his second Cabinet in 1841 as secretary of war, but he had turned it down, probably in frustration that he had not been offered the more senior position at the Treasury.

MACLEOD AFFAIR. This episode marked the reemergence of the *Caroline* **affair** and added to the tension in Anglo-American relations already caused by that matter. In 1840 a British officer, Alexander Macleod, was arrested in New York after boasting of his involvement in the original seizure of the *Caroline*. The New York authorities charged him with involvement in a number of crimes arising from the incident, including murder, and refused to withdraw their prosecution when, goaded by complaints from British authorities, the U.S. government under the successive administrations of **Martin Van Buren**, **William Henry Harrison**, and **John Tyler** attempted to get the state to drop the charges. Only when Macleod was acquitted, after it was proven that he had lied about his involvement, was the crisis resolved. But crisis it had been as Britain had been prepared to break off formal relations if Macleod was convicted, while Congress had voted $10 million for war preparations and had authorized the president to call up volunteers should the need arise.

MADISONIAN, THE. This newspaper was founded in 1837 with the aim of putting forward "**Conservative Democrat**" views on banking and currency. Its first editor was Thomas Allen, and in the 1837-39 congressional session **Whigs** and "Conservative Democrats" combined to reward him with the House printing contract in place of the administration editor **Francis Blair**. In 1841 **John Tyler** began to work with the paper as his unofficial organ under its new editor, J. B.

Jones, and it defended the president in the face of Whig criticism of his veto policy and threats of impeachment. *The Madisonian* advocated Tyler's candidacy for the presidency in 1844, openly calling for a courtship between the president and the **Democratic** Party should that be the necessary avenue to his reelection, but it was also the paper that reported his final withdrawal from the campaign in 1844.

MAINE BOUNDARY DISPUTE. This was one of several disputes over the exact course of the **Canadian boundary** with the United States. In Maine the disputed territory lay in the lower basin of the Aroostook River where the federal government had earlier begun issuing land grants to settlers. In 1832 the King of Holland, the arbiter agreed upon by the United States and Britain, offered a border line with New Brunswick along the St. Johns River, which **Andrew Jackson** and his Cabinet managed to persuade Maine's agents to accept. However, the Senate failed to accept the deal, with opposition Senators adding amendments which made it impossible to ratify. Feelings on both sides of the border were aroused. New Brunswickers and the British were especially angered by the Senate's rejection of the arbitration. Meanwhile, in the absence of a ratified deal Maine called on the federal government to be prepared to use force to support their more exaggerated claims over the territory in question.

   As he entered office, President **Martin Van Buren** was confronted with this still smoldering situation and tried to pacify both sides. He agreed to Britain's request to establish a new arbitration commission but also accepted Maine's position that if the commission failed to establish the line intended by 1783 treaty then there would be no further direct negotiation to reach a compromise. The increasingly extreme stance on both sides of the border resulted in the **Aroostook War** in 1838-39 that could have led to a more general outbreak of Anglo-American hostilities. Afterwards Van Buren sought ways of getting Maine to drop its resistance to a compromise or, failing that, a mechanism by which any settlement by arbitration would be binding upon the state. But none of these approaches proved acceptable to Britain and the issue remained unresolved for the rest of Van Buren's term.

   Ultimately a new boundary commission was established during **John Tyler**'s administration. Its conclusions, awarding Maine 7,000 out of the 12,000 disputed acres (including the Aroostook valley) and granting Americans the right to carry timber down the St. Johns River, were to be accepted as part of the **Webster-Ashburton Treaty** of 1842. Representatives from Maine reluctantly accepted the final compromise worked out in Washington, although only after the efforts of agents, funded from the president's secret account, to sway political and public opinion in the state in favor of some sort of compromise deal. There were also suggestions that less than fair and proper use of a variety of old maps created the wrong impression that Maine would have more to gain from the compromise than from holding out for a better deal.

MANGUM, WILLIE P. (1792-1861). This North Carolinian enjoyed a career in the law before beginning a political journey of considerable variety, including at one time or another being a surprise presidential candidate and effectively acting as vice-president. Like many other supporters of **William Crawford**, Mangum aligned himself with **Andrew Jackson** in the run-up to the **election of 1828** and then supported the president's early activities from his seat in the Senate. However, again like so many other southern **Democrats**, Mangum became alarmed by the direction Jackson took in 1833-34 and opposed the **Force Act** and the **removal of the federal deposits** as examples of **executive usurpation**. He voted with the **Whigs** to **censure** Jackson, only to resign his seat in 1836 when it became clear that his state legislature wanted him to vote to **expunge** the resolutions. In recognition of his solid **States' Rights Whig** credentials, South Carolina awarded Mangum its electoral college votes in the **election of 1836**.

After a short spell in his home state legislature Mangum reentered the Senate in 1841, this time to stay until 1853. It was during the first of these two Senate terms that he assumed the vice-president's responsibilities in the Senate, once **John Tyler** had succeeded to the presidency. By now Mangum was belying his **states' rights** background and aligned with **Henry Clay**, supporting his **bank bill** in 1841 and opposing Tyler's **bank bill veto of 1841**, **Thomas Ewing's** alternative **fiscal corporation** proposal, and the Exchequer plan of the following year. Mangum proved a loyal Whig by supporting the **tariff of 1842** and opposing reductions proposed by the **tariff of 1846** and he demonstrated hostility to Tyler and **James Polk's** moves on **Texas**, Mexico, and **Oregon**. Yet, as if to confirm the chameleon-like nature of his career, he remained a friend of Polk and was used by him to sound out Whig opinion.

MANIFEST DESTINY. This famous ideological strand stemmed from earlier times but came to be encapsulated in the 1840s, first appearing by this name in the *United States Magazine and **Democratic Review***, and later in another **John O'Sullivan** journal, the *New York Morning News*. Manifest Destiny's main thrust, that it was the God-ordained mission of the United States to expand to fill the continental landmass of North America, made it particularly appropriate to the **expansion** experience of that decade. The idea was tinged with religious, racial, and commercial impulses that all suggested that there was something superior about the Protestant, European-American way of life, which justified the idea of spreading principles of American freedom. Manifest Destiny is most famously associated with the process of western expansion, used to explain and justify stances taken during crises over **Texas annexation**, the **Oregon boundary**, and the **Mexican War**. Indeed, **James Polk** integrated ideas of Manifest Destiny into his view of U.S. continental responsibility in the face of European influence in North America. However, there were some Americans who even believed that the sense of American continental mission should stretch from the far North to the extreme South as well, views that colored their attitudes toward Canadian rebel movements and peace efforts with Britain over the Canadian border and that also inspired dreams of territorial acquisitions in the Caribbean and areas south from Mexico.

MANN, HORACE (1796-1859). Mann was a Massachusetts lawyer and legislator who, during terms in his state's House and Senate, inspired legislation on a number of issues, including prohibition of alcohol, insane asylum reform, and, most famously, education. His state Board of Education was the first in the country and he became its secretary in 1837, serving in that post until 1848. In his annual reports and in the *Common School Journal* which he edited, Mann pushed for better pay for teachers and proper teacher-training at colleges and generally he called for state governments to assume responsibility for the provision of education, all with the aim of creating a more responsible citizenry. After a trip to Europe in 1843 he advocated the abolition of corporal punishment in schools and he also attacked denominational schools. In 1848 Mann resigned his position to replace **John Quincy Adams** in the House of Representatives, serving until 1853 as a **Whig** with **anti-slavery** leanings.

MANUFACTURING. During the whole of this period manufacturing industry remained clearly in second place behind **agriculture** as an economic pursuit, although the 1840s did witness a growth of manufacturing and of its importance to the nation as a whole and to certain regions in particular. While the proportion of the **labor** force engaged in manufacturing pursuits stood at just below 10 percent in 1840, the figure had risen to just below 15 percent by 1850, and the relative value of manufacturing production and of exports of manufactured goods also rose during the period. In the northeast of the country, but also in some of the developing urban centers of the Midwest, industrialization was becoming the dominant economic force, with raw metal-working, shoe-making, and, in particular, cotton and woolen textiles standing out as the growth industries of the era.

The period was perhaps more interesting for witnessing the continuation of a range of trends in manufacturing development, in progress since the late 18th century. Increasing amounts of manufactured output were being produced in plants using powered machinery, either water- or, increasingly, steam-driven. There was similarly more processing of raw materials using fuelled methods, such as iron forges and furnaces for lime and tar. Corporate organization's provision of more finance and the wider markets served by improving transportation links together encouraged moves to greater levels of mass production, either through the "putting-out" system in which workers carried out their work in their own homes or workshops on behalf of the owner of the raw materials and of the finished product, or increasingly through a factory style of production. Both also witnessed a specialization of labor in which workers performed a narrower range of processes before passing on their work to others to complete. However, there still remained much variety in industrial location, from domestic manufactures done in the home for family use, through mill villages, mill towns, and industrial plants based on **slavery** in the South, all producing cheap goods for a mass consumption market, to largely urban specialist producers making finer products for bespoke customers.

MARCY, WILLIAM (1786-1857). This **Democratic** politician and statesman rose to prominence in New York after a childhood in Massachusetts, an education at Brown University in Rhode Island, and a period of military service during the War of 1812. His legal career led him into politics, initially as a supporter of **Martin Van Buren** through the **Albany Regency**. Marcy was elected to the Senate in 1831, where he supported **Andrew Jackson**'s attack on the **Second Bank of the United States**, and then he served three terms of office as governor of New York between 1833 and 1839, before suffering defeat at the hands of **William Seward**. During that period Marcy split with Van Buren, mainly over the sense of the **Independent Treasury** proposals, and he became one of the leaders of the New

York Democratic **Hunker** faction. This stance would bring its rewards when he was appointed as secretary of war under **James Polk**, although Marcy was by no means the first New York Democrat suggested for the post. Of course this appointment meant that he occupied the War Department at the crucial period of the **Mexican War**, although much of the credit for American success in that conflict should lie with Polk himself, who took a very hands-on approach to the management of the war effort. Marcy is perhaps most famous for his comment that to the victor should go the **spoils**, providing a notorious label for the business of patronage in the Jacksonian era and thereafter.

MARKET REVOLUTION. This label has been applied by historians to the dramatic changes that occurred in economic practices, social relations, and political economy in the first third of the 19th century. Fired by the **transportation revolution** and much speedier transmission of mail and, through newspapers and pamphlets, of ideas and information, these changes penetrated virtually every aspect of people's lives in those geographical areas most directly affected. In economic terms the revolution brought more people into a position where they made decisions about the production, sale, and purchase of goods on the basis of commercially imposed factors, driven by international market conditions, and, increasingly, by the burgeoning level of internal commerce. Hence more farmers grew for sale for profit rather than just for subsistence, while investors in manufacturing bought new machinery and introduced new methods of getting the most out of their workforces.

Socially, as well as altering the specific relationship of farmers with their neighbors and local merchants, and of masters and industrial capitalists with their employees, the market revolution contributed to the growing distinction between different classes of Americans, whether farm producers or wage-earners, a growing professional middle class, business owners, and those associated with corporations. It wrought changes in gender relations, too.

In the field of politics the revolution was in the behavior of Americans as they responded to the welter of change around them. Those who suffered directly from a less personal and more unpredictable, commercially-driven economy joined with those who were outside it altogether and others involved but suspicious of its worst effects, to propose measures to guard against the more damaging impact of economic change and to oppose measures, such as those forming **Henry Clay's American System**, designed to carry forward that change at even greater speed. Such doubters tended to coalesce in the ranks of the **Democratic** Party of the 1830s. Others, leaning to the **Whigs**, were far more positive about the impact of economic change and supported just the sort of measures they hoped would promote it and bring what they saw as its benefits to an even wider constituency. In its most extreme, and controversial application, as put forward by historian Charles Sellers, the idea of "revolution" is taken to mean a thoroughgoing political revolution in which the proponents of change successfully manipulated popular opinion, religious developments, legal interpretation, education, and culture to secure almost hegemonic status for the increasingly market-dominated political economy.

MARSHALL, JOHN (1755-1835). Marshall had been chief justice of the Supreme Court since 1801 and had presided over 1,000 cases and written decisions in over 500, making him a crucial element in the development of the Court's practices and its interpretative direction. Although he was clearly nearing the end of his tenure by the time the Jacksonian era began, there were still some famous cases to come. The most notable of these was *Worcester vs. Georgia*, in which Marshall ruled in favor of the **Cherokee** against the state of Georgia, allegedly prompting **Andrew Jackson** to call upon him to try to enforce his ruling. Outside the Court's chamber Marshall leaned toward support of **Henry Clay** in the **election of 1832**, and attended the Virginia constitutional convention in 1829 where he opposed extending voting rights to all white men.

MARTINEAU, HARRIET (1802-1876). This writer and observer of things American was born in Norwich, England, and made her name with a number of books on economics. She traveled in the United States in 1834 and 1836, and although many of her observations were made through rose-colored glasses, historians of the Jacksonian era still find useful her 1837 work, *Society in America*. Her American experience also converted her to **abolitionism**, inspiring her to join the **American Anti-Slavery Society**. Her own writings on the subject did much to awaken British opinion on the subject of American **slavery**. She also championed the cause of **women** and prison reform.

MASON, JOHN (1799-1859). This Virginian statesman and politician served in a variety of state positions in the 1830s before coming to prominence in the 1840s as a member of both **John Tyler** and **James Polk**'s Cabinets. Mason attended his state's famous constitutional convention in 1829, where he opposed extension of the suffrage and more equitable representation for newly settled counties. Between 1831 and 1837 he sat in the House of Representatives, supporting **Andrew Jackson** in all matters except the **Force Act**, while between 1837 and 1844 he held a number of state and federal judicial positions. Mason made his true bow on the national stage when he became Tyler's secretary of the navy in 1844. As a friend of Polk since college days, he made the transition into the new president's Cabinet, becoming first his attorney general, then his Navy secretary after the resignation of **George Bancroft** in 1846. During his time in the latter office he served as acting attorney general once more. Throughout he proved a loyal Cabinet member, being in agreement with the president on most issues.

MAYSVILLE ROAD VETO. In May 1830 Congress passed a bill by which the federal government would subscribe in stock in Kentucky's Maysville Road company. The road was designed as an extension of the **National Road** from its Ohio River terminus, and ultimately, it was hoped, would form part of a continuous road through to the Tennessee River in northern Alabama.

Although it was only one of six **internal improvements** bills passed at the time, it is the Maysville bill whose name has lived on as the first example of **Andrew Jackson**'s use of the **veto power** to make a statement on an issue connected with the **American System**. Although as a western senator Jackson had supported similar improvements, as president he had to balance this off against a range of forces. There was his own desire to cut federal expenses as a function of reducing the **national debt**, while there were also important groups among his supporters, and potential supporters, who disliked the bill. Some in eastern states opposed the bill out of a sense of injustice since they had already undertaken many projects using their own and not federal money, while moderate **states' rights** elements throughout the nation and in the South in particular would have constitutional qualms about such measures. In the end Jackson went with these other pressures and decided to veto the bill, avoiding the danger that a western backlash would threaten his greatly desired policy of **Indian removal** by delaying the veto until the day after the **Indian Removal Act** had passed in Congress.

The specific constitutional grounds he gave for the veto, in a message drafted by **Martin Van Buren** and **James Polk**, were that, rather than being truly national in nature, the bill financed a stretch of road entirely within the boundaries of the single state of Kentucky—

significantly the home state of the notional leader of the opposition party, **Henry Clay**, who had strongly supported the measure. Jackson also claimed that the bill would have increased the national debt since all federal money for that session had been appropriated already. The veto and several others that followed soon after halted direct federal subsidy of private roads and **canals**, if not other types of internal improvements, and seemed to reinforce the notion that in the future the funding of roads, canals, and **railroads** would be the business of state and local government. Congress upheld Jackson's action and the public's reaction seemed to suggest that the president had caught the popular mood on this issue, as he would so many other times during his presidency.

MELVILLE, HERMAN (1819-1891). The renowned novelist was born in New York City and after a period of largely self-education served on a packet ship to Liverpool in 1839 and then on whaling ships to the South Seas in 1841. He deserted to live on a number of South Sea islands before joining the crew of a naval vessel until 1843. These early experiences provided him with a wealth of information that dominated his written output of mainly maritime novels and tales. These started with *Typee, or a Peep at Polynesian Life*, published in Britain in 1846. There followed *Omoo: A Narrative of Adventures in the South Seas* in 1847, and *Mardi and a Voyage Thither* and *Redburn: His First Voyage*, both produced in 1849.

MEXICAN WAR, CAUSES. Relations between the United States and Mexico had long given grounds for concern even before immediate tensions on the border between the now U.S. state of Texas and Mexico precipitated war in May 1846. There were long-standing damages claims by American citizens against Mexico, while dispute over the **Mexican boundary** had also been a diplomatic issue since the late 1810s. Undoubtedly, though, the issue of **Texas** exacerbated those boundary issues and when that state became a target for annexation, and then was annexed, opinion on both sides of the border was aroused. Mexico was outraged when some Americans joined Texan adventurers in expeditions into northern Mexico, such as that to Santa Fe in 1841. Later, Mexican hostility to the annexation of Texas led to their suspension of diplomatic relations with the United States in spring 1845. Mexico's refusal finally to recognize either the independence of Texas or then its annexation had led to a number of Mexican raids into Texas, which even before annexation many Americans treated as attacks on U.S. soil, since the raids seemed to threaten their cherished goal of annexation. There was, then, a considerable amount of precedent for anger on both sides of the border, which helps to explain why the immediate crisis of spring 1846 gave rise to war after the posturing of U.S. and Mexican troops led to incursions by the latter over the Rio Grande, with some American casualties.

It is also clear, however, that broader causes lay behind the war. The behavior of individual Americans in Texas and New Mexico betrayed hints of a more general expansionist fervor at work at this time, in line with the spirit of **Manifest Destiny**. American settlers were active in **California** as well, some prominent behind moves for rebellion against the Mexican authorities, and for some time the U.S. government had demonstrated considerable sympathy with such moves, sending secret agents to observe and work with the rebels even before the immediate crisis with Mexico boiled up. Indeed, requests to purchase New Mexico and California had formed part of the faltering efforts to renew diplomatic relations with Mexico in the run-up to the war. In 1845 **John Slidell** was dispatched to offer Mexico treaty terms, including a resolution of the Texan boundary issue and the payment of debts to American citizens as the key demands, although the **James Polk** administration was prepared to assume responsibility for the debts in exchange for the territorial grants it desired.

Not surprisingly the Mexican authorities were greatly offended by such suggestions and Slidell's mission ended in failure, both precipitating the dispatch of **Zachary Taylor**'s troops to the Rio Grande in the first place and strengthening the Polk Cabinet's determination to go to war on the grounds that their key demands had not been met. The Mexican attacks across the border in April 1846 gave the necessary pretext and in response early the next month President Polk called upon Congress for a declaration of war, which was forthcoming on 12 May.

MEXICAN WAR, CONDUCT AND RESOLUTION. The American conduct of the Mexican War was multi-pronged, with at least four discernible phases or theaters of operation. Predictably the initial border incursions which provided the trigger for the actual declaration of war transformed into a significant campaign in northern Mexico, with American efforts being led by **Zachary Taylor**, through the siege at **Monterrey** in September 1846 to a culminating moment with the battle of **Buena Vista** in February 1847. At the same time American forces targeted northwestern Mexico, with **Stephen Kearny** conquering New Mexico in August 1846 before moving on to assist American efforts in **California**, where even before the outbreak of the war agents had been assisting rebellion against the Mexican authorities. Here the efforts of **John Sloat, Robert Stockton, John Frémont**, and Kearny accomplished their goals of helping the **Bear Flag** rebels to succeed and of seizing California for the United States.

While these territorial acquisitions were highly important for immediate American sectional politics and later economic development, it was the final campaign of the war that proved most significant in bringing the conflict to an end and in securing gains already made on the ground. **Winfield Scott**'s great march to the heart of Mexico began when he landed with an army near Vera Cruz in March 1847 and then took that port before leading his troops on a march inland via battles at **Cerro Gordo, Jalapa, Puebla, Contreras**, and **Cherubusco**. His successes brought the Mexican government to the negotiating table, but the campaign resumed when the Mexicans refused to cede territories in any peace deal. Scott pressed on and occupied Mexico City itself in September 1847, the cue for the resumption of peace talks that would ultimately result in the Treaty of **Guadalupe Hidalgo**. In total American deaths from battlefield wounds and other war-related causes numbered over 13,200, most of these occurring off the field of battle where only some 1,800 died. The war is estimated to have cost the United States nearly $100 million.

MEXICAN WAR, CONSEQUENCES. The Mexican War's greatest significance lies in the fact that it secured to U.S. possession huge swathes of new territory in the current Southwest, while also confirming the statehood of Texas as one of the United States. It is hard to imagine the United States without components such as Texas and California, with the important states and natural resources in between, and thus the war played a major role in the nation's long-term physical and economic development as well as bringing to near conclusion its current territorial integrity.

However, at the time of the conflict itself and the decade after, the war and its potential and then actual outcomes had dramatic implications for the political and **sectional** development of the nation. While the war was very popular, it also attracted significant opposition from pacifist and reform groups and from the congressional **Whig** Party. Whigs proved particularly strong in the House of Representatives and in 1848 succeeded in passing resolutions condemning the motivation behind the war. However, they shied away from demanding the recall of American troops behind the Rio Grande and did not succeed in limiting U.S. demands to a concession by Mexico of that river as the accepted boundary and to a Mexican agreement to damages claims. This represented tacit acceptance that U.S. war demands could include territorial claims and clearly it was these that represented the really controversial issue.

The prospect of new territories raised the potential clash between **expansionism** and **anti-slavery** fears that the war was being fought to extend the territory into which **slavery** might spread. While the war continued there were several overt attempts to divorce its conduct and any gains secured out of it from the expansion of slavery, most famously the **Wilmot Proviso** clause which opponents attempted to tack onto a number of measures for the war's prosecution. As the war neared its conclusion there remained many who disagreed about the amount of American territorial gain that should result, with extreme "**All Mexico**" and "**No Territory**" factions emerging. At one stage of the efforts to secure a peace, with an acquisition of lands part of it, the level of disagreement threatened to block progress, but of course the war was finally settled in the Treaty of **Guadalupe Hidalgo** with its significant territorial awards to the United States. However, the political ramifications did not end with the treaty and the sectional fall-out from the debates over new territories would dominate national politics for the whole of the following decade culminating in southern secession in 1860-61.

MEXICO, BOUNDARY NEGOTIATIONS. Dispute over the exact location of the boundary between Mexico and the United States represented one of the festering diplomatic issues of the early Jacksonian era. **Andrew Jackson** inherited a treaty signed with Mexico by Anthony Butler on behalf of **John Quincy Adams'** administration in 1828, which confirmed boundary arrangements set out in the earlier Adams-Onís Treaty of 1818. Jackson would have preferred the 1828 treaty not to have been concluded, since it left unsettled an attempt to purchase Texas from Mexico, part of Butler's original orders, but the new president presented it to the Senate anyway. Opposition senators denied the administration more time to enable the Texas issue to be taken further and the treaty was ratified. In 1835 another convention established a commission for determining the exact boundary between the United States and Mexico, but its work was interrupted and then finally superseded by the **Texan independence** struggle. In 1838 it was now the United States and Texas which agreed to establish a commission to determine the location of their common boundary. But of course, the status of Texas and the new U.S. boundary

with Mexico once Texas had been annexed would recur as destabilizing issues in the run-up to the **Mexican War**.

MIAMI AND ERIE CANAL. This 300-mile **canal** system, in total
costing over $8 million, was built between 1825 and 1845 to link the
Ohio cities of Toledo and Cincinnati, in order to tie the latter city to
the Lakes trading network. As early as 1830 it stretched from Cincinnati to Dayton and, as it developed, helped to encourage the growth
of communities such as Hamilton and Dayton. Tension over the canal's northern terminus played a part in the **Toledo War** incident in
1836-37.

MICHIGAN, STATEHOOD. Michigan was one of the more isolated
parts of the United States at the beginning of the Jacksonian era, but
as the **Erie Canal** helped link this lakeside region to more populous
areas in the East, the territory experienced dramatic population
growth and an acceleration of its course to statehood. The population
grew from under 32,000 in 1830, to 212,000 in 1840, reaching the
minimum required for statehood by 1834. The territory petitioned for
statehood at that time, but a positive congressional response was delayed by a continuing dispute over the boundary with Ohio, with that
state's congressmen attempting to block Michigan's application until
the territory accepted Ohio's version of the line under dispute in the
Toledo strip. In the middle of the **Toledo War** the acting territorial
governor, Stevens Mason, who had officially just been removed from
office by **Andrew Jackson**, refused to countenance any further congressional delays, called a constitutional convention, and was elected
the first governor under the state's new constitution. This forced the
hand of Congress, which reached a compromise settlement with Ohio
and accepted the previously unofficial status of Michigan as a state,
the 26th, in January 1837. Jackson signed the bill admitting the state
to the Union on 26 January.

MILITIA, PROPOSAL TO REFORM. During **Martin Van Buren**'s
administration the U.S. army was faced with new demands on its resources as it fought the **Second Seminole War** in addition to carrying out its usual frontier and other duties. In the face of many failings
it became clear that had war with Britain broken out over either the
Caroline or **Aroostook** affairs the army would have been ill-prepared
to respond. Consequently Secretary of War **Joel Poinsett** made proposals to Congress, suggesting that state militias be brought under a
greater degree of federal control, with regular training with U.S.

troops and some funding from the federal government. The proposal horrified those already worried about **executive usurpation** and the centralizing tendency of the planned **Independent Treasury**, and soon it was being denounced as likely to create a standing army. Although the president had supported Poinsett's scheme, after this hail of protest made clear the likely political cost with a presidential election looming, the proposals were withdrawn.

MILLER, WILLIAM (1782-1849). This self-taught religious thinker was born in Massachusetts, later moving to Vermont. Although notionally a Baptist, Miller won notoriety for his radical ideas, his studies of the Book of Daniel leading him to predict that the world would come to an end in 1843, after the return of Christ. Radical these ideas may have been, but from 1831 onward his preaching, and the promotion of his predictions in published form, led to the development of a large following of Millerites, many of who began to jettison their belongings as 1843 approached. Indeed, nationwide his following numbered in the hundreds of thousands by that time. When 1843 passed without incident, Miller denied that the business of predicting the date of the second coming was an exact science and postponed it until October 1844. A second disappointment led to general disillusionment with his ideas, but he and a few followers persisted and established the Adventist Church in 1845.

MILLS, ROBERT (1781-1855). Born in Charleston, South Carolina, Mills became an architect and engineer of considerable renown, and is generally considered to be the first professional American architect. He spent his early years working with, among others, Thomas Jefferson and Benjamin Latrobe, and he developed a taste for classical revival architecture, although at the same time remaining keen to develop an American vernacular style. In the 1820s Mills was responsible for leading a program of **internal improvements** in Charleston and more widely in South Carolina. He designed a wide range of types of building, including both churches and public works such as customs houses. In 1833 Mills worked on improving the acoustics in Congress and three years later was appointed federal architect and engineer. He guided to completion the construction of the federal Treasury Building, the Patent Office, and the Old Post Office in Washington, D.C. Mills had also designed monuments, including the Washington Monument in Baltimore (1814-29), which prepared him for the commission to design the **Washington Monument** in the nation's capital in 1845. Work on this began in 1848, although some elements of his original design were not to be included in the final project.

MINNESOTA, TERRITORIAL STATUS. At the close of this period the number of people in the future state of Minnesota was around 4,000 but its population had been left in an unorganized limbo by the transition to statehood of both **Iowa** and **Wisconsin**. In August 1848 a group of settlers, merchants, lumbermen, and fur traders met at the Stillwater convention to petition Congress for territorial status, producing a successful outcome when Minnesota was organized and admitted as a territory on 3 March 1849.

MISSOURI COMPROMISE LINE. Although originally it affected only territories acquired through the Louisiana Purchase, some in the 1840s sought to apply the Missouri Compromise dividing line of 36° 30′ across the whole continent as a solution to the issue of the potential expansion of **slavery** into newly acquired western territories. Only moments after **Wilmot's proviso** made its first appearance in Congress a follower of **John Calhoun** suggested that **Oregon** would be free of slaves because it lay north of the Missouri Compromise line. As an idea this came to be championed most fervently by **James Buchanan**, with occasional support from the rest of **James Polk**'s Cabinet, from the *Washington Union*, and at times from the president himself, although by December 1847 both Polk and the party organ leaned more to the **popular sovereignty** method. Eventually the compromise line was by-passed as a method for determining the question of slavery's expansion, because after the Oregon territory was organized without slavery, no application of the compromise line would offer enough potential free areas to be attractive to northern opinion as a compromise. Ultimately, of course, it would even be overturned in its application to areas of the Louisiana Purchase as well, by the Kansas-Nebraska legislation of 1854.

"MONEY POWER." This was a label forming part of the **Jacksonian** critique of the prevailing financial system, warning that banking, the **credit system**, and **paper currency** all conspired to benefit a numerically limited and legally privileged class at the expense of farmers, planters, and laborers. It was extended to express the fear that this privileged class might use its economic clout to pervert the political system in the same way as **Nicholas Biddle** had once attempted, by bank loans to politicians and by contraction of the credit system in 1833-34.

"MONSTER BANK." This was a negative epithet given to the **Second Bank of the United States** by its opponents, who warned of its corrupting power and entangling influence.

MONTERREY, BATTLE OF. This **Mexican War** battle was the first major engagement involving **Zachary Taylor**, when he besieged the town of Monterrey, over 100 miles south of the Rio Grande, in September 1846. The town surrendered to him after three days.

MOORE, ELY (1798-1860). This **labor** leader rose from an obscure background in New Jersey and New York to become one of the first representatives of his class in Congress. Moore had moved to New York City in the 1820s and there joined the printers' union, as well serving as delegate to the city's General Trades Union in 1833. In addition to his active labor membership he also wrote for the cause, editing the *National Trades' Union* journal and writing for the Democratic *Evening Post*. The highpoint of his career came when he was elected to the House as a labor man in 1834, and then secured re-election in 1836, this time as a **Democrat**. After Moore suffered defeat in 1838 **Martin Van Buren** appointed him to a customs house job, only for Moore to be ousted again in 1841 with the regime change. He ran unsuccessfully for Congress in 1844, but again was rewarded by his party with the post of U.S. marshal in southern New York.

MORMONISM. This distinctively American religion grew out of the fertile religious soil of the **Burned-Over District** of western New York, when **Joseph Smith** published a series of revelations as the **Book of Mormon**. Founded by Smith in Fayette, New York, in April 1830, Mormonism shared many of the tenets of Christianity and indeed claimed to be the true primitive Christian church, in the place of other denominations that had strayed from the right path. It departed from Christianity in its profession of many doctrines based upon post-biblical revelation.

The early history of Mormonism was one of persecution and flight, as it moved from New York, through Kirtland, Ohio, and **Independence**, Missouri, and eventually, in 1839, to Illinois and the more deeply rooted settlement at **Nauvoo**. Although arousing local hostility from non-Mormons, the religion did succeed in attracting many converts from both America and abroad, with the result that by 1845 the community's population had risen to some 12,000. After further problems, culminating in the murder of Smith in 1844, **Brig-**

ham Young in 1846 led the majority of the Mormons from Illinois to the Great Salt Lake valley where they established their own town and state of Deseret. However, several splinter groups remained in the Midwest.

MORSE, SAMUEL (1791-1872). Best known as the inventor of the **telegraph** and the author of the telegraphic code that bears his name, Morse began his varied professional career as a painter. Born in Massachusetts and educated at Yale, he had followed the common course for young American artists, combining work at home with a period of travel abroad between 1829 and 1832. In 1825 he had established the American Academy of Design and in 1832 became professor of painting and sculpture at New York University. It was during this period that a darker side to Morse's character was revealed as he demonstrated himself to be a raving **nativist**, who under the name "Brutus" published anti-Catholic letters in the *New York Observer* in 1834, with attacks on Catholic schools and office-holding.

    Morse's experimentation leading to the production of a telegraph machine began in the mid-1830s, and despite initial difficulties he eventually succeeded in securing a patent for it in 1837. After demonstrating the telegraph to the Cabinet in 1838 it was not until 1843 that Congress awarded him a grant for a first experimental line between Washington, D.C. and Baltimore. This was the start of Morse's years of good fortune, as the line proved a great success in 1844, while with the help of his new business manager **Amos Kendall** he was now winning most disputes as to who exactly was responsible for the design of the telegraph.

MORTON, WILLIAM (1819-1868). Born in Massachusetts, this dentist trained in medicine at Harvard and dentistry at Baltimore. Morton was best known for his experiments with ether as a general anesthetic and gave the first public demonstration of its use in 1846 in an operation on a neck tumor. He received a patent for its use, despite the fact that others, such as **Crawford Long**, had been using ether for some time beforehand.

MOTT, LUCRETIA (1793-1880). Lucretia Mott was born Lucretia Coffin, in Nantucket, Massachusetts, and became influential in Quaker circles as a preacher and social reformer. She and her husband were friends of **William Lloyd Garrison** and helped to establish the **American Anti-Slavery Society** in 1833. Both were believers in practical measures to undermine **slavery**. Her husband had abandoned the trade in cotton in 1830, while Lucretia refused to buy anything that had had slave labor involved in its manufacture. Their practical approach extended to support for runaway slaves.

Mrs. Mott also valued the role of **women** in **abolitionist** circles, founding the Philadelphia Female Anti-Slavery Society in 1833 and the Anti-Slavery Convention of American Women in 1837. When both she and her husband went to an international anti-slavery convention in London in 1840, the refusal to seat Mrs. Mott on the grounds of her gender propelled her into a fight for equal rights for women, alongside her continuing support for abolitionism. Together with **Elizabeth Cady Stanton** she convened the meeting at **Seneca Falls** in 1848.

MOUNT, WILLIAM SIDNEY (1807-1868). This artist was born on Long Island, and spent a period apprenticed to his own brother, another artist, before going on to study at the National Academy of Design, to which he was admitted in 1832. Mount's work included both portraiture and landscapes. His portraits of statesmen such as **Daniel Webster** helped to pay the bills, while his landscapes and popular studies of rural life and African-Americans have probably left the greater impression. His major works from the period include *Rustic Dance after a Sleigh Ride* (1830), *Dancing on the Bare Floor* (1831), *Bargaining for a Horse* (1835), *Cider Making* (1840), and *Eel Spearing at Setauket* (1845).

– N –

NATIONAL DEBT. This period witnessed, if only for a short time, the virtual elimination of the national debt. **Andrew Jackson's** stated main fiscal priority was to pay off the debt, and through policies of administrative **retrenchment** and careful monitoring of **internal improvements** expenditure, with the aim of not allowing increases in spending to exceed the ability of the government to pay for them in any one year, he just about managed to achieve that goal. Helped by increasing revenue from land sales in particular, his administration oversaw a fairly steady fall in the national debt, to a figure of just over $37.5 million by 1835 and virtually nothing by 1836. Even after the **panics of 1837 and 1839** reversed the falling trend in the debt, in 1840 it still stood at only around $4 million, one of the lowest levels in American history at 21 cents per capita.

However, the fall in the national debt did create new political problems, notably what to do with any potential or actual surplus in federal revenue. Some proposed distributing any surplus to the individual states for them to spend on such developmental projects as they chose to pursue. Indeed, when many states were hard hit by the depression of the late 1830s, finding themselves with less revenue to honor debts they had already incurred on such projects, the **Whigs** considered that it was politic and economically essential for the federal government effectively to assume such debts, using the **distribution** of surplus federal revenue as the means for doing so.

NATIONAL INTELLIGENCER. This Washington D.C. newspaper became the main organ of the **National Republican** and **Whig** parties during the Jacksonian era. Its consistency in attacking the **Democratic** administrations and policies of **Andrew Jackson** and **Martin Van Buren** earned its editors, Joseph Gales and William Seaton, congressional printing contracts whenever the opposition parties succeeded in controlling one house or the other. The *Intelligencer* continued to operate into the 1840s, when, after early optimism about the prospects of **John Tyler**'s administration, it watched with regret as the Whig Party tore itself apart over the banking issue and Tyler's other vetoes. Subsequently the paper acted neither as the organ of the president, nor was particularly hostile to him, although it clearly supported the regular candidacy of **Henry Clay** for the **election of 1844**. The *Intelligencer* remained a thorn in the side of the Democratic administration of **James Polk**, criticizing most aspects of its performance but especially its foreign policy exploits.

NATIONAL REPUBLICANS. This political party developed out of that portion of the Republican Party which, under **John Quincy Adams** and inspired in particular by **Henry Clay**, began to advocate a more activist approach by government, and especially by the federal government, to fostering economic development and growth through a strong banking system, **protective tariffs**, and federally-funded **internal improvements**. The party's organization became more established in opposition to **Andrew Jackson** and it often displayed greater unity in congressional roll calls on economic issues than did the evolving Jacksonian coalition, only to be thwarted by the president's veto.

However, the party's main weakness lay in a lack of electoral success, as it found problems winning much support in the deeper South. It marshaled a strong platform of issues in support of Clay for the **election of 1832**: support for a national bank and other economic policies which they accused Jackson of being inconsistent or negative about; criticism of the president's handling of administrative matters and of the **Cabinet reshuffle**; and particularly harsh condemnation of his policy of **Indian removal**. However, the party's efforts proved largely powerless in the face of Jackson's popularity and the apparent sympathy of many people for his **Bank bill veto**. After 1832 the influence of new party groupings, such as the **Anti-Masonic** Party, and personnel shifts combined to produce the **Whigs** as the main opposition to the Jacksonian Democrats, although the new party shared much of the National Republicans' optimistic nationalism and appeal to the higher social classes.

NATIONAL ROAD. This important project was a product of the boom for **internal improvements** sweeping the nation in the 1820s and 1830s. It consisted of a road starting at Cumberland, Maryland, designed to reach into the developing midwestern states. During this period it extended from Wheeling, Virginia, through Zanesville, Ohio, to reach Columbus, Ohio, by 1833. By 1850 it had been extended into Indiana. Almost inevitably the broader National Road project was caught up in debates over the use of federal funding for improvements when in 1830 **Andrew Jackson** vetoed bills supporting feeder roads between Washington and Cumberland and from Zanesville south into Kentucky. However, in line with his avowal that he would support genuinely national projects, the president did approve an extension of the main road from Zanesville westward. At the same time Congress rejected proposals for a second national road running north-south between Buffalo and New Orleans.

NATIONAL TRADES UNION. The first National Trades Union, convened in 1834, was part of the trend among skilled **labor** groups to organize across different skill and industry boundaries. Already there had been attempts to create community-wide general **trade unions**, and the association of such groups on the wider national level was the next logical step. However, the national union only offered its fairly slim membership a chance for discussion of issues rather than active trade union measures and ultimately it proved short-lived, suffering a decline during the **panic of 1837** and ensuing hard times of the late 1830s.

NATIVISM. Nativism was the attitude of favoring native-born Americans over immigrants, with support for government policies to the same effect. This less attractive side of the American **immigration** experience has been almost ever-present in the nation's history, rising to prominence during times of particularly high immigration or general social tension.

In the second quarter of the 19th century nativism formed part of the surge of Protestant revivalism, directing its hostility mainly at Roman **Catholics**. However, it became the foundation of a more general attitude toward immigrants, and especially the Catholic Irish, whose numbers increased so dramatically as the period developed. Nativist proposals included restricting immigrants' civil and political rights, by lengthening the period of residence necessary to obtain citizenship from five to 25 years, blocking immigrants from holding public office, and removing public funds from Catholic schools.

Nativism appealed to Americans in many different walks of life, producing both institutional and populist responses, as well as drawing out figures more famous for other things—for example, under the pen-name "Brutus" **Samuel Morse** wrote "Foreign Conspiracy against the Liberties of the United States." Institutionally nativism was especially strong in the cities of the eastern seaboard and Midwest, in groups like the Protestant Reformation Society of 1836, the New York-based Native American Democratic Association of 1836, which won the mayoral election for Aaron Clark in 1837, the American Protestant Union of 1841, and the American Republican Party of 1843, which won municipal elections in New York a year later. Also in 1844 nativists voted into office three of Philadelphia's four congressmen. It was perhaps no surprise that nativism surged during the hard economic times of the late 1830s and early 1840s, and the culmination of this trend came in 1845 when delegates from New England and the mid-Atlantic states met in Philadelphia to form the national Native American Party. More populist expressions of nativism were to be seen in attitudes toward Catholics in general and in particular in the attack on the **Ursuline convent** in 1834 and in the **Philadelphia riots** a decade later. Immigrants and their living conditions were also readily blamed for the spread of **cholera** in 1832.

While receiving little public condemnation from figures of either of the main political parties, nativism seemed to appeal more to the same groundswell of opinion that sustained the **Whig** Party. Locally it tended to be Whigs who proposed limitations on immigrants' rights, while **Democrats** favored easier terms for citizenship for recent immigrants and in some states proposed that voting rights be given to all white male residents whether or not they were officially citizens. Whether more repelled by the Whigs or attracted by the

Democrats, foreign-born voters tended to vote for the latter and in the **election of 1844** some leading Whigs blamed **Henry Clay**'s defeat on the loss of crucial eastern states where foreign-born voters had swung to **James Polk**. These claims enhanced the nativist trend within those local branches of the Whig Party, although its national leadership was wary of pushing the issue too far. Of course, nativism would rise to even greater prominence in national and local politics in the period immediately after the end of the longer Jacksonian era, with the emergence of the Know-Nothing Party.

NAT TURNER'S REVOLT. This was perhaps the most threatening and certainly the most influential revolt by slaves in the American South during the period. In August 1831 a slave preacher, Nat Turner, prevailed upon between 60 and 80 slaves in Southampton County, Virginia, to rise up against the white community. Although the revolt was quashed within three days, some 60 white people were killed, including Turner's own master and his family, while some 100 African-Americans died during the revolt or by execution afterwards. Among the latter was Turner, who had remained on the run for six weeks before his capture led to his trial and hanging.

As well as inspiring vicious white retaliation against African-Americans, the revolt also led many white southerners to draw their own conclusions about its chronological proximity to the publication of the *Liberator* a mere eight months earlier and it hardened their resolve to resist **abolitionist** activity. The revolt was also partly responsible for eroding any remaining inclination on the part of southerners to abolish **slavery** from within, the Virginian assembly voting to reject a bill to get rid of the peculiar institution, albeit by a narrow margin. Instead many of the institutional underpinnings of slavery were strengthened and made harsher.

NAUVOO. Joseph Smith established this Illinois community in 1839 on the site of the town of Commerce, after he had led the **Mormons** out of Missouri. Smith regarded it as the base of the Mormon religion and by 1840 it had become the largest city in Illinois, with several substantial buildings and a population nearing 20,000 by 1845.

NAVAL REFORM. After some attempts at cost-cutting and greater efficiency during **Martin Van Buren**'s administration, it was really under **John Tyler**, and especially his secretary of the navy, **Abel Upshur**, that major efforts at reform in both the navy and Navy Department were attempted. Upshur called for an expansion and modernization of the navy, to enable it to cope with technological change and with greater commitments across the two main oceans. He demanded the repair of older vessels and advocated steam-powered, screw propeller-equipped ships, often in defiance of supporters of more traditional naval practices. In addition he called for the establishment of a proper naval academy, for changes in the navy's ranking system, and for better central administrative facilities for the navy, including the creation of naval bureaus at the expense of the old Board of Naval Commissioners.

Congress blocked the naval academy proposal at this stage—that would have to wait until legislation in October 1845 established such an institution at Annapolis—while the creation of new ranks never did reach the Senate for consideration. Congress did, though, vote to replace the Board with five new bureaus, to increase the number of Navy Department administrative staff, and to establish better facilities for the keeping of charts and naval instruments, which ultimately, in 1844, would also house the Naval Observatory. Increased appropriations also allowed for the development of steam-driven iron warships, such as the U.S.S. *Princeton*. Finally there was also to be reform in the treatment of sailors in the navy, especially with regard to its punishment regimes, in part thanks to exposures of the practice of flogging in works such as **Richard Henry Dana**'s *Two Years before the Mast,* and in the controversy surrounding the *Somers* **mutiny**.

NEW ECHOTA, TREATY OF. Representatives of the United States signed this fraudulent treaty with a minority of the **Cherokee** tribe at their northern Georgian capital on 29 December 1835. By its terms the Cherokee agreed to cede all their remaining lands east of the Mississippi, in exchange for $5 million and seven million acres of land in the far West. The treaty was used by the federal government as the pretext for removing all the Cherokee who remained in the East, including those not party to it, and it led directly to the infamous "**trail of tears.**"

NEW ENGLAND ANTI-SLAVERY SOCIETY. This group, set up in Boston in 1831 by a meeting of over 70 **abolitionists**, including **William Lloyd Garrison**, was the first publicly to espouse immediate abolition while at the same time attacking earlier proposed solutions for the issue of **slavery**, such as colonization.

NEW MEXICO, TERRITORIAL STATUS. The New Mexico lands formed a significant part of the acquisitions resulting from the **Mexi-**

can **War** and the debate as to their future size and territorial status almost inevitably became tinged with dispute over the possibility of **slavery**'s extension. **James Polk** was keen for an early resolution of these issues, but despite his prompting in his annual message of December 1847 no progress was made on arrangements for New Mexico in the 1847-48 congressional session. In December 1848 Polk repeated his recommendation for a settlement, most likely on terms of **popular sovereignty**, out of the conviction that the spread of slavery to the region was improbable in the first place. However, the House of Representatives chose to back a settlement along the lines of the **Wilmot Proviso** and, as Polk had previously made clear that he would veto any southwestern territorial bill with the proviso attached, a rocky road lay ahead. Various alternatives were considered, including one in which New Mexico would be combined in a single state with **California**, but by the end of Polk's term no territorial bill for New Mexico had yet been passed.

NEW YORK CITY FIRE. In December 1835 a devastating fire swept through New York City, destroying over 600 buildings in the financial district and causing damage to a cost of around $22 million. It bankrupted many New York insurance companies and provoked many calls to national politicians for relief. The fire was only one of several in the period between 1835 and 1845, which collectively destroyed most of the city.

NEW YORK SAFETY FUND. This system was established during **Martin Van Buren**'s brief term of office as governor of New York, 1828-29. Under its terms all the state's banks joined an association and contributed 3 percent of their capital to a common fund, later called the "safety fund," which could be drawn from to refund the creditors of any bank that defaulted. In view of the fact that the system was run by a commission that occasionally inspected member banks, the Safety Fund effectively assumed the role of a central bank, in the process lessening the direct impact of the **Second Bank of the United States** in New York. The Fund soon rose to $30 million and helped to provide a more stable and secure banking system for the people of New York.

NEW YORK SUN. The *New York Sun*, created in 1833 by Benjamin Henry Day, was the first successful example of a "**penny press**" daily. It appealed to a much wider audience than was traditionally the case and featured stories on crime, violence, and entertainment. In the

1840s it would be edited by Moses Beach, who not only played a part in forming the New York Associated Press in 1848 but also was caught up in events in Mexico City in the lead-up to the outbreak of the **Mexican War**.

NEW YORK TRIBUNE. Although an example of the "**penny press**," the *Tribune* was founded by **Horace Greeley** in 1841 with the intention of establishing a mid-market paper, between the sensationalism of **James Gordon Bennett**'s *New York Herald* and the detachment of the *Evening Post*. Within only a couple of months the *Tribune*'s readership had grown into the thousands and soon it had become the most popular **Whig** newspaper around. It opposed **John Tyler** when he began to veto many of the preferred Whig policies, and it adopted a cautious approach to the **Mexican War**, warning against it going on too long. The *Tribune* was to become one of the foremost northern newspapers in the period leading up to the outbreak of the Civil War.

NICHOLSON LETTER. Issued in December 1847, this was the public communication by which **Lewis Cass**, the **Democratic** Party hopeful for the presidential nomination in 1848, set out his opposition to the **Wilmot Proviso** and promulgated what would become the dominant Democratic solution to settling the question of slavery in the territories, **popular sovereignty**.

NILES, JOHN (1787-1856). This **Democratic** politician from Connecticut sat in the Senate for most of the 1830s before being promoted to the position of postmaster general in the last year of **Martin Van Buren**'s administration, after the resignation of **Amos Kendall** in 1840. Niles' promotion was in part reward for his loyal support for the administration on issues like the **Independent Treasury**, a reflection of his own leaning to the more radical wing of his party. He was genuinely hostile to the financial self-interest of the commercial classes and at the state level favored strict measures for the regulation of banks and corporations. After leaving office in 1841 Niles played a less prominent part in the national politics of the 1840s, although he still exercised some influence on patronage in his home state during **James Polk**'s administration. By this time Niles was becoming disenchanted with the regular Democratic Party, opposing the administration's **tariff bill in 1846**, and two years later he joined the **Free Soil** coalition and headed their ticket in Connecticut.

"NO TERRITORY" MOVEMENT. The **Whig** Party adopted the "No Territory" position as a means of expressing their opposition to the **Mexican War**. Their rather unreasonable demand that the United States should not benefit territorially from the sacrifices made in any successful war effort was born of a desire to find a common ground upon which all Whigs could agree. While the more extreme call by **anti-slavery** elements for no expansion of **slavery** as a result of the war was too inflammatory for conservative and southern Whigs, it could be accommodated within a party-wide agreement not to take any territory at all, which would ensure that the issue of slavery's extension would not arise in the first place.

The "No Territory" stance reached its zenith in Senate debates on the Treaty of **Guadalupe Hidalgo**, when 15 Whigs voted for an amendment offered by **George Badger** deleting any territorial acquisitions from the treaty. But, just like their opponents on the other extreme who called for greater territorial gains from the war, even to the extent of "**all Mexico**," the "No Territory" group could not hope to secure the necessary two-thirds majority to allow the treaty to pass with their amendment attached. So, rather than continuing to block the treaty and perpetuating a war they opposed so strongly, eight of the 15 swallowed the fact that it was better to have an early peace with limited territorial acquisition than to have no peace at all or a later peace with even greater territorial gains. Their votes for the final unamended treaty allowed it to pass.

NOYES, JOHN (1811-1886). Born in Vermont, Noyes was educated at Dartmouth and began legal training before a personal religious conversion took him to Yale Divinity School instead in 1832. He was a revivalist and liberal theologian whose belief in a free church and advocacy of perfectionism lost him his license as a Congregational minister and caused him to be expelled from Yale. Noyes went on to found a Bible community based on perfectionist principles in Putney, Vermont in 1836 but in 1847 was forced to abandon it as the local neighborhood objected to the community's practice of complex marriage. The following year he established a new, longer-lasting community at **Oneida**.

NULLIFICATION. Nullification was the extreme **states' rights** assessment of how any individual state should deal with what it considered to be an unconstitutional expression of federal power. Drawing on long theoretical roots back to Thomas Jefferson and James Madison's Virginia and Kentucky resolutions, several states had flirted with nullification in the past. At the start of the Jacksonian era, Georgia came close to nullifying federal authority by its treatment of Native Americans, often in defiance of Supreme Court rulings.

However, in the late 1820s and early 1830s nullification came to be associated most strongly with the single state of South Carolina and its leading political figure, **John Calhoun**. In response to federal **tariff** laws, which many South Carolinians claimed were unconstitutional because they included elements of **protection**, Calhoun and others produced a series of position papers articulating the steps states could take against what they judged to be oppressive and unconstitutional federal legislation. Should all other remedies fail, the ultimate step was the state's right to declare the alleged unconstitutional laws null and void within its boundaries. The depth of South Carolinian feeling on this issue, generally agreed to be bound up with fears of possible federal action against other southern institutions such as **slavery**, if ever Congress should decide to use similar flexibility of constitutional interpretation to address that issue, confronted the nation with its most threatening **sectional** moment of the Jacksonian era, in the **Nullification crisis** in the winter of 1832-33. *See also* FORT HILL ADDRESS; SOUTH CAROLINA EXPOSITION AND PROTEST.

NULLIFICATION CRISIS. This episode of heightened **sectional** tension arose out of southern discontent with the policy of the **protective tariff**, as exemplified in particular by the **tariffs of 1828 and 1832**. Many southerners had hoped that **Andrew Jackson** would sympathize with their opposition to protection, especially as their leading advocate, **John Calhoun**, was vice-president. However, these hopes were dashed as Calhoun's influence with Jackson waned between 1829 and 1831, to the point that he seemed to be out of the running to succeed **Old Hickory**. Moreover, the president proved willing to sign the tariff of 1832, leaving the more extreme opponents of protection in South Carolina little choice, in their thinking, but to resort to **nullification**.

Inspired by Calhoun's ideas, but driven by more radical nullifiers such as George McDuffie and **James Hamilton**, South Carolina elected a legislature with a two-thirds majority in favor of calling a special convention to espouse nullification. The convention issued its **Nullification Ordinance** in November 1832, setting a date after which it would nullify the tariff laws should the federal government not respond first. Then the state's regular legislature passed the measures necessary to implement nullification, should the final need arise, and to provide for military readiness. At the same time it emphasized its defiance by selecting Calhoun as Senator, after he had first resigned as vice-president, and by casting its electoral college votes for **John Floyd**. James Hamilton resigned as the state's governor, to take charge of military preparations, a sensible step as President Jackson soon issued his highly confrontational **Nullification Proclamation** in which he effectively called the nullifiers traitors. Congress also passed the **Force Act** authorizing the president to use force to implement federal laws.

With the Union teetering on the brink of break-up, and possibly even Civil War, more cautious and moderate opinions intervened. South Carolina nullifiers became alarmed at the prospect of violence, as both federal troops and **Unionist** supporters in their own state expressed a willingness to stand up to them. It also seemed unlikely that they would be able to attract substantial support from other southern states sympathetic to their views. While many other southerners were as angry about the protective tariff as South Carolinians were, and certainly were most alarmed at the prospect of the use of federal force against another state, they were not yet ready to go to the same lengths as the nullifiers. The next most extreme state, Georgia, was reluctant to dishonor the debt it owed to the president over the issue of **Indian removal**.

In the face of such pressures the South Carolina state legislature moderated its position by putting the emphasis on protecting those merchants who refused to pay import tariff duties rather than punishing those who might choose to continue paying them. The new state governor, **Robert Hayne**, refrained from calling militia troops into Charleston, for fear of being thought too provocative. Finally, when it seemed that Congress might offer some reform of the tariff laws, South Carolina's legislature eased the situation by extending the deadline by which nullification would come into force until such time as Congress had made up its mind.

Meanwhile, despite his stance in the Nullification Proclamation, Jackson proved willing to encourage these moves, using his 1832 annual message to call for a modification of the tariff. The result was the **tariff of 1833**, often portrayed as being part of a wider legislative **compromise** putting a seal on the end of the Nullification crisis. The crisis only officially ended when South Carolina's reconvened nullification convention abandoned the Nullification Ordinance against the tariff, but even then it made the token gesture of nullifying the Force Act, safe in the knowledge that the very reason for the act's possible implementation had been removed anyway.

NULLIFICATION ORDINANCE. When a special convention called by South Carolina met in November 1832 it precipitated the start of the **Nullification crisis** by issuing the Nullification Ordinance. The Ordinance declared that the state would nullify the **tariffs of 1828 and 1832** and stated that its decision would not be subject to Supreme Court review. It also asserted that any attempt to enforce the tariff acts would push South Carolina into seceding from the Union.

NULLIFICATION PROCLAMATION. This presidential message represented **Andrew Jackson**'s specific response to South Carolina's decision to nullify federal tariff laws in 1832. Written in conjunction with **Edward Livingston**, the proclamation marked the high point in the president's rhetorical **unionism**, putting great emphasis on the value of the Union as a single nation and as a government of people as much as of states. More practically, the proclamation expressly denied that the Constitution sanctioned the right of any state to nullify federal legislation or to secede from the Union, declaring the latter step as tantamount to treason. Its unionist tone made Jackson temporarily very popular with the likes of **Daniel Webster** but also alarmed those in the **states' rights** fraternity and many old Republicans within the Jacksonian coalition. Several southern states, including North Carolina, Mississippi, Georgia, Alabama, and, eventually, Virginia, shared their alarm and refused to endorse the proclamation.

– O –

OBERLIN COLLEGE. This educational establishment was founded in Lorain County, Ohio in 1833 as the Oberlin Collegiate Institute. It admitted its first students in December of that year, and from the very first included **women** in its student body, initially in a separate ladies' institute but subsequently in the regular undergraduate program as well. Indeed, the College produced the first four female B.A. graduates in the United States. Oberlin was also one of the first colleges to admit African-American students, from 1835. Already receiving funding from **Arthur Tappan**, in 1834 the College attracted several students and faculty from the **Lane Seminary** in Cincinnati, which, along with the arrival of **Charles Grandison Finney** from New York a year later, helped to bring Oberlin and the community around it into the ranks of those taking a more active **abolitionist** stance against the institution of **slavery**.

OFFICE OF INDIAN AFFAIRS. The Office of Indian Affairs began life as a bureau of the War Department in 1824 and assumed the title Office in 1830 when the position of commissioner of Indian affairs was formalized. Four years later all this was given a legislative basis by congressional act, establishing the Office as the main center of responsibility for handling the federal government's relations with Native Americans. Of course this was the period when **Indian removal** was at its height, and in recognition of the growth of the Office's workload its staff was increased in 1836, with some transferred in from the War Department. In 1849 the Office was part of the administrative reorganization that witnessed the creation of the **Department of the Interior**, to which branch the Office of Indian Affairs was now transferred from the War Department.

OHIO AND ERIE CANAL. This **canal** system, planned in the mid-1820s, was completed in 1832 and contributed tremendously to the economic development of Ohio. Its 300-plus miles ran between terminal points close to Portsmouth in the south and Cleveland in the north, and by linking the Ohio River to Lake Erie and beyond, via the **Erie Canal** system, it allowed the state's trade to take a much shorter route than it had once had to via the Ohio and Mississippi Rivers. A feeder canal, completed in 1831, also linked the state capital, Columbus, to the main canal and its trade. The canal fostered the state's **agricultural** and industrial enterprise and helped to change Cleveland from frontier town to thriving commercial center. At the same time it reinforced the influence of the Erie Canal in reorienting the main patterns of trade between the Midwest and the Atlantic coastal communities.

"OLD FUSS AND FEATHERS." This was a popular nickname for General **Winfield Scott**, which played on his belief in meticulous procedure and military etiquette and his preference for ostentatious dress uniform.

"OLD HICKORY." This was a nickname assumed by **Andrew Jackson** in the War of 1812 when his troops likened him to hickory wood because of his endurance and strength.

"OLD ROUGH AND READY." This was a popular nickname for General **Zachary Taylor**, which derived from his informal leadership style and contempt for dress uniform.

ONEIDA COMMUNITY. This was one of the most prominent American experiments in cooperative, communitarian living. It was founded by **John Noyes** in northern New York in 1848 and was governed by weekly public committees, which oversaw its principles of common ownership of property, cooperative economic activities, polygamous marriage, equality of rights for **women**, and eugenics through efforts at birth control. As well as producing its own food, the community produced manufactures in smithies and textile facilities.

OREGON, TERRITORIAL STATUS. Even before the **Oregon Treaty** of 1846 established the boundary line between the territory and British Columbia, there had been several moves to organize Oregon. In 1842-43 an Oregon promoter in the Senate, the Missourian Lewis Linn, proposed a bill establishing territorial government as well as offering land grants to settlers there. His bill failed, but in the 1844-45 congressional session David Atchison called for the political organization of "**all Oregon**," with an allocation of land and resources for building U.S. forts. Meanwhile, in July 1843 settlers in Oregon had drafted their own constitution, called the organic law, which proposed a provisional three-part government, voluntary taxes, and regulation of land settlement.

It was such extralegal efforts on the ground, as well as the difficult problems facing the Oregon settlers, as exemplified by the **Whitman massacre**, which accelerated congressional efforts at organizing Oregon once the boundary had been settled. Straight after the Senate's approval of the treaty over Oregon, President **James Polk** in August 1846 called on Congress for a bill to organize the new territory and, after that session ran out of time, repeated his call in his 1846 annual message. The fact that virtually the same pattern occurred the following year revealed that the urgency for organization was being outweighed by other considerations, and it would only be in August 1848 that appropriate legislation was passed.

Given the priorities of the time it is not surprising that debates over the extension of **slavery** proved to be the stumbling block, although few believed that the peculiar institution would ever be established in Oregon. Rather than the free status of Oregon being the problem, it was the method used to legislate for it that aroused the passions, as representatives of both sections looked to how other territories would be established in the future. A House bill of summer 1846 organized Oregon without slavery by reference to the Northwest Territorial Ordinance of 1787, but this failed to win Senate support. The following year some in the House now suggested that slavery be prohibited in Oregon according to the **Missouri Compromise** settlement rather than the Northwest Ordinance, but this time the Senate removed the prohibition altogether as southerners denied Congress' right to legislate on the matter of slavery extension at all.

At this point Polk stepped in to hurry things along by putting pressure on congressmen to accept a Missouri Compromise-style arrangement, but still Congress delayed and instead a special Senate committee proposed a compromise by letting the existing provisional free status of the region stand. Rather than forcing Congress to legislate on the matter, John Clayton proposed that in the fullness of time the courts could decide on the legality of the territory's own prohibition, should anyone choose to take a slave there. The Senate backed this proposal and was prepared to extend it to the **California** and **New Mexico** territories as well, but the House rejected the compromise and passed its own bill with a simple prohibition of slavery in the Oregon territory. The Senate finally voted to accept that bill, allowing Polk to approve it, although the president made clear in a special message that he did so only because it fitted in with the spirit of the Missouri Compromise.

OREGON TRAIL. This fur traders' route from the Missouri River to the Columbia River became in the 1840s the main trail for successive parties of missionaries and pioneers moving through Wyoming and Idaho to the western territories of **Oregon** and **California**. Some 2,000 miles long, it ran from **Independence**, Missouri, via Fort Hall to Fort Vancouver. It played a major practical role in the popular application of **Manifest Destiny**.

OREGON TREATY. A long-standing dispute over the exact location of the far northwestern border between the United States and British North America came to a point of crisis in the mid-1840s, at one point threatening war between the two countries. The disputed territory, stretching from the Rockies to the Pacific between the 42° and 54° 40′ parallels, encompassed lands in the current states of Washington, Oregon, and Idaho as well as the province of British Columbia. Although the specific point at issue was the course of the boundary westward to the ocean from the point where the Columbia River and the 49th parallel diverged, growing tension between both countries' settlers on the ground combined with the American feelings of **Manifest Destiny** and Anglophobia to encourage wilder rhetorical claims on the part of the United States which deepened the crisis.

Before both sides began to consider the issue more seriously during the administration of **John Tyler**, the broader **Oregon** region was subject to arrangements laid down by conventions of 1818 and 1827, which had allowed joint occupation and settlement in the disputed territory in the absence of a firm agreement on the boundary line. After the issue was once more left untouched by the **Webster-Ashburton Treaty**, from 1843 on there was an acceleration of diplomatic attempts to settle the matter. In London the British offered the more southerly line of the Columbia as the border, which **Edward Everett** countered with the suggestion of the 49th parallel all the way to Vancouver Island, which the British would retain. However, although Tyler was keen to use a success over Oregon as an **expansionist** triumph favorable to northern interests to balance **Texas annexation**, his secretary of state at that time, **Abel Upshur**, did not invest the same energy in it, with the result that the matter was left unresolved. British calls for further arbitration of the line were now met by more extreme claims by Tyler, who, no doubt pandering to an emerging **"All Oregon"** movement in the **Democratic** Party of the old Northwest, called in his 1843 annual message for a much more northerly **54° 40′** boundary line. **James Polk** perpetuated this more extensive claim during his campaign for the **election of 1844** with an aggressive call for a "reoccupation" of all Oregon, and at the same time Congress resolved to end the earlier conventions by which both parties jointly occupied the disputed region and to allow Americans to form their own government in the territory.

Although Polk softened his demands in his inaugural address, his tone was still sufficiently belligerent to alarm the British, especially as he continued to reject further arbitration of the matter. Unfortunately the calming diplomacy needed at this point was not to be and instead the rather clumsy efforts of the British minister, **Richard Pakenham**, only deepened the crisis. Contrary to his orders Pakenham rejected Polk's more realistic offer of a boundary based on the 49th parallel, causing Polk to withdraw the offer in the misguided belief that the British government would not accept it and to recommend to Congress in December 1845 that it pass a resolution giving notice to the British that the joint occupation would be terminated.

In the five months it took Congress to debate and then pass the notice resolution, albeit it with a clause still holding out the hope of compromise, both governments frantically sought to calm things down. Polk returned to his offer of the 49th parallel, inspired by the sense that a **Mexican war** was becoming increasingly likely and by the information that British ships had embarked for North America.

When it became clear that Britain was also ready to agree to that line as the boundary, with a dividing line through the waters east and south of Vancouver Island, an actual treaty on those terms was drafted in June 1846. It also allowed American and Hudson's Bay Company vessels to navigate the waters of the Columbia River in common.

The settlement was still not quite finalized. The treaty went before the Senate a few days after it had been signed and looked likely to receive rough treatment in that body at the hands of the "All Oregon" Democrats. William Allen resigned as chair of the Foreign Relations Committee in protest, and when it came to the final vote nearly all the northern Democrats voted against ratification. Ultimately it was only because most **Whigs** voted in favor alongside southern Democrats that the treaty was ratified on 18 June. So it was that after a crisis of tough words and brinkmanship the Oregon boundary issue was settled, ironically along lines suggested by the United States as early as 1827.

OSCEOLA (ca. 1800-1838). Osceola was born in Alabama, of mixed British and **Creek** parentage, but gained renown as a leader of the Florida **Seminole** at the time of the **Second Seminole War**. Having opposed the 1832 Treaty of Payne's Landing by which some of the Seminole had agreed to the U.S. policy of **Indian removal**, Osceola became the leader of the faction that continued to reject negotiation with the U.S. government. In many ways it was his actions that precipitated the war, after murdering an Indian agent at Fort Drake in 1835 and inspiring others to abandon talks that were taking place with **Thomas Jesup**. In October 1837 he was arrested under a flag of truce and imprisoned for the rest of his life, dying in Fort Moultrie in Charleston harbor.

O'SULLIVAN, JOHN (1813-1895). Born at sea, of Irish stock, O'Sullivan was educated at Columbia before training as a lawyer. While he did pursue some legal work and enjoyed a political career at state level, he is best known as a newspaper journalist and editor. With the support of leading **Democrats** he founded the *United States Magazine and Democratic Review* in Washington, D.C., which, more commonly known as the *Democratic Review*, became a leading Democratic intellectual organ of the 1840s. He later moved the paper to New York City, and there also co-edited, with Samuel Tilden, the **James Polk** campaign paper *Morning News* in 1844. Despite his support for **expansionism**, demonstrated by his first published use of the term **Manifest Destiny** and by his support for the annexation of **Cuba** in 1847, he supported the **Barnburner Martin Van Buren** in 1848.

OVERBANKING. This was the term given to a sense that in the mid-1830s a mixture of international monetary flows and government policy was fuelling too fast a proliferation of banking. Given that not all banks were as sound as others, this raised the danger that any change of circumstances could cause the American economy to collapse. Already from 1830 to 1835 the number of state-chartered banks had doubled, as some states invested public money to buy bank stock, underwrote state banks with public credit, or, in the West in particular, established wholly state-owned banks. The expansion in banking was in part justified by the greater amount of Mexican silver in circulation and by British investment, causing the amount of money supply in 1836 to reach a level two-and-a-half times greater than that in 1829. On top of that, speculation in the purchase of public lands reached a high in 1835-36, creating further expansionist pressure within the banking system. Although not solely responsible, nor intentionally so, **Andrew Jackson**'s attack on the **Second Bank of the United States** and his policy of depositing federal revenue with state banks undoubtedly encouraged these trends by providing greater assets upon which banks could lend more and increase the circulation of **paper money**. While again not entirely responsible for the **panic of 1837**, overbanking clearly did exaggerate the impact of the collapse that followed.

OVERSEAS COMMERCE. Even in the face of increased **manufacturing** development in the United States and growing levels of domestic commerce, overseas trade remained a significant feature of the American economy in this era. It is true that internal commerce did grow faster than international trade, the former exceeding the latter for the first time in 1831 and reaching a level three times greater by 1847. This encouraged a sense among some merchants that their resources were better placed in burgeoning **internal improvements** and manufacturing companies at home. Nevertheless overall exports and imports more than doubled in value between 1829 and 1849, with particularly healthy increases in the years before the **panic of 1837** and again, after a fall-off and slower recovery in the late 1830s and early 1840s, between 1846 and 1849.

　　Certain significant trades experienced greater growth than others, notably all trade with Britain, the sugar trade with Cuba, and trade with China. Exports of staple, especially southern, products such as **cotton** still accounted for most of the foreign income coming into the United States and there was a massive explosion in the volume, if not always the value, of cotton exports in the period. In exchange for exports America received mainly British manufactured imports and investment capital. Naturally the increases in exports and imports boosted the amount of carrying trade to be conveyed across the oceans, and America's native merchant and **shipping** communities were profitably involved in this work, as well as in tramp shipping between other countries.

Overseas commerce rarely raised issues of specific significance in the era's politics and diplomacy, but clearly general debates over the level of **tariff** duties were of importance to producers, merchants, and shippers involved in overseas business, while the U.S. diplomatic community was charged with securing as favorable conditions as possible for Americans involved in overseas commerce by means of **commercial treaties**. Just occasionally episodes of special significance brought overseas trade into the political or diplomatic spotlight, as occurred with the reopening of trade with Britain's **West Indian** and North American colonies, the negotiation and then Senate rejection of a commercial treaty with the German **Zollverein**, and the **Treaty of Wanghia** with China.

OWEN, ROBERT DALE (1801-1877). This Scottish-born writer, editor, and intellectual, the son of Robert Owen, had become involved in the idealistic community at New Harmony in Indiana in the 1820s. After its collapse, he and his associate, **Fanny Wright**, remained in the United States, moving to New York City, where together they established the *Free Enquirer* in 1829. Owen advocated a range of popular causes, including **labor** rights, rotation in office, anti-clericalism, and public school education, as well as the wilder suggestion that all children be taken under state responsibility at the age of two to ensure equal opportunities for all. In 1833 he returned to New Harmony and two years later he entered the Indiana legislature, before going on to serve his state in Congress between 1843 and 1847. Owen's interests in this later period included the **Smithsonian Institution**, some of whose committees he worked on, as well as legal reform, with special attention to more liberal divorce and property rights for married **women**.

– P –

PAKENHAM, RICHARD (1797-1868). This British diplomat, of Irish background, had served a long diplomatic career, including a tour of duty in Mexico, before he became the British minister to the U.S. government in 1844. Pakenham entered the post at a crucial moment in the developing crises over **Texas annexation** and the **Oregon** border and he would go on to play a role in both, unwitting in the case of the former and witting in the latter.

In 1844 Pakenham was the recipient of a letter from the new secretary of state, **John Calhoun**, who warned against the influence the British might exercise in Texas in helping **abolitionists** to end **slavery** there and to create a free rival to southern U.S. states. Although the **Pakenham letter**, as it came to be known, failed to draw the British minister into a debate on **slavery**, he did advise his government not to interfere with U.S. annexation of Texas or the later crisis of relations with Mexico.

Pakenham was also the man in Washington charged with the difficult task of negotiating on the Oregon issue, first with Calhoun, and then with **James Buchanan** under **James Polk**'s administration. On several occasions he offered a settlement of the border by arbitration, hinting that the British might be prepared to make concessions, but he was continually rebuffed. His frustration led him in turn to reject American offers that might have been acceptable to his own government, which only added to the growing sense of crisis between the two countries. However, eventually it was Pakenham who drafted the final Oregon Treaty with Buchanan.

PAKENHAM LETTER. This letter was written on 18 April 1844, by **John Calhoun** to the British minister to the United States, **Richard Pakenham**, in the midst of **John Tyler**'s administration's efforts to secure **Texas annexation**. In it Calhoun warned the British government not to get involved and explicitly linked American possession of Texas with the preservation of **slavery**, saying that annexation was the best way to protect Texan (and southern U.S.) slavery against otherwise irresistible British pressure for abolition. The letter was in part responsible for the defeat of the annexation treaty in the Senate, which had a secret view of it in documentation sent for consideration alongside the treaty itself, and when it was leaked to the public by the **Tappan** brothers the letter aroused fears that **expansion** was being pursued in order to spread slavery.

PALO ALTO, BATTLE OF. This was the first major battle of the **Mexican War**, fought on 8 May 1846 between the time of the initial border affrays and the actual declaration of war a few days later. It was one of two great successes for **Zachary Taylor** as he confronted Mexican troops who had crossed the Rio Grande in greater numbers hoping to crush him. Together with the battle of **Resaca de la Palma** the following day, the victory at Palo Alto ended this immediate threat and laid the foundation for Taylor's successful northern Mexico campaign.

PANIC OF 1834. This short-term downturn in American economic fortunes in the winter of 1833-34 was caused by the necessary, but also deliberate, temporary contraction of loans by **Nicholas Biddle's Second Bank of the United States** in response to **Andrew Jackson's removal of the federal deposits**. The tightening of credit damaged many companies, caused others to fail, and brought a degree of unemployment to commercial centers, especially New York City. But overall the panic's impact was fairly shallow as most forms of trade in goods increased during this period, and as, contrary to expectations, the money supply was not greatly contracted, because foreign metal imports into the country increased and state banks extended their lending, to some extent compensating for the reduced credit of the Second Bank. The panic was also short-lived, ending when Biddle abandoned his efforts at contraction. Even so it generated some political effect as memorials flooded to Congress calling for relief, the majority blaming the president's removal policy for the worsening situation. The episode also gave Jackson even more ammunition for his attack on the "**monster bank**," since the panic seemed to demonstrate the dangerous influence that Biddle could exercise over the economy. So it was then that Jackson advised delegations of businessmen coming to Washington for relief to go to Biddle in Philadelphia instead.

PANIC OF 1837. In spring 1837 the United States shared in a sudden but short-lived global economic crisis, which interrupted what was otherwise a period of expansion for the American economy between 1830 and 1839. A range of domestic factors contributed to and exacerbated the panic, which effectively burst a bubble of economic overconfidence. Generally it was an excess of speculative activity that endangered the health of the economy: land speculation between 1833 and 1837; banking speculation as financial institutions extended their note issues through a greater volume of loans; state governments getting more into debt to fund improvements; all these contributed to a heavy dependence on credit that would be damaging should economic confidence collapse. Federal government policies of **removal of the federal deposits** and **distribution** had indirectly contributed by offering state **deposit banks** and state governments greater reserves upon which to base loans or to invest in projects. However, this expanded economic activity was mainly founded upon international trading patterns, which caused larger amounts of metallic currency, in the form of Mexican silver, to enter and remain in the United States rather than be channeled through to Britain. Moreover, British interests also invested more in the United States, mainly in loans to a range of state improvements projects.

These trends to some extent justified the expansion of the mid-1830s but also emphasized its dependence upon external circumstances, and it was a change in these circumstances that precipitated the panic. In 1836 a rise in British interest rates caused the curtailment of credit extension to American importers of British goods and made it more profitable for British investors to keep their silver in Britain than to invest it in the United States. Indeed, specie actually began to bleed from the United States, removing the main buttress to credit and note issue, and causing banks to contract their loans in the spring of 1837.

At the same time state banks nationwide, but especially those in the seaboard states, were also squeezed by the **1836 Deposit Act** whose regulatory provisions and **distribution** feature reduced their reserves. Indeed, the incidental timing of the implementation of this act, and of the **Specie Circular**, could hardly have been worse for combining with existing pressures to exaggerate the contraction of loans and of the currency.

Finally, in February 1837 the price of **cotton** began to fall, leaving many merchants with overextended commitments and with no means to honor their loans as banks contracted their note issues. Commercial failures occurred in New Orleans and then in New York City and Philadelphia, as importers failed to meet their commitments. As panic started to spread merchants and the public rushed to get hard money in their own pockets by attempting to redeem notes from banks. In May 1837 several New York banks suspended payment of specie in exchange for notes, followed soon after by banks across the country, leaving only a handful operating normally.

A crisis that climaxed with pressure on banks to suspend specie payments and with failures of importing companies soon developed wider implications. Some corporations went bankrupt, manufacturing production shuddered to a halt, and unemployment rose, precipitating some urban riots in protest at the cost of rents, food, and fuel. Many state governments defaulted on the loans taken out to fund their improvements projects. Property values slumped and land sales fell by over two-thirds. However, it is important not to exaggerate the impact of the crisis, which was for the most part isolated to the narrower international trading sector of the United States. Business activity did continue, especially in **agriculture** and domestic trade, and although specie went out of circulation, **paper money** still provided a means of exchange between individuals and also in transactions involving state and local governments. Indeed within six months of the panic's outbreak manufacturing began to pick up, and a further six months later credit and specie flows from Britain resumed, allowing a revival of business and a resumption of specie payments by banks by April 1838.

The resumption came amidst encouraging sounds from **Martin Van Buren**'s administration over the opposition of the still influential banker **Nicholas Biddle** who hoped to make the abandonment of certain **Democratic** policies the price for bank resumption. Yet although things began to steady economically for the administration, considerable political damage had been done. Already Van Buren had been forced into calling one of the very rare **special sessions** of Congress, in the summer of 1837, in part to solve practical problems of how to handle the federal government's financial resources when the suspension of so many banks had activated the Deposit Act's regulations relating to the liquidity of deposit banks. More importantly, whether rightly or wrongly, the panic called into question many of the financial policy decisions adopted by **Andrew Jackson**'s administration and left a tricky inheritance for Van Buren. For, while on one side the panic only confirmed the sense of the Democratic attack on banks and inspired them to new plans for cutting government off from all banks and from dangerous internationally-influenced credit fluctuations (as seen in plans for the **Independent Treasury**), on the other the lived experience of economic hardship recruited more supporters for **Whig** plans to safeguard enterprise and the **credit system**, including, perhaps, even the creation of a new national bank, which they claimed would have been able to navigate the country through the economic fluctuations of the previous few months. Mid-term elections in 1837 signaled this popular disquiet as Whigs both prevailed in many states won by Van Buren only the previous year and secured bigger margins of victory than in their own previous triumphs. The impact of another, and this time more long-lasting economic crisis after the **panic of 1839** only exaggerated this trend.

PANIC OF 1839. The panic of 1839 is generally less feted among historians than its famous predecessor two years earlier and at the time it failed to provoke the same sort of immediate political impact. However, ultimately the panic of 1839 was a more serious financial downturn than the **panic of 1837**, as it marked the real conclusion of the boom economy of the 1830s and as such had a greater impact on people's lives and businesses. As in 1837 the crisis began when banks came under pressure to contract their loans and issue of **paper money**, once again because of international pressures: the British needed money to pay for grain imports from Europe, deflecting investment in American projects, while a rise in British interest rates began to drain specie out of the United States. As confidence fell in the health of the economy and the banking system in particular, banks started to suspend payments of specie when presented with their notes, beginning in October 1839 in Philadelphia. Hundreds more banks across the country followed suit, and this time some suspensions lasted until the 1840s.

Following close on the heels of the panic of 1837, this new crisis ushered in a period of genuine depression that lasted until 1843. This time there was no quick resumption of the flow of British capital into the United States and this fact, combined with state policies generated through the **bank wars**, caused a fall in the number of banks and in the amount of currency in circulation until around 1843-44. **Overseas commerce** struggled as levels of imports fell and as the cost of buying food in Britain deflected some money away from the cotton textile manufacturing that provided such an important market for exported American **cotton**. Although economic output in the United States actually increased by 16 percent during the period, the level of prices fell by 46 percent, which made it hard for producers to generate enough profit to meet their commitments. Unemployment rose in urban areas, while many still in employment had to endure wage cuts. Southern and western regions were also badly hurt.

Many called on governments for relief measures and for protection from the less palatable legal consequences of depression, such as imprisonment for debt and forced sales of their property to recover moneys owed, but for the most part these calls were in vain. State governments were also struggling, many teetering on the edge of bankruptcy, and this limited their ability to help those suffering during the depression. Meanwhile, **Martin Van Buren**'s administration made it an item of policy to tell the people not to expect relief from governments, in the hope that such a stance would encourage Americans to return to more careful economic practices in future, less governed by credit and by the risky drive for personal advancement. This stance won the **Democrats** little favor and, although in the short term the panic may have helped their push for the **Independent Treasury** scheme in 1840, the administration did not manage to overcome the fact that it was in office when the panics and depression had occurred, this contributing to their defeat in the **election of 1840**.

PAPER CURRENCY. Paper money, issued by banks in the form of loans, made up a significant part of the circulating currency in Jacksonian America, despite strictly speaking lacking any legal status. Paper money was no doubt an essential lubricant for a commercializing economy, making it easier to complete transactions and loans than would have been the case with a metal-only currency. But in the mid-1830s the expansion of paper money, as part of a more general growth in banking (and some thought **overbanking**), became both a significant economic force and a political issue. Notes in circulation, supported by greater levels of specie in the American economy at the same time, rose from $10.2 million in 1833 to $149.2 million in 1837. Once the vital circumstance of plentiful foreign metal sustaining the level of note issue was removed, as it was in late 1836 and again in 1839, the resulting contraction in note issues caused major slumps in economic confidence and heralded the **panics of 1837 and 1839** respectively.

Even before this, though, many in the ranks of **Jacksonian Democracy** had adopted the "**hard money**" position of warning of the dangers of too much, and maybe even any, reliance on paper money. **Andrew Jackson** himself considered the issue of notes by state-chartered banks unconstitutional, while to others it was little more than a dangerous and fraudulent practice, feathering the nest of banks and corporations, while weakening the country's economic foundations. These analyses were translated into a series of measures to reduce the attractiveness of paper money as a means of exchange, as seen in the **Specie Circulars** and provisions within the 1836 **Deposit Act** and 1840 **Independent Treasury Act**. However, despite the impact of the panics and depression of the late 1830s, paper money remained an essential element of the American financial system for the rest of the period and beyond.

PARKMAN, FRANCIS (1823-1893). Parkman was one of the first great American narrative historians. Born in Boston and educated at Harvard, he had gained considerable experience while traveling in Europe and the American West. His trip on the **Oregon Trail** to Wyoming in 1846 generated his first great work, *The Oregon Trail* (1849), a combination of realism and **romanticism** and of history and personal journal.

PATENT OFFICE ACT. As part of a wider trend in **administrative reform** this act, passed in July 1836, completely rewrote U.S. patent law, regularized earlier arrangements on patents, and established the Patent Office as part of the State Department. The act created the post of commissioner to head the office, the first incumbent being Henry Ellsworth, and it also increased the office's staff to a level more appropriate to the amount of business demanded by an increasingly technological society. After 1836 the office had the duty of checking whether applications for patents met the requirements of patent law, including innovation, usefulness, and workability, and of issuing to successful applicants patents for 14 years, or 21 years if it were felt that a device faced particular problems of development and marketing. In 1839 the office took on a slightly different brief when it was authorized to disseminate seeds and useful **agricultural** information to farmers.

PAULDING, JAMES K. (1778-1860). Paulding hailed from the same upstate New York background as his friend **Washington Irving**, whose career Paulding's own as a writer and naval official almost mirrored. His literary output included the play *Lion of the West* (1831), *Westward Ho!* (1832), a *Life of Washington* (1835), the apologetic *Slavery in the United States* (1836), *The Old Continental* (1846), and *The Puritan and his Daughter* (1849). At the same time Paulding worked as secretary to the navy's Board of Commissioners and as a navy agent in New York between 1824 and 1838. These posts gave him the experience needed to serve as **Martin Van Buren**'s navy secretary between 1838 and 1841, but only after Irving had turned down an offer of the post. Paulding's other credential for the post was a loyalty to the **Democratic** Party and its controversial policies such as the **Independent Treasury**, an allegiance that also led him to write for the ***Democratic Review***.

PENNSYLVANIA MAINLINE SYSTEM. This **internal improvements** scheme, consisting of over 600 miles of **canals** and 100 miles of **railroad** by 1840, was Pennsylvania's answer to the **Erie Canal**, and was designed to tap the immediate, and indeed more far-flung, hinterland of Philadelphia. A railroad between that city and Columbia, completed in 1834, combined with a series of canals to create a continuous transportation system from Philadelphia to Pittsburgh, cutting the journey time between the two cities to four days. Other canal spurs, completed in 1831 and 1832 respectively, linked the Susquehanna and Delaware Rivers to the Mainline system. In all the system cost over $32 million to complete, at one point bringing the Pennsylvanian government to the point of defaulting on the interest payments on the bonds issued to finance the works, and it included some novel technological innovations, such as the Allegheny Portage railroad, which conveyed freight over the difficult mountainous region between two canal termini. Altogether the system spurred on the exchange of raw materials and manufactured goods between East and West, as well as encouraging the carriage, and hence production, of anthracite coal in Pennsylvania. The construction of a railroad all the way between Philadelphia and Pittsburgh, begun in 1846, promised to supplement if not challenge the significance of the Mainline.

"PENNY PRESS." Inspired by the publication of the *New York Sun* in 1833, costing only one cent, a number of other cheap newspapers emerged in New York in the 1830s and 1840s, including the *Herald*, the *New York Tribune*, and the *Times*. The development was made possible by mass printing methods such as rotary presses and cheaper wood pulp paper, which made larger circulations and print runs feasible. The "penny press" also expanded the definition of the age's newspaper audience with its choice of stories, adding tales of entertainment and of more salacious crime and violence to the usual fare of politics and business. As the population grew and spread, so examples of the "penny press" were also to be found in other eastern, and then western, cities.

PEOPLES' CONVENTION. This was a meeting of some 1,000 **Free Soilers** in Columbus, Ohio, in June 1848. Inspired by the likes of **Salmon Chase**, it attracted many who were wary of the two main parties' positions on the issue of **slavery** expansion and who preferred a clear-cut stance advocating the **Wilmot Proviso**. The convention came under the influence of 15 **Conscience Whigs**, rebelling against their party's nomination of **Zachary Taylor**, and their plea to convene another meeting at **Buffalo** was heeded. In this move lay the roots of the Free Soil coalition party in the **election of 1848**.

PERRY, MATTHEW (1794-1858). Perry was born in Newport, Rhode Island, and began a lifelong service in the navy when he enlisted in 1809. He was present on a number of significant diplomatic missions in the late 1820s and early 1830s, including treaty expeditions to Turkey and Russia and the mission to settle **spoliation claims** from Naples in 1832. Perry moved on to press for technological change during periods in the New York naval yard, where he became captain in 1837 and commodore in 1841, and in 1837 he commanded the U.S.S. *Fulton*, one of the navy's first steamships. After a period commanding the African squadron between 1843-45, where his duties included helping to police the illegal international **slave trade**, Perry rose to true prominence during the **Mexican War**, when as commander of the Gulf squadron he contributed to the strategy for capturing Vera Cruz prior to **Winfield Scott**'s landing there. He spent the rest of the war conducting further raids on Mexico's gulf ports.

"PET BANKS." *See* DEPOSIT BANKS.

PETITIONS, ANTI-SLAVERY. *See* GAG RULES.

PHILADELPHIA RIOTS. This series of armed conflicts between Protestants and mainly Irish **Catholics**, in May-June 1844, represented one of the most extreme examples of populist violence resulting from the cultural clash between **nativism** and **immigration** during the period. Outbreaks occurred predominantly among weavers in the city's manufacturing districts, with the Irish usually defending themselves against nativist-inspired attacks. Three Catholic churches and several blocks of Irish neighborhood housing were burned and the nativists even fired cannon on Irish rioters. Overall some 20 people died in the outbreak.

PHILLIPS, WENDELL (1811-1884). After studying at Harvard and Harvard Law School this Bostonian followed up a mediocre career as a lawyer by becoming one of the leading orators of the **abolitionist** movement, when he married a friend of **William Lloyd Garrison**. Phillips first came to prominence during a debate at Faneuil Hall during which he denounced the actions of the mob that had killed **Elijah Lovejoy** in 1837. A staunch Garrisonian, Phillips stood by both Garrison and the **American Anti-Slavery Society** after 1840, especially after his wife had been prevented from attending an international **anti-slavery** convention in London. Like Garrison he eschewed political action, denounced the Constitution, and held out little hope for abolitionists for as long the United States remained a union of northern and southern states. Indeed in his pamphlets, *The Constitution—A Proslavery Document* (1842) and *Can an Abolitionist Vote or Hold Office under the United States Constitution?* (1843), Phillips called for the dissolution of the United States. He showed a genuine concern for the fate of African-Americans, being prepared to take action to support fugitive slaves and attacking discriminatory race laws in Massachusetts. He also supported a range of other reform causes including **women's** rights, penal reform, the eight-hour day, and prohibition.

PIERCE, FRANKLIN (1804-1869). Even before rising to the heights of the presidency in the 1850s, this New Hampshire-born **Democratic** lawyer and politician had enjoyed a substantial public career. After studying at Bowdoin, where he befriended **Nathaniel Hawthorne**, and in the law office of **Levi Woodbury**, Pierce followed his father, the governor of his home state, into politics, sitting in the New Hampshire state legislature. In 1833 to 1837 he sat in the House and then moved to the Senate for the next six years, and in both demonstrated solid loyalty to his party, supporting **Andrew Jackson**'s stance in the **bank wars** and the **gag rules** and opposing federal funding of **internal improvements**. Pierce's time in the Senate was remarkable only for his being the youngest sitting Senator, most of his time spent voting the Jacksonian line and courting the friendship and support of the older, mainly southern, members of his party, as well as younger senators such as Jefferson Davis. On leaving the Senate, Pierce returned to his law practice for a short time before becoming the U.S. attorney in New Hampshire, although in 1846 he did decline **James Polk**'s offer of the position of attorney general. This period of law practice and loyal party service in his state continued into the 1850s, but was punctuated by his decision to enlist as a private in the **Mexican War** army. Pierce rose to the rank of brigadier general by 1847 and was injured during **Winfield Scott**'s march on Mexico City.

POE, EDGAR ALLAN (1809-1849). This renowned poet and author was born in Boston but was orphaned at the age of three and subsequently spent long periods living with his guardian in Virginia and Britain. After a debt-ridden career at the University of Virginia, Poe joined up in the army as an under-age recruit in 1827 and proved quite successful, rising to the highest rank possible for noncommissioned men, sergeant major. He did not replicate this success at West Point between 1830 and 1831 and was dismissed for neglect of duty. By this time he had already been writing poems for some years, and in 1831 he published two volumes of these. The next 18 years witnessed an ultimately tragic course for Poe's career, moving between New York, Baltimore, and Philadelphia, combining editorial work and critical writing for a series of magazines with his own fictional output. Among the publications he worked for were the *Southern Literary Messenger* between 1835 and 1837 and the Philadelphia *Burton's Gentleman's Magazine* and *Graham's Magazine.*

While Poe was a talented literary critic, one of the finest American purveyors of the genre ever, he is best remembered for his short-story writing, especially in the realms of the macabre. Examples of these were published collectively as *Tales of Grotesque and Arabesque* in 1839. But Poe also wrote a novel, the *Narrative of Arthur Gordon Pym*, in 1838 and was a pioneer in the genre of detective fiction, with his tales "Murders in the Rue Morgue" and "The Mystery of Marie Roget." He regarded himself first as a poet, writing prose only to survive financially, and his great poems include "The Raven" written in 1845. While pursuing his erratic career, Poe was also involved in a number of scandalous relationships, including his marriage to his 12-year-old cousin, and attempted suicide in 1848 before dying of alcohol poisoning in 1849.

POINSETT, JOEL (1779-1851). This South Carolinian had a wide range of interests that led to a number of different public careers. However, after diplomatic postings in the 1820s to the Argentine Republic, Chile, and Mexico, where he made good use of his skills in foreign languages, Poinsett rose to particular political prominence during the **Nullification crisis**. At this crucial moment for his state he remained a friend to **Andrew Jackson** and led the **Union** cause in South Carolina, being prepared to raise militia troops loyal to the federal government should the need arise. Four years later Poinsett became secretary of war under **Martin Van Buren**, serving a full four years during which he suggested controversial **militia reforms**, supervised the army in its many active commitments, from police actions along the **Canadian border** to the **Second Seminole War**, and also supported several exploring expeditions to the American frontier and across the seas. The scientific implications of these expeditions appealed to Poinsett's earlier interests and in retirement he returned to such pursuits as a founding supporter of the **Smithsonian Institution** and also as a backer of the privately chartered National Institute for the Promotion of Science. Of course his name is best remembered for the red-leaved plant, the poinsettia, which he brought back with him after his service in Mexico.

POLK, JAMES K. (1795-1849). Just as the Jacksonian age began with a man from Tennessee in the White House, so the era of **Manifest Destiny** drew to a close with another, **Young Hickory** following in the footsteps of **Old Hickory**. James Polk's career was filled with superlatives, having come to office as the first successful dark horse candidate and departing Washington for retirement, and what turned out to be a tragically early death, after a term that placed him among the most successful presidents on record.

Polk was a North Carolinian by birth and, after moving to Tennessee at the age of 11, returned to his native state to study at the University of North Carolina. He left that institution to take up legal training under **Felix Grundy** and was admitted to the bar in 1820. After marriage to **Sarah Childress** in 1824, Polk embarked on a political career which suggested that his later dark horse status arose only from his not being earlier linked to the nomination process rather than from any lack of political prominence.

Polk sat as a **Democrat** in the House of Representatives between 1825 and 1839, with stints as chair of the Ways and Means Committee at the crucial moment when the House considered the **removal of the federal deposits** and as speaker from 1835 to 1839. He left Washington to fight and win the election for Tennessee governor in 1839, only to lose the position in 1841 and fail to win it back two years later. But by this time he was already being considered for higher things: **Andrew Jackson** would have liked Polk to become **Martin Van Buren**'s running mate in the **election of 1840**, while in 1843 **John Tyler** offered him Cabinet rank as secretary of the navy, a position Polk declined. It was, then, perhaps not such a shock that, when the Democratic Party sought a pro-**Texas annexation** candidate with loyalty to and support from the **Jacksonian** faithful and from Jackson himself, they turned to Polk. After the close-fought **election campaign of 1844**, Polk entered the White House with less than a majority of the popular vote.

Polk's administration was notable for its stability and apparent lack of acrimony. After the frequent Cabinet changes of his predecessor's term, Polk's witnessed very few, four of the six members remaining in office for the whole term and the navy secretary and attorney general changing one and two times respectively, one of the latter being the switch of John Mason to the navy office. For the most part, though, it was Polk who mattered. He was a dominant figure within the administration, taking a close personal interest in the business of all the Cabinet offices, but especially the State and War Departments that dealt with the crucial international issues that occupied so much of his presidency. He kept a close eye on expenditure and generally ran his presidency as a very tight ship. Only matters of patronage, exacerbated by increasing factional rivalries within the Democratic Party, posed any significant problems for the administration.

The achievements of the Polk administration were many and, when compared with intentions stated early in the presidency, account for the usually positive assessment of his time in office. In 1846 Congress passed two financial measures of lasting significance: the **Independent Treasury**, reviving the Van Buren policy that had been overturned under Tyler, only this time laying the foundations of a system that would last well into the 20th century; and the **1846 tariff** which remained in force until 1857. In addition the 1846 Warehouse Act eased the procedures and immediate financial demands upon merchants importing goods into the United States. Polk also maintained the spirit of Jackson, if not of all Americans in this era of **expansionism**, by using his **veto** against several bills granting federal funds for **internal improvements**.

Of course, expansion is what Polk's term is most renowned for, witnessing as it did the near completion of the main continental landmass of the United States. Polk had won the election on the back of support for Texas annexation, and although this had pretty well been settled by the time he entered office, he still helped the process along. First he left in place Tyler's decision to press for immediate annexation rather than to delay matters until another treaty was negotiated with Texas. Then Polk used careful diplomacy on the ground in Texas to ensure as smooth a transition to statehood as possible. While the final steps to statehood might have been smooth for Texas itself, they did bring with them increasingly tense relations with Mexico, which would eventually spiral downward to war in 1846. However the motives behind the **Mexican War** and its overall morality are assessed, it cannot be denied that the war allowed Polk once again to fulfill significant ambitions, both in the resolution of the immediate triggers for the war, the Texas-Mexican border and unpaid debts, and in the acquisition of substantial territories in **New Mexico** and **California**. Finally Polk used a combination of caution and brinkmanship to bring a largely satisfactory conclusion to the long dispute with Britain over the **Oregon** territory boundary in 1846.

While the successful acquisition of territories represents the most significant achievement of Polk's presidency in terms of its contribution to the long-term development of the United States, the final months of his term witnessed the failure to deal with some of the consequences of success. Bitter debates over the extension of **slavery** blocked arrangements for the territorial organization of the lands recently acquired from Mexico, while the same debates delayed any such arrangement for Oregon until late in the day. In the course of these disagreements lay the beginning of the end of the **second party system** that had been so effective in sheltering the political establishment from the growing storm of **sectionalism**. It was probably for the good of Polk's own sense of well-being, and certainly of his historical reputation, that his decision to hold office for one term only, and then his early death, removed from him the need to deal with these developments and to witness the break-up of the Union that they precipitated.

POLK, SARAH CHILDRESS (1803-1891). Sarah Childress was born into a wealthy and socially prominent Tennessee family and married the rising politician **James Polk** in 1824. Remaining childless, she was able to accompany her husband throughout his political career, whether at Washington or during his time as governor of their home state. While her influence was not always guaranteed to assist her husband's career, especially when she figured prominently among the Washington wives who shunned **Peggy Eaton** during the **Eaton Affair**, her contribution to the White House routine was invaluable. As well as running the social side of the presidential office, although not necessarily to everyone's taste as she insisted upon strict Sabbath observance and banned dancing, she also helped to communicate political news to her husband.

POPULAR SOVEREIGNTY. Alongside the **Wilmot Proviso** and an extension of the **Missouri Compromise line**, popular sovereignty was the third major method proposed by which Congress could determine the status, slave or free, of new western territories. In point of fact the adoption of popular sovereignty by Congress would actually take specific decisions out of the national government's hands and leave them instead for the people within each territory to make for themselves. This sense of allowing the local democratic will to prevail proved particularly attractive to the **Democratic** Party in the late 1840s, especially since the uncertainty as to each territory's future decision would allow the party to appeal to supporters in both **sec-**

tions of the nation with the claim that popular sovereignty would result in a territorial settlement acceptable to them and not to the other section. So then popular sovereignty came to be associated most closely with leading Democrats.

The idea was first put forward in explicit terms by **Lewis Cass** in December 1847 in debates on **California, Oregon,** and **New Mexico** and in his **Nicholson letter**, and formed part of his stance during the **election of 1848**. By the end of 1847 **James Polk** and the majority of his Cabinet were also beginning to lean toward popular sovereignty as the most suitable compromise on the issue. However, the proposal held within it the seeds of considerable controversy, most notably over its ambiguity about the precise stage in a territory's development at which it would be applied, and of course it would become one of the more explosive issues of the deepening sectional crisis of the 1850s when applied to territories already thought to have been organized by other methods.

POST OFFICE REFORM. As befitted its importance as one of the biggest employers of federal office-holders and as the body responsible for some 15 percent of the federal budget, the Post Office received considerable attention amidst other efforts at **administrative reform** throughout the period. In part this was also a reflection of the increased demands made on the Office by the **expansion** of the United States and the wider settlement of its lands.

The major figure in the early reform of the Office was **Amos Kendall**, who became postmaster general in 1835. Although **Andrew Jackson** had earlier recognized the need for some change by according the position Cabinet status in 1829, Kendall's predecessor, **William Barry**, had proved at best inefficient and at worst corrupt in his oversight of the department. However, within only a few months Kendall had applied more careful administrative methods and better checks against corrupt practices to enable him to wipe out the Office's debt of about $600,000. Within two years the Office was turning a profit even bigger than that figure. But Kendall was also keen that the Office be reformed on paper as well as through the energy of the incumbent postmaster general and so in 1836 he helped to draft the Post Office Act, which provided for greater oversight of the Office's revenue and expenditure, both by the Treasury which received its funds and audited its accounts and by Congress which made appropriations to it. Kendall remained postmaster general for most of **Martin Van Buren**'s term as well, overseeing an increase in the

postal network by over half, so that by 1841 its annual mileage had
reached 36 million miles.

Congress at that time turned down some other proposals that
Kendall made, notably a reduction in the rate of postage for letters, an
increase for newspapers, and a restriction of the federal government's
special franking privilege to the executive branch alone. However,
the report of George Plitt, a postal worker sent by Kendall to investigate postal reform in Britain, did influence the work of Post Office
reform in the 1840s.

While again Congress initially turned down calls for a reduction
of postal rates, fearing that it would cut the revenue of an Office already in debt again during the hard times following the **panic of
1839**, by 1845 there were signs that the deficit was falling and Congress now proved sympathetic to Postmaster General **Charles Wickliffe**'s request for a reduction in rates, including it in the Postal Reform Act of that year. That act also authorized federal subsidies to
steamship lines carrying the mail between American and certain foreign ports and gave to the Post Office jurisdiction over **Samuel
Morse**'s **telegraph** line between Washington and Baltimore (although this would only last for a year in practice). In the meantime
Wickliffe's term in the post had witnessed a continued growth in the
postal network, with the opening of some 700 new post offices, and
he had also tried to assume Post Office control over private mail
companies that had arisen in competition to the Office. An idea cop-
ied from one of those companies provided a postscript to reform in
the era, when in July 1847 the Post Office introduced its first postage
stamps, to be paid for by the sender, replacing the system by which
the recipient paid for postage. *See also* INCENDIARY MAIL; SAB-
BATARIANISM.

POWERS, HIRAM (1805-1873). Powers was born in Vermont but
moved to Ohio in 1817, beginning work in a mechanics workshop. In
Cincinnati he made his name sculpting figurines for the Western Museum and he later moved to Washington in the winters of 1834-35
and 1835-36 to develop his skills as a serious sculpting portraitist. He
spent those months modeling busts of prominent Americans, including **Andrew Jackson, John Calhoun, John Quincy Adams, Daniel
Webster, Martin Van Buren**, and **John Marshall**. In 1837 Powers
left America for permanent residence in Florence, Italy, producing in
1845 a nude statue of a Greek slave that both scandalized and excited
his American audience. The most prominent examples of his work in

America were statues of Thomas Jefferson and Benjamin Franklin for the Capitol in Washington, D.C.

PREEMPTION. This was a **land policy** favored by those more sympathetic to the fast opening of western lands by genuine settlers. Preemption would guarantee squatters favorable terms when buying land they had already settled on and improved, most notably the right to purchase it direct rather than being forced to bid against others for it at auction. Congress granted preemption to squatters on surveyed lands on five separate occasions in the early Jacksonian era, including acts of 1830, 1838, and 1840, before the 1841 Preemption Act, passed in the **special session** of Congress of that year, established preemption terms that would remain in effect for the next 50 years. Again applying only to surveyed lands, and not to unsurveyed or Indian reservation land, it allowed any squatter to buy 160 acres at a minimum price of $1.25 per acre. The act specifically limited the amount of land that could be bought by any one land agent, in order to discourage land speculation companies from dominating land purchases.

PRIGG VS. PENNSYLVANIA. This Supreme Court ruling of 1842 left an ambiguous legacy for the contentious **sectional** issue of runaway **slaves.** On the one hand, it favored the rights of slave-holders by ruling as unconstitutional a Pennsylvania law prohibiting the return of fugitive slaves, because it directly contravened the federal Fugitive Slave law. But at the same time the ruling denied that any state had a responsibility to actively assist in the enforcement of that law, which encouraged many northern states to pass personal liberty laws forbidding state authorities from helping federal officers to implement the Fugitive Slave law.

PRINCETON, U.S.S. At the request of Secretary of the Navy **Abel Upshur** Congress had authorized the construction of the U.S.S. *Princeton* as the world's first steam-driven iron warship with an under-water propeller. She was also to be armed with the world's largest single-cast iron gun, nicknamed "The Peacemaker." Pride in the achievement turned to tragedy on 28 February 1844, when a special gala cruise took place to mark the official launch of the vessel. The third firing of the gun brought a terrible misfire killing many of those standing on one side of it. Abel Upshur, now secretary of state, and his replacement in the Navy Department, **Thomas Gilmer**, were among the several leading government and military officials who died in the explosion, while **John Tyler** survived only because he was below decks at the time. The incident, and particularly the death of Upshur, may well have altered the course of political and diplomatic events in the mid-1840s as Tyler was forced into yet another Cabinet reshuffle, including the introduction of **John Calhoun**, who as secretary of state now had responsibility for the vital issue of **Texas annexation**.

"PROCLAMATION TO THE PEOPLE OF SOUTH CAROLINA." *See* NULLIFICATION PROCLAMATION.

PRO-SLAVERY. In the face of **anti-slavery** activity of various kinds, whether in the actions of slave rebels like **Nat Turner** or in the developing **abolitionist** movement, southerners from many walks of life began to adopt a principled defense of the institution of **slavery** in this period. Pro-slavery thinking had at its core the idea that slavery was at the very heart of southern society: to some the peculiar institution was an economic necessity; in the eyes of others it helped to civilize a primitive people fit for no other condition; for others still, slavery was a means to a racially-defined equality, in which all whites could at least rest assured of being raised above the slave masses. Paradoxically other pro-slavery ideologues also claimed that slavery was the bastion of an aristocracy of talent and virtue and of traditional values in the face of the type of riot and disorder that democracy seemed to encourage in the rest of American society. As well as history, economics, and politics, the pro-slavery tradition drew heavily upon the Bible to support its stance, in response to the strongly moralistic tone of the abolitionist message. Southern Methodists and Baptists denounced as false Christians their once fellow evangelists in the North who now espoused abolition. Southerners believed it to be their duty to instruct masters and slaves to make slave society even better and to demonstrate, in part by converting the African race through slavery, the superiority of a Christian civilization.

Pro-slavery thought formed an important part of a developing schism in ideas between North and South in the 1830s and then of a growing **sectionalism** in politics in the 1840s, as it inspired a more energetic assertion of the right of slave states to be heard in national debates on issues such as the organization of territories.

PROTECTION. *See* TARIFF, PROTECTIVE.

PUEBLA. This Mexican town was captured as part of **Winfield Scott's Mexican War** march on Mexico City, on 15 May 1847. It marked the successful completion of half the journey from the port of Vera Cruz to the capital and Scott remained there for the better part of three months for recuperation and reinforcement before moving further toward the capital.

– Q –

QUALLAH BATTOO. In spring 1832 the U.S. frigate *Potomac* attacked and destroyed the Sumatran village of Quallah Battoo, killing some 100 native Malays. Although the frigate's captain had exceeded his orders with the degree of force he used, the action had been sanctioned by **Andrew Jackson** as a response to an attack by natives against a Salem ship involved in the pepper trade the previous year, in which three Americans had been killed. The president received political criticism for the resort to force and for the disproportionate nature of the response, notwithstanding the captain's clear breach of orders.

QUIDOR, JOHN (1801-1881). Quidor was born in New York State and early in his life trained to be a painter. He was particularly famous for paintings based on historical and literary themes drawn from works by the likes of Cervantes, **James Fenimore Cooper**, and **Washington Irving**. Between 1828 and 1839 Quidor made his living depicting episodes from Irving and Cooper's books, including representations of Ichabod Crane and the Headless Horseman and several studies of Leatherstocking. In these paintings humans were often caricatured figures while natural features such as trees and rocks took on an almost animated appearance. In 1836, after the **New York City fire** of 1835, Quidor moved to Illinois to continue this work.

QUINCY, JOSIAH (1772-1864). Prior to the Jacksonian era, Quincy had been a lawyer and important statesman and reformer in Boston, following stints in the Massachusetts legislature and House of Representatives with six years as mayor of the city between 1823 and 1829. In 1829 he returned to his alma mater to become president of Harvard College, reforming the curriculum and faculty and instilling a greater level of discipline among the student body. He held the post until 1845, writing a bicentennial history of the college in 1836.

QUINTUPLE TREATY. *See* SLAVE TRADE.

– R –

RAILROADS. Railroads became an increasingly important form of **internal improvement** during this period, joining with roads, maritime vessels, and **canals** in fostering the **transportation revolution**. The first railroads consisted of horse-drawn wheeled vehicles used on tracks in mines, but as early as 1828 construction of the first railroad proper began with the **Baltimore and Ohio**. When that railroad started carrying passengers in 1830 the nation only had 23 miles of track, but within five years this had risen to 1,098 miles, by 1840 to 2,800 miles, and, despite a dip in construction between 1842 and 1848, to 5,996 miles by the latter year, with all the eastern coastal and most midwestern states having at least some stretch of railroad within their borders. By that time the total mileage was already double that of canals, reflecting the relative ease of building railroads. However, for the most part railroad traffic in this era was limited to the carriage of passengers, as the relative expense of carrying goods by train wagons compared to barges meant that only in the 1850s did railroads start to undermine canal traffic in those areas well served by canals.

In this first period of railroad construction Americans began to develop certain distinctive approaches that contrasted with those in the original place of inspiration for railroads, Britain. American engineers tended to seek out cheap and easy construction techniques, with sharp curves, steep gradients, and wooden construction materials (apart from the rails), and they developed locomotives to suit.

At this stage the development was anything but coordinated, as community competed with community, state with state, as well as railroad against canal and other railroad companies to produce a piecemeal spread of track systems, often with different gauges that hampered the emergence of a fully integrated rail network. The whole process was funded by a combination of private and public investment. Half the money came from state governments and, especially after the **panic of 1837**, from local sources. However, the federal government did assist, by imposing lower **tariff** duties on imported railroad iron, by allowing military engineers to participate in the surveying and construction of lines, and by awarding mail contracts to railroad companies in 1838. *See also* PENNSYLVANIA MAINLINE SYSTEM.

RALEIGH LETTER. This represented **Henry Clay**'s first attempt to make public his views on the issue of **Texas annexation** during his presidential candidacy in the **election of 1844**. Probably issued in agreement with **Martin Van Buren** as a result of a cross-party attempt to keep the question of Texas out of the election, Clay warned that annexation of Texas without Mexico's agreement would lead to war with that country and as such was a dangerous and inexpedient measure. He attributed its emergence solely to the ambitions of **John Tyler** and his hangers-on, desperate for a means to create an election-winning issue. Together with the **Whig** platform's silence on expansion, the letter suggested that under a Clay presidency there would be little chance of immediate annexation. As the developing campaign demonstrated the popularity of Texas, producing a pro-annexation **Democratic** opponent rival in the form of **James Polk** instead of the expected Van Buren, Clay would later amend his stance in his **Alabama letters**.

"RED FOX OF KINDERHOOK." This nickname for President **Martin Van Buren** derived from a number of personal references, including his home, his sandy-colored hair, and his reputation, especially among his enemies, for a sly and devious approach to political activity.

REMOVAL OF FEDERAL DEPOSITS. This action, contemplated as early as September 1832 in the wake of the **bank bill veto** but finally implemented in 1833, formed part of **Andrew Jackson**'s developing project of untying the link between the federal government and the **Second Bank of the United States**. In some respects the decision to stop depositing federal revenues with branches of the Bank was as vital an action as the veto itself in influencing the short-term economic fortunes of the country and the longer-term development of the **second party system**.

Jackson decided to end the Bank's responsibility for receiving deposits of federal revenue in order to weaken the Bank's economic influence and to undermine **Nicholas Biddle**'s ability to use that influence to prevail upon Congress to pass another re-charter bill that would override any further presidential veto. The question that remained was where to deposit federal revenue in future. The Jacksonians were several years of difficult political wrangling away from taking the logical final step to a system of **Independent Treasury** facilities to hold the deposits, and so, for lack of any alternative, Jackson had to overcome his innate suspicion of all banks and agree that selected state banks would receive and hold federal revenue in the future.

Initially **Amos Kendall** negotiated agreements with seven **deposit banks**, or "pet banks" as political opponents began to call them, to receive the federal deposits and, after the removal of two secretaries of the treasury, **Louis McLane** and William Duane, effectively for refusing to comply, a third, **Roger Taney**, finally implemented the "removal." Contrary to the impression left by the label given to the policy, no deposits were actually "removed" from the Second Bank's keeping, but rather its existing deposits were used to defray federal expenditure while any new deposits went to the chosen seven.

So began years of political debate and historical controversy about the motives behind the removal and indeed the whole course of Jacksonian banking policy. Some historians, notably Bray Hammond, point to the facts that deposit banks were resorted to at all, and that those initially selected were run by sympathizers of the **Democratic Party**, as proof that the Bank veto and subsequent policies were inspired by a state bank driven campaign to free the economy from the restraint of the Second Bank. Although this may have been the motivation of some Democrats, most historians are now agreed that **Jacksonian Democracy**'s attack on the Bank was at heart the first part of a wider attack on all banks, as would be revealed by the trajectory of the party's policies at both state and federal level into the later 1830s and beyond.

Where there is no doubt is that the removal policy represented a crucial element in the developing party battles of the mid-1830s. Jackson's political opponents were able to appeal to those who felt disquiet at the measure on a range of levels. To some the argument was purely economic as they warned against the implications of removing from the Second Bank a substantial proportion of its resources and with them its ability to regulate the economy effectively. They also pointed to the fact that a House report had previously declared the deposits safe in the care of the Bank.

However, the significance of this report perhaps lay even more in its political implications. The fact that Jackson had chosen to ignore the report's findings, combined with his treatment of two secretaries of the treasury and, indeed, with his decision to work through the Treasury in the first place, a department Congress claimed special authority over, aroused fears about the president's exercise of power. Indeed, it could be said that removal, alongside Jackson's earlier use of the **veto** and his stance during the **Nullification crisis**, created the whole issue of **executive usurpation** that did so much to strengthen the ranks of the **Whig** opposition party. It was this that led the Senate to pass formal resolutions **censuring** the president, ushering in a bitter period in which his supporters and opponents sought to **expunge** or defend the attack on his reputation. Jackson's own defense, that his actions were justified by the recent election that stood almost as a plebiscite in favor of attacks on the Bank, held sway in the House, where his supporters succeeded in passing resolutions rejecting both re-charter of the Bank and a restoration of the deposits. In this way, the removal of the deposits became almost the key issue that determined an individual's political loyalty.

Finally, removal had a degree of economic impact. Biddle retaliated against the removal policy by flexing the Bank's muscles. In part a sensible response to the looming reduction of its reserves, the resulting contraction in its loans in the winter of 1833-34 caused the temporary economic downturn known as the **panic of 1834**. That Biddle hoped this would inspire a business and popular outcry for restoration of the deposits and for a new charter for the Bank is revealed by the fact that he contracted loans by almost double the amount that was demanded from the Bank's branches by other banks in the form of drafts. Removal was also blamed, by some, for **overbanking** and overextension of credit in the mid-1830s, and hence indirectly for the **panic of 1837**. However, although removal did give large amounts of federal money to less well-regulated and managed state banks, which they then used as a foundation for greater levels of note issue through loans, the main impetus behind the expansion in banking were changing patterns of international flows of metallic currency.

RENWICK, JAMES (1818-1895). This architect and engineer was educated at Columbia and was also inspired by his father, and namesake, an engineer who encouraged his son's innovative designs incorporating new technology and materials. James Jr. made his name with the plans and construction of Grace Church in New York City, between 1843 and 1846, as well as with the Congregational Church in the city's Union Square in 1846. Although mainly involved in the design of churches, Renwick also produced a number of important commercial and public buildings, including the commission for the **Smithsonian Institution** in 1848-49. Here the red, castle-like appearance perpetuated his preference for a Gothic style that challenged the neo-classicism of most of the prevailing Washington architecture.

RESACA DE LA PALMA, BATTLE OF. Like its sister battle at **Palo Alto** the day before, this military action happened before news of the American declaration formally beginning the **Mexican War** had reached **Zachary Taylor**. On 9 May 1846 Taylor pressed home the advantage won at Palo Alto and crossed the Mexican border for another victory which helped to lay the foundations for his later successes in the northern Mexican theater of the war.

RETRENCHMENT. **Andrew Jackson** instituted a policy of retrenchment of federal government spending as part of his broader goals of **administrative reform** and in particular reduction of the **national debt**. With the specific aim of not allowing expenditure to exceed revenue in any given session, the administration made temporary savings at the start of Jackson's presidency by reducing the number of treasury officials, which had the dual effect of slashing the wage bill and lowering the potential for corruption, and by making savings in the Navy Department. However, such an effort proved hard to sustain as the level of administrative business increased and within two years most federal departments were experiencing a rise in expenditure again. Luckily for Jackson, revenue increased during this period as well, which allowed him to fulfill his ambition of reducing the debt. Later in the 1830s **Martin Van Buren** treated the **panic of 1839** as a wake-up call to the American people to force them to exercise retrenchment in their own and in their governments' affairs. By withdrawing from the **credit**-driven expansion of the mid-1830s the people would reduce their own indebtedness and the economy's exposure to uncontrollable fluctuations.

RHETT, ROBERT BARNWELL (1800-1876). Rhett was a South Carolinian politician and supporter of **John Calhoun**. After a time at Beaufort College and some legal training he went on to represent one of most densely **slave**-populated areas of the American South, first in the state legislature to 1833, and then, after a period as state attorney general, in the House of Representatives between 1837 and 1849. Throughout Rhett adopted a strict **states' rights** stance, as befitted someone who feared the potential use of federal power against the peculiar institution. Not surprisingly he supported all the moves for **nullification** and even resigned from the South Carolina legislature when it accepted the **compromise tariff in 1833**. His support for Calhoun and a low **tariff** led Rhett to repeated expressions of an extreme states' rights position, and when Calhoun failed to win the **Democratic** Party's presidential nomination in 1844 so worried was

Rhett that **James Polk** would not be safe on the tariff that he issued the famous Bluffton proclamation demanding that South Carolina should secede if the federal government continued to ignore the state's interests. As the acquisition of new territories changed the sectional agenda in the mid-1840s Rhett took the fairly predictable position of attacking the **Wilmot Proviso** and indeed avowing that Congress did not have any power at all to legislate on the future status, free or slave, of the territories.

RHODE ISLAND, NEW CONSTITUTION. In the wake of **Dorr's Rebellion** Rhode Island produced a new state constitution that was eventually accepted by the majority of the people. While it improved somewhat the representative apportionment given to the state's urban areas, its main provisions brought about **suffrage extension**. Property-less native-born U.S. citizens would in future be able to vote in federal and state-wide elections if they paid a registration tax of one dollar, while recent immigrants had to own property equivalent to $134 before they could vote in such elections. Non-property owners and non-taxpayers would still not be allowed to vote in local elections.

RICE. Rice was a significant crop in the development of **agricultural** units along the creeks and river inlets of the South Atlantic coastal states of South Carolina, Georgia, and northern Florida. It was grown to produce starch and was mainly consumed by the domestic market, although around 25 percent found markets in Europe and the Caribbean. It required a great amount of capital outlay and intensive labor use, making it almost entirely the business of plantations worked by **slave** labor. The late 1830s and 1840s were particularly successful years for the production of rice.

RICHMOND ENQUIRER. This newspaper, edited by **Thomas Ritchie**, the head of the **Richmond Junto**, became one of the leading organs of the early **Jacksonian** movement, and helped to cement the coalition that led to **Andrew Jackson**'s **election in 1828**. The *Enquirer* remained loyal to both Jackson and **Martin Van Buren** despite some difficult times during the **Nullification crisis** and debates over the **Independent Treasury**. However, when Van Buren announced his opposition to immediate **Texas annexation** in 1844, the *Enquirer* called on him to withdraw his candidacy for the **election of 1844**, and when he did not, abandoned him in favor of **James Polk**. It also called on **John Tyler**, whom it praised for his efforts to annex

Texas, to end his own challenge for election and to throw in his lot with Polk and the regular **Democratic** Party.

RICHMOND JUNTO. This political "machine," headed by **Thomas Ritchie**, publisher of the *Richmond Enquirer*, dominated Virginia **Democratic** politics for more than 25 years. The Junto assumed a **states' rights** stance on most issues, which attracted it to the growing coalition behind **Andrew Jackson** in the late 1820s. Indeed many regard its alliance with the **Albany Regency** as the heart of the developing **Jacksonian** movement. The Junto continued supporting Jackson for the term of his presidency and, despite a strong challenge from the Virginian **Conservative Democrat William Rives** in the late 1830s, remained loyal to **Martin Van Buren** during his presidency, before switching its allegiance to **James Polk** in 1844.

RIPLEY, GEORGE (1802-1880). This important literary critic and social reformer was born in Massachusetts and attended both Harvard and its Divinity School. Although ordained as a **Unitarian** minister, Ripley revealed himself in writings published in the *Christian Examiner* to be even more liberal than most other Unitarians were and he went on to become one of the founding **Transcendentalists** in 1836. Together with **Margaret Fuller** he established *The Dial* in 1840, and, after leaving the church in 1841, was the leading light behind the **Brook Farm** community. During his time there, from 1841 to 1847, he oversaw its transition from fairly liberal Transcendentalism to a much stricter Fourierite approach in which members were subjected to a more disciplined series of routines. He also edited the Fourierite magazine, *The Harbinger*, between 1845 and 1849.

RITCHIE, THOMAS (1778-1854). Ritchie worked as a schoolteacher and bookseller before becoming a journalist, a career move that would see him rise to become one of the most important local political organizers in the country. In 1804 he became editor of the *Richmond Enquirer*, a position he would hold for the next 41 years. At the same time he was a leading member of the **Richmond Junto**, and used his influence to take Virginian Republican **Democrats** on a journey through support for **William Crawford** to advocacy of **Andrew Jackson**. Indeed, together with **Martin Van Buren** and the **Albany Regency** Ritchie helped to form the vital North-South coalition that sustained Jackson in the **election of 1828** and in the early years of his presidency. As a Democratic loyalist he supported Jackson in his attacks on federally-financed **internal improvements** and on the **Second Bank**, while his cautiously moderate **states' rights** position caused Ritchie to stick by the Union and Jackson during the **Nullification crisis** when others were abandoning the president in horror at his apparent shift to **unionism**.

When Van Buren became president, Ritchie found it harder to keep the Junto's influence strong in the face of the opposition of **Conservative Democrats** like **William Rives** to the **Independent Treasury**, but he remained loyal to the president nonetheless. Ritchie and Van Buren's political relationship eventually foundered, however, on the issue of **Texas annexation** in 1844. The Virginian editor supported annexation and wanted a Democratic candidate who could deliver it. When Van Buren expressed his opposition to it, Ritchie abandoned him in favor of **James Polk**, after also helping to persuade **John Tyler** to drop his own candidacy. Ritchie's reward was the invitation to create the Polk administration's newspaper organ at the capital, the *Washington Union*, and he went on to become an important channel of communication to and from the new president.

RIVERS AND HARBORS CONVENTION. In summer 1847 some 20,000 Americans attended a convention in Chicago to call for continued federal support for **internal improvements** projects. Despite **James Polk**'s vetoes of **harbors and rivers** legislation in 1846 and 1847, and despite the absence from Chicago of some leading **Democrats**, such as **Lewis Cass**, signaling their opposition to federally funded improvements, the convention demonstrated that there was still considerable public support for such measures. The convention also spent some time considering the idea of a transcontinental **railroad**.

RIVES, WILLIAM CABELL (1793-1868). Rives was Virginian **Democratic** politician whose course seriously endangered the unity of his party in the late 1830s. After graduating from William and Mary, he received legal training from among others Thomas Jefferson and developed a taste for political service. In the run-up to the **election of 1828** Rives helped **Thomas Ritchie** organize Virginia for **Andrew Jackson**, and his reward was an appointment as U.S. minister to France from 1829 to 1832. It was he who negotiated the important first deal on **spoliation claims**, even if it would be several years before the French government actually paid up. On his return he embarked upon a period of interrupted terms in the Senate, between 1832 and 1834, 1836 and 1839, and 1841 and 1845.

Initially Rives proved a loyal Democrat, backing the attacks on the **American System**, **internal improvements**, and the **Second Bank**. He even resigned in 1834 rather than having to follow his state legislature's orders to back the **censure** of President Jackson for his **removal of the federal deposits**. Considered a vice-presidential possibility for 1836, Rives was actually offered the post of secretary of war by **Martin Van Buren**, a post he declined. But within a few months Rives found himself completely at odds with the new administration over its proposed financial policies: he opposed the **Specie Circular** and Van Buren's efforts to sustain it during the panic year of 1837; but in particular he was hostile to the **Independent Treasury**, being a fervent supporter of state banks and worrying that the policy would be so disastrous as to allow **Whigs** to push through a new national bank, his worst fear of all. And so began an odd alliance, in which he led other **Conservative Democrats** into backing Whig opposition to the Independent Treasury.

After an uncertain couple of years in which he lost his Senate re-election battle in 1838 but then won again in 1840, he found kinship with **John Tyler**, the **States' Rights Whig** whose own attack on a new national bank Rives supported. Indeed as part of Tyler's "**corporal's guard**" he defended the **bank vetoes of 1841**. Ironically, by 1844 his desire for moderation on the question of **Texas annexation** led him to support the pro-Bank **Henry Clay**'s election bid.

ROGERS, ISAIAH (1800-1869). Born in Massachusetts, Rogers was the man who replaced Charles Bulfinch as Boston's leading architect. He made his name with works such as the Tremont Theater in 1827 and the Tremont House hotel in 1829, and then pursued his profession in New York, Cincinnati, and Washington. In the latter he served as supervising architect at the Treasury Department. New York was the site of probably his most famous work, including the Astor House hotel (1832-36), the Bank of America building (1835), the Merchants' Exchange (1836-42), and the Astor Place Opera House in 1847. Rogers also designed the Harvard Astronomical Observatory.

ROMANTICISM. Romanticism was a broad cultural movement, international in its spread and influencing different strands of artistic endeavor. Flourishing in the late 18th century through to the middle of the 19th, it acted as a corrective to Enlightenment values of reason and order by emphasizing personal sensibility, imagination, and the value of individual experience. In American art the **Hudson River School** was the foremost manifestation, reflecting Romanticism's drive for reflecting the primitive force of real nature. Developing trends in architecture, and in particular a Gothic style, as exemplified by the work of **James Renwick**, also fitted in with a Romantic admiration for the Middle Ages in preference to Classical examples. In thought and literature the emphasis on self and sensibility was reflected in the **transcendentalist** movement, while the work of **Nathaniel Hawthorne** and **Edgar Allan Poe** emphasized the more introspective and at times darkly macabre side of human nature. **Washington Irving** and **James Fenimore Cooper** also demonstrated to varying degrees a Romantic approach to landscape and the human spirit.

ROSS, JOHN. *See* COOWESCOOWE.

ROTATION OF OFFICE. This was the principle that there should be a frequent turnover of public office-holders, in order to guarantee a better, more democratic government by limiting the possibility for corruption and avoiding the creation of an entrenched group of officials. Although **Andrew Jackson**'s renowned commitment to the pursuit of this principle is probably exaggerated, he did make genuine attempts to remove known corrupt officials early in his administration, and went on to replace nearly half of the officers appointed directly by the president and to oversee the removal of around 10 percent of all federal officers. Of course, while rotation fitted in with his more general assault on the privileged in the name of the many, he was also guided in this by the natural and politically realistic desire to reward his party faithful. *See also* SPOILS SYSTEM.

– S –

SABBATARIANISM. This was an **evangelically** inspired moral reform stance, calling for an end to the exercise on Sundays of all practices worldly and commercial. Sabbatarianism had been advocated by **Congregationalists** and Presbyterians as early as the 1810s but it was given extra force by the surge of revivalism of the late 1820s, when groups like the General Union for the Promotion of the Christian Sabbath, and individuals like Ezra Stiles Ely and Jeremiah Evarts, came to the fore. For example, in 1829 Ely called on **Andrew Jackson** not to choose a Sunday to begin his journey from Tennessee to Washington D.C. to take up the presidency.

The leading political manifestation of Sabbatarianism was the campaign to get the federal government to stop the mail service on Sundays, as sympathetic reformers became one of the first groups to use the pressure group technique of petitioning to achieve their aim. Along with the treatment of Native Americans, the push for Sabbath observance became one of the cultural issues that separated the political parties to some extent. For instance, although Jackson had indeed delayed the journey to his inauguration until a Monday, generally he and his supporters were cool to the aims and demeanor of the Sabbatarians. Opponents of the movement, accusing its supporters of suggesting an infringement of the constitutional separation of church and state, tended to lie more with the **Democratic** Party, with future Vice-President **Richard Mentor Johnson** to the fore. Meanwhile, like many other reform issues Sabbatarianism appealed more to members of the **National Republican** and later the **Whig** parties. At this time, though, it was the opposition to Sabbatarianism that prevailed.

SALMON, ROBERT (ca. 1775 - ca. 1848). This British-born painter was famous for his maritime scenes, in particular those depicting the seafront of Boston, which he had adopted as his home town in 1828. So accurate were Salmon's representations that historians have often used his work as detailed historical evidence, while in his own time insurance companies employed him to paint pictures of ship fires to help with their claims procedures.

SAN JACINTO, BATTLE OF. Fought on 21 April 1836, the battle of San Jacinto proved to be the conclusive last engagement of the **Texan independence** struggle. Although in retreat and considerably outnumbered, **Sam Houston**'s army, pretty well the last hope of the Texas cause, made a surprise attack on the army of **Santa Anna** and succeeded, at the cost of only nine of their own number, in killing or capturing almost the entire Mexican force of about 1,500. Santa Anna himself was among those captured and as a result he was prevailed upon to sign a peace treaty giving Texas its independence.

SANTA ANNA, ANTONIO LOPEZ DE (1794-1876). The foremost Mexican general and frequent president of his country was twice involved in major matters involving the future state of Texas and the United States. After supporting Mexico's own independence struggle against Spain, Santa Anna had risen to a position of virtual dictatorship by 1833 and it was he who led Mexican opposition to **Texan in-**

dependence in 1835-36. Although successful in overwhelming the Texan garrison at the **Alamo**, his defeat and capture at **San Jacinto** resulted in acceptance of Texan independence, although he, like many other Mexicans, was never fully reconciled to the idea. Certainly on his return to the presidency in 1841 after a period of retirement, Santa Anna set the tone for the next two years by threatening war against the United States should **John Tyler**'s administration press for **Texas annexation**. Although practically a dictator again by 1844 Santa Anna was deposed the following year and began a period in exile in Cuba, during which he maintained secret and unofficial negotiations with the United States, suggesting that if he were to return as president he might be willing to concede Mexican territory and a boundary settlement over Texas in exchange for $30 million. After the **Mexican War** had started he returned to Mexico and took control of the army once more. He became provisional president in 1847 and led the resistance to **Winfield Scott**'s advance on the Mexican capital. Indeed Santa Anna kept fighting to the very end at **Puebla**, upon which he resigned as president, was dismissed as commander of the army, and fled his country.

SCHOOLCRAFT, HENRY ROWE (1793-1864). Schoolcraft was a New Yorker whose work in a glass factory allowed him to develop a strong interest in mineral science. It was as a mineralogist that he participated in a number of exploring expeditions in the 1820s and 1830s, including one he led in 1832 that is renowned for discovering the source of the Mississippi River. However, Schoolcraft also served as a federal officer overseeing frontier affairs with various Native American tribes. He worked as Indian agent in the Lake Superior region between 1822 and 1836, and then was Michigan's superintendent of Indian affairs from 1839 to 1841, before being ousted by the incoming **Whig** regime. These duties led him to take a keen, if rather patronizing, interest in native societies, producing a number of written works including *Algic Researches* (1839) and *Notes on the Iroquois* (1846). In 1847 Schoolcraft's efforts inspired Congress to support the taking of a census of all Native American tribes to assist future policy-making.

SCOTT, WINFIELD (1786-1866). Scott was a military man of Virginian background, whose rise to senior ranks after serving in the army since 1808 led him to be present at nearly every actual or potential warring moment of the period. Although personally on very bad terms with **Andrew Jackson**, whom he had criticized in an earlier career for the actions that led to the **Florida report**, Scott was entrusted by the president with negotiations with the Sac and Fox Natives during **Black Hawk's War** in 1832 and took a role in the early stages of **Second Seminole War** in 1835. Scott had also commanded army forces in South Carolina during the **Nullification crisis** winter of 1832-33, when many feared there would be an outbreak of violence. President **Martin Van Buren** recognized Scott's talents and on two occasions sent him to act as a peacekeeper on the **Canadian border**, first in New York in 1837 after the *Caroline* incident and then in Maine during the "**Aroostook war**" in 1838. In between Scott also undertook the job of overseeing the removal of the **Cherokee** along the infamous "**trail of tears.**"

However, his moment of greatest service to his country came after he had risen to the position of general in chief of the army in 1841. Although a **Whig**, twice considered as a possible presidential candidate in 1840 and 1844, and as such never fully trusted by the **Democratic** administration of **James Polk**, Scott commanded the American armed forces from Washington D.C. during the early stages of the **Mexican War** and then personally led the final successful push on Mexico City in 1847. Even so, Polk refused to entrust him with the job of negotiating a peace treaty, and Scott's behavior in advising **Nicholas Trist** led to his replacement as commander in Mexico. His reputation was assured, though, and of course in 1852 he would at last stand as the Whig candidate for president, albeit unsuccessfully.

SECOND BANK OF THE UNITED STATES. This central banking institution was chartered by the federal government in 1816 as part of a nationalist effort to strengthen the nation's economic institutions in the wake of the War of 1812. As a national bank it had specific responsibility for managing the national debt and for receiving and disbursing the federal funds, but at various times, and especially under the presidency of **Nicholas Biddle**, it had used its dominant financial position to attempt to regulate the activities of state banks. In total the Bank held about one third of the nation's specie reserves and bank deposits. It also made loans amounting to about 20 percent of the nation's total, and issued a similar proportion of the bank notes in circulation in the United States. This level of activity, combined with sound running and a very conservative level of note issue relative to specie reserves, enabled the Bank to regulate the amount of note issues by local banks and the conditions under which they made loans. From the Bank's Philadelphia base its influence spread out across most of the states through a number of branches (25 of them by

1830), limited only in those areas that had introduced their own forms of bank regulation, such as the **New York Safety Fund** and the **Suffolk system**.

However, the Bank was never far from political controversy. In addition to doubts as to the constitutionality of the Bank's charter, the Bank's activities occasionally brought criticism down upon its own head. During the hard times following a major economic panic in 1819 the Bank came in for a large share of the blame, arousing deep and long-lasting hostility to it in many parts of the nation, but especially in the West. There were also grave suspicions about whose interests this federally-chartered national bank best served, since four-fifths of the stock was in private hands. Moreover there were many who simply feared the level of influence the Bank's strong position might allow it to exercise. So then, when Biddle applied for a new charter for the Bank in 1832, four years before the old charter's 20-year term expired, this latent and not-so-latent opposition combined to make the Bank's very existence one of the defining features of party politics in the Jacksonian era.

Andrew Jackson set the ball rolling by vetoing the **1832 bank bill** and then attempting, albeit unsuccessfully, to sell off the remaining government stock in the Bank in spring 1833. Later that year, however, he took the steps of running down the remaining federal deposits from the Bank's safekeeping and of depositing federal revenue with state **deposit banks** from that point on. Biddle's retaliatory contraction of loans, partly demanded by the loss of reserves but also inspired by the crude political calculation that it would create pressure for an end to the removal policy and for a new re-charter effort, led to the **panic of 1834** and only seemed to confirm the worst fears of opponents of the Bank's potential influence. Jackson was unequivocal in blaming Biddle for the problems of the panic, and the president's view seemed to prevail. The Second Bank never did receive a renewed charter and became defunct as a national institution in 1836, taking on a Pennsylvania status instead, as the **United States Bank of Pennsylvania**. *See also* REMOVAL OF FEDERAL DEPOSITS.

SECOND GREAT AWAKENING. This period of religious revival began in the late 18th century but reached its climax in the second and third decades of the 19th century, inspiring a genuine **evangelical** fervor among many Christian denominations, but especially the Methodists, Baptists, and Presbyterians. It arose from the same groundswell of religious excitement that allowed the likes of **Joseph**

Smith and **William Miller** to flourish and it swept across New England and other areas recently settled by New Englanders, such as the **Burned-Over District** of western New York. Inspired by leading evangelical preachers like **Charles Grandison Finney**, the awakening led to efforts of individual self-improvement and generated many of the reform movements of the era associated with the **benevolent empire**.

SECOND PARTY SYSTEM. This is the label given by political scientists and historians to the competitive system of electoral politics that emerged in the 1830s and reached near maturity by the **election of 1840**. Following a period of less clear-cut party divisions in the period 1815 to 1832, the system heralded a return to some of the features of the first party system between Republicans and Federalists in the first two decades of national history. In particular this was marked by fairly close organizational and electoral competition between two major parties across most of the nation's regions and states. Parties began to use nominating conventions to select their candidates for the presidency and to draw up platforms of party principles. Close communication and chains of partisan newspapers tied together party followers from different states and party loyalty was rewarded by means of patronage when power was won. Even the new parties' names, the **Democrats**, the **National Republicans**, and their eventual heirs the **Whigs**, increased the party feel of the period when compared to earlier personalized labels such as **Jackson** men or **Clay** men.

The level of popular voting and the prevalence of competitive elections in most states or constituencies in the period from 1836 on suggest that this was truly the first genuinely national party system. In this system voters usually proved loyal to their first choice of party and elections were more often a contest of getting a party's supporters to vote (rather than not vote) and trying to appeal to new voters, than of converting supporters away from the opposition. On a legislative level, too, there were increasing signs of party regularity in roll calls, as parties fought for their preferred measures and for control of legislative offices. Both parties had a range of policies for cementing and advancing the benefits of American civilization, and both framed them in a world view relevant to the experiences and attitudes of their supporters. At the same time each also presented their opponents as dangerous forces within the nation, ironically occasionally using **anti-party** rhetoric to attack their activities.

SECOND SEMINOLE WAR. This seven-year long conflict beginning in November 1835 represented the most violent example of Native American resistance to **Indian removal**. When Florida **Seminoles** hostile to earlier removal treaties killed U.S. Indian agents in November 1835, and then attacked and killed most of a group of soldiers sent to pacify the region, they sparked off a major effort of military retaliation. Led by **Osceola**, the Seminole forces engaged in unconventional but very successful tactics that initially devastated parts of northeastern Florida, inflicted significant casualties, and managed to pin down half the U.S. army. It was only when **Winfield Scott** was replaced by **Thomas Jesup** that U.S. troops had greater success, by resorting to a type of guerrilla warfare themselves. A truce was signed in March 1837, but was again rejected by Osceola and also broken by white planters who were allowed into Seminole lands to claim runaway slaves in contravention of the truce's terms. The war burst into life again and became one of the less pleasant military actions in American history, with Jesup eventually seizing Osceola under a flag of truce in October 1837. His capture took the momentum out of the Seminole effort, and they suffered a further setback at Lake Okeechobee in December of that year. Although fighting would drag on for a further five years until August 1842, high casualties eventually brought the Seminoles to the point of submission.

Some 3,000 people were killed during the War, which cost over $30 million. Afterwards most of the Seminoles were relocated across the Mississippi, although a small band of 300 was allowed to remain in southwest Florida and some remained as fugitives. As a political issue it provided just one more example of over-harsh treatment of Native Americans for **Whigs** and reform groups to point to as a sign of the moral corruption of the **Democratic** administrations responsible for it.

SECTIONALISM. There were many causes of tension between different sections of the nation and between each section and the federal government. Northeast, South, and West had different economic and social trajectories and expressed this diversity politically in attempts to secure control of the nation's elected offices, or to form alliances with other sections, so that policies in their favor could be implemented. At times it was western interests that looked the most distinctive, as that region pushed for support over **Indian removal, internal improvements, land policy**, and expansion into **Oregon**. The West's views became increasingly significant as that section assumed a greater weight in the nation, in terms of number of states, size of population, and, concomitantly, number of representatives and electoral college votes. Certainly at the beginning of the Jacksonian era some southern politicians recognized this growing status and attempted to forge a **South-West alliance** in defiance of a Northeast that seemed to be becoming increasingly alien to both.

Still, this period also provided the continuing signs that the most prominent and enduring sectional divide was that between those areas with and those without the institution of **slavery**, especially as the rise of the **abolitionist** movement took criticism of slavery to new levels of urgency. Accepting the peculiar institution and now also the more explicit **pro-slavery** defense became associated with a pro-southern attitude, while to doubt, question, or attack slavery was seen as anti-southern. Admittedly, after reaching a high point during the **Nullification crisis** in 1832-33, for the rest of that decade sectional issues were not allowed to threaten the political stability of the Union. Indeed most major politicians of both parties strove to keep likely sectional issues submerged for fear of damaging the young and potentially still fragile national alliances of the **second party system**. In particular **Democrats** adopted this stance, with their consistent support of the **gag rules**, their stance on **incendiary mail**, and their initial reluctance to allow recognition of **Texan independence** and **annexation** to arouse sectional fears.

Nevertheless, sectionalism continued to lurk beneath the surface of regular party politics and could influence its rhetorical concerns at least, as was the case in the **election of 1836**. Increasing abolitionist activity and corresponding pro-slavery statements refused to allow slavery to disappear, and in the 1840s issues such as seizure of slave-trading ships like the *Amistad* and the *Creole*, the operation of the fugitive slave law, and especially territorial **expansion**, with its potential for spreading the peculiar institution into the far West, all propelled the North-South sectional division to the forefront of most aspects of public life. Religious denominations like the Methodists and Baptists split into sectional wings, in 1844 and 1845 respectively, while the national Presbyterian church rid itself of abolitionist members. Party politicians found it hard to steer a steady course without reference to sectional issues, as the dynamic provided by the frequency of elections pushed them to appeal to the sectional concerns of their immediate constituencies, in the process weakening ties between different wings of the national parties and further inflaming sectional suspicions and discord. Indeed by the end of the 1840s there were even signs of a fledgling southern nationalism willing to contemplate the idea of a separate southern nation, while the more extreme abolitionist stance called for an end to union with slaveholders.

SEMINOLE. This tribe of the southeastern corner of North America, deriving from the **Creek** confederacy, became closely associated with Florida during its period of Spanish rule. Their presence there had made them the target of American hostility even before Florida became part of the United States, as they appeared likely to support British and Spanish interests in that region, and at times also gave refuge to fleeing **slaves**. It had been to check such cross-border activities that the United States had already fought a war with the Seminole, in the late 1810s, General **Andrew Jackson**'s vigorous actions there earning the opprobrium of some in the **Florida expedition report**. Once Florida was ceded to the United States, there began a steady process by which the Seminole surrendered most of their tribal lands, latterly by treaties signed under the auspices of the 1830 **Indian Removal Act**. Many, perhaps most Seminole, opposed removal, encouraged in part by the African-American population among them, who feared being left vulnerable to enslavement or reenslavement should the Seminole leave. The refusal by a majority of Seminoles to contemplate leaving Florida led to the **Second Seminole War** between 1835 and 1842. However, after defeat by attrition in this violent conflict, most of the Seminole had to endure removal, with the exceptions of a small group allowed to stay and of some renegades who managed to escape removal and remained in the Everglades.

SENECA FALLS CONVENTION. In July 1848 between 100 and 300 delegates gathered at the first major American convention in support of **women**'s rights, held in the Wesleyan Methodist chapel of Seneca Falls, the home town of **Elizabeth Cady Stanton**. She, along with **Lucretia Mott**, had been planning such a meeting since they had made each other's acquaintance at an **anti-slavery** convention in London in 1840. Although the convention was presided over by Mott's husband, and despite the presence of other male luminaries, including **Frederick Douglass**, the convention was very much the work of Stanton and Mott. They presented it with a Declaration of Sentiments, modeled after the Declaration of Independence and calling for greater levels of legal and political equality for women. Stanton also made what was the first public call for voting rights for women. Male-dominated newspapers generally ridiculed the convention, with the notable exception of the reform-sympathetic *New York*

Tribune, but women's rights supporters took some momentum from the convention and reconvened in Rochester just two weeks later.

SERGEANT, JOHN (1779-1852). This 1795 Princeton graduate was born in Philadelphia and rose to prominence as a lawyer and politician. As a friend of **Nicholas Biddle,** Sergeant represented the **Second Bank of the United States** in a number of Supreme Court cases, and he was also part of the legal team that put the case of the **Cherokee** in *Worcester vs. Georgia.* His advocacy of these causes reflected views that put him firmly in the political camp in opposition to the Jacksonian **Democrats.** Indeed, Sergeant was one of the **National Republicans** who had advised Biddle of the political advantages of seeking an early re-charter of the Bank in 1832, and later that year he stood as his friend **Henry Clay**'s running mate in the presidential election. Later in the decade Sergeant sat as a **Whig** in the House of Representatives between 1837 and 1841, still holding out hope for the creation of a new national bank and vigorously opposing the **Independent Treasury** proposal of **Martin Van Buren**'s administration.

SEWARD, WILLIAM HENRY (1801-1872). Seward followed the common route of a legal career into New York politics before becoming one of the most influential leaders of the **Whig** Party. In the early 1830s he had sat in New York's state senate for the **Anti-Masonic Party,** and ran unsuccessfully for them as gubernatorial candidate in 1834. Four years later, as a Whig, he did win election as governor, his victory over **William Marcy** representing a major triumph against the previously dominant New York **Democrats.** During his four years as governor between 1839 and 1843 Seward supported public works, such as more **railroads** and an expansion of the **Erie Canal** network. His advocacy of educational reform, including opposition to an imposition of Protestant religion on the public school system, earned him the favor of **Catholics** such as Archbishop **John Hughes.** He also diverged from many Whigs in expressing doubts about the usefulness of a new national bank and instead supported a well-regulated free banking system in New York. After his term as governor Seward was without elected post until he entered the Senate in 1849, having begun by the late 1840s to reveal hints of **antislavery** views which would cause him to feel some disillusionment when his party nominated the southerner **Zachary Taylor** and Seward's own New York factional rival, **Millard Fillmore,** as its candidates for **election in 1848.**

SHEEP FARMING. Sheep farming became an important northern **agricultural** pursuit during this period, flourishing as a result of the demand for wool from both British and American textiles **manufacturing** industries. For much of the period some 60 percent of sheep were farmed in New England and the mid-Atlantic states, often taking over in areas where difficult soil conditions and competition from further west had made staple crop production less viable. In turn, by 1850, the center of sheep-farming had itself begun to shift into the Ohio Valley.

SHIPPING. This was a period of generally steady growth in America's maritime industries, although there could be occasional, local downturns in shippers' and shipbuilders' fortunes, notably in New England in the 1837 to 1843 period. A large proportion of the maritime carrying business undertaken by Americans occurred between U.S. ports, a burgeoning trade reserved exclusively for American-owned vessels. But Americans were also involved internationally in **overseas commerce** on the major routes across the Atlantic with Britain and other parts of Europe, to the colonial possessions of Britain and Spain in the western hemisphere and to the developing independent nations of Latin America, and increasingly in more exotic trades with parts of Africa and the Far East. As well as direct trades and return journeys via a third country, there was also considerable American involvement in tramp carriage between other countries. Most of these trades suffered a downturn in the aftermath of the **panic of 1837** and particularly of the **panic of 1839**, creating financial difficulties for some of those involved. Indeed, the depression produced a concerted, if ultimately unsuccessful attempt to change the **commercial treaty** terms enjoyed in American ports by foreign vessels.

The period also witnessed considerable technological change in shipping, with the introduction in the 1830s of regular steam-driven ocean-going packet services. Internally, river steamboats reached their period of greatest importance, carrying passengers on ferry and longer-haul trips in the Northeast, while on the Mississippi and other great river systems of the South, Southwest, and Midwest, they became essential carriers of people and goods both up- and downstream. However, on the high seas sailing vessels still performed the vast majority of carrying business, and the later years of the period saw the development of the great clipper fleets, in the tea trade from 1843, and later in trade with **California**.

SIR ROBERT PEEL CASE. See *CAROLINE* AFFAIR.

SLAVE TRADE. The continuing existence of **slavery** in the United States and in other current and former colonial possessions in the Americas, such as Cuba and Brazil, meant that in the Jacksonian era there was still business to be done in the buying and selling of human beings. While the official banning of the importation of slaves into the United States had been in place since 1808, this did not make the nation immune to debates and issues arising from the slave trade, since internationally illegal trading still continued, while domestically there was still a burgeoning slave trade both within and between individual states and regions.

At a domestic level the trade in slaves proved vital to the growth of the peculiar institution and its expansion westward. Although many slaves traveled west when their masters took up new lands, without the slave trade the significant growth of the slave-based **cotton** agriculture in the Southwest would have been less likely. A whole industry, encompassing slave traders, markets, credit arrangements, and advertising, developed as economic pressures and opportunities encouraged the movement of human property around the American South.

Predictably, as **abolitionists** raised the level of their attacks on slavery as a whole, so too they pointed to the slave trade as perhaps the most distasteful aspect of the slave regime, with its potential for splitting up "married" couples, parents and children, and broader slave family networks. An end to the trade in slaves obviously formed part of the broader aim of abolishing slavery itself, but more moderate **anti-slavery** elements also demanded the end of the slave trade in the District of Columbia as one of their constitutionally more achievable aims. The domestic trade in slaves also provided two of the more celebrated legal and diplomatic incidents relating to slavery in this period, in the cases of the *Enterprise* and *Creole*, both ships having been involved in the legal coasting trade between two U.S. ports when they were seized by British colonial authorities and their cargoes declared free.

Of course the most famous case of slaves being freed when on a slave trading vessel came with the *Amistad* affair. In this case, though, the slaves were Spanish-owned and the *Amistad* was involved in the illegal transatlantic trade in slaves. The case was also something of a contradiction of U.S. attitudes to the international slave trade in the 1830s, because although the American involvement in the trade had been legally over since 1808 and Congress had gone so far as to declare the trade piracy in 1820, rarely had the United States given much support to the job of policing the illegal trade. In

1839 Congress did authorize U.S. naval vessels to seize ships clearly equipped as slave carriers, but intolerance of the international slave trade did not stretch to adhering to the terms of the Quintuple Treaty of 1841 by which five European powers agreed to mutual rights of searching each other's flagged vessels for evidence of the trade. Indeed, when **Daniel Webster** and **Edward Everett** even hinted that the United States might sign up to the treaty, southerners and Anglophobes like **Lewis Cass** responded angrily, claiming that the treaty masked British efforts to undermine rivals to East Indian cotton growers and to continue the much hated policy of impressment. Some ground was made a year later, however, when in an exchange of letters at the same time as the **Webster-Ashburton Treaty**, Britain and the United States agreed to the establishment of joint squadrons of naval vessels off the coast of Africa, which would cooperate with each other in searching vessels of their own national flags. American implementation of this agreement in practice proved less active, with few vessels sent and an often less than serious participation in the agreed duties by those commanding officers who did go.

SLAVERY. Slavery was the distinctive institution that provided much of the labor force of the American South, producing those crops, such as **tobacco**, **rice**, **sugar**, and especially **cotton**, that accounted for a very high proportion of the nation's entire economic output and export goods. This period saw the continuing remarkable increase of the slave population almost exclusively by means of natural growth, rising from between 2 and 2.5 million at the beginning of the period to over 3.2 million by 1850. At the same time the distinctively southern numerical preponderance of slaves had become mirrored by legal provisions, as terms providing for the immediate or gradual abolition of slavery in all northern states had by this time almost wiped out slavery in the North altogether. But within the South there was a significant change during this period, as the balance of the slave population shifted westward. States like Alabama, Mississippi, and Louisiana became the heart of the cotton kingdom and the movement of planters and slaves together, and of slaves on their own in the internal **slave trade**, nearly equalized slave numbers in the Southeast and Southwest.

As a political issue slavery assumed the paradoxical position of being much talked about but also largely relegated from the center of national party politics during the first half of the period. The rise of the **abolitionists** and the corresponding shift in emphasis in **proslavery** thought clearly intensified debate about slavery and made its presence the likely heart of future **sectional** disagreement and tension. However, although the issue of slavery was implicitly linked to the crisis over **nullification** and the **tariff in 1832**, politicians of both major parties succeeded in keeping it off the national political stage after that, by means of the **gag rules**, federal acquiescence in the blockage of **incendiary mail**, and hesitation in accepting the **Texas annexation**. However, the 1840s dawned to new, more bitter debates about the international slave trade, the fate of fugitive slaves, and in particular the question of slavery's **expansion** to new territories. These would challenge the ability of the **second party system** to hold back sectional tensions in future and perhaps its very survival itself.

SLIDELL, JOHN (1793-1871). This New York-born lawyer, educated at Columbia, moved to Louisiana to practice law in the 1820s and 1830s. Slidell served **Andrew Jackson** as U.S. district attorney in New Orleans, but suffered defeat in his attempts in 1834 and 1836 to represent his state in the Senate as a **states' rights Democrat**. However, he would go on to serve in the House of Representatives between 1843 and 1845, before resigning the position when he was appointed as minister to Mexico with the mission of restoring formal diplomatic relations with that country in late 1845. As well as having orders to sort out the outstanding Texas border problem and the issue of claims, it was rumored that Slidell was empowered to offer $40 million for the purchase of New Mexico and **California**. Outraged at this presumption, two Mexican administrations refused formally to receive Slidell and the resulting failure even to begin talks on what **James Polk**'s administration considered the non-negotiable issues of the Texas border and claims led to both Slidell's departure in March 1846 and Polk's decision to make the declaration that officially began the **Mexican War**.

SLOAT, JOHN (1780-1867). Sloat was born in New York and until 1816 alternated service between the naval and commercial marines. His later onshore and sea postings included command of the Portsmouth Naval Yard, but it was as the officer in command of the Pacific Squadron at the outbreak of the **Mexican War** that his name became famous. Sloat played a part in supporting the **Bear Flag** rebellion against Mexican rule in **California** and then in July 1846 ordered the U.S. flag to be raised in Monterey, before going on to capture San Francisco. Ill health forced him to transfer his command to **Robert Stockton**, and after the war Sloat went on to command the Norfolk Naval Yard.

SMITH, GERRIT (1797-1874). Gerrit Smith was a New Yorker from Utica, whose management of his father's highly successful land speculation business brought him great wealth. He put this wealth to philanthropic uses, backing a number of different **benevolent** institutions, including the American Bible Society, the American Tract Society, and the American Sunday School Union, and reform movements such as **temperance**, prison reform, peace, **sabbatarianism**, and **women**'s rights. He also gave practical assistance to New York's freed slaves, in the form of land grants and calls for an end to racially discriminatory legislation. It is no surprise, then, that it was Smith's support for and involvement in **abolitionism** that brought him most renown.

Like so many abolitionist sympathizers Smith began in support of the **American Colonization Society** but increased in radicalism along with others in the **anti-slavery** movement. His financial contributions formed a major part of the income of the New York Anti-Slavery Society and he also gave backing to **William Lloyd Garrison**, eventually joining the **American Anti-Slavery Society** in 1835. Toward the end of the 1830s Smith parted ways with Garrison over the legitimacy of political action against **slavery** and he became one of the organizers of the **Liberty Party** in New York, even being reputed to have been the one who gave it its name. He stuck with the Party for the rest of the 1840s and 1850s, refusing to join many of his colleagues in moving to the **Free Soil** coalition on the grounds that he regarded it as a watering down of the attack on slavery. His close Liberty Party supporters even put him forward as an independent presidential candidate in the **elections of 1848**, 1852, and 1856.

SMITH, JOSEPH (1805-1844). Born in Vermont, Smith was one of several religious figures to emerge from the exciting revival years in upstate New York and probably has had the longest influence in terms of his specific legacy. After claiming that he had witnessed revelations from the angel Moroni and had received from him a series of golden plates in 1827, Smith became the prophet and founder of the **Mormon** Church. Smith's two-year translation of the plates resulted in the *Book of Mormon*, published in 1830, which proved the inspiration for the foundation of the Church the same year. It was Smith who led the Mormons on their numerous travels, from New York west to Ohio, to Missouri, and finally to Illinois, in a search for their perfect community and in flight from local suspicion and hostility. Meanwhile he reinforced the establishment of the Mormon Church, with the production in 1835 of the *Doctrines and Covenants*, one of several publications alongside a number of biblical biographies and even an attempted revision of the Bible. In 1844 Smith's increasing intolerance of critics from within his own Church led to accusations against him of treason and to his imprisonment, during which time he was attacked and killed by a mob. Although arousing strong passions, both positive and negative, his contribution in establishing a new and lasting religion is undeniably significant.

SMITHSONIAN INSTITUTION. The Smithsonian, founded by Congress in 1846, had been inspired in 1829 by English scientist James Smithson's will, which, were his own nephew to die childless, bequeathed his money for the establishment of an institution for the "increase and diffusion of knowledge." Although he had never visited America, Smithson's admiration for the likes of Tom Paine and Ben Franklin and his preference for democracy, social equity, and individualism over monarchy, made the United States, rather than Britain, his beneficiary. When his nephew duly died without heir, Congress accepted the money in 1836, but it would take a further decade of debate before it agreed upon the nature of the institution. In the early stages of the debate some **Democrats** resisted the idea of founding another big federal entity, having only recently rid the country of the **Second Bank**. Eventually, though, a committee chaired by **John Quincy Adams** made recommendations that were enacted and signed into law by **James Polk** in August 1846. This act established the Institution's organizational structure and provided for its running independent of the federal government. **Joseph Henry** was appointed its first secretary and **James Renwick** was soon after commissioned to design the Institution's distinctive first building. From these roots would emerge one of the world's most important and influential centers for scientific and artistic endeavor.

***SOMERS* MUTINY.** This revolt by apprentices on board a naval training ship, the *Somers*, in 1842 resulted in the execution of three ringleaders by their commander, Alexander Mackenzie. Mackenzie's court-martial was the legal sensation of its day, not so much for its judgment, which was to find the commander not guilty, but more because one of the executed apprentices was the son of the secretary of war, **John Spencer**. He refused to accept the court's decision and came into bitter conflict with the secretary of the navy, **Abel Upshur**, who upheld it. President **John Tyler** tried to sit on the fence between his two Cabinet officers by allowing the decision to stand but failing to give it his formal approval by his signature. The episode demonstrated problems in the apprenticeship system in the navy and precipitated necessary **naval reform** in the creation of a naval academy.

SOUTH CAROLINA EXPOSITION AND PROTEST. John Calhoun's "Exposition" was his first important expression of **nullification** views. Written in response to the **tariff of 1828**, it attacked the principle of **tariff protection** as infringing the constitutional powers of Congress to raise revenue by import duties and to protect commerce. At the time, South Carolina's legislature considered the "Exposition" too extreme and hoped that Calhoun's position as vice-president in the incoming administration of **Andrew Jackson** would help to bring about tariff reform in Congress anyway. Indeed, Calhoun's position led him to try to keep his authorship of the "Exposition" secret. However, the legislature did print the "Exposition" for public consumption and in addition passed a formal "protest" against the tariff of 1828.

SOUTH-WEST ALLIANCE. As part of the playing out of **sectional** rivalries within early Jacksonian politics, some southern and western politicians regarded a tactical alliance between their two sections as the most likely means for securing their respective policy objectives, more so than pinning their hopes on **Andrew Jackson** himself, who might have been expected to be sympathetic to some of their aims. So then while the president was more than likely to prove accommodating on the policy of **Indian removal**, it was the western ambition of cheaper **land** and the southern desire for a **tariff for revenue** that pushed these groups together, most publicly in the playing out of the **Webster-Hayne** debate.

However, such an alliance as there was rarely produced concrete results and indeed representatives of both sections were more than happy to work for their own interests when it suited them. In 1830 some westerners who favored **internal improvements** decided to support **distribution** in defiance of southern hostility, while southerners did not vote for land measures cherished by the West, such as **graduation** and **preemption**. Nor did many southerners vote for improvements bills in the 1829-30 congressional session. Nevertheless, the alliance did at one time pose a genuine threat to the existing Jacksonian coalition, a threat that contributed to the president's decision to break with **John Calhoun** and to force his followers to choose between the two men. As Jackson's administration went on, and especially after the **Bank veto** and **Nullification crisis**, national party lines began to replace sectional alliances as the main structures of political activity.

SPECIAL SESSIONS. The difficult economic conditions witnessed during the **panics of 1837 and 1839** and the ensuing longer-term depression in the wake of the latter precipitated the relative rarity in early American history of two special sessions of Congress, summoned for the summers of 1837 and 1841 by **Martin Van Buren** and **William Henry Harrison** respectively. Both were designed to allow incoming presidents to prevail upon Congress to respond to what were considered emergency conditions, avoiding the need to wait until the next regular session of Congress met, in December of each of those years.

In September 1837 Congress met to deal with problems arising from the suspension of specie payments by most of the banks in the nation, which damaged the provision of credit and the availability of circulating currency. Some specific relief measures were passed for eastern importing merchants and western **deposit banks**, while Congress also authorized a temporary issue of **Treasury notes** to help ease the currency difficulties. In the face of a fall-off of many types of business, including land sales and imports, the decision to postpone the final installment of **distribution** provided for by the **Deposit Act** was also sensible, since the federal government might otherwise have found itself short of revenue. However, it was the initial introduction of the **Independent Treasury** proposal that dominated the session, marking out the direction that Van Buren's administration aimed to take during this phase of the **bank wars**. However, that bill and a bankruptcy bill both failed to pass Congress.

Four years later Harrison and **Whig** grandee **Henry Clay** almost came to blows when the president initially turned down the senator's request for a special session in the summer of 1841, casting his tie-breaking vote in a split Cabinet poll on the issue on 11 March. Yet only a couple of weeks later, after Congress had adjourned and many legislators, including Clay, had left for home, Harrison responded to dire warnings from his Treasury secretary, **Thomas Ewing**, about the financial standing of the government by calling for a special session to meet in May.

By the time the session convened, Harrison's death had brought **John Tyler** into the White House and he called for measures for the immediate financial relief of the Treasury, which, it was anticipated, would not to have enough funds to cover its own expenses that year. A loan was secured to cover the federal government's debts, but strangely, given its own precarious position, Tyler also proposed, and Congress passed, the **1841 Distribution Act**, a measure that would pass on any surplus federal revenue from land sales to indebted state governments. Again, though, banking proved the dominant issue, with Clay pressing for the passage of some kind of new national banking institution against the opposition of Tyler, who felt unprepared for consideration of such a contentious issue. Although Whigs succeeded in repealing the Independent Treasury Act passed only the previous year and in passing a **Bankruptcy Act**, the executive and legislative wings of the party practically fell apart over Tyler's vetoes of a range of bank bills. These events led to the **Cabinet resignation** of September 1841 and set the tone for the relationship between Tyler and his nominal party for the rest of his term. *See also* BANK BILL AND VETO, 1841.

SPECIE CIRCULARS. The circulars were a number of orders issued by the Treasury during **Andrew Jackson**'s administration as part of the "**hard money**" agenda of discouraging the overissue of **paper currency**. Each aimed to do this by banning the payment of dues to federal government agencies in paper money below certain denominations, or even in paper money at all. So then in November 1834 federal revenue receivers, such as customs collectors, were ordered, from 1 January 1835, not to accept as payment any money that was not mentioned in a congressional resolution of 1816, a clear attempt to prohibit payment of federal charges in drafts on the **Second Bank**. Then in April 1835 land offices and deposit banks were ordered not to accept payment in notes worth less than five dollars, while after March 1836 that lower limit for acceptable paper money was raised to 10 dollars.

The most famous Specie Circular was that issued on 11 July 1836, which ordered that after August of that year all land purchases were only to be paid for in metal coinage. A four-month window was left open to genuine settlers seeking to purchase land, allowing them until the end of 1836 to use paper money to buy up to 320 acres. This most notorious order was roundly criticized by opposition politicians who pointed to it as yet another example of **executive usurpation**. Many bankers warned that metallic money would be drained away to the West for land purchases, reducing the amount of reserves held by eastern banks and, as a result, their ability to make loans. These forces combined in an effort led by **Whig Henry Clay** and **Conservative Democrats Nathaniel Tallmadge** and **William Rives** to legislate for the Specie Circular's repeal. The Senate did indeed vote for its repeal but failed to win support for this in the House, but neverthe-less both chambers did support a call for the federal government to accept as payment the paper money of any bank that did not issue notes under $20. Their hope that this would help to relieve the pres-sured banking and commercial community was thwarted by Jack-son's pocket veto in March 1837.

When the currency contraction prior to the **panic of 1837** hit, from late 1836 onward, critics of **Democratic** banking and monetary policies predictably claimed that their warnings about the Circular's potential for causing a disruption in the currency flows of the country had come true. Some historians have repeated this assessment, but al-though the Specie Circular might have contributed to the credit con-traction that precipitated the panic, in truth such drain as there was was at levels so insignificant when compared to the amount of money in circulation as not to be a major cause of the panic. Nevertheless, the panic only further fuelled the political debate over whether to re-voke or retain the Circular. Opponents continued to call for it to be terminated or at least revised, in order to ease its impact on eastern banks. Supporters of the Circular and extreme "hard money" advo-cates called for its retention and even for its extension to cover all payments to the federal government. The new president, **Martin Van Buren**, deliberated long and hard on what to do about the Circular and in May 1837 stood firm in his support for its continued operation. However, Democrats and even his own Cabinet were divided on the issue, as some of the party began to see it less as a check on inflation than as a dangerously deflationary measure. Finally, in May 1838, a joint resolution of Congress, offered by Clay, rendered the Circular inoperative, leaving Treasury officials to use their own discretion in deciding which banks' notes were acceptable.

SPENCER, JOHN C. (1788-1855). This New Yorker was educated at Union College before his legal training took him into a number of administrative and legal positions in his home state, including post-master, district attorney, and member of a commission that drafted the revised statutes of the state of New York in 1829. By that time Spencer had also served in the House of Representatives in the late 1810s as well as in both chambers of the state legislature.

Toward the end of the 1820s Spencer was attracted to the **Anti-Masonic** movement and, although appointed by Governor **Martin Van Buren** to a commission investigating the death of William Mor-gan, found the lack of state support for the commission symptomatic of a suspected involvement of the authorities in Morgan's demise.

Spencer resigned and, his Anti-Masonic position reinforced, was elected to the state legislature once more and presided at the **Anti-Masonic Party**'s first national convention in 1831. By the late 1830s Spencer had followed the course of many other New York Anti-Masons and had shifted into the **Whig** Party. There he served as secretary of state under Governor **William Seward**, backing his educational reforms in particular. It was also during this period that Spencer edited an English edition of **Alexis de Tocqueville**'s *Democracy in America*, in 1839.

Spencer's next move was a dramatic one, into **John Tyler**'s second Cabinet in 1841. Since his days as an Anti-Mason, Spencer had resisted the political charms of **Henry Clay** and this now made him attractive to **His Accidency**. Spencer enjoyed an effective period of national executive office, first as secretary of war and later as secretary of the treasury. In the first of those offices he oversaw the end of the **Second Seminole War**, a conflict that moved him to oppose future **Indian removal**. He also attempted to improve internal military communication and coastal defenses. He proved efficient in the position and even had time to help out other, less talented Cabinet officers including the useless **Walter Forward** at the Treasury. This experience stood Spencer in good stead when, after the Senate had rejected his nomination as a Supreme Court justice, Tyler switched him to Forward's department. Again, he proved a good administrator, helping to balance the budget and to reduce the national debt a little.

Nevertheless, Spencer's period in the Cabinet also had its bitter moments, including his dispute with **Abel Upshur** over the fate of his son in the *Somers* mutiny and his growing disenchantment with the growing southern influence within the Cabinet and the moves for **Texas annexation**. Increasingly uneasy, he resigned in protest at what he considered Tyler's illegal use of a special executive account to fund activities in Texas. Tyler at least tried again to appoint Spencer to the Supreme Court in 1844, but once more Clay's supporters in the Senate blocked the nomination, leaving Spencer effectively to retire from public life.

SPOILS SYSTEM. This term was coined by **William Marcy**, a member of the **Albany Regency** and later a leader of the New York **Hunker** faction, to encapsulate the view that supporters of successful political parties, or factions within parties, should expect to benefit in the form of appointive office. The theory was that the use of patronage to reward party loyalists with posts likely to have financial remuneration as well as status and influence would result in better party discipline and more cohesive governance. In a healthy democracy the spoils system would also facilitate a **rotation of office-holders**, allowing a greater number of qualified people to share in the business of administration and as a result providing more responsible government.

Political opponents charged **Andrew Jackson** as having conducted a corrupt and narrowly partisan appointments policy and he is usually considered by historians to have adopted the spoils system to a wide extent. However, he only changed about 10 percent of office-holders during his eight years as president, many of these changes resulting from natural wastage and his reluctance to reappoint men who had ended set terms of office. Nevertheless, Jackson did remove more officials, more quickly, than his immediate predecessors had done and it was hardly surprising that when changes were made the beneficiaries were his friends, personal and partisan, and the nominees of his coalition supporters.

Ironically, in the light of Jackson's reputation, removals were actually greater in number during the more volatile party politics of the 1840s. Although the **Whigs** and their incoming president in 1841, **William Henry Harrison**, pledged to put right the abuses in the patronage system, the pressure to remove opponents and, more heavily, to reward long-suffering party followers meant that large numbers of removals did occur with the transition in party regime. Harrison and **John Tyler**'s Cabinet officers oversaw many changes during the months before their collective **resignation** of September 1841, and then a new set of department heads meant even more opportunity for removal and replacement.

Despite the fact that in his own "inaugural" statement in April 1841 Tyler had said removals would not come thick and fast, he soon veered away from that position, realizing the political value, in his own very peculiar circumstances, of rewarding his friends. Eventually he removed something like 50 percent of civil officials in positions at his disposal. He also made quite a feature of appointing to a range of offices members of his own family, by blood and marriage. There was a particular rash of appointments in the last year of Tyler's term, when he ousted regular Whigs in favor of his own and **Democratic** allies, in the hope that this would assist his **election in 1844**, or if not his then that of a Democratic candidate. He even hoped that **James Polk** would retain these men in office, were he to win that year. Meanwhile, Polk also went on to engage in extensive removals from office when he came to power, only reinforcing the sense that the spoils system was around to stay.

SPOLIATION CLAIMS. One of the ongoing features of U.S. diplomacy during the Jacksonian era and beyond was an effort to resolve the claims for damages incurred by American citizens during European wars in late 18th and early 19th centuries, usually as a result of seizures of trade goods and merchant vessels. While treaties were also successfully negotiated settling claims against Denmark (1830), the Kingdom of the Two Sicilies (1832), Portugal (1832), and Spain (1834), the most significant and prolonged negotiation took place with France. Similarly claims arising from damages incurred during wars for independence in Latin America were settled with Brazil (1830) and Peru (1841), but those against Mexico stand out, even playing a part in the outbreak of the **Mexican War**.

Three earlier administrations had attempted redress from France before **Andrew Jackson** entered the White House and he called for a vigorous approach to the matter. After revolution brought a new regime to power in France in 1830, **William Rives** succeeded the following year in securing a claims treaty, by which it was agreed that 25 million francs were to be paid in six annual installments. However, in 1833 and 1834 the French parliament failed to levy sufficient money to fund the installments, and as late as 1836 none had been paid. This delay prompted some of Jackson's Cabinet to call for reprisals against the property of French citizens and Jackson seemed to sympathize with this more bellicose approach. However, in December 1834 the Senate counseled caution, members of both parties preferring a more circumspect approach to the one proposed by the president. The House was keener to take action and passed a bill that would have provided $3 million in defense appropriations in anticipation of their being needed, but again the more circumspect Senate intervened and blocked the measure. Nevertheless, Franco-American relations became tense as Jackson's inflammatory language and a new French refusal to pay the money until Jackson had explained his behavior led to a suspension of official contacts in 1835-36. But, threatened with the humiliation of being forced to accept the British government as a mediator, the French finally accepted the slightly more moderate tone Jackson adopted in his 1835 annual message. In 1836 they agreed to pay the missing four installments and the remaining two when the time came.

The dispute over claims against Mexico, initially lasting for most of the 1830s, also reached the point of possible violent resolution, especially when it became caught up with the **Texan independence** struggle and the ambitions of some American statesmen to push for **Texas annexation**. In the mid-1830s Jackson again adopted a vigorous stance on the claims, while later others even hoped that pushing Mexico on the claims issue might precipitate a war, which would in turn terminate U.S. treaty commitments not to try to annex Texas. Cooler heads in Congress prevailed and **Martin Van Buren** also desired peaceful relations. In 1838 he accepted an arbitration commission as the means by which to settle the claims and, although the Mexican government's slowness in ratifying the agreement resulted in the commission only being established in 1840, this ultimately agreed recompense of $2 million to American citizens. As in the case of France, though, delays in making the payments prolonged the dispute. Demands for payment of the damage claims formed a non-negotiable part of **John Slidell**'s orders in 1845 and, after he had been forced to leave empty-handed, the claims were included in the list of causes for the war and in later peace negotiation demands.

STANTON, ELIZABETH CADY (1815-1902). Born to the family of a New York congressman and judge, Elizabeth Cady had a strict Presbyterian upbringing and was educated at Troy Female Seminary, graduating in 1832. From early adulthood she mixed in reform circles and developed an interest in the **temperance** and **anti-slavery** movements. She was first cousin to **Gerrit Smith** and reinforced her links with the anti-slavery fold when she married the **abolitionist** Henry Brewster Stanton in 1840. Despite giving birth to and raising three of her seven children in the 1840s it was during this decade that she rose to prominence as an early advocate of **women**'s rights. She was one several American women refused admission at the London Anti-Slavery convention of 1840, an experience which sharpened her sense of injustice and introduced her to a long-term collaborator in the movement, **Lucretia Mott**. For the remainder of the decade, and especially during a period of residence in Boston, Mrs. Stanton developed a network of reforming women, including the **Grimké** sisters and Mott herself. Stanton's organizational efforts culminated in the 1848 convention for women's rights, held at **Seneca Falls**, her home town since 1847. She was the one who wrote and presented the Declaration of Sentiments, calling for equal rights for women, and she also made the first public call for women to share the suffrage.

STATES' RIGHTS. This long-standing constitutional position, in this period more usually associated with the American South, aimed to defend local and state interests against dangers from the perceived overcentralization of government. Many Americans, including President **Andrew Jackson** and most of the **Democratic** Party, shared the more moderate states' rights view that the federal government should not contravene a strict interpretation of the Constitution in its consideration of measures that might affect the individual states. However, the more extreme manifestation of the states' rights doctrine, such as in **nullification** and state secession, failed to win the same level of support. Ironically Jackson's own firm stance against the nullifiers of South Carolina caused many to doubt his own states' rights credentials and, together with some of his actions against the **Second Bank of the United States** and **Martin Van Buren**'s **Independent Treasury** and **militia reform** proposals, helped to shape a distinctive **States' Rights Whig** party faction.

STATES' RIGHTS WHIGS. This group, mainly southern in nature, constituted an important part of the developing **Whig** coalition in the mid-1830s, driven to the party by those actions of **Andrew Jackson**'s administration that offended their **states' rights** opposition to centralized national power. Although many of them had supported Jackson in 1828 in the expectation that he shared their views to some extent, the States' Rights Whigs gradually deserted him and a presidency that they accused of **executive usurpation**. Predictably Jackson's tough stand against South Carolina's nullifiers, in particular his **Nullification Proclamation** and the **Force Act**, provoked the greatest criticism, although his actions in the **removal of the federal deposits** and the **Specie Circular**, and his successor **Martin Van Buren**'s **Independent Treasury** and **militia reform** proposals also aroused fears of too great an exercise of executive or federal power. Although never entirely comfortable alongside regular Whigs, with their espousal of more active federal government involvement in the economy, the States' Rights Whigs' strong ties to the commercial planters of the South did create some common ground with other Whig supporters, such as manufacturers and merchants, behind support for a flourishing, **credit**-driven, and internationally-linked economy.

STEVENS, ROBERT (1787-1856). Robert Stevens was the son of John Stevens, an engineer and steam engine pioneer of an earlier generation. Stevens junior was also involved in steamship construction until becoming president and chief engineer of the Camden and Amboy Railroad in 1830, the first steam rail service in New Jersey. His lasting contribution to **railroad** technology came with his invention of the "t-bar" rail, of fishplates, and of the hooked spike used to hold rails in place. Stevens was also one of the first to experiment with burning anthracite in steam engine boilers. In the 1840s he returned to shipbuilding and designed an armor-plated vessel for the federal government.

STEVENS, THADDEUS (1792-1868). This Vermont-born politician and statesman was educated at Dartmouth College and later moved to Pennsylvania where he made his political career. With early sympathies for **Anti-Masonry**, Stevens shifted to the **Whig** Party during a period in the state legislature between 1833 and 1841. While in that body he was one of those targeted by the rebels during the **Buckshot war**. He was also suspected of having played a major part in swinging the 1840 Whig presidential nomination to **William Henry Harrison**, by leaving incriminating evidence for Virginian delegates to find, implying that the rival candidate, **Winfield Scott**, favored **abolition**. Despite his involvement in the party's affairs at that moment, Stevens' support for a range of reforms, including education, **antislavery**, and changes in racially discriminatory laws, and his generally progressive attitude all made him uncomfortable among the more socially conservative elements of the Whigs. This, and his failure to secure Cabinet office under Harrison, led him to abandon national politics for much of the 1840s, until he entered the House of Representatives with anti-slavery backing in 1849.

STEVENSON, ANDREW (1785-1857). This Virginian **Democratic** politician held two significant posts during the 1830s. As speaker of the House between 1827 and 1833 he favored Democrats in the selection of congressional committees and backed **Andrew Jackson**'s position on the key issues of **Indian removal**, the **Second Bank**, and **nullification**. Stevenson's prominence in the party won him the chair of the Democratic national convention in 1835, during which he helped to draw up the party's platform for the **election of 1836**. Before the election took place, Stevenson had moved to London to take up the post of U.S. minister to Great Britain, a position confirmed only at the second attempt, after the Senate had first rejected his nomination in 1834. He would remain in London until 1841, serving through a difficult period of Anglo-American relations, dominated by tensions over various parts of the **Canadian border**. After his return Stevenson was not such a prominent figure, although he did fail to win election for governor of Virginia by only one vote in 1842. **James Polk** considered him as a possible candidate for the position of secretary of war but opted instead to reward the New Yorker **Wil-**

liam **Marcy**. Stevenson's final bow for the period came at the 1848 Democratic national convention, where he again served as chairman.

STOCKTON, ROBERT (1795-1866). Stockton was born in New Jersey and, after leaving Princeton without graduating, embarked in 1811 upon a career in the navy, interspersed with periods during which he pursued personal business and political and diplomatic activities as well. For instance, between 1828 and 1838 he took time out of the navy to manage interests he had inherited, including the Delaware and Raritan Canal and the Camden and Amboy Railroad. Stockton also campaigned for **William Henry Harrison** in 1840 and in 1843 was offered the position of secretary of the navy by **John Tyler**. Of course the latter offer, which Stockton declined, arose only after effective experience as a naval officer. Before his sabbatical for business purposes, he had commanded squadrons involved in policing the **slave trade** and he had also been present at negotiations for securing land for the establishment of Liberia as a community for the **colonization** of freed slaves.

Upon his return to the navy Stockton oversaw the construction of the ill-fated U.S.S. *Princeton* and its "Peacemaker" gun, luckily surviving both the gun's explosion and the inquiry that cleared him of personal responsibility for the disaster. However, his main claims to fame came during the presidency of **James Polk**. First Stockton served as an agent in **Texas**, trying to arouse pro-annexation sentiment there. Then, during the **Mexican War**, he took over command of the Pacific fleet when **John Sloat** became ill. After appointing **John Frémont** as civil governor of California, Stockton became embroiled in a spat with **Stephen Kearny**, the latter winning out in retaining government recognition of his position. However, no official sanction was taken against Stockton and he would remain in the navy until 1850.

STORY, JOSEPH (1779-1845). Story was born in Massachusetts, educated at Harvard, and went on to become, behind **John Marshall**, the second most significant jurist of the early republic. He had sat on the Supreme Court bench since 1811 and, although many of the 268 majority opinions he wrote were in minor cases, he was largely responsible for the idea that Supreme Court decisions are superior to those of the highest court of any individual state. After Marshall's death Story felt increasingly isolated in the Court, out of line with many of **Roger Taney**'s positions, such as in the *Charles River Bridge* case. This was hardly surprising since Story was also politically conservative and felt deep unease at the statements and actions of **Andrew Jackson**. He proved equivocal on **slavery**-related issues, putting his assessment of the law above any personal feeling about the peculiar institution. He supported the judgment in favor of the *Amistad* rebels, but also stood along with the majority in *Prigg vs. Pennsylvania* ruling that personal liberty laws were unconstitutional.

Story also left a lasting impression as an educator, returning to his alma mater as professor of law from 1829 to 1845 and succeeding in increasing the popularity of Harvard's law program. Moreover, he wrote significant legal works, including *Commentaries on the Constitution of the United States* in 1833, *Commentaries on the Conflict of Laws* (1834), and *Equity Jurisprudence* (1836).

STOURBRIDGE LION. This was the first steam locomotive to be tested on railroad track in the United States, at Honesdale, Pennsylvania, in 1829. Designed originally to haul coal for the Delaware and Hudson Canal company, the *Lion* was built in England to the plans of an American civil engineer.

STRICKLAND, WILLIAM (1788-1854). Strickland was born in Philadelphia and became an important engraver, engineer, and architect. In the latter role he studied as an apprentice to Benjamin Latrobe and went on to share in the Greek revival in American architectural design. Included among Strickland's works were the **Second Bank** building, built before this period, and others in the Philadelphia area, including the U.S. Mint in 1829, the Merchants' Exchange in 1834, and a redesign of the spire of Independence Hall. He also designed the Mints at Charlotte in 1835 and New Orleans in 1835-36, the Athenaeum in Providence in 1836, and the state capitol in Nashville in 1844-49. He was entrusted with designing George Washington's sarcophagus at Mount Vernon. As an engineer Strickland had prepared an extensive study of the British transportation system and this prepared him well for jobs such as a survey of the route of the Chesapeake and Delaware Canal, and the construction of the Delaware breakwater, built between 1828 and 1840.

SUB-TREASURY. *See* INDEPENDENT TREASURY.

SUFFOLK SYSTEM. Established in 1828, the Suffolk system provided a means of bank monitoring for New England. Under its auspices notes of one bank were interchangeable for those of all other banks in the region, which allowed notes to circulate at par throughout New England. Its existence limited the degree to which the **Second Bank of the United States** could be said to operate as a central bank across the whole nation.

SUFFRAGE EXTENSION. A persistent element of the mythology surrounding the Jacksonian era is that **Andrew Jackson**'s election heralded great changes in both the level of qualification for voting and the sort of **elections** that were open to popular votes. While it is now generally acknowledged that Jackson was more the beneficiary of earlier changes in suffrage levels than he was responsible for further advances, it was the case that several states did make constitutional revisions in this period, extending the rights of white men, while leaving **women** and free African-Americans further outside the community of voters. Mississippi, Louisiana, Rhode Island, and Virginia were the states with most restrictions on white voting as the era began and each took steps toward broadening the suffrage, although not always comfortably or peacefully. In 1831 the Virginia constitutional convention left about one third disfranchised despite extending the vote to some lease- and householders. A similar convention in Mississippi in 1832 prohibited property qualifications. Meanwhile, as late as 1840 Louisiana still disqualified half its white males from voting, and Rhode Island had to endure the **Dorr Rebellion** before introducing better, if not perfect levels of suffrage. Even after these, and the earlier changes, many states still went through the period with some degree of property-owning or tax-paying qualification for the right to vote.

SUFFRAGE FOR FREE BLACKS. Symptomatic of the prevalence of **slavery** and of racism throughout the Union, most states had denied free African-Americans the vote in the period before the Jacksonian era. Things were unlikely to change in the following 20 years, with attitudes like those expressed by Supreme Court Chief Justice **Roger Taney** prevailing, it being his view that the separate and degraded condition of free African-Americans should always disqualify them from being American citizens. So then, however limited **suffrage extension** was for white men in this period, African-Americans did not share in it and, indeed, in places experienced a reduction in their rights. Whereas in the past African-Americans had claimed the right to vote in some states under the term "all men" if they met the necessary qualifications, now many states put in place discriminatory rules that effectively excluded them from voting altogether. Other states, such as Tennessee in 1834 and North Carolina in 1835, overtly denied African-Americans their right to vote. Elsewhere custom and intimidation kept them away from the polls. In all only Maine, Massachusetts, New Hampshire, and Vermont allowed their black citizens to vote, these four states accounting for a mere 7 percent of the free black population of the North.

SUGAR. Sugar was a crop grown for its syrup in many southern states, but it was only in Louisiana, and later Texas, that it became a mainstream **agricultural** industry. Sugar was distinctive in requiring a greater degree of mechanization on the plantation for its processing than was the case for most other staple crops. It also was a particularly hard crop for the labor force involved in its growth and harvesting. The level of investment these features demanded ensured that, like **rice**, sugar was almost exclusively a plantation-based crop. In their position as both suppliers for a domestic market and competitors with sugar producers in relatively local neighbors, notably in Cuba and Brazil, Louisiana's sugar planters were among the few Southern producers who supported **tariff protection** of their industry. By 1850 American producers were providing around half the sugar the nation consumed.

SULLY, THOMAS (1783-1872). This English-born painter had moved to the United States as a child, before training with some of the leading American and English artists of his day. Sully's study became the most prolific and popular center for portraiture in America and he produced famous renditions of leading statesmen, including **John Quincy Adams**, **Andrew Jackson**, and **Daniel Webster**, and cultural figures such as **Fanny Kemble**, **Edgar Allan Poe**, and **Washington Irving**. In 1847 the University of North Carolina commissioned Sully to paint a portrait of their most famous alumnus, **James Polk**. Sully also painted historical portraits including *George Washington Wearing the Order of the Cincinnati* (1840).

SUNDAY MAILS. *See* SABBATARIANISM.

SUTTER, JOHN (1803-1880). Having arrived in the United States as a German **immigrant** Sutter became a western pioneer and a leading settler in the **California** territory, both before and after its conquest. After engaging in trade in the far West, in Santa Fe and Oregon, in 1839 Sutter had moved to California to found a colony at New Helvetia, the future Sacramento. Although he received a land grant from the Mexican government and even became a Mexican citizen and official, Sutter sided with the Americans during the **Mexican War**. A wealthy and powerful man in his own right, his renown stems primarily from the fact that gold was discovered on his land in 1848, inspiring the gold rush when **James Polk** referred to the find in his 1848 annual message to Congress.

SWARTWOUT, SAMUEL (1783-1856). This former associate of Aaron Burr was a New York merchant and speculator, who as a friend of both **Andrew Jackson** and **John Calhoun**, gave his support to the developing **Jacksonian Democratic** coalition at the start of the era. Against the advice of **Martin Van Buren**, Jackson appointed Swartwout to the position of collector of the port of New York in 1829, planting the seed for one of the most notorious examples of official corruption in American history. Indeed, Van Buren's advice, although tinged with political bias, had been well-considered, as Swartwout's corruption culminated in him fleeing for Europe in 1839 with some $1 million of public money. His flight created a major scandal and exposed the Democratic Party to criticism for their use of the **spoils system** and for their management of financial and fiscal affairs.

– **T** –

TALLMADGE, NATHANIEL (1795-1864). This New York senator was a strong supporter of state **deposit banks**, **paper money**, and the **credit system**, believing all to be vital to the health of a developing economy. Tallmadge combined with fellow **Conservative Democrats** like **William Rives** in attacking the **Independent Treasury** proposals and "hard money" stance of **Martin Van Buren**'s administration. Although Tallmadge also supported a **protective tariff** and **distribution** and was attracted by the **Whig** Party's attacks on **executive usurpation**, feeling his own party's demands for discipline were overbearing, he only allied with the Whigs rather than joining them full-time. Indeed, by the 1840s he felt more comfortable with the increasingly independent position adopted by **John Tyler** against the regular Whig Party.

TAMMANY HALL. This was the home of New York City's **Democratic** political machine, and consequently the label "Tammany" has been used to refer to New York Democrats.

TANEY, ROGER B. (1777-1864). Roger Taney was a lawyer, statesman, politician, and, most significantly, a jurist of long-term importance after **Andrew Jackson** appointed him chief justice of the Supreme Court in 1836. Born in Maryland, Taney had once been a Federalist but had supported the War of 1812 and then gravitated to the developing coalition of support that would back Jackson in 1828 and become the foundation of the **Democratic** Party. After a stint as his state's attorney general from 1827 to 1831, Taney took up the same position in Jackson's Cabinet in the latter year. A strong supporter of the president's stance on the **Second Bank**, Taney helped to draft the **bank veto message** and then in 1833 he took over at the Treasury Department to oversee the **removal of the federal deposits**. However, partly as a result of his willingness to implement that controversial policy, he was denied Senate confirmation both of the Treasury post in 1834 and of the position of associate justice of the Supreme Court in 1835. Only when appointed to succeed **John Marshall** did Taney finally win the approval of a newly elected Senate.

Taney's most momentous decision came with the Dred Scott case in 1857, but his term as chief justice had by then already witnessed significant rulings, important for specific cases as well as for the power of the federal government and of the Court. Generally his rulings, most notably in the *Charles River Bridge* case, expanded the scope of government to regulate affairs in a way favorable to popular interests against the influence of accumulated wealth and corporations. He also promoted the responsibility of the federal government for the exercise of foreign policy. On one significant issue, the constitutionality of **John Tyler**'s succession and his exact status as president, Taney declined to give advice, officially because he had been approached through the wrong channels but as much because of his own past enmity with both Tyler and **Henry Clay** and an unwillingness to be seen to be taking sides.

TAPPAN, ARTHUR (1786-1865). Arthur Tappan was one of three Massachusetts-born brothers prominent in business and politics during the era. His main influence derived from the substantial fortune he acquired from a dry goods import business in silk products, wealth he put to a range of philanthropic purposes. He supported the creation of **Oberlin College** and helped to establish the New York City Tabernacle for the evangelist preacher **Charles Finney**. But, from early support of **colonization** Tappan's main preoccupation was with the attack on the institution of **slavery**. His money had once bailed **William Lloyd Garrison** out of jail and was also important in helping to found the **American Anti-Slavery Society** and in funding many of its propaganda activities. Indeed, the damaging impact of the **panic of 1837** upon Tappan's business indirectly also hampered the Society's progress, so reliant was it on his financial backing. Together with his brother, **Lewis**, Arthur later moved away from Garrison's immediatist **abolitionism** in 1839, helping to found the **American and Foreign Anti-Slavery Society** in 1840 and backing the **Liberty Party** and its more political agenda in the 1840s. *See also* TAPPAN, BENJAMIN.

TAPPAN, BENJAMIN (1773-1857). The life of Benjamin Tappan took a slightly different trajectory from that of his brothers, **Arthur** and **Lewis**. He had moved to Ohio from Massachusetts in 1799 and found himself drawn more to academic life, law, and politics than to business. In 1831 he became the first president of the Ohio Historical and Philosophical Association and then between 1839 and 1845 he sat as an anti-banking **Democrat** in the Senate, supporting **hard money** and the **Independent Treasury** proposals. Although less driven by religious belief to the strong **abolitionist** position adopted by his brothers, Benjamin was **anti-slavery** in sentiment and acted accordingly in 1844 when he leaked the **Pakenham letter** into the public domain during the Senate's consideration of the **Texas annexation** treaty, in the hope that it would at least provide the opportunity for open rather than secret consideration of the potential slave-expansion ramifications of annexation. His anti-slavery stance reinforced his sympathy with the **Barnburner** wing of his party and led him to support **Martin Van Buren** in his fight for the Democratic presidential candidacy in 1844 and again, as the **Free Soil** candidate, in 1848.

TAPPAN, LEWIS (1788-1873). Like his brothers, **Arthur** and **Benjamin**, Lewis Tappan was born in Massachusetts and then moved on, with Arthur, to become a partner in their New York-based silk import business. His career paralleled that of his brother and business partner in other ways, as he too was involved in the creation of the **American Anti-Slavery Society**, before later splitting from it to participate in the founding of the **American and Foreign Anti-Slavery Society** in 1840. In the meantime he had been prominent in efforts to raise money in support of the *Amistad* rebels, through the *Amistad* Committee that later became the American Missionary Association. He also collaborated with his other brother, Benjamin, in the leaking of the **Pakenham letter** at the time of the **Texas annexation treaty** debates in the Senate in 1844. His own business recovery from the **panic of 1837** was based on his establishment in 1841 of the first commercial credit rating agency in the United States, the Mercantile Agency, which later would become the famous firm of Dun and Bradstreet.

TARIFF, PROTECTIVE. This was the policy stance of those who hoped to use the imposition of federal customs duties upon imports as a means of supporting new or existing domestic **manufactures** and raw materials. By imposing prohibitively high import duties upon similar goods manufactured, grown, or exploited by foreign producers, it was hoped that the United States could create a protected market· for its own citizens. The policy's supporters justified their position with a range of arguments. Initially protection was necessary to develop infant industries, in recognition of the fact that start-up costs and the difficulty of introducing new technology meant that foreign rivals were often in a more competitive position. In the face of such circumstances protection would help young American industries to find their feet and ultimately become competitive, free of the challenge of overseas rivals. However, as articulated as part of the **American System**, protection was advocated more generally as a way of strengthening the United States economy by making the nation independent of foreign suppliers (especially in times of war) and by providing employment for workers and markets for American raw materials.

From the moment it was first legislated, in the tariff of 1816, the principle of protection became a controversial issue, forming the central debating point for **tariffs** during this period, in **1828, 1832, 1833, 1842**, and **1846**. Protection's main supporters came from those regions with a clear and direct interest in it, such as Pennsylvania's metal producing districts and, eventually, New England with its burgeoning textiles production. The **sugar** producers of Louisiana also favored protection against Caribbean and Latin American competitors. Gradually the issue came to be one decided more along party lines, as first the **National Republicans** and then the **Whigs** became protection's strongest advocates. Even so, **Democrats** from those states most in favor of protection occasionally broke party ranks on the issue. The most concerted level of opposition came from the South, a region that worried that protection would harm it both as a consumer of protected, and hence more expensive, goods and as the nation's major exporter, their fear being that other countries would retaliate by imposing high duties on southern products. Opposition to protection also assumed a constitutional dimension, with many southerners claiming that if the federal government exercised unconstitutional power by prohibiting **overseas commerce** rather than promoting or merely regulating it, then other interest groups, such as **abolitionists**, might prevail upon Congress to make other unconstitutional laws. This proved to be the key motivating force behind the popularity of **nullification** in South Carolina.

TARIFF, REVENUE. This was the position adopted by those who believed the first purpose of the tariff was to raise revenue for the federal government. Although often seen as a justification for raising duties to **protective** levels, clearly this stance was not compatible with support for all-out protection which aimed to block importations and which would therefore, in theory, not have brought in any revenue at all. So it was that most protectionists supported a tariff combining higher duties on those goods they desired to protect with revenue-producing levels of duty upon other imports. Opponents of protection, more usually based in the South but also in commercial communities of the Northeast and parts of the Northwest, preferred duties to be set at levels as low as possible to encourage importation and, indirectly, the raising of revenue. Few doubted the constitutionality of a revenue-raising tariff.

TARIFF OF 1828. Also known as the "tariff of abominations," the name given it by anti-tariff groups, the tariff of 1828 set import duties at their highest and most **protective** levels up to that time. The original bill was pushed by **Martin Van Buren**'s followers in Congress with a view to promoting the interests of **Andrew Jackson** in the run-up to the **election of 1828**. The bill placed protective duties on imports of raw materials that also were produced in the Mid-Atlantic and Upper South as well as Louisiana, notably wool, **hemp**, and molasses. Van Buren hoped that by putting high duties on the latter product, and others traditionally imported by New England, such as the iron, rope, and sailcloth used by shipping industries, the tariff would place President **John Quincy Adams** in the difficult position of having to decide whether to veto a policy he generally supported or to accept a bill injurious to the interests of his own section. Van Buren's plan backfired, however, when Jacksonians found the bill less than attractive, while Adams followers were willing to support it, especially when it was amended to provide greater levels of protection for manufactured goods such as **cotton** and woolen textiles. The generally high level of duties and the element of protection aroused

outrage in the agricultural South, making the 1828 tariff one of those
that triggered South Carolina's move toward **nullification**.

TARIFF OF 1832. Almost immediately after the passage of the **tariff
of 1828**, there were calls for a revision to its terms, pressure coming
especially from southern states and supporters of the new president
Andrew Jackson. Although his position on the tariff had never been
completely clear, Jackson realized that the 1828 version was unacceptable to many and he was also prepared to accept general reductions in duty levels now that he was less desperate for revenue to pay
off a diminishing **national debt**. So then when it came, tariff change
emerged from a coalition between Jackson's Secretary of the Treasury **Louis McLane** and the chairman of the House Committee on
Manufactures, former President **John Quincy Adams**. The 1832 tariff removed most of the specific objectionable features of the 1828
tariff and returned general duties to around their 1824 levels, about
33 percent. Meanwhile the bill did retain some **protective** features,
pleasing textiles manufacturers by not reducing duties on most finished cloth products while lowering the duties on their raw materials.
As a gesture to the South, duties on the coarse woolen cloth used for
slaves' clothing were reduced. However, for many in the South the
reductions were still not sufficient and southern Congressmen voted
heavily against the bill's passage. Nor did the bill ease the pressure
for **nullification** in South Carolina, where the continuation of any
degree of protection was sufficient to propel affairs to crisis point.

TARIFF OF 1833. This act continued the process of revising levels of
tariff duty in response to the discontent expressed against the **tariff of
1828**, but it also formed a crucial part of the **compromise of 1833**
that brought to an end the dangerous **Nullification crisis** of 1832-33.
Although as in 1832 **Andrew Jackson**'s administration supported
further tariff revision, it was not surprising that key elements of the
work to achieve it were carried out by the leading **protectionist** and
nullification advocates in Congress, respectively **Henry Clay** and
John Calhoun, since only they could hope to carry their supporters
with them in passing the bill.

     Clearly the key to its success lay in persuading anti-protection
nullifiers that the tariff would be stripped of its protective features.
This was achieved by increasing the number of items to be considered free of duty and by holding out the prospect of a top rate for duties of 20 percent by the year 1842. Protectionists were to be con-
soled by the process by which the 20 percent rate would be reached.

All duties above that level in 1833 would be reduced gradually, one tenth every two years, with any remaining duties over 20 percent to be equalized at that level in 1842, which meant that protection on some items could in theory continue for another 10 years. The bill also legislated for the valuation of imports at their port of entry, this being seen as the best way of establishing their true value and of allowing the remaining element of protection to work better.

Even so, the most ardent protectionists opposed the bill, with **Daniel Webster** and the Pennsylvanian Democrat **George Dallas** to the fore, and it eventually passed only by a regionally divided vote, the South winning enough backers from the Northwest to overcome opposition from the Northeast. Although successful as part of the compromise that calmed the sectional tension of the Nullification crisis, the 1833 tariff is usually considered at best neutral in its economic impact or perhaps as damaging, especially to the confidence of manufacturers. It also left a legacy of considerable doubt as to how the final elements of its implementation should be carried out, causing unnecessary haste in the early stages of debates on the **tariff of 1842**.

TARIFF OF 1842. For different, less sectionally charged reasons, the debates culminating in the passage of the tariff of 1842 were almost as dramatic as those surrounding its predecessor, the **tariff of 1833**. Indeed, the latter act to some extent created the drama, since uncertainty as to whether its prescription for a final reduction of duties above 20 percent would leave any active tariff duties in place heightened the belief that it was necessary to pass a new act. This circumstance actually led to attempts to pass the **Little Tariff** bill in order to allow more time for producing an acceptable longer-term measure, but **John Tyler**'s veto of the temporary bill blocked its implementation and should have warned **Whigs** of the problems to come.

At the start of the 1841-42 session of Congress supporters of **protective tariffs** were heartened by the admission of Tyler and even of some of his more extreme **states' rights** supporters, such as **Abel Upshur**, that in the dire financial situation facing the federal government an upward revision of import duties was necessary and that incidental protection would be an acceptable outcome of this. **Millard Fillmore** had introduced a bill early in the session, proposing to increase duty levels back to where they had stood by the **tariff of 1832** and, although some Whigs delayed debate on the measure to embarrass Tyler in retaliation for his veto of the **Bank bill of 1841**, eventually Congress passed the bill by narrow majorities in both houses, with voting largely on sectional lines.

Tyler's earlier statements gave the bill's supporters reason to hope that it would meet with the president's approval when he received it in August 1842, but as in the case of the Little Tariff two months earlier, the new bill failed to suspend **distribution** even though it would have raised import duties above the 20 percent set out as a trigger level by the **Distribution Act of 1841**. Predictably Tyler's response was the same too and his veto precipitated political uproar in the House. A special committee dominated by Whigs even suggested that the president had committed acts that could be declared impeachable and although ultimately it shied away from formally adopting that step, the Whig majority in the House did support the committee's report. However, they lacked the strength to override the veto and so were forced to accept a revised tariff bill without a clause perpetuating distribution, against the express instructions to his followers from **Henry Clay**, who looked on in dismay from his temporary retirement. The amended bill passed both houses only by one vote, having twice been voted down in the House by the casting vote of the Clay loyalist speaker. Tyler now felt able to sign the bill, but by this time near irreparable damage had been done to his relationship with the rest of the Whig Party.

TARIFF OF 1846. As a long-term **free trader** it was expected that **James Polk** would push for a downward revision of the tariff when he became president in 1845. His inaugural and first annual messages reinforced a reputedly "scientifically" compiled report from the secretary of the treasury, **Robert Walker**, calling for a **tariff for revenue** only, with any incidental **protection** to be enjoyed by all sectors of the economy. The end of the post-**panic of 1839** depression and good victories for the **Democratic** Party in elections to both congressional chambers also seemed to presage the replacing of the **tariff of 1842**. Walker's bill, proposing to establish seven categories of product and to set the levels of duty in each that would maximize revenue, has often been labeled a free trade measure, but in truth it only reduced duties to on average around 25-30 percent, higher than legislated for by the compromise **tariff of 1833**. Even so, debate on the bill was fierce, as protectionists sought to defend their principle and as some northern Democrats revolted against the administration over it. However, final voting on the bill was predominantly partisan in nature, with Vice-President **George Dallas** sealing its success by means of several casting votes despite the fact that he came from the protectionist state of Pennsylvania. The act, which passed in July, proved to be one of the longest surviving pieces of tariff legislation of the 19th century, lasting until 1857.

TAYLOR, ZACHARY (1784-1850). Taylor was a military man of considerable bravery and inspirational qualities who rose to prominence in the **Mexican War**, during which he never lost a battle. Born in Virginia, he spent most of his youth in Kentucky before joining the army in 1808 after a short period of militia service. For most of the early part of his career Taylor was stationed in frontier posts, taking part in the War of 1812, **Black Hawk's War**, and the **Second Seminole War**. He rose in rank from major to colonel, and to brigadier general by the time he defeated the **Seminole** at the battle of Lake Okeechobee in 1837. Promoted again to commander of the army's southern department in 1840, Taylor took up residence in Louisiana and there combined his military duties with efforts to expand upon earlier ventures as a planter and slaveholder by buying a sizable plantation near Natchez. As a planter he proved no radical on the **slavery** issue, regarding the peculiar institution only as an economic necessity which should not be extended into those areas where it was not economically viable or necessary. To this effect he personally opposed **Texas annexation** and the drive for more territories from Mexico.

It was somewhat ironic, then, that it was the presence of troops under Taylor's command, defending the border of the recently annexed Texas, that triggered the Mexican War, and that his efforts helped to win a conflict that did indeed bring new territories into American ownership. Taylor's victories at **Palo Alto** and **Resaca de la Palma** in May 1846 earned him promotion to major general and inspired him to push the campaign into Mexico proper, where he won the battle of **Monterrey** in September 1846. Despite being stripped of a large part of his army, which was sent to reinforce **Winfield Scott**'s campaign, and despite being outnumbered four to one, Taylor then successfully defeated **Santa Anna** at the battle of **Buena Vista** in February 1847.

Taylor returned to a hero's welcome in the United States in November 1847, and **Democratic** fears that this stature would create in him a dangerously popular **Whig** military hero candidate for the **election of 1848** were borne out. Although personally still reluctant and also lacking any previous public statement of party commitment, Taylor was nominated by the Whigs, with **Thurlow Weed** prominent in the efforts to overcome the doubts of some northern party members about the sense of nominating a slaveholder as their candidate.

Taylor duly rode to the White House on the back of his popularity but, again ironically, spent most of his shortened term in the presidency managing problems created by the acquisition of new lands won in the war.

TELEGRAPH. This important system of communication, using electric pulses along wires to pass signals from one location to another, was first introduced during the Jacksonian era and began to be exploited for commercial purposes in the 1840s. The necessary knowledge and technology had been available for some time, but it took the vision of **Samuel Morse** to appreciate the social and economic value of such a development and, with the assistance of chemist Leonard Cole and engineer Alfred Vail, to produce the first working telegraph system. Although Morse conceived of the telegraph in 1832, the first demonstration only occurred six years later, in 1838, and it would be another six years after that before a working line would be in place, when Morse and Vail gave the first successful public exhibition of its powers in 1844. The federal government had provided some of the finance for the trial line but declined to take up Morse's offer to buy the rights for the invention. As a result Morse established his own Magnetic Telegraph Company instead, which eventually made him a significant fortune. The telegraph began to change the very culture of communication and even of politics, as politicians now awaited immediate news of major events such as conventions and elections.

TEMPERANCE. In the face of high levels of public drinking in the United States temperance was a reform movement committed to convincing or even compelling individuals to moderate or to end their consumption of alcohol. Although initially inspired mainly by medical fears, temperance developed a moral imperative as religious revivals demanded that Americans be self-disciplined individuals. The year 1826 saw the creation of the American Society for the Promotion of Temperance, which, starting in New England, built up a network of support throughout the country, by 1834 featuring local associations in every state and numbering 5,000 societies and some one million members in total. Individual religious denominations and businesses promoted their own temperance efforts. Methodists tightened their rules on drink and eventually called for total abstinence in 1831. Meanwhile some temperance-supporting employers organized boycotts against the trade in drink and insisted that their employees stop drinking. Diminishing levels of alcohol intake suggest that temperance campaigns did meet with some success, but there was still impetus for a further revival of the temperance movement in the 1840s, as groups like the Washington Temperance Society used tactics similar to **evangelical** religious revivals to draw in converts. That decade witnessed both New York and Maine adopting a statewide prohibition of the retail sale of alcohol, in 1845 and 1846 respectively, although in the former it was repealed again by 1847.

TEN-HOUR DAY CAMPAIGN. The **labor** campaign for a 10-hour working day was an important part of workers' responses to their decreasing autonomy in the workplace, one of the significant consequences of trends in **manufacturing** development in the period. By 1835 labor activity had inspired the end to working days longer than 10 hours in most regions outside New England, and the movement gained even more strength both from **Andrew Jackson**'s ruling that this limit should prevail in the Philadelphia Naval Yard and from **Martin Van Buren**'s executive order in 1840 that laborers on federal public works were to toil no more than 10 hours a day. During the 1840s and 1850s seven states followed suit in introducing such restrictions.

TEN REGIMENTS BILL. This bill, considered by the 1846-47 congressional session, proposed the creation of larger military resources with which to prosecute the **Mexican War**. Opponents of the war and of **James Polk**'s administration made the bill's legislative career a difficult one and, with **John Calhoun** prominent, the Senate actually rejected it in February 1847. This provoked the administration's newspaper organ, the *Washington Union*, to such levels of criticism of the Senate that its representatives were expelled from the Senate floor. However, the bill was reconsidered and eventually passed.

TEXAS ANNEXATION, IMPLEMENTATION. Following congressional adoption of the compromise allowing the president to choose whether to offer **Texas annexation by legislative settlement** or by a renegotiated treaty, on 3 March 1845 **John Tyler** quickly notified the Texas government that immediate annexation would take place, so long as Texans accepted. Angered that Tyler had taken the decision out of his hands, the incoming president, **James Polk**, initially instructed the American chargé in Texas, **Andrew Jackson Donelson**, to ignore Tyler's orders, but later was persuaded by his Cabinet that Tyler had acted correctly and that the new administration could now only accept the action.

Polk's next task was to nudge Texans away from the renegotiation option that some still favored and toward acceptance of immediate annexation. At one point dramatic events seemed likely to obstruct this process, when Mexico, under the influence of Britain, finally agreed to recognize Texan independence as long as annexation to the United States did not follow. However, Polk sent special agents, including **Robert Stockton**, to work with Donelson in strengthening the Texan resolve for annexation, with promises of federal financial and perhaps military support. Finally the Texan Congress, and then a special convention, agreed to annexation in June-July 1845. A state constitution won approval from the Texan people and was accepted by the U.S. Congress, allowing Texas to enter the Union as a single slave state on 29 December 1845.

TEXAS ANNEXATION, LEGISLATIVE SETTLEMENT. After the Senate rejection of the **Texas annexation treaty** in June 1844, **John Tyler** and his main advisors remained determined that annexation would occur sooner rather than later. At the time the treaty was signed, Tyler had hinted to Texan representatives that, if necessary, the United States could admit a state by congressional action, which would require only simple majorities in both houses rather than two-thirds support in the Senate, significantly increasing the chances of success. So, two days after the treaty's rejection Tyler sent it and the accompanying documentation to the House for their consideration, expressing the view that annexation was vital to the national interest and that negotiations with a view to achieving it did not infringe any international commitments to Mexico or other nations. Finally the president called upon the House to consider admitting Texas as a new state by joint resolution with the Senate. Meanwhile opponents of this approach in the Senate, led by **Thomas Benton**, switched their line of attack, calling for a new treaty so amended as to deflect the dangers they believed to be inherent in the treaty just rejected. Specifically, they proposed admitting Texas as two separate areas, one free and one slave, in order to ease **sectional** fears, while they also insisted that Mexico should participate in the new negotiations to avoid the possibility of any retaliatory war on that country's part.

The 1843-44 session closed without further movement on the issue and Tyler endured a worrying summer, awaiting the outcome of the **election of 1844** and fearing how Texans would react to the treaty's rejection. Some, no doubt, were angry and **Sam Houston** bade farewell to the Texan presidency with a message to his Congress raising once more the possibility of seeking from Mexico its formal recognition of Texas as an independent and separate nation. However, his successor, Anson Jones, appeared more willing to give the United States time to approve annexation. This, together with **James Polk**'s election, which seemed to demonstrate popular support for annexation among the American people, encouraged Tyler to repeat his call for the joint resolution approach in his final annual message to Congress.

Congress proceeded to debate a range of issues connected to annexation, such as the assumption of Texan debts and the definition of boundaries with other states and Mexico. These issues the administration was keen to postpone until annexation was actually accomplished. However, potentially more damaging to the project were claims by some opponents that the constitutional arguments used to justify annexation by joint resolution could only be applied to territories or states that were already part of the United States, and not to an independent state like Texas. Ultimately, though, the House voted in favor of annexation by resolution alone, albeit with some interesting provisions for dividing the state into four parts, two to be free of **slavery** and two to decide for themselves whether or not they would have slavery in future. However, the Senate stood fast in support of Benton's resolution calling for a renegotiated treaty, although even he had by now agreed that Mexico need not be involved.

This stalemate was eventually resolved when in March 1845, under pressure from president-elect Polk, Congress accepted **Robert Walker**'s compromise resolution allowing the president to choose which of the two approaches to take. In one of the last acts of his presidency Tyler, not surprisingly, opted for admission by congressional resolution and so ushered in the implementation of annexation in practice. *See also* TEXAS ANNEXATION, IMPLEMENTATION.

TEXAS ANNEXATION, SIGNIFICANCE. Efforts to secure annexation made the Texas issue one of the most influential forces for political change in the 1840s, affecting **sectional** relations, electoral politics, and international relations. As many party politicians in the later 1830s had feared it would, annexation aroused sectional tensions, with southerners like **John Calhoun** defending **slavery** and the right of slavery to expand into Texas, while many northerners feared that the intention to acquire Texas was more the result of a slaveholders' conspiracy to expand the area of slavery than it was a response to national objectives. Of course, ultimately the absorption of Texas into the Union did not precipitate an immediate sectional crisis. No doubt this was mainly because it involved the admission of only one new slave state and so did not greatly threaten the representative balance between free and slave states. It also could be said not to have extended the institution into new territory, since slavery already existed in Texas. Nevertheless, the tensions that arose during the diplomacy and debates over the admission of Texas signaled likely problems for the integration of new, more widespread and slavery-free territories in the future.

The combination of those sectional tensions and the undoubted popularity of annexation also propelled Texas onto the electoral stage in the run-up to the **election of 1844**. Although the initial candidates of both main parties, **Henry Clay** and **Martin Van Buren**, tried to shy away from the matter and agreed to issue letters stating that they would not push for annexation, the policy's clear popularity forced individual candidates and parties to adopt more active positions, with an eye to where each drew their main support bases. Clay eventually expressed a qualified support for annexation, while the **Democratic** Party convention preferred to jettison Van Buren altogether and nominate instead the dark horse, pro-annexation **James Polk**.

Finally, annexation provided the background for one of the major causes of the later conflict between the United States and Mexico. Since 1843 Mexican rulers had been warning that annexation would be considered grounds for war. Polk's refusal to reject the course toward annexation caused Mexico to break off diplomatic relations, while American demands that Mexico recognize both the legality of annexation and the line of the Rio Grande as the new border between the two countries were the major sticking point in the efforts to restore more peaceful relations before the outbreak of the **Mexican War**. Ultimately it would be Mexican military activity across the Rio Grande in response to the U.S. army presence in Texas, under General **Zachary Taylor**, that sparked off hostilities in the war itself.

TEXAS ANNEXATION, TREATY NEGOTIATIONS. The prospect of U.S. annexation of Texas became a political issue almost from the moment of **Texan independence** from Mexico in 1836. Many Texans were keen on annexation and petitioned the United States to that effect as early as August 1837. However, it would not be until the middle of **John Tyler**'s term that political realities forced it to the center stage of politics.

Even though early in his term as president **Andrew Jackson** had made noises about purchasing Texas from Mexico, the question of how to respond to an independent Texas was a totally different one.

The United States, as a neutral nation, still had treaty obligations with Mexico, which, even after **Santa Anna**'s acceptance of Texan independence, was still officially at war with the state. Many in the United States also doubted the constitutionality of any attempt to annex Texas. Foremost, though, were the same fears that had led Jackson to delay recognizing Texan independence until his last day in office. Both he and his successor, **Martin Van Buren**, feared that annexing Texas might let the genie of **sectional** discord over **slavery**'s expansion out of the bottle, threatening the newly forged national **second party system** and ultimately the nation's stability. So it was, then, that Van Buren followed Congress in turning down the formal Texan approach for annexation. When Tyler broached the idea with his first secretary of state, **Daniel Webster**, in December 1841, he received a cool response, and this, as well as the prediction that the Senate would block any annexation treaty, caused the president to turn down two subsequent Texan offers in 1842.

However, Tyler certainly found the idea of annexation an attractive one and even perceived in it a possible popular issue upon which he could mount a successful reelection campaign, either as an independent candidate or for the **Democrats**. Many of his Virginian entourage were long-standing supporters of annexation too, although for some of them the hope was that **John Calhoun** would be the main electoral beneficiary. Either way, Tyler leaned closer toward a pro-annexation position, appointing the like-minded Waddy Thompson and **Abel Upshur** as minister to Mexico and secretary of state respectively. Along with Calhoun, **Duff Green** in London, and the influential **Robert Walker**, these officials pushed the cause of annexation. A strong refrain was a warning that if annexation did not occur soon, British influence would force Texas to abandon slavery, endangering either the American South's own slave and **cotton** interests (as claimed by Upshur, Calhoun, and Green) or any hope that Texas might act as a sink through which slavery might drain out of the United States into Latin America (as suggested by Walker). Unlike many of his advisors, Tyler was probably suspicious of the veracity of and intentions behind the information he was receiving about British ambitions, but nevertheless he initiated several diplomatic missions to secure annexation, beginning in November 1843, although it was likely that Upshur had already begun unauthorized talks a month earlier.

Of course it would take two parties to make this marriage and at times Texas proved a not entirely willing bride, influenced to some extent by European powers keen to support a buffer state between the

United States and Mexico. In June 1843 Britain had helped Texas and Mexico to sign an armistice and a month later Texas had declared that it was withdrawing its offer of annexation. Again, when approached by Upshur later that year it held back from making commitments, fearful that the U.S. Senate would reject any annexation treaty. It took assurances from Upshur, that he believed the Senate would approve a treaty and that the United States government was prepared to use military force to protect Texans against Mexican reprisals, to calm those fears, but ultimately Mexico's own reluctance to carry on peace talks was what pushed **Sam Houston** and Texas back to all-out efforts at annexation.

Negotiations now continued apace, under first Upshur and then, after his death, under acting Secretary John Nelson and Calhoun. Finally the annexation treaty was signed on 12 April 1844, proposing to admit Texas as a territory whose public lands would accrue to the U.S. government, which in turn would assume the independent state's debts. That slavery would persist in line with property rights of Texans was left unwritten, while it was agreed that later negotiations would sort out the exact line of the boundary between Texas and other states and Mexico. Calhoun also repeated oral assurances that American troops would be made ready to meet any Mexican reprisals.

However, subsequent events proved the hollowness of Upshur's earlier claims that the Senate would support an annexation treaty. After nearly a month-long debate a combination of Whig partisanship and northern suspicions about the intentions behind annexation came together to block the treaty in the Senate on 8 June 1844, by a vote of 35 to 16. Only one **Whig** supported the treaty while seven **Democrats**, six northern and the Missourian **Thomas Hart Benton**, opposed it. Tyler's attempts to dress the treaty up in clothing of national significance failed to outweigh his former party colleagues' obstruction and the sense of danger that annexation might precipitate war with Mexico. In addition, the inclusion of Calhoun's **Pakenham letter** in the documents accompanying the treaty made it almost impossible for northerners to support the treaty. Texas annexation would, then, have to await a legislative resolution and further diplomatic activity before it was implemented. *See also* TEXAS ANNEXATION, IMPLEMENTATION; TEXAS ANNEXATION, LEGISLATIVE SETTLEMENT.

TEXAS INDEPENDENCE. The proximity to the United States of the Spanish Central American and then independent Mexican province of

Texas made it the focal point for many settlers from the north in the 1820s. At times consciously encouraged by the Mexican government, this American immigration caused the population of Texas to grow dramatically, from 5,000 in 1821 to between 35,000 and 50,000 by 1835. It also changed the very nature of the province as these new-comers spoke English, only pretended at Catholicism and, true to their mainly southern roots, kept **slaves** at a time when the peculiar institution had been abandoned in the rest of Mexico. From the start many Anglo-Texans were unhappy with the Mexican government's legal procedures, linguistic demands, and commercial regulations, but Texan noises of complaint and even of possible separation from the rest of Mexico only brought repression upon their heads, including the prohibition of slavery and of Anglo-American immigration. Fur-ther strict measures were introduced under the rule of the newly emerged dictator, **Santa Anna**, and these led to all-out revolt in Texas, first in the name of a return to rights enjoyed in the 1820s, and then, in March 1836, for independence itself, as Texans formed their own, constituted government.

Texan independence was ultimately won on the battlefield. There were early rebel victories in late 1835 at Gonzales, Goliad, and San Antonio, and then, after the loss of the garrison at the **Alamo**, the Texan army regrouped and won a conclusive victory at **San Jacinto**. Santa Anna's capture at that battle forced him to accept Texan inde-pendence and to agree to the establishment of the Rio Grande as the border between the two countries.

Despite the efforts of the Texan commissioner to the United States, **Stephen Austin**, and the fact that many Americans had been attracted to join the rebel movement, **Andrew Jackson**'s administra-tion maintained a steady neutrality during the independence struggle. Even the presence of personal friends, such as **Sam Houston**, among the Texan leadership, could not sway Jackson from his stance of avoiding giving any cause for discontent to the Mexican government. This and the delay in according official U.S. recognition of the newly independent Texas until the final day of his term in 1837 were no doubt the result of Jackson's reluctance to arouse **sectional** discord over the issue of Texas at home, something that would also dampen any early enthusiasm for **Texas annexation**.

Nevertheless, U.S. recognition represented one of the early suc-cesses of the fledgling independent Texas, matched by acknowledg-ment of its status by France in 1839 and Britain in 1840. Meanwhile, elections had been held in 1836, returning Sam Houston as the first president, between 1836 and 1838. Houston and his successor, **Mira-**

beau Lamar, both faced economic problems while Lamar proved especially energetic in removing the **Cherokee** from Texan lands, succeeding in this endeavor after the battle of the Neches in 1839. However, tension with Mexico remained the main issue facing the Texan government, as many Mexicans were still reluctant to accept the state's independence. Lamar did little to help by offering his support to potential rebels in other Mexican states. These problems would continue into the 1840s until an armistice in 1844 brought a temporary end to violent actions across the border. Thereafter, the slow move toward annexation into the United States came to dominate both the internal and external affairs of the state.

THOMPSON, SMITH (1768-1843). Thompson was a New Yorker who, after an education at Princeton, went on to a distinguished juridical career, culminating in a position as Supreme Court justice between 1823 and his death in 1843. He had a brief flirtation with party politics in 1828 when he ran as the **National Republican** candidate for governor of New York, only to be defeated by **Martin Van Buren**. Never a leading figure on the bench, Thompson did play a role in the *Amistad* affair with his initial ruling in 1839 that the U.S. government had no jurisdiction in prosecuting the rebels for murder. He did not, though, make any final ruling on the status of the *Amistad* rebels in 1841.

THOREAU, HENRY DAVID (1817-1862). This famous writer and naturalist was born in Concord, Massachusetts, and, after a lengthy, interrupted education, graduated from Harvard in 1837. Thoreau worked variously as a schoolteacher, both during and after his college years, as a surveyor, and as an assistant in his father's pencil factory, helping to make its pencils among the best in America. As one of the original **Transcendentalists** he published some poems in *The Dial*, but generally his writing did little to support him financially. Thoreau is most famous for his period of self-sufficient retreat near Walden Pond, between 1845 and 1847, which would inspire a later book of his experience in 1854. But by then he had already published *A Week on the Concord and Merrimack River* in 1849 and his famous essay "Resistance to Civil Government" in which he justified his conscientious non-payment of taxes in 1846, for which he had been briefly imprisoned. Among others he met and took ideas from were **Orestes Brownson** and **Ralph Waldo Emerson**, the second of whom Thoreau lived with for large parts of the 1840s.

THREE MILLION ACT. Like its predecessor in the previous congressional session, the **Two Million Bill**, this appropriation act considered by the 1846-47 session of Congress had been requested to provide the money needed to prosecute peace negotiations with Mexico and, in particular, to pay for any territorial acquisitions secured in the **Mexican War**. This act, too, became the focus for debates over the **Wilmot Proviso**, whose supporters tried to attach it to the bill, but unlike its predecessor the Three Million Act was eventually passed, without any amendment providing that **slavery** should not be allowed to spread into any territories acquired in the war.

"TIPPECANOE AND TYLER TOO." This was perhaps the most famous campaign slogan used by the **Whigs** in the **election in 1840**, making reference to their choice of candidates, **William Henry Harrison**, victor of the 1811 Battle of Tippecanoe, and **John Tyler**. One predictably critical **Democratic** observation of the slogan was that it was all rhyme and no reason!

TOBACCO. This important staple **agricultural** crop, a long-term fixture in the American Upper South, continued to undergo shifts in usage and growing patterns occurring throughout the wider period of which the Jacksonian era formed part. Cigar and chewing-tobacco started to replace snuff and pipe-tobacco as the main markets for the crop. Meanwhile there were also some changes in production techniques and a geographical shift in the balance of tobacco-growing away from traditional centers, like Virginia and Maryland, to Kentucky, Tennessee, Ohio, and other southwestern and even northwestern regions. In the face of these developments representatives from older tobacco states made a concerted effort to promote overseas markets for their crop, through congressional efforts and diplomatic initiatives.

TOCQUEVILLE, ALEXIS DE (1805-1859). Alexis De Tocqueville was a French peer after 1827, a statesman, and a political writer whose trip to the United States in 1831, to study the country's penal system, generated one of the classic commentaries on American society and politics. For, on his return to France in 1832, in addition to producing his report on penitentiaries, he began to write *Democracy in America*, published in two volumes in 1835 and 1840. Although critical of some aspects of American life, including what he feared was a tyranny of the majority, De Tocqueville celebrated the way in which the American political environment had allowed a diffusion of the best European social ideas, the result being a steady development toward a more democratic society without the need for recourse to violent revolution. In addition to this, his most famous work, he also wrote on aspects of European and, specifically, English life.

TOLEDO WAR. This border dispute between Michigan and Ohio in 1835-36 at one point led to minor outbreaks of violence between settlers from the territory and the state respectively and also caused a delay in the admission of **Michigan to statehood**. The dispute, over a 400 square mile area around Toledo, arose out of inaccurate mapping of the Northwest Territory, Ohio having accepted one interpretation on becoming a state in 1803 while Michigan accepted another when it was organized as a territory two years later. The disagreement became more urgent in this period as Michigan neared statehood but also when it became clear that both the community of Toledo and the company responsible for the construction of the **Miami and Erie Canal** saw the economic benefits of making Toledo the northern, lake terminus of the canal. However, for that to happen Toledo had to be declared part of Ohio, since the canal's founding charter, issued by that state, demanded that the terminus lie within her boundaries.

Both states sent surveyors into the disputed land in order to prove their ownership of it, but their jobs were made more difficult when both Governor Robert Lucas and Territorial Governor Stevens Mason ordered militia posses into the area, resulting in minor clashes and the arrest of some of the Ohio surveyors. In another incident a Michigan sheriff was stabbed in a barroom brawl. Although Lucas did not ease the tension when he declared the disputed region a county of Ohio bearing his own name, President **Andrew Jackson**'s only available realistic course of action to resolve the crisis was to remove Mason from office. Mason did continue to lead his militia in irregular actions against Toledo, but his Jackson-appointed successor, John Horner, and Lucas now managed to establish much friendlier relations. This paved the way for a congressionally-sanctioned settlement that confirmed Ohio's tenure of the Maumee bay and Toledo strip but also compensated Michigan with a large area of the Upper Peninsula south of Lake Superior, some 9,000 square miles of what would turn out to be timber- and mineral-rich lands. The same deal provided for Michigan's admission as a state.

TOM THUMB. This was the first American-built steam locomotive to operate on a passenger **railroad** line. Designed by **Peter Cooper** in 1830, it was built to compete in a contest to prove whether steam-power could provide a faster and stronger service than a horse-drawn train. Although it broke down in the trial, the locomotive proved that it could work at greater speeds and went on to run on the **Baltimore and Ohio Railroad**.

TOUCEY, ISAAC (1792-1869). This **Democrat** rose to prominence in the more conservative faction of the Connecticut party, rivaling the likes of **Gideon Welles** and **John Niles**. Toucey's career was fairly unexceptional, including stints as a representative in the House between 1835 and 1839 and later as his state's governor between 1846 and 1847. But then as a New Englander and personal friend of **James Polk** he became the president's first choice to replace **Nathan Clifford** as attorney general, taking up the office in June 1848.

TOWN, ITHIEL (1784-1844). Town was born in Connecticut and rose to become one of the first professional architects in America. Because he did most of his work in collaboration with partners, such as **Alexander Davis**, his personal contribution to developments is not always easy to gauge, but he certainly helped further the Greek revival style of architecture in buildings like the Connecticut Capitol in New Haven (1829), the New York Customs House (1833), New York University (begun 1833), the North Carolina Capitol in 1833-40, and the Wadsworth Athenaeum in Hartford in 1842. Together with his friend **Samuel Morse**, Town founded the American Academy of Design in 1825 and although he officially retired in 1835 he was also made an honorary member of the Royal Institute of British Architects in 1836. With money made from patenting a style of truss-structure bridge, he proved a liberal supporter of education, helping to establish an impressive library.

TRADE UNIONS. As one means by which American **laborers** were represented, trade unions underwent a roller-coaster ride of experience during the Jacksonian era in the face of continuing **manufacturing** development and fluctuations in the nation's economic health. Single-trade unions in more traditional workshop-based industries flourished in the early years of the period as workers attempted to organize in response to significant changes in working practices, such as putting-out and de-skilling, that threatened both their pockets and sense of self-worth. Increasingly competitive employment practices also alienated those laborers who still worked on site with master craftsmen, the latter now coming to be excluded from union ranks. In addition to complaining about new working practices and fighting for shorter working hours and the very right to organize in the first place, generally it was the bread-and-butter issues of better pay and conditions that concerned unions most of their time, as workers found that their wages tended to rise less quickly than prices in the inflation years of the early 1830s. The majority of the around 200 strikes in the period 1833-36 were in response to such issues. However, some trade unions shared with other labor groups a broader reform agenda of better education, militia reform, and abolition of the practice of imprisonment for debt.

Part of the rise in influence and numbers of trade unions in the early Jacksonian era came with the emergence of other trends. There were attempts to organize workers, including **women**, in some of the newer industrial environments such as textiles factories. As well as single-trade unions, the growth of general unions representing workers of various trades in a particular city continued in this period, with New York and Philadelphia workers' groups experimenting with such bodies in 1833 and 13 cities having city-wide unions by 1836. It is estimated that by that year the New York General Trade Union had over 60 percent of workers in Manhattan enlisted on its books. Meanwhile some took this trend to its logical, if ultimately not very influential, conclusion with the creation in 1834 of the first **National Trade Union**.

These bodies, as well as the single-trade unions, suffered badly toward the end of the 1830s as the **panic of 1837** and especially the depression following the **panic of 1839** produced mass unemployment among urban and manufacturing workers. Union activity declined as numbers in work fell and as many workers realized that in the face of such hard times any job was better than no job. *See also COMMONWEALTH VS. HUNT.*

"TRAIL OF TEARS." This was the critical label applied to the forced exodus of **Cherokee** tribes from their homeland in the Southeast to new territories across the Mississippi River. After most Cherokee refused to accept the process of **Indian removal** which a few of their colleagues had agreed to in the Treaty of **New Echota** of 1835, the U.S. government took steps to implement their removal by force if necessary, backed by military involvement under the command of **Winfield Scott**. The experience proved a terrible one, as about one quarter of the 16,000 who made the journey in 1838-39 died en route. Already inadequate rations were pilfered, while poor clothing and insufficient means of transportation exaggerated the impact of both disease and very cold weather. Although Scott is usually thought to have handled the matter as sensitively as possible, even giving Cherokee chiefs responsibility for the final removal from intermediate camps, the nature of the venture and the failure to resource it adequately throw a bad light on the general motives of the Jacksonian policy toward Native Americans.

TRANSCENDENTALISM. Transcendentalism was a philosophical and intellectual movement whose American manifestation emerged in and around Boston in the 1830s and 1840s. Part of the broader movement of **Romanticism**, Transcendentalism drew on European roots, but its immediate American spiritual parent was **Unitarianism**, with which it shared a rejection of the strictness of Puritan Calvinist theology and, indeed, of the ritualism and dogma of most established religions. This stance accorded with Transcendentalism's support for individualism, part of its general belief that intuitive approaches to thought, more than observation and reason, would allow the individual to fulfill his/her potential by facilitating an awareness of nature's beauty and truths. Institutionally the movement came to be based around the Transcendental club, founded in Boston in 1836, and the important periodical, *The Dial*, whose production involved leading associates such as **Ralph Emerson** and **Margaret Fuller**. Other prominent Transcendentalists included Theodore Parker, **Bronson Alcott**, **George Ripley**, and, latterly, **Henry Thoreau**, several of whom were involved in the **Brook Farm** community in the 1840s.

TRANSPORTATION REVOLUTION. The transportation revolution represented the combined impact in the first half of the 19th century of the development of improved means of river and ocean-going travel and of **internal improvements** in the form of roads, **canals** and **railroads**. Such developments had a massive influence on the distance, speed, and cost of movement of people, products, and ideas and information around the United States. In some cases the very direction of transportation, for goods in particular, was reoriented as new improvements made viable some shorter routes previously impossible for reason of impassibility, slowness, and cost. For example, a lot of trade that previously was floated from the Midwest down the Mississippi River to New Orleans, for trans-shipment to the Atlantic coast, now took the more direct route through canals feeding into the Great Lakes and then along the **Erie Canal** and Hudson River. While such reductions in the distance to be traveled clearly helped to cut costs, so too did improvements in speed on already viable routes. So then it has been estimated that on some journeys freight rates fell between 75 and 90 percent as a result of transportation improvements.

In addition to its geographical impact, both in encouraging the physical opening of new parts of older states and regions as well as frontiers in the Southeast, Northeast, and especially the whole of the West, and in promoting the development of **urban** centers as hubs of improved communications, the transportation revolution is also judged to have generated a wider revolution in economic and social behavior and patterns, known as the **market revolution**.

TRAVIS, WILLIAM (1809-1836). Travis was a South Carolinian who moved, via Alabama in 1818, to settle in Texas in 1832, where fame and historical immortality awaited him. After being temporarily imprisoned by Mexican authorities for defending a slave-owner in a legal case, he became a focus of early Texan complaints against Mexican central rule in 1832. Travis went on to support the **Texas independence** struggle and became a colonel in the army in 1835. As co-commander of the forces at the **Alamo** in spring 1836 he died with all his men during the attack and victory by **Santa Anna**.

TREASURY NOTES. On several occasions in the hard times following the **panics of 1837 and 1839** Treasury notes were resorted to as a way of helping to ease problems of a contracted circulating currency. In the summer of 1837 Secretary of the Treasury **Levi Woodbury** allowed Treasury drafts to circulate as currency when **deposit banks** proved unable to redeem them with specie. In its **special session** later that summer Congress agreed, over **Whig** opposition, that the Treasury could issue $10 million more of such notes. Four years later, as the nation struggled through the longer-term depression that followed the 1839 panic, **John Tyler** recommended to the 1841 special congressional session that more Treasury notes be authorized in order to meet an anticipated Treasury deficit of $11 million, and the issue of such notes was also considered as one of the powers of the Tyler administration's unsuccessful **Board of Exchequer** proposal in December 1841. Despite the fact that by 1844 the improved state of the economy and currency meant that there was no longer a need for Treasury notes, some **Democrats** were starting to regard them as a safer form of currency than notes issued by banks and thus agreed at the time of the passage of the **1846 Independent Treasury Act** that Treasury notes would be acceptable in payment of dues to the federal government. In the following two years some $32 million in Treasury notes were issued.

TRIST, NICHOLAS P. (1800-1874). Trist was a Virginian who had moved to New Orleans at quite a young age. Throughout his early life he met and befriended several future Jacksonians, such as **Andrew Jackson Donelson** at West Point and **Edward Livingston**, under whom he studied law in New Orleans. These acquaintances would help to shape his future career and political allegiance, for, even though he was appointed to a State Department post late in 1828 by **Henry Clay**, Trist had supported **Andrew Jackson** in the **election of 1828** and would receive **Old Hickory**'s appointive favor after he became president. For example, during the **Eaton Affair**, when Donelson left Washington for the more peaceful surroundings of Tennessee, Trist moved from the State Department to act as Jackson's private secretary. In 1834 he became consul at Havana, remaining there after relinquishing the office to a **Whig** in 1841.

However, it was under **James Polk** that Trist rose to a position of considerable prominence, first as chief clerk to the State Department and then most famously as the man sent to negotiate the end of the **Mexican War** in April 1847. As a Spanish-speaker he was a good choice for the job, but he ran into numerous problems, first with General **Winfield Scott**, who had himself coveted the task of negotiating, and then, after making his peace with the general, with the Polk administration itself. Keen to push on with the job in hand, Trist ignored orders to desist from carrying on the negotiations and successfully concluded the Treaty of **Guadalupe Hidalgo** in 1848. On his return to Washington he was fired by the administration, shunned by its members, and would not receive any pay until he was compensated some 25 years later.

TRUCK FARMING. The production of vegetable crops on a larger scale than ever before was a significant **agricultural** development in the hinterlands of some major American cities during this period, as farmers sought to take commercial advantage of the opportunity to supply rising **urban** populations. New England began to grow fruit and vegetables on a commercial basis but it was the mid-Atlantic states that were prominent in this production. As yet transportation was not fast enough, nor preservation or refrigeration techniques available, to allow areas further west to challenge these centers of vegetable crop production.

TRUTH, SOJOURNER (ca. 1799-1883). This New York-born slave was freed when her native state's slaves were finally emancipated in 1828. She became a household servant and an itinerant preacher,

variously influenced by the teachings of the prophet Mathias and the
millenarian **William Miller**. In the 1840s she lived for a time with
the Northampton Association communal society and while there embraced the **abolitionist** cause. She went on to tour the country, speaking on behalf of abolition and **women**'s rights.

TURNER, NAT (1800-1831). *See* NAT TURNER'S REVOLT.

TWO MILLION BILL. At the same time as **James Polk**'s administration called upon the 1845-46 session of Congress for resources to
prosecute the **Mexican War**, the president pressed for passage of a
financial appropriation with which to pay for territories acquired
from Mexico, whether secured by war or by peaceful means. Even after the war had started Polk was determined to follow the stipulation
first made in his orders to **John Slidell** before the war, that the United
States should pay Mexico for any territorial acquisition in the far
Southwest (excluding **Texas**).

The Two Million Bill was intended to provide the financial
wherewithal to support that negotiating stance, but on its appearance
in August 1846, two days before the scheduled end of the congressional session, it ran into trouble from the gathering forces of **Whig**
partisan opposition and northern **anti-slavery** opinion. Although the
Senate quickly passed the bill, the House voted to amend it with the
addition of the **Wilmot Proviso**, making it the first bill to become the
focus for **sectional** debates on this dangerous point of political principle. Indeed, both Whigs and **Democrats** in the House split along
sectional lines in their voting on the amendment. The Senate had neither the inclination to support the Proviso nor the time, in the one remaining day of the session, to push the bill through without it, as the
Proviso's supporters successfully filibustered until the scheduled end
of the session. Efforts at funding territorial acquisition would now
have to wait until the next session and debates on the **Three Million
Act**.

TYLER, JOHN (1790-1862). John Tyler was a prominent Virginian
politician and statesman who in 1841 became the first vice-president
to succeed to the presidency after the death of the sitting president.
After graduating from the College of William and Mary he began a
political career and served as his state's governor in the 1820s before
going on to sit as senator for Virginia from 1827 until 1836. Although once a personal supporter of **John Quincy Adams**, Tyler became a leading opponent of that president's nationalist agenda on

economic policies that offended his own hostility toward a national bank, the **protective tariff**, and federal assistance with **internal improvements** projects. He joined with **Andrew Jackson** in 1828 and backed the new president's vetoes of the **Maysville Road** bill and of the **Second Bank** re-charter bill, as well as his **Indian removal** policy. Tyler's support was rewarded when he easily won renomination to the Senate in 1832 from Virginia's **Democrat**-dominated legislature.

However, not long after that Tyler came into conflict with the president as he alone among senators voted against the **Force Act** during the **Nullification crisis**. He also considered unconstitutional Jackson's further attacks on the existing role of the Bank through the **removal of the federal deposits**, and he stood true to his principles by resigning as senator rather than following his state's instructions to vote for **expunging the censure** by the Senate of Jackson in February 1836. These positions led Tyler to become a **States' Rights Whig** and his status and experience soon made him prominent within the party. After being on two states' tickets as **Whig** vice-presidential candidate in 1836, losing both times, he was nominated vice-presidential candidate for the whole party for the **election of 1840**, running alongside **William Henry Harrison**. Success in the election, followed by Harrison's untimely death, unexpectedly propelled Tyler into the White House in April 1841.

Tyler's **states' rights** background almost immediately created difficulties for the mainstream of the Whig Party. A series of vetoes of key measures in 1841, including two of new **Bank** bills, left Tyler largely isolated from major party support in Congress and reliant on a few, albeit significant, fellow travelers. His own proposal of a **Board of Exchequer** got nowhere in Congress, while his further use of the veto, most notably of the **Little Tariff** and first **tariff bill of 1842**, led to an unsuccessful attempt to impeach him.

Nor were relations with his Cabinet much easier. Most of the Cabinet Tyler inherited from Harrison had resigned in the wake of the Bank vetoes, which at least allowed him to select his own supporters, some of whom had already been advising him in the context of a "**corporal's guard**," a form of **Kitchen Cabinet**. Fortune continued to elude him as early deaths and then an accident on board the U.S.S. *Princeton* forced him into further Cabinet changes. There were also strong suspicions that even Tyler's closer Cabinet colleagues were secretly trying to promote the interests of **John Calhoun**, at least until Calhoun himself entered the Cabinet in 1844.

Even Tyler's personal life failed to provide much relief during the early stages of his presidency, as his first wife, Letitia, suffered the effects of a stroke before dying in September 1842. But, in this respect, as well as in more political affairs, the year 1844 promised to bring an upturn in fortunes. The president remarried, the much younger **Julia Gardiner Tyler** bringing energy and vivacity to administration circles.

By that time Tyler also held within his grasp potential political triumph and long-term historical fame. Keen to find an issue with which to win a party following of his own or to make himself attractive to the Democratic Party as a candidate, he had earlier agreed to moves to secure **Texan annexation** to the United States. Other foreign policy successes during his term, including the **Webster-Ashburton Treaty** and the **Treaty of Wanghia** with China, seemed to suggest diplomacy was an area where he might make political capital. Now Texan compliance and the signing of a treaty with **Sam Houston** in 1844 promised much, but Tyler's dreams then fell apart. The U.S. Senate rejected the treaty and even though this did not automatically spell the end of all hopes for annexation, as other methods were explored, Tyler found his thunder had been stolen anyway when the Democrats nominated the pro-annexation **James Polk** for the presidency, leaving Tyler without adequate support to pursue his own reelection. Even his ultimate act as president, declaring that the United States would admit Texas as a state as soon as possible, in line with a joint resolution of Congress, had its downside insofar as Tyler's long-term reputation has been concerned. Annexation has been seen as one of the major events reigniting **sectional** tensions over **slavery**'s expansion that would lead ultimately to the outbreak of the Civil War, a development Tyler would witness from a retirement begun immediately after he left the presidency in 1845.

TYLER, JULIA (1820-1899). Julia Tyler was the second wife of President **John Tyler**, 30 years her senior. Born Julia Gardiner in New York State, she became a noted figure in the Washington social circle, known to have been courted by numerous other men before her association with the president. Having survived both the explosion on board the U.S.S. *Princeton* and the shock of losing her father in that accident, she married Tyler in June 1844. As well as bringing lavish entertainments and dancing to the White House, she proved a useful supporter to the president in other public matters.

TYLER DOCTRINE. This diplomatic position was incorporated in a message sent to Congress in December 1842, relating to the growing influence of European and especially French interests in the Sandwich Islands, the present-day state of Hawaii. **John Tyler**'s secretary of state, **Daniel Webster**, reflected his own region's maritime perspective by stating how vital the islands were to all Americans involved in transpacific voyages, and in particular to New England's whaling and other mercantile vessels. The facts that U.S.-flagged **shipping** constituted a majority share of maritime activity in the islands and that American citizens had more investments there than did any other foreign group gave the U.S. government good cause to warn against any attempts by Europeans to control affairs in the Sandwich Islands. In effect the message represented an extension of the application of the Monroe Doctrine into the Pacific.

– U –

UNIONISM. **Andrew Jackson**'s love of the United States as a union stood in an at times precarious balance with his stance in favor of a moderate **states' rights** interpretation of the Constitution. The president's advocacy of unionism peaked at the time of the greatest **sectional** challenge to the Union witnessed in his administration, during the **Nullification crisis**. In both his **Nullification Proclamation** and his second inaugural address in March 1833, just days after the resolution of the crisis, Jackson expressed strong support for the concept of the nation as a union of the American people rather than just as a compact of states.

At that time Jackson turned for advice to the more nationalist members of his coalition of supporters, such as **Edward Livingston** and **Louis McLane**, and other former Federalists at the expense of his more traditional old Republican backers. Moreover, some opposition nationalist figures such as **Daniel Webster** and **John Quincy Adams** so admired Jackson's firm unionist stance on nullification that there were suggestions of a new party alignment, with Webster featuring as a possible successor to **Old Hickory**. Indeed, both the president's plans to tour the Northeast, the most recent home of more nationalist expressions, and Webster's own tour wooing unionist feeling among both administration and opposition ranks only seemed to encourage such rumors. However, the end of the Nullification crisis and the resumption of the **bank wars**, with the debate over **removal of the federal deposits**, brought home to Jackson the incongruity of any formal arrangement with Webster, one of the **Second Bank**'s greatest champions. Any thought of a unionist party was scotched and remained so, as long as banking and financial issues continued to forge the new party lines emerging in the mid-to-late 1830s.

UNION PARTY. The Union Party was a movement that arose in South Carolina to oppose the direction taken by the state's supporters of **nullification**. Although hailing more from mercantile and up-country farming regions of the state, most Union Party followers came from the same social and political milieu as the nullifiers and often shared personal friends with them, but disagreed on the best tactics for resolving the problems faced by the state. Led by the likes of **Joel Poinsett**, Langdon Cheves, William Drayton, and Daniel Huger, the Union Party strove to persuade more moderate nullifiers against taking dangerous steps toward nullification. However, in the face of the more successful leadership and organization of extreme nullifiers, the Union Party found themselves on the back foot and in the run-up to elections to the state legislature that would decide whether or not to call for a nullification convention, they became victims of violent intimidation on the streets of Charleston.

　　Once South Carolina's decision in favor of nullification had precipitated the **Nullification crisis**, President **Andrew Jackson** pinned great hopes upon the Union Party as his eyes and ears in South Carolina and as potential allies should more overt action be needed to enforce federal law in the state. However, despite Jackson's promise of military support, the Union Party shied away from creating their own militia to challenge that of the nullifiers. Nevertheless their representations did bring about some modification of the means to be used to enforce nullification, with the state's legislature reducing the emphasis upon punishment of those South Carolinians who might choose to abide by federal tariff laws.

UNITARIANISM. Unitarianism was a liberal form of Protestant Christianity that denied the doctrines of the Trinity and maintained that God exists in one person only. From roots in colonial New England, arising as a challenge to strict Calvinism, Unitarianism became particularly prevalent by the first quarter of the 19th century, with over 100 **Congregational** churches in New England turning to Unitarian principles after 1815. In the latter part of the Jacksonian era, Unitarianism was closely linked to **transcendentalism**, with which it shared a view of humanity far removed from the Calvinist doctrine of

innate depravity, preferring instead to see the potential for spiritual
growth in all through education and self-discipline.

UNITED STATES BANK OF PENNSYLVANIA. After its demise
as a federally-chartered institution in 1836 the **Second Bank of the
United States** continued its operations as the United States Bank of
Pennsylvania. Its Pennsylvania charter incorporated all the Second
Bank's stockholders and allowed the U.S. Bank to assume all its remaining assets and liabilities, confirming it as still the largest bank in
the country, albeit with less influence over state banks than was previously the case. Predictably this strong position continued to arouse
the hostility of the **Democrats**, with President **Martin Van Buren**
challenging the unfair advantage the U.S. Bank seemed to enjoy by
continuing to receive so-called "resurrection notes," notes originally
issued when it was still the Second Bank. Commitments to make
loans to the Pennsylvania government, to purchase state utility
stocks, and to pay the state a bonus of $2 million did not represent the
same level of public responsibility as **Nicholas Biddle** and the
Bank's other directors had felt under its federal charter, and so they
embarked upon a course of rather more risky policy choices. The
Bank began to borrow heavily from abroad during good times, but
consequently experienced increasingly difficult times in the **panics of
1837 and 1839**, until an attempt to sustain falling **cotton** prices by
keeping a significant amount of cotton out of the market caused a loss
of confidence among its investors. Their decision to jettison their
stock holdings forced the Bank to shut its doors for the last time in
1841.

UNITED STATES SOUTH SEAS EXPLORING EXPEDITION.
The idea of an expedition to explore the regions around the two poles
with a view to establishing if there were any habitable land there was
first floated by **John Quincy Adams**. Congress authorized the expedition in May 1836, but after two years of delay and neglect by the
secretary of the navy, **Mahlon Dickerson**, its brief was amended to
include an exploration of the whole Pacific. Secretary of War **Joel
Poinsett**, whose department adopted supervision of the project, appointed **Charles Wilkes** to command it, and in August 1838 six ships
finally embarked from Hampton Roads on a voyage that would last
until 1842. The expedition's course took it to islands off the northwest coast of Africa, before recrossing the Atlantic, rounding Cape
Horn, and then sailing up the western side of South America, charting
the coast as it went. It then crossed the Pacific to Australia and

headed south to Antarctica, before returning to explore the northwest coast of North America. The final leg of its journey carried it once more across the Pacific, this time to East Asia, and then on around the Cape of Good Hope to the Atlantic coast of the United States.

In the course of this epic voyage the expedition charted 200 islands, the northwest coast of North America, and San Francisco bay, and claimed to have made the first proper discovery of Antarctica. It also generated scientific data and made important collections of artifacts, substantially adding to knowledge of botany and astronomy, and of the sea's bottom. Ultimately the exhibits gathered across the globe would form part of the collection of the **Smithsonian Institution**. In addition to its scientific significance, the expedition aroused interest in the lands forming the Pacific rim, including the promising markets of East Asia, which later **commercial treaties** with China and Japan would attempt to exploit. Moreover, in a separate report suppressed by **John Tyler**'s administration out of fear of alienating the British at the time of the delicate **Webster-Ashburton** negotiations, Wilkes also recommended that the United States stand firm in a demand for a boundary line along the **54° 40′** parallel between British Columbia and the **Oregon territory**.

UNITED STATES TELEGRAPH. **Duff Green**'s Washington-based newspaper helped **Andrew Jackson**'s campaign in the presidential **election of 1828** and became the first official journalistic organ of **Old Hickory**'s administration in 1829-30. As a **John Calhoun** loyalist, however, Green and his paper shared the fate of the vice-president in losing Jackson's favor. Cabinet wrangles and the *Telegraph*'s failure to adopt as strong an anti-**Second Bank** line as the president desired led to the administration abandoning the *Telegraph* as its organ in 1830 in favor of **Frank Blair**'s *Washington Globe*. Thereafter the *Telegraph* continued to be a flag-waver for Calhoun and issued some of the most bitter personal charges against Jackson, including publication of Calhoun's view of the break-up over the **Florida report** and accusations about the influence upon the president of the **Kitchen Cabinet**, the first public use of the term. The *Telegraph* remained an important newspaper, continuing to attract printing contracts from Congress well into the mid-1830s.

UPJOHN, RICHARD (1802-1878). Upjohn was the English-born head of a family of architects, who emigrated to the United States in 1829, settling in New Bedford and then in Boston in 1834. After designing houses for clients primarily in Maine and also street furniture for Boston Common, he moved to New York City in 1839, where he became famous for his commissions for church designs, including that for rebuilding Trinity Church. This achievement in red sandstone, considered by some the first Gothic building in the United States, led to commissions for a series of further Episcopalian churches in the city, as well as more small-scale parish churches in suburban areas, Upjohn having taken up residence in Brooklyn in 1842. He also designed buildings for Bowdoin and Harvard Colleges. He had been naturalized as an American citizen in 1836.

UPSHUR, ABEL (1790-1844). Upshur was born into a prosperous family from the Virginian eastern shore region. After brief spells at both Yale and Princeton, the latter ending when he was expelled for supporting a student protest, Upshur went on to study law with the prominent lawyer and later statesman and jurist, **William Wirt**. In the 1830s Upshur's political career was entirely focused on Virginia, as he sat in the state General Court between 1826 and 1841 and attended the state's constitutional convention. As a **states' rights** man he opposed President **Andrew Jackson**'s firm stance during the **Nullification crisis**, and this, as well as support for state banks and hostility to the **Independent Treasury** scheme, led him naturally into the arms of **States' Rights Whigs** during the presidential **election of 1840**. As much as anything it was his friendship for **John Tyler** that caused him to adopt a Whig stance, and he went on to serve his friend well, first as part of Tyler's **"Corporal's Guard,"** and then in 1841 as secretary of the navy after the president's first Cabinet resigned en masse. Upshur proved an energetic department head, only to find his efforts at **naval reform** often thwarted by resistance from within the department and Congress.

Two years later Upshur replaced **Daniel Webster** as secretary of state and embarked upon undoubtedly the most influential period of his career. Partly out of his own conviction and partly out of loyalty to **John Calhoun**, Upshur was a fervent advocate of **Texan annexation** and now found himself in a position to do something about it. He was the one who really set in motion negotiations with a view to annexation in 1843, initially in secret and even without Tyler's immediate knowledge. Keen to protect the interests of **slavery**, especially against British intentions as reported to him by **Duff Green** in London, Upshur pushed the project through to near diplomatic triumph, when, on the point of finalizing the treaty, he was killed by the explosion of the Peacemaker gun on board the U.S.S. *Princeton*.

URBAN DEVELOPMENT. Fired by the **transportation** and **market revolutions**, American cities grew in number, size, and energy during this period. Although the balance of the population was still overwhelmingly rural, numbers in cities grew at twice the rate of those in the countryside. Moreover, while cities were still primarily residential and commercial centers, their population increase and the expansion of market activities contributed to their continuing development of **manufacturing**, with a distinctive mixture of working environments, including tenement rooms, workshops, and factories. For many Americans, however, the city also came to be a place of danger and problems. Poor construction contributed to the collapse of some buildings while several cities experienced damaging fires, mostly notably **New York**. It was cities, also, that usually acted as the channel through which epidemics entered the country, as was the case with the spread of **cholera**. Other critics considered cities increasingly dangerous because of their social and ethnic mix, which only became more diverse as the period went on. Crime, vice, and gang activity all seemed to betoken a degree of social decline in the city, made all the worse by often inadequate municipal government and the extra pressures brought by economic downturns in the **panics of 1833, 1837, and 1839.**

URSULINE CONVENT. On the nights of 11 and 12 August 1834 this **Catholic** establishment, in Charlestown, Massachusetts, was attacked by a Protestant mob, which ransacked and burned down the convent buildings and tore up its gardens. Notionally acting in defense of a woman who, it was claimed, was being held in the convent against her will, the rioters actually betrayed a heady combination of motives, including anti-Catholicism, **nativism**, and male suspicion of the independent, educated **women** that the convent housed. It spoke much of the tense relationship between traditional New England society, with its newly fervent **evangelical** tone, and the beginnings of cultural diversity introduced by **immigration** and the growth of different religions.

– V –

VAN BUREN, MARTIN (1782-1862). Van Buren was one of the leading statesmen and politicians of the age, who as well as helping to forge the **Democratic** Party and the **second party system** within which it operated, held a number of executive posts, including the presidency between 1837 and 1841, making him the first president to have been born after 1776.

Martin Van Buren was raised in Kinderhook, New York, situated on the road between New York City and Albany. After a practical education in law offices he began a successful legal career and entered the world of local politics. He served terms as state senator, state attorney general, and judge advocate, but was perhaps best known for his factional and party activities, first in alliance with the Clinton family and then in bitter opposition to De Witt Clinton in a struggle to assume leadership of the state's Republican Party for his own "Bucktail" faction. Van Buren drew on this experience to found the **Albany Regency**, the political machine that dominated the state's Democratic politics, and he would prove influential in the creation of the political coalition carrying **Andrew Jackson** into the White House.

During this period Van Buren's political service was at a national level, as one of New York's senators between 1821 and 1829. He supported the strict construction candidate **William Crawford** in the 1824 election, and then tried to lead Crawford's followers and other "old Republicans" into support for Jackson in 1828, based upon an opposition to what he considered the executive and nationalist excesses of **John Quincy Adams**' administration. At the same time as he helped Jackson to the presidency, Van Buren secured gubernatorial election in his home state, only to resign the position in 1829 in order to become Jackson's secretary of state. Even in his short term in the top office in New York, however, he did inspire the **Safety Fund System**, as a means of providing security for depositors in the state's banks.

Van Buren held his post in the Cabinet until 1831 and during his tenure in the State Department oversaw a settlement of the long-standing **West Indian trade dispute**, as well as making progress in the case of French **spoliation claims**. He also proved an increasingly valued advisor to the president, assisting in the draft of the message accompanying the **Maysville Road bill veto**, and sticking by the president in the midst of the **Eaton Affair** when the rest of the Cabinet family seemed to be defying the president's wishes. It was Van Buren's offer to resign that allowed the **Cabinet reshuffle** of 1831, with its resulting purge of **John Calhoun** aficionados, and the former secretary of state's reward was nomination to the post of U.S. minister to Great Britain. He sailed to take up that post before learning that his nomination had been rejected by the Senate, but even at this moment of apparent political adversity Van Buren's star was on the rise.

The Senate vote to reject his nomination numbered the days of his rival Calhoun as Jackson's vice-president, since it was the South Carolinian who had, as sitting president of the Senate, cast the decisive vote against Van Buren and virtually assured Van Buren of the president's preference for him as running mate for 1832. Van Buren did indeed become vice-president and remained an influential advisor to Jackson on most issues for the rest of his presidency.

Jackson's preferred running mate for 1832 turned into his virtually hand-picked successor as presidential candidate in 1836. However, despite winning the election, Van Buren's own personality and inferior popularity (at least as compared to Jackson's) combined with the maturing two-party system that was generating a more powerful and coordinated opposition party to substantially reduce his margin of victory. These forces would manifest themselves again in 1840, when after a disappointing term of office marked by two economic **panics, in 1837 and 1839**, the latter heralding a longer-lasting depression, Van Buren was defeated by **William Henry Harrison's "Log Cabin" campaign**. Van Buren's term had been marked by bitter debates over the **Independent Treasury**, which was delayed for three years before finally being passed by Congress; by the culmination of efforts to remove the **Cherokee** along the "**trail of tears**"; by the vicious prosecution of the **Second Seminole War**; by continuing efforts to discourage both meddling with **slavery** and the emergence of issues that might challenge **sectional** harmony, including the **Texas annexation**; and by threatening concerns over **Canadian border** relations with British interests in Upper Canada and New Brunswick.

After relinquishing the presidency, Van Buren remained a leading political figure, although increasingly troubled by the splits that sectional issues began to cause within his party. Still hopeful of a return to the White House, he turned down the offer of a Supreme Court seat from **John Tyler**, and in the early stages of the 1844 nomination process his chances looked good. Indeed Van Buren was the majority candidate at the Democratic Party's nomination convention. However, his refusal to countenance an immediate annexation of Texas prevented him from securing a substantial enough majority to secure the nomination and so he was passed over in favor of "dark horse" **James Polk**.

Having turned down Polk's offer of a return to London as U.S. minister, Van Buren became a figurehead for New York's **Barnburner** faction and their northern allies, who were becoming increasingly frustrated by southern influence within the Democratic Party and by their lack of patronage rewards from Polk. As such, when the Barnburners began to turn to the **Free Soil** coalition in 1848, Van Buren was their choice, adopted by the party as a whole, as presidential candidate. While ultimately, and unsurprisingly, unsuccessful in the election, it is thought that votes for Van Buren reduced Democratic support sufficiently to account for the electoral success of **Zachary Taylor** over **Lewis Cass**.

VANDERBILT, CORNELIUS (1794-1877). Vanderbilt was a **shipping**, and later **railroad**, magnate born into much humbler surroundings on Staten Island, New York. Lacking formal education, he worked on his father's farm before establishing his own ferry line between Staten Island and Manhattan in 1810. In 1829 he bought his first steam-boat and set up a service on the Hudson River between Albany and Manhattan. Through both of these lines Vanderbilt made a considerable fortune, consolidated only further when he sold his interest in both ventures. Now, instead, he established packet lines between New York and Providence, and later to Hartford, Boston, and Portland, before turning his attention south to lines with Washington, D.C., and Charleston. By this stage Vanderbilt probably owned more steamships than any other man alive, a circumstance that helped earn him the nickname "commodore." He extended his maritime interests into shipping round to California and across the Atlantic Ocean, and later involved himself in the railroad business, especially in plans to build a trans-isthmus railroad to connect the Pacific and Atlantic oceans.

VANDERLYN, JOHN (1775-1852). Vanderlyn was born in New York State and underwent a classical education and an early exposure to art and design. Under the patronage of Aaron Burr he made several trips to Europe to pursue training in painting. After returning to the United States he displayed in New York City a number of works completed in Europe and as a result was able to make a living as a professional painter thereafter. From the 1820s on, portraiture was Vanderlyn's main line of work, with his commissions including a full-length painting of George Washington. However, he was also commissioned to decorate the Capitol Rotunda in Washington, D.C. with a mural entitled *The Landing of Columbus*, completed in 1837.

VAUGHAN, CHARLES (1774-1849). This British diplomat was born in Leicester, England, and after many European travels was appointed a privy councillor and minister to the United States in 1825.

Vaughan spent much of his time in office making extensive tours of his host nation, in 1826 and 1829, while he also had a long term of absence between 1831 and 1833 before finally relinquishing the post in 1835. Nevertheless, in the meantime he had used his personal connections with the likes of **Joseph Story** and **Henry Clay** to seek resolution of a range of Anglo-American issues and had helped in particular to settle the **West Indian trade dispute** through negotiations with **Andrew Jackson**'s administration.

VERPLANCK BILL. This was the first attempt at tariff adjustment considered by Congress in the midst of the **Nullification crisis** in 1832-33. Drafted with the assistance of the secretary of the treasury, **Louis McLane**, and hence thought to have President **Andrew Jackson**'s approval, the bill was put before the House by the chairman of its Ways and Means Committee, the New York Democrat Gulian Verplanck. The bill proposed a sharp reduction of duties, by as much as half, over the next two years, with the intention of returning duty levels to around where they had been in 1816, albeit with a degree of **protection** left in place. The latter satisfied neither protectionists, who considered the reductions too severe and too precipitate, nor nullifiers, who opposed any degree of protection appearing to be left in the tariff and who were hostile to the fact that it had been produced by the Jackson administration. Already lacking support, the Verplanck bill came to be supplanted by **Henry Clay**'s proposed compromise **tariff bill of 1833**.

VETO POWER. Andrew Jackson was the first to use the president's constitutionally-granted veto power to any great extent, being responsible for around one third of all the vetoes issued before the Civil War. Jackson usually claimed that he vetoed bills out of concern for their constitutionality, but policy considerations also clearly came into play. Here, too, he justified his actions on the grounds that he was the only political figure to be able to claim a national mandate for his position. While the veto of the **Bank re-charter bill**, with its classic accompanying message, stands out as the most famous of his vetoes, Jackson also vetoed a number of important **internal improvements** bills, including the **Maysville Road bill**. Meanwhile, to his opponents the use of the veto power was an example of a growing record of **executive usurpation** and provoked a stance in support of much greater independence for the legislative branch. Later **Democratic**-leaning presidents also made similar use of the veto, **John Tyler** against bank and tariff bills in 1841 and 1842, much to the frustration of his nominal party, and **James Polk** against two improvements bills in 1846-47.

VIRGINIA BILL TO ABOLISH SLAVERY. In the late 1820s and early 1830s Virginia went through a process of self-definition in matters political and constitutional. Already in 1829 the state's constitutional convention had altered the allocation of legislative seats to produce a more geographically representative state legislature. Now in 1831-33 the General Assembly discussed the future of **slavery** in the state. Governor **John Floyd** had proposed a plan of gradual abolition as a means of reducing the likelihood of slave rebellions of the type recently led by **Nat Turner** in Southampton County. Discussing other options such as **colonization**, the Assembly only narrowly rejected a motion declaring that action against slavery would be expedient, by 73-58. However, the Assembly then opted instead to reinforce the slave system as the preferred means of controlling their black population. Floyd's abolition proposal was defeated and a more rigid slave code was enacted.

– W –

WABASH AND ERIE CANAL. This Indiana **canal** was planned in the late 1820s with the intention of linking the navigable stretch of the Maumee River, at its Toledo junction with Lake Erie, with the Wabash River at Huntington. After receiving a grant of federal land to encourage its construction, work on the canal began in 1832 at Fort Wayne. Huntington, the original intended terminus of the western portion, was reached in 1835, but when it became clear that the Wabash was not truly navigable from that point, it was decided to take the canal on to Lafayette instead, this extension being completed in 1841. Two years later the eastern stretch to Toledo was finished. Later spurs, including one to Terre Haute, completed in 1849, and extensions south to the Ohio River, made it the longest canal in the United States. It proved effective in encouraging the economic development of northern Indiana.

WALKER, ROBERT J. (1801-1869). Walker was a Pennsylvanian lawyer who went on to forge a political career in Mississippi, rising to Cabinet status during the presidency of **James Polk**. From early days Walker was a loyal **Democratic** supporter of **Andrew Jackson**, sharing both his opposition to the **Second Bank of the United States**

and his strong nationalism, as shown when he supported Jackson's stance against **nullification**.

Walker's nationalism was perhaps best manifested in his advocacy of **expansion**, and while serving as senator from his adopted state between 1836 and 1845 he spoke fervently and cogently in favor of **Texas annexation**, arguing that it would provide a sink through which **slavery** might drain away into Latin America. Indeed, he acted as President **John Tyler**'s pro-annexation spokesman in the Senate. However, come the **election of 1844** Walker advised Tyler to stand down and effectively ran the Polk campaign, having also helped to secure the nomination of his own uncle, **George Dallas**, as Democratic vice-presidential candidate. Walker's expansionist priorities still shone through, though, his influence being apparent in the Democratic platform's famous stance on both Texas and **Oregon**, and once the election was won it was his suggestion that helped to bring about the congressional compromise over Texas in late 1844-early 1845 that left the president to decide whether to push for immediate annexation or to renegotiate a treaty with Texas.

Walker's reward for his prominent role in the 1844 campaign was the position of secretary of the treasury and here he remained loyal to his earlier economic policy stances by managing the passage of both the revived **Independent Treasury of 1846** and in the same year the **tariff act** that often bears his name. He also played a role in the creation of the **Department of the Interior**, as well as remaining true to his major desire for expansion, calling at the end of the **Mexican War** for the conquest and acquisition of the whole of Mexico and expressing ambitions for **Yucatan** and **Cuba** as well.

WALTER, THOMAS (1804-1887). Walter was a Philadelphia-born architect, whose course to his profession took him through periods of apprenticeship to his father, a bricklayer and stonemason, and of study at the drawing school of the Franklin Institute. After working with **William Strickland**, he made his reputation in 1833 with the design of a temple for Philadelphia's Girard College. Walter went on to work on the Philadelphia county prison and also won the patronage of **Nicholas Biddle**, whose private house he remodeled. His most prominent work, the dome on top of the U.S. Capitol, was designed and completed in a later period.

WANGHIA, TREATY OF. Prompted by the news that Britain had recently gained access to four Chinese ports previously not open to foreign trade, in 1842 **John Tyler**'s administration initiated a diplomatic mission with the aim of securing rights at least equal to those enjoyed by the British. After Tyler's first choice of special minister, **Edward Everett**, turned down the post, the job went to **Caleb Cushing** who sailed for China in 1843. In July the following year, Cushing succeeded in signing a treaty that opened five Chinese ports to American commerce on the same terms as were enjoyed by the most favored nation trading with China. The treaty would encourage further the existing trade between China and the United States, with New England to the fore, and would increase American interest in the potential of Asian markets in general. *See also* OVERSEAS COMMERCE.

WAR DEPARTMENT. The War Department experienced a period of considerable activity during this time, both as the focus of **administrative reform** and as the overseer of several important military operations. Largely through executive action, **Andrew Jackson** instituted a number of changes in the department, including the creation of a special office for dealing with the burdensome level of pension claims, a reorganization of the quartermaster's office, and a sideways shift to the Treasury of the office responsible for the coastal survey. As befitted Jackson's hostility to federally sponsored **internal improvements**, he abolished the army board of engineers responsible for assisting in the surveying and construction of such projects.

Under **Martin Van Buren** the department became one of the most significant in the government and certainly the most expensive, as it combined continued responsibility for **Indian removal**, active service in the **Second Seminole War**, and border peace-keeping in both North and South. In 1838 Congress approved an increase in the size of the army, creating an extra regiment and adding numbers to existing units. Even with these increases **Joel Poinsett** deemed the level of military readiness inadequate and proposed controversial **militia reform** plans. Despite their failure, Poinsett's was a successful tenure in the department, witnessing improvements in its activities at a lower cost than previously.

In the **John Tyler** administration, after the end of the Seminole war, the army establishment was reduced by about one third, but the onset of the **Mexican War** brought new challenges to the department, for the most part successfully met.

WAREHOUSE ACT. Coming out of the debates that culminated in the passage of **Robert Walker's** **tariff of 1846**, the passage of the warehousing provision was seen by some as a concession to the interests of American manufacturers worried by reductions in levels of **tariff protection**. By ruling that imported goods be housed in government warehouses for the purpose of valuation, the measure at least gave manufacturers the consolation of knowing that duties would not be calculated on the basis of importing merchants' underestimates of the value of goods.

WASHINGTON GLOBE. This newspaper was founded in the fall of 1830 by **Francis Preston Blair** with the express purpose of replacing the Calhounite *United States Telegraph* as the organ of **Andrew Jackson**'s administration. As a business venture the *Globe* struggled in its early years. Even with the promise of an exaggerated level of executive printing contracts, offered by **Amos Kendall**, Blair still had to battle with the offices of the *Telegraph*, the *National Intelligencer*, and later *The Madisonian* for congressional favor when it came to the award of its printing contracts. Indeed in the *Globe*'s first five years of existence its returns from such contracts never exceeded those of its rivals as its fortunes fluctuated in rhythm with changes in party dominance in the two houses of Congress. However, its circulation levels fared better, as a variety of pressures caused many of the *Telegraph*'s subscribers to shift to the *Globe*, and from May 1831 Blair considered it established enough to begin daily production, soon making it one of the most widely read newspapers, through its own columns and through the network of local papers across the nation that printed its articles and editorials.

As well as becoming the organ through which Jackson issued news of his administration, the *Globe* soon emerged as the major advocate for the **Democratic** Party, backing the candidacies of Jackson and **Martin Van Buren** in their election campaigns and putting forward the main elements of the cases in favor of **Indian removal** and against **nullification**, banking, and **paper money**. It also provided a space within which different factions of the party could debate the merits of particular policies, most notably in the summer of 1837 as options for an **Independent Treasury** scheme were considered prior to the **special session** of September of that year. Overall, the *Globe's* motto, "The world is governed too much," succinctly encapsulated the developing Jacksonian opposition to artificial interference in the economic affairs of the country through governmental action.

Although the *Globe* was still the Democratic Party's main organ when **James Polk** entered the White House, **Young Hickory** began to doubt Blair's loyalty and chose to work with a newspaper that was more of his own making. Already personally cold to the editor, who he felt had never given his political career the support it was due, Polk considered the possibility of allowing the paper to continue under Blair's ownership but with a more acceptable editor such as **Andrew Jackson Donelson, Thomas Ritchie**, or Aaron Brown. Ultimately, though, Polk and Blair reached an agreement that the paper would be sold to Ritchie and three others, with Blair's participation ending for good. The last edition of the *Globe* was issued in April 1845, while its offices, its machinery, most of its staff, and even its subscription list were taken over by the *Washington Union*.

WASHINGTON MONUMENT. The idea of building a monument to George Washington in the nation's capital had been mooted for some years and in September 1833 the Washington National Monument society was established to push the project forward. Under the presidencies of such prominent figures as **John Marshall**, James Madison and, after 1839, **Andrew Jackson**, the society made slow progress toward its goal. In an effort to make the commemoration an expression of democratic spirit, subscriptions were limited to one dollar per year per person, with the result that only $28,000 had been raised by 1836. Even so this was enough to launch the competition to find a suitable design for the monument, a competition won by **Robert Mills**. His original design, including a colonnade of columns, would be amended by the time the cornerstone was laid in 1848, but the familiar obelisk at its center was retained and would become a stunning feature of the Washington skyline.

WASHINGTON TURNPIKE BILL AND VETO. *See* INTERNAL IMPROVEMENTS.

WASHINGTON UNION. Established in May 1845 to replace **Francis Blair**'s *Washington Globe*, the *Washington Union* became **James Polk**'s own journalistic organ. Under the editorship of **Thomas Ritchie** it quite literally replaced the *Globe*, taking over many of its staff as well as its premises, machinery, and circulation list. Polk saw it as his means of managing the news by putting across his views on many of the key issues of the day (including **Oregon**, southwestern **expansion**, and changing positions on the means by which to arrange the **slavery** question in the territories) and at times he personally wrote editorials for the *Union*. Moreover, although Ritchie never became as trusted an advisor to Polk as Blair had been to **Andrew Jackson**, occasionally the relationship between the president and the newspaper was thought to be too close. For example, the *Union*'s overstrident criticism of Congress in 1847 was interpreted as an attempt to put pressure on the legislative body on Polk's behalf in an infringement of the constitutional separation of powers. As a result the paper's representatives were expelled from the Senate for several months in 1847-48.

WEBSTER, DANIEL (1782-1852). This New Hampshire-born lawyer and statesman rose to become one of the most prominent political figures of the age, as a great orator, as a leading opponent of **Jacksonian Democracy** during two periods of service in the Senate from 1827 to 1841 and 1845 to 1850, and as a successful secretary of state in the first half of the **William Henry Harrison/John Tyler** presidency.

Webster marked his arrival on the national political stage in the famous **Webster-Hayne debate** of 1830, in which he propounded the idea of **unionism** in the face of threats of **nullification**. Although this stance drew him closer to **Andrew Jackson** during the **Nullification crisis**, Webster found himself opposed to the president on most other issues and in particular those relating to banking, finance, and western expansion. His support for the **Second Bank of the United States** drew him into the ranks of the **Whig** Party, and he was one of their three candidates for the presidency in the **election of 1836**. Following his appointment by Harrison in 1841, Webster was the only Cabinet member not to resign after Tyler's obstruction of Whig measures in the **special session** in 1841. While he remained in the Cabinet in part out of the hope that Tyler and the followers of **Henry Clay** would reach a compromise over the key issue of a national banking institution, Webster's decision mainly derived from his desire to bring to completion negotiations with Britain that culminated in the **Webster-Ashburton Treaty** of Washington in 1842.

After that, Webster resigned as secretary of state in 1843 and returned to the Senate in 1845, where he strongly opposed both **Texas annexation** and moves toward the **Mexican War**. After the war broke out Webster did not vote to withhold funding for the war effort, but he did assert that no territorial gain should accrue to the United States and he went on to resist the Treaty of **Guadalupe Hidalgo** for the reason that it did include such acquisitions. In later debates on **sectional** matters he supported the compromise of 1850 in the hope of preserving the Union and earned a "**cotton Whig**" label for his pains. A final brief tenure in the office of secretary of state followed his resignation from the Senate and took him through to his death in 1852.

WEBSTER-ASHBURTON TREATY. The Webster-Ashburton Treaty of 1842 represented, perhaps, the single greatest achievement, domestic or diplomatic, of **John Tyler**'s administration. In the face of considerable Anglophobia, born of extremely tense conditions across the **Canadian border** in the late 1830s, the United States and Britain took advantage of the fact that both countries had undergone recent changes in administration to try to restore more pacific relations. Recognizing that such an improvement would be beneficial in making it easier to attract much needed British investment, Tyler and his secretary of state, **Daniel Webster**, responded favorably when the more conciliatory British foreign minister, Lord Aberdeen, proposed to send a special mission to the United States to attempt to resolve outstanding issues. Aided by the fact that Webster found it easy to work with the special British minister, **Alexander Baring**, Lord Ashburton, for whose family banking firm he had done legal work, the negotiations went well and ended in August 1842 in a treaty and several agreements by correspondence that resolved many, if not all, of the problems troubling Anglo-American relations.

One set of solutions concerned the location of the Canadian border with the United States in several places. The treaty's main focus was a settlement of the boundary between **Maine** and New Brunswick, in the hope of ending the tension that had resulted in the **Aroostook war**. Guided by the work of a new boundary commission, including the input of commissioners from Maine and Massachusetts, Webster and Ashburton agreed upon a division of the territory in which the United States gained 7,000 out of the 12,000 disputed acres, including the Aroostook valley, as well as the right to carry timber down the St. Johns River. The treaty also determined the boundary between Canada and Vermont and New York, with the United States receiving Rouse's Point on Lake Champlain in exchange for land ceded in Maine. Further west still the United States gained Sugar Island between Lake Huron and Lake Superior as part of Michigan's northern border, while in the Minnesota territory the agreed river boundary conceded considerable territory to the United States, land ultimately discovered to conceal massive iron ore deposits. Effectively, then, the treaty established the entire current boundary line from Maine in the East to the Lake of the Woods in the upper Midwest.

A second component of the treaty was the inclusion of new terms regulating extradition between possessions of the two countries, with murder, attempted murderous assault, forgery, piracy, robbery, and arson all to be recognized as extraditable offenses. This provision within the treaty was a response to the tensions that had arisen during both the *Caroline* and *Creole* affairs, and had its terms been in place earlier they might have lessened considerably the trouble these incidents caused. As it was, the treaty itself said nothing about either specific episode, but Webster and Ashburton did consider and exchange letters on both, with Britain accepting that it should apologize for the attack on the *Caroline* and assuring that nothing like the *Creole* seizure would be allowed to happen again, since governors of British islands would be ordered to respect international law when ships were driven into their waters by inclement weather or by mutiny. Compensation for the owners of the *Creole* and of its human cargo was left to later diplomats to settle.

Another such issue ultimately left unresolved in the treaty but with enough agreement in exchanges of correspondence to be acceptable to both parties was the problem of impressments. Britain could not be forced into making a public renunciation of the practice but effectively assured the United States that it was unlikely ever to use it again. Finally both nations agreed to cooperate in the use of naval force off the coast of Africa to stop traders in the international **slave trade** using the American flag to cover their operations.

Predictably the treaty did not please everyone. Most **Whigs** would have been reluctant to give the Tyler administration credit for it anyway. Some suggested that Webster too easily surrendered land that rightly belonged to Maine and that he had been able to do so by referring to an inadequately drafted map. Later the treaty would be indirectly attacked when Tyler was accused of inappropriate use of secret federal funds in attempting to sway opinion in Maine in favor of the compromise. Clearly the failures to get reparations for the *Creole* or to secure a treaty-based surrender of the British claim to the right to impressments were also disappointing to many. Yet despite these problems and the fact that the omission of any settlement of the **Oregon** boundary left a potentially open sore in relations with Britain, the treaty comfortably secured its two-thirds approval from the Senate and went on to be greatly celebrated for securing a continuation of peaceful, if not always trustful, relations between the two countries.

WEBSTER-HAYNE DEBATE. This classic debate in January 1830 grabbed the attention of the press and political classes as power relations between the different **sections** of the United States were played out on the floor of the Senate. From a fairly innocuous beginning, Samuel Foote's December 1829 resolution that measures for surveying and selling federally owned western land should be postponed until all lands further east had been sold, the debate exploded into a bitter expression of conflicting interpretations of the fundamental nature of the American Union, with **Robert Hayne** expressing the extreme **states' rights** or **nullification** view that the Union was akin to a treaty between sovereign states, while **Daniel Webster** portrayed it as a single nation.

Hayne made the first move when he called for a **South-West alliance** in opposition to federally imposed **tariffs** and land regulation, hoping to appeal to westerners of a mind similar to **Thomas Hart Benton** who had attacked Foote's resolution. Webster countered that the Northeast had always been a far better friend to the West than the South had been, supporting a clear policy on land sales and also having backed the prohibition of **slavery** from the Northwest Territory and the Louisiana Purchase. If by mentioning slavery Webster had been trying to force Hayne out on the issue of nullification, then he succeeded, as the South Carolinian jumped to the defense of slavery and the Carolina doctrine of nullification. This in turn allowed Webster to attack nullification and to paint a dreadful picture of what might ensue should the Union be compromised by the triumph of that principle. Instead, Webster supported the idea of "Liberty *and* Union now and forever, one and inseparable!"

The debate revealed how politics early in **Andrew Jackson**'s term was still being played out according to the interests of sections, more than along firm party lines, with the president himself leaning toward Webster's view of **unionism** during the debate, as he would again during the **Nullification crisis** a couple of years later.

WEED, THURLOW (1797-1882). After spending much of his early life in the western part of New York State, Weed was apprenticed to a printer and learned the trade of journalism. His *Albany Evening Journal*, produced throughout the Jacksonian period, became one of the leading opponents of the state's **Democratic** Party, paralleling his own course from the ranks of the **National Republicans**, through the **Anti-Masonic Party**, to the **Whigs**. In addition to his journalistic support for the party, Weed became an active Whig member and organizer and earned the nickname "Wizard of the Lobby" for his influence on the party's electoral processes. For the most part this involved personal support for the political fortunes of **William**

Seward, whom he helped to wrest the governor's position from the Democrats in 1838 and then to secure a Senate seat in 1839. However, he also backed the winning horses in the Whig successes in the **elections of 1840 and 1848**, being an early proponent of **William Henry Harrison** and **Zachary Taylor** respectively, and it is generally agreed that he played a major part in the greater popularization of Whig election tactics that led to the 1840 triumph in particular.

WELD, THEODORE (1813-1893). This Connecticut-born educator and reformer rose to prominence after experiencing personal conversion under the influence of **Charles Finney**. Weld became one of the early **abolitionists** and went to the **Lane Seminary** where he led student abolitionists and helped to train abolitionist workers for the **American Anti-Slavery Society**, a group he had helped to found. After marrying his fellow abolitionist and co-author of some of his anti-slavery writings, **Angelina Grimké**, in 1838, he devoted himself more to his work as a teacher in New Jersey and hence became rather less prominent as a public figure in the 1840s.

WELLES, GIDEON (1802-1878). Welles was a Connecticut-born journalist and politician whose career path followed that of many northern **Democrats** as the new issues of the 1840s put pressure on existing party loyalties. While editor of the *Hartford Times* from 1826 to 1836, he served a couple of terms in the state House. He was a close colleague of fellow Jacksonian **John Niles** and at this stage in his career won political preferment from his party of choice. Welles was postmaster at Hartford between 1836 and 1841 and was three times elected state comptroller of public accounts. His career highpoint during this period came in 1845 when he became the first civilian chief of the new Bureau of Clothing and Provisions in the recently reformed Navy Department. However, even while in that office Welles was showing signs of a forthcoming break with his party, covertly working for the **free-soil** candidacy of **Martin Van Buren** during the **election of 1848**, a stance that was in part responsible for his dismissal from the post in the same year. *See also* NAVAL REFORM.

WEST INDIES TRADE DISPUTE. The success of **Andrew Jackson**'s administration in securing a diplomatic settlement of this longstanding issue with Britain represents one of only a handful of truly significant foreign policy developments during **Old Hickory**'s presidency. Trade between the United States and Britain's possessions in the western hemisphere had been variously open or closed ever since American independence had been sealed in 1783, as the two sides disagreed over how vessels of each country and of Britain's colonies would be received in the other's ports. Most recently **John Quincy Adams** and Secretary of State **Henry Clay** had resolved upon a firm stance on the issue and consequently had ushered in a period of total closure of the direct trade between the United States and British West Indies, a situation upon which the British government seemed reluctant to treat further, even though Adams and Clay were eventually to moderate their stance.

On his accession to the presidency Jackson, through Secretary of State **Martin Van Buren** and the U.S. Minister in London **Louis McLane**, immediately adopted a generally more conciliatory approach, although still holding the stick of possible retaliatory action over British heads, as he warned that Congress might restrict trade with Britain's Canadian provinces if a settlement were not reached. Britain agreed to negotiate and a deal was struck, in which, by means of mutual legislation in October 1830, U.S. ports were opened to British vessels coming from the island colonies and colonial ports were opened to American vessels sailing from the United States. In surrendering the earlier stricter claims that would have provided better terms for the shipping interests of New England, the Jackson administration seemed to be favoring the more localized interests of southern shippers and southern and western producers. Certainly representatives of New England's maritime industries continued to moan about the deal into the late 1830s and early 1840s and even through to 1849 when Britain's repeal of her navigation system removed any remaining grounds for American complaint.

As an issue the settlement also attained significance for the bitter domestic after-taste it left behind. The surrender of terms favorable to New England's shippers provided one point upon which the Jackson administration endured criticism of the deal from opposition politicians. However, the fact that Adams and Clay had eventually been prepared to accept similar terms to those finally won by Jackson weakened this means of attack. Nevertheless, opposition forces still tried to make political capital out of the deal, by accusing Van Buren of humbling the United States before the British lion through his assertion that his predecessors had adopted too extreme a stance. The secretary of state's punishment, meted out after he had resigned as part of the **Cabinet reshuffle of 1831**, was to see the Senate reject his nomination as minister to Britain in January 1832, with his arch-rival,

Vice-President **John Calhoun** casting the decisive vote. *See also* OVERSEAS COMMERCE.

WESTERN EXPANSION. *See* EXPANSIONISM.

WHEAT. Along with **corn,** wheat represented the main crop of the moving northern frontier, with Ohio becoming the main wheat producer in 1840. However, it remained a crop of major importance in eastern states as well, such as Virginia, New York, and Pennsylvania, and indeed the latter wrested back the title of leading wheat producer by 1849. National production rose from around 85 million bushels in 1839 to 100 million in 1849, figures well below those for corn, but the nature and price of wheat made it clearly the leading northern cash crop.

WHIG MANIFESTO. In September 1841 a caucus of some 50-60 congressional **Whigs** met to approve a document drafted by **John Pendleton Kennedy** in response to **John Tyler**'s veto of the **Bank bill of 1841.** The Manifesto expressed public regret at how Tyler's action had denied the regular Whig Party one of their preferred policies, but also specifically accused the president of acting with the same level of **executive usurpation** as **Democratic** presidents had displayed in the past. It called for firmer restrictions on presidential power, and effectively wrote Tyler out of the party that had nominated him to the vice-presidency.

WHIGS. The Whig Party emerged as the main party of opposition to the **Democrats** in the mid-1830s and, together with them, made up the constituent parts of a truly national **second party system.** Drawing heavily upon the leadership and support base and economic nationalism of the **National Republicans,** the Whigs also absorbed much of the emotional drive and organizational ability of the **Anti-Masonic Party.** However, it was their emergence as a genuinely competitive force in southern states that was most dramatic, and here the appeal of Whig economic policies combined, for a small number, with **states' rights** hostility to **Andrew Jackson**'s tenure as president and, for more, with a general disquiet at **executive usurpation,** to win a substantial support base. Although slower to adopt the more overt methods of party organization and discipline of the Democrats, and also despite being more avowedly **anti-party** in their expressed views, in 1840 the Whigs ran what was probably the most populist campaign seen to that date, with its popular rallies and slogans, including the one that gave the **"Log Cabin" campaign** its name.

The victory of **William Henry Harrison** in that year's election, alongside Whig majorities in both houses of Congress, marked the highpoint in the party's fortunes, although for brief periods in the 1830s it had joined with disgruntled **Conservative Democrats** in wresting occasional legislative control in the Senate, while in 1847 Whigs would grab control of the House and a year later would win the presidency again for **Zachary Taylor**. The party's national electoral fortune was not always matched by the best of personal luck, however, as on both occasions it lost its triumphant presidents to early deaths. This proved of more immediate damage to the party in 1841, when the succession of **John Tyler**, a minority **states' rights Whig**, ruined its first, and probably also its best and last, chance to implement its policy agenda on the national stage. By the later 1840s the party was already experiencing the same problems generated by the **sectional** issue of **slavery**'s expansion that were bedeviling the Democrats, and in the case of the Whigs the impact proved more terminal more quickly.

To a great extent the ideas and issues adopted by the Whig Party sat at the opposite extreme to those of the Democrats, although it is dangerous to generalize about the whole party across the whole nation. Certainly the party's ideas appealed to those of a more conservative bent in their social attitudes, although these were by no means the party's only support group. Many Whigs, especially those coming out of the Anti-Masonic tradition, shared the dreams of opportunities for the many espoused by Democrats, but where they differed from followers of the party of Jackson was in their willingness to pursue this progressive vision through the machinery of government intervention at local, state, and federal levels, along the lines of **Henry Clay**'s **American System**. This brought them firmly into line with other Whigs in their support for policies such as the **protective tariff**, government support for **internal improvements**, including direct or indirect use of federal money in such projects, and sound policies on banking, currency, and the **credit system**, such as, at various times, the defense of state **deposit banks** (against proposals for an **Independent Treasury**) and the idea of a new national bank.

The Whig taste for government intervention stretched beyond economic matters to the realm of cultural and social policy, where their ideas could be seen as more restrictive than progressive, in their methods if not in their motivation. They drew heavily from the ranks of **evangelical** reform groups and were more likely than the Democrats to advocate the use of government authority alongside voluntary efforts to reform certain aspects of Americans' lives in the hope of liberating them from sin, such as in their calls for proper observance of the **Sabbath** and for changes in drinking habits.

This tendency to impose a set of cultural values upon others again set the Whigs apart from the Democrats with their greater acceptance of multiculturalism, albeit a white version of it. For that reason Whigs proved less attractive to arriving groups of **immigrants**, who despised efforts to change their personal behavior and came to associate some Whigs with measures of a **nativist** leaning. Ironically the reform spirit also made Whigs generally more sympathetic to those other patches in the American multicultural quilt, Native Americans and African-American slaves. Whigs inherited from National Republicans the duty of opposing the worst excesses of **Indian removal** while many Whigs in the North also sympathized with the **antislavery** message. This, along with a concern about the potential consequences, international and sectional, also inspired their opposition to the main policy trend of the 1840s, territorial **expansion**, as seen in their blocking in the Senate of the **Texas annexation** treaty and in their consistent opposition to a declaration of war against Mexico. *See also* MEXICAN WAR.

WHITE, HUGH LAWSON (1773-1840). White was born in North Carolina, only to move via Virginia to Tennessee, where he made his name as a fighter of Native Americans, a lawyer, and ultimately as a prominent politician and unsuccessful presidential candidate. His first roles were mainly legal, serving as district attorney for the United States and as a Tennessee judge, but he also pursued business interests such as the presidency of the State Bank of Tennessee. Initially attracted to the camp of **Andrew Jackson**, White was actually offered the position of secretary of war by **Old Hickory**, but he preferred to express his support for Jacksonian policies such as **Indian removal** and the **Bank veto** from the seat in the Senate he occupied between 1825 and 1840. However, by 1834 he was starting to part company with the Jacksonians, expressing reservations about the **removal of the federal deposits** and the campaign to **expunge the censure** against Jackson's actions.

White reserved his main doubts for **Martin Van Buren** and so had no qualms when selected to run against him as the **Whig** Party candidate in several southern states in the **election of 1836**. Combining emerging Whig principles and policies with the claim that as a northerner Van Buren could not be trusted on the **slavery** question,

White performed well, securing around 49 percent of the southern popular vote overall and the 14 electoral college votes of Georgia and Tennessee. Thereafter he continued to follow the Whig line through to the **election of 1840**, resigning as senator rather than having to follow orders from Tennessee's legislature to vote for the **Independent Treasury** scheme, and backing **Henry Clay** and then **William Henry Harrison** for the presidency in 1840.

WHITMAN, WALT (1819-1892). The future great poet was born on Long Island and spent the early years of his life moving between a range of jobs in and around the New York area, including periods as an office boy, as a printer, and as a schoolteacher on Long Island once more. While there Whitman resumed work as a newspaper writer and editor, editing the *Long Islander*, before returning to edit a number of minor **Democratic** organs in New York City and then the *Brooklyn Eagle*. After two years he lost that post for supporting the **Free Soil** Party. Whitman traveled in the West and spent a period working on the New Orleans *Crescent* in 1848 but returned to the East to establish the "free soil" *Brooklyn Freeman* in 1849.

WHITMAN MASSACRE. Reverend Marcus Whitman was a Protestant missionary from New York, who had moved to Oregon in 1836 to bring the benefit of his medical training to Native American tribes there. Nevertheless he was also a supporter of greater levels of white settlement in Oregon and indirectly this led to his demise in November 1847. Groups from the Cayuse tribe, increasingly suspicious of the growing numbers of white settlers in their region, murdered Whitman, his wife, and some 12 other members of his mission at its base at Walla Walla. News of this massacre generated greater urgency in demands for the establishment of some sort of territorial government in Oregon. *See also* OREGON, TERRITORIAL STATUS.

WHITTIER, JOHN G. (1807-1892). This Massachusetts poet of Quaker antecedents and beliefs was famous for his **abolitionist** stance. From early in his career Whittier contributed prolifically to **William Lloyd Garrison**'s papers and in return received his support for his own editorial ventures, including the *New England Weekly Review* between 1830 and 1832 and the *Pennsylvanian Freeman* from 1838 to 1840. However, Whittier split with Garrison over the issue of political action, having served as a member of the Massachusetts legislature in 1835 and then aiding in the formation of the **Lib-**

erty Party. His pastoral evocation of the New England of his youth, *Legends of New England in Prose and Verse*, published in 1831, was among his earliest creative works, while later works included *Lays of My Home* in 1843, *Ballads* in 1844, and *Voice of Freedom* in 1846.

WICKLIFFE, CHARLES (1788-1869). Wickliffe was born in Kentucky and, after a private education, combined military service during the War of 1812 with careers in the law and local politics. Having entered the House of Representatives as a Republican in 1823, he served until 1833 and steered a tricky course between early support for **Andrew Jackson**, personal loyalty to **John Calhoun**, and sympathy for the **Second Bank of the United States**. Even when the latter issue brought him into the ranks of the **Whig** Party, Wickliffe's position remained uncomfortable as his fellow Kentuckian **Henry Clay** viewed him with suspicion as a late convert to the ranks of the anti-Jacksonians. For example, Clay was furious when president-elect **William Henry Harrison** consulted Wickliffe on a range of matters relating to Kentucky in 1840-41.

In September 1841 **John Tyler** appointed Wickliffe to replace the resigning **Francis Granger** as postmaster general, the Kentuckian's only previous experience of an executive role having come as replacement governor of his state after the death of the incumbent. Now in the Cabinet, he introduced reforms in the **Post Office**, helping to make the service cheaper. Wickliffe was also the only 1841 Cabinet appointee to survive with Tyler for the rest of his term and became a close friend of the president, supporting his stance on **Texan annexation**. This development caused Wickliffe to follow the course of many Tyler men back to the **Democrats** and in 1845 he was one of the men chosen by **James Polk** as special commissioner to Texas to whip up support for annexation. After successfully accomplishing this he returned to private life in Kentucky.

"WILDCAT BANKS." Earning their name from the perception that they emerged in areas so remote that only wildcats would live there, these banks represented the extreme manifestation of the massive expansion of banking at local and state levels in the 1830s. Most usually associated with southern and western states and territories, their founders often established them upon a fraudulent basis, by borrowing gold to demonstrate to chartering authorities their ability to support their note issue, only to return the gold having succeeded in securing their charter. Predictably, but not entirely accurately, some attributed the overextension of banking and note issue that proved so disastrous in the **panic of 1837** to the rise of "wildcat banks" and blamed both problems upon those who had caused the demise of the **Second Bank of the United States**, which had removed the safest guiding hand over the banking industry.

WILKES, CHARLES (1798-1877). Wilkes was a New Yorker who, after receiving a commission in 1818, made a career in the U.S. Navy. In 1833 he became head of the Depot of Charts and Instruments, a role that made him a suitable candidate to lead his most famous enterprise of the period. In 1838 he was appointed to command the **United States South Seas Exploring Expedition** that is often referred to by his name. Wilkes recorded his experiences on the remarkable voyage between 1838 and 1842 in his *Narrative of the United States Exploring Expedition*, published in 1844.

WILKINS, WILLIAM (1779-1865). Wilkins was a Pennsylvanian lawyer, politician, and statesman who came to prominence in the western part of his state around Pittsburgh. For most of his career he successfully reconciled strong support for **Andrew Jackson** and membership in the **Democratic** Party with his own economic nationalism born of his state's interests and his personal involvement in **manufacturing**, banking (as president of the Bank of Pittsburgh), and **internal improvements**. Up to 1831 when he entered the Senate, Wilkins held a range of judicial and political posts, and at one time was even being considered as a possible Democratic vice-presidential candidate for 1832. Indeed, Pennsylvania did nominate and vote for him instead of **Martin Van Buren**. As chairman of the Senate Judiciary Committee Wilkins supported Jackson through the **Nullification crisis**, backing the **Force Act**, and then he went on to support **removal of the federal deposits**, abandoning more likely ties to the **Second Bank**'s president, **Nicholas Biddle**.

Wilkins' reward for his loyalty was appointment to replace his fellow Pennsylvanian, **James Buchanan**, as U.S. minister to Russia until 1836. Upon his return to the United States Wilkins reentered Congress as a Representative in 1842, albeit only after electoral defeat in 1840, and in 1844 he became **John Tyler**'s last secretary of war. Here he proved himself an aggressive champion of the **Texas annexation** campaign but found himself less in step with the rest of the Cabinet on economic issues. He retired from office in 1845 with the arrival of **James Polk**.

WILMOT, DAVID (1814-1868). After a comfortable childhood and legal study Wilmot embarked upon a career in the law and politics. He remained a relatively minor **Democratic** politician from Pennsylvania, backing successively **Andrew Jackson, Martin Van Buren**, and even **James Polk** despite an earlier preference for Van Buren for the 1844 candidacy. Wilmot's support for **Texas annexation** as a slave state seemed to belie what was to come when his name hit the political headlines during his tenure as representative in the House between 1845 and 1851, most crucially during debates arising from the **Mexican War** and the potential acquisition of territory as a result of the war. It was Wilmot who proposed the famous amendment to funding bills for the war, the **Wilmot Proviso** that became the focal point of **anti-slavery** efforts in Congress.

Historians have long debated Wilmot's intentions in tying the anti-slavery banner to any possible territorial gains of the Mexican War. Perhaps he genuinely believed that American **expansion**, which he supported in principle, was in danger of being tainted by association with a slave power conspiracy to push **slavery** across the continent, a development that would have offended his own view that western lands should be preserved for the enterprise of free white men. Alternatively historians have suggested that he acted to mend fences with his protectionist Pennsylvania constituency, after he alone of the state's Democrats had voted in favor of reducing levels of import duties in the **tariff of 1846**. Nevertheless, after 1846 Wilmot clearly aligned himself with the **barnburner** element of his party, helping to organize the **Free Soil** coalition and backing Van Buren for the presidency again in 1848.

WILMOT PROVISO. In August 1846 **David Wilmot** proposed an amendment to the **Two Million bill** to the effect that **slavery** should not be permitted to expand into any new territory paid for with the money, whether acquired by the United States through military action in the **Mexican War** or through treaty negotiation. While Wilmot's proviso was never actually enacted, either in this and other appropriation bills, such as the **Three Million Act**, or in later measures to organize the new territories of **Oregon, California**, and **New Mexico**, it revealed the increasing northern disquiet at the possible expansion of slavery into territories where it did not already exist. Indeed a mixture of moral, racial, and political concerns so moved northern opinion that numerous northern state legislatures voted their approval for the principle behind the Proviso, while the northern majority in the House also voted in favor of Wilmot's amendment and its successors to other bills. Predictably the Proviso aroused southern hostility and suspicions and this reaction found expression in the Senate, which several times struck out the House's amendments. It also attracted the ire of President **James Polk**, who vowed to veto any bill that included an explicit statement of the Proviso. As such the Proviso contributed considerably to the growing **sectional** tension emerging over the issue of whether and how to stop the spread of slavery into the new territories of the West.

WIRT, WILLIAM (1772-1834). This Maryland-born lawyer and later political leader in Virginia had his most prominent moment in the national spotlight as attorney general under both James Monroe and **John Quincy Adams**. However, retirement to private life in 1829 did not bring with it total isolation from the affairs of state, as Wirt's services as a lawyer remained highly prized. Most famously he was part of the team advocating the cause of the **Cherokee** tribes before the Supreme Court, including the *Cherokee nation* and *Worcester vs. Georgia* cases. Finally, and somewhat ironically considering his own former membership in the Masons, he was nominated as the reluctant presidential candidate of the **Anti-Masonic** Party in 1832, winning the seven electoral college votes of Vermont.

WISCONSIN STATEHOOD. A combination of **Indian removal** and a massive influx of white American settlers, mainly northeasterners in search of farmland, pushed the region beyond Lake Michigan through its territorial stage to statehood by 1848. As the population grew in the 1830s, from 4,000 to over 11,000, residents called for territorial status separate from the Michigan territory. As more settlers arrived, attracted by good prospects in lead mining, **Michigan**'s own push for statehood prompted the creation in April 1836 of a separate Wisconsin territory, at this stage encompassing the future Iowa and Minnesota as well as bits of the Dakotas. Two years later in 1838 those other areas were themselves organized to form the separate Iowa territory, leaving Wisconsin to pursue its own course toward statehood.

By that time the territorial capital had moved from Belmont, near Platteville, to Madison. Although at over 130,000 by 1840 the population was more than enough to be considered for statehood, initially the territorial government rejected such a move on the grounds that it would bring an increase in taxes and make government more intrusive. However, as both the population and economy of the territory continued to grow in the 1840s it was decided that statehood would allow the opportunity to grant incorporated charters and to claim federal support for a range of projects. Voters supported the idea of statehood in 1846 but rejected the first draft proposal of a constitution in 1847, before accepting a new version in 1848. It offered very liberal voting regulations but imposed restrictive provisions on the use of state government power in supporting economic activity, including limits on the level of state debt and a prohibition of the use of state funds for improvements. Finally in May 1848 Wisconsin was admitted to statehood as the 30th state.

WISE, HENRY (1806-1876). This Virginian statesman and politician followed a somewhat maverick political course in the House between 1833 and 1844, although having most in common with other **States' Rights Whigs** in abandoning an earlier support of **Andrew Jackson** in the wake of the **Force Act**. His main influence came as a strong supporter of **John Tyler** and associate of that president's "**Corporal's guard.**" Indeed, Tyler three times appointed Wise U.S. minister to France only to see his nomination blocked on each occasion by **Whigs** in the Senate. By this time Wise had rejoined the **Democrats** as a supporter of **John Calhoun** and eventually secured his reward with appointment as minister to Brazil.

WOMEN. The Jacksonian era witnessed dramatic developments for American women as they shared in the social, economic, and political changes of the day, both as passive members of their immediate family groups and, increasingly, as energetic agents. A combination of a fall in the average birth rate and increasing levels of money to spend on domestic servants and consumer items left many white women from the middle- to upper-middle and wealthy classes with more time on their hands. As the dominant gendered ideas of the day placed women, in most male eyes, in a dependent position, with few if any rights as wives or daughters and certainly none as politically active citizens, some writers, such as **Catharine Beecher** and **Lydia Maria Child,** theorized for American women a significant domestic role as mothers and supervisors of the household. According to this "domestic feminism" good mothers could discourage the development of indigent children and contribute, through the rearing of sons in particular, to the raising of a generation fit for the emerging democratic experiment in the United States. However, significant though these ideas were, they were hardly relevant for the probable majority of women, for whom family circumstances, race, region, or class meant that daily experiences were far more varied than the narrow confines of domestic feminism allowed for. These, and the growing minority of women who pushed at the boundaries of what social convention allowed, contributed to a vastly more diverse picture of female activity during the era.

As with most men the majority of white women would spend a high proportion of their time making a contribution to their family's living. In **agriculture** women combined care for children and domestic chores with working alongside husbands, or fathers, in producing the main subsistence or cash crops. In addition they assumed dedicated roles in gathering certain foodstuffs such as milk and eggs and in spinning, weaving, and making clothes. African-American women took on similar roles, albeit mostly in the very different environment of slave-holdings, where the fact of ownership made even more overbearing the traditional patriarchal leanings of Jacksonian society. An increasing proportion of women, however, were finding employment on other terms, in jobs that were more or less commercialized extensions of their usual economic roles within the family. As wealth expanded the horizons of some households, so this provided opportunities for women, both native-born and recently immigrated, in domestic service. Women worked from home in the shoe-making and textiles industries or in some cases entered developing factories, most famously in the case of the "mill girls" of **Lowell**. More sinister were the increasing levels of prostitution in the growing **urban** areas of the country, whose existence the activities of a generation of **benevolent** reformers uncovered as well as challenged.

The fact that on a daily basis so many women went beyond prescribed feminine roles only points out the historical limitations of theories of domestic feminism. Other women of the time, often from the same middle-class milieu that gave rise to those theories, themselves challenged their relevance in both thought and deed. At their most radical they formed part of communitarian experiments that challenged many of the basic precepts of American society, such as at **Brook Farm** and **Oneida**. **Fanny Wright** often shocked with her rather more liberal ideas on racial and gender relations. The activities of prominent middle-class women more usually represented a less extreme extension of the social or cultural expectations of a woman's role. **Sarah Hale** proved a successful writer and editor, while **Margaret Fuller** assumed a prominent place in not only her own immediate literary circles but also the influential **transcendentalist** movement. The education of women also became a significant aspect, with the emergence of female seminaries, the admission of female students to the first co-educational college at **Oberlin**, and the establishment of the first lasting women's college at Mount Holyoke by **Mary Lyon**. To a large extent, however, the education of women was seen as part of domestic feminism's larger purpose, by equipping future mothers with the values needed to raise their children successfully or by producing a generation of female teachers who would carry on the task in schools. *See also* KEMBLE, FANNY; MARTINEAU, HARRIET.

Most dramatic of all was the involvement of women in the burgeoning benevolent and reform activities so fired up by revived religion of the day. Already prominent in the ranks of the country's religious denominations, many women now combined religious fervor with yet another extension of their feminine role, this time as sympathetic purveyors of charitable good works, to play a significant, albeit usually rank and file, part in the reform societies that so proliferated in the era. So then women were attracted to the **anti-Masonic** movement, women signed petitions against the worst excesses of **Indian removal**, and women were prominent in the **abolitionist** attack on slavery. Just occasionally women even assumed a more active role in reform, such as the leading influence of **Dorothea Dix** for the reform of asylums, the efforts of **Prudence Crandall** on behalf of African-American education, and the abolitionist campaigning of the **Grimké** sisters.

The experience of some women in the abolitionist movement contributed to the emergence of a more concerted challenge to prevailing gender roles in the 1840s. Admittedly there had been occasional earlier expressions of female outrage at their treatment, including what can only be considered nascent trade union ideas arising from the much trumpeted environment of the Lowell mills. The activities of Fanny Wright aside, however, there had previously been few attacks on the political restrictions on women in the early part of the era. Indeed, such political activity as there was, was limited to the witting or unwitting involvement of Washington wives in parlor politics, such as the fulfillment of the presidential entertainment role by the likes of **Emily Donelson**, **Julia Tyler**, and **Sarah Polk**, or the more dramatic events surrounding **Peggy Eaton** at the start of **Andrew Jackson**'s presidency. Women attended in the galleries at congressional sessions, but their direct involvement in political campaigning often reinforced traditional roles, as for instance in the case of support for the **Whig William Henry Harrison** as the best potential shield for the status of women and family.

However, when the actions of abolitionists like the Grimkés generated criticism of the fact that they even dared to participate actively in the movement, some women began to articulate views calling for greater equality of treatment for their gender, making parallels between their own position and that of the entire African-American race. And it would be the treatment of two women, **Lucretia Mott** and **Elizabeth Cady Stanton**, at an international anti-slavery convention that inspired moves that culminated in the **Seneca Falls convention** in 1848 and its call for equal political rights for women. *See also* CALHOUN, FLORIDE; JACKSON, RACHEL.

WOODBURY, LEVI (1789-1851). This New Hampshire statesman was educated at Dartmouth College and after legal training began a political career. An undistinguished term as governor of his state was followed by a period in the Senate, where he stayed until **Andrew Jackson** appointed him secretary of the navy in 1831. Three years later Woodbury was switched to the Treasury, serving in that office for the remainder of Jackson's two terms as well as that of his successor **Martin Van Buren**. As secretary, Woodbury oversaw much of the difficult wrangling over banking, currency, and the **Independent Treasury**, generally following the administration line of **hard money** and hostility to the **Second Bank**. In 1841 he returned to the Senate, where he supported **Texas annexation**, but he left again in 1845 when appointed to the Supreme Court by **James Polk**. Some even considered him a possible **Democratic** presidential nominee for the **election of 1848**, but his perceived lack of popularity with the electorate counted against him.

WORCESTER vs. GEORGIA. This Supreme Court case in 1832 produced the second, and ultimately more important, of two landmark rulings concerning the plight of the **Cherokee** in Georgia. It was generated when several missionaries sympathetic to the Cherokee settled with them in territories over which the state claimed jurisdiction, and broke a state law by refusing either to swear allegiance to the state or to secure a permit to settle there. Supporters of the missionaries claimed that Georgia's law contravened the U.S. Constitution by superseding congressional responsibility for regulating Indian affairs, obstructing foreign treaties (with the Cherokee), and trespassing on the rights of the Cherokee sovereign nation. In a departure from his own ruling in **Cherokee Nation vs. Georgia**, Chief Justice **John Marshall** this time ruled that the Cherokee were a sovereign nation with legitimate title to their lands, and that the Georgian laws were unconstitutional.

Practically the ruling was ineffective at the time, since neither Georgia nor, more significantly, President **Andrew Jackson** was of a mind to follow through its implications. Although Jackson did work behind the scenes for the release of the missionaries, it was only after a guarantee from their chief legal representative, **William Wirt**, that he would not present their case to the Supreme Court again. It could not stop the ultimate fate of the Cherokee, who lost control of their lands and were removed west of the Mississippi River. Nevertheless the precedent set by the ruling would become a bastion of tribal powers to later generations of Native Americans.

WORKINGMEN'S MOVEMENT. Workingmen's Parties represented another means, alongside **trade unions**, by which the interests of American **labor** came to be represented on the stage of public policy debate in Jacksonian America. Broader in its message than were unions, and indeed never fully united, the Workingmen's movement offered an intellectualization of labor issues, drawing on the ideas of radical thinkers such as Thomas Skidmore and **William Leggett**. Its support for equal opportunity for all rather than just better conditions for workers in particular appealed equally to masters and mechanics. Among the movement's varied proposals were universal education, opposition to government-chartered monopoly rights for banking and other corporations, **hard money**, land reform, abolition of imprisonment for debt, opposition to anything competing with free labor (including contract prison labor and exploitation of apprentices and child labor), policies supporting anti-clericalism, and the disestablishment of religion.

In political terms the Workingmen's Parties operated as early examples of third parties. Arising first in Philadelphia in the late 1820s and then in New York City, in the form of the Committee of Fifty, whose members included **Fanny Wright** and **Robert Dale Owen**, the movement had representative parties in most cities throughout the Union by the 1830s. Although they did run their own candidates for local election, such as in New York in 1829, they were also prepared to cooperate with one or other of the major parties. This association meant that, even after local Workingmen's Parties began to fade out of existence in the mid-1830s after many electoral defeats, their influence lived on, with their attacks on aristocracy and privilege reinforcing the ideology of the **Democratic** Party in particular, as evidenced by its policies on banking and currency.

WRIGHT, FRANCES (1795-1852). Born in Dundee, Scotland, Fanny Wright spent periods touring the United States in 1818 and 1824 after inheriting a large fortune. During that period she befriended the Marquis de Lafayette and then spent some time in 1826 living in a communitarian experiment at Nashoba, Tennessee, where she proposed the idea that African-Americans would work more profitably as free men than as **slaves**. In 1829 Wright moved to New York City and made a name lecturing at the Hall of Science on **women**'s rights, religious freedom, and progressive education. While in New York she also published the radical *Free Enquirer* newspaper, in association with her lover, **Robert Dale Owen**. In 1830 Wright returned to Europe and Paris, by way of Haiti, where she had taken her freed slaves. Five years later she settled once again in the United States, at Cincinnati where she expressed herself a **Jacksonian** in her support for **Democratic** financial and banking policies of **hard money** and the **Independent Treasury** and in her opposition to **sabbatarian** campaigns. However, in 1839 she left once more for France and only returned to the United States sporadically as part of more widespread travels during the decade that followed.

WRIGHT, SILAS (1795-1847). Wright was born in Massachusetts, moved with his family to Vermont in 1796 and later took up a career in law in the upstate region of New York. He entered local politics as a supporter of **Martin Van Buren** and went on to become perhaps his most loyal follower over the next 30 years. In the House of Representatives between 1827 and 1829, then as New York state comptroller from 1829 to 1833, and finally in the Senate between 1833 and 1844, Wright proved a loyal **Democrat**, supporting **Andrew Jackson**'s fiscal and banking policies throughout, including opposition to efforts to re-charter the **Second Bank** and to **distribution**, and support, as chair of the Senate Finance Committee, for the **Independent Treasury** scheme. After turning down **John Tyler**'s offer of a Supreme Court position, Wright remained loyal to Van Buren, sharing his reluctance to push for **Texas annexation**. Moreover, even though he was prepared to support **James Polk** once he had been nominated as the regular Democratic candidate for 1844, Wright's loyalty to Van Buren prevented him from allowing himself to be selected as Polk's running mate and from accepting Polk's offer of the post of secretary of the treasury. Instead Wright ran for and won office as governor of New York, only to fail in a bid for reelection in 1846, after his **Barnburner** stance caused a split with the **Hunker** elements

of his party. Thereafter he effectively retired, to die of a heart attack
the following year.

– Y –

YOUNG, BRIGHAM (1801-1877). This Vermont-born religious figure moved to New York State early in his life and there combined
work in the building trades with evangelical worship among Methodists before a conversion experience shaped the rest of his life. In 1832
he joined the Church of Latter Day Saints and rapidly rose to become
a leading figure in the developing **Mormon** religious movement.
Within a year he was an elder in his local Mormon congregation and
soon after led a group to join up with the Mormon leader, **Joseph
Smith**, at Kirtland in Ohio. Smith came to value Young's support and
talents and sent him on tours across many states with the aim of converting more to his religion. In 1835 Young was appointed one of the
12 Apostles with powers second only to Smith, and he was elected
president of the Council of Apostles a year later. After helping to establish **Nauvoo**, he took his evangelizing work to Liverpool in England between 1839 and 1841, before returning to further missionary
work in the eastern United States for the next three years. After Smith
was murdered in 1844, Young took over as acting president of the
main group of Mormons, and it would be he who led them from Nauvoo on their great trek west to the Great Salt Lake valley in present-
day Utah in 1846-47. Thereafter he was formally elected head of the
Mormon Church.

YOUNG AMERICA. Mirroring many similar movements emerging
out of new expressions of nationalism in Europe, the "Young America" idea represented a statement of extreme pride in America's
present and future. First espoused in 1845 by the South Carolinian
Edwin De Leon, it shared with **Manifest Destiny** much of the same
nationalistic fervor for American democratic institutions and for the
economic and social opportunities apparently open to American citizens. As adopted by mainly **Democratic** politicians later in the decade and beyond, it came to be used as a tool with which to counter-
balance **sectional** tensions, mainly through its call for the extension
of the benefits of American nationhood across the western hemisphere and the Pacific.

"YOUNG HICKORY." This nickname, enjoyed by **James Polk**, grew out of the parallels between his own career and that of his Tennessee predecessor in the White House, **Old Hickory** himself, **Andrew Jackson**. Polk's steadfast support of Jackson while a congressman and then the similarity in his attitudes and approach to the presidency only reinforced the political capital to be gained by using the name to make a strong identification with the dominant figure of the age.

YUCATAN. When the Mexican government called for assistance in meeting the challenge of a revolt among the native population of the Yucatan peninsula in early 1848, **James Polk**'s administration was among those forced to assess their position with regard to this request. Several in Polk's Cabinet joined with others in the Senate in expressing a range of **expansionist** views beyond simply offering assistance to the Mexican government, including support either for a military occupation by U.S. troops or for outright annexation of the peninsula by the United States. Polk himself feared inaction might lead to other, European, powers securing a foothold of influence in the Yucatan, but his own wariness of committing American interests to the project prevailed, while the return of peace to the peninsula ended debate on the matter anyway. Even so, the episode provided yet more evidence of the strength and nature of expansionist fervor in the middle and late 1840s.

– Z –

***ZOLLVEREIN*, TREATY WITH.** This commercial treaty, signed in 1844 by Henry Wheaton and representatives of the Prussian government on behalf of the *Zollverein*, or German Customs Union, was one of the few acts of commercial diplomacy in this era to meet with domestic political opposition. In part this was owing to the treaty's particular purpose, to implement a policy of commercial reciprocity, that is the reduction by each country of a range of duties imposed on imported goods coming from the other. While even opponents of the treaty recognized that its promise to reduce German duties on American **tobacco**, lard, raw **cotton**, and **rice** was welcome, they considered the treaty's approach potentially confusing, inappropriate, and even unconstitutional. They claimed that the treaty would set a precedent that, if followed, would lead to partial and confusingly complex customs regulations. They also claimed that other nations enjoying most favored nation status in their trade relations with the

United States would demand the same levels of duty as now to be enjoyed by German exporters, with or without the condition that they offer changes in their own duties similar to those reductions to be made by the *Zollverein*.

Most seriously, many opponents of the treaty regarded it as attacking their preferred policy of a **protective tariff** through the back door of diplomacy rather than allowing the branch of government responsible for revenue raising, namely the House of Representatives and Congress as a whole, to make such decisions. Although President **John Tyler** acknowledged that Congress would formally pass the specific rate reductions called for in the treaty, the Senate Foreign Relations Committee criticized this request as another example of **executive usurpation**, since the House would not be initiating the changes in duties itself.

Accusing the president of leading instead of following Congress on this matter, the Senate allowed the treaty to die without ratification, tabling it by a vote of 26 to 18 on the last day of the 1843-44 congressional session. In addition to the points of principle put forward, the rejection of the treaty also owed much to the desire of regular **Whigs** to prevent Tyler from claiming success for the treaty and to sustain the momentum gained by blocking the **Texas annexation** treaty. *See also* COMMERCIAL TREATIES; OVERSEAS COMMERCE.

Andrew Jackson

John Quincy Adams

Henry Clay

John Calhoun

Daniel Webster

Zachary Taylor

Winfield Scott

Sam Houston

Robert Walker

James Buchanan

Lewis Cass

Martin Van Buren

William Henry Harrison

James Polk

John Tyler

William Lloyd Garrison

Roger Taney

APPENDIX

Presidents and Their Administrations, 1829-1849

ANDREW JACKSON 1829-1837

Presidential Election Results:

Year		Popular votes	Electoral votes
1828	**Andrew Jackson**	**647,286**	**178**
	John Quincy Adams	508,064	83
1832	**Andrew Jackson**	**687,502**	**219**
	Henry Clay	530,189	49
	William Wirt	33,108	7
	John Floyd		11

Vice Presidents: John C. Calhoun (1829-32)
Martin Van Buren (1833-37)

Cabinet:
Secretary of State
  Martin Van Buren (1829-31)
  Edward Livingston (1831-33)
  Louis McLane (1833-34)
  John Forsyth (1834-37)
Secretary of the Treasury
  Samuel Ingham (1829-31)
  Louis McLane (1831-33)

William Duane (1833)
Roger B. Taney (1833-34)
Levi Woodbury (1834-37)
Secretary of War
John Eaton (1829-31)
Lewis Cass (1831-37)
Benjamin Butler (acting, 1836-37)
Attorney General
John Berrien (1829-31)
Roger B. Taney (1831-33)
Benjamin Butler (1833-37)
Postmaster General
John McLean (1829)
William T. Barry (1829-35)
Amos Kendall (1835-37)
Secretary of the Navy
John Branch (1829-31)
Levi Woodbury (1831-34)
Mahlon Dickerson (1834-37)

MARTIN VAN BUREN 1837-1841

Presidential Election Results:

Year		Popular votes	Electoral votes
1836	**Martin Van Buren**	**764,176**	**170**
	William H. Harrison	550,816	73
	Hugh L. White	146,107	26
	Daniel Webster	41,201	14
	W. P. Mangum		11

Vice President: Richard M. Johnson (1837-41)

Cabinet:
Secretary of State
John Forsyth (1837-41)
Secretary of the Treasury
Levi Woodbury (1837-41)
Secretary of War
Joel Poinsett (1837-41)

Attorney General
  Benjamin Butler (1837-38)
  Felix Grundy (1838-40)
  Henry Gilpin (1840-41)
Postmaster General
  Amos Kendall (1837-40)
  John Niles (1840-41)
Secretary of the Navy
  Mahlon Dickerson (1837-38)
  James K. Paulding (1838-41)

WILLIAM HENRY HARRISON 1841

Presidential Election Results:

Year		Popular votes	Electoral votes
1840	**William H. Harrison**	**1,274,624**	**234**
	Martin Van Buren	1,127,781	60
	James G. Birney	7,069	0

Vice President: John Tyler (1841)

Cabinet:
Secretary of State
  Daniel Webster (1841)
Secretary of the Treasury
  Thomas Ewing (1841)
Secretary of War
  John Bell (1841)
Attorney General
  John Crittenden (1841)
Postmaster General
  Francis Granger (1841)
Secretary of the Navy
  George Badger (1841)

JOHN TYLER 1841-1845

Cabinet:
Secretary of State
  Daniel Webster (1841-43)
  Abel Upshur (1843-44)
  John C. Calhoun (1844-45)
Secretary of the Treasury
  Thomas Ewing (1841)
  Walter Forward (1841-43)
  John Spencer (1843-44)
  George Bibb (1844-45)
Secretary of War
  John Bell (1841)
  John Spencer (1841-43)
  James Porter (1843-44)
  William Wilkins (1844-45)
Attorney General
  John Crittenden (1841)
  Hugh Legaré (1841-43)
  John Nelson (1843-45)
Postmaster General
  Francis Granger (1841)
  Charles Wickliffe (1841-45)
Secretary of the Navy
  George Badger (1841)
  Abel Upshur (1841-43)
  David Henshaw (1843-44)
  Thomas Gilmer (1844)
  John Mason (1844-45)

JAMES K. POLK 1845-1849

Presidential Election Results:

Year		Popular votes	Electoral votes
1844	**James K. Polk**	**1,338,464**	**170**
	Henry Clay	1,300,097	105
	James G. Birney	62,300	0
1848	**Zachary Taylor**	**1,360,967**	**163**
	Lewis Cass	1,222,342	127
	Martin Van Buren	291,263	0

Vice President: George M. Dallas (1845-49)

Cabinet:
Secretary of State
  James Buchanan (1845-49)
Secretary of the Treasury
  Robert Walker (1845-49)
Secretary of War
  William Marcy (1845-49)
Attorney General
  John Mason (1845-46)
  Nathan Clifford (1846-48)
  Isaac Toucey (1848-49)
Postmaster General
  Cave Johnson (1845-49)
Secretary of the Navy
  George Bancroft (1845-46)
  John Mason (1846-49)

Bibliography

Contents

Introductory Note

This bibliography errs on the side of inclusiveness and provides a good coverage of some of the classic works on this period as well as some of the more recent historical output produced in monographs and article form. The bibliographical works included in the first section below have been exceptionally useful in compiling this list but it should also be noted that many of the more general surveys and interpretative texts, including Daniel Feller's *Jacksonian Promise* and Harry Watson's *Liberty and Power*, also have excellent bibliographies. These have been supplemented, and can continue to be so by future readers, by reference to journal-based and online bibliographies that constantly alert the scholar to the growing volume of historical writings on all aspects of American history. Other listed reference works have also proven invaluable in the preparation of this book, although Paul Doutrich's *Shapers of the Great Debate on Jacksonian Democracy: A Biographical Dictionary* was published too late to be consulted.

It is to be hoped that the sections within the bibliography are well enough defined to guide readers to most aspects of what they may wish to pursue in further reading. An attempt has been made to avoid repetition where possible. To facilitate this, works covering government policy with regard to specific aspects of the economy have been included in the relevant section in the economy subdivision of the bibliography. However, in some cases single works have had to be included in more than one section, when the material is equally relevant to both. This has been the case in particular with works examining religion, reform, gender issues, and labor.

It seems invidious to pick out particularly important titles from such a long list of valuable scholarship. However, for the reader new to the area Glyndon Van Deusen's *The Jacksonian Era* remains the only, if now very dated, text covering the whole of the specific period of this volume. The four volumes in the generally excellent University Press of Kansas Presidential History series, by Donald Cole, Major Wilson, Norma Peterson, and Paul Bergeron, provide varying degrees of coverage of the main developments of each presidential term and as such are a useful supplement to Van Deusen. If looking for a more interpretative slant on the whole era, the reader should turn to Charles Sellers' *The Market Revolution*, a controversial and at times difficult work whose impact is still being felt among the community of historians working on the period. Alternatively the works by Feller and Watson mentioned above provide more accessible treatments of the era, portraying the achievements and expectations of Jacksonian Americans in respectively more optimistic or pessimistic lights. A forthcoming work in the Longman History of the United States series, by Donald Ratcliffe, should bring up to date the work of synthesizing the historical analysis of the main developments of the period.

Journals still provide space for much of the cutting-edge research into any period of history and the period covered by this book is particularly well served in this regard. Leading the way remains the *Journal of American History*, whose occasional articles on the era are supplemented by excellent book reviews, lists of recently published scholarship, and publishers' notices. Doing much the same job for the earlier part of this period is the *Journal of the Early Republic*, perhaps the premier journal for scholars interested in the Jacksonian era, while the British-based *American Nineteenth Century History* is developing a reputation for solid new scholarship. In addition to the large number of state historical journals, regionally focused journals also provide a platform for useful studies of the period, with the *Journal of Southern History*, the *New England Quarterly*, and the *Pacific Historical Review* being the leaders in the field.

In addition to the printed primary sources listed below there are several collections of manuscript sources that provide essential material for a study of the period. This is especially important given the fact that none of the four leading presidents of the era is served by a modern, edited collection that extends throughout their term as president. Predictably the Library of Congress Manuscripts division to some extent fills this gap, with extensive collections relating to Andrew Jackson, Martin Van Buren, and James Polk, all being accessible in microform, and the former two being extended in that format to include papers held in other collections as well. Most of John Tyler's papers were lost during the Civil War, but the Library of Congress holds most of what remains. The Southern Historical Collection and the Tennessee Presidents Center also hold useful supplementary materials.

Selected primary materials can also be found on a number of relevant Web sites. Once again the Library of Congress is probably the best first port of call, through **http://www.loc.gov** and some of the more specific pages in the American Memory project at **http://memory.loc.gov**. Other sites need to be used with a greater degree of caution, but **http://www.earlyrepublic.net/** does link to some more or less reliable reference sites and primary source collections.

1. General

1.1 Bibliographies, Historiographical Works, and Dictionaries

Bisson, Wilfred J., comp. *Franklin Pierce: A Bibliography.* Westport, Conn.: Greenwood Press, 1993.

Burkholder, Robert E., and Joel Myerson, comps. *Emerson: An Annotated Secondary Bibliography.* Pittsburgh, Penn.: University of Pittsburgh Press, 1985.

————. *Ralph Waldo Emerson: An Annotated Bibliography of Criticism, 1980-1991.* Westport, Conn.: Greenwood Press, 1994.

Cave, Alfred A. *Jacksonian Democracy and the Historians.* Gainesville, Fla.: University of Florida Press, 1964.

Conway, Jill K., with the assistance of Linda Kealey and Janet E. Schulte. *The Female Experience in Eighteenth- and Nineteenth-Century America: A Guide to the History of American Women.* Princeton, N.J.: Princeton University Press, 1982.

Crawford, John E., comp. *Millard Fillmore: A Bibliography*. Westport, Conn.: Greenwood Press, 2002.

Crawford, Mark, David S. Heidler, and Jeanne T. Heidler, eds. *Encyclopedia of the Mexican-American War*. Santa Barbara, Calif.: ABC-CLIO, 1999.

Cronin, John W., comp. *A Bibliography of William Henry Harrison, John Tyler, James Knox Polk*. Washington, D.C.: Riverford Publishing Co, 1935.

Cronin, John W., and W. Harvey Wise Jr., comps. *A Bibliography of John Adams and John Quincy Adams*. Washington, D.C.: Riverford Publishing Co., 1935.

Doutrich, Paul E. *Shapers of the Great Debate on Jacksonian Democracy: A Biographical Dictionary*. Westport, Conn.: Greenwood Press, 2004.

Durfee, David A., ed. *William Henry Harrison, 1773-1841 and John Tyler, 1790-1862: Chronology, Documents, Bibliographical Aids*. Dobbs Ferry, N.Y.: Oceana Publications, 1970.

Farrell, John J., ed. *James K. Polk, 1795-1849: Chronology, Documents, Bibliographical Aids*. Dobbs Ferry, N.Y.: Oceana Publications, 1970.

———. *Zachary Taylor 1784-1850 and Millard Fillmore 1800-1874: Chronology, Documents, Bibliographical Aids*. Dobbs Ferry, N.Y.: Oceana Publications, 1971.

Fehrenbacher, Don E., comp. *Manifest Destiny and the Coming of the Civil War, 1840-1861*. New York: Appleton-Century-Crofts, 1970.

Feller, Daniel. "Politics and Society: Toward a Jacksonian Synthesis." *Journal of the Early Republic* 10 (1990), 135-61.

Formisano, Ronald P. "Toward a Reorientation of Jacksonian Politics: A Review of the Literature, 1959-1975." *Journal of American History* 63 (1976), 42-65.

Jones, Kenneth V., ed. *John Quincy Adams, 1767-1848: Chronology, Documents, Bibliographical Aids*. Dobbs Ferry, N.Y.: Oceana Publications, 1970.

Klein, Martin A. *Historical Dictionary of Slavery and Abolition*. Lanham, Md.: Scarecrow Press, 2002.

Mehaffey, Karen Rae. *Victorian American Women, 1840-1880: An Annotated Bibliography*. New York: Garland, 1992.

Miller, Randall M., & John R. McKivigan, eds. *The Moment of Decision: Biographical Essays on American Character and Regional Identity*. Westport, Conn.: Greenwood Press, 1994.

Miller, Randall M., and John David Smith, eds. *Dictionary of Afro-American Slavery*. Westport, Conn.: Praeger, 1997.

Moseley, Edward H., and Paul C. Clark Jr. *Historical Dictionary of the United States-Mexican War*. Lanham, Md.: Scarecrow Press, 1997.

Moser, Harold D., comp. *John Tyler: A Bibliography*. Westport, Conn.: Greenwood Press, 2001.

Oates, Stephen B., and Buz Wyeth, eds. *The Approaching Fury: Voices of the Storm, 1820-1861*. New York: HarperCollins Publishers, 1997.

Parsons, Lynn H., ed. *John Quincy Adams: A Bibliography*. Westport, Conn.: Greenwood Press, 1993.

368

BIBLIOGRAPHY

Remini, Robert V., and Edwin A. Miles, comps. *The Era of Good Feelings and the Age of Jackson, 1816-1841.* Arlington Heights, Ill.: AHM Pub. Corp., 1979.

Remini, Robert V., and Robert O. Rupp. *Andrew Jackson: A Bibliography.* Westport, Conn.: Meckler, 1991.

Risjord, Norman K. *Representative Americans, The Romantics.* Lanham, Md.: Rowman & Littlefield, 2001.

Ruiz, Ramón Eduardo, ed. *The Mexican War—Was It Manifest Destiny?* New York: Holt, Rinehart and Winston, 1963.

Sellers, Charles Griers. "Andrew Jackson versus the Historians." *Mississippi Valley Historical Review* 44 (1958), 615-34.

Shaw, Ronald E., ed. *Andrew Jackson, 1767-1845: Chronology, Documents, Bibliographical Aids.* Dobbs Ferry, N.Y.: Oceana Publications, 1969.

Sloan, Irving J., ed. *Franklin Pierce, 1804-1869: Chronology, Documents, Bibliographical Aids.* Dobbs Ferry, N.Y.: Oceana Publications, 1968.

———. *James Buchanan, 1791-1868: Chronology, Documents, Bibliographical Aids.* Dobbs Ferry, N.Y.: Oceana Publications, 1968.

———. *Martin Van Buren, 1782-1862: Chronology, Documents, Bibliographical Aids.* Dobbs Ferry, N.Y.: Oceana Publications, 1969.

Stevens, Kenneth R., comp. *William Henry Harrison: A Bibliography.* Westport, Conn.: Greenwood Press, 1998.

Tutorow, Norman E., comps. *The Mexican-American War: An Annotated Bibliography.* Westport, Conn.: Greenwood Press, 1981.

Wilentz, Sean. "On Class and Politics in Jacksonian America." *Reviews in American History* 10 (1982), 43-63.

Wilson, Clyde N. *John C. Calhoun: A Bibliography.* Westport, Conn.: Meckler, 1990.

Wise, W. Harvey, Jr., and John W. Cronin, comps. *A Bibliography of Zachary Taylor, Millard Fillmore, Franklin Pierce, James Buchanan.* Washington, D.C.: Riverford Publishing Co., 1935.

———. *A Bibliography of Andrew Jackson and Martin Van Buren.* New York: B. Franklin, 1970.

1.2 General Surveys and Interpretative Texts

Cunliffe, Marcus. *The Nation Takes Shape, 1789-1837.* Chicago: University of Chicago Press, 1959.

Feller, Daniel. *The Jacksonian Promise: America, 1815-1840.* Baltimore: Johns Hopkins University Press, 1995.

Fish, Carl Russell. *The Rise of the Common Man, 1830-1850.* New York: Macmillan, 1927.

Hofstadter, Richard. "Andrew Jackson and the Rise of Liberal Capitalism." *The American Political Tradition and the Men Who Made It.* New York: Alfred A. Knopf, 1948, pp. 45-67.

Lacour-Gayet, Robert. *Everyday Life in the United States before the Civil War, 1830-1860.* Translated by Mary Ilford. New York: Ungar, 1969.

Larkin, Jack. *The Reshaping of Everyday Life, 1790-1840.* New York: Harper & Row, 1988.

McCormick, Richard L. *The Party Period and Public Policy: American Politics from the Age of Jackson to the Progressive Era.* New York: Oxford University Press, 1986.

Masur, Louis P. *1831: Year of Eclipse.* New York: Hill & Wang, 2001.

Meyers, Marvin. *The Jacksonian Persuasion: Politics and Belief.* Stanford, Calif.: Stanford University Press, 1957.

Nye, Russell Blaine. *Society and Culture in America, 1830-1860.* New York: Harper & Row, 1974.

Pessen, Edward. *Jacksonian America: Society, Personality and Politics.* Homewood, Ill.: Dorsey Press, 1969.

Potter, David M. *The Impending Crisis, 1848-1861.* New York: Harper & Row, 1976.

Schlesinger, Arthur M., Jr. *The Age of Jackson.* Boston: Little, Brown & Co., 1945.

Sellers, Charles G., Jr. *The Market Revolution: Jacksonian America, 1815-1846.* New York: Oxford University Press, 1991.

Sobel, Robert. *Conquest and Conscience: The 1840s.* New York: Thomas Y. Crowell & Co., 1971.

Somkin, Fred. *Unquiet Eagle: Memory and Desire in the Idea of American Freedom, 1815-1860.* Ithaca, N.Y.: Cornell University Press, 1967.

Stokes, Melvyn, and Stephen Conway, eds. *The Market Revolution: Social, Political and Religious Expressions, 1800-1880.* Charlottesville, Va.: University Press of Virginia, 1996.

Van Deusen, Glyndon G. *The Jacksonian Era, 1828-1848.* New York: Harper & Row, 1959.

Watson, Harry L. *Liberty and Power: The Politics of Jacksonian America.* New York: Hill and Wang, 1990.

Wilson, Major L. *Space, Time and Freedom: The Quest for Nationality and the Irrepressible Conflict, 1815-1861.* Westport, Conn.: Greenwood Press, 1974.

Wiltse, Charles. *The New Nation, 1800-1845.* New York: Hill & Wang, 1961.

1.3 Printed Primary Source Collections

Belz, Herman, ed. *The Webster-Hayne Debate on the Nature of the Union: Selected Documents.* Indianapolis, Ind.: Liberty Fund, 2000.

Blau, Joseph L., ed. *Social Theories of Jacksonian Democracy: Representative Writings of the Period 1825-1850.* Indianapolis, Ind.: Hackett Publishing Company, 2003.

Bode, Carl, ed. *American Life in the 1840's.* Garden City, N.Y.: Anchor Books, 1967.

Davis, David Brion, ed. *Antebellum American Culture: An Interpretive Anthology*. University Park, Pa.: Pennsylvania State University Press, 1997.

Eaton, Clement, ed. *The Leaven of Democracy: The Growth of the Democratic Spirit in the Time of Jackson*. New York: G. Braziller, 1963.

Freehling, William W., ed. *The Nullification Era: A Documentary Record*. New York: Harper & Row, 1967.

Garrison, George P., ed. "Diplomatic Correspondence of the Republic of Texas." *Annual Report of the American Historical Association for the Year 1908*. 2 vols. Washington, D.C.: Government Printing Office, 1911.

Gatell, Frank Otto, ed. *The Jacksonians and the Money Power, 1829-1840*. Chicago: Rand McNally, 1967.

Gatell, Frank Otto, and John M. McFaul, eds. *Jacksonian America, 1815-1840: New Society, Changing Politics*. Englewood Cliffs, N.J.: Prentice-Hall, 1970.

Graebner, Norman A., ed. *Manifest Destiny*. Indianapolis, Ind.: Bobbs-Merrill, 1968.

Kraditor, Aileen S., ed. *Up from the Pedestal: Selected Writings in the History of American Feminism*. Chicago: Quadrangle Books, 1968.

Lowance, Mason, ed. *Against Slavery: An Abolitionist Reader*. New York: Penguin Books, 2000.

McAfee, Ward, and J. Cordell Robinson, comps. *Origins of the Mexican War: A Documentary Source Book*. 2 vols. Salisbury: Documentary Publications, 1982.

Manning, William R., ed. *Diplomatic Correspondence of the United States: Inter-American Affairs, 1831-1860*. 12 vols. Washington, D.C.: Carnegie Endowment for International Peace, 1932-39.

———. *Diplomatic Correspondence of the United States: Canadian Relations, 1784-1860*. 4 vols. Washington, D.C.: Carnegie Endowment for International Peace, 1940-45.

Morris, Richard B., and James Woodress, eds. *Jacksonian Democracy, 1829-1848*. New York: Webster Division, McGraw-Hill, 1976.

Mullin, Michael, ed. *American Negro Slavery: A Documentary History*. Columbia, S.C.: University of South Carolina Press, 1976.

Ostrander, Gilman M., ed. *The Romantic Democracy, 1835-1855*. University City: Marston Press, 1971.

Pessen, Edward, ed. *Jacksonian Panorama*. Indianapolis, Ind.: Bobbs-Merrill, 1976.

Remini, Robert V., ed. *The Age of Jackson*. Columbia, S.C.: University of South Carolina Press, 1972.

Richardson, James D., comp. *A Compilation of the Messages and Papers of the Presidents, 1789-1902*. 10 volumes. Washington, D.C.: Bureau of National Literature and Art, 1904.

Rose, Willie Lee, ed. *A Documentary History of Slavery in North America*. Athens, Ga.: University of Georgia Press, 1999.

Rozwenc, Edwin C., ed. *Ideology and Power in the Age of Jackson*. Garden City, N.Y.: Anchor Books, 1964.

Schlesinger, Arthur M., Jr., Fred L. Israel, and David J. Frent, eds. *The Election of 1828 and the Administration of Andrew Jackson*. Philadelphia: Mason Crest Publishers, 2003.

———. *The Election of 1840 and the Harrison/Tyler Administrations*. Philadelphia: Mason Crest Publishers, 2003.

Taylor, Clare, comp. *British and American Abolitionists: An Episode in Transatlantic Understanding*. Edinburgh: Edinburgh University Press, 1974.

Thomas, John L., ed. *Slavery Attacked: The Abolitionist Crusade*. Englewood Cliffs, N.J.: Prentice-Hall, 1965.

Thompson, C. Bradley, ed. *Antislavery Political Writings, 1833-1860: A Reader*. Armonk: M.E. Sharpe, 2004.

Welter, Rush, comp. *American Writings on Popular Education: The Nineteenth Century*. Indianapolis, Ind.: Bobbs-Merrill, 1971.

Whitney, Ellen M., ed. *The Black Hawk War, 1831-1832*. 2 vols. Springfield, Ill.: Illinois State Historical Library, 1970-1978.

Wiltse, Charles M., ed. *Expansion and Reform, 1815-1850*. New York: Free Press, 1967.

2. Biographical Material

2.1 Presidents

Bergeron, Paul H. *The Presidency of James K. Polk*. Lawrence, Kans.: University Press of Kansas, 1987.

Burstein, Andrew. *The Passions of Andrew Jackson*. New York: Knopf, 2003.

Chitwood, Oliver P. *John Tyler: Champion of the Old South*. New York: D. Appleton-Century Company, 1939.

Cole, Donald B. *Martin Van Buren and the American Political System*. Princeton, N.J.: Princeton University Press, 1984.

———. *The Presidency of Andrew Jackson*. Lawrence, Kans.: University Press of Kansas, 1993.

Curtis, James C. *The Fox at Bay: Martin Van Buren and the Presidency, 1837-1841*. Lexington, Ky: University Press of Kentucky, 1970.

———. *Andrew Jackson and the Search for Vindication*. Boston: Little, Brown, 1976.

Dusinberre, William. *Slavemaster President: The Double Career of James Polk*. New York: Oxford University Press, 2003.

Goebel, Dorothy B. *William Henry Harrison: A Political Biography*. Indianapolis, Ind.: Historical Bureau of the Indiana Library and Historical Department, 1926.

Green, James A. *William Henry Harrison, His Life and Times*. Richmond, Va.: Garrett and Massie, 1941.

Haynes, Sam W. *James K. Polk and the Expansionist Impulse*. Edited by Oscar Handlin. New York: Longman, 1997.

James, Marquis. *Andrew Jackson: Portrait of a President.* Indianapolis, Ind.: Bobbs-Merrill, 1937.

Kesilman, Sylvia H. "John Tyler and the Presidency: Old School Republicanism, Partisan Realignment, and Support for His Administration." Ph.D. Dissertation, Ohio State University, 1973.

Leonard, Thomas M. *James K. Polk: A Clear and Unquestionable Destiny.* Wilmington, Del.: S.R. Books, 2001.

McCormac, Eugene Irving. *James K Polk: A Political Biography.* Berkeley, Calif.: University of California Press, 1922.

McCoy, Charles A. *Polk and the Presidency.* Austin, Tex.: University of Texas Press, 1960.

Monroe, Dan. *The Republican Vision of John Tyler.* College Station, Tex.: Texas A & M University Press, 2003.

Morgan, Robert J. *A Whig Embattled: The Presidency under John Tyler.* Lincoln, Neb.: University of Nebraska Press, 1954.

Mushkat, Jerome, and Joseph G. Rayback. *Martin Van Buren: Law, Politics and the Shaping of Republican Ideology.* DeKalb, Ill.: Northern Illinois University Press, 1997.

Niven, John. *Martin Van Buren: The Romantic Age of American Politics.* New York: Oxford University Press, 1983.

Parsons, Lynn Hudson. "In which the Political becomes the Personal and Vice Versa: The Last Ten Years of John Quincy Adams and Andrew Jackson." *Journal of the Early Republic* 23 (2003), 421-43.

Peterson, Norma Lois. *The Presidencies of William Henry Harrison and John Tyler.* Lawrence, Kans.: University Press of Kansas, 1989.

Remini, Robert V. *Andrew Jackson and the Course of American Freedom, 1822-1832.* New York: Harper & Row, 1981.

———. *Andrew Jackson and the Course of American Democracy, 1833-1845.* New York: Harper & Row, 1984.

Seager, Robert, II. *And Tyler Too: A Biography of John and Julia Gardiner Tyler.* New York: McGraw-Hill Books, 1963.

Sellers, Charles G., Jr. *James K. Polk: Jacksonian, 1795-1843.* Princeton, N.J.: Princeton University Press, 1957.

———. *James K. Polk: Continentalist, 1843-1846.* Princeton, N.J.: Princeton University Press, 1966.

Silbey, Joel H. *Martin Van Buren and the Emergence of Popular Politics.* Lanham, Md.: Rowman & Littlefield, 2002.

Ward, John William. *Andrew Jackson—Symbol for an Age.* New York: Oxford University Press, 1955.

Wilson, Major L. *The Presidency of Martin Van Buren.* Lawrence, Kans.: University Press of Kansas, 1984.

Wyatt-Brown, Bertram. "Andrew Jackson's Honor." *Journal of the Early Republic* 17 (1997), 1-36.

2.2 Other National and Local Political Figures

Aderman, Ralph M., and Wayne R. Kime. *Advocate for America: The Life of James Kirke Paulding.* Selinsgrove, Penn.: Susquehanna University Press, 2003.

Ambler, Charles Henry. *Thomas Ritchie: A Study in Virginia Politics.* Richmond, Va.: Bell Book & Stationery Co., 1913.

Baker, Elizabeth Feast. *Henry Wheaton, 1785-1848.* Philadelphia: University of Pennsylvania Press, 1937.

Bartlett, Irving H. *Wendell Phillips: Brahmin Radical.* Boston: Beacon Press, 1961.

———. *Daniel Webster.* New York: W. W. Norton, 1978.

———. *John C. Calhoun: A Biography.* New York: W.W. Norton, 1993.

Baxter, Maurice G. *One and Inseparable: Daniel Webster and the Union.* Cambridge, Mass.: Harvard University Press, 1984.

———. *Henry Clay and the American System.* Lexington, Ky: University Press of Kentucky, 1995.

Belohlavek, John M. *George Mifflin Dallas: Jacksonian Patrician.* University Park, Pa.: Pennsylvania State University Press, 1977.

Bemis, Samuel F. *John Quincy Adams and the Union.* New York: Alfred A. Knopf, 1956.

Blue, Frederick J. *Salmon P. Chase: A Life in Politics.* Kent, Ohio: Kent State University Press, 1987.

Brown, Norman D. *Daniel Webster and the Politics of Availability.* Athens, Ga.: University of Georgia Press, 1969.

Campbell, Randolph B. *Sam Houston and the American Southwest.* New York: Harper Collins, 1993.

Cantrill, Gregg. *Stephen F. Austin: Empresario of Texas.* New Haven, Conn.: Yale University Press, 1999.

Capers, Gerald M. *John C. Calhoun, Opportunist: A Reappraisal.* Gainesville, Fla.: University of Florida Press, 1960.

Chambers, William Nisbet. *Old Bullion Benton: Senator from the New West: Thomas Hart Benton, 1782-1858.* Boston: Little, Brown, 1956.

Clifford, Philip Greely. *Nathan Clifford, Democrat (1803-1881).* New York: G.P. Putnam's Sons, 1922.

Coit, Margaret. *John C. Calhoun: American Portrait.* Boston: Houghton Mifflin, 1950.

Cole, Donald B. *A Jackson Man: Amos Kendall and the Rise of American Democracy.* Baton Rouge, La.: Louisiana State University Press, 2004.

Current, Richard N. *Daniel Webster and the Rise of National Conservatism.* Boston: Little Brown, 1955.

———. *John C. Calhoun.* New York: Twayne, 1963.

Dalzell, Robert F., Jr. *Daniel Webster and the Trial of American Nationalism, 1843-1852.* Boston: Houghton Mifflin, 1973.

Duberman, Martin B. *Charles Francis Adams, 1807-1886.* Boston: Houghton, Mifflin, 1961.

Duckett, Alvin Laroy. *John Forsyth: Political Tactician.* Athens, Ga.: University of Georgia Press, 1962.

Dunne, Gerald T. *Justice Joseph Story and the Rise of the Supreme Court.* New York: Simon and Schuster, 1970.

Eaton, Clement. *Henry Clay and the Art of American Politics.* Boston: Little, Brown & Co., 1957.

Fladeland, Betty. *James Gillespie Birney: Slaveholder to Abolitionist.* Ithaca, N.Y.: Cornell University Press, 1955.

Frotheringham, Paul R. *Edward Everett: Orator and Statesman.* Boston: Houghton Mifflin Company, 1925.

Fuess, Claude M. *The Life of Caleb Cushing.* 2 vols. New York: Harcourt, Brace & Co., 1923.

Garraty, John A. *Silas Wright.* New York: Columbia University Press, 1949.

Going, Charles B. *David Wilmot, Free-Soiler: A Biography of the Great Advocate of the Wilmot Proviso.* New York: D Appleton & Co., 1924.

Govan, Thomas P. *Nicholas Biddle: Nationalist and Public Banker, 1786-1844.* Chicago: University of Chicago Press, 1959.

Green, Philip Jackson. *The Life of William Harris Crawford.* Charlotte, N.C.: University of North Carolina at Charlotte, 1965.

Haley, James L. *Sam Houston.* Norman, Ok.: University of Oklahoma Press, 2002.

Hall, Claude H. *Abel Parker Upshur: Conservative Virginian, 1790-1844.* Madison, Wisc.: State Historical Society of Wisconsin, 1964.

Handlin, Lilian. *George Bancroft: The Intellectual as Democrat.* New York: Harper and Row, 1984.

Harlow, Ralph Volney. *Gerrit Smith, Philanthropist and Reformer.* New York: H. Holt & Co., 1939.

Hart, Albert Bushnell. *Salmon P. Chase.* New York: Chelsea House, 1980.

Hatcher, William B. *Edward Livingston: Jeffersonian Republican and Jacksonian Democrat.* University, La.: Louisiana State University Press, 1940.

Herold, Amos L. *James Kirke Paulding: Versatile American.* New York: Columbia University Press, 1926.

Hobson, Charles F. *The Great Chief Justice: John Marshall and the Rule of Law.* Lawrence, Kans.: University Press of Kansas, 1996.

James, Marquis. *The Raven: A Biography of Sam Houston.* Indianapolis, Ind.: Bobbs-Merrill, 1929.

Johnson, Herbert A. *The Chief Justiceship of John Marshall, 1801-1835.* Columbia, S.C.: University of South Carolina Press, 1997.

Kirwan, Albert Dennis. *John J. Crittenden: The Struggle for the Union.* Lexington, Ky: University Press of Kentucky, 1962.

Klein, Philip S. *President James Buchanan: A Biography.* University Park, Pa.: Pennsylvania State University Press, 1962.

Klunder, Willard Carl. *Lewis Cass and the Politics of Moderation.* Kent: Kent State University Press, 1996.

Messerli, Jonathan. *Horace Mann: A Biography.* New York: Knopf, 1972.

Meyer, Leland. *The Life and Times of Colonel Richard M. Johnson of Kentucky.* New York: Columbia University Press, 1932.

Mooney, Chase C. *William H. Crawford, 1772-1834.* Lexington, Ky: University Press of Kentucky, 1974.

Munroe, John A. *Louis McLane: Federalist and Jacksonian.* New Brunswick, N.J.: Rutgers University Press, 1973.

Nagel, Paul C. *John Quincy Adams: A Public Life, A Private Life.* New York: Knopf, 1997.

Nathans, Sydney. *Daniel Webster and Jacksonian Democracy.* Baltimore: Johns Hopkins University Press, 1973.

Newmyer, R. Kent. *Supreme Court Justice Joseph Story: Statesman of the Old Republic.* Chapel Hill, N.C.: University of North Carolina Press, 1985.

———. *John Marshall and the Heroic Age of the Supreme Court.* Baton Rouge, La.: Louisiana State University Press, 2001.

Nichols, Roy F. *Franklin Pierce.* Philadelphia: University of Pennsylvania Press, 1958.

Niven, John. *Gideon Welles: Lincoln's Secretary of the Navy.* New York: Oxford University Press, 1973.

———. *John C. Calhoun and the Price of Union: A Biography.* Baton Rouge, La.: Louisiana State University Press, 1988.

———. *Salmon P. Chase: A Biography.* New York: Oxford University Press, 1995.

O'Brien, Michael. *A Character of Hugh Legaré.* Knoxville, Tenn.: University of Tennessee Press, 1985.

Parks, Joseph H. *Felix Grundy: Champion of Democracy.* University, La.: Louisiana State University Press, 1940.

———. *John Bell of Tennessee.* Baton Rouge, La.: Louisiana State University Press, 1950.

Parsons, Lynn Hudson. *John Quincy Adams.* Madison, Wisc.: Madison House, 1998.

Peterson, Merrill D. *The Great Triumvirate: Webster, Clay and Calhoun.* New York: Oxford University Press, 1987.

Poage, George R. *Henry Clay and the Whig Party.* Chapel Hill, N.C.: University of North Carolina Press, 1936.

Ratner, Lorman. *James Kirke Paulding: The Last Republican.* Westport, Conn.: Greenwood Press, 1992.

Rayback, Robert J. *Millard Fillmore: Biography of a President.* Buffalo, N.Y.: Buffalo Historical Society, 1959.

Reid, Ronald F. *Edward Everett: Unionist Orator.* New York: Greenwood Press, 1990.

Remini, Robert V. *Henry Clay: Statesman for the Union.* New York: W.W. Norton & Co., 1991.

———. *Daniel Webster: The Man and His Time.* New York: Norton, 1997.

Richards, Leonard L. *The Life and Times of Congressman John Quincy Adams.* New York: Oxford University Press, 1986.

Rippy, J. Fred. *Joel R. Poinsett: Versatile American.* Durham, N.C.: Duke University Press, 1935.

Roper, Donald Malcolm. *Mr. Justice Thompson and the Constitution.* New York: Garland, 1987.

Scarry, Robert J. *Millard Fillmore.* Jefferson, N.C.: McFarland, 2001.

Sewell, Richard H. *John P. Hale and the Politics of Abolition.* Cambridge, Harvard University Press, 1965.

Shankman, Kimberley C. *Compromise and the Constitution: The Political Thought of Henry Clay.* Lanham: Lexington Books, 1999.

Shenton, James P. *Robert John Walker: A Politician from Jackson to Lincoln.* New York: Columbia University Press, 1961.

Simpson, Craig M. *A Good Southerner: The Life of Henry A. Wise of Virginia.* Chapel Hill, N.C.: University of North Carolina Press, 1985.

Smith, Elbert B. *Francis Preston Blair.* New York: Free Press, 1980.

Smith, Jean Edward. *John Marshall: Definer of a Nation.* New York: H. Holt & Co., 1996.

Smith, William Ernest. *The Francis Preston Blair Family in Politics.* 2 vols. New York: Macmillan, 1933.

Spencer, Ivor D. *The Victor and the Spoils: A Life of William L. Marcy.* Providence, R.I.: Brown University Press, 1959.

Stewart, James Brewer. *Joshua R. Giddings and the Tactics of Radical Politics.* Cleveland, Ohio: Press of Case Western Reserve University, 1970.

———. *Wendell Phillips: Liberty's Hero.* Baton Rouge, La.: Louisiana State University Press, 1986.

Swisher, Carl Brent. *Roger B. Taney.* New York: Macmillan, 1935.

Trefousse, Hans L. *Thaddeus Stevens: Nineteenth-Century Egalitarian.* Chapel Hill, N.C.: University of North Carolina Press, 1997.

Van Deusen, Glyndon G. *The Life of Henry Clay.* Boston: Little, Brown & Co., 1937.

———. *Thurlow Weed: Wizard of the Lobby.* Boston: Little, Brown & Co., 1947.

———. *Horace Greeley: Nineteenth-Century Crusader.* Philadelphia: University of Pennsylvania Press, 1953.

———. *William Henry Seward.* New York: Oxford University Press, 1967.

Varg, Paul A. *Edward Everett: The Intellectual in the Turmoil of Politics.* Cranbury, N.J.: Associated University Press, 1992.

Wayland, Francis F. *Andrew Stevenson: Democrat and Diplomat, 1785-1857.* Philadelphia: University of Pennsylvania Press, 1949.

Weisenburger, Francis P. *The Life of John McLean: A Politician on the United States Supreme Court.* Columbus, Ohio: Ohio State University Press, 1937.

Williams, John Hoyt. *Sam Houston: A Biography of the Father of Texas.* New York: Simon and Schuster, 1993.

Wiltse, Charles M. *John C. Calhoun.* 3 vols. Indianapolis, Ind.: Bobbs-Merrill, 1944-51.

Woodford, Frank B. *Lewis Cass: The Last Jeffersonian.* New Brunswick, N.J.: Rutgers University Press, 1950.

2.3 Prominent Americans in Other Fields

Abzug, Robert. *Passionate Liberator: Theodore Dwight Weld and the Dilemma of Reform.* New York: Oxford University Press, 1980.

Adams, Bluford. *E Pluribus Barnum: The Great Showman and the Making of U.S. Popular Culture.* Minneapolis, Minn.: University of Minnesota Press, 1997.

Albrecht, Robert C. *Theodore Parker.* New York: Twayne, 1971.

Antelyes, Peter. *Tales of Adventurous Enterprise: Washington Irving and the Poetics of Western Expansion.* New York: Columbia University Press, 1990.

Arrington, Leonard J. *Brigham Young: American Moses.* New York: Knopf, 1985.

Bacon, Margaret Hope. *Valiant Friend: The Life of Lucretia Mott.* New York: Walker, 1980.

Baer, Helene Gilbert. *The Heart Is Like Heaven: The Life of Lydia Maria Child.* Philadelphia: University of Pennsylvania Press, 1964.

Banner, Lois W. *Elizabeth Cady Stanton, a Radical for Woman's Rights.* Boston: Little, Brown, 1980.

Bauer, K. Jack. *Zachary Taylor: Soldier, Planter, Statesman of the Old Southwest.* Baton Rouge, La.: Louisiana State University Press, 1985.

Bernard, Jacqueline. *Journey toward Freedom: The Story of Sojourner Truth.* New York: Norton, 1967.

Bohner, Charles H. *John Pendleton Kennedy, Gentleman from Baltimore.* Baltimore: Johns Hopkins Press, 1961.

Bremer, Richard G. *Indian Agent and Wilderness Scholar: The Life of Henry Rowe Schoolcraft.* Mount Pleasant, Mich.: Clarke Historical Library, Central Michigan University, 1987.

Bringhurst, Newell G. *Brigham Young and the Expanding American Frontier.* Boston: Little, Brown & Co., 1986.

Brodie, Fawn. *No Man Knows My History: The Life of Joseph Smith, the Mormon Prophet.* New York: A A Knopf, 1945.

Brown, Arthur W. *William Ellery Channing.* New York: Twayne, 1961.

——. *Margaret Fuller.* New York: Twayne, 1964.

Brown, Thomas J. *Dorothea Dix: New England Reformer.* Cambridge, Mass.: Harvard University Press, 1998.

Browne, Stephen Howard. *Angelina Grimké: Rhetoric, Identity, and the Radical Imagination.* East Lansing, Mich.: Michigan State University Press, 1999.

Bushman, Richard L. *Joseph Smith and the Beginnings of Mormonism.* Urbana, Ill.: University of Illinois Press, 1984.

Capper, Charles. *Margaret Fuller: An American Romantic Life.* New York: Oxford University Press, 1992.

Carlson, Oliver. *The Man Who Made the News: James Gordon Bennett.* New York: Duell, Sloan and Pearce, 1942.

Chaffin, Tom. *Pathfinder: John Charles Frémont and the Course of American Empire.* New York: Hill and Wang, 2002.

Clifford, Deborah Pickman. *Crusader for Freedom: A Life of Lydia Maria Child.* Boston: Beacon Press, 1992.

Commager, Henry Steele. *Theodore Parker.* Boston: Little, Brown & Co., 1936.

Couslon, Thomas. *Joseph Henry, His Life and Work.* Princeton, N.J.: Princeton University Press, 1950.

Cowdrey, Bartlett, and Herman Warner Williams Jr. *William Sidney Mount, 1807-1868: An American Painter.* New York: Columbia University Press, 1944.

Cromwell, Otelia. *Lucretia Mott.* Cambridge, Mass.: Harvard University Press, 1958.

Crouthamel, James L. *Bennett's New York Herald and the Rise of the Popular Press.* Syracuse, N.Y.: Syracuse University Press, 1989.

Crowe, Charles. *George Ripley: Transcendentalist and Utopian Socialist.* Athens, Ga.: University of Georgia Press, 1967.

Darnell, Donald. *James Fenimore Cooper: Novelist of Manners.* Newark, Del.: University of Delaware Press, 1993.

Davis, William C. *Three Roads to the Alamo: The Lives and Fortunes of David Crockett, James Bowie, and William Barret Travis.* New York: Harper Collins, 1998.

Delbanco, Andrew. *William Ellery Channing: An Essay on the Liberal Spirit in America.* Cambridge, Mass.: Harvard University Press, 1981.

Dillon, Merton L. *Elijah P. Lovejoy: Abolitionist Editor.* Urbana, Ill.: University of Illinois Press, 1961.

———. *Benjamin Lundy and the Struggle for Negro Freedom.* Urbana, Ill.: University of Illinois Press, 1966.

Doughty, Howard. *Francis Parkman.* New York: Macmillan, 1962.

Dunlay, Tom. *Kit Carson and the Indians.* Lincoln, Neb.: University of Nebraska Press, 2000.

Eames, S. Morris. *The Philosophy of Alexander Campbell.* Bethany, W.Va.: Bethany College, 1966.

Eckhardt, Celia Morris. *Fanny Wright: Rebel in America.* Cambridge, Mass.: Harvard University Press, 1984.

Edgell, David P. *William Ellery Channing: An Intellectual Portrait.* Boston: Beacon Press, 1955.

Edwards, William B. *The Story of Colt's Revolver: The Biography of Col. Samuel Colt.* Harrisburg, Penn.: Stackpole Co., 1953.

Elliott, Charles Winslow. *Winfield Scott: The Soldier and the Man.* New York: Macmillan, 1937.

Feller, Daniel. "A Brother in Arms: Benjamin Tappan and the Antislavery Democracy." *Journal of American History* 88 (2001), 48-74.

Field, Peter S. *Ralph Waldo Emerson: The Making of a Democratic Intellectual.* Lanham: Rowman and Littlefield, 2002.

Finlay, Ruth Elbright. *Lady of Godey's: Sarah Josepha Hale.* Philadelphia: J.B. Lippincott Co., 1931.

Foner, Philip S. *Frederick Douglass: A Biography.* New York: Citadel Press, 1964.

Ford, Alice. *John James Audubon: A Biography.* New York: Abbeville Press, 1988.

Fraser, James W. *Pedagogue for God's Kingdom: Lyman Beecher and the Second Great Awakening.* Lanham: University Press of America, 1985.

Gale, Robert L. *Richard Henry Dana Jr.* New York: Twayne, 1969.

Gilchrist, Agnes Eleanor Addison. *William Strickland: Architect and Engineer, 1788-1854.* Philadelphia: University of Pennsylvania Press, 1950.

Gill, John. *Tide without Turning: Elijah P. Lovejoy and Freedom of the Press.* N.p.: 1958.

Gollaher, David. *Voice for the Mad: The Life of Dorothea Dix.* New York: Free Press, 1995.

Gougeon, Len. *Virtue's Hero: Emerson, Antislavery, and Reform.* Athens, Ga.: University of Georgia Press, 1990.

Green, Elizabeth Alden. *Mary Lyon and Mount Holyoke: Opening the Gates.* Hanover, N.H.: University Press of New England, 1979.

Greenberg, Kenneth S., ed. *Nat Turner: A Slave Rebellion in History and Memory.* New York: Oxford University Press, 2003.

Griffith, Elisabeth. *In Her Own Right: The Life of Elizabeth Cady Stanton.* New York: Oxford University Press, 1984.

Grossman, James. *James Fenimore Cooper.* New York: W. Sloane Associates, 1949.

Guelzo, Allen C. "An Heir or a Rebel? Charles Grandison Finney and the New England Theology." *Journal of the Early Republic* 17 (1997), 61-94.

Haeger, John Denis. *John Jacob Astor: Business and Finance in the Early Republic.* Detroit: Wayne State University Press, 1991.

Hague, Harlan, and David J. Langum. *Thomas O. Larkin: A Life of Patriotism and Profit in Old California.* Norman, Ok.: University of Oklahoma Press, 1990.

Hamilton, Holman. *Zachary Taylor, Soldier of the Republic.* 2 vols. Indianapolis, Ind.: Bobbs-Merrill, 1941-1951.

Harding, Vincent. *A Certain Magnificence: Lyman Beecher and the Transformation of American Protestantism, 1775-1863.* Brooklyn, N.Y.: Carlson, 1991.

Hardman, Keith J. *Charles Grandison Finney, 1792-1875. Revivalist and Reformer.* Syracuse, N.Y.: Syracuse University Press, 1987.

Hardwick, Elizabeth. *Herman Melville.* New York: Viking, 2000.

Harnback-Stowe, Charles E. *Charles G. Finney and the Spirit of American Evangelicalism.* Grand Rapids, Mich.: W. B. Eerdmans Pub. Co., 1996.

Hedges, William L. *Washington Irving: An American Study, 1802-1832.* Baltimore: Johns Hopkins University Press, 1965.

Henderson, Daniel. *The Hidden Coasts: A Biography of Admiral Charles Wilkes.* New York: Sloan, 1953.

Hinks, Peter P. *To Awaken My Afflicted Brethren: David Walker and the Problem of Antebellum Slave Resistance.* University Park, Pa.: Pennsylvania State University Press, 1997.

Hirshson, Stanley P. *Lion of the Lord: A Biography of Brigham Young.* New York: Knopf, 1969.

Huggins, Nathan Irvin. *Slave and Citizen: The Life of Frederick Douglass.* Boston: Little Brown, 1980.

Hutchinson, William Thomas. *Cyrus Hall McCormick.* 2 vols. New York: The Century Company, 1930.

Jacobs, Wilbur R. *Francis Parkman, Historian as Hero: The Formative Years.* Austin, Tex.: University of Texas Press, 1991.

Johnson, Deborah J. *William Sidney Mount: Painter of American Life.* New York: American Federation of Arts, 1998.

Johnson, Timothy D. *Winfield Scott: The Quest for Military Glory.* Lawrence, Kans.: University Press of Kansas, 1998.

Karcher, Carolyn L. *The First Woman in the Republic: A Cultural Biography of Lydia Maria Child.* Durham, N.C.: Duke University Press, 1994.

Kirker, Harold. *The Architecture of Charles Bulfinch.* Cambridge, Mass.: Harvard University Press, 1969.

Knapp, Bettina Liebowitz. *Edgar Allen Poe.* New York: F. Ungar Pub. Co., 1984.

Kunhardt, Philip B., Jr., Philip B. Kunhardt III, and Peter W. Kunhardt. *P.T. Barnum: America's Greatest Showman.* New York: Knopf, 1995.

Lapati, Americo D. *Orestes A. Brownson.* New York: Twayne, 1965.

Larkin, F. Daniel. *John B. Jervis, an American Engineering Pioneer.* Ames, Iowa: Iowa State University Press, 1990.

Lawall, David B. *Asher Brown Durand, His Art and Art Theory in Relation to His Times.* New York: Garland Pub., 1977.

Leopold, Richard W. *Robert Dale Owen, A Biography.* Cambridge, Mass.: Harvard University Press, 1940.

Lerner, Gerda. *The Grimké Sisters from South Carolina: Rebels against Slavery.* Boston: Houghton Mifflin, 1967.

Liscombe, Rhodri Windsor. *Altogether American: Robert Mills, Architect and Engineer, 1781-1855.* New York: Oxford University Press, 1994.

Logan, Deborah Anna. *The Hour and the Woman: Harriet Martineau's "Somewhat Remarkable" Life.* DeKalb, Ill.: Northern Illinois University Press, 2002.

Long, Robert Emmet. *James Fenimore Cooper.* New York: Continuum, 1990.

Lumpkin, Katherine DuPre. *The Emancipation of Angelina Grimké.* Chapel Hill, N.C.: University of North Carolina Press, 1974.

Lurie, Edward. *Louis Agassiz, A Life in Science.* Baltimore: Johns Hopkins University Press, 1988.

Mabee, Carleton. *The American Leonardo: A Life of Samuel F. Morse.* Fleischmanns, N.Y.: Purple Mountain Press, 2000.

Mabee, Carleton, and Susan Mabee Newhouse. *Sojourner Truth—Slave, Prophet, Legend.* New York: New York University Press, 1993.

McAteer, John. *Ralph Waldo Emerson: Days of Encounter.* Boston: Little Brown, 1984.

McCracken, Harold. *George Catlin and the Old Frontier.* New York: Dial Press, 1959.

McCuskey, Dorothy. *Bronson Alcott, Teacher.* New York: Macmillan, 1940.

McFeely, William S. *Frederick Douglass.* New York: Norton, 1991.

Mack, Edward C. *Peter Cooper, Citizen of New York.* New York: Duell, Sloan and Pearce, 1949.

McLean, Albert F., Jr. *William Cullen Bryant.* New York: Twayne, 1964.

Madsen, Axel. *John Jacob Astor: America's First Multimillionaire.* New York: John Wiley, 2001.

Marshall, Helen E. *Dorothea Dix, Forgotten Samaritan.* Chapel Hill, N.C.: University of North Carolina Press, 1937.

Martin, Terence. *Nathaniel Hawthorne.* New York: Twayne, 1965.

Meltzer, Milton. *Tongue of Flame: The Life of Lydia Maria Child.* New York: Crowell, 1965.

Merrill, Walter. *Against Wind and Tide: A Biography of William Lloyd Garrison.* Cambridge, Mass.: Harvard University Press, 1963.

Moody, Richard. *Edwin Forrest.* New York: Knopf, 1960.

Morison, Samuel Eliot. *"Old Bruin": Commodore Matthew Perry, 1794-1858: The American Naval Officer Who Helped Found Liberia.* Boston: Little, Brown, 1967.

Motley, Warren. *The American Abraham: James Fenimore Cooper and the Frontier Patriot.* New York: Cambridge University Press, 1987.

Moyer, Albert E. *Joseph Henry: The Rise of an American Scientist.* Washington, D.C.: Smithsonian Institution Press, 1997.

Nevins, Allan. *Frémont: Pathmarker of the West.* New York: D. Appleton Co., 1939.

Nichols, Roger L. *Black Hawk and the Warrior's Path.* Arlington Heights, Ill.: H. Davidson, 1992.

Nye, Russel B. *George Bancroft.* New York: Washington Square Press, 1964.

Odgers, Merle M. *Alexander Dallas Bache, Scientist and Educator, 1806-1867.* Philadelphia: University of Pennsylvania Press, 1947.

Ohrt, Wallace. *Defiant Peacemaker: Nicholas Trist in the Mexican War.* College Station, Tex.: Texas A & M University Press, 1997.

Osborne, William S. *Lydia Maria Child.* Boston: Twayne, 1980.

Painter, Nell Irvin. *Sojourner Truth: A Life, A Symbol.* New York: W. W. Norton, 1996.

Parker, Hershel. *Herman Melville: A Biography. Vol.1, 1819-1851.* Baltimore: Johns Hopkins University Press, 1996.

Parker, Robert A. *A Yankee Saint: John Humphrey Noyes and the Oneida Community.* New York: G. P. Putnams, 1935.

Parry, Ellwood C. *The Art of Thomas Cole: Ambition and Imagination.* Newark, Del.: University of Delaware Press, 1988.

Peeples, Scott. *Edgar Allen Poe Revisited.* New York: Twayne, 1998.

Perry, Mark. *Lift Up Thy Voice: The Grimké Family's Journey from Slaveholders to Civil Rights Leaders.* New York: Viking, 2001.

Peskin, Allan. *Winfield Scott and the Profession of Arms.* Kent, Ohio: Kent State University Press, 2003.

Peters, James S. II. *The Spirit of David Walker, the Obscure Hero.* Lanham: University Press of America, 2002.

Place, Charles A. *Charles Bulfinch, Architect and Citizen.* Boston: Houghton Mifflin Company, 1925.

Pollard, John Albert. *John Greenleaf Whittier: Friend of Man.* Boston: Houghton Mifflin Co., 1949.

Porter, Kenneth Wiggins. *John Jacob Astor: Business Man.* 2 vols. Cambridge, Mass.: Harvard University Press, 1931.

Porterfield, Amanda. *Mary Lyon and the Mount Holyoke Missionaries.* New York: Oxford University Press, 1997.

Quarles, Benjamin. *Frederick Douglass.* Washington, D.C.: Associated Publishers, 1948.

Rash, Nancy. *The Painting and Politics of George Caleb Bingham.* New Haven, Conn.: Yale University Press, 1991.

Remini, Robert V. *Joseph Smith.* New York: Penguin Viking, 2002.

Rhodes, Richard. *Audubon: The Making of an American.* New York: Knopf, 2004.

Rice, Madeleine Hooke. *Federal Street Pastor: The Life of William Ellery Channing.* New York: Bookman Associates, 1961.

Ringe, Donald A. *James Fenimore Cooper.* New York: Twayne, 1962.

Rogers, Sherbrooke. *Sarah Josepha Hale: A New England Pioneer, 1788-1879.* Grantham, N.H.: Tompson and Rutter, 1985.

Rolle, Andrew F. *John Charles Frémont: Character as Destiny.* Norman, Ok.: University of Oklahoma Press, 1991.

Rusk, Ralph L. *The Life of Ralph Waldo Emerson.* New York: C. Scribner's Sons, 1949.

Sampson, Robert D. *John L. O'Sullivan and His Times.* Kent, Ohio: Kent State University Press, 2003.

Schlesinger, Arthur. *Orestes A. Brownson: A Pilgrim's Progress.* Boston: Little Brown, 1939.

Schroeder, John H. *Matthew Calbraith Perry: Antebellum Sailor and Diplomat.* Annapolis, Md.: Naval Institute Press, 2001.

Shackford, James Atkins. *David Crockett: The Man and the Legend.* Chapel Hill, N.C.: University of North Carolina Press, 1956.

Sherwood, Midge. *Frémont: Eagle of the West.* North Hollywood, Calif.: Jackson Peak Publishers, 2002.

Silverman, Kenneth. *Edgar Allen Poe: Mournful and Never-Ending Remembrance.* New York: Harper Collins, 1991.

———. *Lightning Man: The Accursed Life of Samuel F.B. Morse.* New York: Alfred A. Knopf, 2003.

Simon, Paul. *Freedom's Champion—Elijah Lovejoy.* Carbondale, Ill.: Southern Illinois University Press, 1994.

Sklar, Kathleen Kish. *Catherine Beecher: A Study in American Domesticity.* New Haven, Conn.: Yale University Press, 1973.

Slack, Charles. *Noble Obsession: Charles Goodyear, Thomas Hancock, and the Race to Unlock the Greatest Industrial Secret of the Nineteenth Century.* New York: Hyperion, 2002.

Smith, Arthur D. H. *Commodore Vanderbilt.* New York: R. M. McBride & Co., 1927.

————. *Old Fuss and Feathers: The Life of Winfield Scott.* New York: The Greystone Press, 1937.

Snyder, Stephen H. *Lyman Beecher and His Children: The Transformation of a Religious Tradition.* Brooklyn, N.Y.: Carlson, 1991.

Staiti, Paul J. *Samuel F. B. Morse.* New York: Cambridge University Press, 1989.

Stetson, Erlene, and Linda David. *Glorying in Tribulation: The Lifework of Sojourner Truth.* East Lansing, Mich.: Michigan State University Press, 1994.

Streshinsky, Shirley. *Audubon: Life and Art in the American Wilderness.* New York: Villard Books, 1993.

Sullivan, Dolores P. *William Holmes McGuffey: Schoolmaster to the Nation.* Rutherford, N.J.: Fairleigh Dickinson University Press, 1994.

Thomas, Benjamin Platt. *Theodore Weld: Crusader for Freedom.* New Brunswick, N.J.: Rutgers University Press, 1950.

Thomas, John L. *The Liberator: William Lloyd Garrison, A Biography.* Boston: Little, Brown, 1963.

Viola, Herman J. *Thomas L. McKenney: Architect of America's Early Indian Policy, 1816-1830.* Chicago: Sage Books, 1974.

Wagenknecht, Edward. *Washington Irving: Moderation Displayed.* New York: Oxford University Press, 1962.

————. *Edgar Allen Poe: The Man behind the Legend.* New York: Oxford University Press, 1963.

————. *Henry Wadsworth Longfellow: Portrait of an American Humanist.* New York: Oxford University Press, 1966.

Welch, Marvis Olive. *Prudence Crandall: A Biography.* Manchester, Conn.: Jason Publishers, 1983.

Westerhoff, John H. *McGuffey and His Readers: Piety, Morality and Education in Nineteenth-Century America.* Nashville, Tenn.: Abingdon, 1978.

Whicher, Stephen. *Freedom and Fate: An Inner Life of Ralph Waldo Emerson.* Philadelphia: University of Pennsylvania Press, 1953.

Williams, Cecil B. *Henry Wadsworth Longfellow.* New York: Twayne, 1964.

Wilson, Dorothy Clarke. *Stranger and Traveler: The Story of Dorothea Dix, Reformer.* Boston: Little, Brown, 1975.

Wolf, Ralph F. *India Rubber Man: The Story of Charles Goodyear.* Caldwell, Idaho: The Caxton Printers, 1939.

Wright, Nathalia. *Horatio Greenough: The First American Sculptor.* Philadelphia: University of Pennsylvania Press, 1963.

Wyatt-Brown, Bertram. *Lewis Tappan and the Evangelical War against Slavery.* Cleveland, Ohio: Case Western Reserve University Press, 1969.

2.4 Major Printed Primary Works and Papers

Adams, Charles Francis. *Diary.* Edited by Aïda DiPace Donald and David Donald. 8 vols. Cambridge, Mass.: Harvard University Press, 1964-1986.

Adams, John Quincy. *Writings of John Quincy Adams.* Edited by Worthington Chauncey Ford. 7 vols. New York: Greenwood Press, 1968.
———. *Memoirs of John Quincy Adams, Comprising Portions of his Diary from 1795 to 1848.* Edited by Charles Francis Adams. 12 vols. Freeport, N.Y.: Books for Libraries Press, 1969.
Barnes, Gilbert H., and Dwight L. Dumond, eds. *Letters of Theodore Dwight Weld, Angelina Grimké Weld and Sarah Grimké, 1822-1844.* 2 vols. New York: Da Capo Press, 1970.
Beecher, Lyman. *Autobiography of Lyman Beecher.* Edited by Barbara M. Cross. 2 vols. Cambridge, Mass.: Harvard University Press, 1961.
Benton, Thomas Hart. *Thirty Years' View; or, A History of the Working of the American Government for Thirty Years, from 1820 to 1850 ... by a Senator of Thirty Years.* 2 vols. New York: Greenwood Press, 1968.
Biddle, Nicholas. *The Correspondence of Nicholas Biddle Dealing with National Affairs.* Edited by Reginald C. McGrane. Boston, J. S. Canner, 1966.
Birney, James Gillespie. *Letters of James Gillespie Birney, 1831-1857.* Edited by Dwight L. Dumond. 2 vols. New York: D. Appleton-Century Company, 1938.
Boydston, Jeanne, Mary Kelley, and Anne Margolis, eds. *The Limits of Sisterhood: The Beecher Sisters on Women's Rights and Woman's Sphere.* Chapel Hill, N.C.: University of North Carolina Press, 1988.
Brownson, Orestes A. *The Early Works of Orestes A. Brownson.* Edited by Patrick W. Carey. 4 vols. Milwaukee, Wisc.: Marquette University Press, 2000-2003.
Bryant, William Cullen. *The Letters of William Cullen Bryant.* Edited by William Cullen Bryant II and Thomas G. Voss. 6 vols. New York: Fordham University Press, 1975-1992.
Buchanan, James. *The Works of James Buchanan, Comprising His Speeches, State Papers, and Private Correspondence.* Edited by John Bassett Moore. 12 vols. Philadelphia: J.B. Lippincott Company, 1908-11.
Buckingham, J. S. *America, Historical, Statistic, and Descriptive.* 2 vols. New York: Harper & Brothers, 1841.
Butler, William Allen. *A Retrospect of Forty Years, 1825-1865.* Edited by Harriet Allen Butler. New York: C. Scribner's Sons, 1911.
Cain, William E., ed. *William Lloyd Garrison and the Fight against Slavery: Selections from The Liberator.* Boston: Bedford Books of St. Martin's Press, 1995.
Calhoun, John C. *The Works of John C. Calhoun.* Edited by Richard K Crallé. 6 vols. New York: D. Appleton and Co., 1851-56.
———. "Correspondence of John C. Calhoun." Edited by J. Franklin Jameson. *Annual Report of the American Historical Association for the Year 1899.* Vol. 2. Washington, D.C.: Government Printing Office, 1900.
———. *The Papers of John C. Calhoun.* Edited by Robert L. Meriwether et al. 27 vols. Columbia, S.C.: University of South Carolina Press, 1959-2003.
Chase, Salmon P. *Diary and Correspondence of Salmon P. Chase.* New York: Da Capo Press, 1971.

Chevalier, Michael. *Society, Manners, and Politics in the United States; Being a Series of Letters on North America.* New York: B. Franklin, 1969.

Child, Lydia Maria. *Letters of Lydia Maria Child.* New York: Arno Press, 1969.

Clay, Henry. *The Private Correspondence of Henry Clay.* Edited by Calvin Colton. New York, A. S. Barnes, 1856.

———. *Works of Henry Clay, Comprising His Life, Correspondence, and Speeches.* Edited by Calvin Colton. 7 vols. New York: Henry Clay Pub. Co., 1897.

———. *The Papers of Henry Clay.* Edited by James F. Hopkins, Mary W. M. Hargreaves et al. 11 vols. Lexington, Ky: University Press of Kentucky, 1959-1992.

Cooper, James Fenimore. *Letters and Journals.* Edited by James Franklin Beard. 6 vols. Cambridge, Mass.: Harvard University Press, 1960-1968.

———. *The American Democrat and Other Political Writings.* Edited by Bradley J. Birzer and John Willson. Washington, D.C.: Regnery Publishing, 2000.

Cutler, Wayne, ed. *North for Union: John Appleton's Journal of a Tour to New England Made by President Polk in June and July 1847.* Nashville, Tenn.: Vanderbilt University Press, 1986.

Davis, Jefferson. *The Papers of Jefferson Davis.* 6 vols. Baton Rouge, La.: Louisiana State University Press, 1971-1989.

———. *Private Letters, 1823-1889.* Edited by Hudson Strode. New York: Da Capo Press, 1995.

De Tocqueville, Alexis. *Democracy in America; and Two Essays on America.* Translated by Gerald E. Bevan. London: Penguin, 2003.

Dickens, Charles. *American Notes for General Circulation.* Edited by Patricia Ingham. London: Penguin Books, 2000.

Emerson, Ralph Waldo. *The Collected Works of Ralph Waldo Emerson.* Edited by Robert E. Spiller. 6 vols. Cambridge, Mass.: Harvard University Press, 1971-2003.

Fillmore, Millard. *Millard Fillmore Papers.* Edited by Frank H. Severance. 2 vols. Buffalo, N.Y.: The Buffalo Historical Society, 1907.

Finney, Charles G. *The Autobiography of Charles G. Finney.* Edited by Helen Wessel. Minneapolis, Minn.: Bethany Fellowship, 1977.

———. *Lectures on Revival.* Minneapolis, Minn.: Bethany House Publishers, 1988.

———. *The Memoirs of Charles G. Finney: The Complete Restored Text.* Edited by Garth M. Rosell and Richard A. G. Dupuis. Grand Rapids, Mich.: Academie Books, 1989.

Frémont, John Charles. *Memoirs of My Life.* New York: Cooper Square Press, 2001.

French, Benjamin Brown. *Witness to the Young Republic: A Yankee's Journal, 1828-1870.* Edited by Donald B. Cole and John J. McDonough. Hanover, N.H.: University Press of New England, 1989.

Garrison, William Lloyd. *The Letters of William Lloyd Garrison*. Edited by Walter M. Merrill. 6 vols. Cambridge, Mass.: Harvard University Press, 1971-1981.

Gouge, William. *A Short History of Paper Money and Banking in the United States; to which is Prefixed an Inquiry into the Principles of the System*. 2 vols. New York: A. M. Kelley, 1968.

Grimké, Angelina. *Walking by Faith: The Diary of Angelina Grimké, 1828-1835*. Edited by Charles Wilbanks. Columbia, S.C.: University of South Carolina Press, 2003.

Grund, Francis. *Aristocracy in America; From the Sketch-book of a German Nobleman*. Gloucester, Mass.: P. Smith, 1968.

Hamilton, James A. *Reminiscences of James A. Hamilton; or, Men and Events, at Home and Abroad, during Three Quarters of a Century*. New York: C. Scribner & Co., 1869.

Hamilton, Thomas. *Men and Manners in America*. New York: A. M. Kelley, 1968.

Harrison, William Henry. *Messages and Letters of William Henry Harrison*. Edited by Logan Esarey. 2 vols. New York: Arno Press, 1975.

Hawthorne, Nathaniel. *The Letters*. Edited by Thomas Woodson, L. Neal Smith, and Norman Holmes Pearson. 4 vols. Columbus, Ohio: Ohio State University Press, 1984-1987.

Hinks, Peter P., ed. *David Walker's Appeal to the Coloured Citizens of the World*. University Park, Pa.: Pennsylvania State University Press, 2000.

Hone, Philip. *The Diary of Philip Hone, 1828-1851*. Edited by Allan Nevins. 2 vols. New York: Dodd, Mead and Company, 1927.

Houston, Sam. *The Writings of Sam Houston, 1813-1863*. Edited by Amelia W. Williams and Eugene C. Barker. 8 vols. Austin, Tex.: University of Texas Press, 1938-1943.

———. *The Autobiography of Sam Houston*. Edited by Donald Day and Harry Herbert Ullom. Westport, Conn.: Greenwood Press, 1980.

———. *The Personal Correspondence of Sam Houston*. Edited by Madge Thornall Roberts. 4 vols. Denton, Tex.: University of North Texas Press, 1996-2001.

Howells, William Cooper. *Recollections of Life in Ohio from 1813-1840*. Gainesville, Fla.: Scholars' Facsimiles & Reprints, 1963.

Hunt, Gaillard, ed. *The First Forty years of Washington Society in the Family Letters of Margaret Bayard Smith*. New York: F. Ungar Pub. Co., 1965.

Irving, Washington. *Letters*. Edited by Ralph M. Aderman, Herbert L. Kleinfield, and Jenifer S. Banks. 4 vols. Boston: Twayne Publishers, 1978-1982.

Jackson, Andrew. *Correspondence of Andrew Jackson*. Edited by John Spencer Bassett. 7 vols. Washington, D.C.: Carnegie Institution of Washington, 1926-35.

———. *The Papers of Andrew Jackson*. Edited by Sam B. Smith and Harriet Chappell Owsley et al. 6 vols. Knoxville, Tenn.: University of Tennessee Press, 1980-2002.

Kendall, Amos. *Autobiography of Amos Kendall*. Edited by William Stickney. New York: Peter Smith, 1949.

Kennedy, John Pendleton. *Memoirs of the Life of William Wirt.* 2 vols. Philadelphia: Blanchard and Lea, 1856.

Lieber, Francis. *The Stranger in America; or, Letters to a Gentleman in Germany: Comprising Sketches of the Manners, Society, and National Peculiarities of the United States.* Philadelphia: Carey, Lea & Blanchard, 1835.

Longfellow, Henry Wadsworth. *The Letters of Henry Wadsworth Longfellow.* Edited by Andrew Hilen. 6 vols. Cambridge, Mass.: Harvard University Press, 1967-1982.

Mangum, Willie Person. *Papers.* Edited by Henry Thomas Shanks. 5 vols. Raleigh, N.C.: State Dept. of Archives and History, 1950-1956.

Marshall, John. *The Papers of John Marshall.* Edited by Herbert A. Johnson, Charles T. Cullen, et al. 11 vols. Chapel Hill, N.C.: University of North Carolina Press, 1974-2002.

Martineau, Harriet. *Society in America.* Edited by Seymour Martin Lipset. New Brunswick, N.J.: Transaction Books, 1981.

Nelson, Anson, and Fanny Nelson. *Memorials of Sarah Childress Polk, Wife of the Eleventh President of the United States.* Spartanburg, S.C.: Reprint Co., 1974.

Owen, Robert Dale. *Threading My Way; An Autobiography.* New York: A.M. Kelley, 1967.

Poe, Edgar Allan. *Letters.* Edited by John Ward Ostrom. 2 vols. New York: Gordian Press, 1966.

Polk, James K. *The Diary of James K. Polk during his Presidency, 1845 to 1849.* Edited by Milo M. Quaife. 4 vols. Chicago: A. C. McClurg & Co., 1910.

———. *Correspondence of James K. Polk.* Edited by Herbert Weaver and Paul H. Bergeron. 10 vols. Nashville, Tenn.: Vanderbilt University Press, 1969-2003.

Poore, Benjamin Perley. *Perley's Reminiscences of Sixty Years in the National Metropolis.* 2 vols. New York: AMS Press, 1971.

Ryan, Alvan S., ed. *The Brownson Reader.* New York: Arno Press, 1978.

Sargent, Nathan. *Public Men and Events in the United States from the Commencement of Mr. Monroe's Administration in 1817 to the Close of Mr. Fillmore's Administration in 1853.* 2 vols. New York: Da Capo Press, 1970.

Scott, Winfield. *Memoirs of Lieut.-General Scott, LL. D.* 2 vols. Freeport, N.Y.: Books for Libraries Press, 1970.

Smith, Gerrit. *Sermons and Speeches of Gerrit Smith.* New York: Arno Press, 1969.

Smith, Joseph. *Selected Sermons & Writings.* Edited by Robert L. Millet. New York: Paulist Press, 1989.

Stanton, Elizabeth Cady. *Eighty Years and More: Reminiscences, 1815-1897.* Boston: Northeastern University Press, 1993.

Stanton, Henry B. *Random Recollections.* New York: Harper & Brothers, 1887.

Strong, George Templeton. *Diary.* Edited by Allan Nevins and Milton Halsey Thomas. 4 vols. New York: Macmillan, 1952.

Trollope, Fanny. *Domestic Manners of the Americans.* Edited by Pamela Neville-Sington. London: Penguin Books, 1997.

Tyler, Lyon G., ed. *The Letters and Times of the Tylers.* 3 vols. New York: Da Capo Press, 1970.

Van Buren, Martin. "The Autobiography of Martin Van Buren." Edited by John C. Fitzpatrick. *Annual Report of the American Historical Association for 1918.* 2 vols. Washington, D.C.: Government Printing Office, 1920.

Webster, Daniel. *The Writings and Speeches of Daniel Webster.* 18 vols. National edition. Boston, Little, Brown, 1903.

———. *The Papers of Daniel Webster.* Edited by Charles M. Wiltse and Harold D. Moser. 14 vols. Hanover, N.H.: University Press of New England, 1974-1989.

Weed, Thurlow. *Life of Thurlow Weed including His Autobiography and a Memoir.* 2 vols. Boston: Houghton, Mifflin and Company, 1883-84.

Wise, Henry. *Seven Decades of the Únion; the Humanities and Materialism, Illustrated by a Memoir of John Tyler, with Reminiscences of Some of His Great Cotemporaries.* Freeport, N.Y.: Books for Libraries Press, 1971.

3. Politics

3.1 Administration Politics

Bergeron, Paul H. *The Presidency of James K. Polk.* Lawrence, Kans.: University Press of Kansas, 1987.

Cole, Donald B. *The Presidency of Andrew Jackson.* Lawrence, Kans.: University Press of Kansas, 1993.

Crenson, Matthew A. *The Federal Machine: Beginnings of Bureaucracy in Jacksonian America.* Baltimore: Johns Hopkins University Press, 1975.

Curtis, James C. *The Fox at Bay: Martin Van Buren and the Presidency, 1837-1841.* Lexington, Ky: University Press of Kentucky, 1970.

Kesilman, Sylvia H. "John Tyler and the Presidency: Old School Republicanism, Partisan Realignment, and Support for His Administration." Ph.D. Dissertation, Ohio State University, 1973.

Lambert, Oscar Doane. *Presidential Politics in the United States, 1841-1844.* Durham, N.C.: Duke University Press, 1936.

Latner, Richard B. "The Kitchen Cabinet and Andrew Jackson's Advisory System." *Journal of American History* 65 (1978), 367-88.

———. *The Presidency of Andrew Jackson: White House Politics, 1829-1837.* Athens, Ga.: University of Georgia Press, 1979.

McCoy, Charles A. *Polk and the Presidency.* Austin, Tex.: University of Texas Press, 1960.

Marszalek, John F. *The Petticoat Affair: Manners, Mutiny and Sex in Andrew Jackson's White House.* New York: Free Press, 1997.

Morgan, Robert J. *A Whig Embattled: The Presidency under John Tyler.* Lincoln, Neb.: University of Nebraska Press, 1954.

Peterson, Norma Lois. *The Presidencies of William Henry Harrison and John Tyler.* Lawrence, Kans.: University Press of Kansas, 1989.

Preston, Daniel. "The Administration and Reform of the U.S. Patent Office." *Journal of the Early Republic* 5 (1985), 331-53.

Ratner, Lorman A. *Andrew Jackson and His Tennessee Lieutenants: A Study in Political Culture.* Westport, Conn.: Greenwood Press, 1997.

Remini, Robert V. *The Legacy of Andrew Jackson: Essays on Democracy, Indian Removal, and Slavery.* Baton Rouge, La.: Louisiana State University Press, 1988.

Rohrs, Richard C. "Partisan Politics and the Attempted Assassination of Andrew Jackson." *Journal of the Early Republic* 1 (1981), 149-53.

Smith, Culver H. *The Press, Politics, and Patronage: The American Government's Use of Newspapers, 1789-1875.* Athens, Ga.: University of Georgia Press, 1977.

White, Leonard D. *The Jacksonians: A Study in Administrative History, 1829-1861.* New York: Macmillan, 1954.

Wilson, Major L. *The Presidency of Martin Van Buren.* Lawrence, Kans.: University Press of Kansas, 1984.

3.2 Regional, State, and Local Political Studies

Atkins, Jonathan. *Parties, Politics and the Sectional Conflict in Tennessee, 1832-1861.* Knoxville, Tenn.: University of Tennessee Press, 1997.

Benson, Lee. *The Concept of Jacksonian Democracy: New York as a Test Case.* Princeton, N.J.: Princeton University Press, 1961.

Brauer, Kinley J. *Cotton versus Conscience: Massachusetts Whig Politics and Southwestern Expansion, 1843-1848.* Lexington, Ky: University Press of Kentucky, 1967.

Bruce, Dickson D. *The Rhetoric of Conservatism: The Virginia Convention of 1829-1830 and the Conservative Tradition in the South.* San Marino, Calif.: Huntington Library, 1982.

Cole, Donald B. *Jacksonian Democracy in New Hampshire, 1800-1851.* Cambridge, Mass.: Harvard University Press, 1970.

Cooper, William J. *The South and the Politics of Slavery, 1828-1856.* Baton Rouge, La.: Louisiana State University Press, 1978.

———. *Liberty and Slavery: Southern Politics to 1860.* New York: Knopf, 1983.

Dennison, George M. *The Dorr War: Republicanism on Trial, 1831-1861.* Lexington, Ky: University Press of Kentucky, 1976.

Dunaway, Wilma A. *The First American Frontier: Transition to Capitalism in Southern Appalachia, 1700-1860.* Chapel Hill, N.C.: University of North Carolina Press, 1996.

Dupre, Daniel S. *Transforming the Cotton Frontier: Madison County, Alabama, 1800-1840.* Baton Rouge, La.: Louisiana State University Press, 1997.

Eaton, Clement. *The Growth of Southern Civilization, 1790-1860.* New York: Harper, 1961.

Etcheson, Nicole. *The Emerging Midwest: Upland Southerners and the Political Culture of the Old Northwest, 1787-1861*. Bloomington, Ind.: Indiana University Press, 1996.

Folsom, Burton W., III. "Party Formation and Development in Jacksonian America: The Old South." *Journal of American Studies* 7 (1973), 217-29.

Formisano, Ronald P. *The Birth of Mass Political Parties: Michigan, 1827-1861*. Princeton, N.J.: Princeton University Press, 1971.

————. *The Transformation of Political Culture: Massachusetts Parties, 1790s-1840s*. New York: Oxford University Press, 1983.

Gettleman, Marvin E. *The Dorr Rebellion: A Study in American Radicalism, 1833-1849*. New York: Random House, 1973.

Goodman, Paul. "The Social Basis of New England Politics in Jacksonian America." *Journal of the Early Republic* 6 (1986), 23-56.

Gronowicz, Anthony. *Race and Class Politics in New York City before the Civil War*. Boston: Northeastern University Press, 1998.

Huston, Reeve. *Land and Freedom: Rural Society, Popular Protest and Party Politics in Antebellum New York*. New York: Oxford University Press, 2000.

Jeffrey, Thomas E. *State Parties and National Politics: North Carolina, 1815-1861*. Athens, Ga.: University of Georgia Press, 1989.

Kruman, Marc W. *Parties and Politics in North Carolina, 1836-1865*. Baton Rouge, La.: Louisiana State University Press, 1983.

Leonard, Gerald. *The Invention of Party Politics: Federalism, Popular Sovereignty and Constitutional Development in Jacksonian Illinois*. Chapel Hill, N.C.: University of North Carolina Press, 2002.

Levine, Peter, D. *The Behavior of State Legislative Parties in the Jacksonian Era: New Jersey, 1829-1844*. Rutherford, N.J.: Fairleigh Dickinson University Press, 1977.

Link, William A. *Roots of Secession: Slavery and Politics in Antebellum Virginia*. Chapel Hill, N.C.: University of North Carolina Press, 2003.

Lockley, Timothy J. *Lines in the Sand: Race and Class in Lowcountry Georgia, 1750-1860*. Athens, Ga.: University of Georgia Press, 2001.

McCurdy, Charles W. *The Anti-Rent Era in New York Law and Politics, 1839-1865*. Chapel Hill, N.C.: University of North Carolina Press, 2001.

McNeilly, Donald P. *The Old South Frontier: Cotton Plantations and the Formation of Arkansas Society, 1819-1861*. Fayettesville, Ark.: University of Arkansas Press, 2000.

Maizlish, Stephen E. *The Triumph of Sectionalism: The Transformation of Ohio Politics, 1844-1856*. Kent, Ohio: Kent State University Press, 1983.

Sacher, John M. *A Perfect War of Politics: Parties, Politicians and Democracy in Louisiana, 1824-1861*. Baton Rouge, La.: Louisiana State University Press, 2003.

Sellers, Charles G., Jr. "Banking and Politics in Jackson's Tennessee, 1817-1827." *Mississippi Valley Historical Review* 41 (1954), 61-84.

————. "Jackson Men with Feet of Clay." *American Historical Review* 62 (1957), 537-51.

Shade, William G. *Democratizing the Old Dominion: Virginia and the Second Party System, 1824-1861.* Charlottesville, Va.: University Press of Virginia, 1996.

Sinha, Manisha. *The Counterrevolution of Slavery: Politics and Ideology in Antebellum South Carolina.* Chapel Hill, N.C.: University of North Carolina Press, 2000.

Smith, W. Wayne. *Anti-Jacksonian Politics along the Chesapeake.* New York: Garland, 1989.

Snyder, Charles M. *The Jacksonian Heritage: Pennsylvania Politics, 1833-1848.* Harrisburg, Pa.: Pennsylvania Historical and Museum Commission, 1958.

Sydnor, Charles S. *The Development of Southern Sectionalism, 1819-1848.* Baton Rouge, La.: Louisiana State University Press, 1948.

Tallant, Harold D. *Evil Necessity: Slavery and Political Culture in Antebellum Kentucky.* Lexington, Ky: University Press of Kentucky, 2003.

Thornton, J. Mills, III. *Politics and Power in a Slave Society: Alabama, 1800-1860.* Baton Rouge, La.: Louisiana State University Press, 1978.

Watson, Harry L. *Jacksonian Politics and Community Conflict: The Emergence of the Second Party System in Cumberland County, North Carolina.* Baton Rouge, La.: Louisiana State University Press, 1981.

3.3 Elections

Atkins, Jonathan M. "The Presidential Candidacy of Hugh Lawson White in Tennessee, 1832-1836." *Journal of Southern History* 58 (1992), 27-56.

Basch, Norma. "Marriage, Morals and Politics in the Election of 1828." *Journal of American History* 80 (1993), 890-918.

Carwadine, Richard. "Evangelicals, Whigs and the Election of William Henry Harrison." *Journal of American Studies* 17 (1983), 47-75.

Chambers, William Nisbet. "The Election of 1840." In *History of American Presidential Elections, 1789-1968.* Edited by Arthur M. Schlesinger Jr. 4 vols. New York: Chelsea House, 1971. 1: 643-744.

Gammon, Samuel R. *The Presidential Campaign of 1832.* Baltimore: Johns Hopkins University Press, 1922.

Gunderson, Robert G. *The Log Cabin Campaign.* Lexington, Ky: University Press of Kentucky, 1957.

Hamilton, Holman. "The Election of 1848." In *History of American Presidential Elections, 1789-1968.* Edited by Arthur M. Schlesinger Jr. 4 vols. New York: Chelsea House, 1971. 2: 865-918.

Heale, Michael. *The Presidential Quest: Candidates and Images in American Political Culture, 1787-1852.* London: Longman, 1982.

Holt, Michael F. "The Election of 1840, Voter Mobilization, and the Emergence of Jacksonian Voter Behavior." In *A Master's Due.* Edited by William J. Cooper. Baton Rouge, La.: Louisiana State University Press, 1985.

Kleppner, Paul et al. *The Evolution of American Electoral Systems.* Westport, Conn.: Greenwood Press, 1981.

McCormick, Richard P. "Was There a 'Whig Strategy' in 1836?" *Journal of the Early Republic* 4 (1984), 47-70.

Paul, James C. N. *Rift in the Democracy.* Philadelphia: University of Pennsylvania Press, 1951.

Rayback, Joseph G. *Free Soil: The Election of 1848.* Lexington, Ky: University Press of Kentucky, 1970.

Remini, Robert V. *The Election of Andrew Jackson.* Philadelphia: J. B. Lippincott, 1963.

―――. "The Election of 1828." In *History of American Presidential Elections, 1789-1968.* Edited by Arthur M. Schlesinger Jr. 4 vols. New York: Chelsea House, 1971. Volume 1.

―――. "The Election of 1832." In *History of American Presidential Elections, 1789-1968.* Edited by Arthur M. Schlesinger Jr. 4 vols. New York: Chelsea House, 1971. Volume 1.

Sellers, Charles G., Jr. "The Election of 1844." In *History of American Presidential Elections, 1789-1968.* Edited by Arthur M. Schlesinger Jr. 4 vols. New York: Chelsea House, 1971. 1: 747-861.

Silbey, Joel. "The Election of 1836." In *History of American Presidential Elections, 1789-1968.* Edited by Arthur M. Schlesinger Jr. 4 vols. New York: Chelsea House, 1971. 1: 574-640.

3.4 Party Systems and Political Parties

Alexander, Thomas. *Sectional Stress and Party Strength: A Study of Roll-Call Voting Patterns in the United States House of Representatives, 1836-1860.* Nashville, Tenn.: Vanderbilt University Press, 1967.

Altschuler, Glenn, and Stuart Blumin. *Rude Republic: Americans and their Politics in the Nineteenth Century.* Princeton, N.J.: Princeton University Press, 2000.

Ashworth, John. *"Agrarians" & "Aristocrats": Party Political Ideology in the United States, 1837-1846.* London: Royal Historical Society, 1983.

Baker, Jean H. *Affairs of Party: The Political Culture of Northern Democrats in the Mid-Nineteenth Century.* Ithaca, N.Y.: Cornell University Press, 1983.

Bilotta, James D. *Race and the Rise of the Republican Party, 1848-1865.* New York: P. Lang, 1992.

Blue, Frederick J. *The Free Soilers: Third Party Politics, 1848-1854.* Urbana, Ill.: University of Illinois Press, 1973.

Blumin, Stuart M., Glenn Altschuler, et al. "Round Table: Political Engagement and Disengagement in Antebellum America." *Journal of American History* 84 (1997), 855-909.

Bowers, Claude G. *Party Battles of the Jacksonian Period.* Boston: Houghton Mifflin, 1924.

Brock, William R. *Parties and Political Conscience: American Dilemmas, 1840-1850.* Millwood, N.Y.: KTO Press, 1979.

Brown, Thomas. *Politics and Statesmanship: Essays on the American Whig Party.* New York: Columbia University Press, 1985.

———. "From Old Hickory to Sly Fox: The Routinization of Charisma in the Early Democratic Party." *Journal of the Early Republic* 11 (1991), 339-70.

Bullock, Steven C. *Revolutionary Brotherhood: Freemasonry and the Transformation of the American Social Order, 1730-1840.* Chapel Hill, N.C.: University of North Carolina Press, 1996.

Chase, James S. *Emergence of the Presidential Nominating Convention, 1789-1832.* Urbana, Ill.: University of Illinois Press, 1973.

Donovan, Herbert D. A. *The Barnburners: A Study of the Internal Movements in the Political History of New York State and of the Resulting Changes in Political Affiliation, 1830-1852.* New York: New York University Press, 1925.

Ershkowitz, Herbert, and William G. Shade. "Consensus or Conflict? Political Behavior in State Legislatures during the Jacksonian Era." *Journal of American History* 58 (1971), 591-621.

Formisano, Ronald P. "Political Character, Antipartyism and the Second Party System." *American Quarterly* 21 (1969), 683-709.

Formisano, Ronald P. et al. "Round Table: Alternatives to the Party System in the 'Party Period.'" *Journal of American History* 86 (1999), 93-166.

Friedman, Jean E. *The Revolt of the Conservative Democrats: An Essay on American Political Culture and Political Development, 1837-1844.* Ann Arbor, Mich.: UMI Research Press, 1979.

Gatell, Frank O. "Money and Party in Jacksonian America: A Quantitative Look at New York City's Men of Quality." *Political Science Quarterly* 82 (1967), 235-52.

Goodman, Paul. *Towards a Christian Republic: Antimasonry and the Great Transition in New England, 1826-1836.* New York: Oxford University Press, 1988.

Hofstadter, Richard. *The Idea of a Party System: The Rise of Legitimate Opposition in the United States, 1780-1840.* Berkeley, Calif.: University of California Press, 1969.

Holt, Michael F. "The Democratic party, 1828-1860." In *History of U.S. Political Parties.* Edited by Arthur M. Schlesinger Jr. 4 vols. New York: Chelsea House, 1973, 1: 497-571.

———. *The Rise and Fall of the American Whig Party: Jacksonian Politics and the Onset of the Civil War.* New York: Oxford University Press, 1999.

Holt, Michael P. "The Anti-masonic and Know-Nothing Parties." In *History of U.S. Political Parties.* Edited by Arthur M. Schlesinger Jr. 4 vols. New York: Chelsea House, 1973, 1: 575-737.

Howe, Daniel Walker. *The Political Culture of the American Whigs.* Chicago: University of Chicago Press, 1979.

Kohl, Lawrence. *The Politics of Individualism: Parties and the American Character in the Jacksonian Era.* New York: Oxford University Press, 1989.

Kraditor, Aileen. "The Liberty and Free Soil Parties." In *History of U.S. Political Parties*. Edited by Arthur M. Schlesinger Jr. 4 vols. New York: Chelsea House, 1973, 1: 741-63.

Kutolowski, Kathleen Smith. "Freemasonry and Community in the Early Republic: The Case for Antimasonic Anxieties." *American Quarterly* 34 (1982), 543-61.

———. "Antimasonry Reexamined: Social Bases of the Grass Roots Party." *Journal of American History* 71 (1984), 269-93.

Livermore, Shaw. *The Twilight of Federalism: The Disintegration of the Federalist Party, 1815-1830*. Princeton, N.J.: Princeton University Press, 1962.

Lynn, Alvin. "Party Formation and Operation in the House of Representatives, 1824-1837." Ph.D. Dissertation, Rutgers University 1972.

McCormick, Richard P. *The Second American Party System: Party Formation in the Jacksonian Era*. Chapel Hill, N.C.: University of North Carolina Press, 1966.

Marshall, Lynn L. "The Strange Stillbirth of the Whig Party." *American Historical Review* 72 (1967), 445-68.

O'Connor, Thomas H. *Lords of the Loom: The Cotton Whigs and the Coming of the Civil War*. New York: Scribner, 1968.

Pessen, Edward. "Who Governed the Nation's Cities in the 'Era of the Common Man'?" *Political Science Quarterly* 87 (1972), 591-614.

Ratcliffe, Donald J. "Antimasonry and Partisanship in Greater New England, 1826-1836." *Journal of the Early Republic* 15 (1995), 199-239.

Ratner, Lorman, comp. *Antimasonry: The Crusade and the Party*. Englewood Cliffs, N.J.: Prentice-Hall, 1969.

Remini, Robert V. *Martin Van Buren and the Making of the Democratic Party*. New York: Columbia University Press, 1959.

Russo, David J. "The Major Political Issues of the Jacksonian Period and the Development of Party Loyalty in Congress, 1830-1840." *Transactions of the American Philosophical Society* 62 (1972).

Sellers, Charles G., Jr. "Who were the Southern Whigs?" *American Historical Review* 59 (1954), 335-46.

Shade, William G. "Political Pluralism and Party Development." In *The Evolution of the American Electoral System*. Edited by Paul Kleppner et al. Westport, Conn.: Greenwood Press, 1981.

Shields, Johanna Nicol. *The Line of Duty: Maverick Congressmen and the Development of American Political Culture, 1836-1860*. Westport, Conn.: Greenwood Press, 1985.

Silbey, Joel H. *The Shrine of Party: Congressional Voting Behavior, 1841-1852*. Pittsburgh, Penn.: University of Pittsburgh Press, 1967.

———. *The Transformation of American Politics, 1840-1860*. Englewood Cliffs, N.J.: Prentice-Hall, 1967.

———. *The Partisan Imperative: The Dynamics of American Politics before the Civil War*. New York: Oxford University Press, 1985.

———. *The American Political Nation, 1838-1893*. Stanford, Calif.: Stanford University Press, 1991.

Smith, Kimberley K. *The Dominion of Voice: Riot, Reason and Romance in Antebellum Politics.* Lawrence, Kans.: University Press of Kansas, 1999.

Van Deusen, Glyndon G. "The Whig Party." In *History of U.S. Political Parties.* Edited by Arthur M. Schlesinger Jr. 4 vols. New York: Chelsea House, 1973, 1: 333-493.

Vaughn, William P. *The Antimasonic Party in the United States, 1826-43.* Lexington, Ky: University Press of Kentucky, 1983.

Wilson, Major. "Republicanism and the Idea of Party in the Jacksonian Period." *Journal of the Early Republic* 8 (1988), 419-42.

3.5 Legal and Constitutional Developments

Billikopf, David M. *The Exercise of Judicial Power, 1789-1864.* New York: Vantage, 1973.

Dunne, Gerald T. *Justice Joseph Story and the Rise of the Supreme Court.* New York: Simon and Schuster, 1970.

Gawalt, Gerard W. *The Promise of Power: The Emergence of the Legal Profession in Massachusetts, 1760-1840.* Westport, Conn.: Greenwood Press, 1979.

Green, Fletcher. *Constitutional Development in the South Atlantic States, 1776-1860: A Study in the Evolution of Democracy.* Chapel Hill, N.C.: University of North Carolina Press, 1930.

Haines, Charles. *The Role of the Supreme Court in American Government and Politics. Vol.1: 1789-1835.* Berkeley, Calif.: University of California Press, 1944.

Haines, Charles, and Foster Sherwood. *The Role of the Supreme Court in American Government and Politics. Vol.2: 1835-1869.* Berkeley, Calif.: University of California Press, 1957.

Hall, Kermit L. *The Politics of Justice: Lower Federal Judicial Selection and the Second Party System, 1829-1861.* Lincoln, Neb.: University of Nebraska Press, 1979.

Horwitz, Morton. *The Transformation of American Law, 1780-1860.* Cambridge: Harvard University Press, 1977.

Hyman, Harold M., and William M. Wiececk. *Equal Justice under Law: Constitutional Development, 1835-75.* New York: Harper, 1982.

Jessup, Dwight Wiley. *Reaction and Accommodation: The United States Supreme Court and Political Conflict, 1809-1835.* New York: Garland, 1987.

Kutler, Stanley I. *Privilege and Creative Destruction: The Charles River Bridge Case.* Philadelphia: Lippincott, 1971.

Lenner, Andrew C. *The Federal Principle in American Politics, 1790-1833.* Lanham, Md.: Rowman and Littlefield Publishers, 2001.

Newmyer, R. Kent. *The Supreme Court under Marshall and Taney.* New York: Crowell, 1968.

Scalia, Laura J. *America's Jeffersonian Experiment: Remaking State Constitutions, 1820-1850.* DeKalb, Ill.: Northern Illinois University Press, 1999.

Siegel, Adrienne. *The Marshall Court, 1801-1835.* Millwood, N.Y.: Associated Faculty Press, 1987.

Siegel, Martin. *The Taney Court, 1835-1864.* Millwood, N.Y.: Associated Faculty Press, 1987.

Swift, Elaine K. *The Making of an American Senate: Reconstitutive Change in Congress, 1787-1841.* Ann Arbor, Mich.: University of Michigan Press, 1996.

Swisher, Carl Brent. *The Taney Period, 1836-1864.* New York: Macmillan, 1974.

White, G. Edward. *The Marshall Court and Cultural Change, 1815-1835.* New York: Macmillan, 1988.

Wiceck, William M. *The Sources of Antislavery Constitutionalism in America, 1760-1848.* Ithaca, N.Y.: Cornell University Press, 1977.

Williamson, Chilton. *American Suffrage: From Property to Democracy, 1760-1860.* Princeton, N.J.: Princeton University Press, 1960.

Zagarri, Rosemarie. *The Politics of Size: Representation in the United States, 1776-1850.* Ithaca, N.Y.: Cornell University Press, 1987.

3.6 Sectional Issues

Ashworth, John. *Slavery, Capitalism, and Politics in the Antebellum Republic: Vol.1. Commerce and Compromise, 1820-1860.* Cambridge: Cambridge University Press, 1995.

Bailey, David T. *Shadow on the Church: Southwestern Evangelical Religion and the Issue of Slavery, 1783-1860.* Ithaca, N.Y.: Cornell University Press, 1985.

Berwanger, Eugene H. *The Frontier against Slavery: Western Anti-Negro Prejudice and the Slavery Extension Controversy.* Urbana, Ill.: University of Illinois Press, 1967.

Brown, Richard H. "The Missouri Crisis, Slavery, and the Politics of Jacksonianism." *South Atlantic Quarterly* 65 (1966), 55-72.

Daly, John Patrick. *When Slavery Was Called Freedom: Evangelicalism, Proslavery and the Causes of the Civil War.* Lexington, Ky: University Press of Kentucky, 2002.

Dusinberre, William. "President Polk and the Politics of Slavery." *American Nineteenth Century History* 3: 1 (2002), 1-16.

Ellis, Richard E. *The Union at Risk: Jacksonian Democracy, States' Rights and the Nullification Crisis.* New York: Oxford University Press, 1987.

Ericson, David F. "The Nullification Crisis, American Republicanism and the Force Bill Debate." *Journal of Southern History* 61 (1995), 249-70.

Faust, Drew Gilpin. *A Sacred Circle: The Dilemma of the Intellectual in the Old South, 1840-1860.* Baltimore: Johns Hopkins University Press, 1977.

Foner, Eric. "The Wilmot Proviso Revisited." *Journal of American History* 56 (1969), 262-79.

Ford, Lacy K. "Recovering the Republic: Calhoun, South Carolina and the Concurrent Majority." *South Carolina Historical Magazine* 89 (1988), 146-59.

Franklin, John Hope. *The Militant South, 1800-1861.* Cambridge, Mass.: Harvard University Press, 1956.

Freehling, Alison Goodyear. *Drift toward Dissolution: The Virginia Slavery Debate of 1831-1832.* Baton Rouge, La.: Louisiana State University Press, 1982.

Freehling, William W. *Prelude to Civil War: The Nullification Controversy in South Carolina, 1816-1836.* New York: Harper & Row, 1966.

———. *The Road to Disunion: Volume 1: Secessionists at Bay, 1776-1854.* New York: Oxford University Press, 1990.

Genovese, Eugene. *The Slaveholders' Dilemma: Freedom and Progress in Southern Conservative Thought.* Columbia, S.C.: University of South Carolina Press, 1992.

Hendrick, George, and Willene Hendrick. *The* Creole *Mutiny: A Tale of Revolt aboard a Slave Ship.* Chicago: Ivan R. Dee, 2003.

Henig, Gerald S. "The Jacksonian Attitude toward Abolitionism." *Tennessee Historical Quarterly* 28 (1969), 42-56.

Jones, Howard. *Mutiny on the* Amistad: *The Saga of a Slave Revolt and Its Impact on American Abolition, Law and Diplomacy.* New York: Oxford University Press, 1987.

Knupfer, Peter B. *The Union as It Is: Constitutional Unionism and Sectional Compromise, 1787-1861.* Chapel Hill, N.C.: University of North Carolina Press, 1991.

Latner, Richard B. "The Nullification Crisis and Republican Subversion." *Journal of Southern History* 43 (1977), 19-38.

McCardell, John. *The Idea of a Southern Nation: Southern Nationalists and Southern Nationalism, 1830-1860.* New York: Norton, 1979.

McCurry, Stephanie. "The Two Faces of Republicanism: Gender and Proslavery Politics in Antebellum South Carolina." *Journal of American History* 78 (1992), 1245-64.

McFaul, John M. "Expediency vs. Morality: Jacksonian Politics and Slavery." *Journal of American History* 62 (1975), 24-39.

Maier, Pauline. "The Road Not Taken: Nullification, John C. Calhoun and the Revolutionary Tradition in South Carolina." *South Carolina Historical Magazine* 82 (1981), 1-19.

Miles, Edwin A. "After John Marshall's Decision: *Worcester v. Georgia* and the Nullification Crisis." *Journal of Southern History* 39 (1973), 519-44.

Miller, William Lee. *Arguing about Slavery: The Great Battle in the United States Congress.* New York: A. A. Knopf, 1996.

Morrison, Chaplain W. *Democratic Politics and Sectionalism: The Wilmot Proviso Controversy.* Chapel Hill, N.C.: University of North Carolina Press, 1967.

Morrison, Michael A. "Martin Van Buren, the Democracy and the Partisan Politics of Texas Annexation." *Journal of Southern History* 61 (1995): 695-724.

————. *Slavery and the American West: The Eclipse of Manifest Destiny and the Coming of the Civil War.* Chapel Hill, N.C.: University of North Carolina Press, 1997.

Nye, Russel B. *Fettered Freedom: Civil Liberties and the Slavery Controversy, 1830-1860.* East Lansing, Mich.: Michigan State University Press, 1963.

Peterson, Merrill D. *Olive Branch and Sword—The Compromise of 1833.* Baton Rouge, La.: Louisiana State University Press, 1982.

Ratcliffe, Donald J. "The Nullification Crisis, Southern Discontents, and the American Political Process." *American Nineteenth Century History* 1:2 (2000), 1-30.

Ratner, Lorman. *Powder Keg: Northern Opposition to the Antislavery Movement, 1831-1840.* New York: Basic Books, 1968.

Remini, Robert V. "Martin Van Buren and the Tariff of Abominations." *American Historical Review* 63 (1958), 903-17.

Richards, Leonard L. *"Gentlemen of Property and Standing": Anti-Abolition Mobs in Jacksonian America.* New York: Oxford University Press, 1970.

————. *The Slave Power: The Free North and Southern Domination, 1780-1860.* Baton Rouge, La.: Louisiana State University Press, 2000.

Rugemer, Edward B. "The Southern Response to British Abolitionism: The Maturation of Proslavery Apologetics." *Journal of Southern History* 70 (2004), 221-48.

Schwarz, Philip J. *Migrants against Slavery: Virginians and the Nation.* Charlottesville: University Press of Virginia, 2001.

Sewell, Richard H. *Ballots for Freedom: Antislavery Politics in the United States, 1837-1860.* New York: Oxford University Press, 1976.

Shade, William G. "'The Most Delicate and Exciting Topics': Martin Van Buren, Slavery and the Election of 1836." *Journal of the Early Republic* 18 (1998), 459-84.

Sheidley, Harlow W. *Sectional Nationalism: Massachusetts Conservative Leaders and the Transformation of America, 1815-1836.* Boston: Northeastern University Press, 1998.

Snay, Mitchell. *Gospel of Disunion: Religion and Separatism in the Antebellum South.* New York: Cambridge University Press, 1993.

Stewart, James Brewer. "'A Great Talking and Eating Machine': Patriarchy, Mobilization and the Dynamics of Nullification in South Carolina." *Civil War History* 27 (1981), 197-220.

Wender, Herbert. *Southern Commercial Conventions, 1837-1859.* Baltimore: Johns Hopkins University Press, 1930.

Wilson, Major L. "'Liberty and Union': An Analysis of Three Concepts Involved in the Nullification Crisis." *Journal of Southern History* 33 (1967), 331-55.

Wyly-Jones, Susan. "The 1835 Anti-Abolition Meetings in the South: A New Look at the Controversy over the Abolition Postal Campaign." *Civil War History* 47 (2001), 289-309.

3.7 Reform Movements

Abzug, Robert H. *Cosmos Crumbling: American Reform and the Religious Imagination.* New York: Oxford University Press, 1994.

Alexander, Ruth M. "'We Are Engaged as a Band of Sisters': Class and Domesticity in the Washingtonian Temperance Movement, 1840-1850." *Journal of American History* 75 (1988), 763-85.

Barnes, Gilbert Hobbs. *The Anti-Slavery Impulse, 1830-1844.* New York: D. Appleton Century Co., 1933.

Boyer, Paul. *Urban Masses and Moral Order in America, 1820-1920.* Cambridge, Mass.: Harvard University Press, 1978.

Clark, Christopher. *The Communitarian Moment: The Radical Challenge of the Northampton Association.* Ithaca, N.Y.: Cornell University Press, 1995.

Davis, David B., ed. *Ante-bellum Reform.* New York: Harper and Row, 1967.

Filler, Louis. *The Crusade against Slavery, 1830-1860.* New York: Harper & Row, 1960.

Foster, Lawrence. *Women, Family and Utopia: Communal Experiments of the Shakers, the Oneida Community and the Mormons.* Syracuse, N.Y.: Syracuse University Press, 1991.

Friedman, Lawrence J. *Gregarious Saints: Self and Community in American Abolitionism, 1830-1870.* New York: Cambridge University Press, 1982.

Fuller, Wayne E. *Morality and the Mail in Nineteenth Century America.* Urbana, Ill.: University of Illinois Press, 2003.

Goodman, Paul. *Of One Blood: Abolitionism and the Origins of Racial Equality.* Berkeley, Calif.: University of California Press, 1998.

Griffin, C. S. *The Ferment of Reform, 1830-1860.* New York: Crowell, 1967.

Grob, Gerald. *Mental Institutions in America: Social Policy to 1875.* New York: Free Press, 1972

Guarneri, Carl J. *The Utopian Alternative: Fourierism in Nineteenth Century America.* Ithaca, N.Y.: Cornell University Press, 1991.

Hampel, Robert L. *Temperance and Prohibition in Massachusetts, 1813-1852.* Ann Arbor, Mich.: UMI Research Press, 1982.

Harrold, Stanley. *The Abolitionists and the South.* Lexington, Ky: University Press of Kentucky, 1995.

———. *Subversives: Antislavery Community in Washington D.C., 1828-1865.* Baton Rouge, La.: Louisiana State University Press, 2003.

Hershberger, Mary. "Mobilising Women, Anticipating Abolition: The Struggle against Indian Removal in the 1830s." *Journal of American History* 86 (1999), 15-40.

Jeffrey, Julie Roy. *The Great Silent Army of Abolitionism: Ordinary Women in the Antislavery Movement.* Chapel Hill, N.C.: University of North Carolina Press, 1998.

John, Richard R. "Taking Sabbatarianism Seriously: The Postal System, the Sabbath, and the Transformation of American Political Culture." *Journal of the Early Republic* 10 (1990), 517-67.

Kohl, Lawrence F. "The Concept of Social Control and the History of Jacksonian America." *Journal of the Early Republic* 5 (1985), 21-34.

Kolmerton, Carol A. *Women in Utopia: The Ideology of Gender in the American Owenite Communities*. Bloomington, Ind.: Indiana University Press, 1990.

Kraditor, Aileen S. *Means and Ends in American Abolitionism: Garrison and His Critics on Strategy and Tactics, 1834-1850*. New York: Pantheon, 1969.

Lawes, Carolyn. *Women and Reform in a New England Community, 1815-1860*. Lexington, Ky: University Press of Kentucky, 2000.

Lesick, Lawrence T. *The Lane Rebels: Evangelicalism and Antislavery in Antebellum America*. Metuchen, N.J.: Scarecrow Press, 1980.

McKivigan, John. *The War against Proslavery Religion: Abolitionism and the Northern Churches, 1830-1865*. Ithaca, N.Y.: Cornell University Press, 1984.

Magdol, Edward. *The Antislavery Rank and File: A Social Profile of the Abolitionists' Constituency*. New York: Greenwood, 1986.

Mathews, Donald G. *Slavery and Methodism: A Chapter in American Morality, 1780-1845*. Princeton, N.J.: Princeton University Press, 1965.

Melder, Keith E. *Beginnings of Sisterhood: The American Woman's Rights Movement, 1800-1850*. New York: Schocken Books, 1977.

Meranze, Michael. *Laboratories of Virtue: Punishment, Revolution and Authority in Philadelphia, 1760-1835*. Chapel Hill, N.C.: University of North Carolina Press, 1996.

Mintz, Steven. *Moralists and Modernizers: America's Pre-Civil War Reformers*. Baltimore: Johns Hopkins University Press, 1995.

Newman, Richard S. *The Transformation of American Abolitionism: Fighting Slavery in the Early Republic*. Chapel Hill, N.C.: University of North Carolina Press, 2002.

Nissenbaum, Stephen. *Sex, Diet and Debility in Jacksonian America: Sylvester Graham and Health Reform*. Westport, Conn.: Greenwood Press, 1980.

Pierson, Michael D. *Free Hearts and Free Homes: Gender and American Antislavery Politics*. Chapel Hill, N.C.: University of North Carolina Press, 2003.

Rorabaugh, W. J. *The Alcoholic Republic: An American Tradition*. New York: Oxford University Press, 1979.

Roth, Randolph A. *The Democratic Dilemma: Religion, Reform and Social Order in the Connecticut River Valley of Vermont, 1791-1850*. New York: Cambridge University Press, 1987.

Rothman, David J. *The Discovery of the Asylum: Social Order and Disorder in the New Republic*. Boston: Little, Brown, 1971.

Schantz, Mark S. "Religious Tracts, Evangelical Reform and the Market Revolution in Antebellum America." *Journal of the Early Republic* 17 (1997), 425-66.

Smith-Rosenberg, Carroll. *Religion and the Rise of the American City: The New York City Mission Movement, 1812-1870*. Ithaca, N.Y.: Cornell University Press, 1971.

Spann, Edward K. *Brotherly Tomorrows: Movements for a Co-operative Society in America, 1820-1920.* New York: Columbia University Press, 1989.

Staudenraus, P. J. *The African Colonization Movement, 1816-1865.* New York: Columbia University Press, 1961.

Stauffer, John. *The Black Hearts of Men: Radical Abolitionists and the Transformation of Race.* Cambridge, Mass.: Harvard University Press, 2002.

Stewart, James Brewer. *Holy Warriors: The Abolitionists and American Slavery.* New York: Hill and Wang, 1976.

Strong, Douglas M. *Perfectionist Politics: Abolitionism and the Religious Tensions of American Democracy.* Syracuse, N.Y.: Syracuse University Press, 1999.

Tyler, Alice Felt. *Freedom's Ferment: Phases of American Social History from the Colonial Period to the Outbreak of the Civil War.* Minneapolis, Minn.: University of Minnesota Press, 1944.

Tyrrell, Ian R. *Sobering Up: From Temperance to Prohibition in Antebellum America, 1800-1860.* Westport, Conn.: Greenwood Press, 1979.

Voss-Hubbard, Mark. "Slavery, Capitalism and the Middling Sorts: The Rank and File of Political Abolitionism." *American Nineteenth Century History* 4:2 (2003), 53-76.

Walker, Robert H. *Reform in America: The Continuing Frontier.* Lexington, Ky: University Press of Kentucky, 1985.

Walters, Ronald G. *The Antislavery Appeal: American Abolitionism after 1830.* Baltimore: Johns Hopkins University Press, 1976.

———. *American Reformers, 1815-1860.* New York: Hill and Wang, 1978.

Wyatt-Brown, Bertram. "Prelude to Abolitionism: Sabbatarian Politics and the Rise of the Second Party System." *Journal of American History* 58 (1971), 316-41.

———. *Yankee Saints and Southern Sinners.* Baton Rouge, La.: Louisiana State University Press, 1985.

Yellin, Jean Fagan. *Women & Sisters: The Antislavery Feminists in American Culture.* New Haven, Conn.: Yale University Press, 1989.

Zaeske, Susan. *Signatures of Citizenship: Petitioning, Antislavery, and Women's Political Identity.* Chapel Hill, N.C.: University of North Carolina Press, 2003.

Ziegler, Valarie H. *The Advocates of Peace in Antebellum America.* Bloomington, Ind.: Indiana University Press, 1992.

3.8 Expansionism and International Relations

Astolfi, Douglas M. *Foundations of Destiny: A Foreign Policy of the Jacksonians, 1824-1837.* New York: Garland, 1989.

Barr, Alwyn. *Texans in Revolt: The Battle for San Antonio, 1835.* Austin, Tex.: University of Texas Press, 1990.

Bauer, K. Jack. *The Mexican War, 1846-1848.* New York: Macmillan, 1974.

Belohlavek, John M. *"Let the Eagle Soar!": The Foreign Policy of Andrew Jackson*. Lincoln, Neb.: University of Nebraska Press, 1985.

Benns, F. Lee. *The American Struggle for the British West India Carrying Trade, 1815-1830*. Bloomington, Ind.: Indiana University Studies, Vol. 10, 1923.

Binder, Frederick Moore. *James Buchanan and the American Empire*. Selinsgrove, Penn.: Susquehanna University Press, 1994.

Binkley, William Campbell. *The Expansionist Movement in Texas, 1836-1850*. Berkeley, Calif.: University of California Press, 1925.

————. *The Texas Revolution*. Baton Rouge, La.: Louisiana State University Press, 1952.

Brack, Gene M. *Mexico Views Manifest Destiny, 1821-1846: An Essay on the Origins of the Mexican War*. Albuquerque, N.M.: University of New Mexico Press, 1975.

Carroll, Francis M. *A Good and Wise Measure: The Search for the Canadian-American Boundary, 1783-1842*. Toronto: University of Toronto Press, 2001.

Chalfant, William Y. *Dangerous Passage: The Santa Fe Trail and the Mexican War*. Norman, Ok.: University of Oklahoma Press, 1994.

Connor, Seymour V., and Odie B. Faulk. *North America Divided: The Mexican War, 1846-1848*. New York: Oxford University Press, 1971.

Corey, Albert B. *The Crisis of 1830-1842 in Canadian-American Relations*. New Haven, Conn.: Yale University Press, 1941.

Crapol, Edward P. "John Tyler and the Pursuit of National Destiny." *Journal of the Early Republic* 17 (1997), 467-91.

Dawson, Joseph G. III. *Doniphan's Epic March: The 1st Missouri Volunteers in the Mexican War*. Lawrence, Kans.: University Press of Kansas, 1999.

Del Castillo, Richard Griswold. *The Treaty of Guadalupe Hidalgo: A Legacy of Conflict*. Norman, Ok.: University of Oklahoma Press, 1990.

DeVoto, Bernard. *The Year of Decision: 1846*. Boston: Little, Brown, 1943.

Dykstra, David L. *The Shifting Balance of Power: American British Diplomacy in North America, 1842-1848*. Lanham, Md.: University Press of America, 1999.

Eisenhower, John S. D. *So Far from God: The U.S. War with Mexico, 1846-1848*. New York: Random House, 1989.

Foos, Paul. *A Short, Offhand, Killing Affair: Soldiers and Social Conflict during the Mexican-American War*. Chapel Hill, N.C.: University of North Carolina Press, 2002.

Francaviglia, Richard V., and Douglas W. Richmond, eds. *Dueling Eagles: Reinterpreting the US-Mexican War, 1846-1848*. Fort Worth, Tex.: Texas Christian University Press, 2000.

Frazier, Donald S., ed. *The United States and Mexico at War: Nineteenth-Century Expansionism and Conflict*. New York: Macmillan, 1998.

Fuller, John D. P. *The Movement for the Acquisition of All Mexico, 1846-1848*. Baltimore: Johns Hopkins University Press, 1936.

Graebner, Norman A. *Empire on the Pacific: A Study in American Continental Expansion*. New York: Ronald Press, 1955.

Griffin, Eldon. *Clippers and Consuls: American Consular and Commercial Relations with Eastern Asia, 1845-1860.* Ann Arbor, Mich.: Edwards Brothers, 1938.

Hardin, Stephen L. *Texian Iliad: A Military History of the Texas Revolution.* Austin, Tex.: University of Texas Press, 1994.

Harlow, Neal. *California Conquered: War and Peace on the Pacific, 1846-1850.* Berkeley, Calif.: University of California Press, 1982.

Haynes, Sam W., and Christopher Morris, eds. *Manifest Destiny and Empire: American Antebellum Expansionism.* College Station, Tex.: Texas A & M University Press, 1997.

Henry, Robert Selph. *The Story of the Mexican War.* Indianapolis, Ind.: Bobbs-Merrill, 1950.

Hietala, Thomas R. *Manifest Design: Anxious Aggrandizement in Late Jacksonian America.* Ithaca, N.Y.: Cornell University Press, 1985.

Horsman, Reginald. *Race and Manifest Destiny: The Origins of American Racial Anglo-Saxonism.* Cambridge, Mass.: Harvard University Press, 1981.

Hyslop, Stephen G. *Bound for Santa Fe: The Road to New Mexico and the American Conquest, 1806-1848.* Norman, Ok.: University of Oklahoma Press, 2002.

Johannsen, Robert. *To the Halls of the Montezumas: The Mexican War in the American Imagination.* New York: Oxford University Press, 1985.

———. *The Frontier, the Union and Stephen A. Douglas.* Urbana, Ill.: University of Illinois Press, 1989.

Jones, Howard. *To the Webster-Ashburton Treaty: A Study in Anglo-American Relations, 1783-1843.* Chapel Hill, N.C.: University of North Carolina Press, 1977.

Jones, Howard, and Donald A Rakestraw. *Prologue to Manifest Destiny: Anglo-American Relations in the 1840s.* Wilmington, Del.: S. R. Books, 1997.

Lack, Paul D. *The Texas Revolutionary Experience: A Political and Social History, 1835-36.* College Station, Tex.: Texas A & M University Press, 1992.

Lander, Ernest McPherson, Jr. *Reluctant Imperialists: Calhoun, the South Carolinians, and the Mexican War.* Baton Rouge, La.: Louisiana State University Press, 1980.

Langum, David J. *Law and Community on the Mexican California Frontier: Anglo-American Expatriates and the Clash of Legal Traditions, 1821-1846.* Norman, Ok.: University of Oklahoma Press, 1987.

McCaffrey, James M. *Army of Manifest Destiny: The American Soldier in the Mexican War, 1846-1848.* New York: New York University Press, 1992.

McLemore, Richard Aubrey. *The French Spoliation Claims, 1816-1836: A Study in Jacksonian Diplomacy.* Nashville, Tenn.: n.p., 1932.

———. *Franco-American Diplomatic Relations, 1816-1836.* University, La.: Louisiana State University Press, 1941.

Merk, Frederick. *Manifest Destiny and Mission in American History: A Reinterpretation.* New York: Alfred A. Knopf, 1963.

———. *The Oregon Question: Essays in Anglo-American Diplomacy and Politics.* Cambridge, Mass.: Harvard University Press, 1967.

————. *Slavery and the Annexation of Texas.* New York: Alfred A. Knopf, 1972.

Merk, Frederick, and Lois Bannister Merk. *The Monroe Doctrine and American Expansionism, 1843-1849.* New York: Alfred A. Knopf, 1966.

————. *Fruits of Propaganda in the Tyler Administration.* Cambridge, Mass.: Harvard University Press, 1971.

Nance, Joseph M. *After San Jacinto: Texas-Mexican Frontier, 1836-1841.* Austin, Tex.: University of Texas Press, 1963.

Nelson, Anna Kasten. *Secret Agents: President Polk and the Search for Peace with Mexico.* New York: Garland, 1988.

Perkins, Bradford. *The Cambridge History of American Foreign Relations.* Vol. 1: *The Creation of a Republican Empire, 1776-1865.* New York: Cambridge University Press, 1993.

Perkins, Dexter. *The Monroe Doctrine, 1826-1867.* Baltimore: Johns Hopkins University Press, 1933.

Phillips, George Harwood. *Indians and Intruders in Central California, 1769-1849.* Norman, Ok.: University of Oklahoma Press, 1993.

Pierce, Gerald S. *Texas under Arms: The Camps, Posts, Forts, and Military Towns of the Republic of Texas, 1836-1846.* Austin, Tex.: Encino Press, 1969.

Pinheiro, John C. "'Religion without Distinction': Anti-Catholicism, All Mexico and the Treaty of Guadeloupe Hidalgo." *Journal of the Early Republic* 23 (2003), 69-96.

Pletcher, David M. *The Diplomacy of Annexation: Texas, Oregon and the Mexican War.* Columbia, Mo.: University of Missouri Press, 1973.

Price, Glenn W. *Origins of the War with Mexico: The Polk-Stockton Intrigue.* Austin, Tex.: University of Texas Press, 1967.

Rauch, Basil. *American Interest in Cuba: 1848-1855.* New York: Columbia University Press, 1948.

Reeves, Jesse S. *American Diplomacy under Tyler and Polk.* Baltimore: Johns Hopkins University Press, 1907.

Reichstein, Andreas V. *Rise of the Lone Star: The Making of Texas.* Translated by Jeanne R. Willson. College Station, Tex.: Texas A & M University Press, 1989.

Roberts, David. *A Newer World: Kit Carson, John C. Frémont, and the Claiming of the American West.* New York: Simon & Schuster, 2000.

Roeckell, Lelia M. "Bonds over Bondage: British Opposition to the Annexation of Texas." *Journal of the Early Republic* 19 (1999), 257-78.

Schroeder, John H. *Mr. Polk's War: American Opposition and Dissent, 1846-1848.* Madison, Wisc.: University of Wisconsin Press, 1973.

Shurbutt, Thomas Ray, ed. *United States-Latin American Relations, 1800-1850: The Formative Generations.* Tuscaloosa, Ala.: University of Alabama Press, 1991.

Siegel, Stanley. *A Political History of the Texas Republic, 1836-1845.* Austin, Tex.: University of Texas Press, 1956.

Singletary, Otis A. *The Mexican War.* Chicago: University of Chicago Press, 1960.

Smith, Justin H. *The Annexation of Texas*. New York: Baker and Taylor, 1911.
———. *The War with Mexico*. 2 vols. New York: Macmillan, 1919.
Stephanson, Anders. *Manifest Destiny: American Expansionism and the Empire of Right*. New York: Hill and Wang, 1995.
Stevens, Kenneth R. *Border Diplomacy: The* Caroline *and* McLeod *Affairs in Anglo-American-Canadian Relations, 1837-1842*. Tuscaloosa, Ala.: University of Alabama Press, 1989.
Stuart, Reginald C. *United States Expansionism and British North America, 1775-1871*. Chapel Hill, N.C.: University of North Carolina Press, 1988.
Tutorow, Norman E. *Texas Annexation and the Mexican War: A Political Study of the Old Northwest*. Palo Alto, Calif.: Chadwick House, 1978.
Varg, Paul A. *United States Foreign Relations, 1820-1860*. East Lansing, Mich.: Michigan State University Press, 1979.
Walker, Dale L. *Bear Flag Rising: The Conquest of California, 1846*. New York: Forge, 1999.
Watson, Samuel. "United States Army Officers Fight the 'Patriot War': Responses to Filibustering on the Canadian Border, 1837-1839." *Journal of the Early Republic* 18 (1998), 485-519.
Weeks, William Earl. *Building the Continental Empire: American Expansion from the Revolution to the Civil War*. Chicago: Ivan R Dee, 1996.
Weems, John E. *To Conquer a Peace: The War between the United States and Mexico*. Garden City, N.Y.: Doubleday, 1974.
Weinberg, Albert K. *Manifest Destiny: A Study of Nationalist Expansionism in American History*. Baltimore: Johns Hopkins University Press, 1935.
Winders, Richard Bruce. *Mr. Polk's Army: The American Military Experience in the Mexican War*. College Station, Tex.: Texas A & M University Press, 1997.
———. *Crisis in the Southwest: The United States, Mexico, and the Struggle over Texas*. Wilmington, Del.: S. R. Books, 2002.

4. Economy

4.1 National and Local Economic Developments

Arrington, Leonard J. *Great Basin Kingdom: An Economic History of the Latter-Day Saints, 1830-1900*. Cambridge, Mass.: Harvard University Press, 1958.
Barbour, Barton H. *Fort Union and the Upper Missouri Fur Trade*. Norman, Ok.: University of Oklahoma Press, 2001.
Billington, Ray A. *Westward Expansion: A History of the American Frontier*. New York: The Macmillan Company, 1949.
———. *The Far Western Frontier, 1830-1860*. New York: Harper, 1956.
Brooke, John L. *The Heart of the Commonwealth: Society and Political Culture in Worcester County, Massachusetts, 1713-1861*. New York: Cambridge University Press, 1989.

Bruchey, Stuart. *The Roots of American Economic Growth, 1607-1861: An Essay in Social Causation.* New York: Harper and Row, 1965.

Buley, R. Carlyle. *The Old Northwest: Pioneer Period, 1815-1840.* 2 vols. Indianapolis, Ind.: Indiana Historical Society, 1950.

Clark, Christopher. *The Roots of Rural Capitalism: Western Massachusetts, 1780-1860.* Ithaca, N.Y.: Cornell University Press, 1990.

Frazer, Robert W. *Forts and Supplies: The Role of the Army in the Economy of the Southwest, 1846-1861.* Albuquerque, N.M.: University of New Mexico Press, 1983.

Gibson, James R. *Farming the Frontier: The Agricultural Opening of the Oregon Country, 1786-1846.* Seattle, Wash.: University of Washington Press, 1986.

Goetzmann, William H. *Army Exploration in the American West, 1803-1863.* New Haven, Conn.: Yale University Press, 1959.

Gruenwald, Kim Marie. *River of Enterprise: The Commercial Origins of Regional Identity in the Ohio Valley, 1790-1850.* Bloomington, Ind.: Indiana University Press, 2002.

Holliday, J. S. *The World Rushed In: The California Gold Rush Experience.* New York: Simon and Schuster, 1981.

Lamar, Howard R. *The Far Southwest, 1846-1912.* New Haven, Conn.: Yale University Press, 1966.

Lindstrom, Diane. *Economic Development in the Philadelphia Region, 1810-1850.* New York: Columbia University Press, 1978.

McGrane, Reginald C. *The Panic of 1837: Some Financial Problems of the Jacksonian Era.* New York: Russell & Russell, 1965.

Miller, Nathan. *The Enterprise of a Free People: Aspects of Economic Development in New York State during the Canal Period, 1792-1838.* Ithaca, N.Y.: Cornell University Press, 1962.

North, Douglass C. *The Economic Growth of the United States, 1790-1860.* Englewood Cliffs, N.J.: Prentice-Hall, 1961.

Pencak, William, and Conrad E. Wright (Eds). *New York and the Rise of American Capitalism: Economic Development and the Social and Political History of an American State, 1780-1870.* New York: New-York Historical Society, 1989.

Pitt, Leonard. *The Decline of the Californios: A Social History of the Spanish-speaking Californians, 1846-1890.* Berkeley, Calif.: University of California Press, 1966.

Reséndez, Andrés. "National Identity on a Shifting Border: Texas and New Mexico in the Age of Transition, 1821-1848." *Journal of American History* 86 (1999), 668-88.

———. "Getting Cured and Getting Drunk: State versus Market in Texas and New Mexico, 1800-1850." *Journal of the Early Republic* 22 (2002), 77-103.

Rezneck, Samuel. "The Social History of an American Depression, 1837-1843." *American Historical Review* 40 (1935), 662-87.

Rohrbough, Malcolm. *The Trans-Appalachian Frontier: People, Societies and Institutions, 1775-1850.* New York: Oxford University Press, 1978.

Rothenburg, Winifred Barr. *From Market-places to a Market Economy: The Transformation of Rural Massachusetts, 1750-1850.* Chicago: University of Chicago Press, 1992.

Rousseau, Peter L. "Jacksonian Monetary Policy, Specie Flows, and the Panic of 1837." *Journal of Economic History* 62 (2002), 457-88.

Starr, Kevin, and Richard J. Orsi, eds. *Rooted in Barbarous Soil: People, Culture, and Community in Gold Rush California.* Berkeley, Calif.: University of California Press, 2000.

Temin, Peter. *The Jacksonian Economy.* New York: W.W. Norton, 1969.

Unruh, John D., Jr. *The Plains Across: The Overland Emigrants and the Trans-Mississippi West, 1840-1860.* Urbana, Ill.: University of Illinois Press, 1979.

Utley, Robert M. *The Indian Frontier of the American West, 1846-1890.* Albuquerque, N.M.: University of New Mexico Press, 1984.

Walker, Dale L. *Eldorado: The California Gold Rush.* New York: Forge, 2003.

Weber, David J. *The Mexican Frontier, 1821-1846: The American Southwest under Mexico.* Albuquerque, N.M.: University of New Mexico Press, 1982.

Wishart, David J. *The Fur Trade of the American West, 1807-1840: A Geographical Synthesis.* Lincoln, Neb.: University of Nebraska Press, 1979.

4.2 Thought and Practice in Economic Policy

Conkin, Paul. *Prophets of Prosperity: America's First Political Economists.* Bloomington, Ind.: Indiana University Press, 1980.

Dorfman, Joseph. *The Economic Mind in American Civilization.* Vols. 1-2. New York: The Viking Press, 1946.

Einhorn, Robin L. *Property Rules: Political Economy in Chicago, 1833-1872.* Chicago: University of Chicago Press, 1991.

Gunn, Ray. *The Decline of Authority: Public Economic Policy and Political Development in New York, 1800-1860.* Ithaca, N.Y.: Cornell University Press, 1988.

Handlin, Oscar, and Mary Handlin. *Commonwealth: A Study of the Role of Government in the American Economy: Massachusetts, 1774-1861.* Cambridge, Mass.: Harvard University Press, 1969.

Hartz, Louis. *Economic Policy and Democratic Thought: Pennsylvania, 1776-1860.* Cambridge, Mass.: Harvard University Press, 1948.

Heath, Milton. *Constructive Liberalism: The Role of the State in Economic Development in Georgia to 1860.* Cambridge, Mass.: Harvard University Press, 1954.

Kaufman, Allen. *Capitalism, Slavery and Republican Values: Antebellum Political Economists, 1819-1848.* Austin, Tex.: University of Texas Press, 1982.

Novak, William J. *The People's Welfare: Law and Regulation in Nineteenth-Century America.* Chapel Hill, N.C.: University of North Carolina Press, 1996.

Thistlethwaite, Frank. *The Anglo-American Connection in the Early Nineteenth Century.* Philadelphia: University of Pennsylvania Press, 1959.

4.3 Agriculture

Atack, Jeremy, and Fred Bateman. *To Their Own Soil: Agriculture in the Antebellum North.* Ames, Iowa: Iowa State University Press, 1987.
Baptist, Edward E. *Creating an Old South: Middle Florida's Plantation Frontier before the Civil War.* Chapel Hill, N.C.: University of North Carolina Press, 2002.
Barron, Hal S. *Those Who Stayed Behind: Rural Society in Nineteenth-Century New England.* New York: Cambridge University Press, 1984.
Bidwell, Percy, and John Falconer. *History of Agriculture in the Northern United States, 1620-1860.* Washington, D.C.: Carnegie Institution, 1925.
Danhof, Clarence H. *Change in Agriculture: The Northern United States, 1820-1870.* Cambridge, Mass.: Harvard University Press, 1969.
Ellis, David Maldwyn. *Landlords and Farmers in the Hudson-Mohawk Region, 1790-1850.* Ithaca, N.Y.: Cornell University Press, 1946.
Faragher, John Mack. *Sugar Creek: Life on the Illinois Prairie.* New Haven, Conn.: Yale University Press, 1986.
Gates, Paul W. *The Farmers' Age: Agriculture: 1815-1860.* New York: Harper & Row, 1960.
Gray, Lewis. *History of Agriculture in the Southern United States to 1860.* Washington, D.C.: Carnegie Institution, 1933.
Lampard, Eric E. *Rise of the Dairy Industry in Wisconsin, 1820-1920: A Study in Agricultural Change.* Madison, Wisc.: State Historical Society of Wisconsin, 1963.
McMurry, Sally. *Transforming Rural Life: Dairying Families and Agricultural Change, 1820-1885.* Baltimore: Johns Hopkins University Press, 1995.
Moore, John H. *The Emergence of the Cotton Kingdom in the Old Southwest: Mississippi, 1770-1860.* Baton Rouge, La.: Louisiana State University Press, 1988.
Shore, Laurence. *Southern Capitalists: The Ideological Leadership of an Elite, 1832-1885.* Chapel Hill, N.C.: University of North Carolina Press, 1986.
Siegel, Frederick F. *The Roots of Southern Distinctiveness: Tobacco and Society in Danville, Virginia, 1780-1865.* Chapel Hill, N.C.: University of North Carolina Press, 1987.
Wright, Gavin. *The Political Economy of the Cotton South: Households, Markets and Wealth in the Nineteenth Century.* New York: W.W. Norton, 1978.

4.4 Manufacturing Industry

Clark, Victor S. *History of Manufactures in the United States. Vol.1: 1607-1860.* 3 vols. New York: McGraw Hill, 1929.

Cochran, Thomas. *Frontiers of Change: Early Industrialism in America.* New York: Oxford University Press, 1981.

Dalzell, Robert F. *Enterprising Elite: The Boston Associates and the World They Made.* Cambridge, Mass.: Harvard University Press, 1987.

Dawley, A. *Class and Community: The Industrial Revolution in Lynn.* Cambridge, Mass.: Harvard University Press, 1976.

Faler, Paul G. *Mechanics and Manufacturers in the Early Industrial Revolution: Lynn, Massachusetts, 1780-1860.* Albany: State University Press of New York, 1981.

Hawke, David F. *Nuts and Bolts of the Past. A History of American Technology, 1776-1860.* New York: Harper and Row, 1988.

Hindle, Brooke, and Steven Lubar. *Engines of Change: The American Industrial Revolution, 1790-1860.* Washington, D.C.: Smithsonian Institution Press, 1986.

Hirsch, Susan. *Roots of the American Working Class: The Industrialization of Crafts in Newark, 1800-1860.* Philadelphia: University of Pennsylvania Press, 1978.

Hoke, Donald R. *Ingenious Yankees: The Rise of the American System of Manufactures in the Private Sector.* New York: Columbia University Press, 1990.

Hounshell, David. *From the American System to Mass Production, 1800-1932: The Development of Manufacturing Technology in the United States.* Baltimore: Johns Hopkins University Press, 1984.

Jones, Daniel P. *The Economic & Social Transformation of Rural Rhode Island, 1780-1850.* Boston: Northeastern University Press, 1992.

Meyer, David R. *The Roots of American Industrialization.* Baltimore: Johns Hopkins University Press, 2003.

Paskoff, Paul F. *Industrial Evolution: Organization, Structure and Growth of the Pennsylvania Iron Industry, 1750-1860.* Baltimore: Johns Hopkins University Press, 1983.

Prude, Jonathan. *The Coming of Industrial Order: Town and Factory Life in Rural Massachusetts, 1810-1860.* New York: Cambridge University Press, 1983.

Scranton, Philip. *Proprietary Capitalism: The Textile Manufacture at Philadelphia, 1800-1885.* New York: Cambridge University Press, 1983.

Smith, Merritt Roe. *Harpers Ferry Armory and the New Technology: The Challenge of Change.* Ithaca, N.Y.: Cornell University Press, 1977.

Stanwood, Edward. *American Tariff Controversies in the Nineteenth Century.* 2 vols. Boston: Houghton, Mifflin, 1903.

Taussig, Frank W. *The Tariff History of the United States.* New York: G.P. Putnam's Sons, 1888.

Tucker, Barbara M. *Samuel Slater and the Origins of American Textile Industry, 1790-1860.* Ithaca, N.Y.: Cornell University Press, 1984.

Wallace, Anthony F. C. *Rockdale: The Growth of an American Village in the Early Industrial Revolution.* New York: Alfred A. Knopf, 1978.

Ware, Caroline Farrar. *The Early New England Cotton Manufacture: A Study in Industrial Beginnings.* Boston: Houghton Mifflin, 1931.

Weil, Francois. "Capitalism and Industrialization in New England, 1815-1845." Translated in *Journal of American History* 84 (1998) 1334-54.

Zonderman, David A. *Aspirations and Anxieties: New England Workers and the Mechanized Factory System, 1815-1850.* New York: Oxford University Press, 1992.

4.5 Banking and Finance

Balleisen, Edward J. *Navigating Failure: Bankruptcy and Commercial Society in Antebellum America.* Chapel Hill, N.C.: University of North Carolina Press, 2001.

Bodenhorn, Howard. *A History of Banking in Antebellum America: Financial Markets and Economic Development in an Era of Nation-building.* New York: Cambridge University Press, 2000.

Catterall, Ralph. *The Second Bank of the United States.* Chicago: University of Chicago Press, 1903.

Fenstermaker, J. Van. *The Development of American Commercial Banking, 1782-1837.* Kent, Ohio: Kent State University Press, 1965.

Gatell, Frank O. "Spoils of the Bank War: Political Bias in the Selection of Pet Banks." *American Historical Review* 70 (1964), 35-58.

————. "Sober Second Thoughts on Van Buren, The Albany Regency, and the Wall Street Conspiracy." *Journal of American History* 53 (1966), 19-40.

Green, George D. *Finance and Economic Development in the Old South: Louisiana Banking, 1804-1861.* Stanford, Calif.: Stanford University Press, 1972.

Hammond, Bray. *Banks and Politics in America from the Revolution to the Civil War.* Princeton, N.J.: Princeton University Press, 1957.

Martin, David A. "Metallism, Small Notes, and Jackson's War with the B.U.S." *Explorations in Economic History* 11 (1974), 227-47.

McFaul, John M. *The Politics of Jacksonian Finance.* Ithaca, N.Y.: Cornell University Press, 1972.

Meerman, Jacob P. "The Climax of the Bank War: Biddle's Contraction, 1833-34." *Journal of Political Economy* 71 (1963), 378-88.

Remini, Robert V. *Andrew Jackson and the Bank War: A Study in the Growth of Presidential Power.* New York: W.W. Norton, 1967.

Rockoff, Hugh. *The Free Banking Era: A Re-examination.* New York: Arno Press, 1975.

Scheiber, Harry N. "The Pet Banks in Jacksonian Politics and Finance, 1833-1841." *Journal of Economic History* 23 (1963), 196-214.

Schweikart, Larry. *Banking in the American South from the Age of Jackson to Reconstruction.* Baton Rouge, La.: Louisiana State University Press, 1987.

Shade, William G. *Banks or No Banks: The Money Issue in Western Politics, 1832-1865.* Detroit: Wayne State University Press, 1972.

Sharp, James Roger. *The Jacksonians versus the Banks: Politics in the States after the Panic of 1837.* New York: Columbia University Press, 1970.

Timberlake, Richard H., Jr. "The Independent Treasury and Monetary Policy before the Civil War." *Southern Economic Journal* 27 (1960), 92-103.
————. "The Specie Circular and Distribution of the Surplus." *Journal of Political Economy* 68 (1960), 109-17.
Warren, Charles. *Bankruptcy in United States History.* Cambridge, Mass.: Harvard University Press, 1935.
Wilburn, Jean Alexander. *Biddle's Bank: The Crucial Years.* New York: Columbia University Press, 1967.
Wilson, Major L. "The 'Country' versus the 'Court': A Republican Consensus and Party Debates in the Bank War." *Journal of the Early Republic* 15 (1995), 619-47.

4.6 Land Policy

Bronstein, Jamie. *Land Reform and the Working Class Experience in Britain and the United States, 1800-1862.* Stanford, Calif.: Stanford University Press, 1999.
Feller, Daniel. *The Public Lands in Jacksonian Politics.* Madison, Wisc.: University of Wisconsin Press, 1984.
Goodman, Paul. "The Emergence of Homestead Exemption in the United States: Accommodation and Resistance to the Market Revolution, 1840-1880." *Journal of American History* 80 (1993), 470-98.
Morrison, Michael A. "Distribution or Dissolution: Western Land Policy, Economic Development, and the Language of Corruption, 1837-1841." *American Nineteenth Century History* 1:1 (2000), 1-33 .
Oberly, James W. *Sixty Million Acres: American Veterans and the Public Lands before the Civil War.* Kent, Ohio: Kent State University Press, 1990.
Rohrbough, Malcolm J. *The Land Office Business: The Settlement and Administration of American Public Lands, 1789-1837.* New York: Oxford University Press, 1968.
Van Atta, John R. "Western Lands and the Political Economy of Henry Clay's American System, 1819-1832." *Journal of the Early Republic* 21 (2001), 633-65.
Wellington, Raynor G. *The Political and Sectional Influence of the Public Lands, 1828-1842.* Cambridge, Mass.: Riverside Press, 1914.
Zahler, Helen. *Eastern Working Men and National Land Policy, 1829-1862.* New York: Columbia University Press, 1941.

4.7 Transportation and Communication

Allen, Michael. *Western Rivermen, 1763-1861: Ohio and Mississippi Boatmen and the Myth of the Alligator Horse.* Baton Rouge, La.: Louisiana State University Press, 1990.

Baker, Pamela L. "The Washington National Road Bill and the Struggle to Adopt a Federal System of Internal Improvements." *Journal of the Early Republic* 22 (2002), 437-64.

Cullinan, Gerald. *The United States Postal Service*. New York: Praeger, 1973.

Dilts, James D. *The Great Road: The Building of the Baltimore & Ohio, the Nation's First Railroad, 1828-1853*. Stanford, Calif.: Stanford University Press, 1993.

Durrenburger, Joseph A. *Turnpikes: A Study of the Toll Road Movement in the Middle Atlantic States and Maryland*. Valdosta, Ga.: Southern Stationery & Printing Company, 1931.

Fishlow, Albert. *American Railroads and the Transformation of the Antebellum Economy*. Cambridge, Mass.: Harvard University Press, 1965.

Forsyth, David P. *The Business Press in America, 1750-1860*. Philadelphia: Chilton Books, 1964.

Goodrich, Carter, ed. *Canals and American Economic Development*. New York: Columbia University Press, 1961.

Goodrich, Carter. *Government Promotion of American Canals and Railroads, 1800-1890*. New York: Columbia University Press, 1960.

Gruenwald, Kim Marie. *River of Enterprise: The Commercial Origins of Regional Identity in the Ohio Valley, 1790-1850*. Bloomington, Ind.: Indiana University Press, 2002.

Haites, Erik F., James Mak, and Gary M. Walton. *Western River Transportation: The Era of Early Internal Development, 1810-1860*. Baltimore: Johns Hopkins University Press, 1975.

Hunter, Louis C. *Steamboats on the Western Rivers: An Economic and Technological History*. Cambridge, Mass.: Harvard University Press, 1949.

Jackson, Carlton. "The Internal Improvements Vetoes of Andrew Jackson." *Tennessee Historical Quarterly* 25 (1966), 261-79.

John, Richard R. *Spreading the News: The American Postal System from Franklin to Morse*. Cambridge, Mass.: Harvard University Press, 1995.

Jordan, Philip D. *The National Road*. Indianapolis, Ind.: Bobbs-Merrill, 1948.

Kielbowicz, Richard B. *News in the Mail. The Press, Post Office and Public Information, 1700-1860s*. Westport, Conn.: Greenwood Press, 1989.

Larson, John L. *Internal Improvement: National Public Works and the Promise of Popular Government in the Early United States*. Chapel Hill, N.C.: University of North Carolina Press, 2001.

Malone, Laurence J. *Opening the West: Federal Internal Improvements before 1860*. Westport, Conn.: Greenwood, 1998.

Miller, Nathan. *The Enterprise of a Free People: Aspects of Economic Development in New York State during the Canal Period, 1792-1838*. Ithaca, N.Y.: Cornell University Press, 1962.

Mould, David H. *Dividing Lines: Canals, Railroads and Urban Rivalry in Ohio's Hocking Valley, 1825-1875*. Dayton, Ohio: Wright State University Press, 1994.

Owens, Henry P. *Steamboats and the Cotton Economy: River Trade in the Yazoo Mississippi Delta*. Jackson, Miss.: University Press of Mississippi, 1990.

Reed, Merl E. *New Orleans and the Railroads: The Struggle for Commercial Empire, 1830-1860.* Baton Rouge, La.: Louisiana State University Press, 1966.

Salsbury, Stephen. *The State, the Investor and the Railroad: The Boston and Albany, 1825-1867.* Cambridge, Mass.: Harvard University Press, 1967.

Scheiber, Harry N. *Ohio Canal Era: A Case Study of Government and the Economy, 1820-1861.* Athens, Ohio: Ohio University Press, 1969.

Shaw, Ronald E. *Erie Water West: A History of the Erie Canal, 1792-1854.* Lexington, Ky: University Press of Kentucky, 1966.

————. *Canals for a Nation: The Canal Era in the United States, 1790-1860.* Lexington, Ky: University Press of Kentucky, 1990.

Sheriff, Carol. *The Artificial River: The Erie Canal and the Paradox of Progress, 1817-1862.* New York: Hill and Wang, 1996.

Southerland, Henry deLeon, and Jerry Elijah Brown. *The Federal Road through Georgia, the Creek Nation and Alabama, 1806-1836.* Tuscaloosa, Ala.: University of Alabama Press, 1989.

Taylor, George R. *The Transportation Revolution, 1815-1860.* New York: Holt, Rinehart & Winston, 1951.

Thompson, Robert Luther. *Wiring a Continent: The History of the Telegraph Industry in the United States, 1832-1866.* Princeton, N.J.: Princeton University Press, 1947.

Way, Peter. *Common Labor: Workers and the Digging of North American Canals, 1780-1860.* New York: Cambridge University Press, 1993.

4.8 Overseas Trade and Navigation

Albion, Robert G. *The Rise of New York Port, 1815-1860.* New York: Charles Scribner's Sons, 1939.

Gibson, James R. *Otter Skins, Boston Ships, and China Goods: The Maritime Fur Trade of the Northwest Coast, 1785-1841.* Seattle, Wash.: University of Washington Press, 1992.

Goldstein, Jonathan. *Philadelphia and the China Trade, 1682-1846: Commercial, Cultural and Attitudinal Effects.* University Park, Pa.: Pennsylvania State University Press, 1978.

Hidy, Ralph. *The House of Baring in American Trade and Finance: English Merchant Bankers at Work, 1763-1861.* Cambridge, Mass.: Harvard University Press, 1949.

Jenks, Leland. *The Migration of British Capital to 1875.* New York, Knopf, 1927.

Livingood, James W. *The Philadelphia-Baltimore Trade Rivalry, 1780-1860.* Harrisburg, Pa.: Pennsylvania Historical and Museum Commission, 1947.

Morison, Samuel Eliot. *The Maritime History of Massachusetts, 1783-1860.* Boston: Houghton, Mifflin Co., 1921.

Perkins, Edwin J. *Financing Anglo-American Trade: The House of Brown, 1800-1880.* Cambridge, Mass.: Harvard University Press, 1975.

Ronda, James P. *Astoria and Empire.* Lincoln, Neb.: University of Nebraska Press, 1990.

Rowe, William Hutchinson. *The Maritime History of Maine: Three Centuries of Shipbuilding & Seafaring.* New York: W.W. Norton, 1948.

Schroeder, John H. *Shaping a Maritime Empire: The Commercial and Diplomatic Role of the American Navy, 1829-1861.* Westport, Conn.: Greenwood Press, 1985.

4.9 Labor

Blewett, Mary H. *Men, Women and Work: Class, Gender and Protest in the New England Shoe Industry, 1780-1910.* Urbana, Ill.: University of Illinois Press, 1988.

———. *Constant Turmoil: The Politics of Industrial Life in Nineteenth-Century New England.* Amherst, Mass.: University of Massachusetts Press, 2000.

Boydston, Jeanne. *Home and Work: Housework, Wages and the Ideology of Labor in the Early Republic.* New York: Oxford University Press, 1990.

Bridges, Amy. *A City in the Republic: Antebellum New York and the Origins of Machine Politics.* New York: Cambridge University Press, 1984.

Dawley, A. *Class and Community: The Industrial Revolution in Lynn.* Cambridge, Mass.: Harvard University Press, 1976.

Dublin, Thomas. *Women at Work: The Transformation of Work and Community in Lowell, Massachusetts, 1826-1860.* New York: Columbia University Press, 1979.

———. *Transforming Women's Work: New England Lives in the Industrial Revolution.* Ithaca, N.Y.: Cornell University Press, 1994.

Faler, Paul G. *Mechanics and Manufacturers in the Early Industrial Revolution: Lynn, Massachusetts, 1780-1860.* Albany: State University Press of New York, 1981.

Gatell, Frank O. "Roger Taney, the Bank of Maryland Rioters and a Whiff of Grapeshot." *Maryland Historical Magazine* 59 (1964), 262-67.

Gillespie, Michele. *Free Labor in an Unfree World: White Artisans in Slaveholding Georgia, 1789-1862.* Athens, Ga.: University of Georgia Press, 2000.

Gutman, Herbert. *Work, Culture and Society in Industrializing America: Essays in American Working-Class and Social History.* New York: Knopf, 1976.

Hansen, Karen V. *A Very Social Time: Crafting Community in Antebellum New England.* Berkeley, Calif.: University of California Press, 1994.

Hirsch, Susan. *Roots of the American Working Class: The Industrialization of Crafts in Newark, 1800-1860.* Philadelphia: University of Pennsylvania Press, 1978.

Hugins, Walter. *Jacksonian Democracy and the Working Class: A Study of the New York Workingmen's Movement, 1829-1837.* Stanford, Calif.: Stanford University Press, 1960.

Jensen, Joan M. *Loosening the Bonds: Mid-Atlantic Farm Women, 1750-1850*. New Haven, Conn.: Yale University Press, 1986.

Jones, Daniel P. *The Economic & Social Transformation of Rural Rhode Island, 1780-1850*. Boston: Northeastern University Press, 1992.

Kierner, Cynthia A. *Beyond the Household: Women's Place in the Early South, 1700-1835*. Ithaca, N.Y.: Cornell University Press, 1998.

Laurie, Bruce. *Working People of Philadelphia, 1800-1850*. Philadelphia: Temple University Press, 1980.

———. *Artisans into Workers: Labor in Nineteenth-Century America*. New York: Hill and Wang, 1989.

Lazerow, Jama. *Religion and the Working Class in Antebellum America*. Washington, D.C.: Smithsonian Institution Press, 1995.

Morris, Richard B. "Andrew Jackson: Strikebreaker." *American Historical Review* 55 (1949), 54-68.

Murphy, Teresa Anne. *Ten Hours' Labor: Religion, Reform and Gender in Early New England*. Ithaca, N.Y.: Cornell University Press, 1992.

Pessen, Edward. *Most Uncommon Jacksonians: The Radical Leaders of the Early Labor Movement*. Albany, N.Y.: State University of New York Press, 1967.

Prude, Jonathan. *The Coming of Industrial Order: Town and Factory Life in Rural Massachusetts, 1810-1860*. New York: Cambridge University Press, 1983.

Rilling, Donna. *Making Houses, Crafting Capitalism: Builders in Philadelphia, 1790-1850*. Philadelphia: University of Pennsylvania Press, 2001.

Rorabaugh, W. J. *The Craft Apprentice: From Franklin to the Machine Age in America*. New York: Oxford University Press, 1986.

Ross, Steven J. *Workers on the Edge: Work, Leisure and Politics in Industrializing Cincinnati, 1788-1890*. New York: Columbia University Press, 1985.

Shelton, Cynthia J. *The Mills of Manayunk: Industrialization and Social Conflict in the Philadelphia Region, 1787-1837*. Baltimore: Johns Hopkins University Press, 1986.

Stott, Richard B. *Workers in the Metropolis: Class, Ethnicity and Youth in Antebellum New York City*. Ithaca, N.Y.: Cornell University Press, 1990.

Sullivan, William. *The Industrial Worker in Pennsylvania, 1800-1840*. Harrisburg, Pa.: Pennsylvania Historical and Museum Commission, 1955.

Sutton, William R. *Journeymen for Jesus: Evangelical Artisans Confront Capitalism in Jacksonian Baltimore*. University Park, Pa.: Pennsylvania State University Press, 1998.

Tomlins, Christopher L. *Law, Labor and Ideology in the Early American Republic*. New York: Cambridge University Press, 1993.

Wallace, Anthony F. C. *Rockdale: The Growth of an American Village in the Early Industrial Revolution*. New York: Alfred A. Knopf, 1978.

Way, Peter. *Common Labor: Workers and the Digging of North American Canals, 1780-1860*. New York: Cambridge University Press, 1993.

Wilentz, Sean. *Chants Democratic: New York City & the Rise of the American Working Class, 1788-1850*. New York: Oxford University Press, 1984.

Zonderman, David A. *Aspirations and Anxieties: New England Workers and the Mechanized Factory System, 1815-1850.* New York: Oxford University Press, 1992.

4.10 Urbanization

Adler, Jeffrey S. *Yankee Merchants and the Making of the Urban West: The Rise and Fall of Antebellum St. Louis.* New York: Cambridge University Press, 1991.

Binford, Henry C. *The First Suburbs: Residential Communities on the Boston Periphery, 1815-1860.* Chicago: University of Chicago Press, 1985.

Blouin, Francis X., Jr. *The Boston Region, 1810-1850: A Study of Urbanization.* Ann Arbor, Mich.: UMI Research Press, 1980.

Browne, Gary. *Baltimore in the Nation, 1789-1861.* Chapel Hill, N.C.: University of North Carolina Press, 1980.

Chudacoff, Howard P. *The Evolution of American Urban Society.* Englewood Cliffs, N.J.: Prentice Hall, 1975.

Cronon, William. *Nature's Metropolis: Chicago and the Great West.* New York: W.W. Norton, 1991.

Goodstein, Anita Shafer. *Nashville, 1780-1860: From Frontier to City.* Gainesville, Fla.: University of Florida Press, 1989.

Green, Constance McLaughlin. *Washington: Village and Capital, 1800-1878.* Princeton, N.J.: Princeton University Press, 1962.

Knights, Peter R. *The Plain People of Boston, 1830-1860: A Study in City Growth.* New York: Oxford University Press, 1971.

Mahoney, Timothy R. *River Towns in the Great West: The Structure of Provincial Urbanization in the American Midwest, 1820-1870.* New York: Cambridge University Press, 1990.

Pease, William H., and Jane H. Pease. *The Web of Progress: Private Values and Public Styles in Boston and Charleston, 1828-1843.* New York: Oxford University Press, 1985.

Pred, Allan. *Urban Growth and the Circulation of Information: The United States System of Cities, 1790-1840.* Cambridge, Mass.: Harvard University Press, 1973.

———. *Urban Growth and City Systems in the United States, 1840-1860.* Cambridge, Mass.: Harvard University Press, 1980.

Spann, Edward K. *The New Metropolis: New York City, 1840-1857.* New York: Columbia University Press, 1981.

Stilgoe, John R. *Borderland: Origins of the American Suburb, 1820-1939.* New Haven, Conn.: Yale University Press, 1988.

Wade, Richard C. *The Urban Frontier: Pioneer Life in Early Pittsburgh, Cincinnati, Lexington, Louisville and St. Louis.* Chicago: University of Chicago Press, 1967.

Warner, Samuel Bass, Jr. *The Private City: Philadelphia in Three Periods of Its Growth.* Philadelphia: University of Pennsylvania Press, 1968.

5. Society

5.1 Social Structure

Blumin, Stuart M. *The Emergence of the Middle Class: Social Experience in the American City, 1760-1900.* New York: Cambridge University Press, 1989.

Collins, Bruce. *White Society in the Antebellum South.* London: Longman, 1985.

Hahn, Steven, and Jonathan Prude. *The Countryside in the Age of Capitalist Transformation: Essays in the Social History of Rural America.* Chapel Hill, N.C.: University of North Carolina Press, 1985.

Halttunen, Karen. *Confidence Men and Painted Women: A Study of Middle Class Culture in America, 1830-1870.* New Haven, Conn.: Yale University Press, 1982.

Hartford, William F. *Money, Morals, and Politics: Massachusetts in the Age of the Boston Associates.* Boston: Northeastern University Press, 2001.

Kulikoff, Allan. *The Agrarian Origins of American Capitalism.* Charlottesville, Va.: University Press of Virginia, 1992.

McClelland, Peter, and Richard Zeckhauser. *Demographic Dimensions of the New Republic: American Interregional Migration, Vital Statistics and Manumissions, 1800-1860.* New York: Cambridge University Press, 1982.

Mahoney, Timothy R. *Provincial Lives: Middle-Class Experience in the Antebellum Middle West.* New York: Cambridge University Press, 1999.

Miller, Douglas T. *Jacksonian Aristocracy: Class and Democracy in New York, 1830-1860.* New York: Oxford University Press, 1967.

Owsley, Frank. *Plain Folk of the Old South.* Baton Rouge, La.: Louisiana State University Press, 1949.

Pessen, Edward. *Riches, Class and Power before the Civil War.* Lexington, Mass.: D.C. Heath, 1973.

Ryan, Mary P. *Cradle of the Middle Class: The Family in Oneida County, New York, 1790-1865.* New York: Cambridge University Press, 1981.

Vinovskis, Maris. *Fertility in Massachusetts from the Revolution to the Civil War.* New York: Academic Press, 1981.

Wells, Jonathan David. *The Origins of the Southern Middle Class, 1800-1861.* Chapel Hill, N.C.: University of North Carolina Press, 2004.

Wiebe, Robert H. *The Opening of American Society: From the Adoption of the Constitution to the Era of Disunion.* New York: Alfred A. Knopf, 1984.

5.2 Gender and Family

Alexander, Ruth M. "'We Are Engaged as a Band of Sisters': Class and Domesticity in the Washingtonian Temperance Movement, 1840-1850." *Journal of American History* 75 (1988), 763-85.

Allgor, Catherine. *Parlor Politics: In which the Ladies of Washington Help Build a City and a Government.* Charlottesville, Va.: University Press of Virginia, 2000.

Bartlett, Elizabeth Ann. *Liberty, Equality and Sorority: The Origins and Interpretation of American Feminist Thought: Frances Wright, Sarah Grimké and Margaret Fuller.* Brooklyn, N.Y.: Carlson, 1994.

Basch, Norma. *In the Eyes of the Law: Women, Marriage, and Property in Nineteenth-Century New York.* Ithaca, N.Y.: Cornell University Press, 1982.

———. *Framing American Divorce: From the Revolutionary Generation to the Victorians.* Berkeley, Calif.: University of California Press, 1999.

Berg, Barbara. *The Remembered Gate: Origins of American Feminism: The Woman and the City, 1800-1860.* New York: Oxford University Press, 1978.

Blewett, Mary H. *Men, Women and Work: Class, Gender and Protest in the New England Shoe Industry, 1780-1910.* Urbana, Ill.: University of Illinois Press, 1988.

Boydston, Jeanne. *Home and Work: Housework, Wages and the Ideology of Labor in the Early Republic.* New York: Oxford University Press, 1990.

Boylan, Anne M. *The Origins of Women's Activism: New York and Boston, 1797-1840.* Greensboro: University of North Carolina Press, 2002.

Burnett, Constance Buel. *Five for Freedom: Lucretia Mott, Elizabeth Cady Stanton, Lucy Stone, Susan B. Anthony, Carrie Chapman Catt.* New York: Greenwood Press, 1968.

Chambers-Schiller, Lee Virginia. *Liberty a Better Husband: Single Women in America. The Generations of 1780-1840.* New Haven, Conn.: Yale University Press, 1984.

Chused, Richard H. *Private Acts in Public Places: A Social History of Divorce in the Formative Era of American Family law.* Philadelphia: University of Pennsylvania Press, 1994.

Clinton, Catherine. *The Plantation Mistress: Woman's World in the Old South.* New York: Pantheon, 1982.

Conrad, Susan Phinney. *Perish the Thought: Intellectual Women in Romantic America, 1830-1860.* New York: Oxford University Press, 1976.

Cott, Nancy. *The Bonds of Womanhood: "Woman's Sphere" in New England, 1780-1835.* New Haven, Conn.: Yale University Press, 1977.

Cutter, Barbara. *Domestic Devils, Battlefield Angels: The Radicalism of American Womanhood, 1830-1865.* DeKalb, Ill.: Northern Illinois University Press, 2003.

Delfino, Susanna, and Michele Gillespie, eds. *Neither Lady Nor Slave: Working Women of the Old South.* Chapel Hill, N.C.: University of North Carolina Press, 2002.

Dexter, Elisabeth Anthony. *Career Women of America, 1776-1840.* Francestown, N.H.: Marshall Jones, 1950.

Dorsey, Bruce. *Reforming Men and Women: Gender in the Antebellum City.* Ithaca, N.Y.: Cornell University Press, 2002.

Dublin, Thomas. *Women at Work: The Transformation of Work and Community in Lowell, Massachusetts, 1826-1860.* New York: Columbia University Press, 1979.

———. *Transforming Women's Work: New England Lives in the Industrial Revolution.* Ithaca, N.Y.: Cornell University Press, 1994.

DuBois, Ellen Carol. *Feminism and Suffrage: The Emergence of an Independent Women's Movement in America, 1848-1869.* Ithaca, N.Y.: Cornell University Press, 1978.

———. "Outgrowing the Compact of the Fathers: Equal Rights, Woman Suffrage, and the United States Constitution, 1820-1878." *Journal of American History* 74 (1987), 836-62.

Epstein, Barbara Leslie. *The Politics of Domesticity: Women, Evangelism, and Temperance in Nineteenth Century America.* Middletown, Conn.: Wesleyan University Press, 1981.

Flexner, Eleanor. *Century of Struggle: The Woman's Rights Movement in the United States.* Cambridge, Mass.: Harvard University Press, 1959.

Foster, Lawrence. *Women, Family and Utopia: Communal Experiments of the Shakers, the Oneida Community and the Mormons.* Syracuse, N.Y.: Syracuse University Press, 1991.

Fox-Genovese, Elizabeth. *Within the Plantation Household: Black and White Women of the Old South.* Chapel Hill, N.C.: University of North Carolina Press, 1988.

Ginzberg, Lori D. *Women and the Work of Benevolence: Morality, Politics and Class in the Nineteenth-Century United States.* New Haven, Conn.: Yale University Press, 1990.

Hansen, Karen V. *A Very Social Time: Crafting Community in Antebellum New England.* Berkeley, Calif.: University of California Press, 1994.

Hershberger, Mary. "Mobilising Women, Anticipating Abolition: The Struggle against Indian Removal in the 1830s." *Journal of American History* 86 (1999), 15-40.

Hoffert, Sylvia D. *Private Matters: American Attitudes toward Childbearing and Infant Nurture in the Urban North, 1800-1860.* Urbana, Ill.: University of Illinois Press, 1989.

Isenberg, Nancy. *Sex & Citizenship in Antebellum America.* Chapel Hill, N.C.: University of North Carolina Press, 1998.

Jeffrey, Julie Roy. *Frontier Women: The Trans-Mississippi West, 1840-1880.* New York: Hill and Wang, 1979.

———. *The Great Silent Army of Abolitionism: Ordinary Women in the Antislavery Movement.* Chapel Hill, N.C.: University of North Carolina Press, 1998.

Jensen, Joan M. *Loosening the Bonds: Mid-Atlantic Farm Women, 1750-1850.* New Haven, Conn.: Yale University Press, 1986.

Johansen, Shawn. *Family Men: Middle-Class Fatherhood in Early Industrializing America.* New York: Routledge, 2001.

Kierner, Cynthia A. *Beyond the Household: Women's Place in the Early South, 1700-1835.* Ithaca, N.Y.: Cornell University Press, 1998.

Kolmerton, Carol A. *Women in Utopia: The Ideology of Gender in the American Owenite Communities.* Bloomington, Ind.: Indiana University Press, 1990.

Lawes, Carolyn. *Women and Reform in a New England Community, 1815-1860.* Lexington, Ky: University Press of Kentucky, 2000.

Leach, William. *True Love and Perfect Union: The Feminist Reform of Sex and Society.* New York: Basic Books, 1980.

McCurry, Stephanie. "The Two Faces of Republicanism: Gender and Proslavery Politics in Antebellum South Carolina." *Journal of American History* 78 (1992), 1245-64.

McMillen, Sally Gregory. *Motherhood in the Old South: Pregnancy, Childbirth and Infant Rearing.* Baton Rouge, La.: Louisiana State University Press, 1990.

Matthews, Jean V. *Women's Struggle for Equality: The First Phase, 1828-1876.* Chicago: Ivan R Dee, 1997.

Melder, Keith E. *Beginnings of Sisterhood: The American Woman's Rights Movement, 1800-1850.* New York: Schocken Books, 1977.

Murphy, Teresa Anne. *Ten Hours' Labor: Religion, Reform and Gender in Early New England.* Ithaca, N.Y.: Cornell University Press, 1992.

Perdue, Theda. *Cherokee Women: Gender and Cultural Change, 1700-1835.* Lincoln, Neb.: University of Nebraska Press, 1998.

Pierson, Michael D. *Free Hearts and Free Homes: Gender and American Antislavery Politics.* Chapel Hill, N.C.: University of North Carolina Press, 2003.

Portnoy, Alisse Theodore. "'Female Petitioners Can Lawfully Be Heard': Negotiating Female Decorum, United States Politics, and Political Agency, 1829-1831." *Journal of the Early Republic* 23 (2003), 573-610.

Premo, Terri L. *Winter Friends: Women Growing Old in the New Republic, 1785-1835.* Urbana, Ill.: University of Illinois Press, 1990.

Pugh, David G. *Sons of Liberty: The Masculine Mind in Nineteenth-Century America.* Westport, Conn.: Greenwood Press, 1983.

Reinier, Jacqueline S. *From Virtue to Character: American Childhood, 1775-1850.* New York: Twayne, 1996.

Rohrs, Richard C. "'Public Attention for . . . Essentially Private Matters': Women seeking Assistance from President James K. Polk." *Journal of the Early Republic* 24 (2004), 107-23.

Ryan, Mary P. *Women in Public: Between Banners and Ballots, 1825-1880.* Baltimore: Johns Hopkins University Press, 1990.

Spurlock, John C. *Free Love, Marriage and Middle-Class Radicalism in America, 1825-1860.* New York: New York University Press, 1988.

Stansell, Christine. *City of Women: Sex and Class in New York, 1789-1860.* New York: Knopf, 1986.

Varon, Elizabeth R. "Tippecanoe and the Ladies Too: White Women and Party Politics in Antebellum Virginia." *Journal of American History* 82 (1995), 494-521.

———. *We Mean to be Counted: White Women & Politics in Antebellum Virginia.* Chapel Hill, N.C.: University of North Carolina Press, 1998.

Wellman, Judith. *The Road to Seneca Falls: Elizabeth Cady Stanton and the First Woman's Rights Convention*. Urbana, Ill.: University of Illinois Press, 2004.

Wishy, Bernard. *The Child and the Republic: The Rise of Modern American Child Nurture*. Philadelphia: University of Pennsylvania Press, 1968.

Wood, Kirsten E. "'One Woman So Dangerous to Public Morals': Gender and Power in the Eaton Affair." *Journal of the Early Republic* 17 (1997), 237-75.

Yellin, Jean Fagan. *Women & Sisters: The Antislavery Feminists in American Culture*. New Haven, Conn.: Yale University Press, 1989.

Zaeske, Susan. *Signatures of Citizenship: Petitioning, Antislavery, and Women's Political Identity*. Chapel Hill, N.C.: University of North Carolina Press, 2003.

Zboray, Ronald J., and Mary Saracino Zboray. "Whig Women, Politics and Culture in the Campaign of 1840: Three Perspectives from Massachusetts." *Journal of the Early Republic* 17 (1997), 277-315.

5.3 Slavery and Racial Issues

Aptheker, Herbert. *Nat Turner's Slave Rebellion*. New York: Humanities Press, 1966.

Bancroft, Frederic. *Slave Trading in the Old South*. Baltimore: J. H. Furst Co., 1931.

Berlin, Ira. *Slaves without Masters: The Free Negro in the Ante-bellum South*. New York: Pantheon, 1974.

Campbell, Randolph B. *An Empire for Slavery: The Peculiar Institution in Texas, 1821-1865*. Baton Rouge, La.: Louisiana State University Press, 1989.

Curry, Leonard P. *The Free Black in Urban America, 1800-1850: The Shadow of the Dream*. Chicago: University of Chicago Press, 1981.

Dusinberre, William. *Them Dark Days: Slavery in the American Rice Swamps*. New York: Oxford University Press, 1996.

Foner, Philip, and Josephine Pacheco. *Three Who Dared: Prudence Crandall, Margaret Douglas, Myrtilla Miner: Champions of Antebellum Black Education*. Westport, Conn.: Greenwood Press, 1984.

Fox-Genovese, Elizabeth. *Within the Plantation Household: Black and White Women of the Old South*. Chapel Hill, N.C.: University of North Carolina Press, 1988.

Franklin, John Hope, and Loren Schweninger. *Runaway Slaves: Rebels on the Plantation*. New York: Oxford University Press, 1999.

Frederickson, George M. *The Black Image in the White Mind: The Debate on Afro-American Character and Destiny, 1817-1914*. New York: Harper and Row, 1971.

Fuller, Edmund. *Prudence Crandall: An Incident of Racism in Nineteenth Century Connecticut*. Middletown, Conn.: Wesleyan University Press, 1971.

Genovese, Eugene. *Roll Jordan Roll: The World the Slaves Made.* New York: Pantheon Books, 1974.

Goldin, Claudia Dale. *Urban Slavery in the American South, 1820-1860: A Quantitative History.* Chicago: University of Chicago Press, 1976.

Gudmestad, Robert H. *A Troublesome Commerce: The Transformation of the Interstate Slave Trade.* Baton Rouge, La.: Louisiana State University Press, 2003.

Hadden, Sally E. *Slave Patrols: Law and Violence in Virginia and the Carolinas.* Cambridge, Mass.: Harvard University Press, 2001.

Horton, James Oliver, and Lois Horton. *In Hope of Liberty: Culture, Community and Protest among Northern Free Blacks, 1700-1860.* New York: Oxford University Press, 1997.

Johnson, Walter. *Soul by Soul: Life inside the Antebellum Slave Market.* Cambridge, Mass.: Harvard University Press, 1999.

Kolchin, Peter. *American Slavery, 1619-1877.* New York: Hill & Wang, 1993.

Lewis, Ronald L. *Coal, Iron and Slaves: Industrial Slavery in Maryland and Virginia, 1715-1865.* Westport, Conn.: Greenwood Press, 1979.

Litwack, Leon F. *North of Slavery: The Negro in the Free States, 1790-1860.* Chicago: University of Chicago Press, 1961.

Lott, Eric. *Love and Theft: Blackface Minstrelsy and the American Working Class.* New York: Oxford University Press, 1993.

Mahar, William J. *Behind the Burnt Cork Mask: Early Blackface Minstrelsy in Antebellum American Popular Culture.* Urbana, Ill.: University of Illinois Press, 1999.

Melish, Joanne Pope. *Disowning Slavery: Gradual Emancipation and "Race" in New England, 1780-1860.* Ithaca, N.Y.: Cornell University Press, 1998.

Miller, James David. *South by Southwest: Planter Emigration and Identity in the Slave South.* Charlottesville, Va.: University Press of Virginia, 2002.

Nash, Gary B. *Forging Freedom: The Formation of Philadelphia's Black Community, 1720-1840.* Cambridge, Mass.: Harvard University Press, 1988.

Oakes, James. *Slavery and Freedom: An Interpretation of the Old South.* New York: Knopf, 1990.

Phillips, Christopher. *Freedom's Port: The African-American Community of Baltimore, 1790-1860.* Urbana, Ill.: University of Illinois Press, 1997.

Rael, Patrick. *Black Identity and Black Protest in the Antebellum North.* Chapel Hill, N.C.: University of North Carolina Press, 2002.

Reed, Harry. *Platform for Change: The Foundations of the Northern Free Black Community, 1775-1865.* East Lansing, Mich.: Michigan State University Press, 1994.

Saxton, Alexander. "Blackface Minstrelsy and Jacksonian Ideology." *American Quarterly* 27 (1975), 3-28.

Schwartz, Marie Jenkins. *Born in Bondage: Growing Up Enslaved in the Antebellum South.* Cambridge, Mass.: Harvard University Press, 2000.

Stanton, William R. *The Leopard's Spots: Scientific Attitudes toward Race in America, 1815-1859.* Chicago: University of Chicago Press, 1960.

Starobin, Robert S. *Industrial Slavery in the Old South.* New York: Oxford University Press, 1970.

Strane, Susan. *A Whole-Souled Woman: Prudence Crandall and the Education of Black Women.* New York: W. W. Norton, 1990.

Tadman, Michael. *Speculators and Slaves: Masters, Traders and Slaves in the Old South.* Madison, Wisc.: University of Wisconsin Press, 1989.

Wade, Richard C. *Slavery in the Cities: The South, 1820-1860.* New York: Oxford University Press, 1964.

5.4 Native Americans

Champagne, Duane. *Social Order and Political Change: Constitutional Governments among the Cherokee, the Choctaw, the Chickasaw and the Creek.* Stanford, Calif.: Stanford University Press, 1992.

Cotterill, Robert S. *The Southern Indians: The Story of the Civilized Tribes before Removal.* Norman, Ok.: University of Oklahoma Press, 1954.

De Rosier, Arthur H., Jr. *The Removal of the Choctaw Indians.* Knoxville, Tenn.: University of Tennessee Press, 1970.

Dippie, Brian W. *Catlin and His Contemporaries: The Politics of Patronage.* Lincoln, Neb.: University of Nebraska Press, 1990.

Foreman, Grant. *Indian Removal: The Emigration of the Five Civilized Tribes of Indians.* Norman, Ok.: University of Oklahoma Press, 1932.

Garrison, Tim Alan. "Beyond Worcester: The Alabama Supreme Court and the Sovereignty of the Creek Nation." *Journal of the Early Republic* 19 (1999), 423-50.

Green, Michael D. *The Politics of Indian Removal: Creek Government and Society in Crisis.* Lincoln, Neb.: University of Nebraska Press, 1982.

Hershberger, Mary. "Mobilising Women, Anticipating Abolition: The Struggle against Indian Removal in the 1830s." *Journal of American History* 86 (1999), 15-40.

Hurt, R. Douglas. *The Indian Frontier, 1763-1846.* Albuquerque, N.M.: University of New Mexico Press, 2002.

Kidwell, Clara Sue. *Choctaws and Missionaries in Mississippi, 1818-1918.* Norman, Ok.: University of Oklahoma Press, 1995.

Laumer, Frank. *Dade's Last Command.* Gainesville, Fla.: University of Florida Press, 1995.

Littlefield, Daniel F. *Africans and Seminoles: From Removal to Emancipation.* Westport, Conn.: Greenwood Press, 1977.

McLoughlin, William G. *Cherokees and Missionaries, 1789-1839.* New Haven, Conn.: Yale University Press, 1984.

———. *Cherokee Renascence in the New Republic.* Princeton, N.J.: Princeton University Press, 1986.

Mahon, John K. *History of the Second Seminole War, 1835-1842.* Gainesville, Fla.: University of Florida Press, 1967.

Martin, Scott C. "Interpreting Metamora: Nationalism, Theater and Jacksonian Indian Policy." *Journal of the Early Republic* 19 (1999), 73-101.

Missal, John, and Mary Lou Missal. *The Seminole Wars: America's Longest Indian Conflict.* Gainesville, Fla.: University of Florida Press, 2004.

Norgren, Jill. *The Cherokee Cases: The Confrontation of Law and Politics.* New York: McGraw-Hill, 1996.

O'Brien, Greg. *Choctaws in a Revolutionary Age, 1750-1830.* Lincoln, Neb.: University of Nebraska Press, 2002.

O'Brien, Sean Michael. *In Bitterness and in Tears: Andrew Jackson's Destruction of the Creeks and Seminoles.* Westport, Conn.: Praeger, 2003.

Perdue, Theda. *Slavery and the Evolution of Cherokee Society, 1540-1866.* Knoxville, Tenn.: University of Tennessee Press, 1979.

———. *Cherokee Women: Gender and Cultural Change, 1700-1835.* Lincoln, Neb.: University of Nebraska Press, 1998.

Peters, Virginia Bergman. *The Florida Wars.* Hamden, Conn.: Archon Books, 1979.

Prucha, Francis Paul. *Broadax and Bayonet: The Role of the United States Army in the Development of the Northwest, 1815-1860.* Madison, Wisc.: State Historical Society of Wisconsin, 1953.

———. *American Indian Policy in the Formative Years: The Indian Trade and Intercourse Acts, 1790-1834.* Cambridge, Mass.: Harvard University Press, 1962.

———. "Andrew Jackson's Indian Policy: A Reassessment." *Journal of American History* 56 (1969), 527-39.

———. *The Great Father: The United States Government and the American Indians.* 2 vols. Lincoln, Neb.: University of Nebraska Press, 1984.

Remini, Robert V. *Andrew Jackson and His Indian Wars.* New York: Penguin Viking, 2001.

Rogin, Michael Paul. *Fathers and Children: Andrew Jackson and the Subjugation of the American Indian.* New York: Alfred A. Knopf, 1975.

Satz, Ronald N. *American Indian Policy in the Jacksonian Era.* Lincoln, Neb.: University of Nebraska Press, 1975.

Wallace, Anthony F. C. *The Long Bitter Trail: Andrew Jackson and the Indians.* New York: Hill and Wang, 1993.

Williams, David. *The Georgia Gold Rush: Twenty-Niners, Cherokees and Gold Fever.* Columbia, S.C.: University of South Carolina Press, 1993.

Wright, J. Leitch. *Creeks & Seminoles: The Destruction and Regeneration of the Muscogulge People.* Lincoln, Neb.: University of Nebraska Press, 1986.

Young, Mary Elizabeth. *Redskins, Ruffleshirts and Rednecks: Indian Allotments in Alabama and Mississippi, 1830-1860.* Norman, Ok.: University of Oklahoma Press, 1961.

———. "Conflict Resolution on the Indian Frontier." *Journal of the Early Republic* 16 (1996), 1-19.

5.5 Immigration, Ethnicity, and Nativism

Berthoff, Rowland T. *British Immigrants in Industrial America, 1790-1950.* Cambridge, Mass.: Harvard University Press, 1953.

Billington, Ray A. *The Protestant Crusade, 1800-1860: A Study of the Origins of American Nativism.* New York: Macmillan, 1938.

Blegen, Theodore. *Norwegian Migration to America: 1836-1860.* Northfield, Minn.: Norwegian-American Historical Association, 1931.

Conzen, Kathleen Neils. *Immigrant Milwaukee, 1836-1860: Accommodation and Community in a Frontier City.* Cambridge, Mass.: Harvard University Press, 1976.

Daniels, Roger. *Coming to America: A History of Immigration and Ethnicity in American Life.* New York: Harper Collins, 1990.

Dolan, Jay. *Immigrant Church: New York's Irish and German Catholics, 1815-1865.* Baltimore: Johns Hopkins University Press, 1975.

Erickson, Charlotte, ed. *Invisible Immigrants: The Adaptation of English and Scottish Immigrants in Nineteenth Century America.* London: London School of Economics, 1972.

———. *Leaving England: Essays on British Emigration in the Nineteenth Century.* Ithaca, N.Y.: Cornell University Press, 1994.

Ernst, Robert. *Immigrant Life in New York City, 1825-1863.* New York: King's Crown Press, 1949.

Feldberg, Michael. *The Philadelphia Riots of 1844: A Study of Ethnic Conflict.* Westport, Conn.: Greenwood Press, 1975.

Gerber, David A. *The Making of an American Pluralism: Buffalo, New York, 1825-1860.* Urbana, Ill.: University of Illinois Press, 1989.

Gleeson, David T. *The Irish in the South, 1815-1877.* Chapel Hill, N.C.: University of North Carolina Press, 2001.

Gribben, Arthur, ed. *The Great Famine and the Irish Diaspora in America.* Amherst, Mass.: University of Massachusetts Press, 1999.

Handlin, Oscar. *Boston's Immigrants, 1790-1865: A Study in Acculturation.* Cambridge, Mass.: Harvard University Press, 1941.

Hueston, Robert Francis. *The Catholic Press and Nativism, 1840-1860.* New York: Arno Press, 1976.

Jones, Maldwyn. *American Immigration.* Chicago: University of Chicago Press, 1960.

Knobel, Dale T. *Paddy and the Republic: Ethnicity and Nationality in Antebellum America.* Middletown, Conn.: Wesleyan University Press, 1986.

Miller, Kerby A. *Emigrants and Exiles: Ireland and the Irish Exodus to North America.* New York: Oxford University Press, 1985.

Mitchell, Brian C. *The Paddy Camps: The Irish of Lowell, 1821-61.* Urbana, Ill.: University of Illinois Press, 1988.

Nadel, Stanley. *Little Germany: Ethnicity, Religion, and Class in New York City, 1845-1880.* Urbana, Ill.: University of Illinois Press, 1990.

Niehaus, Earl F. *The Irish in New Orleans, 1800-1860.* Baton Rouge, La.: Louisiana State University Press, 1965.

Nolt, Steven M. *Foreigners in Their Own Land: Pennsylvania Germans in the Early American Republic.* University Park, Pa.: Pennsylvania State University Press, 2002.
Van Vugt, William E. *Britain to America: Mid-Nineteenth Century Immigrants to the United States.* Urbana, Ill.: University of Illinois Press, 1999.
Wyman, Mark. *Immigrants in the Valley: Irish, Germans, and Americans in the Upper Mississippi Country, 1830-1860.* Chicago: Nelson-Hall, 1984.

5.6 Crime and Disorder

Dennison, George M. *The Dorr War: Republicanism on Trial, 1831-1861.* Lexington, Ky: University Press of Kentucky, 1976.
Feldberg, Michael. *The Philadelphia Riots of 1844: A Study of Ethnic Conflict.* Westport, Conn.: Greenwood Press, 1975.
———. *The Turbulent Era: Riot and Disorder in Jacksonian America.* New York: Oxford University Press, 1980.
Gettleman, Marvin E. *The Dorr Rebellion: A Study in American Radicalism, 1833-1849.* New York: Random House, 1973.
Gilje, Paul A. *The Road to Mobocracy: Popular Disorder in New York City, 1763-1834.* Chapel Hill, N.C.: University of North Carolina Press, 1987.
Grimsted, David. "Rioting in Its Jacksonian Setting." *American Historical Review* 77 (1972), 361-97.
———. *American Mobbing, 1828-1861: Toward Civil War.* New York: Oxford University Press, 1998.
Huston, Reeve. *Land and Freedom: Rural Society, Popular Protest and Party Politics in Antebellum New York.* New York: Oxford University Press, 2000.
Johnson, David R. *Policing the Urban Underworld: The Impact of Crime on the Development of the American Police, 1800-1877.* Philadelphia: Temple University Press, 1979.
Lane, Roger. *Policing the City: Boston, 1822-1885.* Cambridge, Mass.: Harvard University Press, 1967.
McCurdy, Charles W. *The Anti-Rent Era in New York Law and Politics, 1839-1865.* Chapel Hill, N.C.: University of North Carolina Press, 2001.
Masur, Louis P. *Rites of Execution: Capital Punishment and the Transformation of American Culture, 1776-1865.* New York: Oxford University Press, 1989.
Miller, Wilbur R. *Cops and Bobbies: Police Authority in New York and London, 1830-1870.* Chicago: University of Chicago Press, 1977.
Prince, Carl E. "The Great 'Riot Year': Jacksonian Democracy and Patterns of Violence in 1834." *Journal of the Early Republic* 5 (1985), 1-19.
Ratner, Lorman. *Powder Keg: Northern Opposition to the Antislavery Movement, 1831-1840.* New York: Basic Books, 1968.
Richards, Leonard L. *"Gentlemen of Property and Standing": Anti-Abolition Mobs in Jacksonian America.* New York: Oxford University Press, 1970.

Steinberg, Allen. *The Transformation of Criminal Justice: Philadelphia, 1800-1870.* Chapel Hill, N.C.: University of North Carolina Press, 1989.

5.7 Religion

Barkun, Michael. *Crucible of the Millennium: The Burned-Over District of New York in the 1840s.* Syracuse, N.Y.: Syracuse University Press, 1986.

Bennett, Richard E. *Mormons at the Missouri, 1846-1852: "And Should We Die . . ."* Norman, Ok.: University of Oklahoma Press, 1987.

Bilhartz, Terry D. *Urban Religion and the Second Great Awakening: Church and Society in Early National Baltimore.* Rutherford, N.J.: Fairleigh Dickinson University Press, 1986.

Bratt, James D. "Religious Anti-Revivalism in Antebellum America." *Journal of the Early Republic* 24 (2004), 65-106.

Brooke, John L. *The Refiners' Fire: The Making of Mormon Cosmology, 1644-1844.* New York: Cambridge University Press, 1994.

Bruce, Dickson. *And They All Sang Hallelujah: Plain-folk Camp-Meeting Religion, 1800-1845.* Knoxville, Tenn.: University of Tennessee Press, 1974.

Butler, Diana Hochstedt. *Standing against the Whirlwind: Evangelical Episcopalians in Nineteenth-Century America.* New York: Oxford University Press, 1995.

Butler, Jon. *Awash in a Sea of Faith: Christianizing the American People.* Cambridge, Mass.: Harvard University Press, 1990.

Calhoon, Robert M. *Evangelicals and Conservatives in the Early South, 1740-1861.* Columbia, S.C.: University of South Carolina Press, 1988.

Carwadine, Richard J. *Transatlantic Revivalism: Popular Evangelicalism in Britain and America, 1790-1865.* Westport, Conn.: Greenwood Press, 1978.

———. *Evangelicals and Politics in Antebellum America.* New Haven, Conn.: Yale University Press, 1993.

Cole, Charles C. *The Social Ideas of Northern Evangelicals, 1826-1860.* New York Columbia University Press, 1954.

Conkin, Paul K. *The Uneasy Center: Reformed Christianity in Antebellum America.* Chapel Hill, N.C.: University of North Carolina Press, 1995.

Conser, Walter H. *God and the Natural World: Religion and Science in Antebellum America.* Columbia, S.C.: University of South Carolina Press, 1993.

Cross, Whitney R. *The Burned Over District: The Social and Intellectual History of Enthusiastic Religion in Western New York, 1800-1850.* Ithaca, N.Y.: Cornell University Press, 1950.

Doan, Ruth Alden. *The Miller Heresy, Millennialism, and American Culture.* Philadelphia: Temple University Press, 1987.

Eslinger, Ellen. *Citizens of Zion: The Social Origins of Camp Meeting Revivalism.* Knoxville, Tenn.: University of Tennessee Press, 1999.

Field, Peter. *The Crisis of the Standing Order: Clerical Intellectuals and Cultural Authority in Massachusetts, 1780-1833.* Amherst, Mass.: University of Massachusetts Press, 1998.

Foster, Charles. *An Errand of Mercy: The Evangelical United Front, 1790-1837.* Chapel Hill, N.C.: University of North Carolina Press, 1960.

Franchot, Jenny. *Roads to Rome: The Antebellum Protestant Encounter with Catholicism.* Berkeley, Calif.: University of California Press, 1994.

Grasso, Christopher. "Skepticism and American Faith: Infidels, Converts and Religious Doubt in the Early Nineteenth Century." *Journal of the Early Republic* 22 (2002), 464-508.

Griffin, C. S. *Their Brothers' Keepers: Moral Stewardship in the United States, 1800-1865.* New Brunswick, N.J.: Rutgers University Press, 1960.

Gutjahr, Paul. *An American Bible: A History of the Good Book in the United States, 1777-1880.* Stanford, Calif.: Stanford University Press, 1999.

Hanley, Mark Y. *Beyond a Christian Commonwealth: The Protestant Quarrel with the American Republic, 1830-1860.* Chapel Hill, N.C.: University of North Carolina Press, 1994.

Hatch, Nathan O. *The Democratization of American Christianity.* New Haven, Conn.: Yale University Press, 1989.

Hill, Marvin S. *Quest for Refuge: The Mormon Flight from American Pluralism.* Salt Lake City, Utah: Signature Books, 1989.

Hood, Fred J. *Reformed America: The Middle and Southern States, 1783-1837.* University: University of Alabama Press, 1980.

Howard, Victor B. *Conscience and Slavery: The Evangelistic Calvinist Domestic Missions, 1837-1861.* Kent, Ohio: Kent State University Press, 1990.

Howe, Daniel Walker. *The Unitarian Conscience: Harvard Moral Philosophy, 1805-1861.* Cambridge, Mass.: Harvard University Press, 1970.

———. "The Evangelical Movement and Political Culture in the North during the Second Party System." *Journal of American History* 77 (1991), 1216-39.

Hutchison, William R. *The Transcendentalist Ministers: Church Reform in New England Renaissance.* New Haven, Conn.: Yale University Press, 1959.

Johnson, Curtis D. *Islands of Holiness: Rural Religion in Upstate New York, 1790-1860.* Ithaca, N.Y.: Cornell University Press, 1989.

———. *Redeeming America: Evangelicals and the Road to Civil War.* Chicago: I. R. Dee, 1993.

Johnson, Paul E. *A Shopkeeper's Millennium: Society and Revivals in Rochester, New York, 1815-1837.* New York: Hill and Wang, 1978.

Knight, George R. *Millennial Fever and the End of the World: A Study of Millerite Adventism.* Boise, Idaho: Pacific Press, 1993.

Kuykendall, John W. *Southern Enterprize: The Work of National Evangelical Societies in the Antebellum South.* Westport, Conn.: Greenwood Press, 1982.

Lazerow, Jama. *Religion and the Working Class in Antebellum America.* Washington, D.C.: Smithsonian Institution Press, 1995.

Le Sueuer, Stephen C. *The 1838 Mormon War in Missouri.* Columbia, Mo.: University of Missouri Press, 1987.

Light, Dale B. *Rome and the New Republic: Conflict and Community in Philadelphia Catholicism between the Revolution and the Civil War.* Notre Dame, Ind.: University of Notre Dame Press, 1996.

Loveland, Anne C. *Southern Evangelicals and the Social Order, 1800-1860.* Baton Rouge, La.: Louisiana State University Press, 1980.

Macauley, John Allen. *Unitarianism in the Antebellum South: The Other Invisible Institution.* Tuscaloosa, Ala.: University of Alabama Press, 2001.

Mathews, Donald G. *Religion in the Old South.* Chicago: University of Chicago Press, 1977.

Meenagh, Martin L. "Archbishop John Hughes and the New York Schools Controversy of 1840-43." *American Nineteenth Century History* 5:1 (2004), 34-65.

Numbers, Ronald L., and Jonathan M. Butler, eds. *The Disappointed: Millerism and Millenarianism in the Nineteenth Century.* Bloomington, Ind.: Indiana University Press, 1987.

Rokicky, Catherine M. *Creating a Perfect World: Religious and Secular Utopias in Nineteenth-Century Ohio.* Athens, Ohio: University of Ohio Press, 2002.

Sassi, Jonathan D. *A Republic of Righteousness: The Public Christianity of the Post-Revolutionary New England Clergy.* New York: Oxford University Press, 2001.

Schantz, Mark S. "Religious Tracts, Evangelical Reform and the Market Revolution in Antebellum America." *Journal of the Early Republic* 17 (1997), 425-66.

———. *Piety in Providence: Class Dimensions of Religious Experience in Antebellum Rhode Island.* Ithaca, N.Y.: Cornell University Press, 2000.

Strong, Douglas M. *Perfectionist Politics: Abolitionism and the Religious Tensions of American Democracy.* Syracuse, N.Y.: Syracuse University Press, 1999.

Sweet, William Warren. *Religion in the Development of American Culture, 1765-1840.* New York: Scribner, 1952.

Taylor, Anne. *Visions of Harmony: A Study in Nineteenth Century Millenarianism.* New York: Oxford University Press, 1987.

Thomas, George M. *Revivalism and Cultural Change: Christianity, Nation Building and the Market in the Nineteenth Century United States.* Chicago: University of Chicago Press, 1989.

Wills, Gregory A. *Democratic Religion: Freedom, Authority and Church Discipline in the Baptist South, 1785-1900.* New York: Oxford University Press, 1997.

Winn, Kenneth H. *Exiles in a Land of Liberty: Mormons in America, 1830-1846.* Chapel Hill, N.C.: University of North Carolina Press, 1989.

6. Culture and Science

6.1 Thought

Boller, Paul F., Jr. *American Transcendentalism, 1830-1860: An Intellectual Inquiry.* New York: Putnam, 1974.

Buell, Lawrence. *Literary Transcendentalism: Style and Vision in the American Renaissance.* Ithaca, N.Y.: Cornell University Press, 1973.

Capper, Charles. "'A Little Beyond': The Problem of the Transcendentalist Movement in American History." *Journal of American History* 85 (1998), 502-39.

Capper, Charles, and Conrad Edick Wright. *Transient and Permanent: The Transcendentalist Movement and Its Contexts.* Boston: Northeastern University Press, for Massachusetts Historical Society, 1999.

Cayton, Mary Kupiec. *Emerson's Emergence: Self and Society in the Transformation of New England, 1800-1845.* Chapel Hill, N.C.: University of North Carolina Press, 1989.

Ekirch, Arthur A. *The Idea of Progress in America, 1815-1860.* New York: AMS Press, 1969.

Francis, Richard. *Transcendental Utopias: Individual and Community at Brook Farm, Fruitlands and Walden.* Ithaca, N.Y.: Cornell University Press, 1997.

Gilmore, Michael T. *American Romanticism and the Marketplace.* Chicago: University of Chicago Press, 1985.

Grossman, Jay. *Reconstituting the American Renaissance: Emerson, Whitman, and the Politics of Representation.* Durham: Duke University Press, 2003.

Howe, Irving. *The American Newness: Culture and Politics in the Age of Emerson.* Cambridge, Mass.: Harvard University Press, 1986.

Matthieson, F. O. *American Renaissance: Art and Expression in the Age of Emerson and Whitman.* New York: Oxford University Press, 1941.

Meyers, Marvin. *The Jacksonian Persuasion: Politics and Belief.* Stanford, Calif.: Stanford University Press, 1957.

Norton, Anne. *Alternative Americas: A Reading of Antebellum Political Culture.* Chicago: University of Chicago Press, 1986.

Ostrander, Gilman M. *Republic of Letters: The American Intellectual Community, 1776-1865.* Madison, Wisc.: Madison House, 1999.

Rose, Anne C. *Transcendentalism as a Social Movement, 1830-1850.* New Haven, Conn.: Yale University Press, 1981.

———. *Voices of the Marketplace: American Thought and Culture, 1830-1860.* New York: Twayne, 1995.

Saum, Lewis O. *The Popular Mood of Pre-Civil War America.* Westport, Conn.: Greenwood Press, 1980.

Smith, Henry Nash. *Virgin Land: The American West as Symbol and Myth.* Cambridge, Mass.: Harvard University Press, 1950.

Tuchinsky, Adam-Max. "'Her Cause against Herself': Margaret Fuller, Emersonian Democracy, and the Nineteenth-Century Public Intellectual." *American Nineteenth Century History* 5:1 (2004), 66-99.

Welter, Rush. *The Mind of America, 1830-1860.* New York: Columbia University Press, 1975.

Widmer, Edward L. *Young America: The Flowering of Democracy in New York City.* New York: Oxford University Press, 1999.

6.2 Literature

Baym, Nina. *Woman's Fiction: A Guide to Novels by and about Women in America, 1820-1870.* Ithaca, N.Y.: Cornell University Press, 1978.
————. *Novels, Readers and Reviewers: Responses to Fiction in Antebellum America.* Ithaca, N.Y.: Cornell University Press, 1984.
Brooks, Van Wyck. *The Flowering of New England.* New York: E. P. Dutton, 1936.
————. *The World of Washington Irving.* New York: E. P. Dutton, 1944.
Brown, Herbert Ross. *The Sentimental Novel in America, 1789-1860.* Durham, N.C.: Duke University Press, 1940.
Buell, Lawrence. *New England Literary Culture from Revolution through Renaissance.* New York: Cambridge University Press, 1986.
Burns, Rex. *Success in America: The Yeoman Dream and the Industrial Revolution.* Amherst, Mass.: University of Massachusetts Press, 1976.
Callow, James T. *Kindred Spirits: Knickerbocker Writers and American Artists, 1807-1855.* Chapel Hill, N.C.: University of North Carolina Press, 1967.
Charvat, William. *Literary Publishing in America, 1790-1850.* Philadelphia: University of Pennsylvania Press, 1959.
Clark, Robert. *History and Myth in American Fiction, 1823-1852.* New York: St. Martin's Press, 1984.
Current-Garcia, Eugene. *The American Short Story before 1850: A Critical History.* Boston: Twayne, 1985.
Davis, David Brion. *Homicide in American Fiction, 1798-1860: A Study in Social Values.* Ithaca, N.Y.: Cornell University Press, 1957.
Kelley, Mary. *Private Woman, Public Stage: Literary Domesticity in Nineteenth Century America.* New York: Oxford University Press, 1984.
Kiefer, Monica Mary. *American Children through their Books, 1700-1835.* Philadelphia: University of Pennsylvania Press, 1948.
MacLeod, Anne Scott. *A Moral Tale: Children's Fiction and American Culture, 1820-1860.* Hamden, Conn.: Archon Books, 1975.
Mott, Frank Luther. *A History of American Magazines. Vol. 1: 1741-1850.* New York: Appleton, 1930.
Patterson, Mark R. *Authority, Autonomy, and Representation in American Literature, 1776-1865.* Princeton, N.J.: Princeton University Press, 1988.
Siegel, Adrienne. *The Image of the American City in Popular Literature, 1820-1870.* Port Washington, N.Y.: Kennikat Press, 1981.
Tompkins, Jane P. *Sensational Designs: The Cultural Work of American Fiction, 1790-1860.* New York: Oxford University Press, 1985.
Zboray, Ronald J. *A Fictive People: Antebellum Economic Development and the American Reading Public.* New York: Oxford University Press, 1993.

6.3 Art and Architecture

Boime, Albert. *The Magisterial Gaze: Manifest Destiny and American Landscape Painting, c.1830-1865.* Washington, D.C.: Smithsonian Institution Press, 1991.

Callow, James T. *Kindred Spirits: Knickerbocker Writers and American Artists, 1807-1855.* Chapel Hill, N.C.: University of North Carolina Press, 1967.

Early, James. *Romanticism and American Architecture.* New York: A.S. Barnes, 1965.

Flexner, James Thomas. *The Light of Distant Skies, 1760-1835.* New York: Harcourt Brace, 1954.

Gardner, Albert Ten Eyck. *Yankee Stonecutters: The First American School of Sculpture, 1800-1850.* New York: Columbia University Press, 1945.

Gayle, Margot, and Carol Gayle. *Cast-iron Architecture in America: The Significance of James Bogardus.* New York: W.W. Norton, 1998.

Gerdts, William H. *American Neo-Classic Sculpture: The Marble Resurrection.* New York: Viking, 1973.

Harris, Neil. *Artist in American Society: The Formative Years, 1790-1860.* New York: G. Braziller, 1966.

Matthieson, F. O. *American Renaissance: Art and Expression in the Age of Emerson and Whitman.* New York: Oxford University Press, 1941.

Maynard, W. Barksdale. *Architecture in the United States, 1800-1850.* New Haven: Yale University Press, 2002.

Miller, Angela. *The Empire of the Eye: Landscape Representation and American Cultural Politics, 1825-1875.* Ithaca, N.Y.: Cornell University Press, 1993.

Miller, Lillian B. *Patrons and Patriotism: The Encouragement of the Fine Arts in the United States, 1790-1860.* Chicago: University of Chicago Press, 1966.

———. "Painting, Sculpture and the National Character, 1815-1860." *Journal of American History* 53 (1967), 696-707.

Novak, Barbara. *Nature and Culture: American Landscape and Painting, 1825-1875.* New York: Oxford University Press, 1980.

Voorsanger, Catherine Hoover, and John K. Howatt, eds. *Art and the Empire City: New York, 1825-1861.* New York: Metropolitan Museum of Art, 2000.

6.4 Performing Arts and Popular Culture

Adelman, Melvin L. *A Sporting Time: New York City and the Rise of Modern Athletics, 1820-1870.* Urbana, Ill.: University of Illinois Press, 1986.

Ahlquist, Karen. *Democracy at the Opera: Music, Theater and Culture in New York City, 1815-1860.* Urbana, Ill.: University of Illinois Press, 1997.

Bank, Rosemarie K. *Theatre Culture in America, 1825-1860.* New York: Oxford University Press, 1997.

Cook, James W. *The Arts of Deception: Playing with Fraud in the Age of Barnum.* Cambridge, Mass.: Harvard University Press, 2001.

Dormon, James H., Jr. *Theater in the Antebellum South, 1815-1861.* Chapel Hill, N.C.: University of North Carolina Press, 1967.

Grimsted, David. *Melodrama Unveiled: American Theater and Culture, 1800-1850.* Chicago: University of Chicago Press, 1968.

Harris, Neil. *Humbug: The Art of P.T. Barnum.* Boston: Little Brown, 1973.

Hodge, Francis. *Yankee Theatre: The Image of America on the Stage, 1825-1850.* Austin, Tex.: University of Texas Press, 1964.

Kirsch, George B. *The Creation of American Team Sports: Baseball and Cricket, 1838-1872.* Urbana, Ill.: University of Illinois Press, 1989.

Lehuu, Isabelle. *Carnival on the Page: Popular Print Media in Antebellum America.* Chapel Hill, N.C.: University of North Carolina Press, 2000.

Lott, Eric. *Love and Theft: Blackface Minstrelsy and the American Working Class.* New York: Oxford University Press, 1993.

Mahar, William J. *Behind the Burnt Cork Mask: Early Blackface Minstrelsy in Antebellum American Popular Culture.* Urbana, Ill.: University of Illinois Press, 1999.

Meserve, Walter J. *Heralds of Promise: The Drama of the American People during the Age of Jackson, 1829-1849.* New York: Greenwood Press, 1986.

6.5 Education

Cremin, Lawrence A. *American Education: The National Experience, 1783-1876.* New York: Harper and Row, 1980.

Foner, Philip, and Josephine Pacheco. *Three Who Dared: Prudence Crandall, Margaret Douglas, Myrtilla Miner: Champions of Antebellum Black Education.* Westport, Conn.: Greenwood Press, 1984.

Fuller, Edmund. *Prudence Crandall: An Incident of Racism in Nineteenth Century Connecticut.* Middletown, Conn.: Wesleyan University Press, 1971.

Gilmore, William J. *Reading Becomes a Necessity of Life: Material and Cultural Life in Rural New England, 1780-1835.* Knoxville, Tenn.: University of Tennessee Press, 1989.

Howe, Daniel Walker. "Church, State and Education in the Young American Republic." *Journal of the Early Republic* 22 (2002), 1-24.

Kaestle, Carl F. *Pillars of the Republic: Common Schools and American Society, 1780-1860.* New York: Hill and Wang, 1983.

Simpson, David. *The Politics of American English, 1776-1850.* New York: Oxford University Press, 1986.

Strane, Susan. *A Whole-Souled Woman: Prudence Crandall and the Education of Black Women.* New York: W. W. Norton, 1990.

Walsh, Julie M. *The Intellectual Origins of Mass Parties and Mass Schools in the Jacksonian Period: Creating a Conformed Citizenry.* New York: Garland, 1998.

6.6 Science and Medicine

Bieder, Robert E. *Science Encounters the Indian, 1820-1880: The Early Years of American Ethnology.* Norman, Ok.: University of Oklahoma Press, 1986.

Boland, Frank K. *The First Anesthetic: The Story of Crawford Long.* Athens, Ga.: University of Georgia Press, 1950.

Bruce, Robert V. *The Launching of Modern American Science, 1846-1876.* New York: Knopf, 1987.

Burleigh, Nina. *The Stranger and the Statesman: James Smithson, John Quincy Adams, and the Making of America's Greatest Museum: The Smithsonian.* New York: Morrow, 2003.

Cassedy, James H. *American Medicine and Statistical Thinking, 1800-1860.* Cambridge, Mass.: Harvard University Press, 1984.

———. *Medicine and American Growth, 1800-1860.* Madison, Wisc.: University of Wisconsin Press, 1986.

Daniels, George H. *American Science in the Age of Jackson.* New York: Columbia University Press, 1968.

Davies, John Dunn. *Phrenology, Fad and Science: A 19th-Century American Crusade.* New Haven, Conn.: Yale University Press, 1955.

Hafertepe, Kenneth. *America's Castle: The Evolution of the Smithsonian Building and Its Institution, 1840-1878.* Washington, D.C.: Smithsonian Institution Press, 1984.

Hovenkamp, Herbert. *Science and Religion in America, 1800-1860.* Philadelphia: University of Pennsylvania Press, 1978.

Kett, Joseph F. *The Formation of the American Medical Profession: The Role of Institutions, 1780-1860.* New Haven, Conn.: Yale University Press, 1968.

Philbrick, Nathaniel. *Sea of Glory: America's Voyage of Discovery: The U.S. Exploring Expedition, 1838-1842.* New York: Viking, 2003.

Porter, Charlotte M. *The Eagle's Nest: Natural History and American Ideas, 1812-1842.* University: University of Alabama Press, 1986.

Rosenberg, Charles E. *The Cholera Years: The United States in 1832, 1849 and 1886.* Chicago: University of Chicago Press, 1962.

Shafer, Henry Burnell. *The American Medical Profession, 1783 to 1850.* New York: Columbia University Press, 1936.

Stanton, William. *The Great United States Exploring Expedition of 1838-1842.* Berkeley, Calif.: University of California Press, 1975.

Viola, Herman J., and Carolyn Margolis, eds. *Magnificent Voyagers: The U.S. Exploring Expedition, 1838-1842.* Washington, D.C.: Smithsonian Institute Press, 1985.

About the Author

Terry Corps was born in 1962 in the English market and commuter town of Bedford. After completing his school education in the town, he attended the University of Durham between 1980 and 1983, graduating with first-class honors in Modern History. Two years as a University Fellow and graduate assistant at the Ohio State University produced an M.A. in American History, after which he returned to Durham to undertake doctoral research on Jacksonian America. In 1992 he was awarded his Ph.D. for a thesis on "Reciprocity Revised: The Jacksonians, Navigation and the Shaping of United States Commercial Policy, 1815-50."

While still completing his thesis Dr. Corps was appointed Lecturer in Historical Studies at the College of Ripon & York St. John (from 2001, York St. John College), where he developed and taught courses in American History and American Studies on the College's York campus. In 1994 he was promoted to Senior Lecturer and took over leadership of the American Studies program, a role he held until 1999. In 2001 he left full-time employment to embark on a combined career of part-time teaching, freelance writing, and parenting. Spells of part-time work followed at the University of Durham and York St. John College, and currently he teaches at the Universities of Sheffield and Leicester.

In addition to preparing the manuscript for the *Historical Dictionary of the Jacksonian Era and Manifest Destiny*, Dr. Corps is working toward publication of a series of article-length studies on various aspects of U.S. commercial policy in the 1840s, as part of a longer-term project examining the place of overseas trade in the context of the "market revolution." He has also written reviews for a number of British journals on American History and American Studies.

435